Fodor's THIRD New EDITION
Healthy
Escapes

Bernard Burt

Previously published as *Health & Fitness Vacations*

Fodor's Travel Publications, Inc.
New York • Toronto • London • Sydney • Auckland

Fodor's Healthy Escapes

Editors: Denise Nolty, Carolyn Price
Contributors: Cherie Burns, Marcy Pritchard
Art Director: Fabrizio La Rocca
Cartographer: David Lindroth
Illustrator: Karl Tanner
Cover Design: Tigist Getachew
Cover Photograph: William Thompson

Design: Vignelli Associates

About the Author

A resident of Washington, D.C., Bernard Burt has written two guidebooks to that city and contributed articles to *American Health*, *The Washington Flyer*, and *Maturity News Service*. The State of Maryland honored him as Travel Writer of the Year in 1985. He is also a founder of the International Spa & Fitness Association.

Special Sales

Fodor's Travel Publications are available at special discounts for bulk purchases (100 copies or more) for sales promotions or premiums. Special editions, including personalized covers, excerpts of existing guides, and corporate imprints, can be created in large quantities for special needs. For more information write to Special Marketing, Fodor's Travel Publications, 201 East 50th Street, New York, NY 10022. Inquiries from the United Kingdom should be sent to Fodor's Travel Publications, 20 Vauxhall Bridge Rd., London, England SW1V 2SA. Inquiries from Canada should be sent to Random House of Canada, Ltd., Marketing Department, 1265 Acrowood Drive, Mississauga, Ontario L4W 1B9.

Contents

Foreword

The appeal of the fitness vacation—holiday time used for maintaining or achieving new levels of physical or mental well-being—continues to widen as new facilities, new programs, new technology, and new ideas attract health-conscious individuals.

Where yesterday's working men and women saw vacation time as an opportunity to escape and relax, today's traveler looks for opportunities to expend additional effort in pursuit of a stronger body, a better self-understanding, perhaps a new self-image. Those who invest vacation time to achieve health and fitness goals may groan about getting up before dawn to go on a hike, yet they tend to return home relishing the natural high it brings them.

Fodor's Healthy Escapes surveys the entire range of fitness holiday opportunities in North America. In the pages of this guide, the in-depth profiles of 250 resorts and facilities and 16 cruise ships provide the detailed information anyone needs to begin to plan a vacation with a purpose.

The fees and prices quoted in the resort and cruise ship profiles are based on tariffs that were current in 1992 and early 1993 and are subject to change as costs rise and the contents of program and package offerings are reformulated. Where applicable, taxes and gratuities are additional. Deposits must usually be received in advance of the guest's arrival, and a cancellation charge applies to most bookings. Each resort makes its own policy with respect to accepting payment by personal check, traveler's check, money order, or credit card. The following abbreviations are used in the resort profiles in noting credit card acceptance: AE, American Express; D, Discover; DC, Diners Club; MC, MasterCard; V, Visa.

Fees for medical services may be covered by health insurance and under some circumstances may be tax deductible; consult the resort's program director and/or your tax advisor for further information.

While every care has been taken to assure the accuracy of the information in this guide, the passage of time will always bring change, and consequently the publisher cannot accept responsibility for errors that may occur.

All prices and schedules quoted here are based on information available to us at press time. The availability of programs and facilities is subject to change, however, and the prudent fitness vacationer will confirm the details of resort or cruise line offerings before beginning to make serious plans.

Fodor's wants to hear about your travel experiences, both pleasant and unpleasant. When a resort or hotel fails to live up to its billing, let us know and we will investigate the complaint and revise our entries where the facts warrant it.

Send your letters to the editors of Fodor's Travel Publications, 201 East 50th Street, New York, NY 10022, or 20 Vauxhall Bridge Rd., London, England SW1V 2SA.

Acknowledgments

The author is grateful for the assistance of Naomi Wagman of Custom Spas Worldwide, Frank van Putten of Spa-Finders Travel Arrangements Ltd., J. J. Reynolds of the Association of Retail Travel Agents cruise ship committee, Judith Singer of Health Fitness Dynamics, Inc., Frank LaFleche of the Canadian embassy's tourism division, Augustin Ballina of the Mexican Government Tourist Office, and all the concerned professionals who worked out with him and contributed to the research and development of the original concept for this book.

The insights shared by T George Harris, founding editor of *American Health* and *Psychology Today* magazines, were a constant source of encouragement.

For personal support and advice, the author is indebted to Denise Austin, Jeffrey Burt, Nancy Love, and Duncan Farrell. Travel was facilitated by American Airlines, Continental Airlines, Mexicana Airlines, and USAir.

For editorial direction through two editions, special thanks to Vernon Nahrgang.

Additional information on programs and therapies is available from the International Spa and Fitness Association (6935 Wisconsin Ave., NW, Washington, D.C. 20815).

Directory 1: Alphabetical Listing of Resorts

Directory 2:
Listing of Resorts
by Program

Holistic Health

Kid Fitness

Life Enhancement

Luxury Pampering

Non-program Resort Facilities

Nutrition and Diet

Preventive Medicine

Spiritual Awareness

Sports Conditioning

Cliff Lodge at Snowbird *86*
Club Med–Huatulco *320*
Doral Saturnia International Spa Resort *160*
Doral Telluride Resort and Spa *68*
Fontainebleau Hilton Resort and Spa *163*
Four Seasons Resort and Club *123*
Global Fitness Adventures *269*
Gray Rocks Inn *311*
The Hard & the Soft *355*
The Inn at Manitou *304*
Le Sport *361*
Mohonk Mountain House *248*
MountainFit (Hawaii) *283*
MountainFit (Montana) *103*
MountainFit (Utah) *90*
MountainFit (Washington) *109*
New Age Health Spa *251*
PGA National Resort & Spa *169*
Pro Muscle Camp *37*
Saddlebrook Sports Science *175*
Sanibel Harbour Resort & Spa *179*
Smith College Adult Camp *242*
Sports/Spa & Clinic at Sandestin *181*
Strong, Stretched & Centered *286*
Swept Away *352*
Tai Chi Farm *258*
Topnotch at Stowe *265*
The Zane Intensives *50*

Stress Control

Akia *117*
The Ashram Health Retreat *12*
The Aspen Club *66*
Black Hills Health and Education Center *120*
Canyon Ranch in the Berkshires *234*
Chateau Elan *183*
Cliff Lodge at Snowbird *86*
Dr. Wilkinson's Hot Springs *19*
Doral Saturnia International Spa Resort *160*
Filhoa Meadows *72*
Global Fitness Adventures *74*
Grand Hyatt Wailea Resort and Spa *273*
Heartland Health and Fitness Retreat *130*
Hilton Head Health Institute *195*
The Himalayan Institute *217*
The Integral Health Center *205*
Nemacolin Woodlands *219*
Northern Pines Health Resort *231*
Omega Institute *252*
The Option Institute *240*
Puerto Vallarta Grand Spa *326*
Sans Souci Health Resort *143*
Topnotch at Stowe *265*
The Zane Intensives *50*

Taking the Waters

Aqua-Mer Center *307*
The Arlington Resort Hotel & Spa *153*

Weight Management

Vibrant Maturity

Introduction

By T George
Harris

Mr. Harris, the
founding editor of
American Health
and Psychology
Today *magazines,
is executive editor
of* The Harvard
Business Review.

Americans are working harder than ever. In the past 15 years the leisure time of the average adult has shrunk by one-third to just 18 hours a week. The work week has grown longer by 20%, and for many working men and women it now approaches the 50-hour week once condemned in sweatshops.

This is not blue-collar sweat. The higher you rise in professional and executive ranks, the longer and harder you work. Then you labor still more hours learning new things, such as computer uses, that you need to do your job better. For many successful working men and women the stress of overload has become a badge of achievement: It comes with the territory. And those who in a previous generation might have been the idle rich often spend inherited wealth today on opportunities to try harder.

Stress has become the common cold of the busy classes. Fighting it, many strive to get into shape for peak performance. Fitness of body becomes the metaphor and means to fitness of mind. Gallup surveys for *American Health* magazine find that two out of three Americans now aim to do weekly exercise (though we don't always do as much as we intend). One in three of us considers health facilities in planning a vacation trip.

In fact the short, healthy trips become the turning point in many lives. When you go on vacation, it's foolish not to return in better shape than when you left. Travel is an investment in yourself, your productive capital. More and more people expect to get some good out of their trips. More people now take shorter and shorter vacations, and they vacation more often. Millions look for places where they will get the body back into motion, places where they will learn about fresh, tasty foods that are not larded down with fat, sugar, salt, and excessive calories.

That's the reason for this book. It fills the need for a detailed, easy-to-use guide to hundreds of places that now strive to provide meaningful recreation for the mind as well as the body. Moving far beyond the concept of the old European spa—those Marienbads where the elderly elite went to take the waters and be attended by doctors—some of the typically North American spots even offer specific programs to tone the brain and the spirit. The Golden Door in California invites a special few into "The Inner Door" to try the meditative lifestyle of serenity. Arizona's Canyon Ranch offers electronic feedback gear to help you tune in on your brain's alpha waves, long associated with meditation and creativity.

The Fodor's guides published by Random House have earned a reputation for practical, hard-to-get information. While other publishers bring out exotic volumes on "spas," this book provides the essential facts about healthy travel in a systematic way. *Fodor's Healthy Escapes* not only gives you prices and the details of programs, it provides such down-to-earth specifics as the kind of workout gear available in the exercise room.

The purpose is simple: to help you find the kind of place you want, nearest where you want to be. You will probably be astonished to discover that among the 250 resorts profiled in this book, several are an easy drive from your home or workplace. Then there are the spas at sea, 24 cruise ships that sail in Caribbean and Pacific waters.

The resorts described in this guide are grouped by region; if you want to find a facility in a specific area, the *Table of Contents* will tell you where to look. If you already have the name of a resort and want to learn what it has to offer, look for it in the alphabetical listing in *Directory 1*. If you want to find a resort that offers a particular kind of program or treatment, turn to *Directory 2*, which lists resorts under 11 categories of fitness program:

- Luxury pampering
- Life enhancement
- Weight management
- Nutrition and diet
- Stress control
- Holistic health
- Spiritual awareness
- Preventive medicine
- Taking the waters
- Sports conditioning
- Non-program resort facilities

I n the search for an author, it was clear that this book did not want a health-food zealot, a weight lifter, a spa devotee, or an exotic travel writer who loves only funky or pricey places. We needed someone who could represent the needs of the hardworking woman or man with a limited time to spend on vacation.

The ideal choice turned out to be Bernard Burt, a marketing consultant out of the University of Pennsylvania's Wharton School, a prizewinning travel writer and a practical-minded executive who had managed programs for Philadelphia's Civic Center. Like many a manager who strives for health, Burt had quite a few naive ideas about health behaviors and healthy food—and found himself totally unprepared, as most executives do, when his doctor told him his life would be shorter than normal if he did not get his weight down. At 58, Burt was ready to study the kinds of places that might help him change his lifestyle, and he signed on to research the new *Fodor's Healthy Escapes*.

Burt began with a test run for the April 1988 issue of *American Health*, an article on the most innovative places then rising in the U.S. spa world. Eager to discover the ancestry of such places, Burt investigated one of Europe's great spas, Brenner's Park Hotel in Baden-Baden, Germany. The historic Friedrichsbad, the emperor's bathhouse, had just been restored at great expense and was drawing Europe's and Japan's water-takers. Striding into the baths, Bernard paid little attention to the sign *Gemischt* (literally, "mixed"). Only when nude women and men appeared together did he realize the meaning of *Gemischt*. Being a gentleman of poise, he eased into the ancient European customs with hardly a blush.

Returned to the United States, Burt's poise underwent a more severe test at the Canyon Ranch in Arizona, one of the most innovative of American health centers. Mel Zuckerman, the founder and owner, has a missionary zeal about providing state-of-the-art programs, seminars, and nutrition. He and Dr. Bill Day, one of the fitness pioneers out of the national YMCA, have made Canyon Ranch the practical testing site for the fitness education.

Bernard Burt realized a clear break between the European spa tradition and American ideas. In different ways, the American industry strives to serve the individual's strong need for the enhancement of physical and mental resources. For most Americans, health means being the best each of us can be at the things we care about, from work to parenting to spiritual growth.

Burt found that other hardworking people seeking healthy turnarounds make wonderful companions. On his first dawn walks up a mountain, he learned that ordinary city clothes do not keep one warm in the desert. His feet seemed to be freezing until a companion executive dug out and passed on an extra pair of Brooks Brothers wool socks. In the supportive environment of the health resorts, guests as well as staff soon develop more than the customary concern for one another's welfare. The general feeling is, We're all in this together.

The most startling discovery Burt made concerned the cuisine. A gourmet who cares deeply about food, a wine lover and an honorary member of Washington's Sommelier Society, he expected to find tasteless brown things to eat, the bran-and-bean-sprout cuisine of the early health-food restaurants. Not so; in almost every resort he found the food so fresh "you don't need a lot of seasoning. And the beautiful presentation of the food always gets to me. Everything is low-fat. Part of the learning process is to find that you can enjoy these things without a lot of butter. All the intelligent and enthusiastic young people cooking in the resorts make it a pleasure to eat."

With help on his personal turnaround, Burt became even more faithful in his daily workouts at the Watergate Health Club in Washington, D.C. The grinding work of the writer does not often lead to exercise, but Burt got his cholesterol and his triglycerides under control. He dropped 30 pounds before he finished this book, and his doctor no longer threatens him. His single purpose now as a writer is to guide you toward the place you'll choose for your own turnaround.

1 Health & Fitness Programs

Planning a fitness vacation is a two-part process that involves determining one's personal fitness goals and finding the right program or resort. You can begin by setting very specific goals for yourself and then look for the program that best suits your needs. Or you can start by surveying the resort offerings to learn what's available and then decide what you want to achieve. This chapter will help in both parts of the planning process: it identifies and describes 11 categories of fitness program and explains what each attempts to do and what participants can hope to accomplish.

Never before have there been so many varied and challenging opportunities for exercising the mind, the spirit, and the body in a vacation with a purpose. The range of programs and facilities is wide, both for healthy men and women who want to stay in shape and for those who are determined to address a problem or improve a condition.

Since the first edition of this book was published in 1989, significant changes have evolved in spa programs. Several trends are expected to accelerate during the '90s: emphasis on preventive medicine and holistic health; less emphasis on weight loss but more education in nutrition and weight management through healthy eating and good exercise habits; and wider use of European hydrotherapy. What this promises are more practical approaches to a total fitness vacation, and more vacation spots that can be enjoyed year-round.

Some pleasure seekers may choose to relax amid the luxurious furnishings of a posh resort; others will find gratification in a week-long hiking adventure or the rugged atmosphere of a ranch that resembles a boot camp. New Age retreats and yoga ashrams, naturopaths and natural healing ranches offer health and healing based on combinations of ancient therapies and the latest concepts in behavior modification. Some establishments preach preventive medicine, taking a holistic approach toward strengthening the body against illness through improved nutrition and an understanding of the relationship between mind and body. Others address such problems as the need to lose weight, to stop smoking, and to deal with stress; these programs educate participants, reinforce motivation, and provide the regime not for quick results but for effective long-term improvement.

Increasingly sophisticated and often specialized resorts offer programs to help guests change their lifestyles at home. The establishment of new eating and exercise habits is now considered preferable to crash courses and 700-calorie daily diets. Techniques such as biofeedback have advanced to patterning weeks that can have even longer term effects. Hydrotherapy equipment from Europe appears alongside mud, seaweed, or algae for body cleansing to accompany the latest in toning, shaping, and weight loss technique.

Computer technology is now applied at nearly all levels of fitness training and understanding. Interactive exercise machines analyze calories expended, adjust themselves to increase your effort, and calculate when your body is functioning best. These machines are a valuable aid to staff members in designing health regimens to suit individual goals and physiology. But they don't take the sweat out of conditioning; the results of a fitness vacation remain yours to achieve.

Basically, your choices fall into two categories: all-inclusive or self-contained destinations that focus on wellness and resorts that feature a spa or health club along with sports and other diversions. In the wellness programs, you'll gain group support and camaraderie from like-minded participants in a structured daily schedule. At the resorts, you'll have more options and temptations.

The costs of a fitness holiday vary widely throughout North America. Where luxury and personal attention are the formula and the staff outnumbers the guests, you can expect to pay premium prices. At the same time, the budget-conscious traveler will find options at $25 a day (including meals) and opportunities to use various resort facilities (without participating in a program) for a small daily fee. Many resorts will offer, for a set price, a package of services to complement the principal program you have chosen. In some areas the off-season brings markedly reduced rates and bargain packages.

Because rate policies differ widely among resorts, the wise traveler will want to have a clear understanding of precisely what features are included in a program rate and what taxes and tipping will be added to the rate quoted. The prices given in the resort profiles in this book were accurate at the time of writing, but they should be used only as a preliminary guide; they will vary throughout 1993 and 1994 as increases go into effect, new combinations of services are offered, and new programs and packages are formulated.

Regional trends also became evident as this edition was updated. Experiencing the greatest growth were Florida, California, and the Southwest. Noteworthy additions to this guide include the Doral Telluride Resort and Spa and the Great Sand Dunes Inn in Colorado; the Sea Spa at The Cloister, and Chateau Elan in Georgia; Sanibel Harbour Resort & Spa in Florida; the Ocean Place Hilton Spa in New Jersey; Skylonda Fitness Retreat in California; the Four Seasons Resort on Nevis; and the newly opened Phoenician Centre for Well-Being in Scottsdale, Arizona. Also added are several exceptional values at spas in Mexico, notably the Avandaro Golf & Spa Resort, in a mountain valley 80 miles from Mexico City.

In the following pages, the descriptions of the 11 categories of fitness program explain in general terms what you can expect to find in the individual programs. Each description concludes with the Fodor's Choice of leading resorts that offer that program. Look up the leading resorts in *Directory 1* and turn to the profiles in the next section of this guide for details of the program offerings at each of the resorts. *Directory 2* gives the complete list of resorts for every program category and indicates the page on which each of the facilities is profiled.

Among those travel agents that are specialists in arranging spa packages are **Custom Spa Vacations** (tel. 800/443–7727), **Spa-Finders Travel Arrangements** Ltd. (tel. 800/255–7227), and **Spa Trek** (tel. 212/779–3480).

Kid Fitness

Programs to motivate children and teenagers to enjoy fitness through fun and exercise are designed to involve youngsters and their parents in a series of health-oriented experiences, complete with nutritious meals, sports, and excursions.

Kid Fitness: Aesculapia, Oregon
Fodor's Choice Doral Telluride Resort and Spa, Colorado
Green Valley Fitness Resort and Spa, Utah

Holistic Health

The theme of **holistic health** programs is that, in order to be truly fit and healthy, you must develop your emotional, intellectual, and spiritual self as well as your body. The nontraditional therapies seek to achieve a sense of wholeness with the world and oneself that will help the body to fend off illness.

Holistic health training can be vigorous or mellow; it is usually a combination of exercise, nutrition, stress control, and relaxation. Activities include walking, hiking, biking, cross-country skiing, tennis, swimming, and aerobics classes. A wide range of alternative healing therapies stretches from massage to yoga, and the body can be cleansed with herbs, enemas, or psychic diagnoses.

The credo of holistic health retreats is that illness results from a lack of balance within the body, whether caused by stress or physical conditions, and that the balance can be restored without the use of medicine. When secluded in places of great natural beauty, the healing process may draw on spiritual sources as well as natural energy to help participants find inner strength.

Holistic Health: Hawaiian Wellness Holiday, Hawaii
Fodor's Choice La Casa de Vida Natural, Puerto Rico
Murrieta Hot Springs Resort, California
New Age Health Spa, New York
Northern Pines Health Resort, Maine
Omega Institute, New York
The Plantation Spa, Hawaii

Life Enhancement

The **life enhancement** program aims for long-term physical and psychological benefits. It involves a total assessment of one's condition, with medical tests and personal consultations on nutrition and fitness. Some programs have a spiritual element, others emphasize an educational approach through exercise, diet, and behavior modification.

Developed in many cases at specialized centers, life enhancement programs usually require complete commitment from participants. The size of the group is generally limited to about a dozen men and women, each working one-on-one with a team of health and behavioral specialists in an intensive experience that little resembles a resort-style program.

Life Enhancement: Duke University Diet and Fitness Center, North Carolina
Fodor's Choice Esalen Institute, California
La Costa Resort & Spa, California
Palm-Aire Spa Resort & Country Club, Florida
The Phoenician Center for Well-Being, Arizona
Rancho La Puerta, Mexico

Luxury Pampering

Usually found at resorts where the staff members outnumber the guests, **luxury pampering** is intended for those who long to be herbal wrapped, massaged, and soaked in bubbling pools fragrant with chamomile. The height of survival chic is lounging in an elegant robe and discussing a delicious spa meal; exercise classes and a weight loss diet can be part of the program, but there will be no activity to put too much strain on the body.

An abundance of options makes luxury pampering a highly personalized regimen, designed for men as well as women. The services include exotic body and skin care treatments and the latest image-enhancers at the beauty salon, among them thalassotherapy tubs, loofah body scrubs with sea salts and almond oil, and paraffin facial masks for dehydrated skin. Recent advances have joined European spa treatments with American fitness concepts, such as an underwater massage followed by a mud pack.

Deluxe accommodations and lots of amenities are basic to luxury pampering. Some resorts have Sunday-to-Sunday schedules, most offer pampering à la carte. To those who say, "No pain, no gain," the pampered reply, "No frills, no thrills."

Luxury Pampering: Avandaro Golf & Spa Resort, Mexico
Fodor's Choice Cal-a-Vie Health Resort, California
Charlie's Spa at the Sans Souci, Jamaica
Doral Saturnia International Spa Resort, Florida
Doral Telluride Resort and Spa, Colorado
The Fontana Spa at The Abbey, Wisconsin
The Golden Door, California
Grand Hyatt Wailea Resort and Spa, Maui, Hawaii
The Greenbrier, West Virginia
The Greenhouse, Texas
Maine Chance, Arizona
Marriott's Spa at Camelback Inn, Arizona

Non-program Resort Facilities

Non-program resort facilities—often a health club that adds the fitness element to a vacation resort—can be just the place for weekend getaways or family vacations. Some fill a gap in areas where fitness resorts are not available; others are close to cultural and historical attractions. Most offer outstanding facilities and special services geared to the fitness-oriented traveler.

Non-program The Claremont Resort, California
Resort Facilities: Le Meridien Hotel & Villas, Bahamas
Fodor's Choice Scottsdale Princess, Arizona
Sonesta Beach Hotel & Spa, Bermuda
Woodstock Inn & Resort, Vermont

Nutrition and Diet

Nutrition and diet programs maintain that well-being begins in the kitchen, that understanding the relationship between nutrition and diet can enhance one's lifestyle and promote sound, healthy habits. Here you may learn to evaluate product labels ("high in fiber," "low in cholesterol") and to cope with the variety of advertising claims.

Participants, both vegetarians and newcomers to macrobiotics, gain a new perspective on nutrition through lectures and first-hand experience in food preparation. How foods affect your health, how to shop, how to choose from restaurant menus, how to plan and prepare meals are among the subjects covered. Classes are designed to generate menus and recipes for nutritious dining that participants will then take home with them.

Designed as an educational experience, with no attempt to provide a crash diet plan, the nutrition and diet program provides the fundamentals for following a regimen of eating healthy natural foods. And participants get to enjoy the meals prepared in class.

Nutrition and Diet: Canyon Ranch at the Berkshires, Massachusetts
Fodor's Choice Duke University Diet and Fitness Center, North Carolina
Jolimar Summit Plantation, Mississippi
The Kushi Institute, Massachusetts
La Costa's Resort & Spa, California
New Life, Vermont
Pritikin Longevity Center, California
Pritikin Longevity Center, Florida

Preventive Medicine

Preventive medicine centers take a scientific approach to health and fitness by combining traditional medical services with advanced concepts for the prevention of illness. Designed for healthy people who want to stay that way, the programs involve medical and fitness testing, counseling on nutrition and stress control, and a range of sports and exercise activities along with massage and bodywork.

Conceived as a regenerative experience for healing and relaxation, the programs can also treat problems associated with obesity, aging, and cardiovascular disease. These programs, usually developed in consultation with your personal physician at home, are carefully structured, supervised at all times, and require full participation.

Participants work with a team of physiotherapists and doctors in learning new techniques for survival; they discover how to eliminate negative habits and modify a lifestyle. The one-on-one training with fitness instructors, nutritionists, and psychologists can reveal ways of accomplishing personal goals.

Along with hospital-related programs, specialized centers for preventive medicine can now be found at leading fitness resorts and at retreats under the auspices of Seventh-day Adventist medical services organizations. They bring together specialists in all fields of health and nutrition to provide a comprehensive prescription for healthy living.

Preventive The Canyon Ranch Health and Fitness Resort, Arizona
Medicine: The Greenbrier, West Virginia
Fodor's Choice Maharishi Ayur-Veda Health Center, Massachusetts
Omega Institute, New York
Poland Spring Health Institute, Maine
Weimar Institute, California
Wildwood Lifestyle Center, Georgia

Spiritual Awareness

In celebrating the human potential, **spiritual awareness** programs strive to stretch the individual's limits both mentally and physically. They try to foster a process of personal growth and transformation through workouts that synchronize mind and body and make one aware of one's inner resources. Specializing in alternative education, vegetarian diets, and natural therapies, they offer psychic tools for living.

The experience may draw on any number of Eastern and Western philosophies, and it might focus on yogic training or sensory awareness. Body therapies, visualization, and shamanism are among the healing processes that can be explored. Private counseling and group sessions are usually available for both beginners and advanced meditators.

Retreats rather than resorts, these centers for spiritual training are situated in places where nature's beauty can be enjoyed without distraction or tension.

Spiritual Awareness: Fodor's Choice
Breitenbush Hot Springs and Retreat, Oregon
Feathered Pipe Ranch, Montana
Kripalu Center for Yoga and Health, Massachusetts
Maharishi Ayur-Veda Health Center, Massachusetts
Omega Institute, New York
Sivananda Ashram, Quebec
Sivananda Ashram Yoga Retreat, the Bahamas
Vista Clara, New Mexico

Sports Conditioning

For the active vacationer or the athlete seeking new challenges, **sports conditioning** programs offer advanced training in a variety of sports, workouts with experts, and high-tech training with the latest in exercise equipment.

The current buzzword is *cross-training*, which denotes a varied program that teaches the benefits of alternating sports such as tennis or swimming with exercises such as walking or weight lifting. Mountain hikes, beach runs, and cross-country skiing are programmed to stretch your endurance limits.

Mental training techniques can also be incorporated in sports conditioning programs. Following the lead of Olympic athletes and professional golfers, trainers are offering courses in guided relaxation, affirmations (positive statements), and visualization to improve the competitive edge. These practices are more than morale boosters; the visualization of successful performance may create neural patterns that the brain will use in telling the muscles what to do.

Therapy for sports-related injuries is a feature of some resorts. Others specialize in the mind-body relationship, with disciplines to promote both physical and spiritual development. Martial arts, yoga, and croquet are newly popular vehicles for integrating exercise and mental concentration.

Sports Conditioning: Fodor's Choice
The Aspen Club, Colorado
Chateau Whistler Resort, British Columbia
Doral Telluride Resort and Spa, Colorado
Global Fitness Adventures, Colorado
Le Sport, St. Lucia

MountainFit, Hawaii
PGA National Resort & Spa, Florida
Swept Away, Jamaica
Topnotch at Stowe, Vermont

Stress Control

Gaining control of the causes of stress is a basic element in the programs of most health and fitness resorts. The approaches to **stress control,** however, are varied; they include relaxation techniques, behavior modification, biofeedback, and meditation.

As a total experience, with a physical setting and food to lift one's spirits, stress control programs can create a strong feeling of well-being. Some are offered as an executive retreat within a resort, as an antidote for job burnout, or as a recipe for self-renewal. The opportunity to work one-on-one with advisors, away from the causes of stress, can enhance the individual's ability to cope with the stress factors of daily life.

Stress Control: The Ashram Health Retreat, California
Fodor's Choice Heartland Health and Fitness Retreat, Illinois
The Himalayan Institute, Pennsylvania
The Integral Health Center, Virginia
The Option Institute, Massachusetts

Taking the Waters

The practice of bathing at hot springs gave rise to the fashionable spas of Europe and America, where people congregated as much for social as for therapeutic purposes. Today **taking the waters**—which may involve drinking six to eight glasses of mineral water daily—is a practice enjoyed for health and relaxation.

The introduction of water-based therapies and mud baths at American fitness resorts is a recent phenomenon. The cross-fertilization of European and American approaches to maintaining a healthy body and a glowing complexion has revived interest in bathing at grand old resorts where natural waters are available free for the asking. Related but different treatments that involve seaweed, algae, and seawater are offered at spas that specialize in thalassotherapy.

For the purist, a secluded hot spring promises the best kind of stress-reduction therapy. Others need the added stimulation of body scrubs with sea salts by a masseur armed with a loofah sponge—or a whirlpool bath bubbling with herbal essences.

Taking the Waters: Aqua-Mer Center, Quebec
Fodor's Choice The Arlington Resort Hotel & Spa, Arkansas
Berkeley Springs State Park, West Virginia
Glenwood Hot Springs Lodge & Pool, Colorado
Harrison Hot Springs Hotel, British Columbia
The Homestead, Virginia
Hotel Ixtapan, Mexico
Kah-Nee-Ta Resort, Oregon
Murietta Hot Springs Resort, California
Saratoga Spa State Park, New York
Spa Hotel and Mineral Springs, California

Weight Management

Learning how to lose weight properly and how to maintain a healthy balance in body mass is the basis of a **weight management** program. This is not a course for a dramatic loss of weight; rather, it teaches proper eating habits, beginning with what to buy in the supermarket and how to prepare meals.

The weight management resort integrates motivational sessions with exercise, diet, and pampering, reeducation with recreation. Some programs involve fasting on juices and water. Some resorts are residential retreats for the seriously obese; some offer a full range of sports and outdoor activities.

Carefully controlled and supervised, the typical regimen is tailored to the individual's fitness level and health needs. A team of specialists—therapists and nutritionists—coaches you on the basics of beginning and maintaining a personal program. Additional motivation and support arise in the camaraderie of being with a group of like-minded dieters.

Weight Management: Fodor's Choice
Canyon Ranch Health and Fitness Resort, Arizona
Green Mountain at Fox Run, Vermont
National Institute of Fitness, Utah
New Age Health Spa, New York
Sans Souci Health Resort, Ohio
Structure House, North Carolina

Vibrant Maturity

The ageing of America, documented by Ken Dychtwald in his book *Age Wave*, has resulted in health and fitness programs designed for specific needs of men and women over age 50. Combining elements of spa vactions with medical services and lifestyle education, these programs can help achieve a healthier way of working, exercising, and eating. The emphasis is on prevention of illness by staying fit.

Vibrant Maturity: Fodor's Choice
The Cooper Wellness Program, Texas
Duke University Diet and Fitness Center, North Carolina
Green Valley Fitness Resort and Spa, Utah
Structure House, North Carolina
Hilton Head Health Institute, South Carolina
Sans Souci Health Resort, Ohio
Maine Change, Arizona
The Oaks at Ojai, California
Weimar Institute, California

2 Health & Fitness Resorts

California

A trendsetter in food, fashion, and fitness, California has been luring health-conscious visitors since the Spanish explorers first landed in San Diego. The 150 miles of coastline between Los Angeles and Mexico boasts more varieties of health spa than will be found in any other part of the nation: mud treatments, mineral waters, vegetarian diets, luxury pampering, and spiritual retreats are widespread.

Northern Californians consider themselves residents of a different state, one with San Francisco at its center. For them the wine country to the north is a principal attraction, and taking mud baths at Calistoga ranks with visiting the vineyards of Napa and Sonoma counties to taste and select one's own private reserve. Inland, the natural grandeur of Yosemite National Park vies with the dry heat and luxury resorts of Palm Springs.

The Ashram Health Retreat

Life enhancement
Stress control
Weight management

California
Calabasas

Barbra Streisand called the Ashram "a boot camp without food." Others have found it a rite of passage to a new self-image; Shirley MacLaine described it in *Out on a Limb* as "a spiritually involved health camp."

The Ashram displaces old stresses with new ones. Most of the fairly affluent achievers who come here have high-pressure jobs, and by challenging themselves to a week of enormous physical exertion and minimal meals, they can experience what some speak of as a transcendent, positive change in attitude.

Living together in close quarters, 10 to a group, guests follow a routine of mountain hikes, exercise, and yoga. A daily massage and a few hours of relaxation are the only respite. Everyone joins in; participation in every activity is required.

Not everyone can handle the discipline. Defections will occur, yet group support and personal counseling work for most participants. There is considerable joking about deprivation training—and serious talk about loving yourself for what you are rather than pursuing a new image.

Turning the concept of a retreat (the original meaning of ashram) into the ultimate challenge was an idea tested in a Guatemalan jungle by the Ashram's owner, Anne-Marie Bennstrom. A cross-country skiing champion in her native Sweden, she tested her personal limits by spending five months alone in the jungle. The mystical clarity of life's essentials, as opposed to the nonessentials, is what she shares with her guests in this retreat high above the Pacific Ocean.

The unpaved entrance road winds uphill to a plain, two-story stucco house. Surrounded by towering eucalyptus trees, the garden contains a small heated swimming pool, a solarium for sunbathing, and a geodesic dome where yoga and meditation sessions take place.

The day begins at 6:30 AM with stretching and breathing exercises that help take the kinks out of sore muscles and build energy for a strenuous hike into the hills. Breakfast is a glass of orange juice. The morning schedule usually includes an hour of weight lifting followed by an hour of exercise in the pool; it winds down with a game of water volleyball.

During the afternoon each guest has a one-hour massage. Calisthenics and a two-hour walk complete the day. The personal traits and individual techniques of the program leaders enhance the experience and guarantee that each guest's physical and psychological needs are attended to.

The Ashram Health Retreat
Box 8009, Calabasas, CA 91372
Tel. 818/222–6900

Administration	Owner-manager, Anne-Marie Bennstrom; program director, Catharina Hedberg
Season	Year-round, scheduled weeks.
Accommodations	Guests double up in 5 simply furnished bedrooms in the ranch house with shared bathroom facilities, library, lounge, and weights room. Exercise clothes and robe provided.
Rates	$2,000 per week, all-inclusive. $900 in advance. No credit cards.
Meal Plans	The three lacto-vegetarian meals include fruit, vegetables, sprouts, seeds, and nuts. Lunch can be a yogurt-and-cottage-cheese blend with fruit slices, dinner a green salad. Snacks of raw vegetables and juices throughout the day.
Services and Facilities	**Exercise Equipment:** Free weights. **Services:** Massage, nutritional counseling, yoga, meditation. **Swimming Facilities:** Outdoor pool. **Recreation Facilities:** Water volleyball. **Evening Programs:** Lectures on developing healthy habits, spirituality, energy centers of the body.
Getting Here	One hour from Los Angeles. Not accessible by private car; all guests picked up by van at locations in the area. Free pickup to and from Los Angeles International Airport and local hotels.
Special Notes	No smoking.

Bon Réussite

Weight management
Life enhancement

California
Lancaster

An hour from Los Angeles, this former fat farm was transformed by new owners in 1991 into one of the most affordable spas in the area, emphasizing a comprehensive plan for "good results" (hence the resort's name). Exercise is available nonstop all day, and the 900-calorie-a-day diet is designed to help you shed pounds while working out, but there is no strict regimen. After a fitness check, the staff plan an agenda for you to stimulate weight loss, lower cholesterol and blood pressure, and increase your energy level.

California

CALIFORNIA

Eureka

Redding

Sacramento R.

Lake Tahoe

Sacramento

San Francisco

San Jose

Modesto

S. Joaquin R.

Monterey

Fresno

Santa Maria

PACIFIC OCEAN

Davis

Sacramento

Napa

Vacaville

Sonoma

Vallejo

San Rafael

Berkeley

Oakland

Alameda

Stockton

Livermore

SAN FRANCISCO

San Jose

0 100 miles

0 150 km

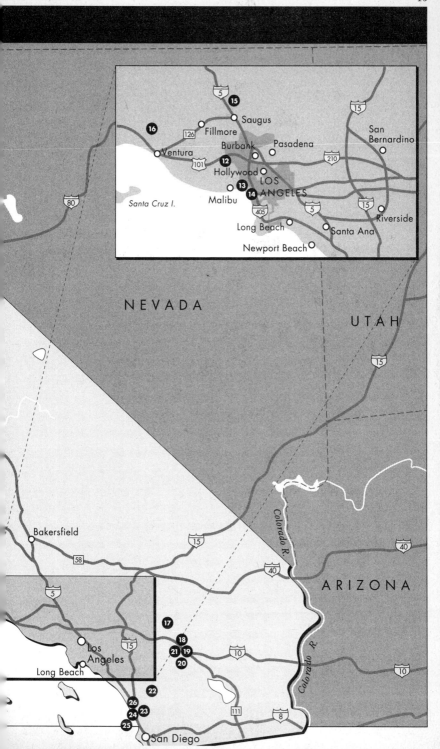

Though the resort vaguely resembles a country motel, the facilities are up-to-date. The pool is the site of aquatics classes and swimming. There is a mirrored gym, a smallish room outfitted with weight training equipment, and a paved jogging/walking course set on 15 acres of desert greenery.

Bon Réussite Health Improvement Center
43109 N. Sierra Highway, Lancaster, CA 93534
Tel. 805/942–1493 or 800/432–5847
Fax 805/942–7115

Administration General Manager, Kevin Keown; spa director, Joan Applegate; medical director, M. M. Mercer, M.D.

Season Year-round.

Accommodations 37 double- or triple-occupancy rooms in a two-story motel complex connected to the spa and dining room. Rooms have modern furnishings, private baths with dressing rooms, air-conditioning, TV, telephones, terrycloth bathrobes.

Rates Daily rate with meals $105–$165. 7-day package $1,125–$1,545. One night paid in advance. Credit cards: AE, MC, V.

Meal Plans Vegetarian fare along with some beef, fish, and chicken. Typical lunch might include soup, Chinese chicken melt, pasta salad, or pita pizza. Dinner entrées include chicken fajitas, vegetable lasagna, broccoli with beef, cheese-stuffed zucchini. Mocktails and vegetable snack breaks daily.

Services and Facilities **Exercise Equipment:** 10-unit Nautilus system, Trotter treadmill, StairMaster, Biobike. **Services:** Aromatherapy; Swedish, shiatsu, reflexology massage; MoorMud, drybrush body scrub, body glo, herbal wrap; health risk appraisal; vibrosaun, accumassage machines. **Swimming Facilities:** Indoor 30-ft. pool, outdoor recreational pool. **Recreation Facilities:** 2 lighted tennis courts, table tennis, putting green; golf nearby. **Evening Programs:** Entertainment, dancing, presentations on beauty enhancement.

In the Area Yosemite National Park.

Getting Here *From Los Angeles.* By car, I–5 north (Golden State Freeway) to I–405 (San Diego Freeway), to Hwy. 14 north, exit at Avenue K onto Sierra Hwy (60 min). By bus from LAX, Antelope Valley Express (tel. 805/945–2529). By plane, Palmdale Airport has scheduled flights; courtesy car pickup.

Special Notes No smoking in public areas and in guest rooms other than private accommodations. Room-sharing service on request.

Cal-a-Vie Health Resort

Life enhancement
Luxury pampering

California Vista Terraced into a Southern California hillside, the 24 country villas of Cal-a-Vie seem lifted from a scene in Provence. Yet the lavish outdoor pool, manicured gardens and streams, and wonderful food are all American. For luxury and weight loss, this is the ultimate escape.

European hydrotherapy and beauty treatments are the specialty of the house. Seaweed wraps to cleanse the pores, lymphatic massage for detoxification, and underwater-massage tubs are part of the sybaritic experience.

"Detoxify" and "cleanse" are terms that are spoken of daily. The program is designed to heal the body by restoring the balance of mind, body, and spirit. No intrusion from the outside world is allowed to disturb the peace and tranquillity of your week of hikes, aerobics classes, and calorie-controlled meals. Designed as a total environment for health and fitness, the 125-acre resort accepts only 24 guests a week for the all-inclusive Sunday-to-Sunday program.

During thalassotherapy, you are cocooned in a mixture of algae and seawater, coated with clay, and gently scrubbed and massaged. Another popular treatment, the aromatherapy massage, is intended to fight tension and its consequences and is also geared to rid the body of cellulite. Essential oils from flowers and herbs are blended and applied to points of the body in varying combinations. As many as 25 oils can be combined for particular trouble spots. A dry brush body scrub sloughs off old skin.

Guests soon learn to relax as they receive total care. A toothbrush and personal things are all you need to bring; sweat suits, robes, shorts, and T-shirts are provided. As you go on to another activity, a fresh set of clothes is supplied. The staff has raised mothering to a fine art, and its members do seem to care. With a ratio of four accredited staff members to each guest, little is left to chance.

The first step is your personal fitness evaluation. Your vital statistics and the results of a battery of tests to determine flexibility, cardiovascular capability, and upper and lower body strength are fed into a computer; your personal diet and exercise regimen will be based on the printout. Meals total between 1,200 and 1,400 calories per day on the maintenance diet, though you may opt for the cleansing or reduction programs.

The day begins with a prebreakfast hike into the hills—long or short depending on your preference—followed by cooling down exercises, and workouts with a group in the swimming pool or in the gym with a personal trainer. Yoga, tai chi chuan, and aerobics are scheduled. Sparring in the "Boxercise" class builds finesse and stamina.

The peace of mind and well-being a guest achieves are contagious. With its freedom from stress, the experience takes on the aspect of joining a big, happy family. There are men-only, women-only, and coed weeks; the resort is for adults only.

Cal-a-Vie Health Resort
2249 Somerset Rd., Vista, CA 92084
Tel. 619/945-2055

Administration	Founder/owners William F. and Marlene Power
Season	Year-round except mid-Dec.–Jan. 2.
Accommodations	24 private villas with heat, air conditioning, French provincial furnishings, beam ceilings, stone fireplaces, flowered chintzes, carved wooden armoires.
Rates	$3,950 per person per week, all-inclusive, includes service charge but not room tax; $1,000 in advance. Credit cards: MC, V.

Meal Plans 3 meals served to order daily, based on suggested calorie intake. Lunch can include a seafood salad, whole wheat pizza with *chèvre* cheese, sautéed tofu, and lentils. Dinner entrees can include sautéed free-range chicken with rosemary and roasted garlic, a pilaf of lentils and brown rice, and grilled swordfish. Fresh herbs from the garden; lemon and grapefruit juice enhance flavors without salt; breads, sorbets, and desserts are made from scratch. Special diets accommodated.

Services and Facilities **Exercise Equipment:** 2 StarTrak treadmills, 2 StairMaster 4000, 2 Windracer bikes, 5 Bodymaster units, step aerobics, free weights. **Services:** Massage (Swedish, shiatsu, aromatherapy), thalassotherapy, hydrotherapy, water exercise class, Boxercise, dry brush body scrub, reflexology, pedicure, manicure; facial, hair and skin care. **Swimming Facilities:** Heated outdoor pool. **Spa Facilities:** Indoor sauna and steam room; recessed Roman whirlpool. **Recreation Facilities:** Tennis court, volleyball; golf, horseback riding nearby. **Evening Programs:** Lectures on current topics, fitness, and nutrition; cooking demonstrations; movies.

In the Area Morning hiking; San Diego museums, theaters, and waterfront; Sea World; herb farm; Mount Palomar Observatory.

Getting Here *From San Diego.* By car, Rte. 163 to I-15 to Vista (1 hr). Free pickup on Sunday to and from San Diego International Airport. Limousine, taxi, rental car available.

Special Notes No smoking on the property except in designated areas.

The Claremont Resort

Luxury pampering
Non-program resort facilities

California **Oakland** The San Francisco Bay area's premier urban getaway traces its origins to a romantic builder's 1915 Victorian castle. The white-turreted hotel presides over 22 acres of landscaped grounds in the hills of Oakland and Berkeley. Fitness programs, a spa, and a restaurant offering a low-calorie menu were added in the resort's major face-lift in 1989.

The spa has 32 massage therapists who do deep-tissue sports massage, shiatsu, and aromatherapy, and there's also a personal trainer on staff to help restyle both your tennis game and your physique. The spa programs include aerobics classes, weight training, and biofeedback. A multipurpose aerobics gym, fully equipped weights room, outdoor exercise and lap pools, and 10 day/night tennis courts are open to all guests.

Therapy treatments and massage are major features here. In the hydrotherapy area are rooms with specialized equipment for underwater massage, herbal wraps, and loofah body scrubs. Herbal and floral essences are used in baths and aromatherapy massage to detoxify the body. Separate locker rooms for men and women are equipped with steam room, sauna, and whirlpool; workout clothing is provided daily.

Weekend packages, focus weeks, and local membership privileges are offered; guests may undertake a total spa program or use some of the facilities as desired. Downtown San Francisco is just a 20 minute ride on the BART train.

The Claremont Resort
Ashby and Domingo Aves., Box 23363, Oakland, CA 94623
Tel. 510/843-3000 or 800/551-7266, Fax 510/843-6239

Administration	General Manager, Leonard Fisher; spa director, Cindy Rudin
Season	Year-round.
Accommodations	239 spacious rooms with oversize beds (some are four-posters) and sitting areas; public rooms for art displays and social and business functions.
Rates	1- to 4-day spa packages with meals $372–$1,419; without meals $305–$1,150; deluxe weekend package for two $1,825; rooms $149–$189 single, $169–$209 double, junior suites $245. One night payable in advance or credit card guarantee. Credit cards: AE, D, DC, MC, V.
Meal Plans	Cross-over cuisine served in the hotel's Pavilion Room and poolside cafe, is calorie-controlled, low in cholesterol and sodium. Specialties have included mesquite-grilled swordfish with papaya chutney, grilled and steamed vegetables, grilled marinated prawns on linguini.
Services and Facilities	**Exercise Equipment:** 3 computerized Lifecycles, 2 Schwinn Air-Dyne bikes, Turbobike, 2 Concept II rowers, 2 Challenger treadmills, Bioclimber, Climbax stairclimber, 22-unit Nautilus circuit, dumbbells (3–50 lb); **Services:** Swedish, sports, and underwater massage, shiatsu, acupressure, aromatherapy, thalassotherapy, herbal wrap, loofah body scrub, facials; classes in aerobics, yoga, tai chi chuan, aquacise, body sculpting, stretching; biofeedback; salon for hair, nail, skin care; nutrition counseling; tennis and swimming lessons. **Swimming Facilities:** Olympic-size outdoor pool, lap pool. **Recreation Facilities:** Water volleyball, 10 tennis courts; golf, horseback riding nearby; hiking, parcourse.
In the Area	San Francisco; Bay Area museums, beaches, water sports. Wine country tours. Oakland's Jack London Square (entertainment, shopping, arts).
Getting Here	*From San Francisco.* By Bay Area Rapid Transit, Rockridge Station (20 min). By car, Bay Bridge to Rte. 24, Claremont Ave. exit (30 min). Taxi, rental car available.
Special Notes	Specially equipped rooms, ramps, and elevators provide complete access to the spa for the disabled. Tennis and swimming clinics for children. No smoking in the spa; smoking permitted in some guest rooms and public areas. Spa hours: Monday–Saturday 8:30 AM–8:30 PM, Sunday 8:30 AM–6:30 PM.

Dr. Wilkinson's Hot Springs

Taking the waters
Stress control

California *Calistoga*	Mud, mineral water, and massage, as offered in Dr. Wilkinson's Hot Springs resort, are the reasons for visiting this historic spa town at the northern end of the Napa Valley. Whether you suffer from arthritis or simply want to relax in the dark warmth of a mud bath, the therapy is reasonably priced.

Half a dozen downtown hotels advertise mud baths and mineral-spring water swimming pools. Their unpretentiousness makes them the antithesis of Southern California's most celebrated spas; neither The Golden Door nor La Costa can offer the combination of treatments found here. The baths attract a young group that includes many European visitors. Compared with bathing in the mud at Ischia or Terme di Saturnia in Italy, Calistoga is a bargain.

What does mud bathing accomplish? The heat and the weight relax muscles and increase circulation. Joints loosen and the nervous system slows down. Between layers of mud and hot mineral water, you feel suspended and soothed. A healthy sweat follows your initial immersion in the primal ooze, and the body detoxifies as pores open and the skin softens.

In the mid-1940s, a chiropractor, Dr. John Wilkinson, developed mud-bath treatments for arthritis and bursitis; the regimen gained popularity in the '70s as interest in holistic health blossomed. Dr. Wilkinson's building still looks like an ordinary motel, but under the management of Wilkinson's son Mark, the services and treatments maintain a standard of excellence. Appointments must be made well in advance during summer months because the baths are open to the public.

Like most places in town, there are separate facilities for men and women (coed baths are available at the Golden Haven, 1713 Lake St.). After you disrobe and drape yourself with a towel, an attendant leads the way to a large, skylighted room that smells of sulfur. Two tiled tubs, each about four feet high, bubble with mud in one corner; showers and soaking tubs complete the scene. Sinking into the mud is easier than it looks, and the attendant gently pats it around your chin. A board under your neck keeps your head up.

Stuck in the mud, you commune with nature for about 12 minutes. The 105-degree mix of volcanic ash, peat, and mineral water works its magic soon enough (people with heart conditions or high blood pressure are advised to stay immersed only a few minutes). After a shower and cooling bath, you are swaddled in sheets and instructed to rest. A whirlpool or steam bath is suggested before your massage.

The final touch is a cool swim in the outdoor pool, filled with the same mineral water sold nationwide for drinking. Use of the swimming pool, large indoor whirlpool, and outdoor hot tub is restricted to motel guests. Health precautions at the baths are meticulous. The mud is drained nightly and sanitized with boiling water.

The bath routine can be varied, if you wish, with a treatment imported from Japan. Available only at the International Spa, 1300 Washington Street, it's a soak in a tub filled with cedar fibers (read "sawdust") and plant enzymes that give off natural heat as they ferment. The soothing process takes about 20 minutes and is followed by a similar cooling process.

Dr. Wilkinson's Hot Springs
1507 Lincoln Ave., Calistoga, CA 94515
Tel. 707/942–4102

Administration Manager, Mark Wilkinson

Season Year-round.

Accommodations 43 modern motel rooms facing a garden courtyard. Private bungalows with complete kitchens. Contemporary and Victorian furnishings, king- or queen-size beds, private baths. TV, telephone, air-conditioning, coffee maker, mini-refrigerator, bottled mineral water.

Rates $49–$84 single, $64–$94 for 2 persons. Larger rooms for up to 4 persons. Mid-week overnight "Stress Stopper" package with treatments $163 single, $145 for 2. Advance payment $100. Credit cards: AE, D, MC, V.

Services and **Services:** Massage (Swedish, Esalen, shiatsu, acupressure,
Facilities deep tissue), blanket wraps, facials. **Swimming Facilities:** Outdoor pool. **Spa Facilities:** Private tubs for mud and mineral water baths, whirlpools (indoors and out). **Recreation Facilities:** Hiking; nearby tennis courts, racquetball courts, golf course.

In the Area Yountville 1870 (historic town); the Sharpsteen Museum (local history), Sam Brannan Cottage (Victoriana), Robert Louis Stevenson House at the Silverado Mine, geysers, vineyards.

Getting Here *From San Francisco.* By car, Rte. 101 to Novato, Rtes. 37, 121 to Napa, Rte. 29 to Calistoga (1½ hr). Taxi, rental car available.

Special Notes Limited access for disabled. No smoking in spa or pool areas.

Esalen Institute

Life enhancement

California The "human potential" movement nurtured in these clifftop
Big Sur gardens and hot springs is alive and well after more than 25 years. Once considered a hippie haven, the Esalen Institute became an American utopia for seekers of ancient wisdom and new truths. Those gave birth to the Esalen style of sensuous massage and turned encounter therapy into an art form.

Secluded above the rocky surf of the Pacific Ocean, this idyllic retreat is surprisingly accessible. Seminars and workshops on holistic health, esoteric religions, and such emerging sciences as Gestalt therapy, psychosynthesis, shamanic healing, and neurolinguistics are offered throughout the year.

Many who come here simply want to unwind, and accommodations are available on a daily basis when rooms are not filled by program participants. Overnight guests can book a massage, hike in the Ventana wilderness, and soak in natural rock pools filled by hot mineral springs.

The Esalen catalogue details various ways to experience learning and personal growth here. Introductory weekends, five-day workshops, work-study programs, and special events open to the public are listed. The institute also offers a hiking trip to Tassajara Zen Monastery.

Esalen Institute
Big Sur, CA 93920
Tel. 408/667–3000 (408/667–3005 for reservations)
Fax 408/667–2724

Administration Chairman, Michael Murphy; president, Steven Donovan; general manager, Brian Lyke

Season   Year-round.

Accommodations   107 beds in rustic lodges; most rooms for 2, some with bunk beds. Comfortably casual furnishings with ocean views and the sound of the surf. No TV, radio, telephone, air-conditioning. Guests share rooms and baths.

Rates   Weekend workshops $350, 5-day seminar fee with lodging $675. Daily rate with meals $95–$115; bunk beds $75–$80. $100 deposit for weekends, $200–$300 for longer programs. Credit cards: AE, MC, V.

Meal Plans   3 meals daily, served buffet style; meat, fish, and poultry, salads and fresh vegetables grown on the property served at lunch and dinner, with a vegetarian entree such as spinach lasagna.

Services and Facilities   **Services:** Massage (Esalen, Heller, Feldenkrais, deep-tissue), rolfing, cranial-sacrial work; special studies. **Swimming Facilities:** Heated outdoor pool. **Recreation Facilities:** Hiking, tai chi chuan, morning exercise class, hot mineral baths. **Evening Programs:** Lectures, concerts.

In the Area   Wilderness experiences (5 days or more); Hearst Castle at San Simeon, Mission of San Antonio de Padua (1771), Tassajara Zen Monastery in Los Padres National Forest (May 1–Labor Day), Big Sur State Park.

Getting Here   *From San Francisco.* By bus, Greyhound via Monterey connecting with Esalen van (3 hr). By car, Rte. 101 south to Monterey, Rte. 156, Coast Rte. 1 (2½ hr). Limousine service Fri. and Sun. from Monterey airport or bus station ($25).

Special Notes   Limited access for the disabled. Special activities and dining plan for children; limited child-care facilities. Nonsmoking cabins, nonsmoking areas in dining room.

The Golden Door

Life enhancement
Luxury pampering
Nutrition and diet
Spiritual awareness

California   The doyen of fitness resorts in Southern California, the Golden
Escondido   Door opened in 1959 a mile from its present location, which now encompasses 177 acres of canyon and orchard. Beyond the ornate brass door lies an enchanted realm of oriental gardens and inns. Guests in standard issue sweat suits and *yukata* robes step peacefully to aerobics classes or massage appointments. The setting and the incredibly thoughtful staff create an air of calm order. The experience is restorative and regenerative.

The process of transforming yourself from sloth to sylph begins on your arrival Sunday afternoon with an interview about your fitness level, diet, and preferences. Do you prefer tennis, instruction in lap-swimming techniques, or a cooking class? A massage with a therapist, who gets to know every muscle in your body, is scheduled every day at the same time.

On the orientation tour for first-time guests, one can't help but be impressed by the attention to detail and devotion to comfort that have been incorporated into the spa's impressive design, a cross between a first-class resort and a Japanese country inn. The four spacious gyms have sliding glass walls that open to fresh air and the beauty of the lush gardens. A graceful bath-house, tiled and topped with gray oriental carving, contains a modern sauna, steam room, Swiss shower, whirlpool, and body wrap.

Each day begins at 6 AM with a brisk mountain hike led by staff members who, Sherpa-like, supply flasks of cool water and fruit to sustain you until you are served breakfast. On the beautifully laid wooden tray is a paper fan with your schedule for the day. All decisions have been made for you, so it is simpler to go with the flow. If you miss an appointment, a kimono-clad staffer will come searching for you.

Camaraderie grows as new friends discuss their dance routines with a diminutive Japanese choreographer and do Dynamic Dumbbells together with a weight lifter. Personal trainers are assigned to help you improve both form and content in the workouts so you can take home an exercise plan tailored to fit your needs. Classes are designed for three fitness levels.

The 50-minute exercise periods fill most of the morning; afternoons are for pampering and personal pursuits. You can have lunch by the pool, in the dining room, or in the privacy of your room. Massages can be alfresco or in your room, with a choice of shiatsu, traditional Swedish, deep-tissue, or aromatherapy. Daily beauty treatments are included in the program cost.

There might be a final session of yoga in the garden, or aquaerobics in the pool. A social hour with nonalcoholic cocktails precedes dinner, and interesting talks are scheduled in the evening.

For fit guests who return whenever they need to recharge, there is now an Inner Door program. It is an advanced course for a small group in problem solving, meditation, and body movement. For four days there are two-hour sessions for exploration of spiritual and inner forces, even tai chi chuan, designed for inner serenity.

Most guests are middle-aged and success oriented; about half are in their 30s and 40s. Eight weeks are reserved for men only, five for couples; the rest of the time is for women only.

The Golden Door
Deer Springs Rd.,
Box 463077, Escondido, CA 92046
Tel. 619/744–6677
Fax 619/471–2393

Administration Manager, Rachel Caldwell; program director, Judy Bird

Season Year-round except Christmas week.

Accommodations Single rooms for 36 guests in buildings patterned after old Japanese honjin inns. 1-story ocher stucco buildings have 2 to 14 bed-sitting rooms overlooking private gardens. Decorated with muted colors and Japanese wood-block prints. Parquet floors with carpets, sliding shoji screens and jalousie windows. Private baths stocked with Golden Door skin-care products. Guest units cluster on courtyards, a short walk from the main building. One private cottage.

Rates $3,950 weekly. $1,000 with reservation, balance due before arrival. No credit cards. Gratuities included; add tax.

Meal Plans Three meals plus snacks served daily. 1,000 calories per day calculated for maximum energy with weight loss, 1,200 for maintenance. Low-cholesterol meals, rich in fiber and whole grains, low in salt, sugar, and fat, served with oriental flair. Lunch can include miso soup, stir-fry vegetables with tofu, or fresh Pacific shrimp sautéed with orange and ginger. Dinner entrees include boneless breast of chicken with wild mushrooms; whole wheat crepes filled with a mixture of spinach, mushrooms, and ricotta cheese; or cabbage rolls stuffed with bulgur pilaf and vegetables. Options: decaffeinated coffee, herbal tea; ulcer diet, diabetic diet, hypoglycemic diet, vegetarian or lacto-ovo vegetarian diet. Mid-morning juice or broth, veggie snacks, and nonalcoholic cocktails served.

Services and Facilities **Exercise Equipment:** 12 Hoggan Camstar weight training units, 6 Trotter treadmills, 3 Cardioaerobikes, 2 StairMasters, PTS/Turbo bike, rowing machine, free weights. **Services:** Massage (Swedish, Trager, shiatsu, and others), aromatherapy, herbal wrap, body scrub, daily skin care, facials, manicure, pedicure, hair styling. Instruction in tai chi chuan, yoga, swimming, circuit training; fitness evaluations and submaximal stress test. **Swimming Facilities:** 2 outdoor pools. **Recreation Facilities:** 2 tennis courts, hiking, classes in flower arranging, crafts, gardening. **Evening Programs:** Lectures on nutrition, stress management, sports medicine, other health-related topics; movies.

In the Area Sea World, San Diego Safari Park, La Jolla.

Getting Here *From San Diego.* By car, Hwy. 163 to I-15, north to Deer Springs Rd. exit (40 min). Free pickup to and from San Diego Airport.

Special Notes Ramps and one-story structures make the entire complex accessible to the disabled. No smoking in public areas. Remember to bring appropriate shoes for hiking, walking, sports.

Green Gulch Farm Zen Center

Spiritual awareness

California Standing amid pines and open fields that stretch to the Pacific
Sausalito only 25 minutes from San Francisco, the wooden guest house at Green Gulch Farm seems far removed from the rest of the world. A peaceful retreat for study and work, the center is suffused with the spirit of Zen.

Buddhist tradition is experienced here in many ways. You can join classes to study Zen texts on basic teachings and the bodhisattva spirit, practice playing the *shakuhachi* (Japanese bamboo flute), or partake of an ancient meditative tea ceremony. Workshops offer instruction in raku tea-bowl making (using clay dug on the farm), flower arranging, and organic gardening.

Guests are welcome to come and go as they please, joining in communal life and work on the organic farm or quietly meditating on long walks through the nearby woods and on Muir beach. Miles of hiking trails surround the 200-acre Green Gulch, leading to Mount Tamalpais and Mill Valley.

As you enter the Lindisfarne Guest House, you'll gain an immediate sense of ageless serenity. Constructed in the Japanese temple style of handmade woodcraft, it has 12 rooms surrounding an atrium that rises to a traditional sloped roof.

A combination of vacation with partial participation in community work and practice is available from Sunday through Thursday nights. The morning schedule includes meditation, work, classes and group discussions; afternoons and evenings are free. Called a Practice Retreat, this program involves a minimum stay of three nights and earns you a modest reduction on the daily rate, plus meals.

Newcomers are invited to a "sitting" that introduces the forms, spirit, and detail of the Soto Zen way. After instruction in *zazen* and *kinhin* (sitting and walking meditation), you'll join members of the community in discussion followed by a silent period before lunch. Looking inward, you'll begin to understand the bodhisattva spirit of kindness and support.

Green Gulch Farm Zen Center
Star Route, Sausalito, CA 94965
Tel. 415/383–3134

Administration	Spiritual leader, Abbot Tenshin Anderson; director, Nancy Schrader
Season	Year-round.
Accommodations	12 rooms with shared baths, 1 suite. Simple wooden furniture, 2 beds in each room. No air-conditioning; central heat. Each room has outside patio or balcony.
Rates	$35–$50 per person in small room, $50–$65 daily double occupancy. $50–$65 daily single in large room, $65–$80 for 2 persons. Meals $5 each. Practice Retreat includes meals, $30 per day single, $50 double occupancy (3-night minimum). Beginner's "sitting" $15, includes lunch; no lodging. Weekend workshop: $100 tuition includes all meals, $170 for shared accommodations, $200 for single room; add tax. Deposit: 1 night, plus $10 per person for each additional night. No credit cards.
Meal Plans	3 vegetarian meals daily, served buffet style, include eggs and dairy products. Organically grown vegetables from the farm are steamed, served with brown rice, miso soup.
Services and Facilities	**Services:** Instruction in Japanese arts, Zen, gardening, herbs. **Swimming Facilities:** Ocean beach, outdoor pool. **Evening Programs:** Lectures on Japanese arts in conjunction with scheduled workshops.
In the Area	Muir Woods, Napa Valley, Marin County Civic Center (Frank Lloyd Wright architecture, art galleries, theater), Sausalito harbor (restaurants, boutiques).
Getting Here	*From San Francisco.* By car, Hwy. 101 to turnoff for Mill Valley, Rte. 1 (Shoreline Hwy.) toward Muir Beach (25 min). By ferry, frequent bay crossings from the Embarcadero to Sausalito, taxi.
Special Notes	Scheduled program for workshops/retreats varies weekly.

Heartwood Institute

Life enhancement
Spiritual awareness

California
Garberville

Set on 240 acres in the mountains on California's North Coast, this rustic complex is a vocational school for practitioners in the healing arts that also welcomes weekend visitors and participants in wellness retreats. The retreat programs are designed for healthy people seeking to become even more healthy. A full schedule of classes, exercise, and bodywork is offered during retreats by experts in Hatha Iyengar yoga, TM, and nutrition.

The wilderness setting is perfect for walks in the woods and mountain biking. In the community center, a picturesque log lodge, are eight private treatment rooms, an outdoor hot tub, wood-fired sauna, and bedrooms. Meals are taken in the cozy dining room or on a spacious deck in nice weather.

Heartwood Institute
220 Harmony Lane, Garberville, CA 95440
Tel. 707/923–2021; Fax 707/923–4906

Administration Co-owners/managers, Robert Fasic, Roy Grieshaber; retreat coordinator, Susie Yong

Season Year-round.

Accommodations 15 rooms in 3-story dormitory, 36 campsites. Simple amenities include sheets, towels, comforters on beds, and shared bathrooms. No air-conditioning or maid service.

Rates Rooms $50–$60; campsite $30. Vitality fasting week, $695–$745 room, $605 campsite. Advance payment $50. Credit cards: MC, V.

Meal Plans 3 meals daily, served buffet style. All meals are primarily vegetarian: organic vegetables, grains, fruits, and nuts are supplemented with dairy products and eggs. Fish is served once a week. There is a snack kitchen for personal use in the community center. Special diets are accommodated.

Services and Facilities **Services:** Yoga classes daily, Swedish/Esalen massage, Polarity Therapy, hypnotherapy, deep-tissue massage, shiatsu, acupressure, breathwork, Jin Shin Jytsu, Transformational Therapy, nutritional counseling. **Swimming Facilities:** Outdoor heated swimming pool. **Evening Programs:** Lectures, dances.

In the Area Sinkyone Wilderness State Preserve, Humboldt Redwoods forest, Eureka and Arcata (Victorian architecture, museums, galleries).

Getting Here *From San Francisco.* By car, Hwy. 101 north to first Garberville exit (3 hr). By bus, Greyhound to Garberville (6 hr). By plane, American and United Airlines to Eureka/Arcata Airport. Pickup arranged at airport or bus station (fee). Car rental, taxi available.

Special Notes Wellness retreat program is personalized by staff counselor.

La Costa Resort & Spa

Luxury pampering
Life enhancement
Weight management
Nutrition and diet

California
Carlsbad

A megaresort for the fun and fitness crowd, La Costa Resort & Spa has a serious program for change of lifestyle. Nevertheless, the country club ambience is more suited to pampering than to preventive medicine.

When the 1,000-acre complex was renovated several years ago, the idea was to be able to offer something for every taste. The result was overcrowding and lack of privacy in the spa building, which was not expanded. That the attractive dining room for dieters can be reached only by a challenge course through Mexican, Chinese, and French restaurants and several bars seems further evidence of poor planning.

The Life Fitness Center's one-week package is designed to educate and motivate guests to adopt healthy habits. Each day begins with a brisk walk around the golf course. Power walking has now become the preferred exercise, for the fit and the not so fit, because it has none of the stress associated with running and jogging. Mornings are devoted to exercise at the gym, or therapy and massage, followed by workshops and lectures. Optional periods allow opportunities for golf, tennis, or personal counseling.

The lifestyle center across from the spa building has its own demonstration kitchen and discussion area. The casual surroundings feel more like a home than a classroom. A nutritionist and the spa's medical director teach how to cook and to eat better. Everyone learns to make omelets without egg yolk.

Medical and physical evaluations are included in the program. An Aeriel computerized exerciser tests your strength, flexibility, and pulmonary function. Nutritional and body composition analysis determine your diet and measure the percentages of fat and muscle in your body. A take-home program, provided at the end of the week, facilitates follow-up.

Camaraderie exists within the small group of Life Fitness program participants, but most of the time you're surrounded by golf and tennis buffs or the fit-looking local club members. It's wise to schedule early appointments at the spa, especially when a large group is meeting at the convention center across the way.

La Costa can be enjoyed simply as a luxury getaway without adhering to a program. Packages are available for two to seven nights, with a choice of eating in the spa or in the other dining rooms. Gourmets may find their downfall in the sinfully delicious desserts in the Champagne Room. Lunch can be served poolside on a terrace near your room if you would rather avoid the gamut of temptations.

Another option—for women only—is the noon-to-noon makeover, a concentrated course in beauty and fitness. Golf and tennis packages are always available, and they can be combined with a fitness program. Anyone can drop in for an aerobics class without prior registration.

The true luxury of La Costa consists of the personal attention guests receive, even though the place is crowded. Locker-room attendants remember your name and slipper size and hand out fresh towels and robes without being asked; they deserve handsome tips. The separate facilities for men and women add to the clublike atmosphere. Included are a eucalyptus-scented inhalation room, steam room, sauna, Swiss multihead showers, hot and cold plunge pools, and an outdoor Jacuzzi. The gym and salon are coed.

Conceived on a grand scale, with two golf courses, a tennis center, waterfalls, and rambling Spanish-style lodges, La Costa dotes on you while encouraging healthy habits. The new owner, a Japanese conglomerate, has assured continuation of the resort's fame as a fitness center.

La Costa Resort & Spa
Costa del Mar Rd., Carlsbad, CA 92009
Tel. 619/438–9111 or 800/854–5000
(Life Fitness Center 800/426–5483)
Fax 619/438–3758

Administration General manager, Darryll Shaeffer

Season Year-round.

Accommodations 482 deluxe rooms and suites in Spanish-style buildings and a motellike spa complex. Newer rooms overlook the golf course. Fine furnishings. Fitness and spa program guests stay in bedsitting rooms by the pool, unless they request otherwise. Six private residences.

Rates 2-night spa package $600 single, $750 for 2 persons; 7-night Life Fitness program $3,640–$3,990 single, $5,460–$5,810 double; room and meals alone, $250–$325 double per night; 10% tax in addition. Spa and salon service charges included. One night payable on booking. Credit cards: AE, D, DC, MC, V.

Meal Plans You select from daily menus of 600, 800, 1,000, or 1,200 calories. Breakfast options include fruit, muffins, an egg-white omelet with salsa, and an energy mix of grains, apple butter, and raisins. For lunch, cheese blintzes, papaya stuffed with crab, and beef Stroganoff. Chicken stuffed with foie gras, fettucini primavera, salmon fillet with horseradish sauce, and veal with artichoke sauce are dinner entrees, with fresh fruit, sherbet, or custard for dessert; coffee (regular or decaffeinated), tea (herbal or regular), nonfat milk, and Swiss Valser water. Special diets accommodated.

Services and Facilities **Exercise Equipment:** Eagle, Nautilus, and Universal weights units, Lifecycles, computerized treadmills, aerobic trainer, rowing machines, free weights, rebounders. **Services:** Massage (Swedish, shiatsu, sports, aromatherapy, reflexology), Orthion, Myopulse, herbal wraps, loofah body scrub, spot toning, facials. Salon for hair, nail, and skin care. Coed exercise classes $10 (aerobics, rebounder, yoga). Nutrition counseling, medical and fitness evaluations. Personal trainer for exercise, swimming, golf, and tennis. **Swimming Facilities:** 5 outdoor pools. **Recreation Facilities:** 23 tennis courts (8 lighted), 2 18-hole golf courses, driving range, horseback riding. Bike rental. **Evening Programs:** Lectures on health and fitness, stress management; movies and resort cabaret. Cooking demonstration.

In the Area Bus or limousine trips to Sea World, San Diego Zoo, Disney-land; Coronado beaches, San Diego museums and Horton Plaza shops, Laguna Nigel (The Ritz Carlton); Del Mar Racetrack.

Getting Here *From San Diego.* By car, I–5 to Carlsbad, La Costa Ave. exit (40 min). By train, Amtrak to Oceanside (30 min). Limousine, taxi, rental car available.

Special Notes Access available for the disabled. Tennis and golf clinics and summer day-camp programs for children. No smoking in the spa building or the dining room. Spa hours: daily 7 AM–8 PM; minimum age 18.

Marriott's Desert Springs Resort

Luxury pampering

California
Palm Desert
The Desert Springs Resort, the elaborate flagship resort created in the desert by the Marriott Corporation, literally floats you away. Gondolas glide from the main lobby to the health spa, an oasis surrounded by lagoons and a golf course.

Water is involved in the treatments and services offered, from hydrotherapy pools to hot and cold plunges, a Turkish steam room, and a vigorous Aquacize Workout.

Separate facilities for men and women provide privacy while guests pursue a personal regimen. Entrusted to a trainer, guests have a choice of fitness consultations and beauty treatments, including underwater massage, acupressure, and facials. Or you can pay the daily admission of $20, which includes workout clothing and robe. The fee is waived when you book any one-day package that includes lunch, treatments, and two exercise classes.

Guests at this airy 325-acre retreat find its elegance and desert views relaxing. Escape the midday sun at the juice bar or have your hair styled at the José Eber salon. Try the dry flotation unit, a space-age capsule with its own environment appropriately named Superspace Relaxer.

Skin-care products are formulated with natural ingredients that include lavender, chamomile, vitamins, collagen, seaweed, and proteins. Applied by shiatsu acupressure technique, the ointments, gels, and sprays are intended to help prevent sun damage and aging. Experiment with a "Bindi" herbal body scrub. Treatments can be booked as part of a half-day pampering package or on a separate basis.

Natural light floods the indoor gym and aerobics studios, where yoga, stretching, and rigorous calisthenics are scheduled throughout the day. The weights training room nearby allows you to work out with a view. Exercise classes, scheduled from 8 AM to 4:30 PM, include step aerobics and body sculpting.

Although it was designed for conferences, the resort caters to vacationers as well. The self-contained spa has saunas, steam rooms, and an Olympic-size lap pool. Private training and fitness consultations are available. A morning walk or jog around the manicured lawns in the hot, dry climate is a great way to begin a day of work or play. Morning hikes into the desert are frequent; sign up in advance for the Joshua Monument trip.

Marriott's Desert Springs Resort
74855 Country Club Dr., Palm Desert, CA 92260
Tel. 619/341–1856, 800/255–0848, or 800/228–9290
Telex 6712074, Fax 619/341–1872

Administration Manager, Dave Ralston; spa directors, John Defons and Kimberly Matheson

Season Year-round.

Accommodations 892 rooms and executive suites, with oversize beds, private baths. Refrigerator mini-bar, contemporary Southwestern furnishings, balcony, and TV with feature movies.

Rates $215–$359 Jan.–May. Two-night Romance package includes a 30-min massage for $409–$506 double; the 7-night package with daily massage, $1,251–$1,591. One night payable in advance. Credit cards: AE, DC, MC, V.

Meal Plans Three spa meals included in package rates. Lunch can be a salad or cold poached salmon. Main dining room dinner entrees include grilled loin of veal, broiled chicken, pasta primavera. Coffee, herbal tea, dairy products. Special diets on request.

Services and Facilities **Exercise Equipment:** 11-station Bodymaster weight training gym, 4 StairMasters, 6 Lifecycles, 4 Precor treadmills, free weights. **Services:** Massage (Swedish, shiatsu, sports, aromatherapy), full-body masks (aloe, algae, mud), facials, herbal wraps, loofah body scrub, Bindi, reflexology. Nutrition counseling, computerized fitness and body-composition analysis. Beauty salon. **Swimming Facilities:** Outdoor pool. **Recreation Facilities:** 2 18-hole golf courses, 18-hole putting course, 16 tennis courts, croquet, water volleyball. Bike rental, horseback riding, skiing. **Evening Programs:** Resort entertainment.

In the Area Guided mountain hiking, sightseeing tours; aerial tramway to Mt. San Jacinto, ballooning, Desert Fashion Plaza (shopping), Bob Hope Cultural Center, Palm Springs Desert Museum (art), Living Desert Reserve (nature studies), Polo Club.

Getting Here *From Los Angeles.* By bus, Greyhound (4 hr). By car, I–10 to Hwy. 111 (2½ hr). By train, Amtrak to Indio (2 hr). Limousine, taxi, rental car available.

Special Notes Limited access for the disabled. Supervised games, movies, tennis lessons for children. No smoking in the spa; nonsmoking areas in restaurants.

Murrieta Hot Springs Resort

Taking the waters
Holistic health
Vibrant maturity

California
Murrieta A spa in the Old World style, the Murrieta Hot Springs Resort is a place to soak your body in a vat of mud, get a great massage, and enjoy vegetarian meals. The current ownership has given the rooms a face-lift and added a second dining room that features chicken, fish, and wines from local vineyards. The atmosphere remains pleasantly laid-back.

New fitness programs have come with the renovations; low-impact aerobics, exercise classes in the water, weights, and a holistic health course are now offered. A fully equipped fitness center allows you to exercise with personal trainers.

Stretching across 47 acres of landscaped grounds, the tranquil resort was once roamed by the Temecula Indians, more recently by the Teamster Union executives who had the mission-style lodges built for their retreats. Hot springs from the Elsinor fault provide the mineral water of varying temperatures that fills the Olympic-size swimming pool and two smaller baths.

Mud baths, body work, and skin care using natural products come with several spa packages and can be ordered à la carte. The arthritis treatments attract large numbers of seniors, while many guests simply like to mellow out in the cleansing mud, a mineral-rich mixture of fine Betonite clay, sea kelp, and peat moss. The bathhouse, a 1920s-style Spanish villa with mosaics and tiled tubs, has private rooms for soaking with essential oils and Bach flower mixes, Finnish saunas for men and women, and a full range of massage.

This is not a luxury facility, as the prices reflect. A 50-minute treatment with mud bath, herbal wrap, and mineral-water soak costs $35. All services are available à la carte.

A full schedule of aerobics classes, tennis, and workshops in body awareness and makeup design allow you to be as busy as you choose. A resident physiotherapist is available for consultation, and a staff nutritionist will recommend a regimen of vegetables, fruit, tofu, sprouts, and grains for those seeking to shed some weight.

Murrieta Hot Springs Resort
39405 Murrieta Hot Springs Rd., Murrieta, CA 92362
Tel. 714/677-7451 or 800/458-4393

Administration	General manager, Robert Jacquet; spa manager, Lynne Vertrees; fitness director, Earl Maynard
Season	Year-round.
Accommodations	242 guest rooms in private cottages and terraced stone lodges furnished with old oak dressers and new oversize beds. New suites with white wicker furniture, brass fixtures, and 2 queen-size beds. All with private bath, TV, and telephone. Air-conditioning by request.
Rates	$60–$115 a day, single or double. 3-day/2-night midweek spa sampler $177 single, $157 per person double occupancy. Full-week fitness program with all meals, treatments, and classes $975 single, $875 double. One-day admission $10. Taxes additional. One night payable in advance, 25% for packages. Credit cards: AE, MC, V. Add gratuities, taxes.
Meal Plans	Vegetarian buffet, fish, or chicken dishes. Entrees include tofu-cauliflower curry, pasta, vegetarian enchiladas, bean burritos, Mexican-style salad. Mesquite-grilled fish and barbecue chicken served in a separate dining room. Coffee, tea, wine; fresh dairy products and cereals at breakfast.
Services and Facilities	**Exercise Equipment:** 11-unit Fisher weight training gym, 3 Aerosteps, 2 Schwinn Air-Dyne bikes, 3 Windracer bikes, Bodyguard bike, StarTrac treadmill, rowing machine, dumbbells and barbells (5–85 lbs.) with 6 benches, squat machine. **Services:** Massage (Swedish, polarity, lymph drainage), herbal wrap, mud bath, loofah body scrub, back scrub, foot care, fa-

cial. Self-awareness counseling. Beauty salon. **Swimming Facilities:** Outdoor pool. **Spa Facilities:** Outdoor pools, indoor Roman-style pools, and private baths, some with mud mixture. **Recreation Facilities:** 14 tennis courts (4 lighted), badminton, shuffleboard. Hiking, jogging trails. Golf at the nearby Rancho California Country Club's par-72 course. Horseback riding, lake fishing. **Evening Programs:** Workshops on holistic health, body polarity, nutrition; dinner-theater productions, concerts.

In the Area Temecula's old-town district, antiques shops, wine tours, ballooning.

Getting Here *From San Diego.* By bus, Greyhound to Temecula (90 min). By car, Hwy. 163 to I–15 past Temecula, Hot Springs Rd. exit (70 min).

Special Notes Limited access for the disabled. Children are welcome to bathe with parents and participate in some workshops. No smoking in public areas. Fitness Center open weekdays 6 AM–9 PM, Sat. 8 AM–6 PM, Sun. 9 AM–1 PM; $5 daily fee.

The Oaks at Ojai

Nutrition and diet
Weight management
Vibrant maturity

California
Ojai

At The Oaks at Ojai, fitness and weight-control programs are the main attractions for men and women who want to unwind or work out without fancy lodging or physical therapy. When you stick to the basics—up to 17 exercise classes and activities daily and a diet of fresh, natural foods that total only 1,000 calories—The Oaks helps you lose up to a pound a day safely.

The program operates on an all-inclusive American plan, and guests are welcome to stay a few days or weeks and take part in as many of the activities as they please. A number of special packages are available, including a spa-cooking week, and mother-daughter days.

Ojai is an art center and a favorite of the practitioners of several healing faiths. The Oaks is located on the main square of the town, and appointments can be made with psychics, astrologers, pyramid enthusiasts, members of the Theosophy movement, or the Krishnamurti Foundation. All are attracted by the natural beauty of a fertile valley near the Los Padres National Forest, little more than an hour's drive north of Los Angeles.

Built as a country inn in 1918, the dignified wood-and-stone structure gained a new lease on life in the 1970s when Sheila Cluff became its owner. A former professional ice skater and physical fitness instructor, Cluff drew together a team of exercise physiologists. A sister spa in Palm Springs, The Palms, offers a similar no-frills program.

Concerned more with teaching and motivating exercise habits than with pampering or bodywork (available at additional cost), the program includes workouts in the pool, body contouring, intense aerobics, and progressive stretches. There are morning hikes into the hills, brisk walks along country roads, and a stretch-and-relax class at the end of the day.

Most activities are held in the main lodge and garden. The complex includes saunas, an aerobics studio, a large swimming pool, and a cluster of guest bungalows. Classes, rated according to the guests' fitness level, last from 45 minutes to an hour. A nurse is on staff to help plan each person's schedule. Or you can work out on weight machines; facilities are open 24 hours.

The day begins with a challenging aerobic workout at 6 AM. Fruits, muffins, and vitamins are set out at the Winners Circle, a juice bar in the lodge. Lunch can be eaten by the pool or in the dining room. There is a midmorning broth break, and vegetable snacks are served in the afternoon. The program is aimed at burning calories, conditioning the heart and lungs, and toning the body. Guests here are diverse, ranging from young professionals to grandmothers; film industry folk, TV actresses, and housewives drop in to shape up or relax.

The Oaks at Ojai
122 E. Ojai Ave., Ojai, CA 93023
Tel. 805/646-5573 or 800/753-6257

Administration Owners, Don and Sheila Cluff; fitness director, Elizabeth Kinney

Season Year-round.

Accommodations 46 guest rooms in the main lodge and cottages, from small singles to a cottage for 3. Simply furnished with modern beds, all have private bath, color TV, telephone, air-conditioning.

Rates $130–$165 daily per person sharing small double lodge room with shower only; $185 in a cottage. Private rooms from $185 per day. One night payable in advance. Add 14% service charge, 6.25% taxes. Credit cards: MC, V.

Meal Plans 3 meals daily. Natural foods, no additives, salt, white flour, or sugar. Lunch can be soup, tuna salad with egg, mushrooms, and cheese, or vegetable crepes. Dinner entrees: vegetarian lasagna, baked chicken, broiled fish, or pasta salad.

Services and Facilities **Exercise Equipment:** 16-station Paramount weight training system, 2 Trotter treadmills, 2 StairMasters, 2 Lifecycles, hand and ankle weights, stretch bands. **Swimming Facilities:** Outdoor pool. **Recreation Facilities:** Hiking; tennis and golf nearby. **Services:** Massage, facials; salon for hair, skin, and nail care; computerized body analysis. **Evening Programs:** Talks on health and fitness.

In the Area Group hiking every morning; bicycle tours, boating and fishing at Lake Casitas, annual music and dance festivals; crafts boutiques; Bart's Corners book and sheet-music shop.

Getting Here *From Los Angeles.* By bus, Greyhound to Ventura (2 hr). By car, Hwy. 101 (Ventura Freeway) to Ventura, Hwy. 33 to Ojai, Hwy. 150 to center of town (80 min). Taxi, rental car available.

Special Notes No smoking in rooms or inside hotel. Gym open 24 hrs. Mother-daughter spa days in January.

The Palms

Nutrition and diet
Weight management
Vibrant maturity

California
Palm Springs

Finding an informal place in which to exercise and diet in the center of Palm Springs resort life is quite a feat. The Palms is a "come as you are" place, one with few frills, plenty of options, and no attendance requirements.

Activity centers on a large swimming pool, and additional classes are held indoors in a small aerobics studio and outdoors under the palms. With up to 16 activities offered daily, guests are encouraged to take part in as many or as few as they please. Special weeks feature high-powered speakers on health, nutrition, and fitness; a seminar on women in management; a 21-day course on quitting smoking; and, in January and May, a mother-daughter week.

The program operates on an all-inclusive American Plan, regardless of how long you stay, and guests may arrive on any day (unless a workshop is scheduled). The flexibility allows you to enjoy the attractions of the Palm Springs area, some within walking distance.

The regimen emphasizes aerobics and body conditioning. Workouts strive to increase flexibility, burn calories, strengthen the heart, and increase lung capacity. The desert climate, a low-calorie diet, and rigorous exercise work together to build power and energy.

Owned by Sheila Cluff, a former professional ice skater and physical fitness instructor, this is the kind of place that appeals to women and their devoted spouses. Most of the guests are in their middle 50s; many are already in good shape but want to lose a few pounds.

The converted manor house and cluster of private bungalows exude a Spanish-colonial ambience and sit handsomely beneath the dramatic starkness of mountains. Although there is no hydrotherapy, a sauna and whirlpool are tucked into the complex.

The Palms
572 N. Indian Canyon Dr., Palm Springs, CA 92262
Tel. 619/325–1111 or 800/753–7256

Administration Manager, Barbara Nos; fitness director, Marilu Rogers Horst

Season Year-round.

Accommodations 37 rooms in the manor and bungalows, most on the ground floor with private patio. Motel-style furniture, double beds, generous closets. All rooms with private or shared bath, air-conditioning, TV, telephone.

Rates $155 per person, double occupancy, private bath, on a daily program basis; $125 with shared bath. Single rooms $85–$220. 9% tax; 14% service charge additional. One night's lodging in advance. Credit cards: AE, MC, V.

Meal Plans Three meals totaling 1,000 calories served daily in the dining room. Breakfast is fresh fruit, diet muffin, and a vitamin supplement. Lunch includes soup, choice of chicken tostada seasoned with chili and cumin, or vegetable crepes. Veal loaf, broiled red snapper in tomato sauce, turkey divan, or vegetarian lasagna for dinner. No salt, sugar, or chemical additives. Coffee and hot or iced herbal tea all day. Midmorning broth break, afternoon vegetables.

Services and Facilities
Exercise Equipment: 2 Paramount weight training gym units, 3 Bodyguard treadmills, StairMaster, 2 Lifecycles, hand and ankle weights, stretch bands. **Services:** Massage, body scrub, aromatherapy; salon for hair, nail, and skin care. Consultation on fitness, body composition analysis. **Swimming Facilities:** Outdoor pool. **Recreation Facilities:** Hiking. Bike rental, horseback riding, tennis, and golf nearby. Downhill and cross-country skiing in the mountains. **Evening Programs:** Talks on dressing for success, the history of Palm Springs, other subjects.

In the Area
Local sightseeing tours; aerial tram ride. Desert Museum, art museum; ballooning, baths at nearby hot springs; Living Desert Reserve.

Getting Here
From Los Angeles. By bus, Greyhound (4 hr). By car, I–10 to Hwy. 111 (2½ hr). By train, Amtrak to Indio (2 hr). By air, scheduled service on Continental (30 min). Taxi service and rental car available. Desert City Shuttle bus ($65).

Special Notes
Limited access for the disabled. No smoking in designated areas. Mother-daughter weeks in January and May. Third week free July–September.

Pritikin Longevity Center

Nutrition and diet
Weight management
Vibrant maturity

California
Santa Monica
The Pritikin Longevity Center, which occupies an entire beachfront hotel, is dedicated to the diet and exercise regime espoused in the 1970s by the late Nathan Pritikin. It is the development center for programs offered elsewhere around the country, and since 1978 it has offered a vacation that combines the elements essential to preventing degenerative disease and improving the quality of one's life.

The medically supervised programs last for 13 and 26 days. The core curriculum includes daily exercise, nutrition and health education, stress-management counseling, and medical services. The two-week program is recommended for weight loss, reducing cholesterol levels, and managing blood pressure. The four-week program is designed for persons afflicted with physical problems such as heart disease and insulin-dependent diabetes. The full course offers increased individual attention, counseling, and supervision. Optional exercise classes are scheduled daily.

Healthy people, too, come here to maintain their health, learn to control their diet, cook and eat Pritikin-style, and exercise. A free hot line is included for those who need continuing support after they leave the program.

The daily schedule includes cooking classes, lectures, and three exercise sessions. A full physical examination is a major part of the program; it includes a treadmill stress test and a complete blood-chemistry analysis. Depending on your personal history and fitness level, you will be assigned to a specialist in either cardiology or internal medicine who will monitor your progress on the prescribed diet and exercise program.

Ocean views from the dining room are a pleasure at mealtimes. The chefs cook without added fat, salt, or sugar, and no coffee or tea is served. Meals are largely vegetarian, although fish and chicken are served several times a week; there are many fresh fruits and whole grains. (The Pritikin diet is 5% to 10% fat, 10% to 15% protein, and 80% high complex carbohydrates.)

Some nutritionists and doctors consider the diet unnecessarily austere, but the results attained by a loyal legion of followers may be convincing evidence that the concept works. The beachfront location is another attraction. If your spouse or partner is not a participant in the program (you are encouraged to bring a support person and work together), there are plenty of diversions at hand. Treading the boardwalk is exercise everyone enjoys. But the hotel has no pool.

However, the strict regimen demands concentration, so don't expect a purely fun-in-the-sun holiday. Between lectures and classes you'll work out in a well-equipped gym and perhaps on the beach. If you enjoy swimming in the ocean, it can be made part of your exercise routine. (All exercises are subject to your doctor's approval.) Bring workout clothes.

Pritikin Longevity Center
1910 Ocean Front Walk, Santa Monica, CA 90405
Tel. 213/450-5433 or 800/421-9911

Administration Director, Robert Pritikin; program director, David Pole

Season Year-round.

Accommodations 128 rooms, from singles to suites, with desk, reading chair, tiled bath and glass-enclosed shower. Better rooms include a Jacuzzi bathtub ($450–$550 supplement for a 13-day program) and ocean views. Air-conditioning, and just enough quiet comfort to make it feel like a resort.

Rates 13-day program $6,133 single, $2,687 for a participating partner; 26-day program $10,458 single, $5,088 for partner. (Medical costs may be covered by health insurance.) $500 in advance, 13-day program; $1,000 in advance, 26-day program. Add gratuities, taxes. Credit cards: AE, MC, V for deposit only.

Meal Plans 3 meals plus 3 snacks daily. Luncheon buffets include vegetarian lasagna, chili relleno, and salad bar. Mostly vegetarian dinners include seafood crepe or salmon teriyaki.

Services and Facilities **Exercise Equipment:** 51 Trotter treadmills, 9 combi bikes, 7 Schwinn Air-Dyne bikes, 3 recumbent bikes, Concept II rower, 2 Precor rowers, Climbmax, 3 AeroStep, Schwinn Bowflex, 15-station weights system, dumbbells (5–50 lbs.), hand weights. **Services:** Medical, fitness, and nutrition counseling; massage, acupressure, and beauty salon appointments. **Swimming Facilities:** Nearby outdoor pool, ocean beach. **Recreation Facilities:** Tennis, golf, fishing nearby; boardwalk along beach. **Evening Programs:** Lectures and films on health-related topics.

In the Area Shopping centers, museums, guided food shopping, and restaurant dining; J. Paul Getty Museum, Norton Simon Museum, Venice Beach, Santa Monica center (artist colony); concierge service for show and concert tickets.

Getting Here *From Los Angeles.* By Bus, Santa Monica Blue Bus from downtown (tel. 213/451–5444) takes about 45 min. By car, Santa Monica Freeway (Rte. 10) to 4th St. exit, Pico Blvd. (20 min). Taxi, limousine, rental car available. Parking on site. SuperShuttle from LAX airport.

Special Notes Elevator connects all floors. No smoking indoors.

Pro Muscle Camp

Sports conditioning

California Anyone who is at all interested in bodybuilding or has looked
Los Angeles through a copy of *Muscle & Fitness* magazine probably knows that top professionals train at Pro Muscle Camp. Some are involved in all aspects of the camp, hanging out in the dorms and eating with campers; others show up only for scheduled sessions, to the dismay of envious guests.

Set on the Loyola Marymount College campus on the outskirts of the city, this isn't your typical summer camp. Nor are most of the campers bodybuilders but rather men and women who have learned that weight training gets them in shape quicker than other sports. So don't worry about being outclassed if you're not in top form.

The day begins with breakfast at 7:30, followed by a seminar with a celebrity bodybuilder such as Cory Everson, Lee Haney, or Pete Aquilino, who work the upper and lower body. An hour of aerobics is scheduled before lunch, a high-energy class of running, swimming, or using weights in the gym.

During the discussions on training that follow lunch, the stars offer tips and answer questions. After that comes three hours of nonstop training in the gym, and the pros walk about and give advice.

Workout facilities are extensive: You can train to your heart's content. The quality of instruction given by the stars varies, but the counselors, all competitive amateur bodybuilders, are consistently good teachers who have sound advice.

Campers lodge in college dormitories and tend to be rowdy. There is much gossip in this fishbowl environment but few gripes about the meals. For someone who loves working with iron, a week here is like being a kid in a candy store.

Pro Muscle Camp
Box 570, Venice, CA 90291
Tel. 310/822–8696 or 800/648–2267

Administration Program director, Marc Missiopeck

Season 4 one-week sessions.

Accommodations 4 persons share on-campus apartments; each 2-bedroom unit has bath with shower, kitchen, air-conditioning.

Rates $499 tuition, $49–$60 per day for meals and lodging sharing a double room. Credit cards: MC, V.

Meal Plans 3 cafeteria meals daily. Salad bar with lunch and dinner. Entrees include broiled chicken, vegetable lasagna, steamed vegetables. High fiber, balanced menus low in fat, salt, and sugar.

Services and Facilities **Exercise Equipment:** 3 units each of all bodybuilding equipment, plus Lifecycles, Liferowers, VersaClimbers, and the Bally Lifecircuit computerized weight training system. **Services:** Classes and private instruction, consultation on health and fitness. **Swimming Facilities:** Indoor Olympic-size swimming pool, ocean beach nearby. **Recreation Facilities:** Tennis, hiking, jogging, sunbathing. **Evening Programs:** Training sessions.

In the Area Hollywood, Disneyland, Santa Monica, Muscle Beach.

Getting Here Located minutes from the Los Angeles International Airport, the campus is reached via the Santa Monica Freeway. Supershuttle van service at the airport.

Special Notes For the disabled there are access ramps to all facilities. No smoking indoors. Other camp locations are to be announced.

St. Helena Hospital Health Center

Life enhancement
Weight management
Spiritual awareness
Preventive medicine
Vibrant maturity

California Napa Valley vineyards spread for miles around the St. Helena
Deer Park Hospital Health Center complex run by the Seventh-day Adventists. Nondenominational and nonsectarian, the medically oriented programs are designed to teach self-management.

Disease prevention is emphasized here. Following a physical examination and an analysis of your diet, doctors and health professionals prescribe a course of action intended to help you achieve a healthier lifestyle. Their specific recommendations for diet take into account your physical condition, nutritional requirements, and weight-loss goals. Together you devise an exercise schedule and discuss hydrotherapy treatments.

The health center's association with St. Helena Hospital enables it to draw on sophisticated medical facilities and medical consultants appropriate to your special problems. The center offers programs in smoking cessation, lifestyle change through nutrition, alcohol and chemical recovery, pulmonary rehabilitation, pain rehabilitation, personalized health, and plastic surgery.

The 12-day McDougall nutrition and diet program includes group therapy and relaxation techniques, vegetarian cooking classes in a teaching kitchen, and bodywork—massage plus use of the steam baths, sauna, and whirlpool. Also available are a gymnasium, exercise track, swimming pool, and biofeedback equipment.

Like other Seventh-day Adventist health centers across the country, St. Helena is known for its emphasis on nutrition. Its diet of fruits, vegetables, and legumes, plus modest amounts of high-fat natural foods such as nuts, avocados, and olives, is taught in cooking class.

The center supplies you with a new perspective on the state of your health in one of California's most historic areas.

St. Helena Hospital Health Center
650 Sanitarium Rd., Deer Park, CA 94576
Tel. 707/963–6200 or 800/358–9195 (800/862–7575 in CA)

Administration Medical director, John Hodgkin, M.D.

Season Year-round.

Accommodations 54 rooms with private bath, air-conditioning, many with balconies with views of Napa Valley; 2 beds and reading chair in motel-modern style.

Rates 7-day smoking cessation program $2,095 single, $1,795 double; 12-day McDougall program $4,095 single, $3,595 double. Meals included. (Medical insurance may cover part of the cost.) Deposit required for some programs. Credit cards: MC, V.

Meal Plans 3 vegetarian meals daily, buffet style. No tea, coffee, or condiments. Cooking without butter and oil; vegetables sautéed in water. Specialties include vegetarian lasagna with mock cheese topping, baked tofu loaf, and eggplant "Parmesan" without cheese. Whole-grain breads baked without dairy products or eggs served in the McDougall program. Fresh fruit at all meals.

Services and Facilities **Exercise Equipment:** Weights room with treadmill, stationary bikes, rowing machines. **Services:** Massage, exercise instruction, private medical counseling, group discussions, group relaxation. **Swimming Facilities:** Outdoor pool (covered in winter). **Recreation Facilities:** Hiking, cycling, tennis, golf, aerobic dancing; horseback riding and glider rides nearby. **Evening Programs:** Informal lectures on health-related topics.

In the Area Antiques shops, mineral baths in Calistoga, winery tours, Jack London Park.

Getting Here *From San Francisco.* By car, Hwy. 80 north past Vallejo to Hwy. 37 going west, Hwy. 29 through St. Helena to Deer Park Rd., cross the Silverado Trail, turn left on Sanitarium Rd. (90 min). By bus, San Francisco airport shuttle service at fixed prices.

Special Notes No smoking in guest rooms or health center facilities.

Sivananda Ashram Yoga Farm

Spiritual awareness

California
Grass Valley

The Sivananda Ashram Yoga Farm follows the yogic disciplines of Swami Vishnu Devananda. Located in a peaceful valley north of Sacramento, the simple farmhouse provides lodging and space for two daily sessions of traditional postures (*asanas*), breathing techniques, and meditation. The intensive regimen of self-discipline is designed to foster a better understanding of the body-mind connection.

Meditation at 6 begins the morning session, brunch is served at 10, and then your schedule is open until 4 PM. Attendance at classes and meditations is mandatory.

The teachings of Swami Sivananda have been widely documented as promoting both physical and spiritual development. His followers and new students join in practicing the 12 asana positions, from a headstand to a spinal twist, each believed to have specific benefits for the body. Participants learn that the proper breathing (*pranayama*) in each position is essential for energy control.

The 80-acre farm attracts a diverse group, families as well as senior citizens. Guests are asked to share bedrooms and to contribute time to communal activities. You may arrive on any day and stay as long as you wish.

With its clear mountain air, fresh spring water, and unspoiled surroundings, the farm is said to suggest the rural paradise of Lord Krishna, called Vrindavan. Spiritual as well as physical, this is karmic yoga at its best.

Sivananda Ashram Yoga Farm
14651 Ballantree Lane, Grass Valley, CA 95949
Tel. 916/272–9322

Administration Manager, Avoram

Season Year-round.

Accommodations 35 guest rooms have 5 beds each, 5 double rooms, minimal furnishings. Showers and toilets shared. Tent space on the grounds. Private rooms on request. Dormitory beds available.

Rates $30 per person per day includes lodging, program, meals; campers pay $25. Supplemental charges for special programs. $25 in advance. No credit cards.

Meal Plans 2 lacto-vegetarian meals daily, buffet style. Morning meal of hot grain cereal, granola, yogurt, fruit. Stir-fry and steamed vegetables, rice, and scrambled tofu for dinner. Homemade soups, whole-wheat breads, green salads.

Services and Facilities **Services:** Massage. **Swimming Facilities:** None. **Recreation Facilities:** Meditation; skiing at nearby resorts. **Evening Programs:** Lectures on Hindu philosophy, concerts.

In the Area Lake Tahoe, historic gold-mining towns of Nevada City, Grass Valley, old-town Sacramento.

Getting Here *From Sacramento.* By bus, Trailways to Auburn (2 hr). By car, I–80 to Auburn, Rte. 49 (1½ hr). Pickup in the farm van $10 at Auburn, $25 at Sacramento Airport.

Special Notes Limited access for the disabled. Children are welcome to participate with parents. No smoking.

Skylonda Fitness Retreat

Life enhancement
Nutrition and diet

California
Woodside

Skylonda Retreat opened late in 1992 on 16 forested acres of coastal hills south of San Francisco. During the seven-day retreats guests recharge themselves physically, spiritually, and mentally while losing weight. The daily schedule, developed by a staff made up largely of veterans from The Golden Door, incorporates hikes, yoga, meditation, weight training, aerobics, aquatic exercises, and massage.

Hiking the extensive network of trails surrounding the retreat is basic to the rigorous schedule. A morning walk is followed by weight-training class, aquatics, and an afternoon hike. In between are quiet periods, lunch, and an aerobics class in the fully equipped exercise room. Evenings are devoted to discussion of stress management, nutrition, and cooking.

In this highly personalized fitness program all participants are expected to strive for being their best. From the 6 AM wakeup call to the 9 PM close of evening programs, there is intense interaction with other members of the group. An hour of silence is included "to reflect on things that are important."

The spacious lodge contains a multipurpose room for aerobics and yoga/stretching classes, with a view of the glass-enclosed swimming pool and outdoor Jacuzzi. The log-timbered upper floors include a library, dining room, and the main gathering room, which features two 19-foot floor-to-ceiling stained glass windows. Guest rooms feature all the amenities of an elegant country lodge, but since contact with the outside world is discouraged, there are no telephones or TVs.

Skylonda Fitness Retreat
16350 Skyline Blvd., Woodside, CA 94052
Tel. 415/851–4500
Fax 415/363–2235

Administration	Founder, D. Dixon Collins; manager, Janus Gronvold-Gross
Season	Year-round.
Accommodations	16 rooms with private bath in 3-story log lodge. Each room contains 2 double beds, open-beam ceiling, and spectacular view of the redwoods.
Rates	7-day all-inclusive program $2,400 plus 6.5% tax and gratuities. Deposit 10%. Credit cards: AE, MC, V.
Meal Plans	3 meals daily included in program. Breakfast can be fresh fruit, whole grain muffin, or cereal. Lunch is a salad or soup with whole-grain bread. Dinner includes cioppino, vegetarian lasagna or halibut baked in parchment, stuffed potato, or veggie grain-stuffed artichoke. Coffee, herbal tea, and decaffeinated coffee available at all times. Energy breaks include a mid-morning drink (orange juice, yeast, nonfat milk) and an afternoon snack of broth, fruit, vegetables, popcorn, or a cookie. Special diets and alternate menu selections are available on request.
Services and Facilities	**Exercise Equipment:** 30-station HydraFitness system, 4 stationary bikes, rower, step units. **Services:** Swedish massage, facial, bodywrap, manicure, skincare. **Evening Programs:** cooking demonstrations, talks.
In the Area	Jasper Ridge Biological Reserve, Portola Valley, Palo Alto.
Getting Here	*From San Francisco.* By car, I–380W to I–280S, I–92W to Scenic Highway 35 (Skyline Blvd). Complimentary pickup at San Francisco International Airport. Pickup also scheduled at Stanford Shopping Center, Palo Alto, and other points.
Special Notes	No smoking in the lodge.

Sonoma Mission Inn and Spa

Luxury pampering

California *Boyes Hot Springs*	San Franciscans have been "taking the cure" at the Sonoma Mission Inn since the turn of the century, but fitness training

and pampering are modern attractions. The sparkling mineral water, bottled for drinking, is supplied to guests' rooms daily.

The high-tech spa is a favorite escape for young couples from the city as well as a popular stopover on wine-country tours. Its first consideration is health maintenance rather than weight loss, and a few days here can do wonders for your spirits.

Several wings of deluxe rooms and mini-suites have been added to the big pink stucco palace since its new owners restored this grand old hotel in 1980. An old-fashioned country market and restaurant are on the grounds. The resort accepts bookings for corporate conferences and sales meetings and, as a result, can be packed one day, quiet the next. Avoid weekends if you yearn for peace and seclusion.

Midweek spa packages are the best buy; weekend rates are strictly à la carte. All adult guests are allowed free access to the bathhouse, which includes twin exercise rooms (one with Keiser Cam II weight equipment, the other with Dynavit units), sauna, steam room, and indoor whirlpools beside a flower-bordered outdoor exercise pool. Scheduled daily are coed aerobics classes, aquacize groups, and hydrotherapy sessions.

Driving up to the main lobby is like arriving for a party at Jay Gatsby's. Juice, coffee, muffins, and a bowl of apples for early risers sit on a buffet near the great fireplace. The baronial reception hall, awash in pastel pinks and peach against bleached wood, sets the mood of casual elegance. The inn and its fashionable dining room and wine bar seem far removed from the rigors of calorie counting.

Down a path through gardens abloom with camellia and jasmine is the spa building, sandwiched between a conference center and tennis courts. After you check in with the spa director and schedule massage and beauty treatments, you are left pretty much on your own.

An airy, two-story atrium that belies the building's origins as a Quonset hut is the setting for most of the activities. The glass-walled exercise room faces a sunlit marble fountain. Try the Keiser Cam II pneumatic resistance machine that tones muscles while you pump air instead of iron, or pedal a Dynavit exercise cycle outfitted with a biofeedback computer that monitors calorie expenditure and pulse rate while charting your cardiovascular response. Report for treatments upstairs in a rather somber room, where you can sip herbal tea and watch TV while you wait to be summoned.

Hydrotherapy is an important aspect of the spa program. The corrosive nature of the mineral water has caused it to be eliminated from the course of treatments; however, the inn has imported equipment that includes a full-length tub for underwater massage in which 30 bubbling jets and a high-pressure hose work to invigorate you. Then an herbal wrap is applied to relax muscles, soften the skin, and draw out toxins. A young attendant explains how each step increases circulation, stimulates heart and lungs, and eliminates toxins.

Serious swimmers will find the spa's pool too small for laps and often crowded with aquacize groups. The large pool for inn guests is unheated.

Sonoma Mission Inn and Spa
18140 Sonoma Hwy. 12, Boyes Hot Springs, CA 95416
(Reservations) Box 1447, Sonoma, CA 95476
Tel. 707/938–9000 or 800/358–9022 (800/862–4945 in CA)

Administration Manager, Peter Henry; program director, Jill Taylor

Season Year-round.

Accommodations 170 rooms in the main building and garden units. Plantation shutters, canopied beds, and ceiling fans; king, queen, and twin beds. Fireplaces, sun deck, and marble baths in the new Wine Country rooms.

Rates Spa Sampler package 1–5 nights, $290 single, $280 double per night, including 3 meals; deluxe room $425 single, $360 double per night. Package available Sunday–Thursday only. Weekday 1-day Getaway (no lodging) with lunch, 3 treatments $275. Tax and gratuities included. One night in advance, $500 for package. Credit cards: AE, DC, MC, V.

Meal Plans Spa menu with calorie counts in main dining room. Choices at 1,000–1,200 calories per day include salmon poached in Chardonnay with tarragon, breast of free-range chicken and steamed vegetables, grilled veal loin with leeks, whole-wheat pizza topped with wild mushrooms, goat cheese, and tomatoes. Decaffeinated coffee, herbal tea, nonfat milk.

Services and Facilities **Exercise Equipment:** 9 Keiser Cam II pneumatic weight units, 2 Monark bikes, Lifecycle, Schwinn Air-Dyne bike, Concept II rowing machine, StairMaster, recumbent bike, treadmill. **Services:** Massage (Swedish, Esalen), fango clay body pack, herbal and seaweed body wraps, loofah scrub, facials, manicures, pedicures. Aromatherapy massage, underwater hydrotherapy massage. **Swimming Facilities:** 2 outdoor pools for exercise; unheated 40-foot pool. **Recreation Facilities:** 2 tennis courts, hiking. Horseback riding, golf nearby.

In the Area Guided group hiking daily; ballooning and gliding; winery tours, Sonoma Mission historic area, antiques shops, specialty food shops, Calistoga mud baths.

Getting Here *From San Francisco.* By bus, Greyhound to Sonoma (90 min). By car, Golden Gate Bridge, Rte. 101, Hwy. 37 to Sonoma, Hwy. 12 (45 min). Public bus at door; Sonoma Airporter scheduled van service to San Francisco airport; limousine, taxi, rental car.

Special Notes Limited access for disabled. No smoking in the spa or in designated areas of the dining room. Spa open daily 7 AM–10 PM.

Spa Del Mar

Luxury pampering
Weight management
Life enhancement

California
Del Mar Overlooking the Pacific, the Spa Del Mar at the Inn L'Auberge combines the influence of European hydrotherapy with America's zest for exercise. Such diverse body treatments as balnea therapy (therapeutic baths), aromatherapy, and seaweed packs with a brushing massage are available à la carte or as part of a package.

Spa cuisine is served in the resort's Bistro Garden, open to the sunny beach breezes most of the year. The menu changes daily, with the calorie count posted beside each item. Emphasis is on fresh local ingredients, with low amounts of saturated fat, sodium, and cholesterol.

The original Del Mar Hotel was a legendary gathering place for the rich and famous, especially during the summer season at nearby Del Mar Race Track. The new inn on the same site combines the cozy comfort of a small European auberge with California-casual ambience. Built on several levels, each guest room has a balcony with an ocean view. On the first floor, close to the spa, rooms open onto a terrace surrounding the swimming pool.

While upscale La Jolla is only minutes away, the lifestyle in Del Mar is slow-paced and casual; the beach here is broad, uncrowded, and ideal for long morning walks. Guests can get here by Amtrak; the station is just below the hotel grounds.

Spa Del Mar
1540 Camino Del Mar, Box 2078, Del Mar, CA 92014
Tel. 619/259–1515 or 800/553–1336
Fax 619/755–4940

Administration	General manager, Ross Justice; spa manager, Brian Dieal
Season	Year-round.
Accommodations	123 deluxe rooms with balcony, marble bath and vanity, wooden armoire, minibar, TV. Some have a fireplace that ignites at the touch of a button; all are air-conditioned. Amenities include makeup lights in the bathrooms.
Rates	$165–$250 for single or double room per night, $325–$750 suites. One-night Spa Refresher package $195 per couple, $240 weekends. Add state tax. Advance payment for one night. Credit cards: AE, MC, V.
Meal Plans	Spa cuisine totaling 800–1,000 calories per day for women, 1,200–1,400 calories for men. Breakfast includes juice, Meuslix cereal or egg-white omelet. Lunch may be a fruit salad or plate of grilled vegetables (Japanese eggplant, red peppers, zucchini, tomatoes, assorted squash), lightly brushed with extra-virgin olive oil. Dinner entrees include grilled fish or chicken and veal medallions in wine sauce.
Services and Facilities	**Exercise Equipment:** Spectrum I weight training units, SprintRider bike, Challenger rowing machine. **Services:** Swedish massage, shiatsu, acupressure, aromatherapy, fango, thalassotherapy, algotherapy, affusions (hot/cold foot and arm baths), herbal wrap, loofah body scrub, facials; beauty salon for hair, nail, and skin care. Aquacise, yoga. **Spa Facilities:** Underwater massage, coed sauna and steam room, 6 massage rooms. **Swimming Facilities:** Outdoor pool (45 ft.), ocean beach. **Recreation Facilities:** 2 lighted tennis courts (concrete surface); golf nearby. Outings to nearby attractions.
In the Area	La Jolla (art museum, theater, shopping), Sea World, San Diego (zoo, Balboa Park museums and theaters, Old Town), Del Mar Race Track (July 25–Sept. 15).
Getting Here	*From San Diego.* By car, I–5 (San Diego Frwy.) north to Del Mar Hts. Rd., Camino del Mar to 15th St. (30 min). By train,

Amtrak to Del Mar (25 min). By bus, Greyhound. Free transfers on arrival, departure.

Special Notes No smoking in spa. Minimum age 16. Spa hours: daily 9 AM–8 PM. Nonsmoking rooms available, some with access for the disabled.

Spa Hotel and Mineral Springs

Luxury pampering
Taking the waters

California   Here is one alternative to rustic resorts with geothermal pools.
Palm Springs   The Spa Hotel and Mineral Springs boasts marble floors in the bathroom, lush gardens, and spacious rooms. The spa, which bases its fitness program on European hydrotherapy, is built on the site of hot mineral springs used by Native Americans for centuries. The Agua Caliente tribe owns the land and recently acquired the hotel.

Decked out in white slippers and oversize terrycloth towels, guests attend sessions of eucalyptus inhalation and use the sauna or the steam room. After a shower, they are escorted to sunken marble tubs. The "magical water" of the springs soon disposes of tension and promotes relaxation.

Herbal tea or ice water is served in the cooling rooms while guests, wrapped in sheets, wait for the masseur or masseuse. The one-hour treatment helps prepare you for a swim in the Olympic-size outdoor pool or a sunbath in the rooftop solarium (clothes optional). Aerobics classes and aquatic exercise in the mineral-water pool are other options.

Looking dated but well maintained, the spa facilities are open to the public for a daily fee. The hotel is in the center of Palm Springs, close to the shops, restaurants, and recreational attractions for which this desert resort is famous.

Spa Hotel and Mineral Springs
100 N. Indian Ave., Palm Springs, CA 92262
Tel. 619/778–1772 or 800/854–1279 (800/472–4371 in CA)

Administration Manager, David O'Bannon; spa director, Faye Antaky

Season Year-round.

Accommodations 230 rooms (20 suites) in a contemporary 5-story hotel. Fashionable rooms with rattan furnishing, oversize bed, dressing area and bath. Balcony, TV, air-conditioning, and morning paper.

Rates Daily European plan $85–$135 per room, single or double. Add 15% gratuity and tax. One night payable in advance. Credit cards: AE, DC, MC, V.

Meal Plans 3 meals a day total 1,000 calories. Fresh fruit and yogurt at breakfast, cold salmon for lunch, choice of lamb medallions, whole-wheat pasta, or grilled shrimp and vegetables for dinner. Coffee, tea, and regular menu are available.

Services and **Exercise Equipment:** 12-station Paramount weight training
Facilities gym, 3 Lifecycles, Liferower, treadmill, free weights. **Services:** Massage (Swedish, sports, shiatsu), aromatherapy, herbal wrap, body scrub, facial; salon for hair, nail, and skin care. **Bathing Facilities:** 34 private Jacuzzis with mineral water.

Swimming Facilities: 2 outdoor pools. **Recreation Facilities:** 3 tennis courts. Golf and horseback riding nearby. Desert hiking, cross-country skiing nearby.

In the Area Sightseeing tours, bicycle rental (38 mi of trails), ballooning; aerial tramway, Living Desert Museum (nature and art exhibits, concerts), Botanical Gardens, Polo Club.

Getting Here *From Los Angeles.* By bus, Greyhound (4 hr). By car, I–10 to Rte. 111 (2½ hr). By train, Amtrak to Indio (2 hr). Limousine, taxi, airport van service, rental car available.

Special Notes No smoking in the spa and in designated areas of the dining room.

Tassajara

Nutrition and diet
Spiritual awareness
Taking the waters

California Awakened by a bell ringer at 5:40 AM, the day begins with med-
Jamesburg itation in the Japanese-style hall, or Zendo, which is the center of the Zen monastery at Tassajara. Students in black garb and with shaved heads join visitors seeking to become familiar with Buddhist practices.

Surrounded by stern mountains and overlooking the Pacific Ocean, the site has been a place of healing and purification for centuries. Native Americans used the hot springs, and Spanish hunters gathered here. Now Tassajara guests bathe in the slightly sulfurous water until parboiled, then stretch out on the rocks to contemplate nature.

The stone buildings that serve as kitchen, dining hall, and office are vestiges of a 19th-century commercial spa. Some of the original cabins built by Chinese laborers in the 1880s are still in use; the newer guest units, with their surrounding patches of bamboo grove, give off a distinctly Eastern air.

Acquired by the San Francisco Zen Center in 1966, Tassajara maintains the tradition of welcoming overnight visitors as well as practitioners of Zen Buddhism. Guests are invited to join in meditation, receive basic instruction, and attend lectures, but no activity is required. Those who wish to participate in a Practice Retreat are required to perform about a half-day of work on the buildings and farm. Workshops in yoga, poetry, and sensory awareness are also offered.

Zen cuisine is one of the most popular attractions. Those who know Tassajara primarily through its cookbooks on vegetarian food can begin to experience Zen cooking in a one-week workshop dubbed "Cooking as Meditation," led by Ed Brown, former head chef here and author of *The Tassajara Bread Book*. In addition to actually preparing food, guests learn that cooking embodies many of the elements of spiritual practice: "working sincerely with the ingredients available, giving more than you ever thought possible, being patient with the fact that everything has a mind of its own, [and] trusting your own sensibilities."

Tassajara
Jamesburg, CA
Reservations: Zen Center, 300 Page St., San Francisco,
CA 94102
Tel. 415/431–3771

Administration	Guest manager, Barbara Isaacson
Season	Apr.–Sept.
Accommodations	Cabins and a few single rooms accommodate up to 65 guests. Some have beds, others a foam cushion on the floor. No electricity; kerosene lamp provided. Communal bathhouse or shared bathroom. No services.
Rates	$110–$178 single, $75–$115 per person double occupancy, with 3 meals. Practice Retreat (3-night min.) $35–$40 per day. Dormitory $65–$75 per night; 2-room suite with private bath $105–$115 per person (4 or more). Add tax. Workshop $580–$740. Deposit $35–$65. No credit cards.
Meal Plans	3 vegetarian meals served daily, buffet style. Breakfast includes oatmeal, tamari-roasted cashew nuts, French toast, yogurt with blackberries. Different breads baked daily. Organically grown vegetables are steamed, served with tofu and brown rice, and baked.
Services and Facilities	**Services:** Meditation retreats, workshops in yoga, cooking, Japanese arts. **Recreation Facilities:** Natural rock pools with circulating thermal water (clothing optional); steam room, outdoor swimming pool. **Evening Programs:** Meditation.
In the Area	Big Sur State Park (hiking, beaches), Carmel (art galleries, boutiques), San Simeon (Hearst Castle art museum), Monterey (Spanish colonial historic site, aquarium), Esalen Institute.
Getting Here	*From San Francisco.* By car, Hwy. 280 south to Rte. 17, via Monterey to Carmel, Rte. G16 (Carmel Valley Rd.) for 23.2 miles, right on Tassajara Rd. to Jamesburg (3 hr).
Special Notes	Park at Jamesburg for the Tassajara stage ($26 per person round-trip for shuttle from parking to lodge) to avoid steep mountain road. No smoking in compound. Bring bath towel, flashlight, blanket. Day visitors $10–$15.

Two Bunch Palms

Luxury pampering
Taking the waters

California
Desert Hot Springs

Al Capone, so the story goes, had the rock-walled fortress-like house built at the desert oasis called Two Bunch Palms in the late 1920s. His casino became the resort's dining room, but the massage parlor below is still in use. Complete with stained-glass windows and Art Deco furnishings, Two Bunch Palms is like stepping into the past.

Popular as a hideaway for Hollywood stars and writers, the spa offers privacy (only registered guests get past the guardhouse), intimacy (44 villas and suites), and total relaxation. No spa packages are offered (26 services are à la carte), no gym or golf course exists, and no children are allowed. For those who crave exercise, however, there are stationary bikes, yoga classes, and a jogging trail.

The dry heat of the desert induces a certain lethargy. To avoid the sun, guests indulge in the spa's extraordinary repertoire of bodywork and beauty treatments. One innovation is the esoteric massage, "designed to balance and harmonize the physical, emotional, and spiritual bodies." Another specialty is reflexology massage: You float in the hot pool on six inner tubes while undergoing hand and foot massage. For your treatment pleasure, mud and seaweed are imported from France, California contributes pure lemon oil, and crystals are provided for personal energy.

Geothermal springs on the north slope of the Coachella Valley supply hot mineral water (148° F) for the spa's swimming pool. Cooled a bit for comfort, the water splashes over a rock waterfall into a turquoise grotto framed by tropical shrubbery, and under a canopy of fan palms and tamarisk trees.

Desert Hot Springs is a pleasantly old-fashioned town of "spatels" catering to budget-minded vacationers; down-valley lies the glamour haven of Bob Hope and his Palm Springs cronies; but Two Bunch, off by itself at the edge of the desert, remains a solitary oasis.

Two Bunch Palms

6742 Two Bunch Parkway, Desert Hot Springs, CA 92240
Tel. 619/329–8791 or 800/472–4334 in CA

Administration	General manager, Jerry Greenbach; spa director, Dana Bass-Smith
Season	Year-round.
Accommodations	44 guest rooms in villas or motel-like buildings near pool. The 2-bedroom suite No. 14 is popular, at $345 a night, complete with the initials A.C. inscribed in a desktop, plus a bullet hole in a mirror, and lookout tower with wet bar that doubles as a tanning deck. Casa Blanca minisuite with Jacuzzi, $266.
Rates	$100–$345 for 2 persons, includes Continental breakfast. Advance payment for 1 night. 2-night minimum. Add tax, gratuity. Credit cards: AE, DC, MC, V.
Meal Plans	3 meals daily served in the resort dining room. No spa diet, but selections of salads, grilled fish or chicken, and seasonal fresh fruit. Living essence cuisine featured.
Services and Facilities	**Services:** Massage (Swedish, Trager, shiatsu, jin shin do, reflexology, deep-tissue), aromatherapy, 90-minute salt-glow body scrub and herbal steam, facials, herbal wraps, mud baths. **Swimming Facilities:** Outdoor mineral-water pool. **Recreation Facilities:** 2 lighted tennis courts, bicycles. **Evening Programs:** Informal entertainment.
In the Area	Joshua Tree National Monument Park (desert habitat), Palm Springs (shopping, museums, mountain cable ride).
Getting Here	*From Los Angeles.* By car, I–10 to Hwy. 111 (2 hr). By bus, Greyhound (4 hr). By train, Amtrak to Indio (2 hr). Private planes and scheduled air service to Palm Springs.
Special Notes	Limited access for the disabled. No smoking in spa. No children (minimum age 18).

Weimar Institute

Life enhancement
Preventive medicine
Weight management
Vibrant maturity

California
Weimar

A diabetic housewife, a stressed-out doctor, and an overweight retiree are representative of the older generation of fitness converts who come to the Weimar Institute to learn healthy habits. Medically oriented yet devoted to education and exercise, the 19-day Newstart program teaches guests to help themselves through a combination of physical, mental, and spiritual healing.

The doctors and staff, all Seventh-day Adventists, see prevention as the best medicine. With the help of computers, the staff makes specific recommendations for diet based on assessments of your physical condition, nutritional requirements, and weight-loss goals. After you undergo a complete physical, your personal schedule will be set by a physician who continues to monitor your progress throughout the three-week program.

Hydrotherapy and massage are part of the program. Included are a 16-head enclosure of contrasting hot and cold showers, Russian-style steam baths, and whirlpools. Those afflicted with neuromuscular problems learn to relieve themselves of pain.

The Seventh-day Adventists, long known for their interest in health and nutrition, accept anyone willing to adhere to a strictly vegetarian diet and exercise regimen at home. The physicians and educators here encourage patients to get off medication as soon as is safely possible. They believe modern technology has overshadowed simple cures for common ailments. Their programs help participants to quit smoking, control weight, and cope with degenerative diseases such as arthritis, diabetes, cancer, and cardiovascular problems.

The first activity of the day is calisthenics. Everyone is encouraged to walk and enjoy the miles of woodland trail on the 457-acre campus. "Stretchercise" classes that won't strain bodies unaccustomed to exercise are scheduled between cooking classes and private counseling or therapy sessions.

Newstart shares resources with Weimar College, a training institution for health-related ministries that offers an intensive, outpatient type of program with live-in accommodations. Weekend seminars are often scheduled for those who want a refresher course in health cooking or controlling stress. Others come simply to relax at the new Weimar Inn, which also has a weights room.

Located in the Sierra Nevada foothills between Sacramento and Reno, Weimar is a nondenominational and nonsectarian place that renews body and spirit.

Weimar Institute
Box 486, 20601 W. Paoli Lane, Weimar, CA 95736
Tel. 916/637–4111 or 800/525–9192

Administration
President, Paul Roberson; medical director, Warren R. Peters, M.D., F.A.C.S.

Season   Newstart program June–mid-Dec.; weekend seminars year-round.

Accommodations   29-room no-frills country lodge. Large rooms with sitting area and private bath, single or king-size beds. Informal gatherings around the fireplace in the lobby; self-service laundry. 23 rooms with cherry furnishings, quilted bedspreads, mirrored closet doors, and flowered wallpaper at the Weimar Inn.

Rates   19-day live-in Newstart program, including medical fees, $4,275; $3,875 for participating spouse or partners, $2,400 for accommodations only. $38 per night for two, $33 single, without meals, at the Weimar Inn. Newstart program $500 per person in advance; inn accommodations 50% in advance. Credit cards: AE, D, MC, V. Rates include tax, gratuity.

Meal Plans   3 vegetarian meals daily in the Weimar Country Cafeteria. Specialties include a "haystack" of chili, rice, sprouts, lettuce, and tomato on corn chips, vegetarian lasagna, steamed vegetables on rice with oriental sauce. Breads baked daily. Whole and sprouted grains. No eggs, cheese, or dairy products.

Services and Facilities   **Exercise Equipment:** 3 Exercycles, Schwinn Air-Dyne bike, 2 rowing machines, 2 treadmills, cross-country ski machine, tiltboard, free weights, 10-unit hydraulic weight-training system. **Services:** Newstart program includes complete physical and medical history evaluation, blood tests, treadmill stress tests, consultation with physician; hydrotherapy and massage; cooking classes; 24-hour nursing staff. **Swimming Facilities:** River bathing and wading. **Recreation Facilities:** Volleyball; golf course nearby. **Evening Programs:** Music, video presentations, and talks on inspirational and health-related topics.

In the Area   Weekend outings to the Empire State gold mine, the California State Capitol, and the Railroad Museum in Sacramento; sightseeing and shopping in the Lake Tahoe area; Yosemite National Park, the Nevada casinos, Old Sacramento.

Getting Here   *From Sacramento.* By car, I–80 north to Weimar, exit on W. Paoli Lane (60 min). By bus, Greyhound to Weimar (60 min). By train, Amtrak to Colfax (45 min). Weimar Institute provides service from the train and bus station (fee); taxi and rental car available.

Special Notes   One room at the lodge and the inn has access for the disabled. No smoking.

The Zane Intensives

Sports conditioning
Life enhancement
Stress control

California
Palm Springs   Workouts with Mr. Olympia, three-time champion muscleman Frank Zane, and psychological conditioning with Christine Zane, are the focus of an intensive three-day program at their estate in Palm Springs. Cross-training evaluations determine a set of exercises geared to your age and physical condition; exercises are accompanied by the use of Dichotics tapes developed by the Zanes to control stress.

One-on-one training instruction concentrates on helping you achieve proper form; the Zanes incorporate aerobics, stretch-

ing sessions, and weight training (with their own personally selected equipment) into each individually tailored program.
Each three-hour session also includes motivational and relaxation techniques. A computer analysis of your diet will show how
eating habits affect your strength, and may lead to suggestions
for food supplements.

You can concentrate on learning what works best for you. Being
in good shape is not essential; even experienced bodybuilders
can get sore by the end of the day.

The mansion, which once belonged to Cary Grant, has been restored to its 1929 Spanish Santa Fe style and boasts a Jacuzzi
alongside the swimming pool.

The Zane Intensives
Box 2031, Palm Springs, CA 92263
Tel. 619/323–7486 or 800/323–7537

Administration Manager, Christine Zane; program director, Frank Zane

Season Year-round

Accommodations Not included in program. Nearby are The Spa Hotel and The
Autry.

Rates $550 single, $900 for two persons. Credit cards: MC, V.

Meal Plans Meals not included in program.

Services and Facilities **Exercise Equipment:** Icharion, Nautilus, Eagle, and Paramount weight training units, Bodymaster, Legblaster, free
weights, barbells. **Services:** Personalized training, stress-con-
trol workshop. **Swimming Facilities:** 60-foot outdoor pool. **Recreation Facilities:** Basketball and croquet courts, badminton,
parcourse, bicycles; 8 tennis courts in nearby public park, public golf course.

In the Area Aerial Tramway to mountain hiking trails, ballooning, Desert
Museum, hot springs, Living Desert Reserve, Fashion Mall.

Getting Here *From Los Angeles.* By bus, Greyhound (4 hr). By car, I–10 to
Hwy. 111 (2½ hr). By train, Amtrak to Indio (2 hr). By air,
scheduled service by USAir and other airlines; airport van
shuttle service, taxi, rental car available.

Special Notes Not accessible for the disabled. No smoking indoors.

The Southwest

Health resorts are the new bonanza in the Old West. Ranches and lodges in the desert offer the latest in diet, nutrition, and exercise programs, and fitness can be combined with skiing, trail rides, and hiking. Two hours north of the Las Vegas casinos, near the pioneer settlement of St. George, in an area of intense development commonly referred to as Utah's Banana Belt or the Other Palm Springs, are modern, palm-studded oases where stress control and weight-management courses are the major attraction.

The pioneers among fitness resorts in the Southwest are the Canyon Ranch and Maine Chance in Arizona and Vista Clara in New Mexico, each with its own programs and ambience, each offering sophisticated yet refreshingly personal service. In the Rocky Mountain states, Colorado has the new Doral Telluride Resort and Spa for sports conditioning, and summer music festivals in Aspen and Vail bring a further dimension to holidays for healthy bodies and minds. Scottsdale, Arizona, now offers the widest range of spas, from the upscale Marriott Camelback Inn to the new Centre for Well-Being at The Phoenician. With a dry, warm climate to match superb fitness and beauty facilities, these are world-class destination resorts.

Buckhorn Mineral Wells Spa

Taking the waters

Arizona
Mesa
Locals and sufferers from arthritis and skin problems know Buckhorn Mineral Wells Spa, a small resort in the desert near Phoenix that offers treatments on an à la carte basis to guests and day visitors. Bathers enjoy private rooms with tiled tubs into which hot mineral water flows continuously; a whirlpool unit enhances the effect, and a licensed masseur or masseuse is on hand from Tuesday to Saturday 9 AM to 5 PM.

Surrounded by cactus and palm trees, the motel-style lodge looks like a combination of hacienda and gymnasium. Separate men's and women's entrances lead to the cement bathing cubicles. The mineral water, unchlorinated and naturally heated at 106 degrees, flows at the rate of 7,000 gallons per hour. Cooler water can be added, but the nurse in attendance recommends the high temperature to relieve sore muscles and aching bones. Tubs are drained, cleaned, and refilled after each use.

Built in the 1940s, the Buckhorn Spa was expanded by the owner and operator, and now guests can stay in adobe cottages equipped for housekeeping. Restaurants and a shopping center adjoin the resort, and there is a small museum on the grounds displaying native birds and animals.

Buckhorn Mineral Wells Spa
5900 E. Main St., Mesa, AZ 85205
Tel. 602/832–1111

Administration Manager, Alice A. Sliger

Season Year-round.

Accommodations	15 cottages with twin beds, private bath, kitchenette. Dishes and linens provided. Units have Spanish-colonial furnishings, air-conditioning.
Rates	$35 a day for 2, Jan.–Mar.; $225 weekly. Lower rates in summer. One night payable in advance. No credit cards.
Services and Facilities	**Exercise Equipment:** None available. **Services:** Whirlpool mineral baths ($12), Swedish-type massage with vibrator ($20). Series rates and combination treatments. **Swimming Facilities:** Nearby lake. **Spa Facilities:** Hot mineral well water in 27 private rooms. **Recreation Facilities:** Golf courses, horseback riding nearby; fishing, picnic areas, parks, water sports.
In the Area	Scottsdale resorts and restaurants; Phoenix; the Heard Museum (Indian art); Paolo Soleri's Arcosanti village.
Getting Here	*From Phoenix.* By Car, Hwys. 60, 80, 89, Recker Rd. (30 min). Rental car available.
Special Notes	No smoking in the bathhouse.

Canyon Ranch Health and Fitness Resort

Life enhancement
Weight management
Holistic health
Preventive medicine
Vibrant maturity

Arizona
Tucson

A 60-acre spread in the foothills of the Santa Catalina Mountains, the Canyon Ranch Health and Fitness Resort is a hightech emporium of good health that positively radiates energy. From the moment you are welcomed in the big hacienda and shown to your casita, the nonstop pursuit of health and well-being seems to put everyone in a happy, optimistic mood. Even the most stressed-out Type A personalities tend to find the extensive schedule of exercise classes, hiking, bike trips, and bodywork to their liking.

The prebreakfast walk requires rising before dawn. On a typical morning, about 50 men and women dressed for the predawn chill warm up on a playing field. The exercise leader sets a brisk pace on paths through the desert landscape of cacti, mesquite, acacia, and palo verde trees. Conversations come naturally with fellow ranchers, and newcomers quickly learn the lay of the land. Later, over a breakfast of Spanish omelet (made of egg whites), orange juice, and freshly brewed decaf coffee, intense debates on the merits of shiatsu and Swedish massage can develop.

The scope and scale of the sprawling ranch will probably be bewildering until you familiarize yourself with the various activity centers and residential clusters. Unlike more rigidly programmed resorts, the ranch allows you to select your activities. Many activities require signing up in advance to limit the size of the group, and you may find that your appointments clash with outings or classes.

Group psychodynamics, a shared experience that builds synergy as you experience many kinds of exercise and health services, is the philosophy that has guided the ranch's development. Options include holistic healing, a computerized

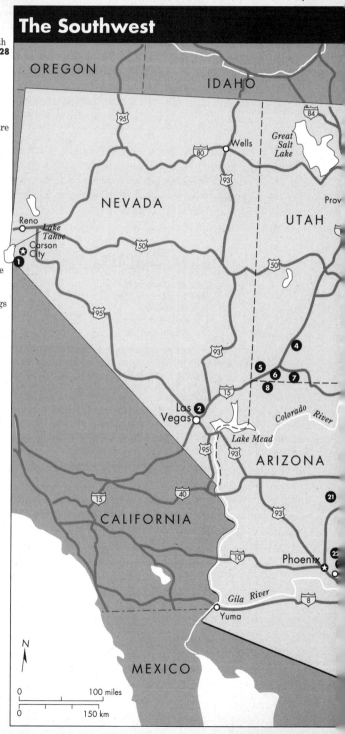

The Southwest

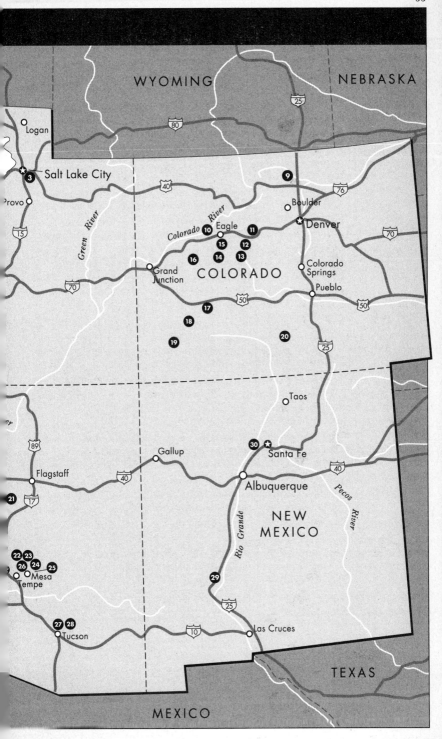

high-impact aerobics. There are also men's aerobics, low-impact aerobics for beginning and advanced groups, water aerobics, and batteries of treadmills and stair-climbers. If the choices prove overwhelming, you can retreat to the privacy of the men's and women's hydrotherapy areas to soak in hot and cold whirlpools and sunbathe in the nude. The saunas, steam rooms, inhalation rooms, and swimming pools, all recently renovated, are open 14 hours a day.

Preventive medicine plays a major role here. Some people return several times a year to combat job burnout or to work on special problems. Programs are scheduled for quitting smoking, weight loss, relief from arthritis, and physical rehabilitation. The resort has a medical/wellness complex with behavioral health professionals and medical services staff, gyms, padded-floor aerobics studios, an indoor swimming pool, and a rest and meditation room in a glass-walled tower with a panoramic view of the mountains.

When you're ready to make a serious commitment to change, head for the Life Enhancement Center. Teamed with specialists, you work on physical and emotional problems. Group support and personal counseling are also available.

You may find that the meals seem suspiciously gourmet. The secret is all-natural ingredients low in salt and saturated fat, high in fiber, and prepared without refined flour or sugar. The cheerful staff will bring seconds and even pack fruit for you to take back to your room. Herbal teas and decaf and regular coffee are available throughout the day; at night there's popcorn in the movie room—unsalted and unbuttered.

Casual in every way, Canyon Ranch attracts an interesting cross section of people, from young executives to grandmothers, from all parts of the Americas and Europe. Up to 40% of the 250 guests in residence at any one time are men.

Canyon Ranch Health and Fitness Resort
8600 East Rockcliff Rd., Tucson, AZ 85715
Tel. 602/749–9000 or 800/742–9000
Fax 602/749–1646

Administration	Founders/owners, Enid and Mel Zuckerman; fitness directors, Linda Marques, Bruce Lesman; medical director, Phil Eichling, M.D., M.P.H.
Season	Year-round.
Accommodations	140 rooms in casitas. Suites and private condominium cottages with kitchen, living room, and laundry. All in desert colors with modern, southwestern furnishings, large beds, TV/radio, and private baths. Year-round air-conditioning.
Rates	5-day Spa Getaway $1,000–$1,860 single, $890–$1,540 per person double occupancy; 11-day Total Lifestyle plan $2,500–$4,550 single, $2,220–$3,610 double. Daily rate $225–$250 single, $220–$345 double. Add 18% service charge and 6.5% tax. Two days payable in advance. No minimum stay. Credit cards: MC, V.
Meal Plans	18-day cycle of calorie-controlled meals (1,200 calories a day for women, 1,500 calories for men). Breakfast selections are french toast, bran muffins, 7-grain waffle; lunch selections are oriental chicken salad, pasta primavera, Mexican spaghetti, bean bur-

rito, stir-fry vegetables, meatless chili; dinner entrees include barbecued chicken breast, cioppino, tomato-basil ravioli, lamb chops, fresh fish. Fresh fruit sorbet, berries in season, blueberry cheesecake are desserts. Fruit-flavored nutrition shakes, crudités, and nonalcoholic drinks served daily. Tea and coffee (regular or decaf) always available. Vitamin supplement at breakfast; alternative vegetarian menu daily.

Services and Facilities **Exercise Equipment:** Full line of weight training machines, 11 stationary bikes, 2 recumbent bikes, 15 treadmills, 8 stair machines, Gravitron, 3 rowing machines, 2 NordicTrack cross-country ski machines, mini-trampolines, free weights. **Services:** 9 types of massage, aromatherapy, herbal wraps, body scrub with crushed pearl; hair salon, nail and skin care. Consultation on nutrition and diet, holistic health, body composition, and fitness level. Biofeedback program, smoking cessation. Cooking class. **Swimming Facilities:** Indoor pool, 3 outdoor pools. **Recreation Facilities:** 8 tennis courts, 3 racquetball courts, squash court, outdoor running track, basketball, volleyball, 21-speed mountain bikes; golf and horseback riding nearby. **Evening Programs:** Talks by psychologists, authors, naturalists, and other specialists.

In the Area Daily hiking, biking trips in Sabino Canyon; Biosphere 2; Arizona-Sonora Desert Museum, crafts market in Nogales, Mt. Lemmon (pine forest); Tucson's old-town arts district, Mission San Xavier del Bac in Santa Cruz Valley.

Getting Here *From Tucson.* By car, Speedway Blvd. east to Kolb Rd., Tanque Verde to Sabino Canyon Rd., Snyder Rd. to Rockcliff (30 min). Free transfer from Tucson airport on arrival and departure; rental car, taxi service available.

Special Notes Limited access for the disabled. Summer program for families; minimum age of guests is 14. Smoking not permitted indoors. Remember to bring completed medical questionnaire, hiking shoes, walking shoes, clothing for warmth, and sun protection. Spa hours: daily 6 AM–10 PM.

Global Fitness Adventures in Sedona

Holistic health
Spiritual awareness

Arizona
Sedona The week-long Global Fitness Adventure in Sedona is a journey of self-awareness, where guests absorb energy from the canyons, towering rock monoliths, and fire-red buttes of the area; visit four primary vortexes—said to emit positive and negative charges that affect human physiology; and take 8- to 15-mile hikes to the remains of ancient settlements.

Most mornings guests begin their days with yoga and tai chi chuan on a rock vortex surrounded by incredible views. A purification ceremony in the traditional Native American Sweat Lodge is optional. The daily schedule also includes a sunset horseback ride, natural healing bodywork, and fitness classes. The group is housed in wooden creekhouses in Oak Creek Canyon, and a private chef cooks organic meals in the main lodge, where evening programs are held.

Global Fitness Adventures in Sedona
Box 1390, Aspen, CO 81612
Tel. 303/927–9593, Fax 303/927–4793

Administration Founder/Director, Kristina Hurrell

Season March–May and September–November.

Accommodations 10 creek houses, each with 2 bedrooms, 2 fireplaces, large living room, kitchen, wood decks. Southwestern decor, shared bathroom. No TV, phone, air-conditioning.

Rates $1,850 per week includes 3 massages, all meals. $500 check deposit, balance due 30 days prior to arrival. Gratuities suggested ($50–$100). No credit cards.

Meal Plan Organic vegetarian meals served family style. Breakfast can be a power drink made from fruit, soy protein powder, and wheat germ or granola. Lunch is a mixed salad or curry tempeh sprout sandwiches. Dinner is Tex-Mex vegetarian chili with jalapeño corn muffins, mixed greens, or vegetable soup with salad.

Services and Facilities **Services:** Massage, natural healing bodywork, fitness classes. **Recreation Facilities:** Horseback riding. **Evening Programs:** Motivational talks, sweat lodge.

In the Area Jerome (Victorian mining town), Tuzigoot and Montezuma's Castle (prehistoric ruins), the Grand Canyon, Sedona arts and crafts shopping.

Getting Here *From Phoenix.* By car, I–17N (90 min). By plane, commuter flights to Sedona airport (20 min). By bus, shuttle service from Phoenix Skyharbor by reservation (tel. 602/282–2066).

Maine Chance

Luxury pampering   *Women only*
Vibrant maturity

Arizona
Phoenix
Maine Chance is Elizabeth Arden's sunbelt showplace, a health retreat for the woman who wants to get away from it all in comfort. Set on a 105-acre estate, the old-world mansion with its views of Camelback Mountain gives guests a sense of being in the middle of a rose garden. The staff of 130 extends lots of personal service to the guests, whose number is limited to 56.

The Sunday–Sunday program is tailored to the individual's needs and fitness level. The full schedule of exercise classes includes workouts in the swimming pool and yoga. Treatments such as the Ardena Wax Bath, manicures, pedicures, and makeup sessions—all using Arden products—require appointments. Focus can be on weight loss or gain, relaxation, or a complete head-to-toe makeover.

Guests are free to do as much or as little as they please. The all-inclusive fee encourages you to try underwater massage as well as the popular Swedish-style soother. Rigorous activities from advanced aerobics to tai chi chuan are also available. You can do laps without exposing sensitive skin to the sun in the newly constructed indoor pool or work out in the newly equipped fitness rooms.

Your exercise can consist of jogging between the manicurist and the hairstylist, or you can participate in the light 30-minute workouts or yoga. Relax in the steam cabinets, sauna, and whirlpool. All the personal attention from the staff makes you feel like a winner.

Maine Chance
5830 E. Jean Ave., Phoenix, AZ 85018
Tel. 602/947–6365

Administration General manager, Judy McGohon

Season Oct.–May. Closed Christmas week.

Accommodations 46 elegant rooms, single or double occupancy, suites in 8 houses, French antique furnishings and modern baths; hair dryer, cosmetics, daily change of wardrobe for spa workouts supplied.

Rates One week $3,170–$3,800 per person double occupancy, $3,400–$4,200 single, all services, gratuities, and tax included. 50% payable in advance. No credit cards.

Meal Plans 3 meals daily begin with breakfast in bed; the personalized diet includes fresh fruit and vegetables, lean meat, fish, coffee or tea. Shrimp mixed salads, cheese soufflés, angelhair pasta with pesto sauce, and filet mignon are among the offerings.

Services and Facilities **Exercise Equipment:** 4 Trotter treadmills, 3 Schwinn Air-Dyne bikes, NordicTrack, Stairlife, Nautilus circuit, free weights, step-aerobics units. **Services:** Massage, facials, skin and nail care, hairstyling, hydrotherapy. **Swimming Facilities:** Indoor pool. **Recreation Facilities:** Tennis, golf, horseback riding nearby. **Evening Programs:** Talks on health, nutrition, fashion.

In the Area Shopping trips to local boutiques; museum tours on request; the Heard Museum (American Indian), Scottsdale, the Desert Museum (natural history).

Getting Here Skyport International Airport 15 min away by car or taxi. Limousine service on arrival and departure.

Special Notes All activities held on ground floor. No smoking indoors.

Marriott's Spa at Camelback Inn

Life enhancement
Luxury pampering
Non-program resort facilities

Arizona Housed in a spectacular hacienda-style structure in the foot-
Scottsdale hills of Mummy Mountain, the Spa at Camelback Inn accommodates fitness buffs as well as the resort's leisure and business guests. Combining the latest technologies and equipment with old-world therapies, the spa has the most complete facilities in the Phoenix-Scottsdale area. Among the features are a health-food restaurant overlooking the lap pool, indoor and outdoor massage rooms, a weights room with video monitors, four types of exercise bicycle, and a comprehensive wellness testing program.

Advancing the art of fitness evaluations, Camelback has linked up with the Cooper Institute of Aerobic Research in Texas, where testing procedures are based on those of aerobics pioneer Dr. Kenneth R. Cooper. FITCHECK is a one-hour assessment of body composition, flexibility, cardiovascular endurance, and body strength. PALS is a comprehensive Personalized Aerobics Lifestyle System that you work on with one-on-one staff instruction and take home in a big binder.

Plan on spending at least a full day at the spa to enjoy some of the exotic bodywork after exercising in the aerobics studio or the fully equipped weights room. Start with a four-mile power walk up the mountainside for grand views of the Phoenix valley and surrounding desert, then through lushly landscaped residential areas. The daily walk at 6:30 AM is open to all resort guests without charge, and if you book at least an hour of services, the daily spa admission charge ($18) is waived.

There is no question that staffers take their work seriously; many have University of Arizona degrees in physiology and some are trained in esoteric massage techniques at workshops in nearby Sedona or California.

Southwestern art and ceramics brighten the locker rooms and lounges, where bottles of water are always at hand to ward off dehydration in the dry Arizona climate. Having a massage outdoors under a crystal-blue sky can be followed by a body scrub with a mixture of sea salts and oils, or an herbal wrap. Specially equipped treatment rooms and the sauna and steam room are in an atrium around a cold plunge pool and hot whirlpool.

Indulging in breakfast and luncheon specialties at Sprouts, the aptly named spa restaurant, won't send you into cholesterol shock. Chefs here have developed menu selections that are suited to the climate—light, tasty, and low in fat. The freshly baked muffins attract resort guests as well as dieters, and Sprouts offers the widest choice of bottled waters in the West.

Supplied with workout clothing, robe, and slippers, all you need to bring is exercise shoes. Classes in the window-walled aerobics studio are enhanced by mountain views; in fine weather workouts take place on the grass. Many forego workouts to simply relax at the sun-shaded outdoor pool and enjoy lunch. The new destination spa for the '90s, Camelback is where fitness and fun are truly well matched.

Marriott's Spa at Camelback Inn
5402 E. Lincoln Dr., Scottsdale, AZ 85253
Tel. 602/948–1700 or 800/242–2635

Administration General manager, Wynn Tyner; spa director, Gayle Moeller

Season Year-round.

Accommodations 423 guest casitas situated on 125 acres. The spa building is surrounded by desert landscaping. Spa packages include deluxe room in private casita, with king-size bed or large twins, decorated in conservative pastels and earth tones. Some have fireplace, upper bedroom and balcony with extra bathroom. All are air-conditioned, have TV, bath amenities, and phones; car parking adjoins casita clusters.

Rates 5-Star Retreat for 2 persons $289 per night, single $239, includes breakfast, unlimited golf, tennis, and spa use, gratuities; 5-day/4-night Calorie Burner program $2,292 for 2 persons, $1,490 single, includes gratuities; add 6.5% tax. Focus on Fitness day with PALS tests $169.65 (no lodging) includes gratuities, tax. All spa services available à la carte. Advance payment by credit card. Credit cards: AE, DC, MC, V.

Meal Plans Choice of spa cuisine in Sprouts Restaurant at the spa building, or Chaparral Room. Breakfast menu offers egg-white omelet, French toast, cereal, freshly squeezed juices, freshly baked muffins, coffee (decaf or regular). Lunch can be a salad, grilled pompano stuffed with crabmeat, or cold skinless breast of chicken. Dinner in the Chaparral Room offers à la carte choices of pasta bow ties with poppy seeds in tomato-basil sauce, poached loin of lamb, grilled aki tuna with papaya relish, and roasted breast of capon stuffed with ricotta cheese. Decaffeinated coffee, herbal tea, and bottled waters are available.

Services and Facilities **Exercise Equipment:** Universal multistation weight training gym, 4 Precor treadmills, StairMaster 4000, Gauntlet, 2 Windracer rowers, 2 Windracer bikes, 2 Schwinn Air-Dyne bikes, Lifecycle, 2 recumbent PTS-Turbo 400 bikes, free weights. **Services:** Swedish, shiatsu, and sports massage, underwater massage (women only), thalassotherapy, aromatherapy, herbal wrap, loofah body scrub, facial; fitness/wellness evaluations, body-composition analysis, nutritional counseling, one-on-one training, beauty salon for hair, nail, and skin care. **Swimming Facilities:** Outdoor lap pool; resort pools. **Recreation Facilities:** 2 golf courses (36 holes), 9-hole pitch-and-putt course, 10 tennis courts (lighted); horseback riding, hiking nearby. **Evening Programs:** resort entertainment.

In the Area The Heard Museum (Native American art and history), Taliesin West (Frank Lloyd Wright home), Cosanti Foundation sculpture garden, Paolo Soleri's Arcosanti, Sedona spiritual energy tour, Buckhorn hot mineral-water baths, Mexican crafts market in Nogales, Biltmore Fashion Park. Big Surf water theme park, Desert Botanical Gardens, equestrian center, Camelback Mountain hiking.

Getting Here *From Phoenix.* By car, north on 44th St., to Lincoln Dr. (30 min). Shuttle bus service from Skyharbor Airport. Taxi, rental car available.

Special Notes Reciprocal guest privileges at Marriott's Mountain Shadows resort and country club. Organized activities for children 5 and older include games, dinner, movies, tennis clinic, tennis day camp. No smoking in the spa. Spa hours: weekdays 6:15 AM–7:30 PM, weekends 6:15 AM–7 PM.

The Phoenician Centre for Well-Being

**Luxury pampering
Life enhancement
Nutrition and diet**

Arizona
Scottsdale Nestled on 130 acres of manicured lawn and desert terrain at the base of Camelback Mountain, The Phoenician combines elegant accommodations, sports, a wide range of spa services, and a wellness center. Though the hotel caters to conferences and family vacationers, the private club atmosphere is maintained. Exceptional service matches the grandeur of the public areas; oversize guest rooms are quiet retreats, with all the amenities of a world-class resort.

Inspired by the therapeutic climate of the Southwest, the center offers treatments using desert plants and minerals. Jojoba, clay, and aloe-vera preparations appear on the menu along with Sothys skin-care products from Paris. Special "signature" programs, including the Desert Adventure and Family Fiesta, are scheduled at select times, and programs are customized to fit the special needs of guests.

The philosophy here is "intuitive choice" in well-being of body, mind, and spirit: guests experience a variety of alternatives in the areas of nutrition, fitness, relaxation, body care, and spirituality, then learn how to integrate these new lifestyle choices into their daily routines at home.

The resort provides a multitude of options for sports and recreation. The two-level Centre for Well-Being is an escape from the desert sun, where you can meditate in a secluded atrium, work out on state-of-the-art equipment, or join an aerobics class in studios equipped with sprung-wood floors. The new exercise facilities, along with beauty salon and barber shop, are on the upper level, enhanced by views of the resort. Activities include walks in the 2-acre cactus garden, picnics by a waterfall, or a traditional English tea. Close to the heart of Phoenix, The Phoenician is a world apart from city life.

The Phoenician Centre for Well-Being

6000 East Camelback Rd., Scottsdale, AZ 85251
Tel. 602/941–8200 or 800/888–8234
Fax 602/947–4311

Administration General manager, Hans D. Turnonzky; director, Josie Feria

Season Year-round.

Accommodations 442 guest rooms in the main hotel, 107 rooms in casitas including 12 parlor suites. Oversize bathrooms in Italian marble, hairdryer, terrycloth robes, 3 telephones. Desert tones accent wooden furniture; suites have hand-carved travertine fireplace. Air-conditioning, TV, daily paper delivery.

Rates Summer: $145–$270, suites $420–$930; winter: $280–$415, suites $775–$1,300. Well-Being program $2,685 (5 nights)–$3,745 (8 nights) for two people. Daily spa admission ($12) waived in conjunction with treatments or program. Tax, gratuity extra. Credit cards: AE, DC, MC, V.

Meal Plans Not included in programs. All resort restaurants and room service offer menu items low in fat, cholesterol, and sodium. Elaine's serves Mediterranean country cuisine, others offer Italian and southwestern specialties.

Services and Facilities Exercise Equipment: Eagle Cybex circuit training, 4 StairMaster 4000 PT, Concept II rower, Liferower, 3 Lifecycle 9500, 2 Schwinn Air-Dyne, PTS Turbo recumbent bike, 5 Precor treadmills, Olympic free weights. **Services:** Massage therapy includes Swedish, shiatsu, sports, reflexology, aromatherapy, jin shin jyutsu, craniosacral, neuromuscular; desert clay, herbal, or aloe-vera body wrap; OJA Shirodhara therapy; facial, eye-lifting, back facial; fitness consultation, body composition analysis, cholesterol testing; scheduled classes for aerobics, tai chi chuan, yoga; salon and barbershop for hair, nail care. **Swimming Facilities:** 7 outdoor pools. **Recreation Facilities:** 18-hole golf course, 11 tennis courts, croquet, lawn bowling, volleyball, badminton, archery, walking, jogging, water basketball and volleyball, bike rental.

In the Area Camelback Mountain hiking, Borgata (shopping), Desert Botanical Garden, Taliesen West (Frank Lloyd Wright Founda-

tion), Heard Museum (Native American art), Sedona arts and
spiritual community, Maine Chance.

Getting Here *From Phoenix.* By car, north on 44th St. to Camelback Rd.,
right to Jokake, left into resort (20 min). Shuttle bus from airport. Taxi, rental car.

Special Notes Funicians Club for children has daily supervised program.
Teenage programs available at certain times of the year.

Scottsdale Princess

Non-program resort facilities

Arizona Rising from the Sonoran Desert like a mirage, the rose-colored
Scottsdale towers and velvet green golf course of the Scottsdale Princess
beckon you to a world of luxury. The 450-acre resort, member
of a hotel chain noted for its upscale facilities in Mexico and
Bermuda, has a king-size health club that enhances the bur-
geoning Phoenix-Scottsdale area. Use of the exercise equipment here and participation in the five daily aerobics classes
come with the daily facility fee ($10).

A fitness staff member sets the pace on a 45-minute morning
walk in the crisp desert air along the grounds and golf course.
The rest of the day is your own to schedule with bodywork and a
bit of luxury pampering. Participating in a wide range of outdoor sports is the major attraction for most guests: walleyball,
Ping-Pong, a fun run, and desert biking are scheduled daily, in
addition to tennis and golf.

Escape the desert sun with a choice of three outdoor swimming
pools, an air-conditioned aerobics studio, and an array of exercise equipment. Other options include nearby hiking trails in
the McDowell Mountains and an equestrian center.

Designed for conventions and sales meetings, the Princess
stays full on weekends by offering special packages. It also organizes a fitness fair and three hours of Olympic-style competi-
tion for corporate groups.

Scottsdale Princess
7575 E. Princess Dr., Scottsdale, AZ 85255
Tel. 602/585-4848 or 800/344-4758
Fax 602/585-0086

Administration Manager, Stephen Ast; health club manager, Jill Eisenhut

Season Year-round.

Accommodations 600 guest rooms and suites range in style from Mexican colonial
to contemporary high-rise. All with living and work areas, terraces, wet bars, and large baths. Casitas with wood-burning
fireplaces near the tennis courts.

Rates $240–$300 single or double occupancy, Jan.–May 14; $90–$120
mid-May–mid-Sept. Packages with the health spa, tennis lessons, and golf (3 days, 2 nights) $319–$575 per person, double
occupancy, high season. One night payable in advance. Credit
cards: AE, DC, MC, V.

Meal Plans The Grill (golf clubhouse) and Las Ventanas (garden atrium
and golf-course view) feature grilled seafood and chicken and
salads. La Hacienda serves Mexican specialties, and the Mar-

quesa features Catalan cuisine. Vegetarian meals are available.

Services and Facilities

Exercise Equipment: 16-station Universal weight training gym, 2 computerized Aerobicycles, 4 Lifecycles, Schwinn Air-Dyne & Monark bikes, Concept II rower, 2 treadmills, free weights, 4 StairMasters. **Services:** Herbal wrap, loofah body scrub, mud wrap, aloe-vera masque, massage (Swedish, aromatherapy, therapeutic, reflexology); salt-glow treatment; beauty salon for facials, hair and nail care. **Swimming Facilities:** 3 outdoor pools, 1 (75 ft) for swimming laps and aquatic exercise. **Recreation Facilities:** 9 tennis courts, 2 18-hole golf courses, racquet and squash courts; nearby equestrian center offers riding, shows, and polo. **Evening Programs:** Resort entertainment.

In the Area

Desert tours by jeep; Sedona arts and spiritual center; hiking trails in the McDowell Mountains.

Getting Here

From Phoenix. By car, north on 44th St. to Camelback Rd., turn right to Scottsdale Rd., then left to Bell Rd. (45 min). By bus, scheduled service from Sky Harbor International Airport.

Special Notes

Some rooms equipped for disabled; ramps and elevators to all areas. No smoking in health club. Hours: weekdays 6 AM–8 PM, weekends 7 AM–7 PM. Kids Klub ($20 per session).

Tucson National Resort & Spa

Luxury pampering
Weight management

Arizona
Tucson

Pleasure pure and simple is the reason to come to the Tucson National Resort & Spa. Set in the desert foothills of the Santa Catalina Mountains, the resort spreads across acres of cultivated gardens and golf courses. Designed on a lavish scale as a country-club community, it has the best little spa in the west.

Hidden within a spectacular clubhouse, the facilities include hydrotherapy rooms for Scotch douches and loofah body scrubs, and a Russian steam bath. The usual collection of saunas and whirlpools for men and women and separate weights rooms are housed here in elegantly tiled and decorated salons, but the special feature is a rooftop deck for alfresco massage that has a spectacular view of the desert.

Mornings begin with a prebreakfast walk along a three-mile path that leads through part of the golf course and over an arroyo. The daily schedule of classes in the aerobics studio is designed for all fitness levels, with stretch-and-flex, water exercise, toning classes, and aerobics. The spa is small and the staff-to-visitor ratio is high. When you want to work out with weights or exercise bikes, someone is always on hand to check your form. There is no required program, and a practical approach to fitness for fun and relaxation prevails.

The resort atmosphere and conference-center activities are not conducive to dieting unless you stick to the daily menu, listed at 1,200 calories. Meals are served in a restaurant with glass walls that overlooks the greens of the former Tucson National Golf Club. It is open to members and guests.

The luxurious resort contrasts sharply with the wasteland that surrounds it. Hiking into nearby Sabino Canyon is an added attraction, opening up a wonderland of boulders, waterfalls, and giant saguaro cacti. The sun-bleached hills take on shades of purple and gold in the early morning.

The trek from your room to the spa building to collect your daily change of shorts and robe is a minor inconvenience. Shower scuffs and towels are also provided. After your workout, try a Swiss shower for a 16-jet water massage, followed by a cold plunge. The women's locker room also has steam cabinets and a recessed Roman-style whirlpool. Both sides have inhalation rooms to clear your sinuses.

Among the treatments in spa packages or à la carte are a vigorous rubdown with sea salts or grated walnuts in sesame seed oil, herbal wraps, and facials. Only at the nearby Canyon Ranch can you find this level of desert-style sophistication.

Tucson National Resort & Spa
2727 West Club Dr., Tucson, AZ 85741
Tel. 602/297-2271 or 800/528-4856
Telex 510-601-5043, Fax 602/742-2452

Administration General manager, Charles Dyke; spa director, Steven J. Waguespack

Season Year-round.

Accommodations 167 rooms and suites in 2-story wings and executive casitas with red-tile roofs and Spanish colonial accents. Rooms have king-size beds, full bath, dressing area, TV, and private balcony. Casitas have wood-burning fireplaces, full kitchen, expansive views. Poolside rooms are closest to the spa.

Rates Spa package $120–$200 single, $90–$130 per person double, per day (2 night minimum); Ultimate Spa package with meals $200–$780 single, $170–$210 double. Add tax and gratuities. Credit cards: AE, DC, MC, V.

Meal Plans 3 meals daily in the Ultimate Spa package. 1,200-calorie (per day) diet low in sodium and cholesterol. Vegetarian lasagna or pizza for lunch, broiled swordfish, pasta primavera, and steamed vegetables for dinner.

Services and Facilities **Exercise Equipment:** 10-station Universal weight training gym, 2 Lifecycles, stationary bikes, free weights, dumbbells (5–45 lb), treadmill, Lifesteps; in women's weights room. Cybex units. **Services:** Swedish massage, herbal wrap, aromatherapy, thalassotherapy, facials, body facials, loofah salt-glow body scrub; manicure, pedicure, hairstyling. Nutritional counseling, private exercise training. **Swimming Facilities:** 75-foot outdoor pool. **Recreation Facilities:** 4 tennis courts (Laykold, lighted), 27-hole golf course, horseback riding, ballooning.

In the Area Sabino Canyon tourmobile, Indian arts and crafts at Mission San Xavier del Bac in Santa Cruz Valley, Mexican crafts in Nogales, Mt. Lemmon observatory, Biosphere 2.

Getting Here *From Tucson.* By car, I–10 north to Cortaro Farms Rd., Shannon Rd. to club entrance (25 min). Airport shuttle service, taxi, rental car available.

Special Notes Elevators provide access for the disabled. No smoking in the spa and in designated areas of the dining room.

The Aspen Club

Sports conditioning
Weight management
Life enhancement
Stress control

Colorado The program here is designed to help you improve your general
Aspen health and fitness level by integrating exercise, healthy eating, and modern medicine. The schedule on a typical Monday in February includes cross-country skiing, tennis, snowshoeing, and downhill skiing, but it's the personal training at the Aspen Fitness and Sports Medicine Institute, the club's high-tech health facility, that sets it apart.

The center for therapy and training employs a comprehensive approach to well-being that considers the individual's personal needs and goals in prescribing short-term lifestyle modifications aimed at making significant health improvements.

The fitness program, which is open to nonmembers, is concerned chiefly with weight loss, stress reduction, and the rehabilitation of sports-related injuries. Visitors stay a few days or a few weeks, scheduling exercise classes and diagnostic appointments among the activities of a world-class resort.

A complete physical evaluation by a team of physicians, physical therapists, and trainers is the first order of business; you undergo a stress test with EKG readings, pulmonary-function tests, and body-fat, strength, and flexibility measurements. A nutritionist evaluates your eating habits and body chemistry (and schedules blood tests when appropriate) prior to recommending a diet that meets your nutritional needs.

Each program is personalized: You work out with a personal trainer, you may be coached on how to order a nutritional meal from a restaurant menu, or enrolled in Pilates training to strengthen muscular resistance. The custom-made character of the program emphasizes the benefits of continuing your new regimen at home. The more immediate benefits tend to be increased energy and improved self-esteem.

Athletes make up a large percentage of the institute's members, as the special equipment attracts pro football players and amateur skiers. Celebrities come, too, and the program director, Julie Anthony, knows how to handle them all: she was formerly team psychologist for the Philadelphia Flyers.

The Aspen Club
Fitness and Sports Medicine Institute
1450 Crystal Lake Rd., Aspen, CO 81611
Tel. 303/925–8900 or 800/882–2582 (800/443–2582 in CO)

Administration Program director, Julie Anthony; medical director, Barry Mink, M.D.

Season Year-round.

Accommodations Studios, 4- and 5-bedroom condominiums, private homes—all with Jacuzzi, fireplace, sun deck—by arrangement with the

Aspen Club Management Company. 91 rooms and suites at the Aspen Club Lodge have oak furnishings, queen-size and twin beds, bath, and kitchen. Maid service, newspaper delivery. Continental breakfast and health-club facilities included.

Rates Aspen Club Lodge rooms $110–$650 single or double, per day; condominium $75–$2,750 per day. The Fitness and Sports Institute services and tests are à la carte or a part of the $650–$800 program. Some costs may be covered by medical insurance. Services and programs billed separately, 15% tax and gratuity added. 50% advance payment within 10 days of booking. Credit cards: MC, V.

Meal Plans Club dining facility; recommended restaurants include Gordon's, Syzygy, Piñons, Cache Cache.

Services and Facilities **Exercise Equipment:** 12-unit David circuit, 4 Keiser Cam III, 3 Nautilus units, Eagle leg press, 2 Polaris units, 7 StairMasters, 5 Quinton, 1 Precor treadmill, 6 Lifecycles, 2 Liferowers, Precor rower, 6 Tunturi bikes, 5 Monark bikes, 2 Schwinn bikes, Turbo and Nautilus recumbent bikes, NordicTrack, free weights, dumbbells and barbells (3–100 lbs). **Services:** Swedish massage, nutritional and food-allergy evaluation, strength and flexibility tests, blood-profile analysis, maximal stress test, body-composition analysis, private exercise training; post-injury therapy. **Swimming Facilities:** Indoor lap pool. **Recreation Facilities:** Skiing, 2 indoor and 7 outdoor tennis courts, 3 racquetball courts, 3 squash courts, basketball, volleyball, wallyball, fencing, cycling, aikido. Golf and horseback riding nearby. **Evening Programs:** Athletics, tournaments, fitness and nutrition seminar.

In the Area Mountain hiking and dogsledding offered by local tour operators. Aspen Music Festival and Ballet/Dance Festival (July–Aug.), ballooning, rafting. Crafts shows and classes at the Anderson Ranch at Snowmass. Nature walks at Hallam Lake Wildlife Sanctuary. Mineral-water baths at Glenwood Springs.

Getting Here *From Denver.* By train, Amtrak to Glenwood Springs (2 hr). By bus, Greyhound to Glenwood Springs (3 hr). By car, I–70 to Dillon, Rte. 91 to Hwy. 24, Rte. 82 via Independence Pass (closed in winter) is scenic route (3½ hr). By plane, flights on United or Continental Express (40 min). Free pickup to and from Aspen airport. Rental car, taxi, limousine available.

Special Notes Full facilities for the disabled. Children's athletic programs in swimming, tennis, squash, racquetball, and dance; nursery and toddler swim class by reservation. No smoking in public areas. Some nonsmoking apartments and rooms. Spa hours: 6:45 AM–10 PM daily.

The Cascade Club at the Westin Hotel

Non-program resort facilities

Colorado Vail Skiers and hikers get a bonus here: a complete sports and fitness facility. Adjacent to the luxurious Westin Hotel, the Cascade Club has a full range of aerobics and sports-training programs plus sports-medicine clinics. In addition to an indoor track and tennis, squash, and racquetball courts, there is a year-round outdoor swimming pool and thermal whirlpool. Daily fee ($10) lets you participate in 5–7 scheduled classes.

After a day on the slopes or the trails, you can have an alfresco soak or enjoy the steam room in the men's and women's pavilions. Tired muscles can be soothed in individual massage rooms, and an aerobics studio allows you to work out any kinks.

The hotel is set in the exclusive Cascade Village, a few steps from the new Ford Amphitheatre, where summer shows range from symphonic pops to rock. To skiers' delight, a new four-passenger chairlift whisks you from the hotel to the upper slopes in eight minutes.

The Cascade Club at the Westin Hotel
Cascade Village, Vail, CO 81657
Tel. 303/476–7111 or 800/228–3000

Administration Cascade Club general manager, Pete Peters

Season Year-round.

Accommodations 322 luxury rooms and suites with king- and queen-size beds, sofas, color TV.

Rates Daily rate per person $89–$375, depending on the season; premier guest rooms and suites higher; value seasons mid-Sept.– mid-Nov., mid-Apr.–June 1. Confirmation by credit card. Add 8.2% tax, 17% gratuity. Credit cards: AE, DC, MC, V.

Meal Plans Robust soups, salads, sandwiches; a skier's breakfast; a "fanny lunch" for mountainside picnics in The Cafe. Alfredo's features rotisserie-grilled meats, chicken, and fish for dinner. No special diet menu.

Services and Facilities **Exercise Equipment:** 17-unit Nautilus circuit, StairMaster, 8 Lifecycles, 4 Lifesteps, 2 StarTrac treadmills, Trotter treadmill, Trackmaster, 2 Schwinn Air-Dyne bikes, UBE, NordicTrack, Concept II rower, Liferower, free weights. **Services:** Swedish massage, fitness and nutritional evaluations. **Swimming Facilities:** Heated outdoor pool. **Recreation Facilities:** 3 outdoor and 4 indoor tennis courts, bike rentals, 3 squash courts, 2 racquetball courts, golf, indoor driving range.

In the Area Vail Nordic and Nature Center and Snowmobile Tours offer various programs. Colorado Ski Museum, Dobson Ice Arena (indoor skating), white-water rafting on the Eagle River.

Getting Here *From Denver:* By car, I–70 to Vail (2 hr). By plane, commuter flights to Avon Airport. Free airport transfers.

Special Notes No smoking in the Cascade Club. Hours: weekdays 6 AM–9 PM, weekends 7 AM–9 PM. Sports clinics for youngsters to age 14.

Doral Telluride Resort and Spa

Life enhancement
Sports conditioning
Luxury pampering
Non-program resort facilities
Kid fitness

Colorado
Telluride The $75 million Doral Telluride Resort and Spa is a luxury retreat catering to both spa lovers and outdoors enthusiasts. Set amid the ski slopes in Southwest Colorado, the 10-story hotel is surrounded by majestic views of the Rocky Mountains. The Alpine Adventures program capitalizes on regional attractions

such as Orvis flyfishing trips, San Miguel river rafting, trail rides, mountain biking and rock climbing, and skiing. Guests can enjoy morning walks in the crisp mountain air, sunrise yoga in a glass-walled studio, and guided hikes.

The Institute di Saturnia is a hushed enclave atop the hotel's 42,000-square-foot spa and fitness center. Offering the widest range of skin-care treatments and bodywork in the area, the 40-room facility is open to both day visitors and hotel guests. Creams and thermal mud packs formulated in Italy are used to prepare for a day on the slopes, or to soothe aches afterward.

Unlike its sister spas in Miami and Italy, the Doral Telluride fitness program is not structured with meals and exercise schedules. The various program packages let you select a course after consultation with the physiotherapist-nutritionist team, and you can have a personal trainer. Arnold Schwarzenegger, who has a condo here, may be pumping iron in the lavishly equipped weights room, and Oprah Winfrey drops in for yoga classes, but it's distinctly low-key.

The weatherproof workouts include both indoor and outdoor swimming pools, cardiovascular deck with inspiring views, and a weight room packed with the latest Cybex equipment. Rock climbing can be practiced indoors, as well as racquetball, squash, and badminton. For family fun there is KidSpa, a new concept in day camps, and a water slide into the indoor/outdoor swimming pool. Workout clothing is provided in locker rooms. The library has books and videos to enjoy in your room. During ski season there is direct access to lifts from the hotel, complimentary van service into historic Telluride, plus ski bus.

Doral Telluride Resort and Spa

624 Mountain Village Blvd., Box 2702, Telluride, CO 81435
Tel. 303/728–6800, 800/223–6725, or 800/285–5050
Fax 303/728–6175

Administration   General manager, Robert Boyle; spa director, Mark Vinchesi

Season   Year-round.

Accommodations   177 deluxe rooms surrounding a four-story atrium. Included are 35 suites with living-dining area. All rooms have balcony, extralarge bathroom with stall shower, southwestern decor, TV, minibar, air conditioning, 2 phones, hair dryer, magnifying mirror, and full amenities.

Rates   4- to 7-night spa packages priced seasonally, from $1,405 single, $1,093 double per person. The Higher Image program includes 3 meals daily, medical screening and high-altitude orientation, unlimited fitness classes, and round-trip transfers from Telluride airport. Add 8.2% tax, 18% gratuity. Daily spa admission $20 for resort guest, $80 if booked with a service by nonresort guest. Daily hotel room tariff $122–$575, suites $225–$900. Deposit for one night by credit card. Credit cards: AE, DC, MC, V.

Meal Plans   Prepared under specific nutritional guidelines for minimal sodium, fat, and caloric content, the exclusive Saturnia Cuisine might include pizza made with tomatoes, fresh mozarella, and basil, or a grilled chicken breast sandwich on a whole-wheat pita for lunch. Dinner may be fresh Atlantic salmon, pasta, and mixed salad. Coffee (regular or decaf), herbal tea, and mineral waters available. Full bar and American-style menu in The Sundance restaurant. Gourmet menu in the Alpenglow room for dinner only (surcharge for spa package guests).

Services and Facilities **Exercise Equipment:** 42-unit Cybex weight training system, 2 Concept II rowers, 2 StairMaster Gauntlets, 3 StairMasters 4000PT, VersaClimber, 6 Precor 9.5 treadmills, 2 Nordic-Tracks, 2 Lifecycles 9500R, 4 Lifecycles 9500, 2 Precor bikes, Pilates, dumbbells (3–100 lbs), free weights. **Services:** Terme di Saturnia body facial, fango, or cellulite treatment, hydrothera-py bath with seaweed, fango, milk whey, aromatherapy; salon for hair, nail, and skin care; personalized training, fitness eval-uation, nutrition plan; stress management using biofeedback, respiration, hemi-sync goggles, "InnerSea" dry float system; Swedish, shiatsu, aromatherapy, sports, and therapeutic mas-sage; herbal wrap, hayflower pack, Ultratone body shaping. **Swimming Facilities:** 25-yard indoor lap pool, heated outdoor/indoor pool. **Recreation Facilities:** 1 racquetball court, 1 squash court, 5 outdoor tennis courts, mountain bike rental, flyfishing, cross-country and downhill skiing equipment rentals, 18-hole golf course; Preferred Peaks room with climbing wall.

In the Area Crested Butte, Black Canyon National Monument, Millon Dol-lar Hwy. (scenic drive), Mesa Verde National Park (Anasazi cliff dwellings), Durango (historic district, narrow-gauge rail-road), Ouray and Pagosa hot springs.

Getting Here *From Denver:* By car, I–70 west to Grand Junction, Hwy. 62 south via Ridegway, Hwy. 145 (6½ hr). By plane, Continental Express and United Express (60 min). Complimentary shuttle service at Telluride Airport to hotel. Car rental, taxi available.

Special Notes KidSpa activities and day care available for half- or full-day fee. High altitude at hotel (9,490 ft. elevation) will require an initial adjustment. Smoking is permitted in all public areas; some guest rooms and designated tables in dining rooms are no-smoking; no smoking in the spa. All areas are accessible for the disabled.

Eden Valley Lifestyle Center

Preventive medicine
Weight management
Spiritual awareness
Vibrant maturity

Colorado This homelike retreat set amid woods, lakes, and streams on
Loveland 550 acres in the foothills of the Rocky Mountains teaches physi-cal conditioning and nutrition in comprehensive programs last-ing seven to 24 days. The Eden Valley Lifestyle Center's approach emphasizes the pursuit of traditional Seventh-day Adventist philosophies of diet and mental and spiritual health under medical supervision.

Following thorough individual physical evaluations by the med-ical director, small groups of guests are counseled on health and disease prevention. Cooking demonstrations show how the vegetarian diet can be adapted to one's own kitchen routines.

The doctor monitors each guest's progress and may suggest ad-ditional activities. Drinking lots of pure water, walking in the clean mountain air and sunshine, and taking hydrotherapy and whirlpool baths are all part of the program.

Personalized strategies for attaining a healthy lifestyle are prepared for those with heart disease, diabetes, degenerative disease, and digestive problems. Chronic fatigue, obesity, arthritis, and high blood pressure are also treated, and there is therapy for quitting smoking.

The Lifestyle program began in 1987 as an extension of services at a nearby home for senior citizens. People of all ages come here to gain new vitality and stamina and to relax in the company of a small supportive group. There is lots of camaraderie here—and a very attentive staff.

Eden Valley Lifestyle Center
6263 N. County Rd. 29, Loveland, CO 80538
Tel. 303/669–7730 or 800/637–9355

Administration	Administrator, Jim Micheff; medical director, Joseph Shidler, M.D.
Season	Year-round.
Accommodations	5 guest rooms with twin beds in a new ranch-style facility, 3 with private bath; 5 rooms in private homes. Draperies and flowered bedspreads. Private sun deck.
Rates	7-day program $745–$795, 14 days $1,395, 21 days $1,995, all per person, double occupancy. Medical costs may be covered by health insurance. $300 in advance for the 14-day and 21-day programs, $100 for the 7-day program, nonrefundable. Credit cards: MC, V. Companion rates available.
Meal Plans	3 vegetarian meals daily, buffet style. Adventist diet of fruit, raw vegetables, legumes, and grains. No butter, oils, or dairy products. Some olives, nuts, and avocado. Vegetarian lasagna with mock-cheese topping. Bean haystack with rice on corn chips, topped with cashew-nut mixture. Green salads, steamed vegetables, and baked tofu for dinner. No coffee, tea, or condiments. Whole-grain bread baked daily.
Services and Facilities	**Exercise Equipment:** Stationary bike, treadmill, trampoline. **Services:** Physical examination, blood-chemistry analysis, computerized lifestyle inventory, daily hydrotherapy treatments with massage, Jacuzzi, sauna. **Swimming Facilities:** Community pool and lakes. **Recreation Facilities:** Mountain trail hiking, fishing, boating; downhill and cross-country skiing. Golf course, tennis courts, horseshoe and picnic facilities nearby.
In the Area	Estes Park (mountain resort), greyhound racetrack, county fair and rodeo, trail rides, ghost towns, antiques shops. Performing-arts and museum exhibitions.
Getting Here	*From Denver.* By car, I–25 north to Loveland, Cty. Rd. 27 to Cty. Rd. 29 (90 min).
Special Notes	No smoking.

Filhoa Meadows

Holistic health
Preventive medicine
Stress control
Taking the waters
Vibrant maturity

Colorado
White River
National Forest

A family-oriented health retreat close to Aspen, Filhoa Meadows offers programs designed to bring your life into equilibrium. Taking a Christian approach, the workshops and private counseling seek to achieve a balance in four areas: mental, physical, spiritual, and social. Coordinated by specialists in physical education and cardiac rehabilitation and medical consultants, activities center around a big wooden lodge close to historic Indian Springs that provide a constant source of hot mineral water for the indoor and outdoor hydrotherapy pools. Guest rooms are divided between the lodge, a private house, and two newly built cabins with duplex apartments, outdoor decks, and hot tubs.

The health education concentrates on understanding diet, exercise, and how our minds work. No meals are served, so come prepared to do your own cooking as well as participate in discussions on nutrition and a healthy lifestyle. Supervised workouts are scheduled in an indoor pool that is equipped with hydrojets and in a small exercise area that has panoramic views of the Rockies.

For couples with marital problems, founder/owner Robert Durham provides conflict-resolution counseling. With the emphasis on personal communications and family relationships, these sessions can involve children as well as adults.

Designed for the person who is at high risk for the lifestyle diseases (cancer, heart problems, arthritis), this is therapy to help change old behavioral habits that are self-defeating and debilitating. In addition to the soothing mineral-water baths, downhill skiing in winter and biking in summer, and the natural scenic beauty at 7,000-foot elevation in the Rockies, you can enjoy a full range of entertainment and sports.

Filhoa Meadows
14628 Hwy. 133, Redstone, CO 81623
Tel. 303/963–1989 or 800/227–8906

Administration Director, Robert Durham; seminar coordinator, Melody L. Durham, R.N.; medical consultant, Bernarr Johnson, M.D., F.A.C.S.

Season Year-round.

Accommodations 4 private bedrooms in the main lodge share 3 bathrooms, kitchen; 2-bedroom River House sleeps 8, has full bathroom, kitchen, family room with additional sofa beds. Choice of single beds, queen- or king-size. 2 rustic cabins with duplex apartments each have queen-size bed, sofabed, kitchenette, bathroom, deck, and hot tub. No air-conditioning, TV, or phone.

Rates $60 per night in the lodge, $50 per night in the River House, single or double occupancy, $65–$70 per couple in cabin. Add taxes. Counseling $40 per hour. Advance payment of 1 night, nonrefundable, by check. No credit cards.

Meal Plans None. Guests do their own cooking.

Services and Facilities **Exercise Equipment:** 2 Schwinn bikes, 2 rowing machines, Sears treadmill, free weights. **Services:** Massage, counseling, cooking demonstration. **Swimming Facilities:** Indoor static lap pool. **Recreation Facilities:** 3 outdoor Jacuzzis, parcourse, running track; nearby downhill and cross-country skiing, trout fishing, hiking, biking, rafting, horseback riding.

In the Area Aspen (summer music and ballet festivals), Glenwood Springs (swimming, golf), jeep tours to the Snowmass Wilderness (ghost towns, nature photography), Colorado River (white-water rafting), Redstone (Victorian mining town).

Getting Here *From Denver.* By car, I–70 to Glenwood Springs, Hwy. 82 to 133 (3 hr). By bus, Trailways to Glenwood Springs (2 hr). By train, Amtrak to Glenwood Springs (1 hr). By plane, scheduled flights to Aspen (30 min). Transportation by prior request to and from Glenwood Springs and Aspen.

Special Notes Limited access for the disabled. No smoking indoors.

Glenwood Hot Springs Lodge & Pool

Taking the waters

Colorado
Glenwood Springs The biggest natural mineral-water pool this side of the Rockies attracts guests to the Glenwood Hot Springs Lodge. Even in subfreezing temperatures the water's lingering warmth should keep you warm long enough to get to the locker room.

Summer and winter, the 130-degree water is cooled for comfort in the 405-foot-long outdoor swimming pool. In a smaller therapy pool equipped with underwater jets for massage, the water temperature is 104 degrees. Together the pools contain 1.1 million gallons of mineral water, changed three times daily. The entire complex is two blocks long.

Lodge guests have direct access to the Hot Springs Athletic Club and can participate in aerobic workouts, use championship racquetball, handball, and wallyball courts, and relax in coed saunas and whirlpools. The club's scheduled fitness classes include water and low-impact aerobics, and Jazzercise.

Located on I–70, the principal east-west route across the state, the Victorian-looking town has motel lodging in every price category as well as camping and RV hookups. The new facility was opened in 1986 for the resort's centennial.

In the nearby vapor caves (coed), the hot springs create temperatures that reach 115 degrees and make for a great sweat. Cold-water hoses are available, but there is no soaking pool. Day visitors are welcome here and at the pools.

Glenwood Hot Springs Lodge & Pool
Box 308, Glenwood Springs, CO 81601
Tel. 303/945–6571

Administration Manager, Kjell Mitchell

Season Year-round.

Accommodations 107 modern rooms furnished with two queen-size beds (some are king-size), private bath and double vanity. Deluxe rooms with balcony or patio overlooking the pools, coffee maker, safe, air-conditioning, geothermal heating.

Rates $46–$73 per day single, $51–$78 double; deluxe rooms $54–$73 single, $59–$78 for 2 persons. Add 7.7% tax. Daily pool admission $6 adults, $3.75 children. Discount on admission to baths and health club for lodge guests. 1 night payable in advance. Credit cards: AE, DC, MC, V.

Meal Plans Meals served at the lodge cafe and nearby motels. Broiled chicken and mountain trout are local specialties.

Services and Facilities **Exercise Equipment:** 10-station Nautilus units, 4 Lifecycles, 2 StairMasters. **Services:** Massage, facials, chiropractic adjustment. **Swimming Facilities:** 4 outdoor pools. **Recreation Facilities:** Hiking, water slide, trout fishing, 4 indoor racquetball courts, 2 handball and wallyball courts.

In the Area Ski resorts, Aspen Music Festival, Wheeler Opera House, Anderson Ranch arts center at Snowmass, galleries and shops in Aspen.

Getting Here *From Denver.* By train, Amtrak twice daily (3 hr). By bus, Greyhound (4 hr). By car, I–70 (3 hr). Rental car available.

Special Notes No smoking in the health club or caves.

Global Fitness Adventures

Life enhancement
Holistic health
Stress control
Spiritual awareness

Colorado
Aspen A Rocky Mountain health retreat for up to 10 participants, this one-week program was designed by former fashion model Kristina Hurrell and her husband, Dr. Rob Krakovitz, author and holistic health authority. Inspired by the majesty and splendor of the Rockies, they designed a life-energizing program filled with fun and activities for guests of all ages.

The picturesque 52-acre ranch is located 45 miles from Aspen and is surrounded by 2 million acres of the White River National Forest. Welcomed at the main lodge, you are assigned to a room or private cabin. A variety of natural healing techniques and bodywork are included in the program. Days begin with an hour of yoga and end with dinner by candlelight.

Outdoor recreation is the focus here. Hiking and touring the backcountry fill most days. Horseback riding continues to be a major attraction at this former dude ranch. The variety of excursions include cross-country skiing, snowshoe hiking, sleigh rides, and downhill skiing (at an additional $45 fee). An optional Vision Quest, involving a 24-hour Indian ceremony, sweat lodge, and drumming, is often available. A daily massage (1-hour) is included in the program rate.

The combination of healthy eating and extensive daily exercise forms a basis for weight loss. Spa-cuisine meals total 800 calories per day. Vegetarian meals and supervised juice or water regimens are also offered.

By adhering to a course of exercise and attending classes on topics ranging from improving communication skills and personal relations to the enhancement of mental, emotional, and physical energies, the sense of well-being you acquire in this magical place will put you on the road to peak vitality.

Global Fitness Adventures
Box 1390, Aspen, CO 81612
Tel. 303/927–9593 or 800/548–2721
Fax 303/927–4793

Administration	Founder/director, Kristina Hurrell; Holistic medicine director, Rob Krakovitz, M.D.
Season	Year-round.
Accommodations	18 rooms in main lodge and guest cabins. Rustic charm, ranch-style furnishings, private modern baths. Lodge with high beam ceiling and open fireplace. Jacuzzi on sun deck.
Rates	$1,700–$2,300 per person, double occupancy for 1 week. $300 per person per day; includes all meals, massages. Deposit $500, balance due 30 days prior to arrival. $50–$100 gratuity suggested. No credit cards.
Meal Plans	3 meals daily, family style, plus snacks. Breakfast is either pineapple or papaya (high in enzymes that aid digestion), granola, or a power drink made from fruit, soy protein powder, and wheat germ. Lunch is either a salad with tofu, nuts, seeds, and sprouts, or lemon garlic tempeh sprout sandwich. Dinner is steamed squash, steamed brown rice with vegetables, grilled trout, or vegetarian lasagna.
Services and Facilities	**Services:** Massage, natural healing bodywork, yoga and meditation training, detoxification techniques, diet plan with nutritional supplement. Personal consultation on medical and health problems, with holistic therapies (fee). Horseback-riding instruction (fee). **Swimming Facilities:** Nearby lake. **Recreation Facilities:** Horseback riding, trout fishing rowing, canoeing, snowshoeing, mountain biking; golf and tennis nearby. **Evening Programs:** Informal workshops on health and nutrition.
In the Area	Cross-country and downhill skiing, trail rides; shopping, summer arts festival in Aspen; mineral baths at Glenwood Springs; Olympic training center at Colorado Springs.
Getting Here	*From Denver.* By car, I–70 to Glenwood Springs, Rte. 82 to Basalt (3 hr). By air, commuter flights to Aspen (40 min). Free pickup in Aspen on Sun.
Special Notes	Laundry service provided. No smoking indoors, smoking discouraged elsewhere. Program also in Sedona, AZ, and Kauai, HI.

Great Sand Dunes Country Club and Inn

Non-program resort facilities
Spiritual awareness

Colorado
San Luis Valley

Opened in 1990, the Great Sand Dunes Country Club and Inn resembles a frontier settlement, with rough-hewn log cabins and 800 head of buffalo roaming the grounds. Don't imagine that you'll have to rough it, however. The native crafts and western antiques scattered about make the accommodations feel authentic, but all the modern conveniences are present as well. Amenities include a sauna, Jacuzzi, ozone-filtered heated swimming pool, glassed-in gym, and 18-hole golf course.

And you can't beat the scenery: The unique sand dunes, waves of ever-shifting sand lapping at the base of snow-capped mountains, cut a 57-square-mile swath through the valley that is clearly visible from every vantage point on the ranch. The atmosphere is conducive to meditation and contemplation, as well as to fun: Children love climbing the sandy slopes, and Nordic skiers often don Arab robes for an outing on a sea of sand.

Surrounding attractions include swims in the warm mineral water at Valley View Hot Springs; old boom towns, like Creed, that retain their frontier spirit; and spiritual retreats such as the Zen Center, Haidakhandi Universal Ashram, Tibetan Buddhist Center, and Carmelite Hermitage.

Great Sand Dunes Country Club and Inn
5303 Highway 150, Mosca, CO 81146
Tel. 719/378–2356

Administration Owner/director, Hisayoshi Ota; General manager, George Kellof

Season July–August.

Accommodations 15 guest rooms in 3 vintage log buildings. Handmade wooden furniture, some king-size beds. Private bathrooms, no air-conditioning, TV, or telephone. Terry-cloth robes provided.

Rates $130–$150 per room for two people, includes Continental breakfast. 2-night golf package $170–$190 per person. Add tax, gratuity. Credit cards: AE, D, MC, V.

Meal Plans The restaurant's à la carte menu features local mountain trout and buffalo steaks and burgers (lower in cholesterol and higher in protein than beef). Specialties include Middle Eastern and Italian dishes. Continental breakfast is included daily.

Services and Facilities **Exercise Equipment:** 8-station Universal gym, StairMaster, Lifecycle, Schwinn Air-Dyne bike. **Recreation Facilities:** 18-hole golf course, stables for guided 2-hour trail rides. **Services:** Swedish massage, shiatsu. **Swimming Facilities:** outdoor pool (heated).

In the Area Rio Grande National Forest, Great Sand Dunes National Monument.

Getting Here *From Denver.* By car, I-25 south to Hwy. 160, west to Colorado Hwy. 150 to County Rd. 6 east (5 hr). By air, Continental Express to Alimosa; complimentary pickup at airport with advance request.

Indian Springs Resort

Taking the waters

Colorado
Idaho Springs At the historic Indian Springs Resort you can swim in mineral water surrounded by tropical foliage beneath a translucent arched roof. Built in 1869, the lodge is a Victorian relic down to its ornate dining room.

The soaking pools cater to guests' naturalist tendencies. Separate caves for men and women have walk-in pools hewn into rock. Water flows from three springs at temperatures ranging from 104 to 112 degrees. No bathing suits are allowed in the caves, and couples and families may soak together. Private tubs are booked by the hour.

Sacred to Native Americans, the hot springs were first developed during the local gold rush, and devotees have traveled from around the world to bathe in them ever since.

Chemical analysis of the water has found that it contains trace minerals essential to good health. While no scientific claims are made for the waters, experts cite the benefits of bathing to those who suffer from arthritis and rheumatism. Unlike most hot springs, the waters here do not smell of sulfur.

Both day visitors and overnight guests are welcome. Located on Soda Creek, with a national forest to the west, this bargain getaway is easily reached from Denver.

Indian Springs Resort
Box 1990, Idaho Springs, CO 80452
Tel. 303/567–2191

Administration Manager, Jim Maxwell

Season Year-round.

Accommodations 32 lodge rooms, single and double, furnished with Victorian antiques and brass beds; few modern conveniences. Deluxe new rooms in the inn with king-size or double beds, color TV, coffee maker, full modern bath.

Rates Lodge rooms $35.95 single, $38.95 for 2 persons; deluxe inn rooms $49.95; campsite $14. Bathhouse admission $9. Weekend package with room, dinner for 2, $41.95. Add 7.2% tax. One night payable in advance by credit card. Credit cards: MC, V.

Meal Plans Rocky Mountain brook trout and fresh vegetables are frequently on the menu; the dining room serves 3 meals daily.

Services and Facilities Services: Massage. **Swimming Facilities:** Indoor pool. **Recreation Facilities:** Hiking, horseback riding, fishing, coed Jacuzzi.

In the Area St. Mary's Glacier.

Getting Here *From Denver.* By car, I–70 east to Idaho Springs exit, Hwy. 385.

Special Notes No smoking in pool area or baths. Pool open daily 9 AM–10 PM. Caves open daily 7:30 AM–10:30 PM.

The Lodge at Cordillera

Luxury pampering
Life enhancement

Colorado
Vail Valley

With its small state-of-the-art spa and expansive views of the Rocky Mountains, the Lodge at Cordillera is an ideal hideaway for those seeking luxury accommodations along with a workout. Built on 2,000 acres overlooking the ultradeveloped ski resort of Vail, the lodge is secluded and intimate. There are just 28 guest rooms, most large enough to rate as suites, in the three-story lodge. With walls of stone and stucco, and a Chinese-slate roof, it has the ambience of an Alpine château. But downstairs within the spa, facilities for fitness and body treatments are the very latest.

The guests (never more than 60) are an interesting mix of seasoned spa goers, sophisticated travelers, and exacting corporate executives. While the staff caters to this upscale clientele, there's still a pleasant air of informality. After all that mountain air and sunshine, even the most fastidious visitor finds it difficult not to relax.

Outdoors are 15 miles of groomed, private trails for hiking, biking, or cross-country skiing, as well as skating and sledding areas, a swimming pool, and tennis courts. Jog about 30 minutes down to the Vail Athletic Club for some indoor action on their glass-enclosed squash court, or try scaling the wall that simulates mountain climbing.

Activities at the spa include fitness classes, aerobics, and morning hikes. The exercise room, with a daunting array of high-tech equipment, adjoins a cushion-floored aerobics studio, atrium-enclosed lap pool, and Jacuzzi with mountain views. Body treatments feature Decleor products, and there is a complete salon for men and women. Programs are available for two to five days, or you can drop in for an afternoon or full-day escape. Plan ahead, because staffers are not prepared for non-program requests.

Adventure-minded guests explore the backcountry on a five-day hiking program led by staff members several times during the summer. Complete with gourmet picnic lunches and soothing spa treatments, the itinerary includes parts of the White River National Forest and the spectacular El Mirador peak. In winter, ski tours of the area are offered.

The lodge's picture-perfect setting against a mountain ridge gives you memorable views without ever having to leave your room. Brushed gold and purple, white with snow or all shades of summer green, the New York mountain range fans out endlessly, and turns burnished amber where the peaks meet a cerulean blue sky.

After a day on the slopes or in the spa, you're ready for an epicurean performance in the Picasso restaurant. First, there are preliminary samplings in front of a carved limestone fireplace in the cavernous lobby. The maple wood-coffered ceilings and plush sofas might be in the home of an oil-industry executive, which is precisely what managing partner William Clinkenbeard planned when he retired from Exxon. This is getting away in style.

The Lodge at Cordillera
Box 1110, Edwards, CO 81632
Tel. 303/926–2200 or 800/548–2721
Fax 303/926–2486

Administration	General manager, Bruce Kendall; spa manager, Dashell Hooper
Season	Year-round.
Accommodations	28 rooms and suites, many with fireplace, balcony, or sun deck. Two queen- or king-size beds, covered with European-style duvets. Handcrafted pine furniture, gemstone-color accents. Spacious bathroom with terry-cloth robes. TV with VCR, air-conditioning.

Rates $145–$260 per night, single or double occupancy for standard room; with fireplace, $170–$230. Suites $225–$385. 2-night Getaway with spa services and meals, $700 single, $525 double; 3-night program $950 single, $700 per person double. 5-day Adventure, $1,950 single, $1,500 per person double occupancy, including gratuities and tax. Advance payment $100 per person. Credit cards: AE, DC, MC, V.

Meal Plans Continental breakfast included in room rate. Nutritionally balanced menus for guests on a fitness program offer such entrees as salmon fillet wrapped in grape leaves, roasted, veal loin Provençale, salad of chicken breast marinated in sherry vinaigrette, and fish of the day steamed with vegetable julienne. Restaurant Picasso has prix-fixe and à la carte menus emphasizing new French *cuisine de qualité.*

Services and Facilities **Exercise Equipment:** 8-unit Keiser Cam II pneumatic weights machines, 3 Trotter treadmills, 3 Lifecycles, StairMaster 4000, PTS Turbo recumbent bike, Precor rowing machine. **Services:** Swedish massage, hydrotherapy, aromatherapy or sea-algae body wrap, body polish, facial, leg-circulation treatment, bust care, waxing, manicure, pedicure; fitness assessment, personal training, endurance testing. **Swimming Facilities:** Indoor 3-lane Olympic (25 m) lap pool, outdoor heated pool. **Spa Facilities:** Separate saunas and steam rooms for men and women, 2 hydrotherapy tubs, lap pool, weights room, aerobics studio, massage rooms. **Recreation Facilities:** 2 outdoor tennis courts, cross-country skiing, ice skating, snowmobiling, dog-sled rides, mountain hiking and biking, bowls, croquet, volleyball, badminton; nearby downhill skiing, golf, trout fishing.

In the Area Vail (cultural center, shopping), Beaver Creek (white-water rafting, skiing), Arrowhead (downhill skiing).

Getting Here *From Denver.* By car, I–70 to Exit 163 at Edwards, Rte. 6 to Squaw Creek Rd., Cordillera Way (2½ hr). By plane, scheduled flights to Avon Airport (25 min); private planes land at Eagle County Airport; helicopter landing pad at Cordillera.

Waunita Hot Springs Ranch

Taking the waters

Colorado
Gunnison National Forest

A family-oriented dude ranch with a thermal water swimming pool, Waunita Hot Springs Ranch offers a taste of the Old West and modern comforts. The 200-acre ranch, family owned and operated, was among the first settlements in western Colorado. Today horseback riding and outdoor recreation are the main attractions.

A log barn houses the riding instruction program, with classes for children and adults. There are corral games and an all-day ride to snow-capped peaks near the Continental Divide. Other activities, scheduled daily, include hayrides and an overnight mountain camp out. Local outfitters offer stream and lake fishing, river floats, and hikes.

Hot mineral water, flowing through the pool and cooled to a temperature of 95 degrees, is soothing and relaxes after riding or hiking. There are heated dressing rooms, and the area is lit at night.

Meals at the ranch house consist of hearty buffets. A bowl of fresh fruit is always on hand, and you can help yourself to coffee, tea, hot chocolate, or punch. Alcoholic beverages are not permitted, and nondenominational religious services are held on Sundays.

Nature lovers and families with children make up most of the 45 guests. You can bird-watch, collect rocks, or hike in the national forest. Bring casual clothes, jeans, and boots and discover real Western hospitality.

Waunita Hot Springs Ranch
8007 County Rd. 887, Gunnison, CO 81230
Tel. 303/641–1266

Administration	Manager, Junelle Pringle
Season	June–Sept.
Accommodations	22 rooms in the ranch house and a log lodge, all with private bath, wood paneling, leather chair. TV in the library. Thermal water heating system. Queen-size beds. Laundry facility.
Rates	$780 a week per person, double occupancy; children's rates on request. $150 deposit per person. No credit cards.
Meal Plans	3 meals daily, buffet style. Cookouts and steak-fry dinners. Home-cooked food to suit any diet. Barbecued chicken and grilled trout specialties.
Services and Facilities	**Swimming Facilities:** 90-foot outdoor pool. **Recreation Facilities:** Hiking, horseshoes, Ping-Pong, corral games, fishing, softball, volleyball. **Evening Programs:** Country-Western Music Hall, movies.
In the Area	Cookout rides, overnight camp out; river float trip, mountain rides, Jeep trips offered by local outfitters; Continental Divide, ghost towns, mining relics.
Getting Here	*From Denver.* By car, Hwy. 285 to Salida, Hwy. 50 to Doyleville, County Rd. 887 (3 hr). By air, Continental Express (40 min).
Special Notes	No smoking indoors.

Wiesbaden Hot Springs Spa & Lodgings

Taking the waters

Colorado
Ouray

Begun as a mountainside motel with mineral water baths, the family owned and operated Wiesbaden Hot Springs Lodge has become a full-fledged health resort in recent years. Its facilities include an exercise room with video monitors but no instructors, a weights room, a sauna, and an indoor soaking pool with rock-walled vapor cave.

The geothermal water that heats the building as well as the swimming pool flows from two springs at temperatures of 111–134 degrees. The mineral water is also circulated through soaking pools, avoiding the need for chemical purification.

Scenic canyons in the national forest are a major attraction for hikers. The makings for a picnic can be found in town, a few blocks away (the lodge has no dining room). Dinner at the

Bon Ton Restaurant in the Victorian St. Elmo Hotel is recommended.

At an altitude of 7,700 feet, the picturesque old mountain town is sheltered from winds by the surrounding forest. Few roads traverse these mountains that are the source of the Rio Grande and several hot springs.

Wiesbaden Hot Springs Spa & Lodgings
625 5th St., Box 349, Ouray, CO 81427
Tel. 303/325–4347 or 303/325–4845

Administration Manager, Linda Wright-Minter

Season Year-round.

Accommodations 18 modern rooms, each with private bath, king-size or twin beds. Private apartments. Glass-walled lounge overlooks the pool and sun deck. Rooms decorated with antiques, some have wood stove. Complimentary morning coffee and tea.

Rates Daily rate per room for 2 persons $75–$130. Add 8.2% tax. 1 night payable in advance. Credit cards: MC, V.

Services and Facilities **Exercise Equipment:** Universal weight training gym, stationary bike, NordicTrack. **Services:** Swedish massage, reflexology, acupressure, aromatherapy, facials. **Swimming Facilities:** Outdoor pool. **Recreation Facilities:** Hiking; bike rental, fitness center at nearby public swimming pool and 3 mineral water pools (pool hours Mon.–Sat. 10 AM–10 PM, Sun. 10 AM–9 PM).

In the Area Antiques shops, Box Canyon falls, Telluride (historical mining town) film festival, Ute Indian reservation, Durango.

Getting Here *From Denver.* By car, I–70 to Grand Junction, Hwy. 550 (4 hr). By air, Continental or United Express to Montrose (1 hr). Car rental and taxis available.

Special Notes No smoking on premises. No pets.

Desert Inn Hotel & Casino

Luxury pampering

Nevada
Las Vegas The combination of a health and fitness club within a country club and casino resort has made the Desert Inn popular. Devoted to exercise and pampering, this well-equipped facility can be enjoyed without entering the casino. Guests pay a daily facilities charge ($18) or sign up for a package plan.

Sunlight streams through floor-to-ceiling glass walls in the central rotundas of the men's and women's pavilions. Dual facilities, including private therapy pools, hot or cold water plunges, and a big central Jacuzzi, are separate and private. The steam rooms, saunas, and hydrotherapy room are a few steps away.

The water-focused treatments include loofah body scrub with sea salts and herbal wraps. Thermotherapy consists of varied applications of heat and cold to soothe and cleanse the body: Moving from Turkish steam room to Finnish sauna, you are wrapped in warm sheets soaked with herbal fragrances.

A private swimming pool for lap swimming and water volleyball is also part of the spa complex. Indoor coed facilities include two gyms: one for weight training and cardiovascular fitness and the other for stretching (no classes).

Set on 200 parklike acres, the Desert Inn offers everything from golf to shuffleboard, plus a ⅟₁₆th-mile parcourse with 10 exercise stations. You can't lose on health even if your luck at the tables isn't up to snuff.

Desert Inn Hotel & Casino
3145 Las Vegas Blvd. S, Las Vegas, NV 89109
Tel. 702/733–4444 or 800/634–6906 (800/634–6906 for
room reservations)
Telex 684481

Administration General manager, Forrest Woodward II; spa director, Winona Sylvia; men's spa manager, Alan Espina

Season Year-round.

Accommodations 821 rooms with a desert theme in a high-rise hotel. Recently refurbished minisuites in the Wimbeldon and Pebble Beach buildings have balconies, full baths, many small amenities and are closest to the spa and tennis complex.

Rates $90–$105 a day, single or double; minisuites $150–$175. Spa packages $149 a day additional, $399 for a deluxe 4-day plan, $99 for half-day. Daily facility charge $18, refunded when services are booked; add 17% gratuity, 7% tax. 1 night payable in advance. Credit cards: AE, DC, MC, V.

Services and Facilities **Exercise Equipment:** 2 Lifecycles, 12 Keiser Cam II units, free-weight dumbbells (2–60 lbs.), 2 StairMaster 4000, Concept II rowing ergometer, 2 StarTrac treadmills, Powerstretch, rebounders. **Services:** Massage, paraffin treatment, salt-glow and loofah body scrub, facials, herbal wrap; nail and skin care. **Swimming Facilities:** Lap pool, Olympic-size recreational pool. **Recreation Facilities:** 10 tennis courts, water volleyball, golf. **Evening Programs:** Celebrity shows in casino.

In the Area Waterworld theme park, Lake Mead recreational area and Hoover Dam, the Grand Canyon. Fashion Show shopping mall.

Getting Here *From Los Angeles.* By bus, Greyhound (5 hr). By car, I–15 (4½ hr). By plane, scheduled flights (1½ hr). Limousine on request; rental car, taxi.

Special Notes Ramps and elevators provide access for the disabled; all facilities are on one level.

Walley's Hot Springs Resort

Taking the waters

Nevada A health club and hot mineral baths are the attractions at the
Genoa charming cluster of Victorian cottages called Walley's Hot Springs Resort. Located in the foothills of the Sierra Nevadas, 12 miles from Lake Tahoe's south shore and 50 miles from Reno, the secluded resort offers a pay-as-you-go treatment plan and free exercise classes.

The main building, a two-story health club, has separate men's and women's sections that contain sauna, steam bath, and massage rooms. A coed weight training room is modestly equipped, but there are plans for expansion.

Mineral water is piped from a pond into the bathhouse, where it continuously flows through the bathing tubs. For an outdoor soak, the 104-degree water is collected in six cement pools, where it is cooled for the swimming pool.

Exercise classes in the pool are scheduled Monday, Wednesday, and Friday mornings and Tuesday and Thursday evenings. Guests can hike the scenic Carson Valley and make daytrips to nearby resorts and casinos. Of special interest are the mud baths and mineral-water treatments at nearby Steamboat Springs, a historic resort that dates from 1904.

Walley's Hot Springs Resort
2001 Foothill La., Box 26, Genoa, NV 89411
Tel. 702/782–8155

Administration	Owner/director, Connie Atwood; Program director, Katherine Vanderbrake
Season	Year-round.
Accommodations	5 private cottages, 1 with queen-size bed, others with twins. Private baths, country antiques, turn-of-the-century ambience. Full hotel service; breakfast delivered.
Rates	$85–$120 per day for 2 with breakfasts; 1 night payable in advance. Credit cards: AE, MC, V.
Services and Facilities	**Exercise Equipment:** 7-station Universal weight training gym, free weights, stationary bikes. **Services:** Massage, herbal wraps. **Swimming Facilities:** Outdoor pool. **Spa Facilities:** Indoor and outdoor mineral-water pools. **Recreation Facilities:** 2 tennis courts, downhill and cross-country skiing nearby. **Evening Programs:** 2 exercise classes weekly.
In the Area	Lake Tahoe resorts and casinos, Reno casinos, historic Carson City.
Getting Here	*From Reno.* By car, Hwy. 395 south to Genoa, Genoa Lane to Foothill Lane (60 min). By bus, Greyhound to Gardnerville (45 min). Rental car, taxi available.
Special Notes	Limited access for the disabled. Children under 12 not permitted in the health club. No smoking in the health club.

Truth or Consequences

Taking the waters

New Mexico
Truth or Consequences

Named after a radio show popular in the 1950s, the town of Truth or Consequences may be the bargain basement of health spas. Springwater is channeled to bathhouses and guest lodges along Broadway and the adjoining streets. Some offer little more than a tub, most do not accept credit cards. A 20-minute soak in unchlorinated 110-degree mineral water typically costs $5, a 60-minute massage with hand-held vibrator costs $25.

Naturopathic treatments are offered at some of the older establishments, but a massage is the principal therapy after bathing. Water sports in mile-long Elephant Butte Lake just outside town, hiking, and tubing on the Rio Grande are mentioned in Chamber of Commerce publications.

What is not mentioned is the run-down appearance of the town and its once famous baths. Yet local operators say the area is picking up, and there are newer motels on the main road.

At the Sierra Natural Healing Center, a former hotel on Broadway, the baths are open daily, 8 AM–8 PM. Brice Callahan, a massage specialist, uses an imported vibrator along with his hands and muscles, and sunken tubs in three private massage rooms are sanitized and filled with fresh, hot mineral water after each use. The older bathhouses rely on nature for water circulation; they have a potential for algae buildup.

Bathers at Ye Olde Hot Springs Bath Haus can exercise in two big pools equipped with metal support bars, or soak in 3 private pools at water temperatures varying from 107° to 110°. Charles Motel in town has separate facilities for men and women. Each has sauna, steam bath, and four individual tubs.

Truth or Consequences
Chamber of Commerce
500 McAdoo St., Drawer 31, Truth or Consequences,
NM 87901
Tel. 505/894–3536

Season   Year-round.

Accommodations   Standard motels on the highway, without mineral baths, include Super 8 and the Western Motel.

Rates $35 a night at the Charles Motel. Confirmation by credit card. Credit cards: MC, V.

Services and Facilities   **Swimming Facilities:** Nearby lake. **Recreation Facilities:** Hiking, tubing.

Getting Here   *From Albuquerque.* By car, I–25 north (2½ hr).

Vista Clara

Life enhancement
Nutrition and diet
Spiritual awareness
Luxury pampering

New Mexico
Galisteo

Attuned to southwestern traditions and lifestyles, Vista Clara provides an energizing experience for just 14 guests. Set on 80 acres in the foothills of the Sangre de Cristo Mountains, it is a completely self-contained environment, designed to integrate body, mind, and spirit.

Each day begins early, with a personalized program that balances vigorous activity, relaxation, and soothing body treatments. Afternoons are dedicated to massage and other treatments included in the program package rate. The spa facilities are housed in authentic pueblo-style adobe buildings equipped with the latest technology.

Meals are a fresh interpretation of spa cuisine. Organic fruits and vegetables grown at Vista Clara, along with southwestern spices, provide a balanced diet that is low in fat, sodium, and cholesterol.

Sharing their philosophy of integrated wellness, staff members explore links between physical and mental well-being, and furnish participants with a rich variety of physical challenges and healthful gratifications.

Vista Clara
HC 75, Box 111, Galisteo, NM 87540
Tel. 505/988–8865 or 800/247–0301

Administration Owners/directors, Christopher and Carmen Partridge; spa director, Minerva Rodriguez

Season Year-round.

Accommodations 10 guest suites in an adobe hacienda with wood-beamed ceilings matched by handcrafted furniture and floors. Persian rugs, original art, and southwestern folk art used throughout. All rooms have private deck or porch, modern bathroom, air-conditioned. No TV.

Rates All-inclusive 3-day package $1,350 single or double, per person; 7-day package $2,695 per person, single or double. Add 15% gratuity and applicable taxes. 50% payment in advance. Credit cards: AE, MC, V.

Meal Plans 3 meals daily included in programs; total 1,200–1,400 calories; special diets accommodated. Breakfast can be banana-buckwheat waffle with blackberries, hot cereal with pecans, almonds, apples, or egg-white omelet with shiitake mushrooms. Lunch entrees include pizza with blue-corn and whole-wheat crust, vegetables and goat cheese, or Mesa Verde salad with chicken, marinated peppers, baked wonton chips. Dinner begins with chilled smoked granny smith apple soup; entree may be pasta and prawns with snow peas and sun-dried tomato pesto, or Pollo Teepee chicken breast with vegetables and accent of charred tomato and red chili sauce.

Services and Facilities **Exercise Equipment:** Universal multistation gym, Challenger treadmill, 2 Lifecycles, StairMaster 4000, free weights (3–50 lbs), Bio-Star hand weights (5–40 lbs), bench press. **Services:** Swedish massage, shiatsu, reflexology, aromatherapy, herbal wrap, clay body mask, body polishing, paraffin hand and foot treatments, polarity facial, and hairdressing. **Activities:** Native American sweat-lodge ceremony, outings to pueblo ruins, guided hikes. **Swimming Facilities:** Outdoor pool. **Spa Facilities:** Coed sauna and steam room, 2 Swiss showers, outdoor Jacuzzi. **Evening Programs:** Astrology reading, dream interpretation, cooking class, mountain folklore, nutrition workshop.

In the Area Santa Fe (museums, galleries, boutiques), Four Corners (energy center), Santa Fe Opera (summer), Indian Market (late August), Chamber Music Festival (summer), Taos Pueblo, Bandolier National Monument, Santuario de Chimayo (healing mud, pilgrimage center), Montezuma (hot springs), Armand Hammer United World College.

Getting Here *From Albuquerque.* Complimentary shuttle service to and from airport (1½ hr). By car, I–25 to Exit 290, Rte. 285 south to Rte. 41 west for 4 miles (1½ hr). Rental car and taxi available.

Special Notes Limited access for the disabled. No smoking on premises. Active-wear clothing provided.

Cliff Lodge at Snowbird

Sports conditioning
Stress control
Luxury pampering

Utah
Snowbird

Alpine views from a penthouse spa, mountaineering courses, and 1,900 acres of groomed ski slopes are the attractions of the sports-oriented Cliff Lodge. Set in Utah's scenic Wasatch Mountains near Salt Lake City, Cliff Lodge is more like a Swiss spa than any other ski resort in America.

The Mountaineering Center complements the spa-and-ski program with rock-climbing classes, overnight backpacking trips, bike tours, and guided treks to the peaks of the national forest. Open from July through mid-October, the center attracts outdoors people and climbers of all achievement levels.

For golfers, there is helicopter service to the courses in nearby Wasatch National Park and at Jeremy Ranch. Skiers can also be whisked up to powder snow conditions on upper slopes.

The active, youthful vacationers here get into shape with stress-management classes and relaxation exercises led by a certified neurolinguistic programmer. The two-story fitness center on the top floors of the 11-story luxury hotel provides a tranquil environment for morning stretch classes, hydrotherapy, or an herbal wrap. Mountains are everywhere you look. After skiing, a hike through Little Cottonwood Canyon, or tennis in the crisp mountain air, you can swim laps in an outdoor pool on the roof. The scenery adds a special dimension to workouts in the glass-walled weights room or relaxation in a whirlpool.

The spa atop the Cliff Lodge, opened in 1987, was the crowning touch in a master plan for year-round recreation developed by Dick Bass, a Texas-born oilman, rancher, and amateur rock climber. There are saunas and steam rooms for men and women and private treatment rooms for sophisticated therapies such as the French Phytomer process of cleansing and toning the bust with marine products. A skin treatment for the back, popular with men, uses steam, a prep scrub, a Phytomer marine peel, and massage cream to deep-cleanse the pores and moisturize the skin.

There's plenty for children to do while their parents exercise or pamper themselves. Special skiing and tennis training are offered for children five and older, and kids stay free in their parents' room. Children's lift tickets are free when children accompany adults on outings.

Another option is the Canyon Raquet Club, a tennis and fitness complex 10 miles from the ski area. Squash, racquetball, and tennis, plus weight training, cardiovascular exercise, and an Olympic-size pool, are open to guests.

Cliff Lodge at Snowbird
Little Cottonwood Canyon Rd., Snowbird, UT 84092
Tel. 801/742–2222 or 800/453–3000
Telex 9102400389 Snowbird UT USA

Administration Manager, John Warner; spa director, Keith Arbon

Season Year-round.

Accommodations 532 rooms and suites with mountain views and balconies that open onto the 11-story atrium. Luxury furnishings and baths, king-size beds, cable TV, full service.

Rates Rooms $69–$157 for 2 persons per day, deluxe bedroom $139–$279 for 2. Mountaineering Center activities charged separately. Deposit: 1 night's rate in summer, 2 nights' rate during winter season. Credit cards: AE, DC, MC, V.

Meal Plans The Aerie's low-fat, low-cholesterol offerings may include vegetarian lasagna or pizza, grilled salmon, broiled chicken, luncheon salads, chicken teriyaki, meatless chili. The Spa Cafe serves fruit smoothies, high-fiber breakfast, and lunch.

Services and Facilities **Exercise Equipment:** 12 Keiser Cam III pneumatic weight-resistance units, Lifecycles, Bodyguard 900 bikes, 2 Stair-Masters, rowing machine, 2 treadmills. Aerobics studio with suspended wood floor. **Services:** Massage, hydrotherapy, herbal wrap, parafango wrap, Phytomer deep-cleansing treatments, manicure, pedicure, facial, hairstyling. Daily classes in aerobics and stretching. Stress-management course (additional fee). **Swimming Facilities:** Outdoor lap pool, Olympic-size indoor pool. **Recreation Facilities:** 23 tennis courts (10 indoor), 2 squash courts, 2 basketball courts; hiking, skiing, rock climbing. Golf and horseback riding nearby. **Evening Programs:** Outdoor adventure films and talks.

In the Area Helicopter rides, Western barbecues, backpacking, mountain bike tours, tram rides; Salt Lake City sports and entertainment centers, Mormon Tabernacle, mineral springs at Heber City, historic Alta (19th-century silver mine).

Getting Here *From Salt Lake City.* By bus, Utah Transit Authority scheduled service from city terminal and airport during winter season (45 min). By car, I–75, I–80, Rte. 210 to Little Cottonwood Canyon (40 min). Free pickup on arrival and departure at Salt Lake City airport with package plans. Limousine, taxi, rental car available. Resort parking; valet service and indoor parking at the lodge only.

Special Notes Ski-training course for the disabled. Ski and tennis instruction, day-care center for children. No smoking in the spa, the 9th-floor guest rooms, and designated areas of the dining room.

Green Valley Fitness Resort and Spa

Nutrition and diet
Weight management
Luxury pampering
Kid fitness
Vibrant maturity

Utah
St. George Discovering a full-service spa along with a concentrated weight-loss and fitness program in the dry desert of southern Utah is reason enough to spend a week or two at the Green Valley resort. Guests can also enjoy full resort facilities plus sophisticated bodywork with locally formulated herbal, mud, and mineral products used exclusively in the spa center's color-coded therapy salons.

Two programs are offered: Basic Fitness and Super Hiking, with options for one-on-one personal training or tennis instruction, including spa services. As you begin to regain energy, you'll appreciate the opportunities to explore the scenic redrock country and hike the canyons that surround the valley. Settled by Mormon pioneers, the area is rich in history, and there are heritage buildings to be visited.

Beginning with an introduction to how the body's weight-regulating mechanism works, your learning experiences include trips to restaurants and supermarkets, cooking workshops, and discussion groups. The nutritious high-energy meals are a revelation regarding the variety and quantity of food that one can enjoy while losing weight. Even exchanging tips with the Green Valley cook in a newly expanded dining room-cum-demo kitchen is encouraged.

Once the mind and body are in sync, the exercise and the hiking become more challenging. Shaping and contouring as weight is lost, the training emphasizes correct posture and body movements. The program is limited to 25 participants per week to maintain personal interaction with staff physiologists and nutritionists. Relax in a private Jacuzzi surrounded by lush greenery and brightly lit candles, and follow it up with a massage or facial.

Sports, too, are a major attraction here. Since this is also the home of the Vic Braden Tennis College, court time can be substituted for aerobics. A glass-covered Olympic-size swimming pool is available for aquacise classes, and there are two golf courses nearby.

Green Valley Fitness Resort and Spa
1515 W. Canyon View Dr., St. George, UT 84770
Tel. 801/628–8060 or 800/237–1068

Administration Owner/director, Alan Coombs; spa director, Carole Coombs; Fitness director, Linda Davis

Season Year-round.

Accommodations Furnished condominium apartments have spacious contemporary interiors with living room, dining counter, kitchen, private bath, balcony. Some have a Jacuzzi on the deck.

Rates Basic Fitness week $1,998 per person, double occupancy; 1-week Super Hiking program, $1,998 per person, double occupancy; with personal trainer, $2,698, with tennis option $1,998. Tax and gratuity included. Single occupancy add $245. $500 deposit. Credit cards: AE, D, MC, V.

Meal Plans 3 meals daily. Low-fat diet, no sugar or salt. Breakfast is scrambled eggs, buttermilk biscuits, turkey sausage, assorted fresh fruit. Lunches include soup, salad, steamed vegetables, a tuna-salad sandwich on whole-grain bread or turkey salad on pita. Typical dinner entrees are baked salmon or orange roughy, stuffed Cornish game hen, beef kebab, or chicken barbecue. Desserts include banana pudding and apple strudel.

Services and Facilities **Exercise Equipment:** Lifecycles, rowing machines, treadmills, stationary bikes, and Universal and Cam Star weight training units. **Services:** Swedish massage, hand and foot reflexology, herbal wraps, facials, powdered-pearl body rub; hair, nail, and skin care. Personal counseling on tension control, wardrobe, coloring and makeup, skin care, shopping. **Swimming Facilities:** Outdoor and enclosed pools, diving pool. **Spa Facilities:** Steam rooms, saunas, whirlpool. **Recreation Facilities:** 15 outdoor and 4 indoor tennis courts, volleyball, shuffleboard, basketball, lawn chess, 9-hole executive golf course, putting green, bowling alley, roller skating, 2 racquetball courts. Rental of bicycles. Horseback riding, downhill skiing, water sports nearby. **Evening Programs:** Talks on health and nutrition.

In the Area Zion National Park excursion with picnic lunch, Vic Braden Tennis College (on site), North Rim of Grand Canyon, Snow Canyon sandstone cliffs, Bryce National Park, Nevada casinos, country and western entertainment, river rafting.

Getting Here *From Las Vegas.* By car, I–15 to St. George (2 hr). By plane, commuter flights on Skywest (40 min). Free pickup to and from St. George airport. Van service from Las Vegas (fee). Car rental, taxi available.

Special Notes Elevators, oversize bathroom facilities for the disabled. Summer fitness/health camp for children, tennis camp at Vic Braden College. No smoking. Bring a medical release from your doctor, casual workout clothing, walking shoes.

The Last Resort

Nutrition and diet
Spiritual awareness

Utah Yoga studies, meditation, and nature walks are the cornerstone
Sunset Cliffs programs for rejuvenating the body and the mind at the Last Resort, an informal mountain retreat. Located in southern Utah about 40 miles southwest of Bryce Canyon, the two-story log building 8,700 feet above sea level boasts spectacular mountain views and accommodates up to 10 guests.

Marked trails attract hikers and backpackers in summer and autumn. In winter the light powder snow makes ideal conditions for cross-country skiing.

As a multidimensional experience, Pujari and Abhilasha offer a seven-day retreat that includes Iyengar yoga workouts twice a day, hiking, and a soak at nearby hot springs. During year-end retreats, total silence is observed for 10 days. A five-day natural-foods cooking course in August teaches meal planning and preparation of tofu, tempeh, whole grains, beans, fresh vegetables, and other healthy ingredients. Spring is celebrated with a 10-day detoxification and spring cleaning of the body.

The Last Resort
Box 6226, Cedar City, UT 84720
Tel. 801/682–2289 or 619/283–8663

Administration Program directors, Pujari and Abhilasha (Ed and Barbara Keays)

Season Year-round, with retreats scheduled in June, July–Aug., Dec., and Jan.

Accommodations Dormitory beds and private rooms for couples. Simple furnishings, communal bath.

Rates 7-day yoga retreat $695 per person, 5-day cooking course $495, 10-day spring retreat $795; year-end Vipassana meditation, 5 days $295, 10 days $495.

Meal Plans Vegetarian meals prepared by a nutritionist, tea, and juice come with retreats. Menus include steamed fresh vegetables, whole grains, rice, casseroles.

Services and Facilities **Swimming Facilities:** Nearby lakes. **Spa Facilities:** Mineral baths at Pah Tempe Hot Springs. **Recreation Facilities:** Hiking, cross-country skiing. **Programs:** Meditation instruction, rebirthing, Iyengar yoga classes, lectures on lifestyle.

In the Area Bryce Canyon National Park. North Rim of the Grand Canyon, Zion National Park, Cedar Peaks. Shakespeare Festival in Cedar City (mid-July–Aug.).

Getting Here *From Las Vegas.* By car, I–15 to Cedar City, Rte. 14 (3 hr).

Special Notes No smoking.

MountainFit

Sports conditioning

Utah
St. George
Hiking the alpine meadows and magnificent canyons of Zion National Park, Pine Valley, and Snow Canyon State Park in southwestern Utah is the focus of the week-long MountainFit program that combines exercise and bodywork with guided wilderness treks.

The hikes, geared to participants' fitness levels, range from relatively rigorous 6-mile walks to a 15-mile, 9-hour endurance challenge. Trails take in the Wiggles (21 short, tight switchbacks), the Subway (a river-carved tunnel), the Icebox (a cold canyon), and the StairMaster (a series of rock wall steps).

Cross-training begins the day; early morning sessions of yoga are followed by a foot massage to prepare muscles for a workout. Then, provisioned with water bottles, lunch, and snacks, groups are taken by van to the trailheads. For safety, hikers also carry emergency equipment and two-way radios, and each day's itinerary is registered with park rangers. At least two staff members accompany each group, one in the lead and one at the rear, and the group sets its own pace. Group members range in age from 30 to 70.

Reaching plateaus at 7,000–10,000 feet, hikers traverse the west and east rims of Zion and encounter vistas of Navajo sandstone formations. The deep-red canyon walls, wind-sculpted arches, and enormous mushroomlike formations called hoodoos provide natural drama, and the vegetation ranges from dry sage flats to mossy deciduous and conifer forests. Guides recount the area's history and geology along the way.

The weekly program begins with an easy two-hour orientation walk. Guides choose subsequent treks from among 16 trails—graded steep to almost vertical—within an hour's drive of St. George. Limbering-up and stretching exercises are done en route, and each participant carries a poncho as protection from storms. The program also includes two one-hour sessions with massage therapists and an afternoon soak at Pah Tempe Hot Springs, an ancient Paiute healing place in Hurricane, Utah. Hard-core hikers finish the week with a 17-mile trek; others may elect to return home early for a massage.

MountainFit
Greene House, St. George, UT 84770
Reservations: 633 Battery St. (5th floor), San Francisco,
CA 94111
Tel. 415/397–6216 or 800/926–5700

Administration	Owner and director, Diane Wechsler
Season	Apr.–May, Sept.–Oct.
Accommodations	7 rooms, some with private bath, have Victorian antiques, brass beds, wood armoires from the time of the Mormon settlers, all in a residential compound centered on a pioneer home of 1872, accommodating 6–12 program participants. Daily maid service.
Rates	$1,850 for the Sat.–Fri. program includes meals, 2 massages, outings. $300 nonrefundable deposit on reservation; balance due 30 days before start of program. Credit cards: AE.
Meal Plans	Daily menu of 1,200–1,500 calories. Breakfast choices are freshly baked muffins, cereals, fruit, French toast filled with strawberry cheese. Trail lunch consists of cold soup, grain salad, peanut butter and jelly sandwiches, fruit. A typical dinner, served family style, includes green salad, salmon poached or baked in pastry, asparagus tips, four-grain pilaf, homemade pasta, blueberry mousse. Coffee, tea, milk are available; dietary needs are accommodated.
Services and Facilities	**Services:** Massage. **Swimming Facilities:** Outdoor lap pool. **Evening Programs:** Lecture-demonstrations, films. Tennis.
In the Area	Zion National Park, Bryce Canyon National Park, St. George Mormon Temple (1877), Chums factory outlet for sportswear.
Getting Here	*From Las Vegas.* By car, I–15 (2 hr). By plane, scheduled service on Skywest (40 min). (Participants' transportation provided on arrival and departure days.)
Special Notes	No smoking in residential compound. Hiking boots required; bathrobe provided. Laundry service on alternate days.

National Institute of Fitness

Weight management
Nutrition and diet

Utah
Ivins

Designed by an exercise physiologist, the National Institute of Fitness's no-frills fitness and weight-loss program is based on nutrition, movement, and recreation in some of the most glorious canyon country in the West. Often called the "Walking Spa," the program includes training with certified coaches on hikes as well as in aerobics classes. 100–150 participants are divided into groups classifed C (most fit), B (average) A (moderate) and Special A (limited fitness).

Vigorous exercise, rather than pampering or bodywork, is central here. On arrival participants are given a fitness evaluation that includes a cardiovascular endurance test. The results-oriented program is designed to get you off diets and drugs and to restore normal cholesterol and sugar levels. Guests with serious weight problems stay a month or more, often shedding 50 pounds. Body work and personal services are optional extras.

The program moves along at a fast pace, and instructors concentrate on teaching techniques that guests can practice on their own at home. The indoor facilities include an aerobics studio, weights room, racquetball court, and covered swimming pool for laps and aquaerobics. New residential and dining rooms added in 1992.

Set in canyons near Zion National Park, the resort complex features dome-shaped housing units that blend in with the ragged terrain. The rolling sand dunes, towering walls of red and buff-colored sandstone, and dark ragged remnants of ancient lava flow all add to the wonder of your daily walk.

National Institute of Fitness
202 N. Snow Canyon Rd., Box 938, Ivins, UT 84738
Tel. 801/673–4905

Administration Founder/director, Dr. Marc Sorenson; program director, Vicki Sorenson; Nutrition director, Ralph Ofcarik, Ph.D.

Season Year-round; program begins Mon.

Accommodations 55 air-conditioned rooms with 1–4 beds each. Also condominium apartments. Modern furnishings, private bath. Semiprivate rooms have partitions, single beds. Daily maid service weekdays.

Rates 1-week program from $564 per person (4 in a room) to $1,074 (single occupancy). $100 (nonrefundable) payable in advance. Gratuities and tax included. Credit cards (3% surcharge): AE, MC, V.

Meal Plans Low-fat weight-loss diet, nutritionally balanced, controlled portions. Low in salt, fat, sugar; high in complex carbohydrates. Pritikin-style entrees for lunch are turkey loaf, tuna sandwich on wheat bread; dinner includes vegetarian lasagna, pizza with turkey. Salad bar daily.

Services and Facilities **Exercise Equipment:** 11-station weight training gym, 2 PT 6000 and 2 PG 4000 StairMasters, 6 Cateye Exercycles, 14 Challenger treadmills, NordicTrak Quinton cross-country unit, 3 Enduricisers, free weights, rebounders. **Services:** Massage, aromatherapy, facials, loofah body scrub; hair, nail, and skin care; fitness evaluation; complimentary makeup session and exercise instruction. **Swimming Facilities:** Heated indoor pool. **Recreation Facilities:** Tennis court, indoor racquetball court; horseback riding nearby. **Evening Programs:** Workshops on nutrition and health.

In the Area Snow Canyon State Park, Las Vegas, Salt Lake City, Zion National Park.

Getting Here *From Las Vegas.* By car, I–15 to St. George, Bluff St. north to Santa Clara, Sunset Blvd. to Ivins (2 hr). By plane, commuter flights on Skywest Airlines to St. George (45 min). Free pickup to and from St. George Airport. Taxi, rental car available.

Special Notes No smoking. Remember to bring exercise clothing, aerobic and hiking shoes. Spa open daily 6 AM–9:30 PM.

Pah Tempe Hot Springs Resort

Taking the waters
Non-program resort facilities

Utah
Hurricane
Deep in a canyon near Zion National Park, hot springs gush from the mud bottom of the Virgin River to fill a series of pools cut into the rocks surrounding the Pah Tempe resort. Here bathing is a sybaritic experience for body, mind, and spirit, and conversation comes easily among guests soaking in the warm, sulfur-rich waters or sinking into the mud for a natural body scrub.

Pah Tempe operates as a bed-and-breakfast lodge; meals are served on a terrace overlooking the river, and the primarily vegetarian menu changes seasonally. The resort and the ambience are completely informal, and the inexpensive lodging and camping sites draw many European campers.

Bodywork is available by prearrangement, and yoga, water aerobics, and health-related workshops are scheduled from time to time, so inquiries and advance planning are necessary for those who want to participate. Travelers who are not staying at the lodge may use the pools, showers, and restaurant for a daily fee ($4). Nature walks, bird-watching and archaeology guides are available to introduce guests to the colorful desert and mountain terrain.

Pah Tempe Hot Springs Resort
825 North 800 East; Box 35–4, Hurricane, UT 84737
Tel. 801/635–2879 or 801/635–2353

Administration
Managing partner, Ken Anderson; director of operations, Maria Monet

Season
Year-round.

Accommodations
Cabins and 7 rooms in the lodge accommodate 24 guests; all are furnished simply (no TV or air-conditioning), all have double bed, some have private bath. Private lodge (capacity 20–30) for groups. RV and campsites.

Rates
$50 per day single, $60–$80 per day for 2, including breakfast; additional person $20, children (age 5 or under) $10. Senior-citizen (63 and older) rates available. RV and camping, $14 single, $20 for 2, $6 additional adult. Rates include use of pools, facilities. Credit cards: MC, V.

Meal Plans
Vegetarian menus for breakfast, lunch, dinner. Entrees include lasagna and a spinach and pinenut spanakopita.

Services and Facilities
Services: Massage, facials, scalp and hair treatments by appointment. Swimming Facilities: Outdoor concrete pool. Spa Facilities: Natural rock pools with circulating thermal water (102–107°), 2 indoor Jacuzzis.

In the Area
Zion National Park, Dixie College Amphitheater, Bit 'n Spur Café for country music, Chums factory outlet for sportswear, St. George Mormon Temple (c. 1877).

Getting Here
From St. George. By car, I–15 to Rte. 9 via Hurricane; entry road at Virgin River Bridge (25 min).

Special Notes
No smoking in pool areas or restaurant. Bring swimwear, beach towel, flashlight.

The Northwest

Native Americans believed long ago that the Great Spirit lived at the earth's center and that steaming hot springs produced "big medicine" waters. Rediscovered by a new generation, the hot springs of the Northwest can be enjoyed in settings of great natural beauty or at large new resort developments. One such sacred spot in Oregon is now the popular resort Kah-Nee-Ta, owned and operated by the Confederated Tribes of the Warm Springs. Wyoming has developed Hot Springs State Park on land purchased from the Shoshone and Arapahoe Indians near Yellowstone National Park. The Sol Duc Hot Springs Resort in Olympic National Park, Washington, is another warm watering spot.

Montana's "big sky" country offers the family-oriented Fairmont Hot Springs Resort and the rustic Chico Hot Springs Lodge, along with 39 ski runs and posh dude ranches. In a verdant valley rich with gold rush lore outside Fairbanks, Alaska, the sulfur sprites of Chena Hot Springs have welcomed homesteaders and "cheechako" travelers since 1905.

Chena Hot Springs Resort

Taking the waters

Alaska
Fairbanks

A soak at the historic Chena Hot Springs Resort near Fairbanks comes accompanied by reminders of pioneer days. There are cabins and pools here that were built in the early 1900s, when the main visitors were gold miners who had traveled by dogsled and on horseback in search of relief from rheumatism and arthritis in the hot springs. Images of the miners still smile from the photographs of the Victorian era that decorate the dining room and lounge.

The old-time character of the resort has not changed, despite recent renovations. The bathhouse was rebuilt recently, with tiled floors and showers in the locker rooms, and expansive use of glass walls in the pool area. The hot mineral water that bubbles to the surface at 156 degrees is cooled to a tolerable 110 degrees in the soaking pools, 90 degrees for swimming. Thermal water also heats the lodge rooms.

The cluster of cabins around the main lodge has the general appearance of a mining camp. In the gardens between the steaming ponds, where the spring waters run into a creek, the machinery, carts, and tools that the miners once used have taken on the role of memorabilia. Moose have been spotted wandering on the grounds, and antlers adorn some of the buildings.

Set in a quiet valley that is part of the state park and recreation system, the hot springs now attract winter and summer vacationers. A lively crowd from the university in Fairbanks 60 miles down the road comes to ski the nearby slopes and well-marked trails, and the springs are popular with Japanese tourists. Yet most guests are Alaskans, and they set the informal tone of the resort. Don't expect calorie-counted food or anything fancy. Wild blueberry daiquiris are the specialty at the bar.

Chena Hot Springs Resort
Chena Hot Springs Rd., Fairbanks, AL 99707
(Reservations) Box 73440,
Fairbanks, AL 99707
Tel. 907/452–7867, Fax 907/456–3122

Administration	Manager, Frank Rose
Season	Year-round.
Accommodations	41 plainly furnished Lodge rooms. Baths private or shared, geothermal hot water, maid service. Cabins with double and single beds, wood-burning fireplace for heat, propane lights, washbasin, chemical toilet. RV hookup, campsites. Single rooms on request.
Rates	$50–$110 per day for 1–4 persons. $25 per night in advance. Credit cards: AE, DC, MC, V.
Meal Plans	Pancakes with berries, hot cereal for breakfast; generous servings of roast beef, ham, roast turkey for lunch and dinner. Fresh produce in season.
Services and Facilities	**Spa Facilities:** 2 indoor whirlpools, swimming pool. **Recreation Facilities:** Volleyball court, croquet, horseshoe pitch; fishing, hiking, mountain climbing; downhill and cross-country skiing, ice skating, snowmobiling, sledding.
In the Area	Chena River cruise, boating, canoeing.
Getting Here	*From Fairbanks.* By car, Rte. 2 (Steese Hwy.) to Chena Springs Rd. (80 min). Rental car available.
Special Notes	Limited access for the disabled. Pool open 8 AM–10 PM ($6 for nonguests).

McKinley Chalet Resort

Non-program resort facilities

Alaska
Denali National Park

Overlooking majestic mountains at a scenic turn in the Nenana River, the McKinley Chalet Resort consists of a cluster of rustic cabins and a modern mountain lodge in an accessible area of the wilderness of Denali National Park. Guests enjoy free use of the only indoor health club and swimming pool this side of Mt. McKinley. Fitness facilities at the resort's Chalet Club include an exercise room with weights, whirlpool, and sauna, and an aerobics studio is used for classes.

Dominated by Mt. McKinley, the Denali experience is a mixture of rugged outdoor treks and guided bus tours.

Naturalists and park rangers accompany trips along park roads that are closed to private cars in the summer. River rafting and a scenic float are other possibilities here.

The Northwest

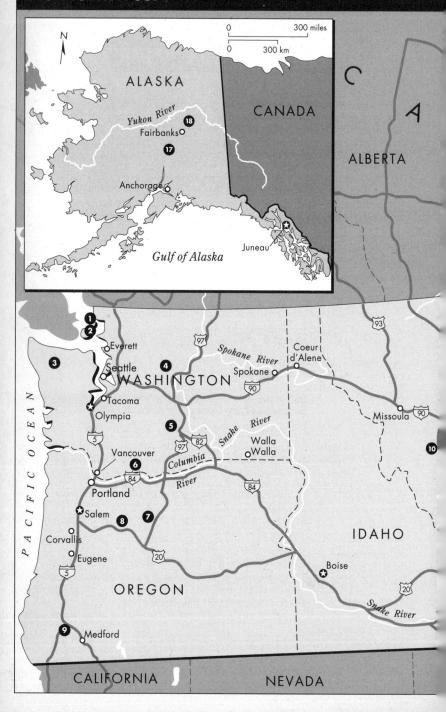

300 miles
300 km

ALASKA

Yukon River

Fairbanks ⊙ **18**

17

Anchorage ⊙

Gulf of Alaska

Juneau ★

CANADA

ALBERTA

C A

1
2

Everett ⊙

3

Seattle
WASHINGTON

4

Spokane ⊙
Coeur
d'Alene ⊙

Spokane River

5 I-90

Tacoma ⊙
Olympia ★

I-5

Missoula ⊙
I-90

10

Snake River

Walla
Walla ⊙

Vancouver

5

6
I-84

Columbia River

I-82
I-97

I-84

Portland

Salem ★

8 **7**

Corvallis ⊙

Eugene ⊙
I-5

Rt. 20

OREGON

Boise ★

IDAHO

Rt. 20

Snake River

9 Medford ⊙

PACIFIC OCEAN

I-97
US-93

CALIFORNIA

NEVADA

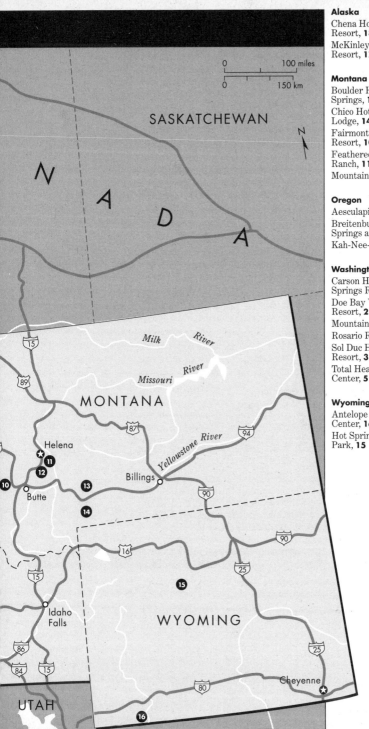

Alaska
Chena Hot Springs Resort, **18**
McKinley Chalet Resort, **17**

Montana
Boulder Hot Springs, **12**
Chico Hot Springs Lodge, **14**
Fairmont Hot Springs Resort, **10**
Feathered Pipe Ranch, **11**
MountainFit, **13**

Oregon
Aesculapia, **9**
Breitenbush Hot Springs and Retreat, **8**
Kah-Nee-Ta Resort, **7**

Washington
Carson Hot Mineral Springs Resort, **6**
Doe Bay Village Resort, **2**
MountainFit, **4**
Rosario Resort, **1**
Sol Duc Hot Springs Resort, **3**
Total Health Lifestyle Center, **5**

Wyoming
Antelope Retreat Center, **16**
Hot Springs State Park, **15**

McKinley Chalet Resort

Milepost 239 Parks Hwy. McKinley Park, AK 99755
Tel. 907/683–2215
Reservations: 825 W. 8th Ave. (240), Anchorage, AK
99501
Tel. 907/683–2215
Fax 907/683–2398

Administration Manager, Carson Fleharty

Season May–Sept.

Accommodations 252 deluxe 2-room suites in an alpine chalet, with hotel service. Units include simply furnished sitting rooms with sofa and reading chair, 2 twin beds (or double with twin), modern bath, wooden balconies and walkways. Dining in the main building (adjoining the Chalet Club).

Rates $147 for 2 persons, double occupancy. Daily 7-hour Tundra Wildlife bus tour, $45 per person. 1-night's lodging in advance. Credit cards: AE, MC, V.

Meal Plans À la carte menu offers fresh salmon baked and grilled, salads, poached halibut, roast leg of lamb, pasta, steaks, chicken, pork. For breakfast, home-baked muffins and breads.

Services and Equipment **Exercise Equipment:** 10-station Universal weight training gym, StairMaster, stationary bikes, rowing machine, free weights. **Services:** Swedish massage. **Swimming Facilities:** Indoor pool. **Recreation Facilities:** River rafting, backcountry hiking. **Evening Programs:** Alaska Cabin Nite buffet $25, children $12.

In the Area Tundra Wildlife bus tour (6 hr), air sightseeing, sled-dog demonstration; Vistadome rail excursion to Fairbanks or Anchorage.

Getting Here *From Anchorage.* By bus, Gray Line of Alaska (5 hr). By train, McKinley Explorer private car, Alaska Railroad scheduled service daily (6 hr). By car, Rte. 3 (George Parks Hwy.) to National Park gateway (5 hr). Free pickup to and from train station.

Special Notes Ramps at health club and some lodging allow access for the disabled. Swimming lessons and nature trail hikes for children. No smoking in the Chalet Club, Chalet Center, and designated areas of the dining rooms. Spa open weekdays 11 AM–10 PM, weekends 9 AM–10 PM.

Boulder Hot Springs

Taking the waters
Holistic health

Montana Mineral-spring baths and mountain hikes at the Boulder Hot
Boulder Springs resort in the foothills of the Elkhorn range of the Rocky Mountains have been an attraction since the early 1800s. Then, in the early 1950s, controversy arose as stories of a radioactive "miracle mine" appeared in the national media.

Operators of the Free Enterprise Radon Mine make no claims for medical benefits. Instead, they point to the documentation of treatments at similar mines near Bad Gastein, Austria, where more than 7,000 patients a year breathe radon under medical supervision.

Those who come to the Free Enterprise mine seeking relief from asthma, arthritis, bursitis, and other forms of chronic, crippling pain bundle up in sweaters and coats and stretch out in deck chairs to breathe the radon gas and drink the radioactive water. Some visitors have claimed to experience improved freedom of movement and relief from pain after a week.

As for the degree of radioactivity involved, the Montana Health Department says that guests are exposed to less than 10% of the maximum legal allowance of radiation to which miners may be exposed. No authoritative medical evaluation of the theraputic value of the mines has been established.

Located three miles from the hotel and 85 feet below ground, the mine is surprisingly dry and comfortable. A large elevator, capable of handling wheelchairs, descends to well-lighted, timbered tunnels equipped with warming lamps. Visits last a maximum of 80 minutes, and a series of up to 32 treatments is suggested (tel. 406/225–3383).

Guests at the big old inn enjoy a variety of therapies from massage to hot and cold plunges, and one may consult with a natural-health specialist. Around the indoor pools is a lounge area with a bar that serves vitamins, mineral supplements, and herbal tea as well as beer. Meals must be ordered in advance; the restaurant is open only on weekends. For those who want to cook for themselves, a central kitchen may be used free of charge. The temperature of the mineral water is 175 degrees when it reaches ground level. Pure enough to drink, it has the effect of a laxative and diuretic. Chemical analysis shows the water to be full of the same medicinal salts used at European spas to treat rheumatism, gout, and some kidney and bladder disorders.

As renovations progress, the resort's owners hope to rejuvenate the health programs. The inn's mission architecture is being preserved.

Boulder Hot Springs
Box 1020, Boulder, MT 59632
Tel. 406/225–4339

Administration	Manager, Barbara Reiter
Season	Year-round.
Accommodations	125-room hotel. Furnishings have a turn-of-the-century look: heavy wooden pieces, oversize beds, old-fashioned baths. Hostel beds, camp sites, RV connections available.
Rates	The hotel could be booked by groups only at press time.
Meal Plans	The Hot Spot Restaurant (hotel) features grilled mountain trout, vegetable lasagna, broiled chicken. Fruit, yogurt, vitamins, distilled water available.
Services and Facilities	**Services:** Massage (acupressure, deep-muscle), biofeedback therapy, consultation on nutrition and health. **Swimming Facilities:** Naturally heated outdoor mineral-water pool. **Spa Facilities:** Separate men's and women's bathhouses have hot and cold plunge pools. **Recreation Facilities:** Hiking, fishing; cross-country skiing.

In the Area Glacier National Park, Lewis & Clark Caverns, Montana State Capitol in Helena, Yellowstone National Park.

Getting Here *From Helena.* By car, I–15 to Boulder, Hwy. 69 to Boulder Springs (40 min). Free pickup to and from Helena or Butte. Service to the radon mine. Rental car available.

Special Notes Limited access for the disabled. No smoking in dining room.

Chico Hot Springs Lodge

Taking the waters

Montana After a day in the saddle, the prospect of a hot soak makes sore
Pray muscles bearable. There's nothing glamorous about the Chico Hot Springs Lodge, but the two hot-springs pools on its 157-acre grounds encourage many visitors to Yellowstone Park to detour. Located about 30 miles from the park's northern gateway, the resort offers horseback riding and pack trips into the Gallatin National Forest and the Absaroka range of the Rockies.

Surrounded by spectacular mountain scenery, the open-air pools are fed by 110-degree untreated mineral water from several springs. Four private areas in the bathhouse have redwood hot tubs large enough for a family of four.

The pools are open to the public as well as to registered guests, and as you soak you might even spot deer on the slopes.

Chico Hot Springs Lodge
Pray, MT 59065
Tel. 406/333–4933

Administration Managers, Michael and Eve Art

Season Year-round.

Accommodations 52 rooms in the main lodge, 12 motel units, several family-size condominium apartments in A-frame cabins. Lodge rooms have Western furnishings, twin beds, private or shared bath.

Rates Lodge rooms $36–$56 for 2 persons per day. Apartment for 2 $64–$74 per day in cabin, $59 in motel unit, $139–$169 in condominium. Confirmation by credit card. Credit cards: MC, V.

Meal Plans Continental fare. À la carte lunch menu includes grilled fish, salad, fruit plate; dinner entrees can be roast venison, saddle of lamb, grilled or sautéed trout.

Services and Facilities **Swimming Facilities:** Mineral-water outdoor pool. **Spa Facilities:** 4 private tubs, 2 outdoor pools, Jacuzzi. **Recreation Facilities:** Boating, trout fishing (private lake), horseback riding; cross-country skiing, snowmobiling, mountain bike rental.

In the Area Trail rides; Yellowstone National Park; Crow Indian Reservation, river float trips.

Getting Here *From Bozeman.* By car, I–90 to Hwy. 89 (2 hr).

Fairmont Hot Springs Resort

Taking the waters

Montana
Anaconda

Big Sky country and big springs come together here. Nestled near the Pintlar Wilderness in an area of boundless views and numerous springs, the Fairmont Hot Springs Resort combines striking modern architecture and Western hospitality. The range of amenities and activities makes it ideal for a family vacation in summer or a skiing holiday in winter.

Native Americans worshiped the "medicine water" of the natural hot springs. The mineral water, 160 degrees when it surfaces, is treated and cooled for the two Olympic-size swimming pools and the indoor and outdoor soaking pools. Resort facilities include men's and women's steambaths but no bodywork.

The family-oriented activities include hayrides and visits to the petting zoo; among the sports options are horseback riding, golf, tennis, and a huge water slide.

Guests have the choice of a fully equipped condominium apartment or rooms and suites in the main lodge. The indoor pool ensures swimming and soaking in comfort year-round.

Fairmont Hot Springs Resort
1500 Fairmont Rd., Anaconda, MT 59711
Tel. 406/797–3241 or 800/443–2381 (800/332–3272 in MT)

Administration Manager, Edward Henrich

Season Year-round.

Accommodations 135 guest rooms in the lodge; time-share condominium apartment rentals. Double beds, quality furnishings, private bath. RV hookup, campsites.

Rates Rooms $59–$72, depending on season; suites $160–$240; condominiums $95–$180 for 1 or 2 persons. 1 night payable in advance. Credit cards: AE, D, MC, V.

Meal Plans Standard American breakfast and dinner in the restaurant.

Services and Facilities **Swimming Facilities:** Outdoor and indoor Olympic-size pools. **Spa Facilities:** Large soaking pools, indoor and outdoor. **Recreation Facilities:** 2 tennis courts, 18-hole golf course, horseback riding, hayrides; trout fishing, cross-country skiing, sleigh rides.

In the Area Yellowstone National Park, Glacier National Park, Discovery Basin (downhill skiing).

Getting Here *From Butte.* By car, I–90 (15 min). Complimentary transportation by lodge van. Rental car available.

Special Notes Limited access for the disabled. Hayrides, sleigh rides for children.

Feathered Pipe Ranch

Holistic health
Spiritual awareness

Montana
Helena

Since 1975 a center for workshops in yoga and holistic health Feathered Pipe Ranch is a magical place that sets spirits soaring, and attracts world-renowned teachers and practitioners.

Almost every week from spring to autumn sees an intensive program here on subjects as diverse as astrology, women's studies, shamanism, massage training, and Iyengar yoga. People from many backgrounds, professionals in the healing arts, and novice students come here to gain new ideas and experience. The number of participants ranges from 35 to 50, and some families attend with young children.

A catalyst for change, the Feathered Pipe Foundation offers vacations that help visitors recognize their wholeness and the interconnectedness of all life. Some even maintain that the ranch wilderness has a healing power.

Located in the Montana Rockies close to the Continental Divide, the retreat sits on land that was once inhabited by a Native American tribe. Climbing to "sacred rocks" for meditation, you gain a panoramic view of the 110-acre ranch. Miles of hiking trails, a sparkling lake and stream, and the dry, clear air make a heady combination that can generate a tremendous feeling of release.

Workshops address many areas of the human-potential movement. There is an annual health and nutrition course; another is devoted to the shamanistic rituals of the Huichol Mexicans. Iyengar yoga is a popular topic in this intimate environment; a one-week course teaches yoga as the means to personal transformation.

Log and stone buildings give the impression of a frontier outpost. Beyond the main lodge are Native American tepees, Mongolian yurts, and basic tents. A cedar bathhouse holds huge hot tubs, a sauna, and a massage room staffed by professional therapists.

The search for insight is the ranch's principal attraction. Serious concentration is the norm here, with little of the fun-and-fitness holiday atmosphere.

Feathered Pipe Ranch
2409 Colorado Gulch, Helena, MT 59601
Tel. 406/443–0430
(Foundation programs) Box 1682, Helena, MT 59624
Tel. 406/442–8196

Administration Executive Director, India Supera; seminars director, Katherine Smith

Season Late Apr.–Sept.

Accommodations 4 dormitory rooms with bunk beds for 2–6 people in the main lodge. Linens, blankets, towels provided. Tents, yurts, campsites, cabins; tepees sleep 2 persons.

Rates 4-day workshop $275–$495, 1-week program $850–$990. Lodging, meals, instruction included. $250 payable in advance. Credit cards (4% surcharge): MC, V.

Meal Plans 3 gourmet vegetarian meals daily, cafeteria style. Organically grown produce. Breakfast includes yogurt, home-baked bread or muffins, fresh fruit; lunch may be tuna-fish salad with pita bread, green salad, or pasta with vegetables; typical dinner selections are baked trout, eggplant and cheese casserole, zucchini baked with tomatoes, baked chicken. Special diets accommodated.

Services and Facilities	**Services:** Massage, bodywork. **Swimming Facilities:** Mountain lake. **Recreation Facilities:** Volleyball, hiking. **Evening Programs:** Talks related to study programs; entertainment.
In the Area	Helena historical area and shopping; Gates of the Mountains boat tour, hot springs.
Getting Here	*From Helena.* By car I–15 (15 min). Rental car and limo available. Van service ($30 round-trip).
Special Notes	No smoking indoors. Remember to bring flashlight, sun protection.

MountainFit

Sports conditioning

Montana
Bozeman

The week-long MountainFit programs in Montana, like those of Utah and Maui, combine strenuous exercise and scenic beauty. Hard-core hikers can enjoy challenging treks in Yellowstone National Park, the Absaroka-Beartooth Wilderness, and along the Bridger Range, where the peaks rise above 9,000 feet. Walkers accustomed to a rigorous pace can also benefit from the program's daily regimen of yoga, conditioning exercises, and sports massages to strengthen leg and body muscles.

Each day's route, selected from among 25 charted hikes, is geared to the average capability of group members, who range in age from 30 to 70 and may include both beginners and experienced hikers. Outfitted with lunch, snacks, and fannypack, their water bottles refilled and frozen nightly, a group of 6–10 hikers sets off daily with a leader and a guide at the rear. Safety is a priority: Each day's route (usually a choice of two destinations) is registered with park rangers, while the staff carries two-way radio equipment and checks hikers regularly for foot blisters or signs of stress.

Based at the Gallatin Gateway Inn, a historic railroad hotel, the six-day program includes spa cuisine with regional produce and perhaps game, two hour-long massages, and yoga instruction. Transportation to the trailheads is provided.

South-central Montana offers forests of tall lodgepole pines, alpine meadows carpeted with rare ferns and bear grass, limestone cliffs with the fossil remains of marine animals, and deer, moose, mountain goats, elk, bison, golden eagles, and cutthroat trout. Staffers recount local lore and identify plants and wildlife en route. A hiking trail in the Gallatin Range passes 11 waterfalls; other outings allow a soak at Chico Hot Springs or rafting on the Yellowstone River.

MountainFit
Gallatin Gateway Inn, Bozeman, MT 59715
Reservations: 633 Battery St., San Francisco,
CA 94111
Tel. 415/397–6216 or 800/926–5700

Administration	Owner and director, Diane Wechsler
Season	July, August; scheduled weeks only.
Accommodations	6 rooms (2 doubles, 4 singles), with brass bed, flowered comforter, and matching curtains; shared baths.

Rates $1,950 for the Sun.–Sat. program includes meals, 2 massages, outings. $300 nonrefundable deposit on reservation; balance due 30 days before start of program. Credit cards: AE.

Meal Plans Daily menu of 1,200–1,500 calories. Breakfast choices are freshly baked muffins, cereals, fruit, pancakes. Trail lunch consists of cold gazpacho soup, couscous salad, peanut butter and jelly sandwiches, fruit. A typical dinner, served family style, includes green salad, homemade pasta, salmon poached or baked in phyllo crust, asparagus tips, four-grain pilaf, sorbet dessert. Coffee, tea, milk are available; dietary needs are accommodated.

Services and **Services:** Massage. **Swimming Facilities:** Outdoor pool. **Recrea-**
Facilities **tion Facilities:** 2 tennis courts, Jacuzzi. **Evening Programs:** Lecture-demonstrations, films.

In the Area Lewis & Clark Caverns, Chico Hot Springs Resort, Yellowstone River; Yellowstone and Grand Teton National Parks; Museum of the Rockies.

Getting Here *From Bozeman.* Participants' transportation provided on arrival and departure (30 min).

Special Notes No smoking in lodge. Hiking boots required; bathrobe provided. Daily maid service.

Aesculapia

Spiritual awareness
Holistic health
Kid fitness

Oregon Created as a community of healers and named after the Greek
Wilderville god of healing and ancient dream temples, Aesculapia is a retreat that teaches self-healing. Visitors take part in shamanistic ritual, hike in the woods, or meditate; help is available from body healers and hypnotherapists, nutritionists and psychotherapists.

Located on 80 acres of mountain wilderness in the Siskiyou Mountains of southwest Oregon, Aesculapia fosters the visionary experience of founder/director Graywolf. Dream-healing workshops for six to eight participants seek to examine visionary experiences. Among special events scheduled are spring and fall weeks devoted to healing communion, weekend retreats, and a two-week combination of spiritual and outdoor adventure that climaxes with a journey on the Rogue River.

Aesculapia
Box 301, Wilderville, OR 97543
Tel. 503/476–0492

Administration Founder/manager, Graywolf/Fred Swinney

Season Year-round.

Accommodations Rustic, comfortable rooms in small mountain houses are shared by community members. Guests bring their own linens, towels, blankets. Campsites available.

Rates $50 a day per person, including meals. 1-week retreat $545, sanctuary only $300. 1 night payable in advance. No credit cards.

Meal Plans Vegetarian meals, fresh fruit and produce in season. Buffets offer salads of sprouts, greens, and grains, vegetarian lasagna, tofu casserole, and home-baked whole-wheat breads.

Services and Facilities **Services:** Massage; counseling on nutrition and health. **Swimming Facilities:** Lake. **Recreation Facilities:** Hiking. **Evening Programs:** Informal workshops, rituals.

In the Area Ocean beaches, vineyard tours, hot springs; Shakespeare Festival (July–Aug.); Rogue River (white-water rafting); Kalmiopsis Wilderness (hiking).

Getting Here *From Eugene.* By bus, Greyhound to Medford (2 hr). By car, I–5 south to Grants Pass (90 min). Rental car available.

Special Notes Programs for children include Emergent Design group sharing of thoughts, feelings, conflicts; outings and adventures.

Breitenbush Hot Springs and Retreat

Taking the waters
Spiritual awareness
Holistic health

Oregon
Detroit The Esalen of the Northwest, the Breitenbush Hot Springs, Retreat, and Conference Center is a holistic community retreat for groups and individuals; its rustic cabins cluster on the banks of the Breitenbush River, surrounded by the Willamette National Forest.

The hot mineral waters are a major attraction: Natural springs and artesian wells supply 180-degree water for the steam bath and outdoor pools. At an idyllic spot in the woods, the water flows through four hydrojet pools for alfresco baths with adjustable temperatures. In the meadow you can dip into footbaths where the hot mineral water flows naturally.

Beyond sybaritic pleasures, the community is dedicated to fostering personal health and spiritual growth. Visitors can join workshops and ceremonies, even experience a meditation pyramid and a Native American sweat lodge. A sanctuary building provides space for a private retreat.

Breitenbush Hot Springs and Retreat
Box 578, Detroit, OR 97342
Tel. 503/854–3314

Administration Manager, Ross McKeen

Season Year-round.

Accommodations 40 cabins for 2–4 people, bath with toilet. 20 tents with mattresses, some bare campsites.

Rates $40–$75 a day per person includes meals. 1 night payable in advance. Credit cards: MC, V.

Meal Plans Ovo-lacto vegetarian diet. Breakfast is granola, hot cereal of mixed grains, yogurt, fruit, and home-baked wheat breads. Lunch can be a salad with sprouts or tuna fish, vegetarian pizza. Dinner entrees may include lasagna, Mexican casserole, or vegetarian pizza.

Services and Facilities **Services:** Massage, hydrotherapy, aromatherapy, herbal wrap; counseling on health and healing. **Swimming Facilities:** Outdoor pool to be renovated; glacial river. **Spa Facilities:** 4 outdoor tiled pools, indoor hot tubs. **Recreation Facilities:** Hiking; cross-country skiing. **Evening Programs:** Workshops on health and nutrition.

In the Area Native American cultural center at Warm Springs Indian Reservation; Mt. Hood National Forest, Mt. Jefferson Wilderness.

Getting Here *From Portland.* By car, I–5 south to Salem, Hwy. 22 to Detroit, Hwy. 46 to Breitenbush (2 hr). By bus, Greyhound (3 hr).

Special Notes Smoking only in designated outdoor areas. Remember to bring bedding, towels, flashlight.

Kah-Nee-Ta Resort

Taking the waters

Oregon
Warm Springs

The Kah-Nee-Ta Resort, owned and managed by a confederation of tribes whose ancestors once worshiped at the springs on their reservation, strikes a delicate balance between tradition and modernity. Guests are invited to tribal ceremonies and festivals and to share a guinea hen baked in clay. Huge swimming pools and bathhouses offer private soaks and a massage. And the tranquillity of the brown hills, the distant snow-covered mountains, and the vast expanse of blue sky where hawks hang like kites on invisible currents of air may seem to have curative powers.

The guest lodge and conference center sit atop a rocky ridge overlooking the Warm Springs River and a recreation complex. Open to the public, this Indian village of tepees and vacation villas offers mineral baths and pools, a golf course, tennis courts, and stables. Trails for biking, hiking, and riding fan out toward the distant Cascade Mountains.

All activities are priced à la carte, and the fees are modest: $20 ($15 for teenagers) for an hour on horseback, $5 for a 25-minute mineral bath. Arrangements can be made on short notice on any day of the week. In the separate men's and women's bathhouses, the five tiled sunken tubs are refilled after each use. The odorless mineral water is piped in at 140 degrees and cooled to suit the bathers.

Named after the Native American spirit of the hot springs, this cheery, family-oriented resort protected by mountains enjoys a dry and sunny climate most of the year. Native Americans say it is a place to make peace with yourself.

Kah-Nee-Ta Resort
Box K, Warm Springs, OR 97761
Tel. 503/553–1112 or 800/831–0100
Fax 503/553–1071

Administration Manager, Ron A. Malfara

Season Year-round.

Accommodations Luxury rooms in the cedar lodge, cottages in the village, and furnished tepees accommodate 325. Lodge rooms have balconies with views, oversize beds, full bath. Campsites, RV and trailer hookup available.

Rates Lodge rooms $89.95–$109.95 per day, single or double; suites (2 bedrooms) $249.95. Cottages $123.95 for up to 4 persons. 1 night payable in advance. Credit cards: AE, DC, MC, V.

Meal Plans Breakfast includes eggs, ham, bacon or sausage, Indian fry bread, huckleberry muffins or croissants. For lunch, salads, pizza, grilled salmon. Dinner selections may be seafood fettucine, Swiss steak, baked salmon, venison steaks, game bird baked in clay. Native salmon bake on Sat., Memorial Day–Labor Day.

Services and Facilities **Services:** Massage. **Swimming Facilities:** Olympic-size outdoor pool (village), outdoor pool (lodge). **Spa Facilities:** 5 tiled Roman tubs in men's and women's bathhouses. **Recreation Facilities:** 2 tennis courts, 18-hole golf course, horseback riding, trout fishing, mountain-bike rental. **Evening Programs:** Drumming, ceremonies, rituals; salmon bake.

In the Area Nature trail walks with resident naturalist; Mt. Hood National Forest, The Dalles recreation area, white-water rafting on the Deschutes River.

Getting Here *From Portland.* By car, Hwy. 26 to Warm Springs (2½ hr). By air, scheduled commercial service to Redmond (30 min); private and charter flights land at Madras Airport 25 miles away. Rental car available.

Special Notes Limited access for the disabled. No smoking in pool area and designated dining areas.

Carson Hot Mineral Springs Resort

Taking the waters

Washington *Carson* The claw-footed enamel tubs are characteristic of the old-fashioned friendliness bathers enjoy at the Carson Hot Mineral Springs Resort. Proud of using "the same bath methods for over 100 years," the management strives to remain unpretentious and comfortable. The rustic cabins, a landmark hotel, and bathhouses located on the banks of the Wind River near its junction with the mighty Columbia date from 1876. The oldest remaining structure, a two-story wood hotel, was built in 1897 to accommodate bathers who traveled by steamboat from Portland, Oregon. The cabins were built in the early 1920s.

Taking the waters is a simple, two-step procedure: a tub soak followed by the traditional sweat wrap, in which an attendant wraps bathers in sheets and heavy blankets to induce a good sweat. Separate bathhouses for men and women offer some privacy.

The 126-degree mineral water is piped directly into the tubs (eight for men, six for women), which are drained and refilled after each use. The water is not treated with chemicals; analysis shows it to be high in sodium and calcium, like springs at principal European spas. The crowning touch is the hour-long massage ($26–$32).

The mountains behind the hotel are laced with hiking trails; there is good fishing nearby, and an 18-hole golf course was recently added. Guests can dine at the hotel or do their own cooking in the cabins.

Carson Hot Mineral Springs Resort
Box 370, Carson, WA 98610
Tel. 509/427–8292

Administration	Manager, Rudy Beilkowsky
Season	Year-round.
Accommodations	9 large hotel rooms, 23 cabins, all simply furnished with double beds. No private bath, TV, or telephone. Cabin rooms have toilet and sink, kitchenette.
Rates	Rooms $29–$34 and cabins $31–$36 for 2 persons, $5 each additional person. 1 night payable in advance. Credit cards: MC, V.
Meal Plans	3 hearty meals daily, à la carte. Lunch menu includes pasta salad, beef lasagna, vegetarian sandwiches. Dinner entrees are a vegetarian "gardenburger," fruit platter, grilled salmon, steak, ham.
Services and Facilities	**Services:** Massage. **Spa Facilities:** Individual tubs in men's and women's bathhouses ($6). **Recreation Facilities:** Hiking, fishing, golf.
In the Area	River trips, The Dalles recreation area, Bonneville Dam, Shakespeare Festival (summer), Portland museums and cultural centers, 18-hole golf course.
Getting Here	*From Portland.* By car, I–84 to Bridge of the Gods, Rte. 14 to Carson (70 min).
Special Notes	Limited access for the disabled. No smoking in the bathhouses.

Doe Bay Village Resort

Taking the waters

Washington
Orcas Island

The hot tubs at the rustic Doe Bay Village Resort afford spectacular views of the San Juan Islands, and the constant 106-degree temperature of the mineral water from nearby springs protects bathers from the chilly mist. Waterfalls, the ocean, hidden beaches, and a sauna with stained-glass windows help to create a special feeling of seclusion and communion.

Native Americans were the first to make a sanctuary here. Loggers and trappers came to enjoy the springs and a tavern in the town, where a general store and post office have operated since the early 1900s. In time the area became an artists' colony and a human-potential center; today the resort is a laid-back haven for lovers of hot springs, hiking, kayaking, and other outdoor life.

The village may strike you as having been caught in a time warp. The old-time general store, listed in the National Register of Historic Buildings, is now a communal kitchen—where you can cook your own meals—and the resort's main dining room. Cabins linked by covered walkways line a grassy slope above the bay.

The paint may be peeling and the plumbing may not always work, but the prices are reasonable. There are campsites (with communal baths and showers) for those who go for seclusion in the woods. Some sites have a dome of plastic sheeting for protection from the rain. Hostel-style dormitory beds at $10, and a Retreat House for $50, accommodate groups and individuals.

Canoe, rowboat, and kayak guided tours are available, and Moran State Park, a large, isolated part of the island, has hiking trails. Its picnic areas and warm-water lakes for fishing and swimming are a few miles from the resort. A large number of day visitors come here by ferry from the mainland for a soak at the springs.

The open-air hot tubs at the resort are equipped with Jacuzzi jets; two have hot water, one is naturally cold. A wood deck surrounds the bathing complex, which is attached to a big sauna hut in which 20 people can enjoy the wood-fired heat comfortably. The price for eight hours is $5 (including parking if you drove over from the ferry), $3 for guests. Bring your own towels.

The tranquilizing effect of the sea air, warm water, and perhaps a massage makes up for the lack of programs or amenities. A modest series of meditation sessions has been scheduled, and this may grow into a permanent program under the resort's new owners, who have established a general store featuring natural foods and a cafe that serves breakfast and dinner.

Doe Bay Village Resort
Star Rte. 86, Olga, WA 98279
Tel. 206/376–2291 or 206/376–4755

Administration	General manager, Cynthia Brancatto
Season	Year-round.
Accommodations	Rustic cabins for up to 100 guests range from duplexes to large cottages with private shower, heat, and bedding. No maid service, TV, telephone. Campsites, tents, RV hookups and dormitory lodging ($10.50) available.
Rates	Cottages $32.50–$85 a day for 1 or 2 persons; $9.50 per additional person. 1 night payable in advance. Credit cards: AE, MC, V.
Meal Plans	Vegetarian cuisine, chicken, seafood à la carte.
Services and Facilities	**Services:** Massage, kayaking instruction. **Swimming Facilities:** Ocean beach, mountain lake. **Spa Facilities:** 3 outdoor tubs, steam room, Jacuzzi. **Recreation Facilities:** Guided kayak tours, fishing, hiking, golf, tennis nearby.
In the Area	Ferry trips to nearby islands; whale-watching boat trips; Seattle museums and cultural life; Olympic National Park.
Getting Here	*From Seattle.* By car, I–5 to Mt. Vernon, ferry from Anacortes. Drive through Olga to east end of the island (3 hr).

MountainFit

Sports conditioning

Washington
Cascade Mountains

Straddling the crest of North Cascades National Park in central Washington, the week-long MountainFit program incorporates a daily itinerary varying between from 3- to 4-hour walks and a rugged 6-hour mountain ascent. Hikers go in groups of 10–13, escorted by four trained guides. After roughing it by day, participants are pampered by night in a mountain lodge surrounded by a forest of evergreens and bright yellow aspens.

The program includes two massages for the week (additional appointments are extra), all meals prepared according to spa cuisine standards, and lodging. Each day begins with a yoga class followed by a hike, for which a day pack with lunch, water bottle, and rain gear are provided. Camaraderie develops quickly; single professionals are among the many repeat visitors.

MountainFit

Reservations: 633 Battery St. (5th floor), San Francisco, CA 94111
Tel. 415/397–6216 or 800/926–5700

Administration Founder/director, Diane Weschsler

Season May, September; scheduled weeks

Accommodations Exclusive mountain lodge with 7 bedrooms; private bathrooms, rustic furniture, living room with huge stone fireplace, and dining room for family-style meals. Bathrobes provided.

Rates $1,750 per person for the one-week program (Sat.–Fri.); supplement for single room $300. $300–$600 payable in advance. Gratuities ($100–$150) extra. Credit cards: AE.

Meal Plan Daily menu of 1,200–1,500 calories based on high-protein energy foods. Breakfast choices include fresh-baked muffins, pancakes with fruit, cereals. Trail lunch consists of gazpacho soup, couscous salad, sandwiches, fruit. Dinners include salad, homemade pasta, poached salmon, four-grain pilaf, sorbet. Coffee, tea, milk available; special diets accommodated.

Services and Facilities **Services:** Massage. **Swimming Facilities:** Outdoor pool. **Recreation Facilities:** Tennis court, volleyball, badminton, horseshoes, Jacuzzi.

In the Area Grand Coulee Dam, Mt. St. Helens National Historic Site, Columbia River.

Getting Here *From Seattle.* Transportation provided to and from SEATAC International Airport.

Special Notes Beginner and advanced hiker trails selected by guides can be challenging, and require proper boots and clothing. Similar program is offered in Montana, Utah, Maui, and British Columbia.

Rosario Resort

Non-program resort facilities

Washington
Orcas Island Sea-inspired treatments for the body and the seaside setting are the lure of the Rosario Resort, built around the former mansion of the shipbuilder Robert Moran. Many of the guest lodges and public rooms have a nautical look; portholes and other parts salvaged from old ships pop up in the indoor swimming pool and other unexpected places. An organ room with a spectacular cathedral ceiling and stained-glass windows is the setting for concerts and lectures.

The carved figurehead of a woman, saved from a sailing ship, looks out to sea from the front lawn of the mansion. Yachters dock here on their trips through the San Juan Archipelago, and the next best way to get here is by seaplane.

Simple pleasures such as hunting for driftwood on the two-mile-long beach, wandering in the pine woods, and relaxing in the sauna attract most visitors. Families with children, senior citizens, and fitness buffs come for a few days or weeks. Canada, the Rockies, and sophisticated Vancouver are a few hours' drive north; charming Victoria is just seven miles away by water.

Orcas Island is protected by hills on one side, warmed by the Japanese current of the Pacific Ocean on the other. The winters are mild and see no snow accumulation.

The resort has a small indoor spa with whirlpool, coed sauna, aerobics studio, and weights room. The daily schedule includes low-impact and aquatic aerobics, dance exercise, stretching and toning (flexercise) calisthenics, and yoga. Spa services are reserved on an à la carte basis.

Guests stay in villas overlooking the water that offer country-home atmosphere and great views. Fresh fish is an important part of the low-calorie spa cuisine option.

Rosario Resort
Eastsound, Orcas Island, WA 98245
Tel. 206/376–2222 or 800/562–8820

Administration Manager, Sarah Geiser; spa director, Pamela Edwards

Season Year-round.

Accommodations 179 rooms, condominium apartments, villas, all with country antique furnishings, modern beds, private bath, color TV, air-conditioning, patio. No room service.

Rates Double rooms $85–$105 a night, studios with fireplace $135. 1 night payable in advance. Credit cards: AE, DC, MC, V.

Meal Plans Menu à la carte in the Orcas Room. Lunch can be a green salad dressed with fresh fruit juice and cayenne pepper or chicken baked in romaine lettuce. Dinner entrees may include grilled salmon with peppercorn, basil, and red-pepper sauce; veal topped with crab and asparagus. Special diets on request.

Services and Facilities **Exercise Equipment:** 4-station Marcy weights unit, 4-station Apollo II gym, Precor rower, stepmachine, 2 Lifecycles, NordicTrack, rebounders, dumbbells (3–50 lbs.). **Services:** Massage (Swedish, shiatsu, reflexology), facials, salt-glow body scrub, pedicure, manicure; full-service beauty salon. **Swimming Facilities:** 2 outdoor pools, indoor pool, ocean beach, mountain lake. **Recreation Facilities:** 2 tennis courts, hiking; 9-hole golf course nearby; marina; kayaking center.

In the Area Whale-watching boat trips, kayaking excursions, ferry trips; island crafts and antiques shops in Eastsound; Orcas Island Historical Museum. Seattle; Vancouver; Olympic National Park, Doe Bay Hot Springs.

Getting Here *From Seattle.* By car, I–5 to Mt. Vernon, ferry from Anacortes to Eastsound (1½ hr). By plane, scheduled flights to Eastsound by Air San Juan; seaplane (20 min). Van service provided to and from Eastsound.

Special Notes Limited access for the disabled; some ground-floor rooms wheelchair accessible. No smoking in the spa or in designated dining areas.

Sol Duc Hot Springs Resort

Taking the waters

Washington
Olympic National Park

Here's the place to bring the family for a soak and a swim after a drive or a hike in Olympic National Park. Located within the park, the Sol Duc Hot Springs Resort maintains public and private pools, including four indoor whirlpools, filled with mineral water that flows from springs on federal land.

Piped into a heat exchanger at a temperature of 123 degrees, the mineral water is cooled for use in the three large outdoor soaking pools. The water's continuous flow into the pools makes chlorination unnecessary. Creek water is heated and treated for the large outdoor swimming pool.

Operating as a concession of the Department of the Interior, the resort has been updated and expanded in recent years. In addition to private cabins, there is a country-kitchen restaurant.

The park's rugged Pacific coastline, forests, and alpine meadows draw more than 2.8 million visitors a year. A short drive from Seattle, it can be visited for a day or an extended stay during the resort season.

Sol Duc Hot Springs Resort
Soleduc River Rd., Olympic National Park, WA
(Reservations) Box 2169, Port Angeles, WA 98362
Tel. 206/327–3583

Administration Manager, Connie Langley

Season May–Oct.

Accommodations 32 cabins with double bed (or twin beds and sofa bed), 6 with kitchen, all with modern bath. RV sites. No TV, telephone, dresser, or air-conditioning.

Rates Cabin with kitchen $84.08 day, without kitchen $75.46, including tax, for 2 persons. 1 night payable in advance. Credit cards: AE, MC, V.

Meal Plans Vegetarian, fish, and chicken dishes. Granola, yogurt, smoked salmon omelet, buckwheat pancakes with fresh berries for breakfast; burgers and deli selections for lunch; charbroiled chicken, baked cod with mushrooms, steaks, steamed vegetable platter, or zucchini-cheese casserole for dinner.

Services and Facilities **Swimming Facilities:** Large public pool. **Spa Facilities:** 4 indoor whirlpools, outdoor soaking pools. **Recreation Facilities:** Fishing, hiking. **Evening Programs:** Talks by park rangers.

In the Area Nature hikes with park rangers. Seattle museums, cultural centers, Pioneer Square (Klondike Gold Rush museum).

Getting Here *From Seattle.* By car, Hwy. 101 to Fairholm, Soleduc Rd. 11 miles to resort (4 hr). By car ferry, scheduled service to Winslow, Hwy. 101 to Soleduc Rd. (2 hr).

Special Notes Ramps at geothermal pools allow access for the disabled; rooms are wheelchair accessible. Nature walks for children with park ranger. No smoking in the bathhouse.

Total Health Lifestyle Center

Life enhancement
Weight management
Spiritual awareness
Vibrant maturity

Washington
Yakima Valley

Coming to the Total Health Lifestyle Center is like visiting elderly cousins in the country. The rambling 50-year-old house has a wide veranda and a green lawn big enough for croquet and badminton, and it is surrounded by apple and pear orchards. The family rooms have a lived-in look. Only the presence of doctors' offices veers from the homelike ambience.

The medically supervised programs of this Seventh-day Adventist natural-healing center are designed to educate guests and restore health; they combine treatments that promote spiritual, mental, and physical well-being. A smoking-cessation program is available. The facilities are nondenominational and nonsectarian, open to everyone, and intended for those suffering from obesity and degenerative disease. Participants, limited to 12 per week, are mostly over 50 and include couples.

Camaraderie develops easily here. Everyone participates in the food and cooking demonstrations, baking bread and learning to prepare vegetarian meals. The Adventists are known for their interest in nutrition, and their "Vegan" diet of fruits, vegetables, legumes, and naturally fat foods like nuts and avocados is observed in the dining room.

The doctors treat angina, high blood pressure, atherosclerosis, diabetes, chronic fatigue, and gastrointestinal disorders. Therapy is structured for each individual. A complete medical checkup is included in the program (separate fee).

Hiking orchard trails and country roads, and hydrotherapy are part of the daily program. The closely monitored participants are expected to maintain an exercise chart and keep a personal record of physical improvement. A steam bath, whirlpool, and Swiss 12-point shower are in the house. Walking is the preferred exercise here, so there's little in the way of exercise equipment.

The personal attention from the doctors and nine staff members (including a registered dietitian) helps motivate guests to help themselves. Lecture notes, reference materials, and recipes are prepared to take home.

Total Health Lifestyle Center
Old Naches Rd., Rte. 1, Box 176, Naches, WA 98937
(Office) Box 5, Yakima, WA 98907
Tel. 509/965–2555 or 800/348–0120

Administration
Administrator, Dr. Fred Hardinge, M.D.; medical director, Dr. Jay Sloop, M.D.

Season
Year-round.

Accommodations
9 upstairs bedrooms with shared and private bath, built-in dressers and closets, old-fashioned furniture, 2 beds.

Rates
19-day all-inclusive program $3,950, includes medical fee; 10-days $2,195, includes medical fee. 50% discount on program for

nonparticipating companion. (Medical insurance may cover some costs.) $450 deposit required. Credit cards: MC, V.

Meal Plans 3 vegetarian meals daily, family style. Lunch may include green salad, cashew chow mein, steamed vegetables. Typical dinner entrees are vegetarian lasagna with mock mozzarella topping, baked tofu, or eggplant Parmesan with cheeseless topping. Lots of complex carbohydrates; no dairy products, eggs, or oils. No coffee, tea, condiments.

Services and Facilities **Exercise Equipment:** Treadmill, stationary bike. **Services:** Guided walks and hikes; medical tests and fitness evaluations; behavior modification program for addictions. **Services:** Hydrotherapy, paraffin handbath, contrast shower, steam bath, massage. **Recreation Facilities:** Community tennis courts and golf course; fishing. **Evening Programs:** Worship hour, health lectures nightly.

In the Area Ginkgo Petrified Forest, Mt. Rainier National Park, Mt. St. Helens Volcanic Monument, Moses Lake, winery tours, Ellensburg Rodeo (Labor Day weekend), Grand Coulee Dam.

Getting Here *From Seattle.* By bus, Greyhound to Yakima (2½ hr). By car, I–90 east to Ellensburg, I–82 south to Yakima, Hwy. 12 toward Naches, Eschbach Rd. to Old Naches Rd. (3 hr). Taxi or prearranged pickup at bus station.

Special Notes No smoking indoors.

Antelope Retreat Center

Holistic health
Spiritual awareness

Wyoming
Savery
An isolated ranch in the foothills of the Continental Divide, the Antelope Retreat Center puts you to work preparing meals, joining in ranch chores, and gardening. Among the special weekly programs are vision quests based on the Native American rite of passage, which include a three-day wilderness fast, and a nature-awareness week devoted to learning survival skills while camping in the Red Desert and Medicine Bow National Forest. Focus programs include a Women's Week with a personal sojourn in the desert, and a Men's Gathering with drumming ritual.

An introduction to the geology of southern Wyoming can include fossil hunting or hiking and riding excursions. Winter activities take guests to Steamboat Springs for downhill skiing and a soak in the hot springs, or into the hills for camping, cross-country skiing, or snowshoeing.

John Boyer grew up on the ranch, founding the retreat center in 1986 to share his love of nature and the inner quiet learned from neighboring Indians. Guests are initiated at a sweatlodge ceremony and taught personal awareness exercises. Some even get to help with lambing the small herd of sheep.

Antelope Retreat Center
Box 166, Savery, WY 82332
Tel. 307/383–2625

Administration General manager, John Boyer; program directors, Gina Lyman and Tom Barnes

Season Year-round.

Accommodations 16 guests in the ranch house, plus two 4-bed native yurts. Shared bathroom; no air-conditioning. Bedrooms have wooden furniture, single or double beds.

Rates $250–$425 weekly plus $100–$200 for special programs (Sat.– Sat.) with all meals. Deposit: 50% of program fee. No credit cards.

Meal Plans 3 meals served daily, family style. Breakfast can be homemade grain cereal with honey, buckwheat pancakes with fruit, or an omelet. Lunch is soup and salad, sandwiches on homemade bread. Dinner main courses are barbecued chicken, baked or grilled fish, spaghetti, tofu casserole, and vegetable stir-fry. Special diets are accommodated.

Services and Facilities **Swimming Facilities:** Stream. **Recreation Facilities:** Hiking, skiing, outings to rodeos and nearby attractions; gardening, ranching.

In the Area Steamboat Springs (downhill skiing, hot springs), Medicine Bow National Forest, Red Desert.

Getting Here *From Denver, Co.* By car, I–70 via Idaho Springs, exit at Dillon, Rte. 9 to Kremmling, Rte. 40 west via Steamboat Springs to Craig, Hwy. 13/789 to Biggs, right on Rte. 70 via Dixon to Savery, left on Creek Rd. (5½ hr). By air, scheduled flights to Steamboat Springs (40 min); van transportation Saturdays ($50 round-trip).

Special Notes Children accompanying program participants charged $75 up to age 4, $200–$362 ages 5–15.

Hot Springs State Park

Taking the waters

Wyoming
Thermopolis
Long before explorers discovered the Big Spring, it was a bathing place for the Shoshone and Arapahoe tribes. When the land was purchased by the federal government in 1896, the deed stipulated that the springs remain open and free to all. Thus there is no charge to bathe in the indoor and outdoor pools maintained by the State of Wyoming. A Holiday Inn, resort apartments, and a rehabilitation center are located within the one-square-mile Hot Springs State Park.

The water wells from the earth at a temperature of 135 degrees and spills down a series of mineral-glazed terraces on its way to the Big Horn River. Some of the flow is diverted to privately operated bathhouses and swimming pools and into the state-run baths. The sparkling clean and airy facilities are patronized by families en route to Yellowstone and by senior citizens from a nearby retirement home. Park and pools are open daily, 9 AM–10 PM.

The Holiday Inn on the bank of the Horn River offers the most complete facilities. There are separate men's and women's bathhouses for private soaks (coed on request), and an outdoor hydrojet pool is filled with warm mineral water. The outdoor swimming pool contains chlorinated tap water. The Athletic Club facilities are free to inn guests.

Located in central Wyoming, the town of Thermopolis is surrounded by high buttes and range land where a herd of bison still roam free; it's a pleasant stop on the way to Yellowstone from Denver and Cheyenne.

Hot Springs State Park
Thermopolis Chamber of Commerce
220 Park St., Thermopolis, WY 82443
Tel. 307/864–2636

Holiday Inn of the Waters
100 Park St., Box 1323, Thermopolis, WY 82443
Tel. 307/864–3131 or 800/465–4329

Administration	Manager, James Mills; program director, Steve Bury
Season	Year-round.
Accommodations	80 rooms with modern furniture, bath, queen-size or twin beds or waterbed. Separate exercise rooms for men and women in the Athletic Club.
Rates	$75 a day for 2 in twin-bed room, $69 single. Meals à la carte. 1 night payable in advance. Add tax (6%) and gratuities. Credit cards: AE, MC, V.
Meal Plans	3 meals daily in hotel restaurant. Special diets accommodated. Western steaks, grilled fish, baked mountain trout, salads in season.
Services and Facilities	**Exercise Equipment:** 9-station Universal weight training gym in men's and women's areas; punching bag, stationary bikes, 2 racquetball courts. **Services:** Massage, beauty shop. **Swimming Facilities:** Outdoor heated pool. **Spa Facilities:** 4 private mineral water tubs, outdoor Jacuzzi; sauna, steam bath, men's and women's bathhouses. **Recreation Facilities:** Bicycle rental (tandem, single); golf, fishing, skiing, snowmobiling nearby.
In the Area	Outfitters offer hunting and fishing trips, scenic tours, river floats. Yellowstone National Park, Wind River Canyon, County Historical Museum (Hole in the Wall Bar), Jackson winter-sports area, Wind River Indian Reservation.
Getting Here	*From Cheyenne.* By car, I–25 to Casper, Hwy. 20 via Moneta (3 hr). By bus, Powder River Line (4 hr).
Special Notes	No smoking in the Athletic Club and designated areas of the dining room. Club hours: weekdays noon–8:30 PM, weekends 10 AM–8:30 PM.

The Central States

Dallas has been in the forefront of recent fitness developments in the Central States. Dr. Kenneth Cooper, who did pioneering research in exercise and nutrition in the U.S. Air Force and at the Cooper Clinic, is the guiding spirit for the Aerobics Center's residential program. In the suburbs, the Greenhouse now offers luxury pampering and body conditioning during mother-and-daughter weeks.

The crossover of European hydrotherapy and American fitness has been introduced at the Spa at Hotel Crescent Court and the Four Seasons resort, where golf, tennis, and a marine body masque can be part of the business day. Kneipp herbal baths and Kur Program from Germany are featured at the new Alamo Plaza Spa in San Antonio, Texas, and at the Lake Austin Resort near Austin.

Akia

Weight management   *Women only*
Stress control

Okalahoma
Chickasaw
National
Recreation Area

A rigid weight-loss diet, and getting lots of exercise are the main ingredients of the no-frills program at Akia, a fitness retreat for a dozen women. Guests participate in full days of hiking, stretching, and body toning in a rigorous dawn-to-dusk schedule that takes advantage of the scenic Arbuckle Mountains and nearby lakes and forests.

The day begins with exercise on the redwood deck that surrounds the main building. The two-mile hike before breakfast is followed by more stretching and toning in a lakeside pavilion.

Aerobics classes, contouring, and relaxation exercises begin the afternoon. Then participants have the option of soaking in the hot tub, getting a massage, walking, bicycling, or swimming in a nearby lake. Private consultation on nutrition with a registered dietitian and one-on-one training with the exercise instructor help you plan a personal fitness program.

Akia guests find the regimented program effective in reducing stress and improving fitness. Participants bring their own linens and towels and help with housekeeping. Lectures on developing healthy habits are given after dinner by candlelight.

Akia
Sulphur, OK
Office: 2316 N.W. 45th Place, Oklahoma City, OK 73112
Tel. 405/842–6269

Administration   Founder/director, Wilhelmina Maguire

Season   10-week spring and fall seasons.

Accommodations   Stone cottages and wood duplex for 11 guests. Cottages have 3 single beds, private bath, carpeting, wooden deck.

Rates $545 for 1-week session; $410 for 5-day session Sun.–Fri.; $355 for 4-day weekend. $150 advance payment. No credit cards.

Oklahoma
Akia, **2**

South Dakota
Black Hills Health and
Education Center, **1**

Texas
The Aerobics Center
Cooper Wellness
Program, **3**
Four Seasons Resort
and Club, **5**
The Greenhouse, **4**
Lake Austin Resort, **6**
The Phoenix Spa at
the Houstonian, **7**

The Central States

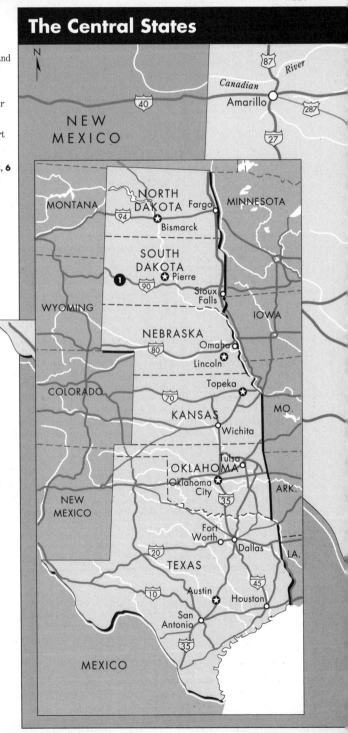

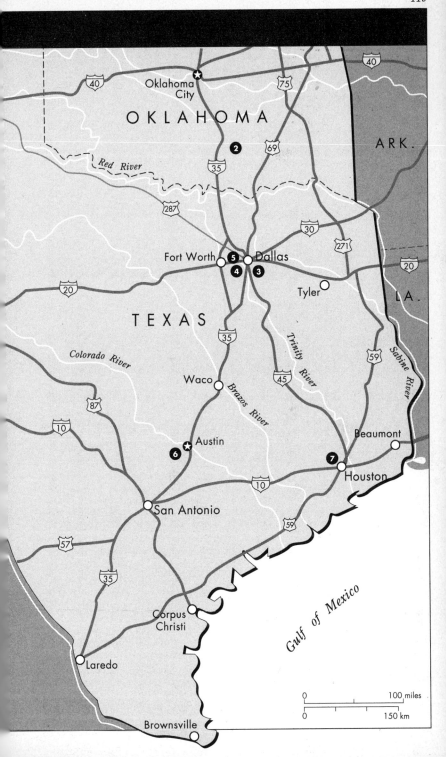

Meal Plans 3 simple meals daily total 950–1,000 calories, with options at breakfast and lunch; 3-course dinner. Breakfast can be cereal with fruit and juice, lunch a high-fiber protein shake. Typical dinner entrees are spinach lasagna, baked fish, eggplant Parmesan, peppers stuffed with lentils and brown rice; ricotta cheesecake is a favorite dessert.

Services and Facilities **Services:** Massage, facial, personal color analysis, body composition test, nutritional counseling. **Swimming Facilities:** Nearby lake. **Recreation Facilities:** Bicycling. **Evening Programs:** Lectures on nutrition, shopping for health food.

In the Area Oklahoma City's Kirkpatrick Center (Native American and African art), National Cowboy Hall of Fame, Guthrie (Victorian prairie capital), Cherokee Heritage Center in Tahlequah.

Getting Here *From Oklahoma City.* By car, I–35 south to Davis, Rte. 12 to Sulphur (2 hr). By bus, free transfers at Oklahoma City Airport, and from Davis, OK.

Special Notes No smoking.

Black Hills Health and Education Center

Life enhancement
Stress control
Spiritual awareness
Vibrant maturity

South Dakota
Hermosa

Across three creeks and up a woodland trail, in a lodge that looks like a mountain resort, you'll find the Black Hills Health and Education Center, a Seventh-day Adventist healing center that offers programs of 12 to 25 days.

Black Hill's medically supervised programs are designed to teach guests to develop healthy habits and to help those who suffer from diabetes, arthritis, hypertension, heart problems, and obesity. Each person's lifestyle is analyzed and a suitable regimen of exercise and diet prescribed. Rehabilitation therapy is provided for persons who have had cardiac surgery.

The program begins with a complete physical examination, blood tests, and medical counseling. Hydrotherapy (included in the program fee) and massage may be recommended; the lodge is equipped with a whirlpool, a Russian steam cabinet, and a shower that alternates hot and cold water from six sprays. Once or twice a week an excursion takes participants to a fitness center and a swimming pool fed by warm springs.

While the lectures cover stress control and nutrition, the central philosophy is one of learning by doing. Everyone joins in bread-making and cooking classes, and outings to a supermarket and restaurant are led by staff members who demonstrate how to shop for and order nutritious foods.

The health center is located in the scenic Banana Belt of the Black Hills, so named for the temperate climate and sunny days that prevail even in winter. Guests explore the canyons, cliffs, and farmlands on daily hikes.

The combined focus on spiritual, mental, and physical health attracts people of all ages to this informal resort, though many of the participants are over 50. They arrive in motor homes that can be hooked up outside, or they stay in the lodge; some bring children and a baby-sitter. Meals are included in rates.

An affiliate of the Black Hills Missionary College, the health center draws on the campus for services. Friday evening is a time when students and guests traditionally gather around the big stone fireplace in the lounge and join in a music program. Included in the program fee are a physical examination, meals, massage, and hydrotherapy.

Black Hills Health and Education Center
Box 19, Hermosa, SD 57744
Tel. 605/255–4101

Administration	President, Willard Werth; medical director, Melvyn Beltz, M.D.
Season	Year-round.
Accommodations	12 rooms in a 2-story lodge, modern furnishings, mostly double beds, private and shared baths. Motor-home services.
Rates	12-day program $1,550 single, $2,395 couple; 25-day program $2,395 single, $3,495 couple. $100–$200 reduction for motorhome use. Daily rate $30–$35 per room. $100 per person advance payment. Credit cards: MC, V.
Meal Plans	3 vegetarian meals daily, buffet style. Fruits, vegetables, legumes, and natural fat sources such as nuts and avocados. Lunch and dinner include salad bar, water-steamed vegetables, entrees such as vegetarian lasagna with mock-cheese topping, baked tofu, cashew chow mein. Whole-grain bread baked daily. No dairy products, eggs, coffee, tea, condiments.
Services and Facilities	**Exercise Equipment:** Schwinn Air-Dyne bikes, Trotter treadmill, rowing machine, trampoline, multipurpose gym. **Services:** Massage, hydrotherapy, medical consultation. **Swimming Facilities:** At nearby fitness center. **Spa Facilities:** Mineral hot springs nearby. **Recreation Facilities:** Gold panning, rock collecting; downhill skiing nearby. **Evening Programs:** Informal talks and films on health-related topics. Music program Fri.
In the Area	Evans Plunge hot springs, a naturally heated indoor mineral-water pool; Custer State Park wildlife preserve; Rapid City; Mt. Rushmore; the Black Hills Passion Play (summer); The Homestead, a working gold mine at Lead; antique train ride from Hill City; Badlands National Park; Wind Cave National Park (caverns); prehistoric excavations. Deadwood casinos.
Getting Here	*From Rapid City.* By car, Hwy. 79 south to Hermosa, Hwy. 40 west to entrance road (40 min). Free pickup to and from Rapid City airport and bus station.
Special Notes	Specially equipped rooms, ramps for the disabled. No smoking indoors.

The Cooper Wellness Program

Weight management
Nutrition and diet
Preventive medicine
Vibrant maturity

Texas A recognized leader in the study of the medical value of exer-
Dallas cise, the Cooper Wellness Program at the Aerobics Center is
designed to help participants achieve permanent changes in
lifestyle. Programs of 7–13 days and a 4-day wellness weekend
teach the adoption and cultivation of healthy habits.

At first look, The Aerobics Center seems more like a country
club than a medical clinic; the stately redbrick mansion is for
the exclusive use of guests, members, and visiting professionals.

Four exercise sessions are part of each day's program. You can
work out on a treadmill or walk and jog on paved and lighted
trails that wind through the 30-acre wooded estate. A gymnasium has basketball and racquetball courts and a three-lane running track. Two heated outdoor lap pools are six lanes wide and
75 feet long. The four outdoor Laykold lighted tennis courts are
equipped with automatic ball machines.

Your stay begins with a full physical examination. The first
day's schedule sees a chest X-ray, a test for pulmonary function, and vision, hearing, and dental exams. A standard
skinfold test and weigh-in on an underwater scale determine
your ideal body weight. Blood pressure is measured during and
after exercise, and an ECG treadmill test measures stress. Before and after the program, 24 blood tests, including HDL and
LDL for cholesterol, are administered. (Your health insurance
may cover this part of the program cost.) The comprehensive
medical report determines the exercise program that will be
recommended for you.

Classes begin on your second day. Specialists lecture on nutrition and health, and you participate in cooking and bread-making demonstrations. Volleyball, aerobics in the swimming pool,
and other forms of group exercise are scheduled. Evenings are
reserved for massages or a walk. The whirlpool, sauna, and
steam room are open every night; participants are entitled to
two 30-minute massages a week.

The combination of a supportive environment, state-of-the-art
equipment and facilities, and the professional staff creates a
disciplined program, and significant results have been seen in
lowering cholesterol and triglyceride levels in only two weeks.
Follow-up calls and return visits have confirmed participants'
success in lowering blood pressure and increasing vitality and
alertness. The center encourages friends and couples to work
together on behavior modification.

Limited to groups of no more than 20, the program appeals to
high-powered executives who have lost control of their health.
Here they work with a team of nine full-time physicians, a den-
tist, nutritionists, and exercise technologists. Guided by Dr.
Kenneth H. Cooper, whose pioneering research on aerobics inspired the founding of the center, these professionals make
wellness meaningful to everyday life.

The Cooper Wellness Program
12230 Preston Rd., Dallas, TX 75230
Tel. 214/386–4777 or 800/444–5192, Fax 214/386–0039
Telex 791578/AEROBICCTR DAL

Administration Program director, Ava Bursau; Founder/president, Kenneth H. Cooper, M.D.

Season Sessions scheduled year-round.

Accommodations 62 rooms, 12 suites, with heavy mahogany king- or queen-size beds, wing chairs, private bath. A grand staircase dominates the marble lobby.

Rates 13-day program $4,795–$5,495 per person all-inclusive, 7-day program $3,295–$3,695 per person, 4-day weekend $2,395–$2,595. With a spouse or companion, 13 days $4,495–$4,795 per person, 7 days $3,095–$3,295 per person, weekend $2,295–$2,395 per person. $800 advance payment, 7-day and 13-day programs; $500 advance payment for 4-day program. Add 13¼% lodging tax, 8¼% meal tax. Credit cards: AE, MC, V.

Meal Plans 3 calorie-controlled meals daily. Low in fat and cholesterol, lunch choices include spinach lasagna or Cajun chicken fillet sandwich on whole-grain bread. Typical dinner entrees are a skewer of sea scallops and fresh vegetables on rice pilaf; medallions of veal with fresh steamed vegetables. Tossed salad and dessert (poached pears, raspberry sorbet) served with lunch and dinner. Decaffeinated coffee and tea.

Services and Facilities **Exercise Equipment:** 10-station Nautilus units, 5-station Universal weights gym, free weights, 5 Lifecycles, 5 Aerobocycles, 13 Schwinn Air-Dyne bikes, 2 recumbent bikes, 4 Pacer treadmills, Bally Liferower, Concept II rowing machine, StairMaster, Versaclimber. **Services:** Personal counseling on fitness, diet, and exercise; medical testing and evaluation. Swedish massage. **Swimming Facilities:** 2 heated outdoor pools. **Recreation Facilities:** 4 25-yard racquetball courts, 4 tennis courts, volleyball, basketball, handball. Golf course nearby. **Evening Programs:** Talks on nutrition and health; walks and massage.

In the Area Dinner at an Italian restaurant; White Rock Lake; the Omnimax film theater in Fort Worth; Dallas Museum of Art, Kennedy Memorial, Fort Worth Science Center, Dallas Arboretum and Botanical Garden.

Getting Here *From Dallas.* By car, Hwy. 635 (LBJ Freeway), Preston Rd. (20 min). Limousine, rental car, taxi available.

Special Notes Ramps and elevator provide access to all areas. No smoking indoors. Remember to bring recent medical records, a watch with second hand, calculator, exercise clothing. Laundry service included.

Four Seasons Resort and Club

Luxury pampering
Life enhancement
Sports conditioning

Texas
Las Colinas Space-age design and Old World architecture meet in the 12,000-acre Las Colinas Urban Center, where the Four Seasons hotel is the centerpiece of a golf-tennis complex sur-

rounded by low-rise corporate buildings. The spa, connected to the hotel and clubhouse by an underground tunnel, offers eight daily exercise classes, weight training, total fitness regimens, stretch groups, water works, and a range of indoor sports and workout facilities. Sophisticated bodywork here includes Phytomer seaweed and kelp products.

Programs can be tailored to suit your needs: You can work out on the advanced Nautilus equipment, do aerobics and body-building exercises, and play a round of golf or team up for tennis. Personal trainers, nutritional counseling, and fitness evaluations are available at an hourly rate that can be combined with any of the resort's special packages.

More than 25 spa treatments and beauty salon services can be booked on an à la carte basis. Services range from massage to aromatherapy, herbal wraps, and baths. There are two sets of Jacuzzis, saunas, steam rooms and hot/cold pools. The spa program assures personal attention from the staff.

Two golf courses, indoor and outdoor tennis courts, and jogging tracks leave little to be desired in the way of sports facilities. Squash and racquetball courts, indoor and outdoor swimming pools, clinics, and private instruction are also available.

The "alternatives" menu served in the main dining room keeps dieters on course. Regular selections are available as well.

Four Seasons Resort and Club
4150 N. MacArthur Blvd., Irving, TX 75038
Tel. 214/717–0700 or 800/332–3442, Fax 214/717–2477
Telex 735319

Administration General manager, Jim FitzGibbon; spa director, Kathryn Waldman; fitness director, Tracy York

Season Year-round.

Accommodations 315 rooms tastefully styled with executive amenities: toiletries, hair dryer, terry robes; comfortable living area, 3 telephones, cable TV, marble bath with separate tub and shower. Private balcony with most rooms; ask for golf course view.

Rates Weekday $185, weekend $115–$135. Spa package 1 night/2 days $230; 6 nights/7 days $1,960 single, $1,546 per person double occupancy. Fresh Start fitness package 2 nights/3 days $745 single, $606 per person double. Credit cards: AE, DC, MC, V.

Meal Plans 3 meals daily in spa packages. Four Seasons Alternative Cuisine is low in cholesterol, fat, calories, sodium. Menu selections are broiled chicken, Mexican chicken enchilada, grilled salmon, roast quail with fresh berry sauce. Daily caloric intake under 1,000; vegetarian meals available.

Services and Facilities **Exercise Equipment:** 12-station Nautilus units, free weights, 6 Lifecycles, 4 StairMasters, 4 treadmills, 2 rowing machines, 10 Schwinn Air-Dyne bikes, 4 ergometers, cross-country ski unit. **Services:** Swedish, shiatsu, reflexology, sports, and aromatherapy massage, herbal and sea-kelp wraps and baths, loofah body scrub, facial. Beauty salon for hair and nail care. **Swimming Facilities:** 25-meter pool, 75-meter outdoor pool, indoor lap pool. **Recreation Facilities:** 8 outdoor, 4 indoor tennis courts, 6 racquetball courts, 3 squash courts, basketball court, 18-hole TPC golf course.

In the Area Dallas Arts District, West End Historic District, shopping malls; Texas Stadium, Market Center, State Fair Music Hall.

Getting Here *From Dallas.* By car, Hwy. 35 to Hwy. 183 (Airport Freeway), MacArthur Blvd. exit. (20 min). Limousine service. Taxi, rental car available.

Special Notes Limited access for the disabled. Professionally managed child-care center (six months to 8 years of age). No smoking in the spa or designated dining areas. Nonsmoking rooms available. Spa hours: Weekdays 6 AM–10 PM, weekends 7 AM–9 PM.

The Greenhouse

Life enhancement *Women only*
Luxury pampering

Texas Privacy and freedom from stress are precious commodities to
Arlington the harried young career women and the celebrities who check into The Greenhouse for a week of physical and emotional rejuvenation. Completely self-contained, with a staff of more than 125 serving just 39 guests, the retreat focuses on well-being and beauty.

You hardly notice the tacky neighborhood as you are whisked from the airport in a chauffeured limousine. Arlington, better known for its Six Flags Over Texas theme park, has been a special destination for the knowledgeable spa set since 1965, when The Greenhouse was built by the fashion trendsetters Neiman Marcus and Charles of the Ritz. While the elegant enclave has maintained its high standard of service and accommodations, it has expanded its program to appeal to the special needs of its guests. Repeaters make up 75% of the clientele.

Thoughtful attention to detail distinguishes a stay here. Each guest is assigned a personal facialist, hairdresser, manicurist, and masseuse for the week. A resident physiologist and nurse help plan a schedule to the individual's needs.

Breakfast in bed begins the day at 7 AM. Your daily schedule comes on the tray, and a fresh leotard and robe await you. A brisk guided walk through the garden is followed by exercise classes to flex and tone the body. Choices include low-impact aerobics, weight training techniques, cardiovascular workouts, and water workouts in the pool. Your personal trainer studies your fitness profile (prepared on your arrival) and works with you at your pace.

Lunch is served poolside, followed by a daily massage and serious pampering. Daily schedules are adhered to unless guests request otherwise. Evenings can be dressy or informal, depending on the guests, yet the setting reflects everything you've ever seen on TV about Texan elegance and style.

Airy, bright, and expensively furnished, The Greenhouse has the look of a semitropical sybaritic hideaway. The skylighted marble-floored atrium for swimming and the luxuriously feminine bedrooms are very much a part of the therapy.

The Greenhouse
107th St., Box 1144, Grand Prairie, TX 76010
Tel. 817/640–4000, Fax 817/649–0422

Administration	Co-directors, Shirley Ogle and Angela Fabry
Season	Year-round except early July and Dec. Programs begin and end on Sun.; 3-day miniweeks sometimes available.
Accommodations	37 single rooms, 2 suites with queen-size half-canopied beds, matching drapes. Hand-embroidered linens, large dressing area, sunken tubs, TV, telephone.
Rates	$3,450–3,700 per week single; suite shared by 2, $3,550 per person; 3 days $2,300–$2,700. $1,000 in advance, nonrefundable. Credit cards: Neiman Marcus card only.
Meal Plans	Choice of weight loss or maintenance: 1,000–1,200 or 1,500 calories a day. 3 meals plus midmorning snack and afternoon fruit frappe. Homemade bran muffin, fresh melon and raspberries, coffee or tea for breakfast; vegetable pizza with green salad, lobster-and-crab salad, cheese soufflé with fruit at lunch; Cornish hens stuffed with shallots and breast meat, broiled lamb chops, grilled salmon at dinner. Gooey chocolate cake or hot apricot soufflé for those not dieting.
Services and Facilities	**Exercise Equipment:** 6-station Universal weight training gym, Nautilus units, 4 Trotter treadmills, 8 stationary bikes, cross-country NordicTrack, 2 StairMaster, body-ball weights, hand weights, poles, elastic Thoro-bands. **Services:** Massage, facials; hair, skin, and nail care; one-on-one workouts. Personal fitness, nutrition, health, beauty, and relaxation programs. Cooking classes. **Swimming Facilities:** Indoor and outdoor pools. **Recreation Facilities:** tennis court, parcourse, jogging track. **Evening Programs:** Discussion topics are stress, wellness, makeup, cosmetic surgery; entertainment, feature films, fashion shows.
In the Area	Neiman Marcus, Dallas Arts District, State Fair Music Hall, Texas Stadium, shopping malls.
Getting Here	*From Dallas.* By car, I-30 to Arlington, Hwy. 360 to Avenue II, left to 107th St. (20 min). Free transportation to and from airport; taxi, rental car available.
Special Notes	No smoking in public areas.

Lake Austin Resort

Life enhancement
Luxury pampering

Texas
Austin

Hill-country walks, water aerobics, and a range of body-strengthening exercise classes make up the week-long program at the Lake Austin Resort. The coed retreat provides a great escape in a part of Texas noted for scenic rolling hills and placid lakes.

European facials with Repechage skin-care products and a full-service salon for hair and skin care are available. Package rates include fitness classes offered daily, meals, and programs on lifestyle enhancement. The back-to-basics ambience appeals to both men and women.

One of the nice touches here is a roommate-matching service. If you want to share accommodations for extra savings, ask about a compatible person who is registered for the program. Stays of less than a week are available, and you can arrive on any day of the week. Programs are offered for 4, 7, 10, and 14 days.

Mornings start at 7 AM with group walks ranging from 2 to 4 miles. The program includes yoga, water aerobics, and step class, though you may decide to just relax by the lake, take out a paddleboat, and indulge in aromatherapy.

The facilities include a lap pool with resistant jets, a coed Jacuzzi, and indoor and outdoor swimming pools. The glass-walled gym overlooks Lake Austin. Hiking and jogging trails plus parcourse extend into the woods.

"Renewal" is the buzzword of the new management that took over the resort in 1983. Staffed by psychologists, kinesi-ologists, and a dietitian, the programs promote personal em-powerment, positive body image, and affirmation through meditation, as well as a fresh approach to wellness.

Lake Austin Resort

1705 Quinlan Park Rd., Austin, TX 78732
Tel. 512/266-2444 or 800/847-5637
Fax 512/266-1572

Administration Manager, Deborah Evans; fitness director, Gayle Moffett

Season Year-round.

Accommodations 40 cabins provide motel-style amenities, TV, air-conditioning, private bath. Bedrooms have 2 full-size beds. Deluxe units available.

Rates 4 days $640–$692 single, $556–$612 double. 7 days $1,120–$1,211 single, $973–$1,071 double. 10 days $1,600–$1,730 single, $1,390–$1,530 double, plus service charge and 6% tax, $200 per person deposit. Credit Cards: AE, MC, V.

Meal Plans 3 meals daily, high in complex carbohydrates and fiber, low in fat, sugar, and salt. Breakfast buffet has muffins, fresh fruit, coffee, tea, juices, choice of tacos, whole-wheat pancakes, blintzes, French toast, cereals. Lunch and dinner entrees may be enchiladas, lasagna, fajitas, pizza, barbecued chicken. Desserts are frozen peach yogurt, sherbet, cheesecake, or rum soufflé.

Services and Facilities **Exercise Equipment:** 6-station Universal weight training gym, 2 StairMasters, 2 Schwinn Air-Dyne bikes, treadmill, rowing machine, free weights. **Services:** Swedish, aromatherapy, shiatsu massage; reflexology; body brushing; polish; Bindi; herbal wrap; clay body masque; seaweed body masque; facials. Salon for hair, nail, care, makeup consultation. Personal consultation on fitness, nutrition, skin analysis, special dietary needs. **Swimming Facilities:** Indoor and outdoor pools. **Recreation Facilities:** Volleyball, badminton, paddleboats, Jacuzzi, tennis; golf and horseback riding nearby. **Evening Programs:** Talks on health and fitness.

In the Area University of Texas, state capitol, L. B. Johnson Library and museum.

Getting Here *From Austin.* By car, Ranch Rd. 2222, FM 620 to Quinlan Park Rd. (45 min). Free transfers to and from Austin Airport. Taxi, rental car available.

Special Notes Smoking and nonsmoking rooms available. Laundry rooms available.

The Phoenix Spa at The Houstonian

Life enhancement *Women only*
Luxury pampering

Texas Providing the motivation for lasting change rather than a quick
Houston fix has been the goal at The Phoenix since 1980. Practical habits
that you can take home are emphasized here, and diet is not
considered synonymous with self-denial.

Until you've had a brisk two-mile morning walk through the
pine trees of this complex, it's hard to imagine that the 22-acre
retreat is just minutes from the city's smoggy freeways. The
combination of the Houstonian Club and the deluxe Houstonian
Hotel makes it possible to enjoy a healthy getaway for a few
days or a full week.

The Phoenix program, held in a former mansion that sits in the
center of the complex, has changed with the times. Pampering
and weight loss are deemphasized now; options include health
and fitness and stress control.

The goal is to improve one's self-image while learning healthy
eating habits and exercising properly within one's limits. Tests
to measure basal metabolism, cardiovascular capacity, body
composition, and muscular flexibility and strength are administered at the medical center upon your arrival. A fitness specialist uses the data to help you formulate a take-home program
during a midweek consultation.

The tightly scheduled program is challenging, but the staff and
exercise instructors give lots of support. And camaraderie develops quickly among the 20 or so participants. The high-tech
exercise system called Powercize, with computerized machines
that greet you by name and keep tabs on calories burned,
brightens workouts. Facilities at the health club include an indoor banked running track, Olympic-size swimming pool,
whirlpools, saunas, steam rooms, and tennis and racquetball
courts.

Each week's program has a different emphasis: A fitness plan
concentrates on exercise, with guest specialists for lectures
and classes; stress-management programs include yoga classes
and aromatherapy massage. All include low-impact aerobic
workouts in a specially designed studio that has a cushioned
floor, exercise sessions in the pool, bodywork, and beauty-salon
services. Additional professional and personal services, available à la carte, can be booked and billed through the hotel.

The Phoenix Spa at The Houstonian
111 N. Post Oak La., Houston, TX 77024
Tel. 713/685–6836 or 800/548–4700 (800/548–4701 in TX)
Fax 713/680–1657

Administration General manager, Neil Sol; director, Sally Kerr-Lamkin

Season Year-round. Coed weeks in May and October.

Accommodations 5 single rooms in the mansion have king-size beds and private
baths; some have fireplaces. Other guests stay in the 300-room
Houstonian Hotel; luxury single rooms have cable TV, private
bath, air-conditioning.

Rates   Basic one-week program $1,300 per person; all inclusive Back-to-Basics Plus week $1,550 per person; 3-night package $850, one-day package $200. Add gratuity and 8¼% tax. Deposit $500, nonrefundable; credit card confirmation for hotel. Credit cards: AE, MC, V.

Meal Plans   Simple meals at a buffet breakfast, table service at lunch and dinner, and juice breaks. 1,000–1,200 calories daily, mainly fresh vegetables, fruits, lean meats, whole grains. No caffeine, sugar, or salt. Low-fat, high-carbohydrate meals include asparagus spears in whole-wheat crepes, baked chicken breast in lemon-saffron sauce, and poached chicken with carrots. Desserts are baked apple in parchment, pumpkin mousse. Vegetarian meals available; special diets accommodated.

Services and Facilities   **Exercise Equipment:** 6-unit Powercise system, 10 David and 7 Keiser pneumatic weight training units, 19 Eagle Cybex units, 5 Universal units, 10 StairMasters, 2 Gravitron, 3 Schwinn Air-Dyne bikes, 8 Windracers, 2 Lifecycles, 15 Trotter treadmills, 2 Concept II rowers, 3 Windrowers, dumbbells (3–125 lb), wrist and ankle weights. **Services:** Massage, manicure, pedicure, facials, aromatherapy, herbal wrap, body scrub, makeup, hairstyling. Medical examination, fitness evaluation, nutritional counseling. Daily spa robe provided. **Swimming Facilities:** 1 indoor, 2 outdoor pools. **Recreation Facilities:** 6 racquetball courts, 5 outdoor tennis courts, parcourse, jogging trail. **Evening Programs:** Talks on health and nutrition; fashion show.

In the Area   Shopping, museums, concerts, opera season, Alley Theater.

Getting Here   *From Houston.* By car, Hwy. 610 N, Woodway Memorial Exit (20 min). Free limousine service on arrival and departure; taxi, rental car available.

Special Notes   Elevators, ramps provide access for the disabled. No smoking. Spa hours: daily 6 AM–8 PM. Daily laundry service included in weekly program.

The Middle West

Fitness resorts are a relatively recent phenomenon in the Middle West; their programs are informal and outdoors oriented, they capitalize on scenic locations, and their focus tends to be on weight loss and general well-being.

Wisconsin offers the widest variety of choices, from the sports-oriented American Club to the sophisticated pampering of the Fontana Spa at the Abbey Resort. In Ohio you can work out in a registered historic landmark at the Kerr House, and Americana and Victorian antiques enhance the ambience of the newly expanded Aurora House Spa. Taking the thermal waters at French Lick Springs in Indiana and the Elms in Missouri has been popular since the turn of the century. At press time, the new Raj health center was under construction in Fairfield, Iowa, devoted to the ancient system of preventative natural medicine known as ayurvedic therapy.

Heartland Health and Fitness Retreat

Life enhancement
Stress control
Nutrition and diet

Illinois
Gilman

Guests are made to feel at home in the Heartland Health and Fitness Retreat's lakefront mansion, which is rather like being at an adult camp in the country. The 30-acre estate boasts a guest list limited to 28, and your day can be as structured or unstructured as you please. You don't need to sign up for scheduled exercise classes, but do make appointments for massage and facials. Since bodywork and beauty treatments are included in the package, most guests take advantage of them—and add further pampering services at their own expense. Workout clothing is provided.

The weekend is the busiest time; van loads of Chicagoans arrive on Friday evening via complimentary transportation from the Loop. Yet the best deal is a five-day stay, from Sunday to Friday noon. Longer, discounted stays can be arranged to concentrate on weight loss or recuperation from illness.

High-tech workouts with weight machines are held in the barn, an impressive three-level fitness center reached through an underground passage from the house. This barn is unlike anything on the neighboring farms; it has a full complement of cardiovascular workout equipment, pneumatic resistance muscle movers, an indoor swimming pool, whirlpool, sauna, steam room, and private massage rooms.

Personal consultation with staff is included in the 5- and 7-day program. They advise you to concentrate on activities you enjoy and to continue them when you return home. (Try yoga and race walking!) Scheduled classes include aerobics, aquacise, step aerobics, martial arts, and self-awareness. Options include a ropes course and Pilates exercises.

Group support is important here. Workout clothing—T-shirts, shorts, sweat suits, and cold-weather gear—serves as a uniform. At 6:30 AM, ready for the brisk morning walk, everyone lines up to massage the shoulders of the person in front. The general-issue sweat suit is acceptable for lounging fireside or watching a movie on the VCR in the evening.

Heartland Health and Fitness Retreat
Rte. 1, Box 181, Gilman, IL 60938
Tel. 815/683–2182 or 800/545–4853
Fax 815/683–2144

Administration Founder, Jerry Kaufman; director, Lynne Myers, R.N.

Season Year-round.

Accommodations 14 pine-furnished rooms, refurbished 1992, have country antiques, down-filled comforters, twin beds, private bath with hair dryer, toiletries, large fluffy towels.

Rates 2-day weekend $500 per person double occupancy, $700 single; 5 days $1,250 double, $1,750 single; 7 days $1,650 double, $2,300 single. Roommate matching on request. Taxes and gratuities included. 50% deposit. Credit cards: AE, MC, V.

Meal Plans 3 meals daily (table service). Snacks and fruit all day. Breakfast includes freshly baked muffins, hot and cold cereal, coffee on request. Vegetarian menu; dairy products, fish served occasionally. No salt, sugar, or added fats. 1,200 calories a day for women, 1,500 for men. Lunch can include hearty soup, vegetable pâté, or Japanese mushroom salad; typical dinner entrees are grilled swordfish with rosemary, Peruvian fish stew, corn crepes with spinach soufflé, fish and vegetable brochettes.

Services and Facilities **Exercise Equipment:** 8 Keiser Cam II pneumatic resistance units, 3 Cybex exercycles, Pilates, 2 Schwinn Air-Dyne bikes, 2 rowers, 3 treadmills, 3 Tunturi exercycles, free weights, hand weights, StairMaster, soft joggers, NordicTrack, trampolines. **Services:** Massage therapy (sports, relaxation, foot), facial, manicure, pedicure, hair and skin care; personal fitness assessment, nutrition evaluation, underwater body composition test. **Swimming Facilities:** 15-meter indoor pool, 3-acre lake. **Recreation Facilities:** 2 lighted outdoor tennis courts, parcourse, hiking, cross-country skiing (equipment provided), 2-person bike, ¼-mile running track. **Evening Programs:** Informal discussions on health-related topics. Guest speakers on stress management, life enhancement, dependency, financial planning.

In the Area Architecture of Frank Lloyd Wright in Oak Park, Abraham Lincoln's home and tomb in Springfield.

Getting Here *From Chicago.* By car, the Dan Ryan Expwy. south, I-57 to Kankakee Exit 308, Hwy. 52/45 (becomes Hwy. 49) to Rte. 24, R.R. 122 (90 min). Free van service to and from downtown Chicago Fri. and Sun. By train, Amtrak to Gilman (1 hr). By bus, Greyhound (2 hr).

Special Notes No smoking indoors.

French Lick Springs Resort

Taking the waters
Non-program resort facilities

Indiana Modeled on the great spas of Europe, the French Lick Springs
French Lick Resort was built in the early 1840s and attracted a wealthy elite

The Middle West

100 miles

150 km

Lake Superior

ONTARIO

N

Sault Ste. Marie

Georgian Bay

Lake Huron

WISCONSIN

3

Green Bay

75

41 43

4

Lake Michigan

MICHIGAN

75

27

Madison

5

Milwaukee

Grand Rapids

96

Lansing

Detroit

90 94

Beloit

6

94

196

94

Ann Arbor

Lake Erie

90

Davenport

90

80

Chicago

7

South Bend

Gary

Toledo

80 90

Cleveland

15

74

River

55

8

Fort Wayne

14

OHIO

71

77

ILLINOIS

57

65

69

75

70

74

41

Columbus

Springfield

70

Indianapolis

Dayton

13

55

INDIANA

Cincinnati

St. Louis

65

52

57

Wabash River

12

64

Ohio River

55

KENTUCKY

who came from all over the country to "take the waters" in as many ways as they could. The sulfurous spring water was bottled and marketed as Pluto Water, and today it is still used in the Pluto Bath in the hotel health club.

Recently restored to its original Victorian elegance in a costly renovation, the hotel has high-ceilinged rooms with ceiling fans, French doors, carved woodwork, and verandas that overlook formal gardens. Its 2,600 acres of lawns and rolling woodland add to the charm and attract families and conventions.

The spa can be enjoyed on a daily-rate basis or with baths and beauty services included in two-night and five-night packages. No formal program of activities is offered; you set your own schedule. The spa director will consult with you on a meal plan, exercise classes, and bodywork. There is a new exercise room, sauna, and whirlpools.

French Lick Springs today is a place to have fun and enjoy a bit of pampering. With 2 championship golf courses, tennis courts, and other recreation facilities at hand, the springs are no longer the sole attraction. Yet you can still have a sip from a well beneath a gazebo or take a bath in spring water piped into a claw-footed tub.

French Lick Springs Resort
French Lick, IN 47432
Tel. 812/936-9300 or 800/457-4042

Administration	General manager, Greg James; spa director, Doris Todd
Season	Year-round.
Accommodations	502 deluxe suites and large double rooms with king- or queen-size bed, antique furniture, modern private bath, color TV.
Rates	$149 spa day package with lunch. Deluxe 5-night spa program, Sun.–Fri. noon, $829 per person double occupancy, $928 single; 2-night midweek package $285 per person double, $325 single. Winter rates lower. Gratuities and tax extra. Credit card confirmation or $100 per person deposit for spa packages. Credit cards: AE, DC, MC, V.
Meal Plans	3 meals daily with spa packages. Low-calorie selections include poached salmon for dinner, shrimp shish kebab and teriyaki chicken for lunch. Vegetarian meals on request.
Services and Facilities	**Exercise Equipment:** 10-unit Universal weight training gym, 2 Air-Dyne bikes, rowing machines, Treadex, Stairobic, Aerobicycle. **Services:** Swedish massage, aromatherapy, reflexology, salt rub, facials, pedicure, manicure, loofah body scrub; makeup lessons, beauty salon for hair and skin care; personal consultation on exercise. **Swimming Facilities:** Indoor and outdoor pools. **Recreation Facilities:** 2 18-hole golf courses, 18 tennis courts (8 indoors and lighted), horseback riding, bicycling, bowling, billiards; fishing, sailing, skiing. **Evening Programs:** Resort entertainment.
In the Area	Surrey rides. Evansville historic district (19th-century homes), Old Vanderburgh County Courthouse, New Harmony colony near Vincennes, Amish farms.
Getting Here	*From Louisville, KY.* By bus, Greyhound (2 hr). By car, I-64 west, Hwy. 150 to Paoli, Rte. 56 west (60 min). Hotel limousine, rental car available.

Special Notes Elevators and ramps connect hotel rooms and spa facilities. Supervised day camp for children during summer; playground, miniature train ride, wading pool. No smoking in the spa.

Indian Oak Resort

Luxury pampering

Indiana Winding hiking paths cut through the woods around Lake
Chesterton Palomar, where the Fitness Center of Indian Oak Resort offers a daily schedule of aerobics and stress-buster massage. There is a full-service salon, two-story lodge, and spa-cuisine menu; training can be personalized to focus on cardiovascular fitness or muscle toning. The two- to four-night all-inclusive spa/accommodations package includes unlimited use of the facilities, meals, and salon services.

Indian Oak Resort
558 Indian Boundry, Chesterton, IN 46304
Tel. 219/926–2200 or 800/552–4232

Administration General manager, Cathy Chubb; spa manager, Wendy Krantz

Season Year-round.

Accommodations 100 rooms, some with king-size beds; modern furniture, private bath, cable TV, phone, air-conditioning.

Rates $64–$119 for 2 persons double occupancy, $59–$94 single; suites $149–$159. 2-night spa package $256 per person double, $341 single; 4-night spa package $405 per person double, $569 single. Add taxes and gratuities. Deposit for first night by credit card. Credit cards: AE, DC, MC, V.

Meal Plans Continental breakfast included in all room rates. Spa package includes 2 meals daily, low in fat, salt, and calories.

Services and **Exercise Equipment:** Universal gym, 2 StairMasters, 2 tread-
Facilities mills, Schwinn Air-Dyne bike, rowing machine, free weights. **Services:** Swedish massage, herbal wrap, facial, shiatsu; salon for hair, nail, and skin care. **Swimming Facilities:** 50-foot indoor lap pool, private lake. **Recreation Facilities:** Boating, fishing, hiking trails.

In the Area Lake Michigan, Dunes National Lakeshore, Indiana Dunes State Park.

Getting Here *From Chicago.* By car, I–80/90 to I–94 (1 hr). By train, Amtrak to Chesterton (80 min). Free shuttle service from train.

Special Notes Fitness Center open Tues.–Fri. 8 AM–8 PM, Sat. 8 AM–5 PM, Sun. 8 AM–1 PM.

The Raj

Life enhancement
Spiritual awareness
Preventive medicine

Iowa The secluded Raj health center, which opened in 1992 in the
Fairfield heart of rolling meadows and woodlands, introduces a new level of luxury to the country's array of destination spas devoted to the ancient system of preventive natural medicine known as ayurvedic therapy. Here, the soothing and refreshing treat-

ments first introduced in America at Massachusetts's Maharishi Ayur-Veda center can be combined with programs incorporating fitness and exercise.

Treatment begins with an assessment of your physiological makeup by a physican concerned with both physical and spiritual health. Maharishi therapies, designed to restore balance in your body, are deeply relaxing. Traditionally known as *panchakarma*, treatments include warm herbal-oil massages, herbal steam baths, and internal cleansing. Aromatic ayurvedic oils are used to enliven engery points (*marmas*) to create a feeling of well-being. As balance develops between your body, mind, and the environment, you practice yoga positions and breathing with staff experts. For stress reduction and to expand inner awareness, you are introduced to Transcendental Meditation and given a mantra. The pace of daily activities is unhurried, the staff comforting. Most participants lose weight on the program without calorie counting.

The Raj
24th St. NW, Fairfield, IA 52556
Tel. 800/248–9050

Administration Owners/directors, Candace and Rodgers Badgett, Jr.; fitness director, Barbara McLaughlin

Season Year-round.

Accommodations 46 deluxe rooms and suites in two-story villas and in the Raj Court Hotel. The Spa Wing of the hotel has 19 standard rooms, while the Hotel Wing has 18 larger deluxe rooms. Each private villa has 3 guest suites. All rooms have queen- or king-size beds, carpeting, air-conditioning, and telephone and are decorated with flowered wallpaper, carved-wood furniture, and silk and cotton draperies. Baths are marble-walled with twin vanities, shower and bath (separate in deluxe rooms and suites), and amenities including hair dryer, robes, and slippers.

Rates $90–$195 single, $47.50–$105 per person double occupancy daily. $1,200 single for 3-day package, $2,500 for 7-day package, $4,500 for 14-day package including meals, treatments, and gratuities. 1-day package without lodging is $210 and includes lunch. Nonparticipating companions stay free on certain weeks. Add 5% tax. Deposit 50%. Credit cards: AE, MC, V.

Meal Plans Three vegetarian meals daily, customized. Dinner may include Indian rice and dal with cooked vegetables, herb seasoning, cooked fruit. Specialties include vegetable pâté. The diet is bland with few fats and no dairy products except milk. Herbal teas and lassi are served as recommended by the doctor.

Services and Facilities **Exercise Facility:** Yoga studio. **Services:** Aromatherapy massage, transcendental meditation, stress management, self-pulse diagnosis, nutrition and diet counseling, internal cleansing. **Recreation Facilities:** Nearby golf, horseback riding, tennis; woodland trails; swimming pool scheduled for completion 1994. **Evening Programs:** Videotapes and lectures on health-related topics.

Getting Here *From Cedar Rapids:* By car, I–380 south, Rte. 1 south to Fairfield airport, right turn on Rural Road 4 (1¼ hrs.). Private planes land at Fairfield Airport, where pickup is on request (fee). Limousine or hotel car picks up at Cedar Rapids Airport (fee).

Special Notes No smoking. Special accommodations available for the physically disabled.

Birdwing Spa

Nutrition and diet
Life enhancement
Luxury pampering

Minnesota The first full-service spa in the upper Midwest, Birdwing Spa
Litchfield blends European therapy and Minnesota traditions. The Tudor-style mansion set on a lakeside estate accommodates up to 25 guests; an exercise studio occupies the former barn/garage, and an outdoor swimming pool and miles of shoreline trails for walks and cross-country skiing are on the grounds. The manor house has a sauna, Jacuzzi, and beauty-treatment facilities.

Oriented to outdoor activity, the spa provides equipment for skiing, canoeing, biking, and circuit weight training. In two daily "image sessions," guests have a choice of facial, massage, or manicure. Aerobic exercise or an hour of yoga completes the daily schedule in the 3,500-square foot fitness building.

Birdwing ranks high as a relaxing experience on a 300-acre country estate. The owners have developed a program to complement a diet regimen of 1,000–1,200 calories daily for women, 1,300–1,500 calories for men. The spa staff includes a registered dietitian, 2 gourmet chefs, and a fitness director. Working with this dedicated team makes sense for those who are just beginning a diet and fitness program. Others will simply enjoy the breakfast in bed, low-calorie gourmet dining, and unabashed pampering. Lake Wobegon this is not.

Birdwing Spa
R.R. 2, Box 104, Litchfield, MN 55355
Tel. 612/693–6064

Administration Owner/directors, Richard and Elizabeth Carlson

Season Year-round.

Accommodations 9 bedrooms (singles and doubles) with Ethan Allen furnishings, draperies, shared baths. The master suite has fireplace, private bath, Jacuzzi, and steam bath.

Rates Full-week program, Sun.–Sun., $1,575 per person in the master suite, $1,350 per person double, $1,095–$1,195 other rooms. 5-day program from Sun. evening, $1,295 per person in the master suite, $1,095 per person double, $895–$995 other rooms. Weekend retreat, Fri.–Sun., $395 per person double in the master suite, $315–$385 other rooms. 1-day overnight package $99–$225. Add gratuities, 6½% tax. $150 in advance for weekends, $300 for other programs. Credit cards: MC, V.

Meal Plans 3 weight-loss meals daily: cinnamon raisin French toast with 3-berry sauce for breakfast, fruit kebabs followed by chicken tacos with salsa or turkey pizza for lunch, chicken asparagus rolls and butterscotch brownies for dinner. Skim milk and dairy products. Vegetarian menu optional.

Services and **Exercise Equipment:** 2 treadmills, 2 Schwinn Air-Dyne bikes,
Facilities StairMaster, free weights. **Services:** Swedish and Esalen massage, facials, hair and nail care, reflexology, paraffin therapy,

back treatment. Nutritional counseling, fitness evaluation, exercise instruction. **Swimming Facilities:** Outdoor pool. **Spa Facilities:** Men's and women's saunas, coed whirlpool, massage room. **Recreation Facilities:** Bicycling, canoeing, cross-country skiing, bird-watching. Tennis and golf nearby. Special weeks for art and nature studies. **Evening Programs:** Guest speakers on stress control, nutrition, cardiac health, and problems of career women. Cooking classes and feature films.

In the Area Minneapolis–St. Paul museums, shopping malls.

Getting Here *From Minneapolis.* By bus, shuttle service morning and afternoon from the Twin Cities airport (80 min). By car, I-394, Hwy. 12 west to Litchfield, Rte. 1 and 23 (90 min). Birdwing makes arrangements for local transportation on request ($50).

Special Notes No smoking in public areas indoors. Minimum age 16.

The Elms Resort

Taking the waters
Non-program resort facilities

Missouri In the 1800s high-living health seekers descended on this
Excelsior Springs sleepy little Missouri town each season to take the mineral waters. The Elms, built to accommodate them in the grand manner, became a tradition that survived two devastating fires; the present limestone and concrete structure was built in 1912 and incorporates the New Leaf Spa.

Ten "environmental rooms" are programmed for jungle rain, wet steam, or dry sauna and equipped with a hot tub for two. The European swim track, which can be mildly claustrophobic, is a one-lane lap pool filled with tap water.

Downtown you'll find the Hall of Waters, an Art Deco treasure that boasts of having the world's longest mineral water bar; other facilities include a large indoor swimming pool and private baths. Built in 1937, the Hall of Waters is run by the city and is open to the public. There's a fee for bathing or swimming, and an appointment is required for a private mineral bath (tel. 816/637–0752). Pool hours are weekdays 8–5, and on summer weekends noon–5.

There's a lot of nostalgic charm about the Elms. Croquet and badminton are played on the lawn, and the tennis court is free to guests. A quaint village of boutiques completes the resort. Popular for conventions and sales meetings, the 23-acre wooded resort is less than an hour from Kansas City.

The Elms Resort
Regent and Elms Blvd., Excelsior Springs, MO 64204
Tel. 816/637–2141 or 800/843–3567
Fax 816/637–1222

Administration Manager, Douglas Morrison; spa manager, Jonlyn Pierce

Season Year-round.

Accommodations 136 rooms furnished with traditional wood dresser and table, desk, ceiling fan, cable TV, old-fashioned tiled bath.

Rates $79 per night for 2 persons Sun.–Thurs., $119 summer weekend package for 2. Suites $95–$130. Condos $150. Add tax (6.975%) and gratuities. Credit cards: AE, DC, MC, V.

Meal Plans American and European cuisine. Salads, fresh fish, meat, or chicken for lunch and dinner. Buffet dinners and brunch included in weekend package.

Services and Facilities **Exercise Equipment:** Nautilus circuit gym, Liferower, Lifecycle, treadmill, stationary bike. Indoor running track circles the lap pool (23 circuits = 1 mi). **Services:** Swedish massage, facial, cosmetology, beauty salon. **Spa Facilities:** Private mineral baths by appointment ($7.50). Hot and cold whirlpools, 3-level spa complex with separate saunas and steam rooms for men and women. **Swimming Facilities:** Outdoor pool; municipal indoor pool. **Recreation Facilities:** Golf, tennis, croquet, badminton, volleyball, horseshoes, shuffleboard; racquetball court nearby; bicycle rental. **Evening Programs:** Resort entertainment.

In the Area Watkins Woolen Mill (19th-century textile factory) in state park; fishing, swimming, hiking, picnicking, camping. Kansas City Zoo, Country Club Plaza (shopping), Crown Center (Hallmark museum), Nelson Atkins Museum of Art.

Getting Here *From Kansas City.* By car, I-35 north to Excelsior Springs, Hwy. 69 to Rte. 10 (30 min). Limo, rental car, taxi available.

Special Notes No smoking in the spa.

Marriott's Tan-Tar-A Resort

Non-program resort facilities

Missouri
Osage Beach
Outdoor recreation is the principal attraction of Marriott's Tan-Tar-A Resort, surrounded by 400 acres in the Lake of the Ozarks region. The lake, created by a dam in 1931, has countless coves for water sports, boating, and fishing. The hotel caters to conventioneers as well as family vacationers.

Guests enjoy use of an indoor/outdoor fitness center. Aerobics classes are offered three mornings a week, aquatics two mornings. The weights room, staffed by fitness specialists, is open daily. Massage and beauty services are available à la carte.

Marriott's Tan-Tar-A Resort
State Road KK, Osage Beach, MO 65065
Tel. 314/348–3131 or 800/826–8272 (800/268–8181 in Canada)

Administration Manager, Bill Bennett; fitness director, Gary DeAngelis

Season Year-round.

Accommodations 1,000 rooms in the hotel and cottages have fireplace, kitchenette, bar (in some rooms and suites), coffee maker, TV, private bath.

Rates Double rooms $129–$149, 1-bedroom suites $239, 2-bedroom suites $319. 2-night golf package for 2 $429–$533 includes breakfast and dinner, unlimited golf. Deposit of 1 night's lodging applied to last night reserved (and forfeited on early departure). Credit cards: AE, DC, MC, V. Rates include tax.

Meal Plans The Cliff Room has Continental cuisine and light fare as well as fried catfish. Windrose on the Water serves fish cooked to order (broiled, baked, sautéed, blackened).

Services and Facilities **Exercise Equipment:** 3 Trotter treadmills, 2 Liferowers, 3 Nautilus stationary bikes, 9-station Universal weight training gym, abdominal-muscle exerciser. **Services:** Swedish massage, reflexology, acupressure, facials; hair, nail, and skin care for men and women. **Swimming Facilities:** 4 outdoor pools, private beach on lake. **Recreation Facilities:** 6 outdoor and 2 indoor tennis courts, 4 indoor racquetball courts, 2 golf courses, 8 bowling lanes, billiards, moped rental, boat rental with fishing guide, trapshooting range, miniature golf, ice skating. **Evening Programs:** Resort entertainment.

In the Area Trail rides, fishing; Bridal Cave, HaHa Tonka Castle monument and state park, antiques shops; Abraham Lincoln home and tomb in Springfield, IL; Harry Truman home and library in Independence, MO.

Getting Here *From St. Louis.* By car, I-44 to Rte. 65 (70 min). Limousine service to and from the airport; rental car available.

Special Notes Supervised morning play camp for youngsters, teenage games and indoor activity in summer. No smoking in the weights room.

Aurora House Spa

Luxury pampering

Ohio
Aurora Clevelanders enjoy formal dinners by candlelight, business executives shift from meetings to massage appointments, and a dozen or so spa guests in terry-cloth robes take tea in a Victorian parlor, all at the Aurora House Spa. Located a few miles from the Ohio Turnpike, the spa gives you a sense of having journeyed back to another century; one of the buildings was a stagecoach inn more than 130 years ago.

In addition to the spa building and a conference center, the complex is headquarters for Mario's International, owned and operated by Mario and Joanne Liuzzo, who have combined their experience in the beauty salon business with a love of Victoriana. Their salon outgrew two Victorian houses in eight years. Planned are an Olympic-size pool in the manner of ancient Roman baths, an enclosed jogging track, and 10 new guest rooms.

Fitness is the focus of the programs for corporate members and health-conscious men and women who come here. Aquaerobics, a Dynastic stretch-and-tone class, weight-loss diets, and thalassotherapy are new features. Recreation includes hiking, biking, and other outdoor sports. The spa has widened its selection of exercise equipment and worked on nutrition with Cleveland Clinic.

Pampering is what the spa does best: eight facial and throat treatments for men and women, massages, pedicures, manicures, makeup application, and a top-quality salon for hairstyling and dressing. Repechage, the house specialty facial, involves a layered thermal mask with applications of concentrated aloe vera juice, powdered seaweed, and clay. When the hardened clay mask is removed, your complexion feels softer and firmer. The price is $70. Also new, is an antistress Vibra Melodic massage.

Therapy, diet, and exercise are intended to work together here. Your day can begin with breakfast in bed, a walk, hike, or jog, and continue in the gym with cardiovascular training. Exercise sessions are tailored to the individual and designed to relax muscles while burning surplus calories. The dining room, known for its low-calorie cooking, looks onto a waterfall.

Aurora House Spa
35 E. Garfield Rd., Aurora, OH 44202
Tel. 216/562–9171, Fax 216/562–2386

Administration	Director, Joanne Liuzzo
Season	Year-round.
Accommodations	14 rooms in the new wing and the original mansion, furnished with period pieces and modern comforts: Jacuzzi, large modern bath, hair dryer, terry-cloth robe. Executive suite has fireplace.
Rates	Spa Escape package with spa meals and aerobics $299 per couple per day, $199 single; 3-day/2-night program $1,619 per couple, $989 single. Tax included, add gratuities. One-third of total payable on booking. Credit cards: AE, MC, V.
Meal Plans	3 meals daily with packages. Oatmeal buttermilk pancake topped with fruit sauce (breakfast), shrimp and vegetable kebab (lunch), ricotta-stuffed zucchini rounds with tomato puree, grilled veal medallions with shiitake mushrooms, and grape mousse made with skim milk (dinner). Controlled use of fats, salt, sugar: yogurt substituted for sour cream, fruit juices and honey for sugar, garlic and citrus for salt.
Services and Facilities	**Exercise Equipment:** Nautilus and Universal weight machines, stationary bikes. **Services:** Massage, facials, body scrub with dulce (a nutrient-packed seaweed) and almond oil, manicure, pedicure, parafango muscle treatment with mud/paraffin mix, aromatherapy, hairstyling, makeup consultation, personalized exercise instruction, Habitat environmental sauna; health and diet analysis. **Recreation Facilities:** Bicycling; golf, tennis, horseback riding nearby; downhill and cross-country skiing. **Evening Programs:** Lectures on health topics.
In the Area	Antiques shops, flea markets, shopping areas, Sea World. Blossom Music Center (Cleveland Orchestra) June–Aug.
Getting Here	*From Cleveland.* By bus, Greyhound (50 min). By car, I-480 to Rte. 91, Rte. 82 and 306; or the Ohio Turnpike (I-80) to exit 13 (40 min). Limousine service from Cleveland Hopkins Airport; rental car available.
Special Notes	Limited access for the disabled. Nonsmoking areas designated.

The Kerr House

Life enhancement
Luxury pampering

Ohio	The Kerr House is an antiques-filled Victorian mansion that
Grand Rapids	functions as a hideaway for men and women who seek privacy

and a complete overhaul. With just eight guests in residence at a time, the facility takes on the atmosphere of a private club. Some weeks are reserved for men only, women only, or corporate groups.

The chatelaine, Laurie Hostetler, sets the program. Breakfast arrives at 7 AM on a wicker tray, and with it comes your personal schedule—massage, facial, nature walk, exercise.

Yoga, the specialty of the house, is taught in a carpeted exercise room on the top floor. Hostetler encourages guests by providing her own book of *asanas*, the exercise positions of Hatha yoga. You can't work out on weight machines or swim laps here, unless you use the community swimming pool. Exercise is limited to low-impact aerobics, walking, and three hours of yoga daily.

Personal counseling makes this spa experience attractive for those who want to learn healthy habits. A good deal of time is spent discussing ways to build self-esteem and to deal with everyday stress. Guests begin to feel a balance between mind and body and to appreciate the excitement of functioning at capacity on natural rather than nervous energy.

Addictions to smoking, caffeine, and sugar can be addressed. Avoiding temptation, changing one's daily routine, and being in a supportive group often inspire success. During the initial chemical withdrawal, positive support and breathing exercises to cleanse the lungs and flush impurities from the body are prescribed. Drinking lots of water, eating natural foods, and cleansing the colon are also advised.

Whirlpool, sauna, and massage sessions are part of the pampering. Guests appear radiant and relaxed by dinnertime in the formal family dining room, where places are set with period china and silver. A harpist plays in the background.

The Kerr House
17777 Beaver St., Grand Rapids, OH 43551
Tel. 419/832–1733

Administration	Director, Laurie Hostetler
Season	Year-round.
Accommodations	5 guest rooms with high ceilings, antiques, lace curtains. The house has massive wood doors, stained-glass windows, a hand-carved staircase.
Rates	$2,150 a week per person double occupancy; $2,550 single. Tax, gratuities, all services included. Weekends $575. 50% payable in advance. Credit cards: AE, MC, V.
Meal Plans	Diet of 750–1,000 calories per day, mainly vegetarian, with fish and chicken. Low in fat and cholesterol; no salt, sugar, refined flour, additives. Lunch can include a Senegalese carrot soup, lettuce salad, pita bread with couscous stuffing, and herbal tea. Typical dinner entrees are eggplant Parmesan with tomato sauce; baked chicken breast on wild rice; shrimp and baked potato. Fresh fruit desserts and sorbets are specialties.
Services and Facilities	**Exercise Equipment:** Rebounders, NordicTrack, backswings. **Services:** Massage, pedicure, facial, hair and skin care, reflexology, polarity, herbal body wraps, mineral baths. **Swimming Facilities:** Community pool nearby. **Recreation Facilities:**

Hiking along the Maumee River and the Miami & Erie Canal towpath; paddleboat rides. **Evening Programs:** Speakers.

In the Area Visit to a glass craftsman's studio, the Ludwig Mill (water-powered saw and grist mill), the restored Fort Meigs, farms and country fairs, hydroplane races (Sept.).

Getting Here *From Toledo.* By car, Ohio Turnpike (I-75) to Rte. 6, Rte. 65 to Rte. 24 (30 min). Complimentary pickup and return at Toledo Express Airport.

Special Notes No smoking indoors.

Sans Souci Health Resort

Weight management
Vibrant maturity
Stress control
Luxury pampering

Ohio On a beautiful, secluded 80-acre estate, a small band of health
Bellbrook seekers follows the owner and director of the Sans Souci Health Resort, Susanne Kircher, on a parcourse fitness trail across the immaculate lawn of the country retreat. Birdsong and gentle breezes enhance the outdoor sessions of stretching, breathing, and wakeup exercises. Miles of hiking trails crisscross the woods and meadows of the estate, which borders a 600-acre wildlife preserve. Classes include step aerobics and yoga.

Kircher, a registered nurse and a former consultant to Olympic athletes, mixes European spa philosophy with no-frills fitness training. The men and women who come here to shed a few pounds learn how to kick the habits that caused them to gain weight. The daily agenda is full of aerobics, from dance steps to slimnastics, and water workouts in the swimming pool during warm months. Meals are mainly vegetarian.

The programs in the spacious country home where the Romanian-born Kircher began her fitness resort in 1978 are devoted to stress management and stopping smoking. The guest list is limited so that programs can be tailored to meet individual needs. An hour a day is set aside for rest and relaxation; meditation walks or yoga classes add another quiet period to the day's schedule, or you may choose to work out in the organic garden that supplies fresh vegetables for summer meals.

Sans Souci Health Resort
3745 Rte. 725, Bellbrook, OH 45305
Tel. 513/848-4851

Administration Director, Susanne Kircher, R.N.

Season May–Oct.

Accommodations Spacious, airy rooms furnished English country style, with private bath, dressing area.

Rates 5-night program Sun.–Fri. $1,180 per person double occupancy, $1,380 single; weekend retreats $550 per person double, $650 single. Daily rate $152 (no room). 30% payable in advance. Tax and gratuity included. Credit cards: MC, V.

Meal Plans 800–1,000 calorie daily diet includes breakfast (sprouted wheat berries in soy milk or homemade granola), snacks, mineral water, lunch (whole-grain crepe, green salad, and steamed vegetables), and dinner such as seafood divan, fruit-garnished chicken served by candlelight. Juice fast recommended on day of arrival.

Services and Facilities **Exercise Equipment:** Stationary bike, rebounder, 18-station parcourse. **Services:** Massage, aromatherapy, acupressure, loofah scrub, facials, herbal wraps, manicures, pedicures, hair and skin care; cooking demonstrations, personal consultation on nutrition and diet. **Swimming Facilities:** Outdoor pool, lake. **Recreation Facilities:** Horseback riding, badminton, volleyball, croquet; golf, tennis, and fishing nearby. **Evening Programs:** Workshops on behavior modification, stress management, nutrition; assertiveness training; therapeutic massage and Jacuzzi relaxation. Guest lecturers and films.

In the Area Picnic lunches, tour of Bellbrook, 600-acre Sugarcreek Reserve.

Getting Here *From Dayton.* By car, I-75 to Rte. 725 East (30 min). Free service to Dayton International Airport; $20 for pickup on arrival.

Special Notes No smoking indoors.

The American Club

Non-program resort facilities

Wisconsin In a town dominated by the nation's leading manufacturer of
Kohler plumbing fixtures and bathtubs, it can be no surprise that luxury and bathing are synonymous at the American Club's 237-room hotel owned and operated by the Kohler Company. With a 36-hole golf course designed by Pete Dye, a Sports Core with indoor and outdoor tennis courts and a spa salon, and a 500-acre nature preserve where country gourmet meals are served in a secluded log lodge, the American Club has become an oasis of fitness in the Midwest.

Whirlpools for two are set on glass-covered terraces and in mirrored baths. For the ultimate in hedonism, ask for a suite equipped the Kohler Shower Tower (similar to Swiss shower) or the Habitat, a master bath with an hour's serenity programmed into it: The sounds of a rain forest, soft breezes, a gentle mist, a steam bath, even desert tanning are simulated.

The club's facilities extend around the village of Kohler and past the factory. Registered guests are issued passes that allow them to charge meals and services and ride a trolley to activities. Part of the club's charm lies in being in a place that looks like a Hollywood vision of middle America yet functions with the precision of a posh resort. The original Tudor-style dormitory, reminiscent of a country inn, has been duplicated across a garden courtyard where a Victorian greenhouse serves as an ice cream parlor.

Checking in at the Sports Core, you get a locker and towel and the opportunity to schedule herbal wraps, massage, and court times. In addition to racquetball courts (used for handball and wallyball, too), six indoor tennis courts are available for an hourly fee, while the outdoor courts are free. The Peter Burwash International staff offers professional instruction. Exercise rooms, aerobics studio, and health services are downstairs. A glass-walled 60-foot swimming pool and the Lean Bean restaurant (a happy discovery for dieters) are off the lobby.

Outdoor and indoor whirlpools and a man-made lake surrounded by a 2-mile exercise parcourse get heavy use from members and guests. The Core is open from 6 AM–11 PM daily. Bodywork, indoor courts, fitness and aquacize classes, and the use of Nautilus and computerized equipment in the weights rooms require additional fees. Racquets and cross-country skis can be rented.

River Wildlife is a place apart, one where the outdoors and good food are celebrated. Marksmen practice, hikers explore more than 30 miles of woodland trails, and canoers and fishermen enjoy the winding Sheboygan River. Horseback rides can be solo or escorted. A rustic lodge with log beams and fieldstone is the centerpiece. Lunch is served daily, dinner on weekends in front of the huge fireplace. In winter the trails are groomed for cross-country skiing, and hot cider is served before a crackling fire. American Club guests need only a $7 pass to use the facilities; the trails are open to all.

As a playground, the American Club and the nearby state parks are tops. Sheboygan, minutes away, offers cultural attractions. The combination of small-scale pleasures, an eager staff, and woodland creatures make this a cozy retreat.

The American Club
Highland Dr., Kohler, WI 53044
Tel. 414/457–8000 or 800/344–2838

Administration	General Manager, Brian R. O'Day; fitness director, Alice Hubbard
Season	Year-round.
Accommodations	237 rooms with a range of whirlpool baths, four-poster brass beds with feather comforters and pillows, wood paneling, carved oak doors, sitting areas, glassed-in terrace with hot tub, wet bar, and mirrored bath in some rooms. Deluxe rooms in the new three-story addition and the renovated Carriage House are reached by crossing the parking lot or using an underground walkway. Free transportation between facilities.
Rates	$114–$550 for 2 in double room, $89–$550 single. 2-day escape packages for 2 persons, including a bubble massage at the Sports Core and some meals, $308 and up. For golfers, 2 rounds at Blackwolf Run, plus amenities, $694 for 2 persons double occupancy. 5-night Fresh Start program (Sun.–Fri.) includes all meals, selection of services, $1,577 single, $2,751 for 2 persons. 1 night payable in advance. Tax and gratuity not included. Credit cards: AE, DC, MC, V.
Meal Plans	Breakfast buffet in the Wisconsin Room, expanded menu at Sunday brunch. Dinner at The Immigrant is a dress-up affair in small rooms dedicated to the club's original European occupants; specialties are Wisconsin whitefish caviar roe, scallops, shrimp, seafood sausage on spinach pasta, mesquite-roasted loin of Iowa pork, Kohler Purelean beef. The River Wildlife menu, changed every weekend, can feature pheasant pâté, grilled rabbit, broiled fresh brook trout stuffed with vegetables, veal scallops with pesto and 5-cheese sauce. Salad of

sprouts and seasonal greens or hamburgers at the Lean Bean or the Horse & Plow pub restaurant for lunch.

Services and Facilities
Exercise Equipment: 14-station Nautilus circuit, 8 Lifecycles, 3 StairMasters, Liferower; 16-station Universal gym, 6 Schwinn Air-Dyne bikes, 2 rowers, Olympic free weights, NordicTrack, 3 step machines. **Services:** Massage, herbal wrap, body wrap, facial, manicure, pedicure; fitness consultation; hydrotherapy. Aerobics classes throughout the day ($6.50 each). Clay marksmanship course, crazy-quail shooting, archery instruction. **Swimming Facilities:** Indoor lap pool, lake with sandy beach. **Recreation Facilities:** 6 indoor and 6 outdoor tennis courts, 2 handball/racquetball courts, fishing, canoeing and boating, bicycle rentals, hiking, cross-country skiing, 2 golf courses.

In the Area
Half-day canoe trip, nature walks, charter-boat fishing on Lake Michigan; Kettle Moraine State Forest (Ice Age formations), dunes on Lake Michigan beaches, nature trail at Sheboygan Indian Mound Park, Kohler Arts Center, Kohler Design Center, cheese plant tour, Kohler Company tour, Manitowac Maritime Museum, shops at Woodlake Kobler.

Getting Here
From Milwaukee. By car, I–43 to Exit 126, Rte. 23 west to Kohler (about 60 min). By bus, Greyhound to Sheboygan (70 min). Sheboygan Limousine Service to Milwaukee's Mitchell Airport, Amtrak, and bus stations.

Special Notes
Elevators link all floors. The Sports Core has supervised activities for children 1½–6. Older children can join week-long summer-camp programs or sign up for tennis and swimming lessons. No smoking in Sports Core athletic and therapy areas.

Aveda Spa Osceola

Luxury pampering
Weight management
Life enhancement

Wisconsin
Osceola
On the banks of the St. Croix river, about an hour's drive from Minneapolis/St. Paul, the Aveda Spa Osceola opened in 1990. A former estate on 80 acres, the prairie-style three-story house dating from 1908 has been rejuvenated with hydrotherapy rooms, European shampoo bed, and a beauty salon.

Owned and managed by the Aveda Corporation, a Minneapolis-based producer of natural products for the hair and skin, the resort serves as both a day spa and a country getaway. In summer, you can enjoy walking, running, or biking on scenic trails surrounding the spa, or spend hours canoeing on the scenic St. Croix River. In winter, cross-country skiing, snowshoeing, and ice-skating outings are organized. You may also choose to visit their Native American sweat lodge.

Spa treatments, enhanced with flower and plant essences and the pure water of St. Croix Springs, are designed to refresh and relax your body. Advanced cellular skin-care technology has been incorporated into the spa's skin-care treatments, which include aromatherapy.

Much of the decor is retained from the 1920s, along with antiques from the 17th century. A mammoth fireplace fills one end of a living room stripped of furniture for use as a yoga salon. Up the wide oak stairway are six bedrooms with polished wood floors; bright Pakistani, Indian, and Turkish carpets; and antique wooden beds laden with down pillows and duvets.

In the lower level of the house, past the sauna and exercise salon, are areas for treatments plus grottolike single bedrooms. Private rooms for massage, facials, and a hydrotherapy tub are reserved for guest use. Additional treatment and guest rooms are in the carriage house.

Programs are individually tailored to each guest's needs. Organized activity is minimal, as are the meals, but if you want the ultimate in skin care while shedding a few pounds, this is the place.

Aveda Spa Osceola
1015 Cascade St., Rte. 3, Box 72,
Osceola, WI 54020
Tel. 715/294-4465 or 800/283-3202
Fax 715/294-2196

Administration General manager/owner, Horst Rechelbacher

Season Year-round.

Accommodations 10 guest rooms, including suites. Furniture ranges from Indian to antiques to Art Deco, with wicker chairs, brass beds. Most rooms have private bath, air-conditioning; no TV or telephones.

Rates A weekend stay with spa services and meals is $510 single, $450 per person double occupancy. 5-day stays are $1,130 single, $1,100 double. Gratuities and taxes included. A one-day package with lunch is $175. Deposit 50% payable in advance. Credit cards: AE, MC, V.

Meal Plans Organic menu includes lunch choices of tomato aspic with guacamole, endive, and nasturtium salad. Dinner entrees include grilled salmon with jalapeño and roasted tomato sauce, stuffed baby artichokes, Peruvian potatoes, and steamed green beans. Dessert can be honey-poached pears with hazelnut-basil bread and fresh fruit sauce. Macrobiotic meals are available.

Services and Facilities **Exercise Equipment:** StairMaster, NordicTrack, Windbike, incline bed. **Services:** Swedish massage, shiatsu, reflexology, aromatherapy, underwater massage; beauty salon for hair, nail, and skin care. **Swimming Facilities:** Community outdoor pool. **Evening Programs:** Speakers on self-management, organic cooking, stress management, personal success, and the science of flower and plant essences.

In the Area Antiques shops in the village of Osceola, canoeing, antique airplane flying (Aug.).

Getting Here **From Minneapolis.** Transportation from the Minneapolis/St. Paul International Airport, $50. By car, I-35 north to Hwy. 97 east, Rte. 95 north to Hwy. 243, east to Rte. 35 north (1 hr). Rental car available.

Special Notes Minimum age in spa is 18. Limited access for the disabled. No smoking in the mansion. Mosquitoes can be annoying between June and September.

The Fontana Spa at The Abbey

Luxury pampering
Weight management
Nutrition and diet
Vibrant maturity

Wisconsin
Lake Geneva

Surrounded by panoramic views of Lake Geneva and the woods, the glass-walled swimming pool and aerobics studio at The Fontana Spa have an indoor-outdoor feeling that is enhanced by the changing seasons. The spa building is separate and apart from the busy resort and convention activities at The Abbey, yet takes advantage of its dining and entertainment facilities.

The spa's opening in 1989 marked a radical innovation for the landmark resort. The ambience here, unlike that of the traditional country inn, is modern with accents in furniture and leaded-glass inspired by Frank Lloyd Wright's prairie designs. At the reception desk you will be directed to separate men's and women's lounges, complete with fireplace, where workout clothing and a robe are issued with your locker key. Your masseur or salon therapist escorts you to the private treatment rooms, where an atmosphere of calm relaxation prevails.

Unexpected amenities add to the feeling of well-being: pitchers of fresh fruit juices along with muffins and fruit are laid out in the morning; the spa salon exudes the aroma of herbs and oils used in the imported French body and skin-care products by Phytomer.

The wide range of services in the spa packages (or on an à la carte basis for resort guests) distinguishes The Fontana as a destination that will appeal to sophisticated spa goers. Treatments range from loofah scrubs, thalassotherapy, and herbal wraps to European hand and foot treatments, from mud masks and aromatherapy facials to massages. In all, 33 different services are offered in combination with aerobic and aquatic exercise classes, and one-on-one training with the latest in exercise equipment.

While the spa is open daily from 7 AM to 9 PM, the number of program participants averages 33. Popular with women who are trying to shed a few pounds, the spa also has programs geared to the special needs of older guests. The staff includes a registered nurse who conducts an initial fitness and health evaluation. Programs are individually tailored to the needs of guests.

One of the quiet gratis pleasures of a holiday at Lake Geneva is the walking trail that follows the waterfront past the summer homes of some of the leading families from Chicago and Milwaukee. A guided walk is scheduled every morning with a staffer to set the pace. Or you can book a cruise on one of the classic yachts moored at The Abbey's marina and get a narrated history of this midwestern Newport.

The Fontana Spa at The Abbey
Hwy. 67/Fontana Blvd., Fontana, WI 53125
Tel. 414/275–5910 or 800/772–1000
Fax 414/275–5910

Administration General manager, Steve Kostechka; spa director, Karen Saia

Season Year-round.

Accommodations 334 rooms in modern lodge (24 new spa wing rooms in 1991). Twin double beds, TV, telephone, air-conditioning. Some locations noisy; lodge has direct entrance to spa building.

Rates 2-night spa sampler midweek $470–$560 single, $405–$450 per person double, weekends $490–$590 single, $415–$465 per person double; 5-night package (Sun.–Fri.) $1,363–$1,513 single, $1,201–$1,276 per person double. Full-day sampler packages $139.80–$221.35. Weekend Unwinder package with breakfast and dinner, $425 for 2. Add 16.5% service charge, 10.5% taxes. 50% advance payment. Credit cards: AE, DC, MC, V.

Meal Plans Menu selections in the spa's dining room are low in calories, saturated fat, and cholesterol. Breakfast can be cinnamon French toast, apple compote, or miniblueberry muffins. 3-course lunch and dinner include barbecued chicken, sea bass wrapped in spinach and served on a bed of saffron couscous, and such desserts as carob mousse, Key lime cheesecake, or fruit brulée and poached pears.

Services and Facilities **Exercise Equipment:** 10-unit Eagle weight training gym, 2 Lifecycles, 2 Turbo bikes, 2 Precor treadmills, StairMaster, 2 rowing machines, free weights, Sierra cross-country ski machine. **Services:** Swedish massage, shiatsu, acupressure, aromatherapy, fango, herbal wrap, loofah body scrub, facials, body polish, mineral baths, Scotch hose/Swiss shower, 3 underwater massage tubs; aerobics and aquacise classes, fitness evaluation; full-service beauty salon. **Swimming Facilities:** Indoor lap pool (18½ yds.), outdoor pool, lake. **Spa Facilities:** Separate men's and women's sauna, steam room, whirlpool; coed Jacuzzis, aerobics studio, pool. **Recreation Facilities:** 6 outdoor tennis courts (lighted), horseback riding, parcourse; golf, boating, racquetball, bike trips nearby; hiking. **Evening Programs:** cooking demonstration, resort entertainment.

In the Area Live theater and concerts, shopping, antiques shops.

Getting Here *From Chicago, IL.* Limousine service (Fee) from O'Hare International Airport. By car, I–94, Rte. 50 and 67 (2 hr). By bus, Wisconsin Lines (2 hr). By air, Delavan Airport handles private aircraft. Rental car available.

Special Notes No smoking in spa or spa dining room. Ground-floor accommodations for the disabled. Minimum age in spa 18; daily charge ($35) for guests not on package plan.

Olympia Village Resort

Non-program resort facilities

Wisconsin
Oconomowoc Olympia Village, a first-class vacation resort for relaxation and rejuvenation, is a good place to escape for a few days or a week. The spa's aerobics studio with a cushioned floor, offers a full schedule of classes that includes a workout in the pool.

A 3-day spa package includes 2 lunches and personal services. You're free to exercise in the weights room or work on your appearance. A personalized fitness program and daily diet will be tailored to your needs and physical abilities by the staff director.

Coed whirlpools and sunken Roman baths allow socializing or a private soak. Separate saunas and steam rooms for men and women and private massage rooms are among the extensive facilities for guests and residents of nearby condominiums. Luxuriously tiled and carpeted, the spa combines glamorous atmosphere and gentle discipline.

Olympia Village Resort
1350 Royale Mile Rd., Oconomowoc, WI 53066
Tel. 414/567–0311 or 800/558–9573

Administration	General manager, Ron Droegmyer; spa manager, Lois Stallman
Season	Year-round.
Accommodations	380 modern rooms facing a lake and ski lifts. Fully carpeted and air-conditioned, all rooms have private bath and color TV.
Rates	2-night spa package $173 per person double occupancy, $260 single. Suites $75 additional per day. Gratuities and tax included. Advance guarantee by credit card. Credit cards: AE, MC, V.
Meal Plans	Dinner choices include broiled herbed chicken, broiled pike in lemon dill sauce, steamed lobster. Luncheon menu changes daily, features spinach quiche, chef's salad.
Services and Facilities	**Exercise Equipment:** 2 Lifecycles, Biocycle, 2 StairMasters, 12-station Universal weight training gym, rowing machine, dumbbells, 30 free weights, wrist weights. **Services:** Exercise classes, massage, herbal wrap, facial, pedicure, manicure, loofah body scrub, hair and skin care. **Swimming Facilities:** Indoor and outdoor pools, private beach on lake. **Recreation Facilities:** Indoor and outdoor tennis, racquetball courts, golf, horseback riding, bicycle rental, water sports; downhill and cross-country skiing. **Evening Programs:** Resort entertainment, movie theaters.
In the Area	Old World Wisconsin (living history village), Octagon House (historic home), fishing, Milwaukee Brewers baseball.
Getting Here	*From Milwaukee.* By car, I–94 to Rte. 67 (40 min).
Special Notes	Elevators and ramps connecting all floors provide access for the disabled. No smoking in the spa and spa dining room. Spa Hours: summer, daily 6:30 AM–10 PM; winter schedule varies.

Sandhill

Life enhancement
Spiritual awareness
Holistic health

Wisconsin	Learning the healing lifestyle at the Sandhill School of Healing
Willard	Arts through scheduled seminars and Health Rejuvenation Weeks includes spa services as well as personal counseling. This is a stress-free, natural environment: surrounded by central Wisconsin farmland, the school is adjacent to and works in close cooperation with a spiritual retreat, The Christine Center for Unitive Planetary Spirituality. Guests sleep close to the healing force of nature, in their own tents or dormitory-style in a barnlike structure.

Independent or guided meditation can be practiced. Seeking an understanding of the whole person, Sandhill brings together Eastern and Western medical studies. Naturopaths and homeopaths come here for workshops that offer practical remedies in family health care. Ayurvedic therapies, as well as yoga, are taught. It is a gentle, nondemanding regimen of exercise, education, and enjoyment of nature.

Weekend seminars include brunch at 10:30 AM and a 4:30 PM meal of vegetables, fruits, grains, legumes, nuts, and seeds. An organic garden on the property supplies seasonal produce, grown and prepared by guests who work along with community members.

Sandhill School and Natural Health Spa
Route 1, Box 261A, Willard, WI 54493
Tel. 715/267-7153

Administration Program directors, Dennis Anderson and Roy Ozanne, M.D.

Season Year-round.

Accommodations Private and semiprivate rooms in cabins; dormitory at the main building. No air-conditioning; community bathrooms. Tent spaces available.

Rates Program fee, including meals and accommodations, $160–$285 weekends, $850 for 7-day Health Rejuvenation Week; for overnight visit, suggested donation is $12 for meals, $12 for dormitory bed, $25 private room, $7 tent site. Advance payment of 20%. No credit cards.

Meal Plan Vegetarian meal served twice daily. A variety of sprouts, baby greens, herbs and spices enhances organic vegetables, grains, and legumes. Dinner includes stirfry, soup, or salad.

Services and Facilities **Services:** Massage, colonic irrigation, yoga; health counseling; rebirths, Chinese acupuncture, acupressure, energy balancing; facial, aromatherapy, myofacial release; nutritional and homeopathic consultation.

In the Area Wisconsin Dells (rock formations), Chippewa Falls, Baraboo (Circus Museum).

Getting Here *From Eau Claire.* By car, I–94 east to Hwy. 10, east to CTH1; northeast for 15 miles to CTHG; north on G to 26 Road; west 1 mi to Bachelors Ave., then south 1 mi (1 hr).

The South

From hot-springs spas to holistic mountain retreats, the range of health facilities in the South includes some of the oldest and some of the newest resorts in the nation. Virginia's Warm Springs baths, Hot Springs National Park in Arkansas, and the ultramodern therapies of the Doral Saturnia International Spa Resort in Florida make dramatic contrasts that show how far the pursuit of fitness has come over the last century.

Advancing programs for health maintenance, Duke University Medical Center in North Carolina sponsors a Diet and Fitness Center, as does the Wildwood Lifestyle Center, a Seventh-day Adventist medical center in Georgia, and the private Hilton Head Health Institute set amid sea pines in South Carolina. For the budget-conscious vacationer, health retreats are available in Tennessee, Mississippi, and North Carolina.

For the combination of fitness facilities and sports opportunities, few resorts can match the programs of the PGA National Resort & Spa, Saddlebrook Sports Science, Sandestin Beach Resort's Sports/Spa & Clinic, and the Safety Harbor Spa and Fitness center, all in Florida.

Uchee Pines Institute Health Center

Preventive medicine
Weight management
Vibrant maturity

Alabama
Seale

This homelike retreat offers health conditioning and special diets in comprehensive 18-day sessions that appeal mostly to persons over 50. Medically directed, the Uchee Pines Institute program treats most degenerative diseases.

The Health Conditioning Center expounds traditional Seventh-day Adventist philosophies on nutrition and mental and spiritual health. Led by three physicians, the staff combines medical and natural healing. A nutritional analysis, aided by computers, gives each patient specific diet recommendations and takes into account each individual's physical condition, nutritional needs, and weight loss goals. Following each guest's complete physical examination (some of which may be covered by medical insurance), a physician prescribes a personal schedule and continues to monitor the patient's progress throughout the program. Treatments to stop smoking, drinking, or other lifestyle problems are also offered.

Diet plays a key role in the cleansing and healing process. The food here is fresh from the farm, and vegetarian meals are totally oil-, salt-, and gluten-free. There are special diets for cancer and menopausal patients.

Secluded in a 200-acre woodland preserve near the Chattahoochee River, the center's live-in accommodations for 14 guests provide privacy and comfort. Walks, gardening, exercise, and hydrotherapy balance out daily lectures on preventive medicine, nutrition, and lifestyle change.

The health center is equipped with a heated, full-body whirl-pool, steam bath, massage tables, and ultrasound therapy units. Special treatments include fomentation—application of moist heat to the body for relief from congestion or pain—and the use of ice packs to slow down circulation or arrest a physical reaction. Only a few pieces of exercise equipment are available to those who want an active program.

The warm, caring atmosphere and small size of the facilities make this an ideal place for older persons who need constant attention and who are searching for a life-restoring experience. It is nondenominational and nonsectarian.

Uchee Pines Institute Health Center
Rte. 1, Box 273, Seale, AL 36875
Tel. 205/855-4764

Administration	Manager, Joseph Anaman; medical director, David Miller, M.D.
Season	Year-round.
Accommodations	7 twin-bedded rooms with modern furniture, flowered bed-spreads, ceiling fans, reading lamps. Private bath.
Rates	$2,595 for an 18-day live-in session, all-inclusive; $2,395 for a spouse as a patient, $1,495 as a nonpatient (includes physical exam and medical consultation). $500 per person advance payment; 5% discount for full payment. Credit cards (4% surcharge): MC, V.
Meal Plans	3 vegetarian meals daily, family style. Adventist diet of fruits, vegetables, legumes, and grains. No fats, butter, or oils. Olives, nuts, and avocado in moderate amounts. Entrees include vegetarian lasagna, whole-wheat pizza, baked tofu.
Services and Facilities	**Exercise Equipment:** Stationary bike, jogger trampoline. **Services:** Massage, showers. **Spa Facilities:** Whirlpool, steam bath. **Recreation Facilities:** Nature hiking, bicycling, gardening, orchard work. **Evening Programs:** Informal discussions of health-related topics.
In the Area	Group outings to Callaway Gardens; Providence Canyon, Tuskegee Institute Museum (history and agriculture).
Getting Here	*From Atlanta.* By bus, Trailways to Columbus, GA (5 hr). By plane, Delta Airlines to Columbus, GA (30 min). By car, I-185 via Columbus, Rte. 80 to Rte. 431, south to Rtes. 24 and 39 (about 5 hr). Free pickup to and from airport and bus station.
Special Notes	No smoking indoors.

The Arlington Resort Hotel & Spa

Taking the waters
Non-program resort facilities

Arkansas	Quiet elegance, spacious accommodations, and old-world
Hot Springs	charm distinguish the landmark Arlington Resort Hotel & Spa, which overlooks Bathhouse Row in the heart of Hot Springs National Park. There are no special programs, but the hotel has men's and women's facilities for mineral-water bathing, including 53 rooms with springwater-filled tubs.

The South

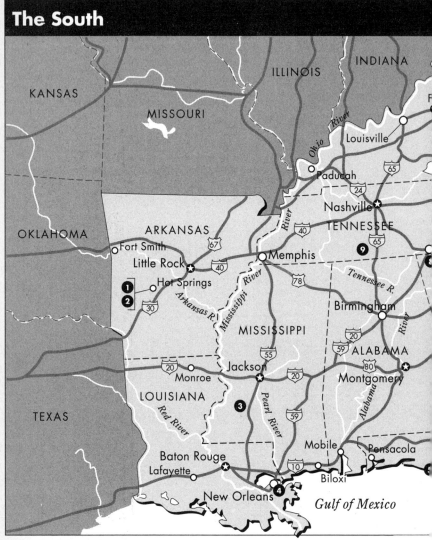

Alabama
Uchee Pines Institute
Health Center, **6**

Arkansas
The Arlington Resort
Hotel & Spa, **1**
Hot Springs National
Park, **2**

Florida
Bonaventure Resort &
Spa, **29**

Doral Saturnia
International Spa
Resort, **32**
Fontainebleau Hilton
Resort and Spa, **30**
Hippocrates Health
Institute, **26**
Lido Spa Hotel, **33**
Palm-Aire Spa Resort
& Country Club, **27**
PGA National Resort
& Spa, **25**
The Pier House
Caribbean Spa, **35**
Pritikin Longevity
Center, **31**

Russell House, **34**
Saddlebrook Sports
Science, **24**
Safety Harbor Spa and
Fitness Center, **23**
Sanibel Harbour
Resort & Spa, **36**
Sports/Spa & Clinic at
Sandestin, **5**
Turnberry Isle Yacht
and Country Club, **29**

Georgia
Chateau Elan, **7**

The Sea Island Spa at
the Cloister, **22**
Wildwood Lifestyle
Center, **8**

Louisiana
EuroVita Spa at the
Avenue Plaza Hotel, **4**

Mississippi
Jolimar Summit
Plantation, **3**

OHIO

WEST VIRGINIA

Frankfort
Lexington
64
KENTUCKY
80
75
Knoxville
40
75
Chattanooga
8
85
26
7
20
Atlanta
85
20
85
6

Chattahoochee River

Flint River

GEORGIA

Valdosta

5

Tallahassee
10
75

FLORIDA

Orlando
4

Daytona Beach

24
23
Tampa

25 26

27
28
Miami
36
41
Fort Myers

Key West 34 35

29
30
31
32
33

Washington, D.C.
95
11
12
64
Richmond
16 15
85
14 13
Norfolk
13
10

VIRGINIA
Roanoke
81
85

Greensboro
17 18
Rocky Mount
19
Winston-Salem
77
Raleigh

NORTH CAROLINA

Charlotte

Greenville

Columbia
20

SOUTH CAROLINA

Augusta
Macon
16

Savannah R.

20
21
Savannah

22

Jacksonville

95

ATLANTIC OCEAN

17

Charleston

N

0   200 miles

0   300 miles

North Carolina
Duke University Diet and Fitness Center, **18**
Structure House, **17**
Westglow Spa, **19**

South Carolina
Hilton Head Health Institute, **20**
The Westin Resort, **21**

Tennessee
Tennessee Fitness Spa, **9**

Virginia
Camp Rediscovery, **11**
Hartland Wellness Center, **12**
The Homestead, **10**
The Kingsmill Resort, **14**
The Integral Health Center, **16**
The Tazewell Club, **13**
Yogaville, **15**

Fort Lauderdale

With the Bath House on the third floor, there's no need to fight the crowds at the public baths outside. The complete treatment takes about 1½ hours, with whirlpool, hot packs, and massage plus optional steam cabinet or sitz bath. The naturally heated mineral water leaves your skin feeling silky smooth and relaxes tense muscles.

Twin cascading mountain pools, where you can swim in the mineral water, and hot tubs are outside. Walking and jogging paths wind through the woods behind the hotel.

Catering to families and convention groups, the hotel has grand lobbies and open loggias, as well as bars and other temptations. For arthritis and neuritis sufferers the Libbey Memorial Physical Medicine Center (within walking distance) offers underwater massage and special hot springs mineral-water hydrotherapy. Also nearby is the Levi Arthritis Hospital, which offers outpatient care.

The Arlington Resort Hotel & Spa
Central Ave. and Fountain St.,
Box 5652, Hot Springs, AR 71901
Tel. 501/623-7771 or 800/643-1502

Administration Manager, Horst Fischer

Season Year-round.

Accommodations 488 guest rooms looking a bit shabby recently, with 2 queen-size beds or 1 king-size, wicker chairs, flowered chintz curtains. Preferred rooms overlook the mountain and National Park, and are those equipped with mineral-water baths.

Rates $50–$88 per room for 2, double occupancy, $44–$76 single. Weekend package for 2, including spa services and $30 food and beverage credit, $90–$125. Family plan $66 per night for up to 4 persons; massage with whirlpool, hot pack $26.50. 1 night advance payment. Credit cards: AE, DC, MC, V.

Meal Plans Breakfast and dinner à la carte in the Venetian Room. Lunch in rustic Captain's Tavern means sandwiches, salads, or seafood selections. Gourmet restaurant open for dinner 3 nights. Dinner entrees include broiled red snapper with red peppercorns, broiled lamb chops, seafood fettuccine, veal marsala, and salads. No diet or low-cal menu, but special diets accommodated.

Services and Facilities **Exercise Equipment:** Weights room with MGI fitness system with curl/high-pull combo unit, knee machine, leg abduction/adduction, overhead press, lats, triceps, and chest units; treadmill, recumbent bike, sit-up bench. **Services:** Massage, hot packs; beauty salon for hair and skin care, including facials. **Swimming Facilities:** 2 outdoor heated mineral-water pools. **Spa Facilities:** Whirlpool and treatment alcoves in separate pavilions for men and women, mineral-water bath. **Recreation Facilities:** Country club golf, tennis, and dining privileges for hotel guests. Three nearby lakes for fishing, boating, and swimming. **Evening Programs:** Resort entertainment.

In the Area Local sightseeing tours, Thoroughbred horse racing at Oaklawn Park (Feb.–April), Magic Springs Family Theme Park, Mid-America Museum (science and history) and outdoor amphitheater, Observation Tower.

Getting Here *From Little Rock.* By bus or scheduled van from the airport. By car, I-30 south, Rte. 70 (45 min). Airport shuttle bus directly to and from hotel ($12 each way). Rental car, taxi available. Parking available on site.

Special Notes Elevator connects all floors to bath house. Game room for children on pool deck. No smoking in bath house.

Hot Springs National Park

Taking the waters

Arkansas Hot Springs National Park was once called the Valley of the Va-
Hot Springs pors. Indians and conquistadores were attracted by clouds of steam from the 47 springs that bring hot mineral water to the surface in what is now a national park within a resort city.

Local lore has it that Hernando de Soto and his explorers relaxed here in 1541. The park rangers tell visitors about the springwater's 4,000-year journey from deep within the earth, where it is heated to 143 degrees, and its mineral content from which its therapeutic properties derive.

In 1832, the federal government set aside four sections of the springs as a health reservation, the first in the country's history. A partnership evolved with private bathhouse and hotel operators, so the National Park Service now regulates operations and maintains the reservoirs, where the springwater cools down to 100 degrees for bathing.

Six bathing facilities are open to the public, and plans are underway for renovation and adaptive reuse of several Art Deco buildings on Bathhouse Row. The most splendid of the eight buildings surviving here, The Fordyce, was built in 1915 by a Colonel Fordyce, who credited the springwaters with saving his life. The interior has stained-glass windows and a skylight with scenes of water nymphs, appropriate for the museum of bathing created as part of the building's restoration in 1989. The gymnasium where Jack Dempsey and Billy Sunday reportedly hoisted wooden dumbbells is again open to the public. Other bathhouses will display art and musical instruments; one will be an exclusive health spa.

In the Buckstaff Bathhouse, a stately three-story brick-and-marble edifice, bathers step into a private porcelain tub filled with mineral water heated to 103 degrees. Plan on about 1½ hours for a soak in the thermal waters, the whirlpools, and a massage. The entire treatment at Buckstaff Baths, including hot packs on sore muscles and a multineedled shower, costs about $23. Reservations are essential.

Vacationing here is like taking a step back in time. Grand old hotels as well as mansions offer bed and breakfast. Hot Springs is also a modern medical center for advanced therapy of degenerative diseases and rehabilitation treatments for postcardiac or surgery patients. The town has the flavor of a 19th-century European spa—all the charm without the exaggerated claims.

Hot Springs National Park
Box 1860, Hot Springs, AR 71902
Tel. 501/623-2308

Hot Springs Convention & Visitors Bureau
Box K, Hot Springs National Park, AR 71902
Tel. 501/321-2835 or 800/543-2284

Administration	Superintendent, Roger Giddings
Season	Year-round.
Accommodations	Bathing facilities in the Arlington, Hilton, Downtowner, and Majestic hotels. Guest houses and camping facilities nearby. Rehabilitation therapy and baths at Hot Springs Health Spa, open daily 9 AM–9 PM.
Services and Facilities	**Swimming Facilities:** Indoor and outdoor pools at hotels; lakes nearby. **Spa Facilities:** 6 bathhouses operate under the auspices of U.S. Department of the Interior. All open Mon.–Sat. 7 AM– 11:30 PM, 1:30 PM–4 PM; hotel hours vary. Arlington open Sun. morning. **Recreation Facilities:** Hiking trails in Ouachita Mountains, boating, fishing, biking, horseback riding; cross-country skiing. Hotels offer tennis, golf. **Programs:** 12-minute slide program scheduled in park headquarters auditorium.
In the Area	Conducted bathhouse tours; Ouachita Lake recreational area, Oaklawn Park (Thoroughbred racing, late Jan.–mid-Apr.), Hot Springs Mountain Tower Ozark Folk Center at Mountain View (concerts, exhibits), Cowie Wine Cellars in Eureka Springs, Alligator Farm, Toltec Mounds State Park (Indian earthworks).
Getting Here	*From Little Rock.* By bus, Greyhound (60 min). By car, I-30 to Hot Springs Exit, Rte. 70 west (60 min).
Special Notes	Ramps and specially equipped rooms in most hotels and Buckstaff Baths. No smoking in bathhouses.

Bonaventure Resort & Spa

Luxury pampering
Weight management
Non-program resort facilities

Florida *Fort Lauderdale*	When you want to go first class on a tight budget, a holiday at the Bonaventure Resort & Spa offers first-rate services à la carte or on a package basis. The difference between the two is in quantity of services, not quality. You can stay a weekend, four days, or a full week; take unlimited exercise classes and enjoy expert bodywork and beauty treatments; or orient your visit around sports—tennis, golf, and horseback riding. But beware adding too many extras to your spa schedule, as your bill will quickly run up.

The hotel also offers a one-day spa sampler—a fixed-price package of pampering and nutritious meals that is popular with people attending conventions. These bookings are limited when spa facilities are crowded. (There is a large local membership, as the residential community around the resort has grown enormously since the spa opened in 1982.)

Separate facilities for men and women, plus a coed gym and pool, are among the features of the free-standing fitness center. Once past the registration desk, you're handed workout clothing and a cotton robe, assigned to a locker where your personal schedule is posted, and then left to your own pursuits.

Sybaritic pleasures aside, management takes a serious approach to fitness here. A staff nurse interviews you on arrival and may suggest consultation on a diet plan. Guests can opt for calorie-controlled meals or dine in the gourmet dining room.

A typical day begins with a walk or jog around the golf course before breakfast, then an hour-long aerobics class. Three levels of conditioning are offered in a dozen different classes that range from easy stretches and energizing routines to deep toning calisthenics. Workouts in the water are popular, especially for people with orthopedic problems. There's no risk to joints and the back while doing aquatics in the pool or in the ocean—the beach is just 30 minutes away by car.

There are cardiovascular exercises for men only, general conditioning and contouring for women only, and separate salons for facials, hair, and skin treatments. One of the specialties, available only here and in California, is Kerstin Florian's complexion revitalizer with fresh cell extracts.

What sets this spa apart from others is the wide range of body and skin-care treatments. Always on the cutting edge, Bonaventure recently introduced a full-body facial and aromatherapy bath to its repertoire of hydrotherapy. An imported line of essential oils is used in the aromatherapy massage.

Families with children have an extra advantage with the sports program for teenagers and day camp for youngsters.

The latest in spa cuisine is served at the hotel in a separate dining room decorated in soft colors, with bamboo screens and mirrors. Dinner dress is casual; meals can be served in your room if you prefer.

Bonaventure Resort & Spa
250 Racquet Club Rd., Fort Lauderdale, FL 33326
Tel. 305/389–3300 or 800/327–8090 (800/432–3063 in FL)
Telex 568–632 (Bonaventure VD), Fax 305/591–9266

Administration Managing director, Vincent Agostino; spa director, Tanya Lee

Season Year-round.

Accommodations 493 luxury guest rooms and suites in nine 4-story buildings; Spacious rooms with balconies overlook lake or golf course with 2 beds (queen-size or twin) or 1 extra-large king-size. Rattan seating and tropical colors. Oversize bath with dressing area.

Rates $150–$250 daily for 1 or 2 persons; Perfect Day package at spa $195 per person (lodging not included), plus tax and gratuity. Boot Camp spa package without services (3-night minimum stay) $228–$302 single, $167–$228 double. 3 day/2 night Spa Sampler with meals, 2 half-hour massages, treatments, and classes: $599–$749 single, $519–$609 double (per person). Additional bodywork and beauty treatments included in 5 day/4 night plan: $1,214–$1,514 single, $1,054–$1,234 double. 8 day/7 night fitness plan $2,040–$2,530 single, $1,725–$2,040 double. Golf and tennis packages available. 1 night's advance payment 7 days after booking or AE confirmation. Credit cards: AE, D, MC, V.

Meal Plans 3 meals with calorie-counted selections served daily in private Spa Dining Room. 1,200 calories suggested for those not on weight-loss diet. Lunch specialties include pasta primavera, curried chicken soup, baked vegetables marinara with tofu, and fresh fruit. Dinner entrees include Maine lobster with asparagus spears, stir-fried chicken and vegetables on cellophane noodles, dessert crepe with blueberry and cheese filling. Decaffeinated and regular coffee and herbal tea; also acidophilus milk. Food is low in fat, cholesterol, refined sugar, and sodium, high in natural fiber, nutrients, and flavor. Dietitian on hand for special requests. Deer Park bottled mineral water.

Services and Facilities **Exercise Equipment:** 10-station Keiser gym, 3 Lifecycles, 5 Quinton treadmills, 3 stationary bikes, 2 StairMasters, Gravitron, 2 Lifesteps, Liferower, free weights (5–50 lb). **Services:** Massage (Swedish, shiatsu, aromatherapy, reflexology), aromatherapy bath, loofah body scrub, herbal wrap, sea-kelp body wrap, thermal back treatment, facials, skin and nail care, hairstyling. Private exercise, golf, tennis, and horseback-riding instruction. Individualized fitness profile, nutrition profile, and body composition analysis. **Swimming Facilities:** Outdoor and indoor pools, ocean beach nearby. **Spa Facilities:** 3½-foot exercise pool, outdoor Jacuzzi, Finnish sauna, Turkish steambath, hot and cold plunge baths. **Recreation Facilities:** 24 tennis courts, 2 18-hole golf courses, 6 racquetball and squash courts, horseback riding, bicycle rental. **Evening Programs:** Lectures on health and stress, psychic readings.

In the Area Shopping trip to Galleria Mall and Fashion Mall, beach shuttle; local sightseeing on request. Everglades tour by airboat, jai-alai fronton, Bahamas cruises, dog and horse racing tracks, Seminole Indian village, Fort Lauderdale museums and performing arts center.

Getting Here *From Miami.* By car, I-75 to Fort Lauderdale, Arvida Parkway Exit, State Rd. 84 (40 min). By plane, scheduled service (15 min). Taxi, rental car available.

Special Notes Ramps, elevators, and specially equipped rooms for the disabled. No smoking in spa building or in designated areas of the dining room. Spa open daily 7 AM–7 PM winter season, summer hours vary.

Doral Saturnia International Spa Resort

Luxury pampering
Life enhancement
Stress control
Sports conditioning

Florida **Miami** Like a vision of Tuscany, the villa's red-tile roof rises above formal gardens, statuary, and cascading fountains at the Doral Country Club. The mood inside is modern, without a trace of sweaty workouts to disturb the calm. Yet the spa is self-contained, with a wing of suites and dining pergola just for those participating in one of the deluxe fitness and beauty packages.

Around the upper levels of the central atrium are the men's and women's locker rooms, equipped with whirlpool, saunas (dry and steam), sun deck, and lounge; 26 private massage rooms with a selection of treatments; a coed beauty salon and skincare treatment rooms that feature an exclusive line of Italian cosmetics; and a running track. Gymnasium and weights room are located below the lobby level.

A grand staircase from a Paris department store provides a grand entrance for lunch in the rotunda. You come as you are; fresh outfits and robes are issued throughout the day in the locker room. Country club and one-day spa guests also dine here. The menu features traditional Italian favorites (pizza and pasta) adapted to meet the standards of the Doral Saturnia Fat Point Nutrition System.

Inspired by the ancient baths at Terme di Saturnia, north of Rome, the Doral Saturnia spa blends European and American health concepts. There are one-on-one workouts with pneumatic resistance equipment imported from Finland, aerobics in two cushion-floored studios, and an indoor pool. Treatments for muscular and skin problems are a specialty; warm mud packs from the same Saturnia volcanic springs used by Italian dermatologists are part of the massage therapy.

Daily regimens are flexible. The classes tend to be jazzy, low-impact workouts that appeal to men as well as women. Refreshing trays of fruits, veggies, and tall frosted fruit drinks are set out on a marble-topped buffet during breaks. For those who prefer tennis, 16 courts are nearby. The spa's signature programs emphasize weight management, health and fitness, sports, or total image. Other programs concentrate on cellulite, peak performance, stress relief.

Appointments for personal services begin in the locker room lounge, where fresh workout clothing is issued. A therapist then escorts you by elevator to private rooms around the lofty rotunda. Serious regimens are planned after consultation with staff specialists who compare your health profile with a computerized model. All this personalized attention—a three-to-one ratio of staff to guests—comes at a price: about $350 per day, including three meals. Treatments are priced individually; various packages focus on fitness and beauty, or on golf, tennis, and horseback riding.

Stress management is taught in a seven-day program scheduled at various times throughout the year. Dr. Eric Goldstein, a psychologist at the University of Miami who has worked with Olympic athletes, developed the program with spa trainers and nutritionists. Biofeedback and respiratory training routines and a "Stress Relief" workout teach participants how to control stress in every aspect of their lives.

The dressy informality of a country house prevails in the spa villa. The mood of prosperity carries into the suites, where you'll find wall-to-wall marble, twin baths (one with Jacuzzi), dressing rooms furnished with robes and cosmetics, and an alcove where fresh fruit and Italian mineral water are supplied daily. Videocassettes are available for those who want to watch a feature film in their living room.

For a fully sybaritic retreat, guests may book one of six suites decorated by Piero Pinto of Milan to evoke regions of Italy. Furnished with original artwork and custom-made seating and beds, the luxury suites are Italian fantasies at an additional $85–$110 on a 2-night package. Additional privacy is offered in T-shaped Grande Suites with two raised bedrooms for an additional surcharge of $55–$70 per night. Some spa patrons book a room in the nearby golf resort and take a one-day package.

Evenings in the glass-walled Villa Montepaldi Ristorante are elegant yet informal. Predinner nonalcoholic drinks are served in the library, where a fast game of billiards might whet one's appetite. The menu combines Tuscan specialties with fresh Florida produce and seafood. You may choose the size of your portion; fat points are listed, and a calorie counter is attached to the menu. One glass of wine or champagne is complimentary with dinner.

Talks by health specialists are scheduled after dinner, but many guests succumb to the temptation to enjoy the luxurious accommodations and prepare for an early morning walk around the golf course. The Spa Villa is air-conditioned, which is essential during the high-humidity summer months. Weather permitting, breakfast is served alfresco, with your choice of newspapers.

Miami's museums, shopping, and nightlife are less than 30 minutes away; Coral Gables and Coconut Grove are even closer. You can take off for the beach in the Doral private bus and use a cabana and exercise room at a sister hotel. Another alternative is a natural massage under cascades of water designed in the spirit of the original Italian spa.

Doral Saturnia International Spa Resort
8755 N.W. 36th St., Miami, FL 33178
Tel. 305/593–6030 or 800/331–7768 (800/247–8901 in FL)
Telex 990471/Doral Saturnia UD
Fax 305/593–6030, ext. 5101

Administration General manager, Offer Nissenbaum; spa director, Carol Upper

Season Year-round.

Accommodations 48 suites, all with twin baths, Jacuzzi, wet bar and refrigerator, VCR, 2 dressing areas, hair dryer, queen- or king-size bed. Suites with private terrace or balcony overlook golf courses or garden.

Rates Spa plan includes suite accommodations, 3 meals daily, and points for choice of services. 2 nights $585–$1,000 per person double occupancy, $935–$1,045 single; 4 nights $1,885 per person double; 7 nights $3,090 per person double. Add taxes and service charge. Spa Day $225 with lunch, classes, massage (1 treatment, no room). Summer rates lower. $500 advance payment within 7 days after booking 7-night plan, balance 14 days before arrival. Full payment within 7 days after booking short stays. Refundable (less $50) up to 14 days prior to arrival date. Credit cards: AE, DC, MC, V.

Meal Plans Specialties include buckwheat waffles with fruit topping or one-egg omelet with spinach. (breakfast), small pizza topped with turkey sausage (lunch), steamed lobster with mussel sauce or grilled honey basil chicken with rice and fresh vegetables (dinner). Saturnia cuisine can be polenta lasagna with layers of smoked chicken, spinach, sliced tomato, or pork loin sautéed with mushroom and marsala sauce. Seafood is offered nightly; special diets accommodated.

Services and Facilities **Exercise Equipment:** 13-station David system, 3–65 lb. free weights, Versaclimber, 2 StairMasters, 2 Lifecycles, 2 Liferowers, 3 Schwinn Air-Dyne bikes, 5 Precor treadmills, barbells (10–50 lb), Hydrofit. **Services:** Fango mud facial and body treatments; facials, herbal wraps, underwater massage, Body gommage cream cleansing, hand and foot therapy, breast firming, leg/hip wrap, Swedish, aromatherapy, acupressure massage. Beauty salon. Cooking class, tai chi. **Swimming Facilities:** Large outdoor pool with cascades, separate Olympic-length lap pool, indoor pool for aquatics. **Recreation Facilities:** 5 golf courses, 15 tennis courts, horseback riding, hiking trail. **Evening Programs:** Lecture and discussion group daily.

In the Area Complimentary use of beach club at Doral Hotel On-the-Ocean; shopping at Bal Harbour, Coral Gables; performing arts seasons and festivals in Miami and Miami Beach; museums and Vizcaya mansion; Orange Bowl games and concerts; jai alai and racetracks; sailing and deep-sea fishing. Major-league baseball and basketball.

Getting Here *From Miami International Airport.* 15 min away, served by major airlines. Amtrak station in Miami. Free limousine service in the spa villa plan (4-day minimum). Taxi, rental car, limo arranged by concierge. Free scheduled shuttle bus to Miami Beach. Free parking, restricted to spa guests.

Special Notes Barrier-free facilities and dining rooms for the disabled; elevators throughout the spa center and villa. No smoking indoors. Spa open daily 8 AM–6 PM.

Fontainebleau Hilton Resort and Spa

Sports conditioning
Luxury pampering

Florida
Miami Beach
Behind the monumental lobby, the half-acre lagoon with rock grotto and cascades, and the deli bar is The Spa. Located in the Fontainebleau's old South building, where convention guests stay, it is developing into a self-contained fitness and health retreat. The ambience is more that of a city club than a fitness resort. The clientele includes local members and visiting businessmen. Access to a health food restaurant and salons for skin care expand the range of this glamorous beach resort.

A computer program measures cardiovascular strength and evaluates diet. It might help beforehand for you to compare notes with your personal physician at home and start working under the supervision of experts on the link between diet, exercise, and health. The spa also organizes workshops for convention groups and half-day seminars in lifestyle management.

The exercise facilities here are perhaps the most extensive to be found in the area. With 105 aerobics classes scheduled weekly, the cushion-floored workout rooms are constantly in action. The array of weight training equipment includes a full line of Nautilus, and the staff includes 30 massage therapists on duty in seven private rooms.

Another attraction is the natural-foods restaurant and its dining terrace overlooking the beach and saltwater swimming pool. Lunch here is not included in the hotel's spa package. Dinner is served in the main dining room.

The Adrian Arpel herbal products are skin-care options. After a dose of Florida sunshine, a fresh herbal and fruit mask has a soothing effect.

Fitness and fun go together. You can get a serious workout in the weights room or get caught up in the many activities offered all guests at the Fontainebleau. Be massaged alfresco or slip into the sauna, steam bath, and Jacuzzi.

Fontainebleau Hilton Resort and Spa
4441 Collins Ave., Miami Beach, FL 33140
Tel. 305/538–2000, 800/445–8667, or 800/548–8886
Spa reservations, tel. 305/865–4101

Administration Spa director, Marc H. Siegel

Season Year-round.

Accommodations 1,224 rooms, all with private bath, and 61 suites. Deluxe bedrooms with king-size or large double beds, TV, and balcony.

Rates 3-day Spa Adventure package $615 single, $840 for 2; Room-only for 2 persons $104–$215 per day in summer, $250–$270 in winter; suites from $375. Add taxes, gratuity. Daily spa pass $12.78. 1 night's lodging advance payment. Credit cards: AE, DC, MC, V.

Meal Plans Paradise Health Bistro (open 8 AM–7 PM) serves sandwiches, pizza, salads, low-cal drinks, juice, and fruit. Heart-healthy items at the hotel's 6 restaurants are the snapper, pasta primavera, and broiled chicken. All meals à la carte.

Services and Facilities **Exercise Equipment:** 20-unit Nautilus circuit, 8 Lifecycles, rowing machines, StairMasters, treadmills, free weights. **Services:** Massage, aromatherapy, loofah body scrub, herbal wrap; personal instruction on exercise, fitness profile, private whirlpool mineral baths, skin-care treatments, manicure, pedicure, hairstyling, skin consultation. **Swimming Facilities:** Exercise pool, free-form recreational pool, and ocean beach. **Recreation Facilities:** 7 lighted tennis courts, Hobie and Catyak catamaran sailboats, windsurfing, beach volleyball. Nearby golf course and horseback riding. **Evening Programs:** Resort entertainment, cabaret.

In the Area Local sightseeing tours and cruises, Caribbean cruises, 1-day Bahamas flights and cruises, Thoroughbred horse races, harness track, dog races, jai alai fronton, Miami Dolphins stadium. Metropolitan Museum (major art shows), Gusman Performing Arts Center (concerts), opera season (winter), chamber music series, theater, baseball, basketball seasons.

Getting Here *From Miami International Airport.* Shuttle van service operates at all times (20 min). Taxi, rental car, limousine, public bus available. Free indoor parking included in spa package.

Special Notes Elevator to all floors and some specially equipped rooms for the disabled. Free children's accommodation with parents. No smoking in spa or designated dining areas. Spa hours: weekdays 6:30 AM–10 PM, weekends 8 AM–7 PM.

Hippocrates Health Institute

Holistic health
Weight management

Florida
West Palm Beach A vegetarian diet, medical consultation, chiropractic therapy, and psychological consultation are central to the health-renewal program at the Hippocrates Health Institute. Sessions three weeks or longer are planned on an individual basis for 15 to 20 participants. Highly structured, the program includes nutritional education, regular exercise, massage, reflexology, detoxification, and relaxation.

Guests stay in a spacious hacienda or at private cottages on the 20-acre wooded estate. A peaceful, healing serenity pervades the grounds, where walkways wind through tropical surroundings to a dry sauna and ozonated swimming pool.

The Hippocrates lifestyle involves learning to be self-sufficient in matters of food and medicine. A typical day begins at 8 AM with light exercise before breakfast, then a blood-pressure check, and discussion session on health and diet. Guests learn and practice how to sprout and grow greens for home use.

Personal counseling comes with the program. A psychologist and an M.D. work closely with the medical director to monitor your progress and advise you on personal problems. Deep-relaxation techniques are taught to enhance healing, creativity, and inspiration. A weekly session with a massage therapist is included in the program. The program is run by health professionals (who moved the institute from Boston) with 30 years' experience teaching vegetarianism.

Hippocrates Health Institute
1443 Palmdale Ct., West Palm Beach, FL 33411
Tel. 407/471–8876 or 800/842–2125
Fax 407/471–9464

Administration Co-directors, Brian R. Clement and Anna Maria Gahns

Season Year-round; scheduled 3-week programs.

Accommodations 12 guest rooms, from luxury suite in Spanish-style hacienda to garden apartments and cottages, some with marble-walled bath and whirlpools. Colonial New England furnishings, views of lush tropical greenery, privacy.

Rates 3-week Health Encounter $5,400–$6,230 private, $1,900–$4,180 shared. Shorter and longer stays on space-available basis. 50% of room rate nonrefundable deposit by certified check or major credit card. Credit cards: AE, MC, V.

Meal Plans 3 meals daily, buffet style, with days designated for juice fasting. Live Food diet of unprocessed organic raw vegetables, fruits, nuts, seeds, sprouts, sea plants and algae, and herbs. Raw juices and legumes in enzyme-rich menu, including combination of red pepper stuffed with cheeselike mix of nuts and seeds or sauerkraut and seed loaf. No dairy products, eggs, fish, meat, coffee, tea, or condiments.

Services and Facilities **Exercise Equipment:** Universal multistation gym, Lifecycle, LifeClimber, treadmill. **Services:** Health consultations, chiropractic treatment, full body massage, facials, supervised exercise program, wheatgrass detoxification schedule. **Swimming Facilities:** Outdoor pool, ocean beach nearby. **Recreation Facilities:** 2 tennis courts, golf and boating nearby. **Evening Programs:** Lectures and discussions nightly.

In the Area Trips to the beach, local museums, shopping excursions.

Getting Here *From Miami.* By bus, Greyhound to West Palm Beach (90 min). By car, Florida Turnpike (I-75) to Palm Beach Exit 40, Okeechobee Blvd. to Skees Rd. (60 min). Free service to and from West Palm Beach airport and bus station. Taxi, rental car available.

Special Notes Ramps provided for the disabled; one specially equipped guest room. No smoking.

Lido Spa Hotel

Vibrant maturity
Weight management

Florida
Miami Beach

An all-inclusive daily rate that covers massage, exercise classes, and nutritional guidance makes the Lido Spa Hotel a good alternative to luxury spas. More a residential hotel than a resort, and occupying choice frontage on Biscayne Bay, it is linked to Miami Beach by the scenic Venetian Causeway, a toll road for Miami commuters.

Family-owned and operated, the Lido has a comfortable, lived-in look, but shows its age. The main building opened in 1962 and is flanked by two-level wings of motel-like accommodations. Garden-level rooms are popular with older guests, who make up the majority of the Lido's regular clientele; they are a friendly community of mature adults, and many return year after year. The managers of the men's and women's spas provide a limited amount of guidance but, at the same time, are responsive to guests' personal needs and interests. If you are self-motivated and can set your own schedule, this could be a pleasant, relaxed vacation.

After an initial consultation on your fitness level, a diet program can be planned with the resident nutritionist. Nobody checks to see whether you comply, but the dietitian lends encouragement during meals. Dieters can avoid temptation by being seated together; otherwise the waiters will serve seconds and dessert orders.

Menu selections (made each morning) are varied, with emphasis on fresh fish and pasta. Lobster is regularly offered. All items are free of salt, sugar, and other additives.

The daily schedule includes two low-impact exercise classes in the air-conditioned gym and occasional workouts in the swimming pool. Otherwise you're on your own to schedule massage appointments, swim in the two outdoor pools (one is filtered salt water), or sunbathe in private cabanas. The Lido is close to Miami Beach attractions, so that a morning walk can include the beach or art galleries on Lincoln Road. Free transportation is provided within a 50-block area for shopping, entertainment, and sightseeing.

Lido Spa Hotel
40 Island Ave., Miami Beach, FL 33139
Tel. 305/538–4621 or 800/327–8363.

Administration Director, Aaron "Chuck" Edelstein

Season Nov.–May.

Accommodations 106 rooms, mostly in one- or two-story garden wings. Fully equipped apartments (15) nearby. Furniture has plastic, 1960s look, well maintained and serviced daily. TV, telephone, air-conditioning; extra charge for refrigerator.

Rates Varies with season, $61–$115 single, $52–$90 per person, double occupancy. Daily rate includes massage (30 min), 3 meals, exercise classes, outings. Add 9.5% tax, gratuities. Deposit $100 per room. Credit cards: AE, MC, V.

Meal Plans Selections from menu include grilled snapper, pasta salad, baked chicken. Eggs, dairy products; coffee and tea available. Kosher food on request.

Services and Facilities **Exercise Equipment:** 2 Precor treadmills, 10 stationary bikes (Tuntori, Monark), StairMaster, Lifecycle, Universal multistation gym, free weights, pulleys, barbells, tiltboard, rebounder. **Swimming Facilities:** Outdoor lap pool, recreational pool. **Spa Facilities:** Steam room, private whirlpools, Swedish massage; loofah body scrub, facial for women only. Beauty salon. **Evening Programs:** musicals or movies.

In the Area Bass Museum of Art, Lincoln Road (arts district), Theater of the Performing Arts (concerts, opera, ballet, musicals), Dade County Cultural Center, Art Deco hotels and cafés, Bayside shops.

Getting Here *From Miami.* By car, Biscayne Blvd. to Venetian Causeway. Free transfer to airport or Amtrak station on departure.

Special Notes No smoking in spa or special areas of dining room.

Palm-Aire Spa Resort & Country Club

Life enhancement
Weight management
Luxury pampering

Florida
Pompano Beach

Surrounded by five 18-hole championship golf courses, 37 clay and hard-surface tennis courts, and condominium apartment buildings, the Palm-Aire Spa Resort has built a clientele of local residents and "snowbird" winter visitors for 23 years. The New York Yankees spend spring training here, and Frank Sinatra reserves a suite when he's performing in nearby Fort Lauderdale.

The spa is beginning to show its age, but it doesn't stint on service. Separate men's and women's pavilions have private sunken Roman baths, Swiss showers (17 nozzles that alternate warm and cool water), and some of the most experienced hands in the massage business. Each has sauna, cold plunge, steam room, and outdoor exercise pool (try aquaerobics in the buff). There's a well-equipped coed gym, racquetball courts, and junior-Olympic-size outdoor swimming pool. Ocean swimming, however, is about a 20-minute ride away.

A typical day begins with 10 minutes of warm-up stretches after breakfast, then a brisk walk on a half-mile parcourse. An instructor monitors your pulse rate on every lap. Fresh workout clothing is handed out in the locker room, and you can relax in the lounge while waiting for your next appointment or class. There's a clublike atmosphere as resident members and regular guests swap gossip and watch the stock market reports. Staff members are attentive and accustomed to gratuities.

Daily aerobics classes range from mild to tough. A fitness exam may be required by an instructor before you may take an advanced class. Many guests mix pampering with their workout, then nap in the afternoon by the pool. The Ultimate Day with lunch is also available.

Calories count in the private spa dining room; the food is portion controlled, high in carbohydrates, and low in fat. The 900-

calorie-per-day plan is sufficient, but second helpings are available. A regular, "fattening" menu is served in the adjoining dining room. Avoid the bar scene and head for the spa guests' lounge, where snacks of raw vegetables and fruit and a videocassette library are available.

Salon services for men and women, in a newly decorated facility adjoining the spa, are charged à la carte. If you plan to stay two nights or longer, ask about package plans, such as the mother-daughter week available June–Sept. A discount is available for repeat visitors.

Palm-Aire Spa Resort & Country Club
2501 Palm-Aire Dr. North, Pompano Beach, FL 33069
Tel. 305/972–3300 or 800/272–5624
Fax 305/968–2744

Administration Hotel director, Marc Mastrangelo; spa director, Kathy Eggleston

Season Year-round.

Accommodations 166 spacious rooms and 18 golf villas. All with separate dressing rooms and some with two baths. Private terraces, about half overlooking golf course. King-size beds and sofas, remote-control TV, built-in wet bar.

Rates Premier Spa Package nightly rate includes meals and spa services. Seasonal prices $378.63–$480.20 single, $325.78–$384.98 per person double. Taxes, gratuities included. Two-night minimum. Ultimate Day (no room) $156 plus tax and gratuity. Golf and tennis packages available. Deposit: one night's advance payment by credit card. Credit cards: AE, DC, MC, V.

Meal Plans 3 meals daily in Spa Dining Room. Breakfast can include poached egg on wheat bread or cottage cheese and a bran muffin. Lunch choices include spinach-mushroom salad followed by baked potato stuffed with cottage and Jarlsberg cheeses or Spanish omelet made with egg whites. Broiled or poached snapper, chicken cacciatore, and vegetable lasagna for dinner. Whipped-mousse dessert or fresh fruit, decaffeinated or regular coffee, herbal tea. The Peninsula Room serves gourmet fare à la carte.

Services and Facilities **Exercise Equipment:** 2 Trotter treadmills, 4 Precor treadmills, 2 StepMasters, 2 Liferowers, 4 Lifecycles, 2 StairMasters, Heartmate bike, 2 Bodyguard ergometer bikes, 3 Schwinn Air-Dyne bikes, 2 recumbent bikes; 16-unit Bodymaster strength conditioning system; complete Olympic free-weight gym, barbells (1–100 lbs.). **Services:** Body massage (Swedish, Trager, deep muscle), thalassotherapy, Sarvar mineral bath, full-body fango mudpack, facial treatments, loofah body scrub, herbal wrap, body composition analysis. Separate men's and women's salons for hair, nail, and skin care. Golf and tennis clinics, personal conditioning. **Swimming Facilities:** 2 outdoor pools; separate men's and women's fitness pools. **Recreation Facilities:** 37 tennis courts, 3 18-hole golf courses, 2 racquetball courts, indoor squash court. **Evening Programs:** Lectures on behavior modification, stress management, nutrition, other health-related topics.

In the Area The Everglades, Fort Lauderdale Museum of the Arts, performing arts center, Parker Playhouse; one-day Bahamas cruise; Pompano Harness Track, Dania Fronton (jai alai), dog and Thoroughbred racing; deep-sea fishing charters, canal cruises; Yankee Stadium (spring training games).

Getting Here *From Miami.* By bus, vans depart from Miami International Airport (60–80 min). By car, I-95 north to Exit 34, Atlantic Blvd., 27th Ave. to second entrance road (45 min). Limousine service (fixed fee) available to and from Fort Lauderdale International Airport and Miami. Rental car, taxi available. Valet service at hotel.

Special Notes Spa facilities on ground level, elevators. No smoking in the spa, the spa dining room, and the lounge.

PGA National Resort & Spa

Luxury pampering
Sports conditioning

Florida
Palm Beach
Gardens

The golf and tennis champions exercise here during tournaments, but the glamour of the new Spa at the PGA National Resort can be enjoyed as a sybaritic getaway combined with sports conditioning year-round. With five golf courses, five croquet courts, a 26-acre sailing lake, biking and jogging trails, and the Health and Racquet Club, the addition of the spa building and a clinic devoted to correcting anatomical dysfunction provides a comprehensive health and fitness program.

The instructors recommend a varied workout program to develop specific muscle groups and cardiovascular strength. Skiers might train on a cross-country exercise machine, a stair-climbing machine, and alternate 20-minute sessions on Nautilus equipment. For the tennis player, there's the treadmill, selected Nautilus units, and tennis aerobics, taught by a tennis pro. Pete Egoscue and his clinic staff address back and posture problems.

The European philosophy of cleansing the body of impurities and toxins is carried through at the new spa building. Hydrotherapy treatments, thalassotherapy, and body masks with natural plants and sea extracts are offered à la carte or in spa packages. The facility is connected to the main resort building and has a private outdoor pool complex, called "Waters of the World," where imported salts and mineral crystals are added to two of the pools. You can experience a soak in the Dead Sea and the French Pyrenees, a hot tub, cold plunge, or just swim.

Even the golf pros are taking to croquet. Since the United States Croquet Association made this their national headquarters in 1987, the game has moved from the backyard to the mainstream. In addition to five tournament-size courts, there is an instruction area where beginners learn the basics of golf croquet. This recreational hybrid can be played by a couple or singles who want a mental workout with mallet and wicket. It looks easy but requires coordination and strategy. Don't forget to bring your whites; all-white dress is required.

Golf, however, is the principal recreation here. The home of the Professional Golfers' Association of America, the five courses challenge any style player, professional or Sunday duffer. Getting in shape for the ultimate golfing experience, a round on the General (a course designed by Arnold Palmer), could be the goal of a fitness regime devised by a team of golf pros and fitness instructors.

There is a specific circuit of Nautilus equipment to help golfers loosen up muscles and gain strength and flexibility. Twenty minutes to an hour on the treadmill will increase cardiovascular endurance. If you're really out of shape, there are daily clinics, private lessons, and three-day golf schools. Or you can go into the advanced PGA National Golf Academy as part of a four-day resort package.

The nutritional needs of a sports regimen are the specialty of resident R. D. Cheryl Hartsough. All restaurants at the resort offer heart-healthy options.

All of these activities are priced separately, with packages offered for golf, tennis, and croquet. There's a $10 daily charge for using the Nautilus equipment and swimming laps at the health club; $12 for scheduled aerobics classes. The full-service spa salon is open to the public.

PGA National Resort & Spa
400 Ave. of the Champions, Palm Beach Gardens, FL 33418
Tel. 407/627–2000 or 800/633–9150
Fax 407/622–0261

Administration Managing director, John Korpi; spa director, Karen Antenucci; fitness director, Sandra Denton

Season Year-round.

Accommodations 335 spacious guest rooms, including 57 suites with tile floors, Mediterranean Revival fabrics and furniture, and 85 cottage units along golf course, each with 2 bedrooms, 2 baths, and kitchen. All rooms with balcony or terrace, private bath, coffeemaker, and walk-in closet.

Rates Daily: $95–$285 for 2, double occupancy. Spa packages of 2 days $500–$828 single, $435–$633 per person double occupancy; 4-day Spa Spectacular $924–$1,516 single, $806–$1,146 per person double; suites $545–$1,038 for 2-day package, $988–$1,896 for 4 days, per person. Full-day spa package with spa cuisine lunch (no lodging) $165–$190. Add 18% service charge, taxes. 1 night advance payment. Credit cards: AE, DC, MC, V.

Meal Plans 3 low-fat spa cuisine meals daily in 2- to 4-day packages. At the Citrus Tree restaurant, menu selections include Florida red snapper grilled over mesquite wood, Cajun blackened beef, grilled chicken. Lunch options are pizza with chicken sausage and fresh tomato marinara, salad with grilled yellow fin tuna, or mixed seafood with Asian noodles and stirfry vegetables. Desserts are Indian River citrus terrine or fresh sorbet. At the health club, salads and "smoothie" fruit drinks available all day.

Services and Facilities **Exercise Equipment:** 2 18-station Nautilus circuits, 5 Trotter treadmills, 4 Lifecycles, 4 StairMasters, 4 Monark stationary bikes, NordicTrack cross-country ski machine, free weights (5–50 lbs.) **Services:** Massage (Swedish, sports, shiatsu, aromatherapy, G-5, reflexology, acupressure, lymphatic, cellulite), algae body wrap, seaweed body polish, aromatherapy wraps, hydrotherapy tubs with sea salts, essential oils, Vichy shower, facials. One-on-one training, The Egoscue

Clinic, wellness lifestyle, stress management, fitness and nutritional assessment, tennis, golf, and croquet instruction. **Swimming Facilities:** Family pool at hotel, health club 5-lane lap pool; outdoor pool and Jacuzzi at the spa. **Recreation Facilities:** 5 golf courses, 19 outdoor tennis courts (12 lighted), 5 indoor racquetball courts, croquet lawn, sailboats, aquacycles, bicycles; walking and jogging trails, horseback riding nearby; fishing in private lake. **Evening Programs:** Disco, resort entertainment; lectures during scheduled golf and tennis programs.

In the Area Palm Beach Worth Avenue shops, Golf Hall of Fame, The Gardens (shopping), Burt Reynolds Dinner Theater, Palm Beach Symphony Orchestra, opera and pops concerts at new performing arts center, Polo Club.

Getting Here *From West Palm Beach.* By car, I-95 to Exit 57, PGA Blvd. west to resort entrance; Florida Turnpike to Exit 44, PGA Blvd. (20 min). Limousine and van service (fixed fee) to and from airport. Taxi, car rental available.

Special Notes Ramps, elevators, and specially equipped rooms provide access for the disabled. Daily baby-sitting, summer day-camp; golf and tennis clinics or private instruction for children. Spa hours daily 8:30 AM–6 PM.

The Pier House Caribbean Spa

Non-program resort facilities

Florida The Caribbean Spa is a special enclave within the popular Pier
Key West House resort. Working out here is both liberating and seductive, mirroring the laissez-faire attitude of Old Town Key West itself. While for most guests the big event of the day is watching the spectacular sunset with beer in hand, you can also indulge in a sybaritic escape.

Decorated in tropical color schemes, the spa building has 22 guest rooms and a boutique spa on the ground floor, where a professional trainer or esthetician will develop your personalized program. Facilities include a coed steam room, sauna, Swiss shower, whirlpool, complete exercise circuit, and salon for hair styling, facials, paraffin, manicures and pedicures.

The beach here is really a small natural cove, to be expanded as the resort grows. Don't be surprised to see nude bathing; local rules are tolerant. Morning exercise classes are held on the beach and in the pool.

A holiday in Key West may bring out the hedonist in you—the Caribbean Spa offers the healthy pleasures.

The Pier House Caribbean Spa
1 Duval Street, Key West, FL 33040
Tel. 305/296–4600 or 800/327–8340 (800/432–3414 in FL)
Fax 305/296–4600

Administration General manager, Don DeFeo; spa director, Betsy Jo Cleveland

Season Year-round.

Accommodations 22 spa rooms; corner minisuite with fireplace, some have Habitat bath with steam/sauna, or bath with marble-topped double vanity, whirlpool tub. White wicker furnishings, sitting area, king-size bed, ceiling fans, French doors opening into a private patio or balcony. Amenities include color TV with VCR, CD players, AM/FM radio, air-conditioning, telephones. The main buildings have 123 guest rooms, including 13 suites.

Rates 4-day/3-night Island Escape package $1,450 for 2 double occupancy, $1,030 single; 3-day/2-night Island Unwinder $580–$890 per couple; 4-day/3-night Stress Breaker Plus $580–$950 per couple. Full-day package with lunch (no lodging) $149, half-day $100. Other rooms from $165–$225 single or double, suites $295–$675. Tax and service charge included. Daily facility charge for resort guests $10. Advance payment for 1 night (longer during holidays). Credit cards: AE, DC, MC, V.

Meal Plans 3 spa cuisine meals daily included in residential package. Breakfast can be tropical fruit with yogurt or egg-white omelet with spinach, onions, and cottage cheese, cereal with skim milk. Lunch choices are grilled seafood; chicken salad; flank steak. Dinner can begin with conch bisque or conch eggroll, salad of field greens in vinaigrette; entrees include Key West shrimp with pasilla chili barbecue sauce, sautéed yellowtail with Key lime sauce, papaya, and avocado; dessert is sliced orange sections and kiwi with passionfruit sorbet.

Services and Facilities **Exercise Equipment:** 9-unit Keiser weight training gym, 2 StairMasters, 2 Precor treadmills, 2 Lifecycles, "Wave Webb" gloves, dumbbells (5–45 lbs.), bench press. **Services:** Massage (sports, therapeutic, aromatherapy, combination), deep pore cleansing, loofah scrub, facial with Key West aloe; salon for hair styling, waxing, manicure, pedicure. One-on-one training. **Swimming Facilities:** 2 outdoor pools, salt-water beach.

In the Area Audubon House and studio, Sloppy Joe's, Hemingway house, Conch Train tour of historic district, Sunken Treasure Museum, Harry Truman Little White House Museum.

Getting Here *From Miami.* By bus, Greyhound (3 hr). By car, Hwy. 1 (Overseas Highway) via 7-mile bridge (3 hr). By air, scheduled service on USAir, American Eagle commuter. Rental car, taxi available; bike and moped rental.

Special Notes No smoking in spa.

Pritikin Longevity Center

Nutrition and diet
Weight management

Florida
Miami Beach Dieting at the Pritikin Longevity Center may be the healthiest holiday in Florida. Everyone, from the doctors on staff to the exercise instructors, eats Pritikin-style.

The revolutionary diet introduced by the late Nathan Pritikin in 1974 is the foundation of 13- and 26-day programs designed to treat and control medical problems. The medically supervised live-in program here provides the support many people need in changing their lifestyles.

The regimen demands discipline, so don't expect a fun-in-the-sun holiday. Along with 50 other participants, you work out in the gym or pool and walk on the beach. If you enjoy ocean swimming, it can be part of your exercise plan. The staff doctor decides what's best.

Exercise, nutrition, stress management, health education, and medical services are the core curriculum. The 13-day program is recommended for sufferers of heart disease, insulin-dependent diabetes, obesity, or uncontrolled high blood pressure. The full course offers individual attention, counseling, and close supervision.

Healthy people come to learn how to safeguard their health. The daily schedule includes cooking demonstrations, lectures, and three exercise sessions. A full physical examination is a major feature of the program and includes a treadmill stress test and complete blood chemistry analysis. Depending on your personal history and fitness level, you are assigned to a specialist in cardiology or internal medicine who monitors your progress on the prescribed diet and exercise program.

Eating the Pritikin meals encourages a taste for food without added fats, salt, or sugar. Caffeine is not permitted. Meals are mostly vegetarian, with lots of fresh fruit and whole grains, and fish is served several times a week. Some nutritionists and doctors consider the diet unnecessarily austere, but the results are proof that the concept works.

The beachfront resort is a bonus. There are plenty of diversions for a nonparticipating spouse or companion.

Pritikin Longevity Center
5875 Collins Ave., Miami Beach, FL 33140
Tel. 305/866-2237 or 800/327-4914 (Flamingo Hotel,
305/865-8645)
Fax 305/866-1872

Administration Executive director, Joan Mikus

Season Year-round, scheduled dates.

Accommodations 100 rooms in beachfront hotel, some facing traffic on Collins Ave., others with an ocean view on penthouse floor, and suites. Smaller rooms included in program with single or double beds, private baths, and comfortable furniture. All with air-conditioning, color TV, telephone, maid service.

Rates 13-day program $5,673 single, $2,587 spouse or companion; 26-day program $9,891 single, $4,445 spouse or companion. More for larger rooms. $500 advance payment for 13-day program, $1,000 for 26-day. Credit cards: MC, V (for deposit only). Discount for repeat visitors.

Meal Plans 3 meals plus 3 snacks daily. Buffet-style breakfast and lunch, table service and menu choices at dinner. Lunch and dinner salad bar. Lunch includes Pritikin vegetarian pizza, eggplant patties with marinara sauce, and rice-tofu *moo goo gai pan;* chicken teriyaki or poached salmon in dill sauce for dinner.

Services and Facilities **Exercise Equipment:** 23 Trotter treadmills, 8 Schwinn Air-Dyne bikes, 2 rowing machines, StairMaster, bench press, hand weights. **Services:** Private counseling on nutrition and health, complete medical and physical examination, including blood tests. Massage, acupressure appointments by request. **Swimming Facilities:** Olympic-size outdoor pool for aerobics; direct access to beach. **Recreation Facilities:** Nearby tennis courts and golf course, boardwalk. **Evening Programs:** Nightly entertainment by local talent; exercises.

In the Area Group trips to shows and jai alai games; Miami museums and sightseeing, deep-sea fishing.

Getting Here *From Miami.* By car, I-95 to Rte. 195, Julia Tuttle Causeway to Collins Avenue (15 min). Public bus, airport shuttle service, taxi, rental car available. Private parking on site.

Special Notes Ramps and elevators provide access for the disabled. No smoking on the premises. Spa hours: daily 6:30 AM–10:30 PM.

Russell House

Holistic health
Weight management

Florida
Key West The juice fasts and 550-calorie diet here have been known to knock off 10 pounds in a week, but most of the guests come for casual relaxation and the laid-back, colorful scene. Located in the historic area where Ernest Hemingway once lived and Harry Truman vacationed, the Russell House is a hideaway at prices well below luxury resorts. The program, like the town, is refreshingly informal.

Consult with staff members on fitness, nutrition, and dieting to set your goals. Activities are divided between active exercise like aerobics in the swimming pool, yoga, and bodywork, including reflexology, acupressure, and herbal wraps. Personal services are à la carte. Don't expect high-tech exercise equipment or spacious rooms at this shocking pink retreat: the concentration here is definitely on shedding pounds.

The low-key atmosphere helps put you in the mood for stress-management workshops and lectures on healthier living. Lifestyle changes are discussed in group sessions on behavior modification, disease prevention, and negative habits. Private counseling and fasting supervised by a staff dietitian help guests lose weight, stop smoking, and change compulsive eating habits.

Russell House
611 Truman Ave., Key West, FL 33040
Tel. 305/294–8787, or 800/851–4111, Fax 305/296–7354

Administration Owner/executive director, James Fischer

Season Year-round.

Accommodations 24 guest rooms for 1–4 persons, with bath, air-conditioning, TV, telephone. Simple, small motel rooms in one-story court with swimming pool. Open-air exercise platform under a banyan tree. One bedroom in tree house.

Rates 1-week program with meals, spa treatments, and accommodations $750–$1,635. Tipping not permitted. $200 advance payment. Credit cards: AE, MC, V.

Meal Plans 3 low-cal vegetarian meals daily. Organic fruit, nuts, seeds, and whole grains. Special diets for hypoglycemia, diabetes, arthritis, and high blood pressure. No salt, sugar, or cholesterol. 550–1,200 calories advised for dieters. Dinner includes a vegetable stirfry or brown-noodle spaghetti; lunch features green salad. Separate facility for juice fast.

Services and Facilities	**Services:** 5 daily exercise classes, body wraps, massage, facials, program to stop smoking, acupuncture, astrology, chiropractice. **Swimming Facilities:** Outdoor pool; beach nearby. **Spa Facilities:** Garden-level sauna and sunken Roman whirlpool. **Recreation Facilities:** Beach, tennis, and golf nearby. Bicycles, snorkeling, and fishing gear can be rented. **Evening Programs:** Informal discussion groups.
In the Area	Local sightseeing by open-air trolley; fishing trips available; Mallory Sq. sunset ceremony in Old Town, Duvall St. boutiques and art galleries, house tours during "Old Island Days" (Feb.–Mar.), Hemingway and Audubon house tours, the Wreckers Museum (maritime history) and Mel Fisher's Sea Salvors exhibit (Spanish treasure), Cuban cultural center and restaurants, Harry Truman Little White House Museum.
Getting Here	*From Miami.* By bus, Greyhound has scheduled daily service (5 hr). By plane, USAir, American Eagle commuter (40 min). By car, Florida Turnpike to Hwy. 1, 7-mile ocean causeway to southern terminus (3½ hr). Taxi, rental car available. Off-street parking.
Special Notes	No smoking.

Saddlebrook Sports Science

Sports conditioning

Florida
Wesley Chapel
(Tampa Bay)

An active, sports-oriented vacation comes in a variety of packages at Saddlebrook. The United States Professional Tennis Association calls this home, as does Harry Hopman Tennis.

The newly emerging field of sports biomechanics underlies Saddlebrook's programs. Directed by sports trainer Dr. Jack Groppel and psychologist Dr. James Loehr, a corrective regimen is designed for business executives interested in improving productivity and athletes seeking peak performance. Both groups learn to handle stress more efficiently while maintaining high levels of energy.

Program flexibility allows you to spend part of the day on the courts or golf course and part of it in consultation with fitness and nutrition specialists. Six services are available, including a psychological profile of how you handle stress in the office or in competitive sports. Based on these assessments, along with your interests and goals, a personal exercise program is designed for you.

Weight loss isn't a top priority here, but the restaurants do have low-calorie items on the menu. A computerized evaluation of your daily food consumption compares your nutritional intake to your recommended dietary allowance. The appraisal takes into account age, sex, weight, and amount of exercise.

Rolling greens and tree-lined fairways surround a traffic-free "walking village" where everything is conveniently located. The centerpiece is a 270-foot Superpool, big enough for racing, water aerobics, or volleyball. The Jockey Club fitness center nearby has ultramodern saunas, whirlpools, steam rooms in separate facilities for men and women, massage rooms, and a fully equipped exercise room.

Families feel comfortable in this community, where there are sports activities for young people as well as competitive-minded parents. Even the convention groups that meet here take time off for sports workshops and a mini-Olympics.

Saddlebrook Sports Science
5700 Saddlebrook Way, Wesley Chapel, FL 33543
Tel. 813/973–1111 or 800/729–8383

Administration Co-directors, Dr. Jack Groppel, Ed.D., and Dr. James Loehr, Ph.D.; General manager, Richard Boehning

Season Year-round.

Accommodations 700 guest rooms in 10 resort clusters, from spacious rooms with large baths to 1- and 2-bedroom suites with fully equipped kitchens. All units have cable TV, modern furniture, queen- and king-size beds, balcony or patio.

Rates Deluxe room, single or double, $145 Jan. 15–Apr. 30, $70 in summer. Suites $145–$270, $85–$120 in summer. 4- and 7-day golf and tennis packages available. 1 night advance payment for short visits, 25% for longer. Sports science program priced separately. Credit cards: AE, DC, MC, V.

Meal Plans Meals not included in packages. The Cypress Room open for Friday night seafood buffet and Sunday brunch. The Little Club features American cuisine. Low-calorie options by special request.

Services and Facilities **Exercise Equipment:** 12-station Nautilus circuit, computerized Biocycle, Monark stationary bike, StairMaster, free weights (2–50 lbs.) and curl bar. **Services:** Swedish massage, facial, manicure. Computerized fitness analysis, health-risk apprais-al, nutrition profile, stress management index, competitive sports profile. Tennis and golf clinics, including videotaped swing analysis. **Swimming Facilities:** 3 outdoor pools. **Recrea-tion Facilities:** 37 tennis courts (hard and clay, some with lights), 2 18-hole golf courses designed by Arnold Palmer. Also fishing (equipment provided), 2-mile jogging trail.

In the Area Busch Gardens (family-oriented theme park and wildlife pre-serve), Sea World (performing whales and dolphins), Disney World, Cypress Gardens, Ybor City (Tampa's Cuban quarter).

Getting Here *From Tampa.* By car, Rte. 275 to I-75, Hwy. 54 (40 min). Lim-ousine, rental car, taxi available.

Special Notes Ground-floor accommodations for the disabled, ramps to fitness center. Programs for children 6–12: tennis and golf instruc-tion, special camps, supervised activities during holidays. No smoking in fitness center and designated dining areas.

Safety Harbor Spa and Fitness Center

Life enhancement
Weight management
Luxury pampering
Taking the waters

Florida
Safety Harbor
(Tampa Bay)
Walking along Bayshore Drive in the morning, swimming laps under swaying palms, and soaking in mineral spring water are among the pleasures of a vacation at Safety Harbor. After a major face-lift in 1992, the Spa & Fitness Center emerged with

new owners, new dining room, conference theater, state-of-the-art exercise equipment, and a Lancôme salon for skin care.

A fountain of youth this is not. Hernando de Soto, the Spanish explorer, supposedly bathed here in 1539 and named the five springs *Espiritu Santu* for their curative powers. Modern chemical analysis shows that each spring has a different proportion of calcium, magnesium, sodium, potassium, and other minerals. Now you can request bottles of mineral water for drinking and a mineral-water bath. The spring water also fills two coed Jacuzzis at a chlorinated indoor pool.

Aquatics is a strong feature of the health-oriented program. Private hydrotherapy tubs in the men's and women's bathhouses are enhanced with blends of herbs and marine algae for stress reduction, relief of muscular tension, and toning treatments. Exercising in the specially designed shallow indoor and outdoor pools burns calories efficiently without straining the body. Specially designed aquatic exercise equipment adds to the resistance against your body as you move in the water, increasing the toning and calorie-burning benefits of the workout. The instructors here specialize in a variety of routines, from gentle to active, to keep you from getting bored. Coed classes attract people of all ages and are specially suited to exercise beginners.

An emphasis on total wellness has come with the new health and fitness orientation. Guests are encouraged to learn health habits and follow a low-fat diet that can be incorporated into their routines at home. The Safety Harbor experience is a good turning point for people who are not fit and need to make changes, though fitness enthusiasts return regularly as well for the sports training programs, including sports triathlon, movement and relaxation, racquetsport conditioning, aerobics circuit training, and bench stepping. The certified instructors accommodate all levels, beginner to advanced, and will outline a personal plan that can be followed at home.

Staff doctors treat cardiovascular and other special problems. A member of the fitness staff will check your overall physical condition, monitor your aerobic heart rate, and analyze your body-fat to muscle ratio. Based on a computer analysis, a specific combination of exercise and diet will be recommended.

Bodywork appointments are made through a guest coordinator, and charged on an à la carte basis. Both men's and women's locker rooms have sauna, steam room, and direct access to the exercise pool, but it's a good idea to bring footwear, even aquatic socks for water aerobics.

There's a view of Tampa Bay from the two well-equipped weights rooms and three aerobics gyms. Exercise instructors promote low-impact routines, and the shock-absorbing floors are specially constructed to help avoid tendonitis and shin splints. However, the workouts are peppy, and the sports training routine is for advanced fitness buffs only.

Both regular and calorie-controlled menus are served in the dining room. Don't be surprised to see a celebrity or two. Performers at nearby Ruth Eckerd Hall often stay here for the workouts and diet meals, and the exercise room is used by professional athletes.

Safety Harbor Spa and Fitness Center
105 N. Bayshore Dr., Safety Harbor, FL 34695
Tel. 813/726–1161 or 800/237–0155

Administration Owner/director, Roger Kumar; spa director, Bina Kumar; medical director, Richard Gubner, M.D.

Season Year-round.

Accommodations 210 bedrooms and suites; 30 full-service apartments in annex across the street. Newer large deluxe units in the towers with balcony or terrace, 2 queen-size beds, dressing room, oversize bath. All air-conditioned, with TV, telephone, robes.

Rates Daily with 3 meals, $215–$298 single, $161–$222 per person double. 3-day/2-night weekend package $424–$576, $337–$471 double; 8-day total fitness plan $1,922–$2,570 single, $1,572–$2,110 per person double. Add 17% service charge, 10% taxes. Spa Day and tennis plan available. Deposit: 1 night advance payment. Credit cards: AE, DC, MC, V.

Meal Plans 3 meals daily in formal dining room. Fitness plan breakfast includes fresh-baked pumpkin muffins, whole-wheat pancakes with raspberry puree, and egg-white omelet with farmer cheese. Lunch includes vegetable chili with white or brown rice, vegetable lasagna, pizza with whole-wheat crust, and breast of chicken with herbed ricotta cheese. Special dinner salads, such as romaine lettuce with Parmesan dressing, then broiled lobster, crab Mornay, shrimp with linguini. Coffee and herbal tea. Suggested daily 900–1,100 calorie menu provides 50% complex carbohydrates, 25% from protein, 20% fat.

Services and Facilities **Exercise Equipment:** Paramount sports trainer system with adductor, abductor, abdominal pullover, pull-down, butterfly back press, lateral raise, leg-kick pulley, bicep/tricep machine. Nautilus hip/back, leg curl, lower back, and abdominal machines. 12 Precor treadmills, 3 StairMasters, LifeStep, Lifecycle, 2 Windracers, 2 Heartmate TV bikes, 2 Schwinn Air-Dyne bikes, Versaclimber, 2 Concept II rowing machines, upper body ergometer, 4 trampolines, Hydra Fitness Total Power machine, Roman Chair abdominal unit. Free weights (1¼–45 lbs.) and dumbbells (3–40 lbs.) with bench press, incline bench, Uniflex unit. 2 speed bags for boxers. **Services:** Medical consultation, fitness evaluation, massage, herbal wraps, salt-glow loofah body scrub. Lancôme Skin Care Institute offers facials, haircuts and styling, makeup consultation, manicure, pedicure. Tennis instruction. **Swimming Facilities:** outdoor and indoor pools. Mineral spring water in all swimming pools and Jacuzzis. **Recreation Facilities:** 7 Har Tru tennis courts, 2 hard courts, putting green, free use of bikes, basketball, water volleyball. Golf and horseback riding nearby for a fee. **Evening Programs:** Lectures on stress management and health-related topics, cooking demonstrations, cultural programs, lounge dancing on weekends.

In the Area Organized outings for beach, biking, fishing (fee). Evening trips to performing arts centers in Tampa and Clearwater, shopping centers, movies; Ybor City (Tampa's colorful Cuban quarter), one-day Bahamas cruise, Busch Gardens (family theme park and wildlife preserve), history museums, Tarpon Springs sponge harvest and sales center, Walt Disney World.

Getting Here *From Tampa.* By bus, scheduled van service from Tampa International Airport. By car, I-275 south to Exit 20, Rte. 60 toward Clearwater, exit on Bayshore Blvd. (20 min). Hotel van to the airport. Taxi, rental car available.

Special Notes Elevators but no specially equipped rooms for the disabled. No smoking in the spa and in designated dining areas. Arrival can be any day; no group program.

Sanibel Harbour Resort & Spa

Luxury pampering
Sports conditioning

Florida Located on 80 wooded acres overlooking island-studded San
Fort Myers Carlos Bay, the resort is memorable for its easy access to Sanibel and Captiva islands and its top-quality tennis courts and fitness facilities. A private beach, marina, and bayfront swimming pool add to recreation options.

Staffed by qualified trainers, the spa's total-body workout room features 20 Keiser pneumatic weight pressure units, 12 free weight stations, and TV viewing while you exercise. More than 40 aerobics classes a week are taught at variable impact levels in a plush studio with carpeted floor. The spa's indoor lap pool is used for an energizing aquafit class. For more active pursuits, four air-conditioned racquetball courts can be booked by the hour. The Racquet Club offers day-long tennis workouts.

A surprising range of body treatments comes with your spa day package: Swiss showers, aromatherapy, salt glow body scrub, herbal and seaweed wraps, and a salon for hair, nail, and skin care. Both men's and women's sections have sauna, steamroom, 5 whirlpools, and hot and cold plunge pools. For a sonic massage, relax on the BETAR bed, a combination of stress-releasing musical energy impulses. A "Sensation" afternoon has sauna, Swiss shower, body buff, mud masque, and reflexology massage. Individually tailored fitness packages can begin any day, as there is no group program. You can also pay the daily facility fee ($10) and use services à la carte.

Sanibel Harbour Resort & Spa
17260 Harbour Pointe Dr., Ft. Meyers, FL 33908
Tel. 813/466–2166
Fax 813/466–2150

Administration Managing director, Bob Moceri; spa director, Susan Brewer

Season Year-round.

Accommodations 240-room hotel in resort complex with 100 2-bedroom luxury condominium apartments facing San Carlos Bay. Hotel rooms offer private balcony, king- or queen-size beds, cable TV, Florida furniture, bath with robes, hair dryer; air-conditioning, telephone, nightly turn-down service. Condominiums in 2 12-story towers have bath with each bedroom, full kitchen, washer/dryer, dining room. Suites available in hotel.

Rates $105–$300 daily per room for 2 persons, suites $225–$840; condominium for 4 persons $130–$495. 6-day/5-night Fitness Retreat package without meals $1,152–$1,777 single in hotel, $1,327–$2,027 single in condo; $915–$1,227 per person double in hotel, $1,002–$1,352 per person in condo. 3-day/2-night Spa Sampler $469–$719 single in hotel, $579–$819 single in condo; $374–$499 per person double in hotel, $429–$549 double in condo. Spa gratuities included in packages, room tax added. Meal plan $61 per person daily (breakfast, lunch, dinner) includes taxes and gratuities. Deposit: 1 night advance payment by credit card. Credit cards: AE, DC, MC, V. Day package (without lodging) $170–$235 includes gratuity.

Meal Plans Breakfast can be buckwheat pancakes or yogurt with fresh fruit, coffee or herbal tea. Light gourmet specials at lunch include chicken terrine appetizer or marinated tuna and grouper carpaccio with baby mixed greens. Entrees are chilled Floridian grouper with lightly spiced papaya coulis, whole-wheat pizza with goat cheese, grilled lamb chop, steamed chicken breast stuffed with mushrooms. "Cuisine of the Sun" nightly special menu uses all natural ingredients might start with lasagna made of blue and yellow corn chips, mozzarella, and peppers; entree can be grilled chicken or steamed salmon; dessert is house-made watermelon sorbet with vanilla sauce.

Services and Facilities **Exercise Equipment:** 18-unit Keiser circuit, 7-station Paramount weights gym, dip station, Icarian 7 station, Smith machine, tricep bar, Preacher curl, 4 Schwinn Air-Dyne bikes, 4 Trackmaster treadmills, 3 Heart Mate computerized bikes, 2 PTS Turbo recumbent bikes, 3 Lifecycles, Liferower, 2 StairMasters. **Services:** Massage (Swedish, reflexology, sports, aromatherapy), loofah salt glow body scrub, herbal or seaweed wrap, facial with paraffin, mud masque, apricot scrub, salon for hair, nail, skin care. Fitness evaluation, nutritional counseling, personal training, tennis instruction. **Swimming Facilities:** Indoor lap pool, outdoor resort pool, bay beach. **Recreation Facilities:** 12 lighted tennis courts (8 clay, 4 Spin-flex), center court stadium, fitness trail, 4 racquetball courts at spa, marina for sailing and fishing charters; golf, horseback riding nearby. Fishing pier. Water sports, canoe rental.

In the Area Everglades National Park (sightseeing boat, overnight canoe trip from Everglades City), Corkscrew Swamp Sanctuary (Audobon Society boardwalk tour) J. N. Ding Darling Wildlife Refuge (naturalist tour), baseball spring training camps, Thomas Alva Edison winter home and laboratory, Henry Ford estate, Burroughs Home (19th-century Georgian Revival mansion), Bonita Springs Dog Track, Seminole Gulf Railway, Sanibel Island, Captiva Island (shelling).

Getting Here *From Fort Meyers or Southwest Florida Regional Airport.* By car, I–75 to Daniels Rd, left at Six Mile Cypress, which becomes Gladiolus Rd., left on Summerlin Rd. to Sanibel Island causeway entrance, right on Harbour Pointe Dr. (20 min). Airport shuttle service on request ($13 per person). Taxi, limousine, and rental car available.

Special Notes Supervised children's program (ages 5–12) daily. No smoking in spa. Spa hours: Mon.–Sat. 7 AM–9 PM, Sun. and holidays 9 AM–5 PM.

Sports/Spa & Clinic at Sandestin

Life enhancement
Sports conditioning
Luxury pampering
Kid fitness

Florida Located on the Gulf of Mexico in Florida's Panhandle, the
Sandestin 2,600-acre Sandestin resort features 45 holes of championship
golf, 14 tennis courts, and water sports along with the spa facility and health center. A health evaluation and assessment at
the Sandestin clinic is based on information about your lifestyle, and a computerized report dictates the steps needed to
improve your exercise and eating habits.

The self-contained health center schedules aerobics classes in a
cushion-floored studio and in the pool, and features a full line of
cardiovascular and weight equipment indoors along with a multipurpose outdoor gym. A water walk on the bay adds water
resistance to your workout (aquatic exercise equipment
provided). Salon services and a restaurant serving heart-
healthy cuisine are included in spa packages.

Participation in spa programs is limited to 20 guests. Resort
vacationers can book classes or clinic services à la carte, daily
or weekly.

The broader concept for seminars at the clinic includes such
topics as cosmetic surgery, lifestyle, and therapy to help you
prepare for surgery as well as postoperative programs to shape
and strengthen the body. The clinic plans to invite leading
health professionals to participate in these seminars. Medical
specialists are available for consultation at the clinic.

Sport-specific training with spa staffers is based on a videotaped analysis of your performance. The Sports Science Laboratory programs professional and amateur athletes as well as
children. The extensive sports facilities at the Sandestin resort
are available to participants in the spa programs.

Located halfway between Pensacola and Panama City, the self-
contained resort is washed on one side by Choctawhatchee
Bay, on the other by the warm Gulf of Mexico, but escapes the
"Redneck Riviera" atmosphere of the Florida Panhandle.

Sports/Spa & Clinic at Sandestin
5500 Highway 98 East, Emerald Coast Parkway,
Destin, FL 32541
Tel. 904/654–5545 or 800/334–6545

Administration Co-directors, Stephanie and Mike Morris

Season Year-round.

Rates 3- to 7-day Fun & Fitness program $595–$1,075, Relax Pak
$575–$1,045, Deluxe Spa package $795–$1,275, 14-day Weight
Management program $2,350. All packages include 3 meals dai-
ly with spa-cuisine options.

Accommodations Lodging not included in spa programs. Options include the
Sandestin Inn ($70–$100 per person double) and the beachfront
Hilton Hotel ($59–$155). Also available are luxury villas and
co-ops. All air-conditioned, with TV and telephone.

Services and **Exercise Equipment:** Nautilus national training center with 25
Facilities units of "Next Generation" weight training equipment, 4
StairMasters, 2 Windracers, 2 Schwinn Air-Dyne bikes, 2
Monark bikes, 4 treadmills, 30 Reebok step aerobics units. **Services:** Swedish and sports massage, aromatherapy, seaweed
bath, facial; salon for hair, nail, and skin care, makeovers; cosmetic surgery postoperative therapy; fitness evaluation, cholesterol screening, nutrition and motivational counseling;

complete physicals, including stress test. **Swimming Facilities:** Outdoor swimming pools, Gulf beach. **Recreation Facilities:** 45 holes of championship golf, 14 tennis courts including grass, Rubico, and hard surfaces, water skiing, snorkeling, sailing, deep-sea fishing; marina with pleasure craft. **Evening Programs:** Seminars on health, lifestyle.

In the Area Big Kahuna Water Park, Eglin Air Force Base (National Armament Museum), Fort Walton Beach, Seaside (New England architecture).

Getting Here *From Pensacola.* By car, Hwy. 98 east (75 min). Rental car available.

Special Notes Specially equipped rooms for the disabled. Children's sports clinic. No smoking in spa. Shape Fitness Week in November.

Turnberry Isle Resort and Country Club

Luxury pampering

Florida
Turnberry Isle
(North Miami)
Here's a luxury hideaway for the executive who wants to shape up in privacy. Boasting spacious accommodations on the Intracoastal Waterway, Turnberry Isle accepts spa guests to share the members' privileges. This well-kept secret maintains a very private club atmosphere.

Clothing for exercise and swimming is supplied daily at the spa reception desk and locker rooms. Bring just leotards and tights. Staff members greet guests by name and quickly make newcomers feel at home.

For a break in the routine, try the beach. There are cabanas, a swimming pool, and light fare for lunch at the private Ocean Club. Relax in a Turkish steam bath and Swedish sauna, or get one-on-one cardiovascular training in the weights room, complete with large-screen TV. The entire array of equipment is top-of-the-line.

Rarely crowded, the club has hydrotherapy, indoor and outdoor whirlpools, and medical consultation. Scheduled aerobics classes in the sprung-wood floor studio are attended by club members, and attract some of the area's best instructors. Yoga also is popular as an afternoon unwinder. And there are a full service salon and cafe poolside.

Turnberry Isle Resort and Country Club
19735 Turnberry Way,
Aventura, North Miami, FL 33180
Tel. 305/932–6200 or 800/223–1588, 800/531–6767 in
Canada, Fax 305/933–3811

Administration General manager, Jon van Ordstrand; spa director, Frederick Benke

Season Year-round.

Rates 2-night mini-spa plan $369–$579 single, $249–$359 per person double occupancy, including taxes and service charges but no meals. 4-night Spa Indulgence plan $1,249–$1,669 single, $909–$1,119 double, 7-night Fitness Plan, $1,949–$2,689 single, $1,249–$1,799 double. One night's advance payment with credit card. Credit cards: AE, DC, MC, V.

Accommodations 271 deluxe rooms in Mediterranean-style country club and hotel complex, all air-conditioned, with king-size beds, marble
bath with hair dryer, whirlpool tub, 3 phones (2 lines), cable TV
with VCR. Also 60 spacious rooms in 5-story Yacht Club hotel
adjoining spa; 27 one- and 2-bedroom villas.

Meal Plans All meals served à la carte. High-carbohydrate luncheon includes grilled swordfish, pasta primavera, and cold shrimp
plate. Typical dinner entrees are steamed lobster tail, tenderloin brochette, eggplant Parmesan, mesquite-grilled redfish
with scallions. Meals in spa café or in the main dining room.

Services and **Exercise Equipment:** 20-unit Nautilus circuit, Plus II Cybex
Facilities units, 2 Liferowers, 5 StairMasters, VersaClimber, 5 Lifecycles, 9 Precor treadmills, Precor 3-D bike, Biocycle, recumbent
bike, 2 Cybex ergometers, 2 Bally Lifesteps, hand weights.
Dumbbells (3–80 lbs). **Services:** Therapeutic massage, Swedish
massage, shiatsu, aromatherapy, reflexology; back cleansing
and heat treatment, Phytomer marine mask, herbal wrap,
loofah body scrub, Swiss shower, Vitabath, skin care. Computerized body-composition analysis, nutrition consultation,
blood cholesterol test, medical consultation. Spa salon for hair,
nail, and skin care. **Swimming Facilities:** 2 pools at spa, Ocean
Club, Country Club. **Recreation Facilities:** 2 championship golf
courses, 24 tennis courts (18 lighted), 2 indoor racquetball
courts, walleyball, basketball, yacht charter.

In the Area Aventura Mall, Thoroughbred races at Gulfstream Park, Dis-
ney World, Miami and Fort Lauderdale museums. Joe Robbie
Stadium (Miami Dolphins), Dania Fronton (Jai Alai), Biscayne
Dog Race Track, baseball.

Getting Here *From Miami.* By car, I–95 to Exit 20, Ives Dairy Rd., U.S.
Rte. 1, Biscayne Blvd. (25 min). By boat, Intracoastal Waterway to Turnberry Isle Marina. Airport shuttle service to Fort
Lauderdale and Miami included in 4- to 7-night plans. Taxi, limousine, rental car available.

Special Notes No smoking in the spa and in designated areas. Spa open daily 7 AM–9 PM. Shuttle bus to beach, mall, country club, and
spa.

Chateau Elan

Luxury pampering
Life enhancement
Stress control

Georgia A new and unique addition to the Atlanta area in 1992, the spa
Braselton at Chateau Elan combines the latest technologies for fitness
and beauty with traditions drawn from European spas. The
chateau is, in fact, a working winery, complete with vineyards
and a reproduction of a 16th-century French manor house.
Follow the woodland trails to a private lake and discover the
elegant retreat where a full-service health and exercise
facility complements beautiful accommodations in 14 guest
rooms.

The professional staff at the spa includes veterans of shuttered
Southwind resort, medical consultants, and specialists in nutrition and smoking-cessation programs. Behavior-modification services also are an option. On arrival you will be offered a

blood lipid screening to check cholesterol/glycerides, and the concierge will make dining reservations in the winery's Le Clos if you're not counting calories.

The spa has its own Cafe Elan and breakfast room where Continental cuisine is served as part of packages for 2–8 days. Meals can also be sampled by day visitors.

A quiet, warm, and friendly atmosphere prevails, encouraging you to discover the best of yourself. Mornings begin with easy stretches, and a short hike is scheduled after breakfast. Nature trails, horseback riding, and golf can be scheduled on your daily program along with aerobics classes and beauty services. Fitness seminars are short consultations with staff members to help set your personal goals.

The completely self-contained spa building has an exercise room staffed by accredited trainers, a beauty salon serving men and women, and private treatment rooms. Also offered are art and sculpture classes, spa cooking demonstrations, and medical consultations ranging from cardiac prevention to imagery and plastic surgery. Special therapy is available for recuperation from illness or surgery and post-holiday recovery.

Having enhanced your image with facial and skin analysis, you may be ready for the weekly shopping excursion to Neiman Marcus or a dinner by candlelight at the winery. Guests here get the royal treatment, southern style.

Chateau Elan
Haven Harbour Drive, Braselton, GA 30517
Tel. 404/867–6200 or 800/233–9463
Fax. 404/867–8714

Administration President, Nancy C. Panoz; fitness manager, Cathy Carroll

Season Year-round.

Accommodations 14 rooms, individually decorated in themes ranging from Oriental to Greek, Western, Art Deco, and Victorian. Antiques and high-tech amenities, queen-size or twin beds, lavish bathroom fixtures. Loft suites feature upper level bedroom with four-poster bed, 2 bathrooms. All air-conditioned, with TV, phone, concierge service.

Rates Daily rate $450–$475 per person, double occupancy, includes lodging, meals, and program. Romantic Getaway (2-night/3-day) $1,000 per couple; golf package with spa services, 2 meals daily (3-night/4-day) $1,424 single, $1,128.50 per person double; luxury week (7-night/8-day) $3,207.90 single, $2,271 double. Day package includes lunch, spa: $175; half-day $100. Add 6% tax, optional gratuities. Deposit $1,000 for a week's stay, $500 for other packages. Credit cards: AE, MC, V.

Meal Plans Basic plan includes 3 spa meals daily, afternoon tea, evening snack. Breakfast specials are blue corn pancakes with fresh homemade quark, yolkless omelet with steamed spinach and mushroom or cheese, salmon gravlax, and cereals, muffins, croissants. Lunch begins with salad or Belgian endive, choice of two soups, entrée choice such as duckling breast, salmon supreme on black noodles, vegetarian goulash. Dinner main course can be petit filet of beef or grilled chicken. Desserts include yogurt fruit ice, fresh fruit, and berry cocktail.

Services and Facilities **Exercise Equipment:** Landice treadmill, 2 Alpine stair-climbers, Preference stationary bike, Bodyguard ergometer, hand weights (complete cardiovascular circuit in Conference Center scheduled to open fall 1993). **Services:** Massage (Swedish, shiatsu, therapeutic, sports, aromatherapy), reflexology, body wrap, salt glow loofah, body gommage, collagen masque, facials, thalassotherapy, paraffin hand and foot moisturizing, mineral bath; salon for hair, nail, and makeup; tanning bed; fitness evaluation, skin analysis, makeup instruction. **Spa Facilities:** Coed sauna, steam bath, whirlpool. **Swimming Facilities:** Outdoor heated pool with resistance jets. **Recreation Facilities:** Bicycles, horseback riding (extra charge), 18-hole golf course (greens fee), 2 tennis courts. **Evening Programs:** concerts.

In the Area Atlanta museums, Buckhead Mall, Atlanta Underground.

Getting Here *From Atlanta.* By car, I–85 north, Exit 48, turn left on Old Winder Hwy. 211 (45 min). Airport shuttle service complimentary on arrival and departure. Limousine, taxi available.

Special Notes Minimum age 16.

The Sea Island Spa at The Cloister

Luxury pampering
Life enhancement

Georgia
Sea Island After 75 years as the grande dame of southern seashore resorts, The Cloister opened its Sea Island Spa at the Beach Club in 1989. Group activity is minimal, because programs are tailored to each guest's fitness level and personal goals. All guests can join a morning beach walk and stretch class. Thalassotherapy by the sea is a major attraction here. Located directly on the pristine Atlantic beach of a private 5-mile-long barrier island, the spa introduced European therapies with seaweed-based products by Repechage. For your body there are seaweed masks and wraps as well as a scrub with salts from the Dead Sea. After an ocean swim, try the honey-and-almond body polish.

In the licensed hands of an esthetician, the facial masque treatment becomes a succession of cleansing and soothing experiences as four layers of aloe, seaweed, and Repechage creams are applied. While your complexion is being detoxified and moisturized to combat the ravages of time and sun, your feet are softened with a paraffin waxing. The final touch may be a reflexology massage, one of 18 different techniques offered by staff therapists.

The aerobics studio and exercise rooms attached to the spa are open to all resort guests for modest daily fees. In the hushed inner suite of treatment rooms you'll find hydrotherapy tubs, wet treatment rooms, 2 Swiss showers, 2 steam rooms, coed sauna, solarium and lounge.

Sports add a special dimension to this seaside escape. The Cloister offers 54 holes of golf at two clubs, plus an acclaimed golf academy with indoor and outdoor training by professionals. In addition to water sports, a tennis club with 18 courts, three skeet ranges, and a biking center with 300 bikes for rent, there are stables with 60 horses, a gun club, and docks for boat rental on the Intracoastal Waterway.

Families as well as mature vacationers make annual pilgrimages, and there are extensive conference facilities. The guest units are in two-story lodges directly behind the sand dunes, where the sound of the sea lulls you to sleep.

The Sea Island Spa at The Cloister
Sea Island, GA 31561
Tel. 916/638–3611 or 800/732–4752

Administration	Managing director, Ted Wright; spa director, Jane Segerberg
Season	Year-round.
Accommodations	264 guest rooms in spacious, modern lodges overlooking the beach and waterway, plus private cottage rental. Choice of twin or king-size bed, patio or balcony. Air-conditioned, with TV, sitting area, walk-in closet, full bathroom, telephone and desk. Original Spanish Mediterranean architecture by Addison Mizner, 1928.
Rates	2-day package $650–$1,018 single, $514–$698 per person double; 5-day $1,740–$2,660 single, $1,400–$1,860 double. Spa Retreat without lodging, $180 full day, $100–$110 half-day. Add 6% tax, 15% service charge, spa gratuities. Deposit $250. No credit cards.
Meal Plans	Full American Plan, 3 meals daily. Limited selection of spa cuisine on menu in main dining room; lunch and breakfast buffet at the Beach Club. Seafood buffet, fresh fish featured daily at beachside restaurant. Formal dinner menu and dancing nightly in main building.
Services and Facilities	**Exercise Equipment:** 12-unit Eagle Cybex weight training circuit, 2 StairMasters, LifeRower, Cycleplus bike, 2 MasterMill treadmills, dynabands. **Services:** Massage including acupressure, deep-muscle therapy, aromatherapy; facial, paraffin hand and foot treatment, herbal or seaweed wrap, body scrub. Fitness evaluation, nutrition consultation, exercise program, personal training and exercise video. **Swimming Facilities:** 2 freshwater pools, ocean beach. **Recreation Facilities:** Horseback trail rides with lunch or evening cookout, 18 tennis courts, 2 golf clubs, skeet range, bike and boat rental.
In the Area	Ft. Frederica (British colonial village, ca. 1740), St. Simons Island (historic church), Jacksonville, FL, Savannah, GA.
Getting Here	*From Jacksonville, FL.* By car, I–95 north, Exit 6, east on Hwy. 17 (45 min). Scheduled van service from Jacksonville Airport ($30). By plane, American Eagle and Delta Express to Brunswick, GA; hotel van on request ($12). Limousine, car rental, taxi available.
Special Notes	Teenage skin care and makeup classes during holidays. Teenage golf clinic. Supervised program for children 3–11 daily and evenings.

Wildwood Lifestyle Center

Life enhancement
Preventive medicine
Vibrant maturity

Georgia	Converts to fitness come here to learn a healthier way of life.
Wildwood	Up to 26 middle-aged professionals and housewives participate

in each session of the Wildwood Lifestyle Program. Medically oriented and devoted to education and exercise, the 24-day program provides a basis for self-help.

Wildwood, a hospital as well as a lifestyle center, has been devoted to preventive medicine for more than 40 years. The doctors, nurses, and staff, all Seventh-day Adventists, see medicine as a means of disease prevention. Their nutritional computer analysis makes specific recommendations for diet and takes into account present physical condition, nutritional requirements, and weight-loss goals. After a complete medical examination a physician—who monitors your progress throughout the three-week program—prescribes a program for you. One-week programs to stop smoking are scheduled at various times during the year. Personal counseling tailored to the health needs of the individual and 10- to 17-day programs are available.

The hospital's live-in accommodations provide privacy and comfort in a secluded valley among the mountains of North Georgia. Each program participant gets a blood chemistry profile, EKG-exercise stress test, lung function evaluation, and chest X-ray. (Health insurance may cover some expenses.) The philosophy is to treat the causes of disease rather than the symptoms. High blood pressure, coronary heart disease, angina, arteriosclerosis, diabetes, stress, constipation, arthritis, and obesity are addressed.

Hydrotherapy and massage may be recommended at extra cost. Hiking twice a day along 35 miles of wooded trails helps guests get in shape. Every afternoon during the week there is a nutrition lecture, followed by cooking classes.

Although it is operated by Adventists, long known for their interest in health and nutrition, Wildwood's program is strictly nondenominational and nonsectarian.

Wildwood Lifestyle Center
Wildwood, GA 30757
Tel. 404/820–1474 or 800/634–9355

Administration	Director, Charles H. Cleveland; Lifestyle Program director, Larry Scott; medical director, Marjorie Baldwin, M.D.
Season	Year-round.
Accommodations	26 mountain lodge bedrooms with twin beds, private patio; some share large bath. Woodland views. Lounge for informal lectures around fireplace, laundry facility.
Rates	24-day program $2,950 semi-private. Private rooms when available. $20 less daily for spouses participating in nonmedical parts of program. Transportation included certain times of year. 7-day stop-smoking program $1,150. $100 per person advance payment, refundable up to 2 weeks before program begins. Credit cards (4% surcharge): MC, V.
Meal Plans	Fruits, vegetables, legumes, and grains. No butter or oil, but nuts, olives and avocados available. 3 daily buffets without dairy products, fish, or meat. Specialties include vegetarian lasagna with melty "cheese" topping of tahini, pimiento, and tomato; oat-burger roll; steamed vegetables with rice; seven-grain bread.

Services and Facilities **Exercise Equipment:** 2 Lifecycles, 2 trampolines, rowing machines. **Services:** Swedish massage, hydrotherapy showers, medical treatment. **Swimming Facilities:** Lake on property. **Spa Facilities:** Sauna and steam room. **Recreation Facilities:** Hiking, boating. **Evening Programs:** Lectures on health-related and spiritual topics.

In the Area Picnics, outings to historical sites and Civil War memorials; Atlanta museums, shopping; Chattanooga museums.

Getting Here *From Atlanta.* By bus, Trailways to Chattanooga (2 hr). By plane, scheduled flights to Chattanooga metropolitan airport. By car, I–24 past Chattanooga, Exit 169 (about 2 hr). Free service to and from Chattanooga airport and bus station. Rental car available.

Special Notes All rooms on ground level; wheelchair patients accepted when accompanied by companion. No smoking indoors. Remember to bring an alarm clock, laundry detergent, umbrella, rain gear.

EuroVita Spa at the Avenue Plaza Hotel

Luxury pampering

Louisiana
New Orleans
Amid Cajun capers and blackened redfish restaurants is an oasis of fitness in New Orleans. The EuroVita Spa is located in a pleasant hotel in the Garden District and is heavily patronized by knowledgeable local fitness buffs and visitors on business. The best deal is a spa plan package for two or four nights.

The fitness facilities spread from a garden patio pool to a mirrored rooftop aerobics studio. An outdoor whirlpool on the sun deck has a view of the city.

Aerobics classes are scheduled daily. Massage, herbal wrap, or loofah body scrub, complete with Swiss shower, are by appointment. Sauna and steam room are available, and robes are provided daily.

The extensive array of exercise equipment is unusual for city spas in this part of the country. The Avenue Plaza is a real discovery.

EuroVita Spa at the Avenue Plaza Hotel
2111 St. Charles Ave., New Orleans, LA 70130
Tel. 504/566–1212 or 800/535–9575

Administration General manager, Marion Rule; fitness director, Donald Henritzy

Season Year-round.

Accommodations 240 1- to 3-bedroom suites in elegant, 12-story stone building. Traditional or Art Deco furnishings, modern baths, air-conditioning, TV. King-size or double beds, foldouts.

Rates $89–$129 single, $99–$129 for 2 in one-bedroom suite, includes spa facilities without program. Spa plan with treatments and meals from 2-night package, $425 single, $350 per person double occupancy, to 5-day/4-night program, $780 single, $1,225 for 2 double occupancy. 25% payable in advance. Credit cards: AE, DC, MC, V.

Meal Plans Breakfast and lunch diet cuisine for spa plan guests (dinner not included). Special menu selections arranged on request. Entrees at lunch include breast of chicken with cognac and raisins, oysters en brochette with chilled seafood salad.

Services and Facilities **Exercise Equipment:** Paramount circuit and Universal multistation unit in weights room open weekdays 7 AM–9 PM, weekends 9–5. Free weights (2–50 lbs.), and barbells (2–50 lbs.), 3 Lifecycles, 3 Schwinn Air-Dyne bikes, Monark ergometer, 2 rowing machines, 2 Precor treadmills, StairMaster, and VersaClimber. **Services:** Massage, herbal wrap, loofah scrub, facial, pedicure, manicure, hairstyling. A health-risk appraisal included in spa plan. **Swimming Facilities:** Heated outdoor pool in garden patio. **Recreation Facilities:** Concierge can make arrangements for tennis, golf, horseback riding.

In the Area Local sightseeing and scheduled tours; bayou tours, antiques shops, Mississippi River cruises.

Getting Here *From New Orleans International Airport.* By bus: Rhodes Public service $8. Taxi or limo: $18 per person (30 min). Rental car available. Private parking for hotel guests.

Special Notes Elevator connects all floors. No smoking in the spa. Remember to bring exercise clothes and tennis shoes.

Jolimar Summit Plantation

Weight management
Nutrition and diet
Life enhancement

Mississippi Set in a mansion on 890 acres of rolling Mississippi hills, the
Summit Jolimar health resort is hardly your typical southern plantation. The reasonably priced programs featured in the spa and fitness center incorporate top-of-the-line exercise equipment, an air-conditioned racquetball court, heated indoor and outdoor swimming pools, and outdoor/indoor Jacuzzis into a personalized weight-loss regimen.

The morning begins with a 2½- to 5½-mile walk along scenic country roads. A range of aerobics classes, from step aerobics to stretch-and-tone, are held throughout the day in the racquetball court and the lap pool, and circuit training with a trainer is scheduled in the weights room after lunch. The resort's practical approach to weight loss even incorporates a field trip to the local supermarket for a lesson in deciphering labels for fat content.

Jolimar Summit Plantation
Rte. 1, Box 237, Summit, MS 39666
Tel. 601/276–9556 or 800/243–3993
Fax 601/276–9578

Administration Director, Michael Tedesco

Season Year-round.

Accommodations 7 rooms furnished individually with twin beds, antiques, flowered wallpaper. All with private bath, TV, air-conditioning. Some have walk-in closet, balcony, environmental bath programmed for climate simulation, or Jacuzzi bath.

Rates Weekend package for 2 nights $380 single, $278 per person double; mid-week 4-night package $728 single, $532 double; weekly $1,215 single, $890 double. Day pass (no lodging) $345. Nightly room rate $146–$235. Rates higher for master bedroom and rooms with special baths, balcony. Add 7% tax; gratuities optional. Deposit $100. Credit cards: MC, V.

Meal Plans 3 meals daily included in program. Dinner can be stirfried vegetables, chicken, or grilled catfish. Fresh spinach, salad, baked potato daily. Home-baked rolls, angel food cake, and frozen peaches are low in salt, fat, and sugar.

Services and Facilities **Exercise Equipment:** 6 Keiser pneumatic weight units, 2 StairMasters, 2 Schwinn Air-Dyne bikes, 2 Precor treadmills, free weights. **Services:** Swedish massage, facial, herbal bath, manicure, pedicure. **Recreation Facilities:** Outdoor tennis court, indoor racquetball court, fishing ponds, canoes; coed sauna, men's and women's steam rooms. **Evening Programs:** Talks, VCR movies with popcorn.

In the Area Natchez (antebellum homes, historic sites).

Getting Here *From New Orleans.* By bus, Greyhound to McComb (3 hr). By train, Amtrak's *City of New Orleans* to McComb (2 hr). By car, I–10 west to I–55 north, Exit 20A to Hwy. 51 north, Guy Barkdull Rd. right to Alford Bridge Rd., Moak's Creek Rd. (2 hr). Airport van ($30 each way) Sunday 3 PM from New Orleans International Airport; complimentary pickup at bus and train station in McComb.

Special Notes Informal dress advised. Exercise clothing available in spa. Roommate matches on request. No smoking indoors.

Duke University Diet and Fitness Center

Life enhancement
Nutrition and diet
Weight management
Vibrant maturity

North Carolina This weight-control program resembles a college course in
Durham healthier living. The combination of lectures, exercise classes, nutrition education, and psychological counseling emphasizes strategies for long-term success and lifestyle change rather than immediate results. For nearly 20 years, the Duke University Diet and Fitness Center has achieved an enviable success rate. In a study of former participants in the program, 70% maintained or lost weight after a one-year follow-up.

Obesity 101 could be the course title of the educational program designed to fit into a two-week vacation period. Many people come for four weeks or longer, hoping to lose from 20 to 200 pounds after unsuccessfully trying various other weight-loss plans without mastering long-term weight management. The average weight loss is two to five pounds per week.

Supervised by a team of doctors, behavioral psychologists, nutritionists, and fitness specialists, the program draws on the resources of Duke University. Housing arrangements, however, are left to the individual, and there are no rooms on campus. The center's staff provides a list of local hotels and furnished apartments.

New participants arrive on Monday. After an initial assessment and evaluation, including laboratory tests and a treadmill stress test, a schedule of classes and lectures is prescribed (about four per day on the two-week program), with free time on weekends to explore the area. Daily check-ins with staff members monitor progress.

The medically supervised part of the program can include psychotherapy on an individual basis and additional laboratory tests. The fitness component—the gym and the swimming pool—enables sedentary types to get some exercise into their lives. Group camaraderie develops in water volleyball, basketball, and badminton games.

Education continues outside the classroom in local supermarkets and restaurants. Duke staffers demonstrate how to shop for the right foods. Cooking classes are popular, and meals made at the center's demonstration kitchen can be eaten. Smokers are given special counseling to help them kick the nicotine habit while adjusting their eating routines.

The improved self-esteem and confidence that comes with weight loss accounts largely for the program's long-term success rate. Instructors illustrate how age, sex, and level of physical activity affect weight and show ways to lower cholesterol, decrease blood pressure, and avoid problems of diabetes.

The center attracts people from all walks of life, of all ages and both sexes. Programs are structured for seriously overweight persons and are without the social strains found in some resorts. A platoon of obese joggers "walking the wall," a 1.6-mile route around the university, is a common morning sight. Later there are water aerobics in the heated indoor swimming pool. It's a full day, from the walk at 7:30 to the after-dinner lecture.

The center encourages family members or close friends to accompany program participants. Arrangements can be made to eat together, attend lectures, and use the exercise facility. Support program costs range from $75 a day to $385 a week.

Durham has been known as a diet and fitness center for more than 40 years. Continuing education at Duke's program is a commitment: Dieters return periodically for reinforcement, and some even move here.

Duke University Diet and Fitness Center
804 W. Trinity Ave., Durham, NC 27701
Tel. 919/684–6331

Administration Medical director, Michael A. Hamilton, M.D.; administrative director, Dawn Schiffhauer, R.D.

Season Year-round.

Accommodations Local inns cater to dieters. Duke Tower, across from center, has furnished apartments with bedroom, living room, kitchen $1,400 per month. Rooms in private homes $100 per week, Holiday Inn $30 per night.

Rates 2-week program $3,350, 4-week program $4,350, 5-day program $1,950. $500 advance payment. $200 deposit Duke Tower suites, refundable. Credit cards: AE, MC, V.

Meal Plans 3 low-calorie, portion-controlled meals daily at Center. Daily diet low in sodium, fat, and cholesterol. Vegetarian and kosher diets accommodated. Seafood gumbo with rice, lamb stew, and eggplant Parmesan for lunch. Italian baked fish, roast barbecued pork, sirloin steak, and black bean tortillas for dinner. Menu published weekly, with calorie counts.

Services and Facilities **Exercise Equipment:** Schwinn Air-Dyne bicycles, treadmills, recumbent bicycles, Paramount exercise equipment, free weights. **Services:** Massage, supervised exercise on bikes, swimming instruction; individual psychotherapy; on-site medical clinic; smoking-cessation program. **Swimming Facilities:** 25-meter indoor pool. **Recreation Facilities:** University campus and city parks provide full range of sports, including tennis, golf, fishing. **Evening Programs:** Lectures on health-related topics scheduled nightly weekdays: Image consultant, dance instructor, Overeaters Anonymous speakers. Duke University performing arts and cultural programs open to participants.

In the Area Low-cost day-trips on weekends include mountains, beach resorts, numerous historic sites. Brevard Music Center concerts late June–mid-Aug., Asheville folk arts. Biltmore Estate near Asheville.

Getting Here *From Raleigh-Durham Airport.* By car, Rte. 70 to I–85, Gregson St. to Trinity Ave. (20 min to center). Duke Towers provides service to and from airport. Taxi, rental car available.

Special Notes Ramps in most buildings provide access for the disabled. Theater, arts, recreational outings for children through community organizations. No smoking indoors and in patio area. Remember to bring appropriate seasonal clothing, exercise and swimming outfits, jogging or walking shoes; notebooks and pens, wristwatch, alarm clock, padlock for gym lockers.

Structure House

Weight management
Vibrant maturity

North Carolina Settling into your apartment in "the village" is like getting a
Durham new lease on life. The cluster of residential units around the new Life Extension Center and the large Georgian-style Structure House, where one goes for meals, classes, and professional services, give off a college campus atmosphere. A healthy lifestyle, in fact, is what you learn here.

Most people come here to lose weight quickly and safely, but the program is designed to teach long-term weight control. The new environment helps, particularly if you have failed to lose weight at home or in other programs. Over 40 qualified professionals help you to understand the reasons behind unhealthy lifestyles and to practice problem solving.

The medically managed program involves mental and physical conditioning. A full physical examination and diagnosis precedes the planning of an individual diet and exercise regimen. For the elderly, the handicapped, and those with health problems, the medical staff consults with patients' private physicians in order to monitor and continue health services.

Therapy does more than reduce stress. Structure House tries to help people understand why they gain weight. Divorce, serious illness, financial setbacks and other major changes often lead to overeating. Everyday stresses, too little activity, depression, and boredom are treated, along with serious cases of obesity, in group sessions with a stress therapist and in private counseling.

A minimum 2-week stay, preferably four to eight weeks, is recommended for serious weight problems. Alumni can return for a week or more of reinforcement; many bring their spouse or a companion.

The integration of medical and psychological aspects of weight loss, alongside dietary and exercise programs, makes this program work for people who need a structured environment. The exercise facilities and classes at the Life Extension Center are the equal of many leading spa resorts. Classes are varied: step aerobics, aquacise and dynabane.

Success stories—losses of 100 pounds and more—are celebrated regularly. The actor James Coco wrote about his experience in a 1984 best-seller; he called it "restructuring."

Structure House
3017 Pickett Rd., Durham, NC 27705
Tel. 919/688-7379 or 800/553-0052

Administration Program director, Gerard J. Musante; medical director, Steven Hirsch, M.D.

Season Year-round; sessions begin 8 AM Mon., new arrivals on Sun.

Accommodations Sixty 1- and 2-bedroom apartments in 9 two-story houses on campus. New modern units, sliding glass door opens onto porch. Washer/dryer, linens, telephone, color TV with HBO, weekly maid service.

Rates $1,300 per week single, $1,170 per person double occupancy, for all-inclusive program and apartment. (Health insurance may cover some services.) $500 per person advance deposit. Credit cards: MC, V.

Meal Plans Selections based on weekly (weeks 1 through 4) system in which each person plans own meals. Suggested 700-calorie menu includes 3-cheese quiche, chef's salad, bean chowder, and French toast. Fri. lunch is a potato bar with toppings. Dinner entrees include sea scallops in wine, baked chicken, and filet mignon. Vegetarian and special diets accommodated.

Services and Facilities **Exercise Equipment:** 5 Nautilus machines, 3 treadmills, 6 Schwinn Air-Dyne bikes, step machine, rowing machine, bench press and free weights, trampoline. **Services:** Massage (Swedish, Trager, deep-muscle, polarity), medical consultation and testing, consultation with clinical psychologist, dietary reeducation workshops. **Swimming Facilities:** Indoor and outdoor pool, lakes nearby. **Recreation Facilities:** Nature trails, basketball, badminton, Ping-Pong, tennis; golf, horseback riding nearby. **Evening Programs:** Occasional parties.

In the Area Eastern Piedmont mountains and lakes, plus numerous historic sites. Minor-league baseball at *Bull Durham* park.

Getting Here *From Raleigh-Durham Airport.* By car, I-40 west (20 min to Structure House). Shuttle service from airport prearranged by Structure House $15. Taxi, rental car available.

Special Notes Ramps for wheelchairs; some apartments equipped for the disabled. No smoking indoors and in designated dining areas. Remember to bring recent medical records, exercise clothing, wristwatch with second hand, walking or jogging shoes.

Westglow Spa

Life enhancement

North Carolina
Blowing Rock
A historic 20-acre mountain retreat overlooking Grandfather Mountain in the Blue Ridge, Westglow was converted in 1991 into North Carolina's first European-style spa resort. The graceful colonial-style mansion built in 1916 now houses six guest rooms and the spa's main dining facility. Additional accommodations are found in two new guest cottages equipped with kitchen, fireplace, TV, and phone. The Life Enhancement Center has an indoor swimming pool, whirlpools, wet/dry sauna, six body treatment rooms, beauty salon, weights room, aerobics studio, and poolside cafe. Health and beauty services range from fitness and nutrition training to massage and body therapy; a daily schedule of classes is posted, though the staff will also do training and aquatics on request.

The miles of forest surrounding the resort provide vacationers with the opportunity to hike, take rafting trips in nearby white-water rapids, or go canoeing. There is a tennis court on the estate, and arrangements can be made nearby for horseback riding, golf, and in winter, downhill skiing.

Westglow Spa
Hwy. 221 South, Box 1083, Blowing Rock, NC 28605
Tel. 704/295–4463 or 800/562–0807

Administration
Founder/directors, Bob and Glynda McPheters; spa manager, Claire Musgrove

Season
Year-round.

Accommodations
6 guest rooms in main house, 2 cottages with 1–2 bedrooms. Vintage furnishings, Oriental rugs, large library retain mansion's original elegance. Modern bathrooms and amenities added in 1989. Cottages have fireplace, air-conditioning, phone, TV, and kitchenette.

Rates
2-night package $499 single, $389 per person double occupancy; 5-night package $1,199 single, $599 double; 7-night package $1,599 single, $1,299 double; day guest (no lodging) $199. Add 6% tax, 10% gratuities. Deposit: 50% in advance. Credit cards: AE, MC, V.

Meal Plans
3 meals daily included in program. Breakfast can be cereal, blueberry pancakes, with herbal tea, decaffeinated or regular coffee, low-fat milk, yogurt. Lunch choices include Oriental pasta, vegetarian sandwich, or sliced pork tenderloin on wheat bread, garden salad, soup. Dinner entrees are mountain trout, mixed grill, vegetarian platter, baked chicken; desserts include homemade lemon sorbet, apple-strudel cheesecake, or seasonal fresh fruit. Mineral water available at extra charge. Afternoon tea served daily.

Services and Facilities
Exercise Equipment: 15-unit Cybex weight training circuit, 12 Cybex Fitron bikes, 4 Lifecycles, 2 Challenger treadmills, 2 Cybex Lifesteps, dumbbells. **Services:** Swedish or deep-muscle massage, aromatherapy, herbal wrap, reflexology, body scrub, facial, cellulite/lymphatic drainage; fitness assessment, exercise, nutrition and diet consultation, personal trainer; salon for hair and nail care. **Swimming Facilities:** indoor lap pool. **Recreation Facilities:** Outdoor tennis court (composition surface),

croquet court, walking trails; horseback riding, 18-hole golf course nearby.

In the Area Tweetsie Railroad and theme park (vintage trains, country music), Blue Ridge Parkway, Great Smoky Mountains National Park.

Getting Here *From Charlotte.* By car, I–77 north, I–40 west to exit 123, Hwy. 321 north to Blowing Rock Bypass exit for Sunset Blvd., Main St. to Hwy. 221 south (2½ hr). By air, USAir Express to Hickory (45 min). Pickup charge $75. Rental car, taxi available.

Special Notes No smoking indoors.

Hilton Head Health Institute

Life enhancement
Stress control
Vibrant maturity
Nutrition and diet

South Carolina
Hilton Head Island
The compact courses held here are concerned with modifying behavior in order to achieve practical results: changes in your daily life and work habits, nutritional education for weight maintenance, and the enhancement of executive stamina.

Health education begins with an understanding of your body. Lectures, workshops, exercise classes, and meals designed to advance that understanding are scheduled in the institute's main building, a short walk from your living quarters. The effect of nutrition and exercise on the body's metabolism and the effect of stress on productivity and health are taught by a team of psychologists, nutritionists, and physical fitness specialists.

The island environment encourages change. Part of the exercise regime is walking on the beach—called a "thermal walk" here because of the effects of sun and air on mood and appetite. The subtropical climate, 12 miles of white, sandy beach, and ample walking and biking trails through local nature preserves go far to enhance and renew the spirit.

Activities center in a campuslike cluster of villas. Participants share well-decorated apartments, fully equipped for laundry or cooking. The island's laid-back atmosphere will certainly ease stress, and the self-management course will help you resist food temptations in high-rise hotels down the beach. The medically supervised programs are suited for individuals and couples who have reached a point in their lives where change is necessary and they need a boost to get started.

Hilton Head Health Institute
Box 7138, Hilton Head Island, SC 29938
Tel. 803/785–7292

Administration Executive director, Peter M. Miller, Ph.D.; medical consultant, Jack M. Catlett, M.D.; fitness director, Robert Wright

Season Scheduled programs year-round; closed during Christmas.

Accommodations Villas in Shipyard Plantation have traditional furniture, fine fabrics, color TV. Each participant has a private bedroom and bath, sharing the living room and fully equipped apartment and laundry facilities with another person in the program. Private porch, parking space, pedestrian walkways.

Rates 6-day program $2,200, 12-day program $3,300, 26-day program $5,200. Deposit: 6-day $500, 12-day $800, 26-day $1,200. All rates are per person; 10% discount for couples. Credit cards: MC, V.

Meal Plans 3 meals and "Metabo" fruit snack daily. Mon.–Fri. diet totals approx. 800 calories daily, more on weekends, when outdoor activity increases. Food high in complex carbohydrates, moderate protein, low fat, no sugar or salt. Lunch can feature pasta primavera with raw vegetables, dinner entrees include chicken enchilada with salsa and brown rice.

Services and Facilities **Exercise Equipment:** 8-station Paramount weight system, 5 Schwinn Air-Dyne stationary bikes, 2 rowing machines, 3 treadmills. **Services:** private massage therapist on request; beauty salon nearby. **Swimming Facilities:** Outdoor pool, ocean beach. **Recreation Facilities:** 24 tennis courts and 3 golf courses within walking distance, for a fee. Nature preserve of subtropical marshes for hiking. Horseback riding, bicycling, windsurfing, sailing, deep-sea fishing available through resort.

In the Area Community theater, cinema, shopping mall. Nature tours by boat; Historic Savannah, GA (1 hr), Beaufort, Charleston (antebellum homes and gardens, 2 hr north).

Getting Here *From Savannah.* By car, I-95 to Rte. 278 (50 min). By plane, Hilton Head Island airport has scheduled service on USAir (via Charlotte) and American Eagle (via Raleigh/Durham). Limousine service hourly from Savannah airport. Taxi, rental car available.

Special Notes Programs for children at community centers. No smoking indoors. Bring an alarm clock, flashlight, medical records. Group size limited to 40.

The Westin Resort

Non-program resort facilities

South Carolina
Hilton Head Island On an island noted for golf, tennis, and fishing, Port Royal Plantation's health facilities at the posh Westin Resort are a happy addition. Equipment, classes, and outdoor recreation on 24 acres of landscaped, subtropical beach are available for a fee; guests in the Royal Beach Club concierge level get complimentary health-club privileges.

The sprawling, five-story hotel has big-city airs and a breezy, Southern Low Country ambience. Enjoy the view of the grand courtyard and three swimming pools from the mirrored weights room. One of the pools is glass-enclosed for year-round swimming and water aerobics classes.

Mornings may begin with a beach walk, recommended by doctors at the Hilton Head Institute. Invigorated by sun, sea, and air, you can join an exercise class or have a personal program planned for you. The club's full-time fitness pro is available for consultation and cardiovascular testing.

Other facilities include a steam room with Swiss shower, a sauna misted with eucalyptus oils, three outdoor whirlpools, and private rooms for massage appointments.

The marriage of low-calorie cooking with Low Country cuisine is a special attraction of the hotel's flagship restaurant, The

Barony. The American Heart Association has honored the menu for low-cholesterol selections of seafood and salads. For informal dining, there's Hudson's Seafood House, on the dock at Skull Creek where the fishing boats unload their daily catch, a few miles from the hotel.

The Westin Resort
2 Grasslawn Ave., Hilton Head Island, SC 29928
Tel. 803/681–4000 or 800/228–3000
Telex 62893418, Fax 803/681–1087

Administration Manager, Patrick Burton; health club manager, Spencer Kurtz

Season Year-round.

Accommodations 410 luxury rooms (including 38 suites), with separate dressing areas, hair dryers, large baths. Furnishings and architecture are reminiscent of grand southern homes. All have balcony.

Rates Room with balcony in Royal Beach Club $315 for 2, with breakfast; other rooms $185–$495 for 2 people in summer. Full oceanfront view $235–$275 for 2; suites $315 and up. 2-night family package $397 for parents' room, $240 for children's. Add 7% tax and $4.50 daily service charge. Rates include spa admission. Golf and tennis packages available. Deposit: one night by credit card. Credit cards: AE, DC, MC, V.

Meal Plans Carolina Cafe buffet serves breakfast, lunch, dinner. Barony Restaurant's low-cholesterol and sodium menu includes free-range chicken with black-pepper pasta and chanterelle mushroom sauce, sautéed shrimp Provençale over angel-hair pasta, and broiled fish of the day. All meals à la carte; dinner in the Barony about $50 per person, including tip, tax, and wine.

Services and Facilities **Exercise Equipment:** Weights room with 14 Universal units, free-weight dumbbells (3–50 lbs.), Lifecycle, rowing machine, 2 StairMasters, treadmill, NordicTrack, Air-Dyne bike, bilateral board equipment, Nautilus abdominal machine. **Services:** Fitness testing, personal instruction on exercise equipment, classes and beach activity; massage by appointment (fee); golf and tennis clinics. **Swimming Facilities:** Indoor pool, 2 outdoor pools (1 with lap lanes); ocean beach. **Recreation Facilities:** Beach runs and walks, volleyball, water polo; 3 golf courses, 16 tennis courts (clay, hard, and grass, 6 lighted), croquet lawn; horseback riding, windsurfing, sailing, and fishing nearby. **Evening Programs:** Resort entertainment.

In the Area Historic Savannah (1 hr), Beaufort, and Charleston (antebellum homes and gardens, 2 hr north).

Getting Here *From Savannah.* By car, I-95 to Hardeeville, Rte. 278 (50 min). By plane, Hilton Head Island airport has scheduled service on Piedmont-Henson (via Charlotte). Also, private aircraft facilities. Hourly limousine service from Savannah airport. Taxi, rental car available.

Special Notes Ramps, specially equipped rooms, elevators to all floors provide access for the disabled. The Kids Korner for children has arts and crafts, games, pool and water activities morning and evening May–Sept., Nov.–Apr. Health club hours: Mon.–Sat. 7 AM–8 PM, Sun. 9:30 AM–6 PM. No smoking in the health club.

Tennessee Fitness Spa

Weight management
Nutrition and diet

Tennessee
Natural Bridge

At this mountain camp for healthy living, guests get back to nature, and back in shape, at the same time. The Tennessee Fitness Spa organizes hikes, swimnastics, canoeing, bike rides, and walks through the area's scenic surroundings to aid in fitness and weight management.

Regularly scheduled classes on nutrition are held in the natural stone dining hall, where the spa chef demonstrates how to cook meals that are low in fat, sodium, and sugar. Most guests are concerned with weight management, and some come for several months to develop a workable weight-loss regimen that they can continue at home.

Guests, who range in age from 20 to 70, join a group leader for a 7 AM hill walk, a 2½-mile warmup followed by stretch class and aerobics. The daily schedule rotates among step aerobics, aquacise, floor work, and lectures. Cross-training can be followed by a soak in the big hot tub or volleyball. Personal services, such as massages and facials, are optional extras.

Tennessee Fitness Spa
Rte. 3, Box 411, Waynesboro, TN
Tel. 615/722–5589 or 800/235–8365

Administration General manager, John Alexander; program director, Wanda Henderson

Season Mid-February to mid-December.

Accommodations 16 double rooms, 2 with 4 beds, in 5 2-story wooden chalets. Simply furnished, with private bathrooms, shower for every two guests, heat. No air-conditioning, TV, or telephone.

Rates $699 per week for private room including meals and program, $449 per person double; $1,299 for 2 weeks in private room, $839 double. Deposit is $100, gratuities optional. No local tax.

Meal Plans 3 meals daily included in program, low in fat, sodium, and sugar. Breakfast can be pancakes, apple spice cake, French toast, or cereal with skim milk. Herbal tea, fruit juices available all day; no coffee. Lunch choices are pizza or black beans and rice, salad bar. Dinner entrées include chicken enchiladas, turkey burgers, Friday night seafood, salad bar.

Services and
Facilities

Exercise Equipment: 3 StairMasters, 3 Precor treadmills, 2 Windracer bikes, free weights. **Services:** Massage, facial, hair styling, manicure/pedicure. **Swimming Facilities:** Covered, heated pool. **Recreation Facilities:** Bicycles, canoes (charge), hiking trails, fishing. **Evening Programs:** Cooking class, cross training, volleyball, pool games, movies, entertainment.

In the Area Natural Bridge (world's only double-span natural rock bridge formation), Natchez Race (scenic highway), Nashville (country music).

Getting Here *From Nashville.* By car, I–65 south, Exit 46 (Columbia), Hwy. 412 via Hohewald, Rd. 20 to Hwy. 99 southwest (2 hrs). By bus, Sunday pickup at 1 PM in Nashville ($25 round-trip). Rental car available.

Special Notes Roommate matching service and 4-person rooms with two bathrooms available.

Camp Rediscovery

Life enhancement
Vibrant maturity

Virginia Designed for adults 50 years and older, Camp Rediscovery
Palmyra blends popular traditional camp activities with personalized health and fitness programs. Challenging participants to expand physical boundaries, the week-long program is a chance to rediscover the simple pleasures of staying fit. The program is scheduled weekdays, spring and fall. Based on personal consultations, camping experiences are geared to the fitness level of participants. You and a staffer choose activities to help meet your goals in terms of physical improvement. At the end of camp, each person is tested again to measure improvement in heart and lung efficiency, flexibility, balance, and strength.

Staffed by members of the Adult Health and Development Program at the University of Maryland, Camp Rediscovery offers one-on-one support in achieving your goals. Warm and enduring friendships develop between campers and staff, all of whom have degrees in health-related subjects.

Taking a multidisciplinary approach, the program imposes no mandatory activities; you can join a supervised canoe trip, play tennis, or practice archery and yoga. Discussions on osteoporosis, loneliness, dental care, stress management, and coping with the psychosocial issues of aging provide mental stimulation during an active week.

As you discover how much physical activity your body can maintain, new challenges appear for those who are capable. Even tree and rope climbing are popular. In addition to scheduled classes in aerobics, staffers conduct walks on the 460-acre woodland preserve along the Rivanna River near Charlottesville. Campers who require more assistance or are in wheelchairs get special attention (some are chauffeured from one activity to another).

Participants come from diverse backgrounds; the average age is 68. After a week of wellness counseling and togetherness, most participants say the camp positively influenced both their physical health and mental happiness.

Camp Rediscovery
Administrative Office: 2007 Pelden Rd., Adelphi, MD 20783
Tel. 301/431–3733

Administration Director, Dr. Daniel Leviton, Ph.D.

Season June, Sept.

Accommodations Shared double room in Hilltop Lodge, or cabin for 4 to 6 occupants. Single room additional. Bathrooms are shared; no heat except in lakeside cabin. Bunk beds supplied with linens.

Rates $350 for 5-day session, shared room; $225 additional for private room if available. Discount for participating group members and camp alumni. No credit cards.

Meal Plans Buffet-style meals served 3 times a day, plus snacks. Prepared with low sugar, salt, and fats, the selections include whole grains and salad, fish, chicken. Fresh vegetable bar at dinner. Seasonal fruit, coffee, tea, and milk available.

Services and Facilities **Exercise Equipment:** Screened gymnasium with exercise mats. **Services:** Group or individual classes in tennis, archery, riflery, yoga, aerobics. **Swimming Facilities:** Lake. **Recreation Facilities:** Volleyball, canoeing, paddleboats; horseback riding nearby (additional fee). **Evening Programs:** Nightly health seminars, folk dancing, or campfire talk.

In the Area Monticello (Thomas Jefferson's Palladian home), Montpelier (home of President James Madison), Ash Lawn-Highland (home of President James Monroe), University of Virginia campus designed by Jefferson, vineyard tours, Ruckersville (antiques shops), McGuffey Art Center (40 studios).

Getting Here *From Washington, DC.* By car, I–66, Exit 10 at Manassas toward Warrenton, Rte. 29 bypass to Culpeper, Rte. 15 south via Orange (2 hr). By train, Amtrak to Charlottesville. Taxi, rental car available. Round-trip van service from Prince Georges or Montgomery counties ($40).

Hartland Wellness Center

Vibrant maturity
Weight management
Preventive medicine

Virginia
Rapidan

The 10- to 18-day program incorporating health, education, and exercise at Hartland Wellness teaches you how to help yourself. The core program consists of cooking school experience, private and group counseling, and physical therapy guided by a team of physicians, dietitians, educators, chaplains, and therapists.

The doctors and staff, all Seventh-day Adventists, focus on disease prevention. Their computer-aided nutritional analysis makes specific recommendations for diet and takes into account physical condition, nutritional requirements, and weight-loss goals. Hydrotherapy treatments and calisthenics also help you get in shape.

The medically-oriented approach and the relaxed, gracious atmosphere in the plantation mansion suit this program to older persons who need personal attention. Spouses are encouraged to participate at a reduced fee. Heart disease, arthritis, cancer, diabetes, and obesity seem manageable on this 575-acre estate in the foothills of the Blue Ridge Mountains.

Activities begin with breakfast at 6:45 on weekdays. A personal schedule is designed after your medical consultation, and you are taught what kind of exercise works best for you. Hydrotherapy, including contrasting hot and cold showers, hot packs, or sitz baths may be recommended.

The program is associated with Hartland College, a small, four-year training program for health professionals. The intensive, outpatient-style program has motellike facilities adjacent to physicians' offices and treatment areas in the mansion. During a 25-day stay, each participant receives a complete physical examination, with EKG test, treadmill fitness test, blood

> This trip we found a road less traveled. And the perfect way to see it.

Vacation Cars. Vacation Prices.

Wherever you travel, Budget offers you a wide selection of quality cars – from economy models to roomy minivans and even convertibles. You'll find them all at competitively low rates that include unlimited mileage. At over 1500 locations in the U.S. and Canada. For information and reservations, call your travel consultant or Budget at **800-527-0700**. In Canada, call **800-268-8900**.

Budget

THE SMART MONEY IS ON BUDGET.®

We feature Lincoln-Mercury and other fine cars. *A system of corporate and licensee owned locations.*

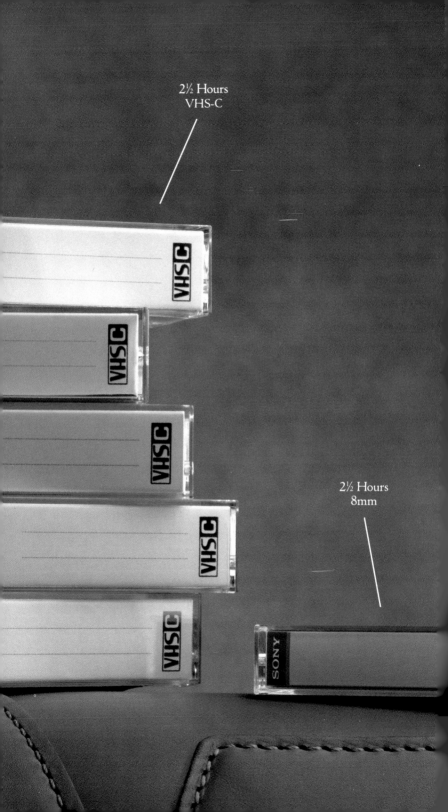

2½ Hours
VHS-C

2½ Hours
8mm

SONY

PACK WISELY.

Given a choice, the seasoned traveler always carries less.
Case in point: Sony Handycam® camcorders, America's most
popular. They record up to 2½ hours on a single tape.
VHS-C tapes record only 30 minutes.* And why carry five tapes
when you can record everything on one? Which brings us
to the first rule of traveling: pack a Sony Handycam camcorder.

SONY
Ⓡ STEREO Ⓛ

8x
Hi-Fi Stereo

video Hi8
Handycam AUTO LOC

AF
PRECISION
CCD

150

FADER

*In standard play mode.

American Express offers Travelers Cheques built for two.

American Express® Travelers Cheques *for Two*. The first Travelers Cheques that allow either of you to use them because both of you have signed them. And only one of you needs to be present to purchase them.

Cheques *for Two* are accepted anywhere regular American Express Travelers Cheques are, which is just about everywhere. So stop by before your next trip and ask for Cheques *for Two*.

Travelers Cheques

chemistry analysis, urinalysis, and body-composition evaluation. (Health insurance may cover some costs.)

The dedicated physicians and educators believe medical technology often overshadows simple ailments that can be pre-
vented with good living habits.

The Seventh-day Adventists, well-known for their interest in
health and nutrition, make their service—nondenominational
and nonsectarian—available to anyone willing to commit themselves to healthy living.

Hartland Wellness Center
Box 1, Rapidan, VA 22733
Tel. 703/672–3100

Administration	Director, William Evert
Season	Sessions monthly except Dec.
Accommodations	15 rooms in a 2-story residential-treatment building. Furnished with antiques, cherrywood dresser and bed; 5 rooms have 2 queen-size beds, 10 have 2 beds. All have private bath.
Rates	10-day program $1,500, spouse $1,350; 18-day program $2,500, spouse $2,250; 25-day medical checkup and program $3,073, spouse $2,766. $100 per person deposit. Credit cards: MC, V (3% surcharge).
Meal Plans	3 vegetarian meals daily. Lunch may include baked tofu loaf, water-steamed vegetables, green salad, baked potato, and homemade bread. Fruit served only at breakfast and dinner, along with grains, cereals, and legumes. No butter or oils. The "Vegan" diet is high in complex carbohydrates. No dairy products, cheese, eggs, meat, fish.
Services and Facilities	**Exercise Equipment:** 2 stationary bikes, 2 treadmills, rowing machine, NordicTrack cross-country ski simulator, free weights. **Services:** Hydrotherapy, massage, stress-management classes, exercise counseling, smoking-cessation program, cardiac and cancer rehabilitation; medical tests, body-composition evaluation, physician's visits; cooking school, weight-control counseling; spiritual guidance. **Swimming Facilities:** Indoor pool. **Recreation Facilities:** Hiking, jogging trails; cross-country skiing (no equipment provided). **Evening Programs:** Medical lectures.
In the Area	Scheduled weekend tours to Monticello (estate of Thomas Jefferson), Montpelier (home of James Madison), museums in Washington, DC; Shenandoah National Park and the Skyline Drive, Colonial Williamsburg, historic Fredericksburg, factory outlets.
Getting Here	*From Washington, DC.* By train, Amtrak to Culpeper (80 min). By bus, Trailways to Culpeper (90 min). By car, I-66 to Lee Highway (Rte. 29) into Culpeper, Rte. 15 toward Orange, to Rte. 614 (about 2 hr). By plane, Dulles International and National Airports, commuter service to Charlottesville. Pickup arranged at airports, bus and train stations for fixed fee. Rental car available.
Special Notes	No smoking indoors. All facilities accessible to the physically impaired.

The Homestead

Non-program resort facilities
Taking the waters

Virginia Style accounts for the enduring popularity of this historic spa.
Hot Springs The mineral springs that made the Homestead famous as long
ago as 1766 still gush in front of the Bath House, furnished with
1920s-style wicker furniture and flowered chintz draperies,
and there are huge marble tubs for mineral-water soaks. The
"spout bath," prescribed here by an advocate of European hydrotherapy in 1937, is faithfully followed today. A doctor's prescription is still required to "take the cure," though not all spa
services come under that category.

Bath, sauna, and massage are spa services outside "the cure."
The Olympic-size indoor swimming pool, built in 1903, is great
for laps and crowded only on weekends. Daily aerobic and
aquacise classes are scheduled. Services are free of charge except baths and body work.

The naturally heated mineral water, high in sulfur and magnesium, reaches your tub at 104 degrees and overflows to keep the
temperature constant. After a few minutes in the sauna or
steam room (the men's side has a Turkish bath), you're led to a
marble slab for a rubdown with coarse salt, then hosed off in the
Scotch spray (hot and cold shower). After cooling down, you're
treated to a massage by an old-timer. The cost is $40–$75, depending on length of the massage. Add aromatherapy ($90) for
the ultimate relaxer.

Most people come here today to bathe for pleasure rather than
therapy. Weekenders are typically family groups from the
South and a few Washingtonians who relish the old-fashioned
ambience and service. Tea is served afternoons to the accompa-
niment of a string quartet in the Edwardian hall. Dinner is a
dressy affair, with a live band for dancing.

The spa will put a spring in your step, but beware the dining
room menu. The Modified American Plan for all guests includes
breakfast and dinner. People have been known to sample all 75
items. Lighter dishes are available in a deli-cafe, located
among the resort boutiques, or you can make a salad at the
luncheon buffet near the tennis courts in summer.

Three golf courses and 19 tennis courts, playable most of the
year, are big outdoor attractions. There's horseback riding,
mountain trout fishing, archery, and trap shooting. Surrounded by a 15,000-acre mountain preserve, the Homestead
has miles of hiking trails. Snowmaking equipment on the slopes
and groomed trails for cross-country skiing are winter attractions.

Despite its rambling size and dated grandeur, the Homestead
makes you feel at home, even as it caters to conventions. Each
season, from blossoming spring dogwood to blazing fall foliage,
has special appeal. The southern hospitality is seasonless.

The Homestead
Hot Springs, VA 24445
Tel. 703/839–5500 or 800/336–5771 (800/542–5734 in VA)

Administration Managing director, Dennis Mills

Season Year-round.

Accommodations 600 guest rooms including 75 suites in main section and tower, built 1902–1929, and South Wing, added with conference center in 1973. Choice rooms and best views in the tower. Mahogany bedsteads, writing tables, lounge chairs, lacy white curtains, damask draperies. Some rooms with French doors that open on to private balconies or screened porches have fireplace, walk-in closet. All are air-conditioned, with TV, telephone, large tiled bathroom.

Rates European Plan daily, $70–$195 single, $95–$220 for 2 double occupancy; 3-day/2-night Vacation Package with spa bath, $189–$289 single, $139–$239 per person double. Children with adults free through age 12, $35 over 13. Packages for golf and tennis. $200 advance payment. Add $7.50 per person daily service, 4½% tax. $45 daily for breakfast and lunch or dinner, plus 16% service charge. Credit cards: AE, MC, V.

Meal Plans Country breakfasts include grits, omelets, steak, mountain trout. Dinner features Virginia ham stuffed with greens, roast beef, broiled chicken, farm produce, sautéed whole trout or smoked fish appetizer.

Services and Facilities **Exercise Equipment:** Universal weights gym, with leg extension, chest press, shoulder press, hip and arm units; StairMaster, 2 treadmills, stationary bikes, abdominal board, rowing machine, free weights. Exercise room open daily 8 AM–7 PM. **Services:** Salt-glow body scrub, mineral tub, therapeutic whirlpool, fitness evaluation, personal trainer, aromatherapy, Swedish massage; salon for facials, manicure, pedicure, and hair styling. **Swimming Facilities:** Large indoor pool with mix of mineral and well water, two outdoor pools. Indoor pool open daily 6 AM–7 PM. **Recreation Facilities:** 3 golf courses, 19 tennis courts (Har-Tru and Gras-Tex), horseback riding, hiking, skeet and trap shooting, archery, fishing, lawn bowling, carriage rides, bowling alley; downhill skiing, ice-skating, cross-country skiing (equipment rental). **Evening Programs:** Movies, dancing.

In the Area Carriage rides. Country boutiques, the baths at Warm Springs (Jeffersonian structure), chamber music concerts at Garth Newel, historic Lexington (Washington and Lee University), Virginia Military Institute (George Marshall Library).

Getting Here *From Washington, DC.* By train, Amtrak from Union Station or Alexandria, VA, to Clifton Forge (4 hr). By car, I–66 west to I–81, at Mt. Crawford Exit, Rtes. 257 and 42 to Goshen, Rte. 39 to Warm Springs, Rte. 220 south to Hot Springs (about 6 hr). By plane, Colgan Airways from National Airport to Ingalls Field at the Homestead, or USAir to Roanoke, VA (1 hr). Private aircraft also land here. Limousine meets train or plane by arrangement (fixed fee). Rental car available. Daily parking charge $10. Valet service.

Special Notes Ramps and elevators in all buildings and some specially equipped rooms provide access for the disabled. Swimming, tennis, and skiing lessons for children; supervised playroom (summer only) and outdoor activity at the spa building (fee). No smoking in the spa and designated areas of the dining room.

The Kingsmill Resort

Non-program resort facilities

Virginia
Williamsburg

For a family vacation combining sports and entertainment, the Kingsmill Resort villas provide an ideal base from which to explore Busch Gardens, Colonial Williamsburg, the scenic Tidewater area, and Atlantic beaches.

Built and managed by Anheuser-Busch, the 2,900-acre resort borders the historic James River, where there's a private marina. Golfers play the River Course, designed by Pete Dye, the Plantation Course, designed by Arnold Palmer, or a 9-hole course. The Sports Club, a 23,000-square-foot structure with indoor and outdoor exercise facilities, restaurant, and adjacent conference center, complements a tennis complex.

There is no charge to registered guests for using the Sports Club facilities. The well-equipped weights room is staffed by instructors. There's an indoor lap pool and an outdoor pool for family play, and complimentary golf, tennis, and fishing also are available.

Located a few minutes from the resort, Busch Gardens, a 360-acre park, has rides, animal acts, Broadway revues, and many activities for families. In Colonial Williamsburg, a few miles up the road, there's plenty of culture to complement your fitness regime. Local museums exhibit everything from Art Deco glass to Fabergé eggs, and a treasure trove of English and American decorative arts dating from 1600 can be seen at the DeWitt Wallace Gallery. Free shuttle bus service operates daily between the resort, the park, and Colonial Williamsburg.

In southeastern Virginia's rolling hills and forests, Kingsmill Resort possesses both cosmopolitan sophistication and Colonial gentility. It's big enough so corporate conferences and vacationers needn't mix. The atmosphere is more residential than resort, and if you enjoy planning your own program, the elements are all here.

The Kingsmill Resort
1010 Kingsmill Rd., Williamsburg, VA 23185
Tel. 804/253–8201 or 800/832–5665

Administration
General manager, Terry Haack; Sports Club manager, Beverly Cutchins

Season
Year-round.

Accommodations
Private villas overlooking river or golf course. 1–3 bedrooms, some complete kitchens, living rooms with fireplace. Residential furnishings, daily maid service. Air-conditioning, king- or queen-size beds, color cable TV.

Rates
Seasonal pricing. $101–$161 for guest room, $394–$539 for 3-bedroom suite in Riverview Rooms. 5-day golf school from $810 per person, double. Add 6.5% tax, optional gratuities. Credit cards: AE, MC, V.

Meal Plans
Sports Club bistro-style restaurant serves light fare, including grilled chicken breast on brioche, pasta salad, and individual pizzas 11 AM–10 PM. Fruit dishes, nut breads, and whipped drinks of yogurt, honey, and fruit prepared daily. Peyton spa

specials at dinner (4–9:30 PM) are sautéed chicken breast over pasta and grilled pork tenderloin with a spicy mango sauce.

Services and Facilities **Exercise Equipment:** 15-station Nautilus exercise machines, 2 treadmills, 2 stationary bikes, 2 Schwinn Air-Dyne bikes, 2 rowing machines, 2 StairMasters, NordicTrack, power rack incline bench, bench press, free weights. **Services:** Aerobic classes and water aerobics ($5 per class), instruction on exercise equipment. **Swimming Facilities:** Indoor 56-foot lap pool, outdoor recreational pool. **Recreation Facilities:** 3 golf courses, 15 tennis courts (Vel-Play, Deco-Turf, lighted), 2 racquetball courts, game lounge with billiards, table-top shuffleboard; coed whirlpool, separate saunas and steam rooms for men and women. **Evening Programs:** Summer season of pop and rock concerts.

In the Area Colonial Williamsburg (88 restored 18th-century buildings, shops, and residences), James River plantation tour, Jamestown Festival Park (replicas of 3 historic ships), Yorktown (Revolutionary War battlefield), Williamsburg Pottery (outlet shops and boutiques), Virginia Beach, Mariner's Museum, Nature Museum and park.

Getting Here *From Washington, DC*. By train, Amtrak from Union Station or Alexandria, VA, to Williamsburg (all seats reserved, 3 hr). By bus, Greyhound (3 hr). By car, I–95 south to I–64 east, Exit 57A to Rte. 199W. By air, commuter service to Norfolk and Newport News on USAir and American Eagle.

Special Notes Interpretive tours for children at historic sites. No smoking in sports club.

The Integral Health Center

Holistic health
Spiritual awareness
Stress control

Virginia
Buckingham Healthy living is taught at the Integral Health Center in a residential setting where small groups focus on programs to achieve and sustain maximum health. Formerly a private home, the center was remodeled to resemble a bed-and-breakfast inn, with accommodations for up to 12 guests.

Week-long programs concentrate on coping with specific physical conditions, including immune deficiency, heart disease, and cancer. Weekend programs address diet and nutrition, weight loss, herbal healing, smoking, and general health and well-being. Chiropractic treatments are available.

Meditation helps guests find quiet and understanding, and breathing techniques build energy. The scenic location, overlooking the James river valley, contributes to a sense of peace.

Spiritual teacher Sri Swami Satchidananda teaches that our whole being can be healed even when it's not possible to entirely heal the body. One young executive came here after undergoing chemotherapy and mastered visualization, a method of directing energy in a conscious manner, to speed her recovery. Others come for a personal retreat or vacation.

Staff members are certified in holistic health sciences. Guest speakers and program leaders add expertise. Yogaville, a residential community for yoga students and monastics on the adjoining Satchidananda Ashram enhances the spiritual atmosphere.

The Integral Health Center
Rte. 1, Box 172A, Buckingham, VA 23921
Tel. 804/969–1451 or 804/969–3121

Administration	Program administrator, Sandra McLanahan, M.D.
Season	Year-round.
Accommodations	7 modern bedrooms, private or shared baths. Sauna, steam room, Jacuzzi.
Rates	Basic daily program, including meals and yoga instruction, $60 single, $100 double. Service charges and tips included. $30 advance payment single accommodations, $50 couples. Credit cards: MC, V.
Meal Plans	3 vegetarian meals served family style in dining room. Rice, dahl, steamed vegetables with brown rice, green salad, tofu dishes, fruit, homemade soups, breads.
Services and Facilities	**Services:** Guided relaxation, medically supervised fasting, instruction in yoga, meditation, cooking, visualization; Swedish massage, shiatsu, herbal wraps, oil baths, chiropractic treatments. **Swimming Facilities:** Outdoor pool, beach on nearby lake. **Recreation Facilities:** Country roads, hiking trails. **Evening Programs:** Meditation.
In the Area	Yogaville and the Light of Truth Universal Shrine; Charlottesville (University of Virginia), Monticello (Palladian villa designed by Thomas Jefferson), Civil War sites (Appomattox Courthouse), Ash Lawn (estate of President James Monroe).
Getting Here	*From Washington, DC.* By train, Amtrak to Charlottesville (3 hr). By bus, Greyhound to Charlottesville (4 hr). By car, I–66 south to Rte. 29, at Lovingston Rte. 56 to Rte. 604 (3½ hr). By plane, commuter flights on USAir to Charlottesville. Service to and from Charlottesville train and bus stations or airport by prior arrangement (fixed fee). Rental car available.
Special Notes	Ashram classes in yoga, meditation, and cooking for children. No smoking. Remember to bring slippers and walking shoes.

The Tazewell Club

Non-program resort facilities

Virginia
Colonial
Williamsburg

The first health club in the old Colonial capital opened in 1988. A part of the Williamsburg Lodge and Conference Center complex, facing a golf course, the Tazewell Club is minutes from the 173-acre historic area. It's an escape to the latest in pampering and exercise after immersing in 18th-century life.

Designed for newcomers to fitness, the club also challenges fitness buffs. The well-equipped weight training room is open from 6 AM to 8 PM, weekdays, til 7 PM on Saturday, and from 11 to 5 on Sunday. Low-impact aerobics classes are taught on weekdays. The swimming pool is popular with families, but certain hours are reserved for lap swimmers; wateraerobics class is scheduled Tuesday, Thursday, and Saturday.

Safety is stressed by the club management, which offers individual instruction on the use of exercise equipment. Aerobics instructors tailor exercise routines to suit your fitness level. It's a shipshape operation with polite, enthusiastic staff.

The workout area has views of the surrounding valley, once part of the Tazewell estate. The swimming pool opens onto a sun deck. The spa, with separate saunas, steam rooms, whirlpools for men and women, and private massage areas, is on the same floor. Try a loofah body scrub or massage.

The club is open to guests staying in any of the five hotels operated by the Colonial Williamsburg Foundation. Two Robert Trent Jones golf courses, eight tennis courts, croquet court, bowling green, and two outdoor swimming pools are nearby. Personal services, court time, and greens fees are extra.

The nation's largest and oldest living history museum is within hiking distance. Williamsburg re-creates the 18th century as it was during the British Colonial era. In the musick master's house, a string quartet may be rehearsing for a concert. At the Raleigh bake shop, you can sample gingerbread and cookies straight from the wood-fired oven.

The Tazewell Club
Williamsburg Lodge
Box C, Williamsburg, VA 23187
Tel. 804/220-7690 or 800/447-7869

Administration Club manager, Cindy Greczek

Season Year-round.

Accommodations 25 Tazewell Club guest rooms in the Williamsburg Lodge, color TV, spacious baths. Also 5 hotels and group of Colonial houses, plus 2 deluxe suites with Jacuzzi, fireplace, wet bar, and private balcony on penthouse level of club. 235 guest rooms in the Williamsburg Inn, a short walk from the health club and 85 rooms in restored homes with Colonial atmosphere. All air-conditioned, with TV, telephone, private bath.

Rates Double or single occupancy in Tazewell wing $188 high season; regular lodge rooms $124–$180; suites $396 for 1–4 persons. Williamsburg Inn $249–$279 suites. House rooms $200–$235. Variable deposits, about $90–$100 per room. Add 8½% tax, optional gratuities. Credit cards: AE, MC, V.

Meal Plans No meals at the Tazewell Club, but guests can charge meals at historic area restaurants. In Regency Dining Room (jacket and tie required) at the Williamsburg Inn, specialties include Chesapeake crabmeat sautéed in wine, picatta of shrimp and veal, and scaloppine of lamb with garlic. Traditional Virginia recipes in the town's taverns—King's Arms, Christiana Campbell's, Josiah Chowning's—run the gamut from peanut soup to stuffed trout. Chesapeake Bay specialties are available at the Friday seafood buffet at the Williamsburg Lodge.

Services and Facilities **Exercise Equipment:** 11 Keiser Cam II stations, Nautilus gym, 2 Lifecycles, 2 Liferowers. **Services:** Massage, loofah scrub, herbal wrap, facial, manicure, pedicure, nonsurgical face-lift, hair/skin care; individual instruction on exercise equipment. **Swimming Facilities:** 60-ft 4-lane lap pool, large outdoor pool. **Recreation Facilities:** 18- and 9-hole golf courses, 8 tennis courts, lawn bowling and croquet, jogging trail, bicycle rentals; badminton, volleyball, and water aerobics on request. Miniature golf. **Evening Programs:** 18th-century concerts, tavern entertainment. Shakespeare productions.

In the Area   Busch Gardens (family-oriented theme park), James River plantation tour, Jamestown Festival Park (replicas of 3 historic ships), Yorktown (Revolutionary War battlefield), Virginia Beach, Mariner's Museum, Nature Museum and park.

Getting Here   *From Washington, DC.* By train, Amtrak from Union Station or Alexandria, VA, to Williamsburg (all seats reserved, 3 hr). By bus, Gold Line or Trailways (3 hr). By car, I–95 south to I–64 east (3 hr). By plane, scheduled flights to Norfolk or Richmond, VA (30 min). Taxi, car rental available; limousine on request. Scheduled van service to airports from Williamsburg hotels.

Special Notes   Elevator to all floors, some specially equipped rooms provide access for the disabled. Tours of historic sites and golf lessons for children. No smoking in club. Remember to bring fitness shoes (white-soled aerobics), workout clothing, leotards. Daily for $7 for guests at other inns.

Yogaville

Spiritual awareness
Holistic health
Vibrant maturity

Virginia   The body-mind connection is strengthened at Yogaville
Buckingham   through in-depth workshops in three essential yoga practices: asana (physical postures), meditation, and pranayama (breathing techniques). A permanent community in the beautiful James River valley near Charlottesville, the ashram welcomes people of all faiths and backgrounds to study and practice the teachings of Integral Yoga under the guidance of the Rev. Sri Swami Satchidananda, who often attends Saturday evening programs, called satangs, when he is in residence. Guests are free to participate or observe, and special training in Hatha Yoga is available for beginners. Classes begin at 6:30 AM, alternating with meals and meditation until 6 PM. Meditation techniques and an understanding of karma also are taught in workshops throughout the year.

Guest accommodations range from a two-story wooden lodge, the Lotus Inn, which has a health food cafe and offers private rooms, to dormitory or tent space. Motor homes can be parked on the grounds of the 750-acre retreat. The main meal is lunch, served in a communal hall. Those who volunteer for work in the organic garden, kitchen, or other areas of the community may earn free meals.

Yogaville
Rte. 604, Buckingham, VA 23921
Tel. 804/969–3121 or 800/858–9642

Administration   Founder, Rev. Swami Satchidananda; program director, Ram Wiener

Season   Year-round.

Accommodations   The Lotus Inn has 6 private rooms with kitchenette, full bath, one double bed and a sofa bed, individually controlled heat and

air-conditioning. 15 dormitory rooms (4–6 beds) have air-conditioning, communal bath, in a 2-story building that includes
classrooms. 8 campsites are in a wooded area, some with plat-
forms, near the dormitory with shower and laundry facilities.

Rates $80 for 2 in private room, $35–$55 per person in dormitory, in-
cluding meals, program. Campers $20 single, $35 couples per
day. Motor home $50 per couple daily, $300 per week. Special
rates for children. Advance deposit for visits of 2 weeks or
more, $100. Credit cards: MC, V.

Meal Plans 3 meals daily included in guest rate. The lactovegetarian diet
includes whole grains, protein sources such as tofu and legumes, fresh fruit, and vegetables. Lunch is the main meal of the
day; breakfast and supper are light buffets with cereals, herbal
tea, yogurt, low-fat milk. Dinner favorites are brown rice pasta
or baked tofu. The Lotus Cafe offers coffee and snacks throughout the day, plus yogurt drinks.

Services and **Services:** Instruction in meditation, Hatha Yoga, daily schedule
Facilities of classes. **Swimming Facilities:** Private beach on 14-acre lake,
river. **Recreation Facilities:** Nature walk, gardening, sauna,
hot tub. **Evening Programs:** Classes or spiritual concert.

In the Area Charlottesville (University of Virginia), Monticello (Jefferson's Palladian villa and orchards), Richmond (Confederacy
museum, historic mansions), Shenandoah National Park, Skyline Drive (scenic highway).

Getting Here *From Washington, DC.* By train, Amtrak to Charlottesville (3
hr). By bus, Greyhound to Charlottesville (4 hr). By car, I–66
west to Rte. 29, I–64 west (toward Lynchburg), 29 Bypass to
I–64 east (toward Richmond), Rte. 20 south, Rte. 655 into Rte.
601, left on Rte. 604 (5 hr). By plane, USAir, United Express,
or Delta, (45 min). Pickup from airport, train, or bus, $15. Ren-
tal car available.

Special Notes Elderhostel for senior citizens, October. Cleaning and linen
service provided twice weekly for guests staying one week or
more at Lotus Inn. Specially equipped facilities for people with
physical disabilities and families. No smoking, alcohol, illegal
drugs, or pets allowed. Bring blanket or towel for yoga, alarm
clock, slip-on shoes.

The Middle Atlantic States

George Washington made taking the waters in West Virginia fashionable at about the same time that Europeans discovered a place called Spa in Belgium. Health resorts flourished over the years in the Poconos, the Alleghenies, and the southern Appalachians. These resorts tend to be small-scale and conservative, emphasizing service and personal attention, and oriented to golf and tennis rather than to high-energy workouts. While the renowned Greenbrier Resort in White Sulphur Springs, West Virginia, recently made the great leap from traditional to contemporary in its health spa, Berkeley Springs—where George Washington bathed—remains a sleepy country town with modest accommodations for spa-goers in a state park. The introduction of snow-making equipment has added a new dimension to resorts throughout the area, with downhill and cross-country skiing now complementing indoor exercise.

In building the nation's first boardwalk, Atlantic City touched off a development boom along the New Jersey shore. The introduction of casino gambling in 1978 brought the town out of a long decline, and when the manufacturer of Lifecycles and other exercise equipment became a Bally company, the shore gained its first full-scale fitness center at Bally's Park Place. Like most spas in the area, it is an amenity rather than a comprehensive health vacation program.

Diversity, however, is what makes the Middle Atlantic states such a rewarding destination for the fitness-oriented traveler. Your choices range from country hotel in the Poconos to the most sophisticated facilities this side of the Alleghenies at Nemacolin Woodlands in the Laurel Highlands of Pennsylvania.

Holistic health programs have not replaced luxury pampering; you can still enjoy bathing in thermal waters throughout West Virginia. At the rustic Coolfont resort on the outskirts of Berkeley Springs, week-long programs for health and fitness, weekend massage workshops, and a smoking-cessation course complement the new spectrum spa.

The Hilton at Short Hills

Luxury pampering

New Jersey
Short Hills
The combination of a luxurious hotel and deluxe European health spa has made the Hilton at Short Hills a popular hideaway for Manhattanites as well as corporate executives visiting the Newark area. With full-service spa facilities—from Roman-style pool to hydrotherapy and fango treatments—and a fitness center and calorie-conscious cuisine, this Hilton offers all the amenities of many fitness resorts. Even complimentary workout attire is provided.

The salon at the spa provides a wide range of face and body programs. Under the direction of Pierre Pellaton, the therapists use European techniques and products for facials, skin rejuvenation treatments, and mud baths. Along with gentle underwater hydromassage, they offer an herbal wrap or an exfoliation combined with seaweed wrap. Completing your new look are hair and nail services, and waxing.

Appointments for all salon services are à la carte, and it's wise to call ahead for a schedule on busy weekends. The hotel offers a Spa Sampler package with a Friday or Saturday night stay that includes health consultation, half-hour massage, aquacise and exercise classes, use of equipment and brunch. A shuttle carries guests to the elegant Short Hills Shopping Mall.

The Hilton at Short Hills
41 JFK Parkway, Short Hills, NJ 07078
Tel. 201/379–0100 or 800/455–8667

Administration General manager, Eric O. Long; spa director, Tony DeLuca

Season Year-round.

Accommodations 300 rooms in a 10-story glass-walled office complex. The Towers has additional amenities in 70 rooms and 37 suites with French doors dividing bedroom and living room. All have TV, 2 phones, marble bathroom with hair dryer, scale, and an array of toiletries. Concierge and private lounge for complimentary breakfast, cocktails, and dessert buffet.

Rates Spa Sampler weekend package $250 for 2 persons. $125–$175 single, $125–$195 for 2 double occupancy per night in standard room; Towers rooms $145–$205 single, $145–$225 for 2 double, suites $235 single, $255 for 2 double. Add 7% tax and gratuities. Deposit: 1 night. Credit cards: AE, DC, MC, V.

Meal Plans No meal plan. Spa cuisine served in the casual Terrace Restaurant. Breakfast choices include eggbeater omelet with salsa, Mueslix cereal, steamed Irish oatmeal; lunch entrees include vegetable frittata, chilled poached salmon with cucumber/onion compote, lobster/angel-hair pasta with mushrooms; dinner menu has shellfish consommé, crispy red snapper with lime-salsa glaze, seared tuna with ratatouille and crisp leeks, grilled chicken breast with pink lentils. Dinner selections also available in The Dining Room prix fixe.

Services and Facilities **Exercise Equipment:** 8 Keiser pneumatic weights units, 2 Concept II rowing machines, 3 Bodyguard treadmills, 2 StairMasters, 4 stationary bikes, free weights (3–50 lbs). **Services:** Massage (Swedish, shiatsu), herbal wrap, facial, body polish, fango, salon for hair, nail, and skin care. Fitness assessment, computerized nutritional analysis, one-on-one training. **Swimming Facilities:** Indoor 50-foot lap pool, outdoor pool. **Recreation Facilities:** Access to racquetball and squash courts (fee); golf, tennis nearby.

In the Area Short Hills Mall (150 shops and boutiques), The Meadowlands (baseball and entertainment complex).

Getting Here *From New York City.* By car, New Jersey Turnpike to Rte. 78N, or Garden State Parkway to Exit 142, Rte. 78 west in local traffic lane to JFK Pkwy (20 min). By bus, NJ Transit from Port Authority Terminal (45 min). By air, complimentary shuttle service to Newark International Airport (15 min.)

Special Notes No-smoking rooms available. Spa hours: weekdays 6 AM–10 PM, weekends 8 AM–8 PM. No smoking in spa; poolside lunch service. Business Center weekdays.

The Middle Atlantic States

Lake Erie

Allegheny River

OHIO

Ohio River

Pittsburgh

Wheeling

Morgantown

Parkersburg

Clarksburg

Potomac River

West Sus

WEST VIRGINIA

Charleston

0   50 miles
0   75 km

NEW YORK

PENNSYLVANIA

Susquehanna River

Williamsport

Scranton

Wilkes-Barre

Easton

Allentown

Reading

Harrisburg

Lancaster

Susquehanna R.

Philadelphia

NEW JERSEY

Newark

Trenton

Wilmington

Delaware R.

Hagerstown

Harpers Ferry

MARYLAND

Baltimore

Washington, D.C.

Annapolis

Dover

DELAWARE

Atlantic City

VIRGINIA

Chesapeake Bay

ATLANTIC OCEAN

N

Ocean Place Hilton Resort & Spa

Luxury pampering

New Jersey
Long Branch

Located within commuting distance of Manhattan, the Ocean Place Hilton's seafront spa is a popular weekend escape for young executives. Skin care to repair damage wrought by the climate and sun is a specialty here. The French moor therapy mud, a black organic natural product by Remy Laure, is used in facials and underwater massage. This is preceded by a vigorous scrubbing with mineral salts and body oils to stimulate circulation, remove dead skin cells, and unclog pores.

For those who prefer a more soothing experience, aromatherapy wraps, facials, or massages are suggested. All treatments can be booked à la carte or as part of one- to three-day packages, with or without hotel accommodations. Fitness classes in the new aerobics studio and the indoor pool can be charged to your bill individually or a program package with spa meals. Over 25 hours of classes are scheduled weekly on the studio's cushioned floor. The spa guests enjoy an ocean front promenade and a nearby state park beach.

Ocean Place Hilton Resort & Spa
1 Ocean Blvd., Long Branch, NJ 07740
Tel. 908/571–4000 or 800/445–8667

Administration General manager, Frank Gaynor; spa manager, Lisa J. Haas

Season Year-round.

Accommodations 254 rooms, all air-conditioned with balcony, TV, phone, modern bath. Contemporary furniture includes desk in oceanfront rooms. Direct access to spa and beach promenade.

Rates $137 single, $204 double for 2 persons. 2-day Spa Escape $149–$189 single, $229–$275 for 2 double occupancy. 3-day Getaway $599–$699, $1,082–$1,172 for 2 double occupancy. Full-day Revitalizer with lunch, no lodging $225. Add tax, gratuities. Daily spa fee $15, class $10. Credit cards: AE, DC, MC, V.

Meal Plans Hilton Food For Life lunch (choice of salads, fruit platters, seafood) included in spa packages. Spa cuisine dinner (additional charge) includes choice of grilled catch of the day, broiled chicken with local vegetables in season, salad bar, fresh fruit.

Services and Facilities **Exercise Equipment:** 11-unit Maxicam circuit, 2 Lifecycles, 2 Stairobic machines, 2 StarTrac 2000 treadmills, dumbbells (3–55 lbs), 2 benches. **Services:** Massage, moor mud hydromassage or wrap, aromatherapy, herbal wrap, French body polish with Vichy shower, salt glow loofah scrub, facials, reflexology, seaweed body masque or facial. Personal goal training, body fat analysis, fitness assessment, circuit training, swimming and tennis lessons. **Swimming Facilities:** Indoor lap pool, outdoor resort pool on sun deck, ocean beach. **Evening Programs:** dancing.

In the Area Monmouth Park Race Trace, Garden State Arts Center, Presidents' Park (beach dunes).

Getting Here *From New York City.* By car, I–95 (New Jersey Turnpike) south to Garden State Parkway, Exit 105 to Rte. 36 (1 hr). By train, NJ Transit commuter services from Penn Station via Newark (2 hr). Taxi, rental car available.

Special Notes Children's day camp Memorial Day–Labor Day. Bike rental available. Specially equipped rooms for physically handicapped guests available. Spa Hours: weekdays 7 AM–9 PM, Sat. 8 AM–10 PM, Sun. 8 AM–6 PM. Beach conditions posted at Presidents' Park.

The Spa at Bally's

Luxury pampering

New Jersey Amid the glitz and glamour of the beachfront casinos, The Spa
Atlantic City at Bally's is a health and fitness oasis. The spacious facilities and top-of-the-line equipment would be the pride of any fitness resort; here they serve as a complement to gambling and entertainment. It's possible not to set foot in the casino, but the majority of the people working out in the weights room also exercise the one-armed bandits.

Four racquetball courts and a complete health-food restaurant flank the reception desk. Anyone may watch the action and enjoy a diet snack. The pool, saunas, whirlpools, and treatment rooms are open to hotel guests and members; others must pay a daily fee. The fee is waived for those who book a minimum of services such as massage or herbal body wrap. The ultimate relaxer is a private session in the MVP Suite, which boasts a marble whirlpool and steam shower; here's where to try aromatherapy, Swedish or shiatsu massage. Exercise classes scheduled 11 AM–3 PM daily include slimnastics, low-impact aerobics, Stretch & Tone, and aquafit. At 8 AM an instructor kicks off the day on the Boardwalk with a complimentary seaside stretch open to all hotel guests.

The spa's exotic gardens and waterfalls and its dramatic view of the Atlantic heighten the sense of luxury. Spa hours are Monday–Saturday 7:30 AM–9 PM, Sunday 8 AM–7 PM.

The Spa at Bally's
Bally's Casino Hotel
Boardwalk and Park Place, Atlantic City, NJ 08401
Tel. 609/340–4600 or 800/772–7777 (800/225–5977 for
room reservations)

Administration General manager, Ronald Mann; spa manager, Michael Angus

Season Year-round.

Accommodations 1,300 rooms with private bath; 110 suites; 9 restaurants. Art Deco touches in the original building, casino luxury in the new tower.

Rates Rooms $115–$205 per day. Spa admission $20 for hotel guests, $30 others. Treatments priced individually. 1-day spa package $99, 6-day/5-night program with caloric-controlled meals $795 double occupancy, $995 single. 3-day/2-night package $395 double. Add tax, gratuities. Payment in advance for packages and weekends. Credit cards: AE, DC, MC, V.

Meal Plans Fresh salads and low-calorie lunches in the Spa Cafe; nonalcoholic drinks. Spa cuisine in the main dining room.

Services and **Exercise Equipment:** 5 Computerized Lifecycle bikes, 10-unit
Facilities Cybex weight training circuit, 5 Precor treadmills, 2 Lifesteps, StairMaster, 2 Nautilus recumbent bikes. **Services:** Massage,

herbal wrap, aromatherapy massage, algae body masque, loofah body scrub, facial; salon for hair, nail, skin care. **Swimming Facilities:** Indoor pool, ocean beach. **Recreation Facilities:** 4 indoor racquetball courts; bike rental on the Boardwalk; golf and tennis nearby. **Evening Programs:** Cabaret and celebrity shows.

In the Area Brigantine National Wildlife Refuge, Farley State Marina, The Noyes Museum (contemporary art), Historic Town of Smithville, Atlantic City Race Track.

Getting Here Atlantic City is served by daily casino bus from points throughout the region. By plane, USAir's commuter flights use close-in Bader Field. By train, Amtrak or commuter service via Philadelphia offers daily service. By car, the Garden State Parkway from points north and south, the Atlantic City Expressway from Philadelphia (60 min). Taxi, rental car, minibus available locally.

Special Notes Facilities for treatments and hotel accommodations available for the disabled. No smoking.

Deerfield Manor

**Life enhancement
Weight management**

Pennsylvania
East Stroudsburg The program at Deerfield Manor takes an individualized approach to diet and nutrition and encourages you to achieve a healthy lifestyle. Participation is limited to 33 men and women who want to unwind and shape up. The daily activities include guided walks, exercise classes, aerobics, yoga, and calisthenics in the heated outdoor pool. Surrounded by mountains, the 12-acre spa retreat stresses moderate exercise and diet amid lots of country charm.

The exercise regimen is complemented by calorie-controlled meals served in a bright, spacious dining room. Each guest selects a menu plan according to personal need and based on the consumption of 750–800 calories per day. One alternative to this is a diet limited to freshly squeezed fruit and vegetable juices at approximately 350 calories daily. Guests make informed nutritional choices when following the "Total Fitness" program introduced in 1980.

The warm, supportive environment is nurtured by a 16-member staff, with occasional visits from lecturers and health professionals. A family-like feeling tends to develop among guests, some of whom return every summer—and some remain for the entire season.

Deerfield Manor
*R.D. 1, Rte. 402N, East Stroudsburg, PA 18301
Tel. 717/223–0160 or 800/852–4494*

Administration Owner/Manager, Frieda Eisenkraft; fitness director, Susan Lipkin

Season Mid-Apr.–mid-Nov.

Accommodations 22 single and double rooms in main country house and deluxe annex rooms with private bath. Furnished with wicker furniture, antiques. Informal lounge with VCR, records. Sauna.

Rates $118–$173 daily per person. Weekly (Sun.–Sun.) $660–$760 per person double occupancy, $875–$960 single. Gratuities included; add 6% tax. Personal services and massage not included. $200 payable in advance. Credit cards: MC, V.

Meal Plans 3 meals daily; fish and chicken, locally grown produce, fresh fruit. Vegetarian meals optional.

Services and Facilities **Exercise Equipment:** StairMaster, treadmill. **Services:** Massage (Swedish, shiatsu, reflexology), facial, wrap. **Swimming Facilities:** Heated outdoor pool. **Recreation Facilities:** 2 tennis courts nearby, golf; roller skating, ice skating, horseback riding. **Evening Programs:** Guest lecturers on health-related topics, handwriting analysis; concerts.

In the Area Shopping tours, summer theater, antique markets, Indian Museum.

Getting Here By car, limousine service on alternate weekends from LaGuardia and Kennedy airports. I-80 from New York, I-84 from New England, I-83 from the Baltimore–Washington area connect with Rte. 402. By plane, major airlines serve Allentown, PA. By bus, Martz Lines to Stroudsburg. Taxi, rental car available locally.

Special Notes No smoking indoors. Ramps and accommodations for disabled.

The Himalayan Institute

Stress control
Weight management
Spiritual awareness

Pennsylvania
Honesdale
Physicians and psychologists at the 422-acre international headquarters of the Himalayan Institute of Yoga Science and Philosophy use biofeedback, aerobic exercise, breathing, meditation, diet, and fasting to train people to live with stress. Their leader is Swami Rama, the Indian yogi who stopped his heart from pumping blood for 17 seconds in a Menninger Foundation clinic experiment in 1970, thereby reinforcing theories about the relationship between the body and the mind.

Biofeedback, a technique that uses machines to teach regulation of the nervous system, is linked with the practice of Eastern philosophy and yoga exercises to form the institute's holistic approach to living. Meditation and relaxation can enable one to gain control of the body and the mind, according to Swami Rama, and the serene atmosphere at this mountaintop retreat provides the appropriate setting for exploring the mind and exercising the body.

Weekday and weekend classes and seminars in stress management, inner growth, and health enhancement are scheduled throughout the year. Some weekend packages include transportation from the institute's branch in New York City.

Research into ancient healing and self-development techniques by the resident faculty is used as the basis for much of the program. Meditation is employed as a systematic method for developing every level of individual consciousness. Sessions of yoga (an hour and 45 minutes) and "silent time" are scheduled throughout the day. Guests are asked to maintain quiet from 10

PM until 8 AM, and to abstain from emotional relationships and other distractions while at the institute.

The day begins at 7 AM with hatha-yoga, and finishes with an after-dinner lecture. You are taught to assume responsibility for your own health. The people who come here are health professionals, families practicing yoga, and students working on degrees. Some guests come just for the weekend retreat in the mountains, the Indian food, and the walking and hiking in the woods that can be the best form of aerobics.

The Himalayan Institute
R.R. 1, Box 400, Honesdale, PA 18431
Tel. 717/253–5551 or 800/822–4547

Administration	President, Rudolph Ballentine, M.D.
Season	Year-round.
Accommodations	100 guests are housed in the main building, a 3-story redbrick structure with austerely furnished rooms with communal toilet and showers. Each room has 1 or 2 beds, a sink, sheets and towels; no lock on the door.
Rates	Health, cooking, nutrition, and meditation seminar weekends $165, including room, meals, herbal tea throughout the day (discount for institute members). 2-week therapy program (Western medical sciences combined with Eastern concepts) $1,750–$2,100 single, $2,550–$3,825 for 2. 4-week weight-loss and self-awareness program $2,500–$3,000. Personal retreat with meals on request. Deposit for seminars. Credit cards: MC, V.
Meal Plans	3 vegetarian meals daily, cafeteria style. Breakfast is oatmeal with apples, fresh banana, whole-grain bread with butter. Lunch can be minestrone soup, hummus, and green salad, or steamed rice with raisins. Dinner includes soup (butternut squash or potato), homemade bread, graham crackers, apples, or tofu-and-lentil casserole. Dairy products, no eggs. Vegetables from organic garden.
Services and Facilities	**Exercise Equipment:** Stationary bikes. **Services:** Biofeedback training (5 sessions $125), aerobics classes, cooking classes, medical and psychological consultations, tennis lessons, breath tests. Massage and body therapies not available. **Swimming Facilities:** Pond on property, with sandy beach and bathhouse. **Recreation Facilities:** Tennis and basketball courts, handball court, hiking trails; cross-country skiing, ice skating. **Evening Programs:** Lectures.
In the Area	Pocono Mountains sightseeing.
Getting Here	*From New York City.* By bus, Short Line from Port Authority (3 hr) or weekend charters from 78 Fifth Ave. (13th St.) by reservation (tel. 212/243–5994). By car, via Lincoln Tunnel to I-80 West, Hwy. 6 through Milford and Honesdale to Rte. 670 (3 hr). By air, scheduled flights to Scranton. Taxi, rental car available.
Special Notes	Preschool, kindergarten, and elementary school programs combine Eastern and Western educational concepts, Montessori methods, and yoga philosophies. No smoking indoors.

Nemacolin Woodlands

Luxury pampering
Weight management
Stress control

Pennsylvania   Atop a scenic bluff in the Laurel Highlands of southwestern
Farmington   Pennsylvania stands the Woodlands Spa, a $6 million addition
to the Nemacolin Woodlands resort and conference center. Despite its name, this is no rustic retreat. The four-level building
of native stone, buff brick, and glass is the best-equipped spa
this side of the Allegheny Mountains.

The range of bodywork available is exceptional—scrubs and
wraps using sea salts, oils, mud, and herbal mixtures;
aromatherapy or Swedish massage; foot reflexology—and facilities in separate wings for men and women provide everything from toothbrushes to workout clothing and robes. After a
session in the steam room or the sauna, you can relax in a glass-
walled whirlpool and enjoy the view of woods and distant mountains.

Downstairs is devoted to exercise: an array of Keiser pneumatic weight training machines, plus bikes, treadmills, and a
StairMaster with video monitors to help you meet your goals; a
four-lane indoor lap pool 65 feet long that's also used for water
aerobics; and a mirrored aerobics studio with cushion-sus-
pended floor that can hold groups of 40 or more.

Upstairs is the beauty salon and a suite of treatment rooms;
both are spacious and airy and warmed in winter by a fireplace.
Dermalogica skin-care system treatments are offered to retard
aging, control blemishes, and rejuvenate your complexion. One
room is specially designed for hydrating pedicures and manicures, a process in which hands and feet undergo a mink-cream
massage followed by a dip into liquid paraffin to build up
"masks" that soften and lubricate the skin.

The basic program includes a prebreakfast walk in the woods
led by staffers, scheduled exercise classes, and energy breaks
for vegetable broth or fruit smoothies. Treatments are included in spa packages of one to six days, or booked à la carte.
Nonprogram guests pay a daily fee for classes. An RN is on
staff.

At the Woodlands Spa you set your own pace: golfers work out
at 6:30 AM prior to heading for the 6,600-yard par-70 course;
spouses limber up with the fitness staff; meeting goers pop in
for an energizer. There's a juice bar with herbal tea, decaffeinated coffee, and snacks, but meals are served in the lodge's posh
dining rooms and cafe.

Spa guests have a choice of accommodations in the alpine lodge
connected to the conference center, or condominiums and cottages in the woods. Either way, you'll have a short hike to the
spa, so come prepared for inclement weather.

The 550-acre resort offers a full range of sports, with equipment supplied at the Activities Center adjoining the spa. The
new indoor Equestrian Center offers dressage training as well
as trail rides and individual horseback outings by the hour.
Outdoor tennis courts, championship croquet, horseshoes, biking, and trout fishing in a stocked lake are among the options.

In winter, trails are groomed for cross-country skiing and snowmobiles, and the lake is filled with ice skaters. The Golf Academy offers instruction most of the year.

Lacking indoor sports facilities, Nemacolin Woodlands allows you to exercise healthy options at the Woodlands Spa. Programs are planned individually for stress management, diet and nutrition. Participants get a fitness evaluation and an optional body-composition and coronary-risk analysis. Personal attention and one-on-one training to assure safety and proper exercise routines add to your learning experience.

Nemacolin Woodlands
Box 188, Farmington, PA 15437.
Tel. 412/329–8555 or 800/422–2736
Fax 412/329–6198

Administration President, Maggie Hardy Magerko; director, Marguerite Lykes Rivell

Season Year-round.

Accommodations 96-room lodge is closest to spa building; new wing with spacious bedrooms and terrace suites furnished in traditional English or Art Deco style. Two queen-size beds are standard, some have 4-posters. Separate bathroom and commode, some with whirlpool bathtub, balcony; TV, 3 telephones, air-conditioning. Also, furnished condominiums and cottages with kitchens.

Rates Varies with season: summer-autumn 4 day/3 night Revitalizer (Sun.–Thurs.) from $915 single or double; suites $1,333–$1,731 single, $1,034–$1,233 per person double occupancy. Meals, services, gratuities, and taxes included in package. Daily room rates include use of spa facilities, from $80 single, $120 per couple, suites $185–$460. Golf and tennis packages available. Deposit $150. Credit cards: AE, MC, V.

Meal Plans Spa dining room in lodge has breakfast buffet with muffins, hot and cold cereals, juices, yogurt, fruit. Lunch, served at spa or in cafe, can be salad with chef's award-winning New England clam chowder. Dinner selections include brook trout stuffed with scallops, shrimp, grilled chicken breast, veal scallops. Menu on 14-day cycle, special diets accommodated.

Services and Facilities **Exercise Equipment:** 10 Keiser pneumatic weight training machines, Biocycle, StairMaster, Trotter and Trakmaster treadmills, VersaClimber, Monark and Rosso bikes, free weight dumbbells (5–50 lbs.). **Services:** Massage (Swedish, sports, aromatherapy, reflexology), facials, back cleansing; body wrap, loofah body polish; hair, nail, and skin treatments. Personalized fitness-assessment, stress-management program, diet and nutrition lectures, body-composition evaluation, one-on-one training. Scheduled walks and group exercise. **Swimming Facilities:** Indoor lap pool, outdoor recreational pool. **Spa Facilities:** Coed weights room, aerobics studio with Reo-Flex floor, treatment rooms, beauty salon, 4-ft.-deep lap pool. Separate men's and women's saunas, whirlpools; workout clothing and robes provided in locker room; juice bar, boutique. **Recreation Facilities:** 4 tennis courts (Omni surface, lighted), bicycle rental, Equestrian Center, 18-hole golf course (2nd course 1994), miniature golf, Golf Academy, croquet, boating, trout fishing, badminton, shuffleboard; winter skating, cross-country skiing, snowmobiles. Racquetball nearby. Greenhouse, table tennis. **Evening Programs:** Music weekends, chess, sports bar.

In the Area White-water rafting at Ohiopyle State Park, Fallingwater (Frank Lloyd Wright architecture), Laurel Caverns, Fort Necessity (French & Indian War), Antietam Battlefield (Civil War), Western Maryland Scenic Railroad (June–Oct.).

Getting Here *From Washington, DC:* By car, Capital Beltway (I-495), I-270 north to Frederick, MD., I-70 west to Cumberland, Rte. 48 to Keyser's Ridge, Rte. 40 (Old National Road) to Farmington, PA. (4 hr). By air, USAir to Pittsburgh (45 min). Transfers on request; private airstrip. Rental car.

Special Notes No smoking in spa or spa dining room. Children's playground, petting zoo, and Family Activities Center open year-round. Plants sold in greenhouse. Pony ride, canoe rental, golf instruction available.

Berkeley Springs State Park

Taking the waters

West Virginia Berkeley Springs State Park has been called the K Mart of
Berkeley Springs spas: An hour-long "tub and rub" treatment costs $25, and in the summer you can swim in the big outdoor pool. All the mineral water you care to drink or take home is free.

Spartan and a bit old-fashioned by today's standards, the state-run facilities offer a down-home Blue Ridge brand of healing. In the original 1815 Roman bath building, step-down tubs rent for $8 an hour per person. Filled with 750 gallons of spring water heated to 102 degrees, the pools hold several people—coed company is fine—in privacy. No reservations are taken; the policy is first come, first served.

Both the main bathhouse and the Country Inn hotel across the street date from the 1920s. Men and women have separate Roman plunge pools; heated mineral water spurts from enormous pipes into a 3-foot-deep tiled tub where patrons soak in privacy. Masseurs operate in open cubicles, steam cabinets line yellow brick walls, and bathtubs provide a relaxing soak. While there's little privacy here, reservations are taken up to two weeks in advance. For beauty salon treatments and private mineral water whirlpools, climb the hillside steps to the Country Inn's Renaissance Spa.

The tiny state park, no larger than a town square, wins high marks for cleanliness and no-frills treatments; bring your jeans and a sense of humor.

Berkeley Springs State Park
Washington St., Berkeley Springs, WV 25411
Tel. 304/258–2711 or 800/225–5982

Administration Superintendent, Robert Ebert

Season Open daily 10 AM–6 PM; Apr.–Oct., Fri. 10 AM–9 PM; Nov.–Mar., daily 10 AM–6 PM.

Accommodations In the Country Inn adjoining the park (tel. 800/222–6300) and several bed-and-breakfast guest houses in town or nearby. The Highlawn Inn, a hilltop Victorian mansion, has rooms with full breakfast for $70–$85 (tel. 304/258–5700). Cabins and lodge rooms at Cacapon State Park (tel. 304/258–1022 or 800/225–5982) 10 mi south of town.

Rates $290 per week for 2 in cabin during summer at Cacapon State Park (sleeps 2–8), rooms in the lodge $48 single, $65 for 2 per day; Country Inn $60–$80 for 1 or 2. Add 9% tax. Discounts for senior citizens. Credit cards: AE, MC, V.

Services and Facilities   **Services:** Massage (30 min), private bath, Roman plunge pool, steam cabinet. **Swimming Facilities:** Outdoor pool open May 30–Sept. 1 ($2 adults, $1.25 children).

Getting Here   By car, the park is located near the intersection of Rte. 522 and Hwy. 9, in the center of town.

Special Notes   Facilities accessible for the physically handicapped. No smoking in bathhouses. Old Roman Bathhouse open weekends only Columbus Day–Memorial Day. Summer concerts at bandstand, Sat. 5 PM.

Coolfont Resort

Holistic health
Life enhancement

West Virginia
Berkeley Springs   A relaxed, informal, budget-priced mountain retreat occupying 1,300 acres in the foothills of the Appalachian Mountains, Coolfont has the laid-back look of a summer camp for adults. With the opening of the Spectrum Spa in 1992, the resident owners culminated 20 years devoted to creating an environment for healthy vacations. In addition to a fitness center with indoor spring-water swimming pool, the spa has private rooms for a wide range of bodywork, a full-service salon, demonstration kitchen, and sprung-floor aerobics studio. In the Swim and Fitness Club are a coed whirlpool and sauna, weights training room with exercise bikes, and a limited selection of Paramount equipment. Group camaraderie builds on prebreakfast walks and afternoon hikes.

Members of the resident staff combine expertise in physical fitness, nutrition, massage, and holistic health for the 6-day health retreat scheduled every month. In addition to regularly scheduled aerobics, yoga, and body-strengthening exercise classes, guest instructors lead workshops on natural nutrition, creative problem solving, and stress reduction. Also offered regularly is a weekend of massage instruction for couples, and a week-long Breathe-Free program for smoking cessation. Programs are limited to 20 participants.

The emphasis is on health awareness, yet there is a cultural dimension to the community. Folk singers, string quartets, and artists in residence perform on weekends. A woodsy lounge bar jumps with country music and sing-alongs. For those not counting calories, bountiful buffets are served; for those who are, the separate (nonsmoking) spa dining room has a fixed menu of low fat/high fiber meals that total about 1,200–1,400 calories daily. It all adds up to fitness with a down-home flavor.

Coolfont Resort

Cold Run Valley Rd., Rte. 1, Box 710, Berkeley
Springs, WV 25411
Tel. 304/258-4500, 202/424-1232, or 800/888-8768
Fax 304/258-5499

Administration	Owners/managers, Martha and Sam Ashelman; program directors, Carolyn Ruos Thomas, Diane Mickelson
Season	Year-round.
Accommodations	240 rooms, some with fireplace and whirlpool bath, in the modern 3-story Woodland Lodge and 20 mountain chalets. The deluxe chalets have 2 bedrooms, double beds, 2 baths, and can be shared as 2 private units. All are air-conditioned, with telephone, daily maid service. Also guest rooms in the historic Manor House (no smoking). Lodge rooms have queen-size or twin beds.
Rates	$67-$107 daily per person double occupancy, $87-$127 single; 2-night Fitness Weekend $300 per person double occupancy, $315 single; 2-night Massage Workshop $550-$600 per couple; 6-night Health Retreat $800 per person double occupancy, $920 single; Breathe-Free program $1,095-$1,295 single. Spa for a Day (no lodging) $99. Add 9% room tax, 6% meal tax, optional gratuities. Deposit: 50% payable in advance (refund when canceled at least 48 hours before start of program). Credit cards: AE, DC, MC, V.
Meal Plans	3 meals daily included in spa packages and daily rate. Breakfast can be omelet, hot cereal, fruits. Lunch is soup or lentil stew, pita sandwich with turkey. Dinner specialties include shrimp stir-fry, salmon baked in parchment, crispy herbed chicken, stuffed baked potato. Salad bar, fruit bowl, herbal teas, decaffeinated coffee available. Juice snacks, "Health Adjustment Hour" in the Squirrel Nest Lounge. Vegetarian meals available; special diets accommodated.
Services and Facilities	**Exercise Equipment:** 14-unit Paramount weight training system, treadmill, Precor rowing machine, 2 Monark bikes, Schwinn Air-Dyne bike, free weights (3-20 lbs.), hand weights. **Services:** Massage (Swedish, reflexology, shiatsu), sugaring or clay body masque, herbal wrap, loofah body scrub, facials; salon for hair, nail, and skin care. Fitness evaluation, nutrition consultation. **Swimming Facilities:** Indoor pool with coed sauna, whirlpool; beach on private lake. **Recreation Facilities:** 8 tennis courts; boating, hiking, horseback riding; team sports; cross-country skiing, ice skating; golf course nearby. **Evening Programs:** Concerts, theme weekends, health lectures.
In the Area	Cacapon State Park, the Castle mansion (1886), Harpers Ferry National Historical Park, Charles Town racetrack, Antietam Battlefield (Civil War), Blue Ridge Outlet Center (shopping), C&O Canal, Berkeley Springs State Park, Prospect Peak Overlook (3-state view), Winchester (apple orchards, festivals).
Getting Here	*From Washington, DC.* By car, I-270/70 to Hancock, MD, Rte. 522 (2 hr); or the Pennsylvania Turnpike (I-76) at the Breezewood exit. By air, USAir has scheduled service to Hagerstown, MD; private planes use Potomac Airport. By bus, Greyhound to Hancock. By train, Amtrak to Martinsburg, WV. Rental car, taxi available.

Special Notes Special accommodations for the disabled. Supervised camp for children, summer only. No smoking in the spa dining room: Swim and fitness club open weekdays 10 AM–8 PM, weekends 8 AM–9 PM. Elderhostel in December.

The Greenbrier

**Luxury pampering
Preventive medicine
Weight management
Taking the waters**

West Virginia
White Sulphur Springs

A legendary resort, The Greenbrier blends old-fashioned comfort with high-tech spa treatments. Opened in 1987, the spa wing has separate soaking pools and therapy rooms for men and women, a mirrored aerobics studio, and interactive exercise equipment. Hydrotherapy comes with mineral water—your choice of sulfur soak or bubbly herbal foam. Sports, riding, and hiking in the foothills of the Allegheny Mountains are significant attractions within the 6,500-acre resort, which includes three golf courses and a rifle club.

While the hotel is a busy scene of conferences and afternoon teas in vast halls filled with "oriental" decor, the spa is serene and small, awash in pinks and greens, with sprigs of rhododendron painted on tiles. The staff includes both old hands and university-trained physiology specialists; they make newcomers feel comfortable about trying some of the exotic-sounding treatments. Seaweed body wraps, aromatherapy, and facials with European floral products are among the à la carte offerings. Ushered into a private dressing room, guests are helped into a step-down tiled tub for a sulfur soak (yes, it smells a bit like rotten eggs but softens the skin) or a bubbly floral bath. Then, in a softly lit room, a massage with herbal aromatic oil and a talc rub follows. The huge indoor swimming pool is open to all resort guests.

The Greenbrier Clinic, established in 1948, occupies a separate building that is completely equipped for diagnostic and preventive medicine. Health examinations can now be combined with spa therapy. Checking in with the resident medical staff, the participant undergoes a comprehensive physical assessment plus advanced fitness evaluation. A doctor will confer with the spa nutritionist and physiologist to plan a personalized diet and exercise regimen.

Spa cuisine is a recent innovation, available to guests in a five-day package that includes breakfast, lunch, and dinner, unlimited exercise classes, luxury pampering, and individual nutrition consultation. The meals contain 30% fat or less, are moderate in cholesterol and sodium, and include high-fiber selections. Presented with classic Greenbrier flair, the menu capitalizes on fresh, natural foods from nearby farms.

As a watering place for southern aristocracy since before the Civil War, the resort has hosted many celebrities. In the President's Cottage (built in 1834), there is a photo of Robert E. Lee at a reunion of his officers. Now a museum, the cottage is full of memorabilia from social seasons past. Tea is still served every afternoon in one of the vast foyers, accompanied by a trio playing on the balcony. Some of the original cottages have been transformed into deluxe accommodations. Constantly refurbished, guest suites are huge, with parlor and walk-in closet, traditional furniture, and Greenbrier green carpet.

The Greenbrier
White Sulphur Springs, WV 24986
Tel. 304/536-1110 or 800/624-6070

Administration   General manager, Ted J. Kleisner; spa director, Judy Stell

Season   Year-round.

Accommodations   650 rooms in main building, deluxe cottages, and guest houses.

Rates $180–$225 daily per person double occupancy, $320–420 single, including breakfast and dinner. Suites from $267 per person. Daily service charge $13.75 plus 6% tax per person. 5-day spa package $2,150 per person double or single, 2-day spa package $950 per person double or single, including 3 meals daily. 5-day Spa and Clinic program $2,150 per person double or single. Deposit: $300 per room payable in advance. Tax and gratuities included in spa packages. Credit cards: AE, DC, MC, V.

Meal Plans   American fare plus low-calorie alternatives at breakfast and dinner in the main dining room. Dinner can begin with smoked duck salad, mushroom consommé, an entree of grilled swordfish or mountain trout with lentil ragout, braised spinach leaves, followed by a salad of red-oak leaf lettuce with tomatoes in yogurt dressing. Dessert is pear strudel in fresh berry sauce. Cafe service for lunch. Tea daily.

Services and Facilities   **Exercise Equipment:** 5-unit Hydra Fitness weight training circuit, 3 Trotter treadmills, 3 Schwinn Dynavit bikes, UBE ergometer, 2 StairMasters, dumbbells (4–40 lb); $10 facility fee includes use of sauna/steam room. **Services:** Full-body massage, back facial, pressure-point facial, herbal wrap, scalp massage, mineral or herbal bath, paraffin hand treatment, aromatherapy; hair, nail, and skin care in salon; one-on-one training, fitness evaluation, personal exercise program. Aerobics class $6. **Swimming Facilities:** Indoor Olympic-size pool, outdoor pool. **Recreation Facilities:** 15 outdoor and 5 indoor tennis courts, platform tennis, 3 golf courses, fishing, skeet- and trapshooting, bowling, croquet, horseback riding, carriage rides, jogging and hiking trails, parcourse, bicycle rental. **Evening Programs:** Feature films, food and wine weekends, dancing.

In the Area   Presidents' Cottage Museum displays memorabilia of famous visitors; crafts studios; mineral water springhouse.

Getting Here   Located just off I-64 and close to the Skyline Drive. By car, I-95 to Richmond. By plane, Lewisburg Airport has scheduled flights by American Airlines via Raleigh/Durham and by USAir via Pittsburgh and Charlotte. By train, Amtrak's Cardinal between New York City, Washington, and Cincinnati stops at the Greenbrier Fri., Sun., and Tues. Private limousine connects with flights at Lewisburg. Rental car, taxi available.

Special Notes   Special accommodations provided for the disabled. Sports school for children June–Labor Day. No smoking in the spa and areas of the dining room. Spa hours: daily 7 AM–7 PM.

Lakeview Resort

Non-program resort facilities

West Virginia
Morgantown

The fitness and sports center of the Lakeview Resort complements an executive conference center and two championship golf courses. Surrounded by woodland and a scenic lake, it's a place for both rigorous workouts and simple relaxation.

The action is continuous in the free-standing fitness center, and registered guests enjoy unlimited free access to facilities. Tennis can be enjoyed year-round, indoors and outdoors. Aerobics classes are scheduled morning and afternoon in a sprung-floor studio. A personal fitness evaluation is offered when you arrive, and the only extra fees are for massage, use of the racquet-sport courts, and aerobics classes. A nursery will take care of the kids while parents work out. Lunch and snacks are available at the spa juice bar.

Lakeview Resort
Rte. 6, Box 88A, Morgantown, WV 26505
Tel. 304/594–1111 or 800/624–8300

Administration Manager, W. G. Menihan; fitness director, Greg Orner

Season Year-round.

Accommodations 2-story inn with 187 well-appointed rooms and 55 2-bedroom condominium units with maid service.

Rates Rooms $75–$125 single, $85–$135 per person double daily, condominium apartments (up to 6 persons) $280 per day. Credit card guarantee for 1 night. Credit cards: AE, DC, MC, V.

Meal Plans Light fare in the lakeview restaurant; juice bar and snacks in the fitness center.

Services and Facilities **Exercise Equipment:** 10-station Nautilus circuit, Marcy weight-resistance gym and recumbent bike, StairMaster, Lifecycle, Liferower, free weights. **Swimming Facilities:** Indoor lap pool and outdoor pool, lake. **Spa Facilities:** Coed whirlpool, separate saunas. **Recreation Facilities:** Racquetball and wallyball courts, indoor and outdoor tennis courts; fishing, boat rentals, horseback riding, waterskiing, 2 golf courses; cushioned indoor running track, aerobics room. **Evening Programs:** Dancing, cabaret.

In the Area Lakeview Theater (summer stock), Cheat River Gorge (whitewater rafting), Star City (glassmaking), Cooper's Park State Forest (hiking trails).

Getting Here Located 75 mi south of Pittsburgh, the resort is accessible by interstate routes and commuter airlines. By car, Rtes. 48 and 79. By plane, Morgantown's Hart Field is served by USAir. Courtesy car pickup to and from airport.

Special Notes No smoking in the fitness center, some guest rooms, designated areas of the dining room.

New England and New York

A return to elegance marked a decade of intensive development throughout the northeastern states. Grand old estates have been rejuvenated, hotels have updated their fitness facilities and introduced European therapies. The result has been a broader range of vacation options for both luxury-minded and budget-conscious travelers.

In Saratoga, New York, where the mineral springs were a prime attraction during the age of Victorian health spas, a state park that encompasses 122 of the city's 163 springs has rejuvenated the Roosevelt Baths and the Gideon Putnam Hotel. In the Berkshires, Arizona's famed Canyon Ranch offers the latest in health programs only minutes away from the Boston Symphony Orchestra's popular summer home at Tanglewood. The facilities at this first destination spa and fitness resort in the Northeast are among the most comprehensive in America.

Advancing the concept of preventive medicine, spas are teaming up with doctors, nutritionists, and psychologists in new programs that address stress control, aging, and lifestyle. In Vermont, Green Mountain at Fox Run has a Liquid Diet Recovery program. At the New Age Health Spa in New York, you can participate in a challenge course designed by experts from Outward Bound, or neurolinguistic training for inner peace. The Kripalu Center for Yoga and Health will operate an executive fitness retreat at Foxhollow in Lenox, Massachusetts.

Norwich Inn & Spa

Luxury pampering

Connecticut
Norwich
Combine a 1920s country inn with a 1980s spa, and you have a perfect weekend escape for city dwellers. Located 2 hours north of New York City, the imposing Georgian-style Norwich establishment took on a new life in 1987 with the addition of the spa. Today the inn blends sophisticated cuisine and beauty treatments with New England tradition.

The spa philosophy of the owner, Edward J. Safdie, is one of nurturing and unadulterated pampering, and this is evident throughout the inn's operation. From flowered chintz and hand-rubbed pine in the old-fashioned bedrooms to high-tech workouts in the gym, the regimen and comfort complement each other.

The 35-foot swimming pool under a soaring cathedral ceiling is the spa's centerpiece. An aerobics studio and an exercise room equipped with Keiser Cam II pneumatic resistance units flank the pool. You can sign up for massages, deep-cleansing facials, body scrubs, hydrotherapy, and a full range of skin and beauty treatments. Classes, scheduled throughout the day, are open to other guests at the inn as well as to program participants.

Because the inn caters to conferences, you may find yourself mingling with a large number of guests who aren't counting calories but have paid $10 for admission to the spa and may sign

New England and New York

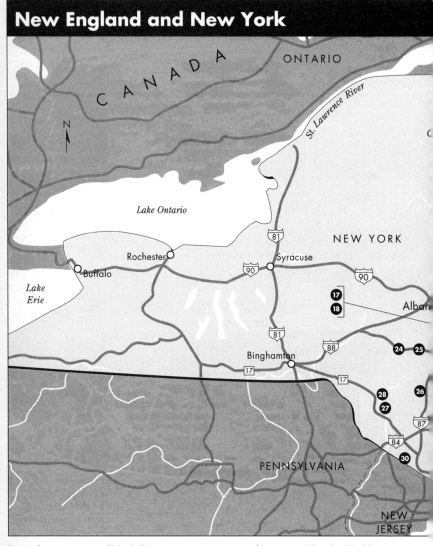

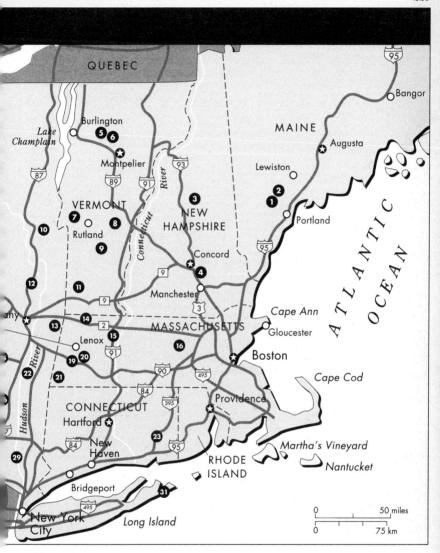

Vermont

The Equinox, **11**

Golden Eagle, **6**

Green Mountain at
Fox Run, **9**

New Life, **7**

Topnotch at Stowe, **5**

Woodstock Inn &
Resort, **8**

up for treatments and classes à la carte. For serious workouts, come on one of the Sunday–Friday packages. Accommodations are in the main building or the villas, just a short distance from the spa.

The range of treatments makes this spa special. Choices include guided imagery, acupressure, thalassotherapy body wraps with algae imported from France, and hydrotherapy in a deep tub with a 60-jet water massage.

Meals are served in a private dining room away from the bar and smoking areas. The author of highly regarded books on spa food, Safdie has given the inn's menu a new look while retaining the classic New England flavor, high in complex carbohydrates—seafood, fresh fruits, local vegetables—and low on fat.

Charm and comfort came with the recent renovation. Antiques, four-poster beds, ceiling fans, handwoven rugs, and lace curtains enhance the bedrooms. A six-foot birdhouse in the lobby is home to a pair of fantail doves. Public areas include a taproom with a large stone fireplace and a quiet sun-room full of palms and wicker. The villas have a clubhouse, gym, and pool.

Surrounded by 37 acres of woodland and situated near a state park, the inn offers rural diversions after workouts.

Norwich Inn & Spa
607 W. Thames (Rte. 32), Norwich, CT 06360
Tel. 203/886–2401
Fax 203/886–9483

Administration	President, Peter Buse; spa manager, Jean Rosaker
Season	Year-round.
Accommodations	65 rooms, 16 suites, all with private bath, furnished with antiques and reproductions. New villas with fireplace, Ralph Lauren prints, and kitchen serviced by the inn.
Rates	Rooms $125–$140 per day for 1 or 2 persons; suites $160–$215. 5-day program $1,350–$2,300 single, $1,140–$1,895 per person double occupancy. 3-day program $820–$1,020 single, $690–$820 per person double. 3 day/2 night Spa Weekend package $345–$485 single, $390–$535 per person double occupancy. $500 deposit for 5-day program. Credit cards: AE, DC, MC, V.
Meal Plans	New England specialties, spa cuisine; no salt, sugar, white flour, fatty oils. Lots of seafood, fresh fruit, vegetables. Menus of 1,200–1,500 calories per day for women, 1,800–2,000 calories for men. Program includes 3 meals daily. Breakfast is scrambled eggs and oatmeal muffin. Lunch includes salad, seafood chowder, and rice pudding. Dinner choice is ossobuco braised in wine, with broccoli, millet, and cantaloupe sorbet.
Services and Facilities	**Exercise Equipment:** 5 Keiser Cam II pneumatic resistance units, 4-station Universal gym, Liferower, 5 Lifecycles, Trotter treadmill, 4 Challenger treadmills, 2 StairMasters. **Services:** Facials, body massage, loofah scrub, hydrotherapy, herbal or clay wrap, fango bath, body brushing, cellulite massage, thalassotherapy, aromatherapy massage; beauty and skincare salon. **Swimming Facilities:** Indoor exercise pool, outdoor lap pool. **Spa Facilities:** Men's and women's sauna and steam room, whirlpool; aerobics classes, private workouts. Closed Sun. afternoon. **Recreation Facilities:** Tennis courts.

Norwich Golf Course and Fort Shantok State Park adjoin the inn's 37 acres. Rental bicycles. **Evening Programs:** Cooking demonstrations, fitness lectures, color analysis.

In the Area Mystic Seaport Maritime Museum, General Dynamics submarine base in Groton, Old Lyme art center and historic homes. Cathedral of St. Patrick in Old Norwich, Essex summer beach colony, Eugene O'Neill Theater Center, Goodspeed Opera House in Haddam, Foxwoods Casino.

Getting Here *From New York City.* By train, Amtrak from Grand Central Station to New London (90 min). By air, scheduled flights to New London by American Airlines and USAir. By car, I-95 to I-395, Rte. 32 to Norwich. Hotel limousine service to the airport and train station in New London ($15 each way). Taxi and rental car available in Norwich and New London. Ample free parking.

Special Notes No smoking in the spa and spa dining room. Spa hours: weekdays 9 AM–6 PM, weekends 8:30 AM–8 PM.

Northern Pines Health Resort

Holistic health
Weight management
Stress control

Maine Getting back to nature can be a healthy experience on the 80
Raymond acres of the Northern Pines Health Resort. The diet and fitness programs, based on a holistic approach, are designed to help participants develop a positive attitude toward weight loss and stress control; the transition is a gradual process, not a quick fix. Lifestyle management, rather than exercise, is emphasized in morning and evening classes.

Essentially a self-help camp with a limited number of optional services, Northern Pines offers a program designed for men and women who want to take control of their lives. Campers range widely in age, a high percentage of them being over 40. The affordable rates make it popular with singles year-round. About 50 guests are resident in summer, 30 during the ski season, which makes for a friendly mix with lots of personal attention from the staff.

Each day begins with stretching exercises and a brisk walk through the woods, followed by a choice of focus sessions or aerobics. Morning and afternoon yoga are optional. Evenings offer more learning activities, from cooking classes to massage demonstrations. Fasting regimens are offered, and about 20% of the guests opt to go on a week-long juice fast.

The camp's lakeside log cabins date from the 1920s and provide total seclusion for couples. New lodge rooms and cabins with two bedrooms are on the hillside amid towering pines, spruce, and hemlock. There are also yurts (earth-covered cabins) for two that have carpeting and modern conveniences.

The informality and laid-back pace appeal to stressed-out professionals who come here to rejuvenate and relax. On a warm summer evening it's not unusual to see swimmers skinny-dipping in the lake after a rap session in the hot tub. Leave your resort clothes at home and bring your old sweatshirts and hiking boots.

Northern Pines Health Resort
Rte. 85, R.R. 1, Box 279, Raymond, ME 04071
Tel. 207/655-7624

Administration Owner/director, Marlee Turner; manager, Susan Lubner

Season Year-round except Nov.–mid-Dec., mid-March–May.

Accommodations Private cabins and lodge rooms for 50. Some share a bathroom, others a communal facility; most have private toilet and shower. Well-worn wood furniture and buildings. Small laundry.

Rates 1-week summer program (Sun.–Sun.) $675–$1,300; weekend (2 nights) $230–$440. Rooms $90–$220 per day. 50% deposit per person, add 10% tax. Credit cards: AE, MC, V.

Meal Plans Modified vegetarian diet, 800 calories per day. 3 meals daily include pasta, salads with home-grown sprouts, poached salmon. Supervised fasts begin with 2 days of raw fruit, vegetables, juices, and broth.

Services and Facilities **Exercise Equipment:** NordicTrack cross-country ski machine, 2 stationary bikes, Solaflex unit, slant board, rebounders, free weights. **Services:** Massage, reflexology, aromatherapy, facials, hair treatment, herbal wrap, floattank sessions, Clearlight therapy. **Swimming Facilities:** Lake with sandy beach. **Recreation Facilities:** Hiking, canoeing, sailing; jogging trails. **Evening Programs:** Cooking demonstrations, massage techniques, sauna baths, salt rubs; videos, storytelling.

In the Area L. L. Bean store, ocean beaches, White Mountain Range; Acadia National Park; ferry trips to Nova Scotia; Portland's restored Old Port, summer theater, Portland Museum of Art; factory outlets in Freeport.

Getting Here *From Portland.* By car, I-95 to Exit 8, Rte. 302 northwest to Rte. 83 (45 min). By air, service to Portland International Airport. Bus station and airport van service for Sun. afternoon arrivals and departures $5 (other times $25–$40). Rental car, taxi available.

Special Notes Summer camp for children, 3½ or 7 weeks. No smoking in public areas. Two rooms accessible for handicapped.

Poland Spring Health Institute

Preventive medicine
Vibrant maturity

Maine
Poland Spring
An extended visit to Poland Spring Health Institute is more like taking a holiday in the country than being at a clinic. The program outlined for you includes drinking the area's world-famous water, a vegetarian diet, and rigorous outdoor exercise.

Just 10 guests are accommodated in old-fashioned comfort in a big New England house; the average stay is two weeks. Run on a nonprofit basis, the group emphasizes Christian traditions. A special program for smoking cessation (14 days) is offered as well.

Guests work closely with specialists on diabetes and stress related ailments. A series of exercises and hydrotherapy treatments is prescribed that is appropriate to your physical condition. Testing by the medical office, when needed, is an additional charge; everything else is included in the weekly fee.

You've Let Your Imagination Go, Now Get Up And Follow Your Dreams.

For The Vacation You're Dreaming Of, Call American Express® Travel Agency At 1-800-YES-AMEX.*

American Express will send more than your imagination soaring. We'll fly you, sail you, drive you to any Fodor's destination and beyond. Because American Express believes the best vacations happen from Europe to the Orient, Walt Disney® World to Hawaii and everywhere in between.

For dependable service, expert advice, and value wherever your dreams take you, call on American Express. After all, the best traveling companion is a trustworthy friend.

AMERICAN EXPRESS Travel Agency

It's easy to recognize a good place when you see one.

American Express Cardmembers have been doing it for years.

The secret? Instead of just relying on what they see in the window, they look at the door. If there's an American Express Blue Box on it, they know they've found an establishment that cares about high standards.

Whether it's a place to eat, to sleep, to shop, or simply meet, they know they will be warmly welcomed.

So much so, they're rarely taken in by anything else.

Always a good sign.

Poland Spring has been synonomous with healthy water for more than a century, largely due to a commercial bottling plant near the institute. Here you drink 8–10 glasses a day directly from the well and bathe in the water, which is piped into the steam room and used for body wraps preceding massage.

The institute's scenic surroundings compensate for a lack of recreational facilities. You can hike, jog, do the parcourse, borrow a bike. In winter there are cross-country skiing and ice skating. An aerobics studio is built into the house, as are the hydrotherapy facilities. After a full day, most guests seem to prefer relaxing on the sun porch and appreciating the view.

Poland Spring Health Institute

RFD 1, Box 4300, Summit Spring Rd., Poland Spring, ME 04274
Tel. 207/998–2894; clinic 207/998–2795
Fax 207/998–2164

Administration Medical director, Richard A. Hansen, M.D.; program director, Ulla Hansen

Season Year-round.

Accommodations 5 large rooms, most sharing a bath.

Rates Semiprivate room $745 a week with meals, private room $950, tax and service charge included. $200 nonrefundable reservation fee. No credit cards.

Meal Plans Salads and steamed vegetbles, fresh fruit, and homebaked bread make up the diet of complex carbohydrates. Dinner buffet may consist of gluten roast, baked potato, green beans, salad. Menu changes daily.

Services and Facilities **Exercise Equipment:** Stationary and outdoor bikes. **Swimming Facilities:** Private lake. **Recreation Facilities:** Boating, canoeing, biking, horseback riding; nearby golf. **Evening Programs:** Lectures on health-related subjects.

In the Area Shopping and sightseeing trips. Shaker village at Sabbathday Lake.

Getting Here By air, Portland International Airport, 30 mi. By car, Boston, about 120 mi. Courtesy transfers.

Special Notes No smoking indoors. Remember to bring sturdy walking shoes, rain gear, and personal medical records as requested.

Camp Lenox for Adults

Spiritual awareness

Massachusetts
Lee

Transformational experiences at Camp Lenox for Adults combine the spiritual and mystical aspects of life. The experiences take some participants to the edge of their ordinary reality, uniting the spiritual and the mundane. Transformation reportedly occurs when the past is incorporated into the present, opening new possibilities for the future.

Campers have full run of the scenic, 250-acre site. The wooden cottages cluster on a hillside overlooking Lake Shaw, and there are 10 tennis courts, a weight training room, and a crafts center as well as water sports facilities. A lakefront dining room, an indoor theater, and newly designed community housing complete the villagelike atmosphere.

Camp Lenox for Adults

Rte. 8, Lee, MA 01238
(Oct.–May 10) 345 Riverside Dr., New York, NY 10025
Tel. 413/243–2223 (212/662–3182 Oct.–May 10)

Administration Program director, Richard M. Moss

Season June and Sept.

Accommodations Community houses and cottages for 8–14 persons, 8 private cottages with twin beds, tent area for 150. Limited bedding.

Rates Tuition $80–$220, meals included. Full payment in advance. No credit cards.

Meal Plans 6 vegetarian gourmet meals are served during the weekend, buffet style. Special diets accommodated with advance notice.

Services and Facilities **Exercise Equipment:** Universal weight training gym. **Swimming Facilities:** Private lake. **Recreation Facilities:** Hiking, jogging, basketball, tennis, sailing, canoeing, kayaking. **Evening Programs:** Concerts, talent shows.

In the Area Summer theater and dance festivals; museums.

Getting Here *From Boston or Albany.* By car, Massachusetts Turnpike (I-90) to Lee (Exit 2), then Rte. 20 and 8. *From New York City and Connecticut.* By car, Rte. 8 North. By bus, daily scheduled service to Lee on Greyhound and Bonanza from Boston and New York. Taxi service in Lee.

Canyon Ranch in the Berkshires

Stress control
Nutrition and diet
Kid fitness
Life enhancement
Weight management
Luxury pampering

Massachusetts
Lenox Canyon Ranch has a mind-and-body approach to fitness that focuses on improving your lifestyle. Skiers can get in shape before tackling cross-country trails, and executives can use the latest biofeedback systems to de-stress. A 100,000-square-foot fitness center includes racquetball, squash, and tennis courts; a running track; a 75-foot swimming pool; and separate spas for men and women with saunas, steam rooms, inhalation rooms, and Jacuzzis.

The Arizona Canyon Ranch's hiking and biking programs have been adapted to the Berkshire terrain, but don't expect to find Southwestern food and lodging. The Boston-based architectural firm of Jung/Brannen (designers of the Doral Saturnia Spa in Florida) has come up with an original design for bringing the outdoors inside. The centerpiece, a mansion that dates from 1897, and its formal gardens, has a restaurant where you dine elegantly on New American cuisine in a replica of Louis XVI's Petit Trianon. Wrapped around the structure are glass walkways that connect to the inn and fitness center.

In addition to daily yoga, meditation, and breathing classes offered in the fitness department, you can schedule private consultations to reduce stress or stop smoking. Centrally located on the second and third floors of the mansions are the medical, behavioral, and movement therapy departments.

Surrounded by majestic views of the Berkshires, the new Canyon Ranch captures the active, informal atmosphere that has been a hallmark of the original in Arizona.

Canyon Ranch in the Berkshires
91 Kemble St. (Rte. 7A), Lenox, MA 02140
Tel. 413/637–4100 or 800/742–9000
Fax 413/637–0057

Administration Manager, Mary Ellen St. John; medical director, Tildabeth Doscher, M.D.

Season Year-round.

Accommodations 120 rooms, mostly gracious units with private patios. New England-style functional furnishings.

Rates $1,130–$1,310 single, $910–$1,100 double occupancy per person for a 4-day/3-night package including 2 services, all meals, and activities. A week costs $2,670 single, $2,220 double, with 5 services, 2 consultations. Service charge (18%) and tax added. 2 nights' deposit in advance. Credit cards: MC, V.

Meal Plans 3 meals and snacks, plus nonalcoholic drinks. Low-cal menus include New England specialties cooked with a minimum of salt and fat. Recipes are 60–65% carbohydrate, 20% protein, and 15–20% fat. 1,200 calories per day recommended for women, 1,500 for men. Vegetarian meals and special diets available. Supervised fasting with doctor's approval. Coffee, tea, milk served; no alcohol.

Services and Facilities **Exercise Equipment:** State-of-the-art treadmills, stair climbers, stationary bikes, rowing machines, free weights, and a full set of Keiser CAM III pneumatic units. **Services:** Herbal wraps, massage (Swedish, shiatsu), aromatherapy, hydrotherapy, herbal wrap, loofah body scrub, acupuncture, and beauty salon; holistic health counseling, biofeedback training; medical checkup and fitness evaluation. **Swimming Facilities:** Indoor and 50-foot heated outdoor pool. **Spa Facilities:** Separate wings for men and women with sauna, steam room, Jacuzzi; studios for aerobics, yoga; aquacise class. **Recreation Facilities:** Cross-country skiing, hiking; bicycles for daily group outings; 3 indoor tennis courts (Har Tru), 3 outdoor courts (clay), 2 racquetball courts, squash court, indoor track. **Evening Programs:** Visiting specialists speak on health and lifestyle topics.

In the Area Optional tours to local museums and festivals. Tanglewood Music Festival, Jacob's Pillow Dance Festival, The Sterling and Francine Clark Art Institute in Williamstown (25 mi), Williamstown summer theater, Appalachian Trail.

Getting Here *From Boston and New York City.* By car, Massachusetts Turnpike (I-90) (3 hrs). By train, daily Amtrak service to Albany, NY; complimentary transfer. By air, scheduled flights to Albany Airport or Bradley International at Hartford/Springfield. Taxi, rental car, limousine for local travel. Complimentary transfers for airports.

Special Notes Ramp entry to all buildings and facilities. Some bedrooms specially equipped for the disabled. A combination of outdoor and supervised fitness training for teenagers called The Young and Restless, July–Aug. No smoking indoors. Spa hours: daily 6:30 AM–10 PM.

Kripalu Center for Yoga and Health

Spiritual awareness
Life enhancement
Preventive medicine

Massachusetts
Lenox

The ancient science of yoga has been synthesized with modern approaches to holistic health and personal growth in a series of programs designed to fight stress and increase well-being. The enormous brick mansion, built for Andrew Carnegie and later enlarged, provides a suitably expansive setting.

On a typical day you have a choice of lectures, workshops, bodywork, and several yoga sessions. Mornings begin in a meditative mood at 5:45 in the main chapel, or with a 6:45 yoga session, followed by breakfast eaten in silence. Most of the guests, who can number to 350, start their day walking about the grounds.

In addition to the daily schedule, there are special programs with such names as Inner Quest Intensive, Relationships that Work, Self-Esteem, Transform Stress, and Getaway Health Holiday. These workshops, lasting four and five days or a weekend, are scheduled throughout the year.

Guiding the focus of all activities is the center's founder, Yogi Amrit Desai, who developed the Kripalu style of yoga. By drawing on the slow performance of classic yoga positions, Kripalu creates a "meditation in movement." Even the aerobic dance class, called DansKinetics, mixes yoga stretches with energetic dance steps.

Classes are divided into beginner, intermediate, and advanced. After dinner, everyone is invited to *satsang*, an evening of meditation and chanting. The theme is not self-denial, but vibrant health.

Participants range in age from 18 to 80 and work together to rediscover themselves through a variety of inner-attunement techniques. Some guests come for a few days of rest and renewal; others seek compassion and healing through private consultation. None of the programs are mandatory, and there's no effort to convert anyone to anything here. Surrounded by 300 acres of forest, this is a peaceful retreat for body and soul.

Kripalu Center for Yoga and Health
Box 793, Lenox, MA 01240
Tel. 413/637–3280 or 800/967–3577

Administration Spiritual director, Yogi Amrit Desai

Season Year-round.

Accommodations Rooms and dormitory bunks for 350. Bedding, sheets, and towels not included. A few deluxe rooms with private or shared baths and a private lounge for breakfast. No maid service.

Lakeview rooms (2 beds) at extra cost. Double beds in forest view rooms. Linens provided.

Rates $120 for a welcome weekend, dormitory accommodations; $420–$900 for 6-night workshops. $60–$145 per day without program. 25% deposit in advance. No refunds, but deposit can be applied to future programs. Credit cards: MC, V.

Meal Plans 3 vegetarian meals daily, buffet style, includes whole grains and vegetables, dairy products. Full salad bar, several entrees, fresh-baked bread, variety of condiments, and hot or cold tea served at noon. Food is low in fat and sweeteners. Special diets accommodated by advance request. Meals eaten in silence to maintain the spiritual atmosphere.

Services and Facilities **Services:** Massage therapies, including Kripalu bodywork, polarity, shiatsu; facial and foot care; medical tests. **Swimming Facilities:** Private lake. **Spa Facilities:** Saunas for men and women, whirlpool, flotation tank. **Recreation Facilities:** Dans-Kinetic aerobic exercise class; skiing in winter. **Evening Programs:** Communal meditation and chanting; Indian dancing and concerts.

In the Area Tanglewood Music Festival (July–Aug.), summer theater and dance; the Sterling and Francine Clark Art Institute in Williamstown.

Getting Here By car, Massachusetts Turnpike (I-90) from Boston, New York City, and the west. Approaching Tanglewood and Stockbridge, look for Richmond Mountain Rd. By air, Bradley International Airport at Hartford/Springfield. By train, Amtrak has 1 train daily from Boston to Pittsfield, with connections to Lenox by Bonanza Bus or Regional Transit. Taxi and limousine service in Lenox.

Special Notes Facilities and rooms specially equipped for the disabled. Day camp for children 4–12, July–Aug., $30 per day. No smoking in or near the center. Remember to bring mat or cushion for meditation and yoga; bedding and towels for dormitory accommodations.

The Kushi Institute of the Berkshires

Nutrition and diet
Spiritual awareness

Massachusetts At the Kushi Institute of the Berkshires, macrobiotics is
Becket taught and experienced as a way of life. The diet is low in saturated fat and high in fiber, natural vitamins, and minerals.

The macrobiotic diet, say its supporters, provides a unifying understanding of life. Since 1978, the Kushi Institute has been in the forefront of macrobiotic research and education. The center offers an intensive seminar in cooking, plus four or five days of instruction on preventing cancer and heart disease. For newcomers to macrobiotics, there is a week-long introductory course that includes exercise and massage.

Secluded on 600 acres of woodlands and meadows, the Berkshire center provides a peaceful, natural environment for study and relaxation. In a former Franciscan abbey, the bedrooms and working kitchen accommodate up to 15 participants in year-round programs. Many of these seminars are taught personally by Aveline and Michio Kushi. In 1986, a spiritual dimension was added, focusing on personal health and transformation, issues of family and society, and global understanding.

The daily activities begin with a session of *do-in*, stretching exercises that are simple and easy to learn. Periods of meditation alternate with lectures and workshops in food preparation. Individuals, couples, and families often participate together.

The Kushi Institute of the Berkshires
308 Leland Rd., Box 7, Becket, MA 01223
Tel. 413/623-5742
Fax 413/623-8827

Administration	Manager, Carolyn Heidenry; program director, Charles Millman
Season	Year-round macrobiotic residential seminar is offered twice a month, beginning on a Sun. and running through lunch the following Sat. Cooking intensives and topical seminars run 4–5 days. Multipart spiritual training seminar scheduled at various times of the year.
Accommodations	10 guest rooms, simply furnished with 1 or 2 beds; 3 rooms have private bath or shower facility.
Rates	7-day residential seminars with meals and a shared bedroom, $795; $595 for room and board only. Private bath $25 additional per day. $100 advance deposit per person. Credit cards: MC, V.
Meal Plans	3 meals daily, family style. Brown rice, miso soup, beans, and cooked vegetables with salads, natural desserts. Specialties include tofu and seitan dishes, sushi, noodles and pasta, amasake pudding.
Services and Facilities	**Services:** Shiatsu massage. Acupressure. **Swimming Facilities:** Nearby lake. **Evening Programs:** Workshops and discussions on diet and nutrition; informal entertainment.
In the Area	Tanglewood Music Festival at Lenox (35 min); summer theater and the Sterling and Francine Clark Art Institute in Williamstown (90 min); Jacob's Pillow Dance Festival in Becket.
Getting Here	*From Boston.* By car, Massachusetts Turnpike (I-90), exit for Lee (2½ hr). By bus, Peter Pan Bus Lines or Bonanza Bus Lines to Lee (3 hr). By air, Bradley International Airport at Hartford/Springfield. Free pickup at bus station in Lee; taxi, car rental available.
Special Notes	No smoking on premises except in smoking lounge.

Maharishi Ayur-Veda Health Center

Spiritual awareness
Preventive medicine
Nutrition and diet

Massachusetts
Lancaster

Ancient Indian healing techniques and modern biofeedback technology are the means to relaxation and good health in the elegant mansion of the Maharishi Ayur-Ved Health Center. Ayurvedic medical treatments are based on an analysis of one's *dosha*, or physical and emotional type. The therapy includes a special diet related to body type, massage with warm oil and herbal essences, and total relaxation.

The healing process of *panchakarma* begins with a physical examination, pulse measurement, and a thorough questionnaire to determine whether you are *vata* (quick, energetic, movement prone), *pitta* (enterprising and sharp), or *kapha* (tranquil and steady). Therapy and diet are prescribed accordingly.

While the system is based on Ayur-Veda, as practiced in Asia, the center's doctors and registered nurses are trained in both Eastern and Western medicine. Cancer and other disease sufferers frequently come for treatment.

A daily two-hour session to rid the body of impurities includes massage, heat application, and a gentle laxative. Neuromuscular training may be recommended through yoga exercises. Aromatherapy is also available, and a course in transcendental meditation is taught for an extra fee. Sound therapy is the focus of the stress-reduction program. Listening to primordial sounds re-created by musical instruments and the human voice, or to tapes of musical rhythms (called *gandharveda* sounds), induces relaxation.

Furnished with large beds and heavy but comfortable chairs, the high-ceiling rooms retain a look of luxury from the 1920s, when this was the country cottage of a shipping magnate involved with the *Titanic*.

Maharishi Ayur-Veda Health Center
679 George Hill Rd.,
Box 344, Lancaster, MA 01523
Tel. 508/365–4549

Administration	Director, Dee Miller; medical director, Deepak Chopra, M.D.
Season	Year-round.
Accommodations	14 bedrooms with several suites. Some small single rooms share a bath. All rooms air-conditioned.
Rates	1-week program $2,850–$3,950 single or double occupancy. Week-long deluxe Royal Program with suite $4,000–$4,300. No credit cards.
Meal Plans	3 vegetarian meals daily in the formal dining room or guests' rooms. Indian rice and dal with cooked vegetables, herb seasoning, and cooked fruit. Specialties include vegetable pâté. Bland diet with few fats and no dairy products other than milk. Herbal teas and lassa as recommended by the doctor.
Services and Facilities	**Services:** Transcendental meditation (TM) instruction in stress-management techniques, psychophysiological audio program, self-pulse diagnosis, aromatherapy. Most programs include massages, heat treatments, and internal cleansing. **Evening Programs:** Videotapes and lectures on health-related topics.
Getting Here	*From Boston:* By car, Massachusetts Turnpike (I-90) west to Rte. 495 North, exit on Rte. 117 West to Rte. 70. Entrance is on George Hill Rd. (about 3 hr). Limousine, rental car for local use.
Special Notes	No smoking.

The Option Institute

Life enhancement
Holistic health
Stress control
Spiritual awareness

Massachusetts The approach at the Option Institute, a mountain retreat, is to
Sheffield nurture healthy attitudes toward life rather than emphasize
physical fitness. Personal attitudes, beliefs, and feelings are
examined to develop a fuller understanding of how to improve
one's physical and mental health. Working in group sessions
and private consultations, participants are taught to be more
accepting of themselves, to learn to find alternatives, and to
form more loving relationships.

Founded in 1983 by Barry Neil Kaufman and Suzi Lyte Kaufman, who have written and lectured on interpersonal relationships, the Option Institute sets out to provide a stimulating
environment for people from all walks of life. Young professionals as well as families of children with special needs come for
weekends and intensive programs of up to eight weeks. A participant is expected to gain a profound sense of energy and vig-
or from the release of tensions. The 85-acre campus set amid
grassy meadows, forests, and streams provides the setting
that can inspire a fresh attitude toward life.

The Option Institute
R.D. 1, Box 174A, Sheffield, MA 01257
Tel. 413/229–2100
Fax 413/229–8831

Administration Program directors, Susan Abrams and Richard Magan

Season Year-round.

Accommodations Cottages have 18 bedrooms, each with 2 beds, shared bath, and
shower. The simply furnished, newly constructed cottages use
natural wood and lots of windows for an open, rustic feeling.

Rates 3-day weekends (Thurs.–Sun.) $395 per person double occu-
pancy, meals included. 1-week intensives exploring the impact
of attitude on body and health $995–$1,125. Specially designed
programs, about $150 per day. Some kitchen-equipped cot-
tages for families with autistic or learning-impaired children.
50% deposit. Credit cards: MC, V.

Meal Plans Vegetarian meals 3 times daily, buffet style. Specialties include vegetarian lasagna, whole-grain casseroles, legumes,
seasonal vegetables, Greek salad, pasta. Limited amounts of
eggs, cheese, milk.

Services and **Services:** Swedish massage; private counseling. **Swimming Fa-**
Facilities **cilities:** Pond. **Recreation Facilities:** Hiking the Appalachian
Trail; downhill skiing at Butternut and Catamount, cross-
country skiing. **Evening Programs:** Workshops and group discussions on health, personal relationships, communication.

In the Area Tanglewood Music Festival at Lenox; summer theater; the
Sterling and Francine Clark Art Institute in Williamstown;
Jacob's Pillow Dance Festival in Lee.

Getting Here *From New York City.* By car, I-95 to the Massachusetts Turnpike, exit for Sheffield (3 hr). By bus, Bonanza Bus Line from

Port Authority Terminal to Sheffield (3 hr). By air, Bradley International Airport at Hartford/Springfield. Free pickup at bus station in Sheffield; private limousine service from airport.

Special Notes Limited access for the disabled. Special training for children who are brain impaired, autistic, or have learning problems. No smoking indoors.

Rowe Conference Center

Spiritual awareness

Massachusetts Weekend programs to stimulate the mind on spiritual and
Rowe health topics are the specialty of the Rowe Conference Center, a mountain retreat affiliated with the Unitarian Universalist Association. The white clapboard farmhouse and two new buildings host a small, nondenominational community that offers a warm, uncompetitive atmosphere for personal and spiritual growth.

Surrounded by 1,400 acres of forest in western Massachussets, Rowe provides a quiet place to discuss current health issues. Topics include clinical and spiritual healing, mastering the mind-body connection, and shamanism. The discussion leaders are on the leading edge of new ways to live full and productive lives. Special weeks are devoted to adult recovery from alcohol problems, for women's issues, and single parents.

Operated like a camp, the center offers no organized fitness program and lets visitors take advantage of natural attractions on their own schedule. Recently expanded guest accommodations provide basic comforts, including a coed sauna. Guests do their own housekeeping and supply their own bedding (available at extra charge).

Rowe Conference Center
Kings Highway Rd., Rowe, MA 01367
Tel. 413/339–4216

Administration Manager, Emmy Howard

Season Year-round.

Accommodations 10 private bedrooms, all with semiprivate bath and 2 beds (bedding at additional cost). Also dormitory rooms for 6–8 people.

Rates Weekend program $90–$165 (depending on guests' financial situation). Room and meals $110 double occupancy, $130 single, $90 dormitory. All require advance payment of $60. Credit cards: MC, V.

Meal Plans Meals from Fri. dinner to Sun. lunch. Vegetarian food served in ample quantities, family style. Seasonal specialties include lentil loaf, squash casserole, and pasta primavera. Eggs and dairy products served, meat on request; special diets accommodated.

Services and Facilities Services: Swedish massage. **Swimming Facilities:** Lake. **Recreation Facilities:** Hiking, cross-country and downhill skiing. **Evening Programs:** Discussion groups, sweat lodge.

Getting Here *From Boston.* By car, I-91 or Rte. 2 to Greenfield, MA, then west on Rte. 2 (the Mohawk Trail) 19 mi to Rowe (3 hr). By bus, Englander Line to Charlemont (2¾ hr).

Special Notes Guest house accessible for wheelchairs. Summer camp for children; weeks for 4th graders to high school seniors. No smoking indoors. Remember to bring sheets and blanket for dormitory rooms.

Smith College Adult Camp

Sports conditioning
Vibrant maturity

Massachusetts Based on the campus of Smith College in the scenic Berkshire
Northampton Mountains, this one-week program offers cross-training with professionals and faculty members in a variety of sports. In addition to tennis, squash, swimming, and track there is a fully equipped gym.

Scheduled activities include aerobics classes, yoga, tai chi chuan, and group hikes. Organized bike trips and outings to nearby attractions are available at no additional charge. Also offered is an introduction to stress control using biofeedback equipment.

Nutrition and dietary consultations with the staff nutritionist helps those concerned with weight loss. Meals are served cafeteria style in the college dining hall; vegetarian meals can be provided with advance request.

Limited to 35 participants, the program attracts a mix of men and women. Average age, 50; minimum age, 22.

Smith College Adult Camp
Northampton, MA 01063
Tel. 413/585–3975

Administration Manager, James A. Johnson

Season June.

Accommodations Dormitory rooms with 2 beds, shared bathroom. Laundry room.

Rates $585 for the 6-day program, includes room, meals, activities, 50% advance payment. No credit cards.

Meal Plan 3 meals daily.

Services and **Services:** Massage. **Exercise Equipment:** Eagle weight training
Facilities gym, indoor and outdoor running tracks. **Swimming Facilities:** 25-yd. indoor pool, lake. **Recreation Facilities:** 12 indoor tennis courts (lighted, Mondo surface), 4 outdoor tennis courts, 6 squash courts. **Evening Programs:** Orienteering, panel discussions, dances, cookouts.

Getting Here *From Boston, MA.* By car, Mass. Turnpike to Hwy. 91, Northampton exit (2½ hr).

DoveStar

Spiritual awareness
Holistic health

New Hampshire The Alchemian Institute, a professional training center for
Hooksett bodyworkers, offers weekend workshops and single-day visits for massage, meditation, and relaxation at DoveStar. Learning

who you are and how to make life more pleasurable and productive is the focus of the experience. Workshops and classes are open to visitors, and individual sessions for instruction or treatment can be scheduled. Vacationers, however, are not accommodated.

Alchemia, the art of personal transformation, is practiced in many ways. You can try rebirthing, creative visualization, and hypnotherapy; you can learn massage techniques. An in-depth session of spiritual counseling looks at how you deal with the issues in your life and offers a new perspective on personal problems.

Getting a massage is perhaps the best part of the day. Powerful yet gently energizing, it can release physical and emotional tensions. Specialists in several techniques work on the areas of your body that need energy balancing. For mental and physical weariness, an Esalen full-body massage is advised; Reiki works on the life-support system. The cost of an hour-long session is $30–$40.

Refreshingly down to earth, this New Age outpost provides rejuvenation on a budget. Overnight guests are accommodated in one of the antiques-filled bedrooms in the old farmhouse. This is a place where professionals in bodywork and stress management come for a retreat of their own.

DoveStar
50 Whitehall Rd., Hooksett, NH 03106
Tel. 603/669–9497

Administration Manager, Kamala Renner

Season Year-round.

Accommodations 2 rooms with antique furniture; air mattress in classroom (linens and towels provided). Shared bath.

Rates $15–$25 nightly for lodging; tuition for weekends $125–$160. 50% payable in advance. Credit cards: MC, V.

Meal Plans No meals. Restaurants include the Swiss Cafe and Spatts, which feature fresh seafood, salad bar, and such seasonal specialties as baked chicken, roast pheasant, duckling.

Services and Facilities **Services:** Alchemia bodywork combination, Reiki, Esalen massage, acupressure, foot reflexology, salt rub, astrology, regressions, hypnotherapy, Ortho-Bionomy, rebirthing. **Swimming Facilities:** Outdoor, heated swimming pool. Naturists welcome. **Recreation Facilities:** Hiking, cross-country skiing, ice skating. **Evening Programs:** New Age tapes and videos; meditation.

In the Area Manchester industrial area redevelopment (arts and crafts), Currier Gallery (New England arts).

Getting Here *From Boston.* By car, north on I-93 to Manchester, Exit 7 onto Rte. 101 East to Bypass 28 for Hooksett, Rte. 27 to the Earth-Star Center (60 min). By bus, Vermont Transit to Manchester, NH (80 min). By air, major airlines serve Manchester. Complimentary transfers at Manchester.

Special Notes Limited access for the disabled. No smoking indoors.

Waterville Valley Resort

New Hampshire
Waterville Valley

Non-program resort facilities

Surrounded by mountain peaks and forests of green fir and silver birch, this 500-acre recreational complex became a four-season resort in 1987 with the opening of a $2-million sports center. The use of the facilities is a bonus for guests at the deluxe lodges and condominiums of the Waterville Valley Resort. In warm weather, you can play tennis on one of 18 clay courts (modest fee), golf, hike, or cycle. In winter, world-class downhill and cross-country skiing covers 225 acres. Services and classes at the center are offered on an à la carte basis.

At the foot of Mt. Tecumseh a full-service ski shop rents equipment and offers instruction. Thirty-five downhill trails are ranked for beginner, intermediate, and advanced skiers. Snowmaking equipment assures good snow conditions from mid-November through mid-April.

The Cross Country Ski Center at one end of the valley is another attraction. Fourteen trails lead into the heart of the forest. Inside the center are two restaurants and a barn where large, shaggy horses wait to be hitched to a wagon that treats children to an old-fashioned sleigh ride.

The Sports Center, open every day of the year, offers indoor and outdoor tennis and swimming, racquetball, squash, and a weights room. A coed sauna and Jacuzzi are available in addition to separate facilities and steam rooms for men and women.

The range of activities makes Waterville Valley a good choice for family vacations. A community bus service provides free transportation all day. While the kids are enjoying a fleet of boats on the pond or taking ski lessons, parents can exercise their options at the Sports Center.

Waterville Valley Resort
Box 417, Waterville Valley, NH 03215
Tel. 603/236–8303 (800/468–2553 for lodging)

Administration Sports center manager, William Travis

Season Year-round.

Accommodations 4,000 beds in quarters that range in variety from deluxe chalet-style inns to modest condominium apartments. Leading choices are Snowy Owl Inn, Black Bear Lodge, and fully equipped 2-story houses. Bookings through the lodging bureau.

Rates 1-bedroom apartments at the Black Bear $89–$99 daily for 1 to 2 persons, 3-day package $255 per couple, includes unlimited midweek golf, tennis, boating, and use of Sports Center. ($5 weekend charge at Sports Center). Add 8% tax. 50% advance payment. Credit cards: AE, DC, MC, V.

Meal Plans No meals in ski or spa packages. Spa food at 2 restaurants: O'Keefe's has vegetarian burgers, fitness salads; the Finish Line has light fare such as broiled fish, fruit plate with cottage cheese, roast chicken.

Services and Facilities **Exercise Equipment:** 4 Nautilus, 1 lats unit, 2 Monark bikes, rowing machine, free weights. **Services:** Swedish massage, aerobics classes, aquacise. **Swimming Facilities:** Indoor and

outdoor 25-meter pools, pond. **Recreation Facilities:** 2 indoor
tennis courts, 2 racquetball courts, squash court, indoor running track, golf, canoeing, horseback riding, skiing, ice skating, hiking, sailing, biking. **Evening Programs:** Seasonal
entertainment.

In the Area   Mt. Washington cog railway.

Getting Here   *From Boston.* By car, Rte. 3 to I-93, exit for Waterville (28),
then 11 miles on Rte. 49 (2½ hr). By bus, Greyhound to North
Conway, NH (3 hr). By air, scheduled flights to Manchester,
NH. Rental car, Valley shuttle bus available.

Special Notes   Ramps and elevator in Sports Center. Ski camps, tennis
camps, and outdoor wading pool for children. No smoking in
sports center.

Aegis

Spiritual awareness

New York
New Lebanon

A philosophy of the interrelatedness of all spiritual traditions
is at the heart of the study programs offered by Aegis in historic Shaker buildings on the grounds of a 430-acre mountaintop
compound. Life is celebrated here in all its diversity with topics
ranging from Taoist healing to Zen dance. A visit is an experience in living together harmoniously and learning how to share
life's bounty.

Founded in 1975 as an esoteric school for the Sufi Order in the
West, the permanent community here is known as the Abode of
the Message. The teachings of their spiritual leaders, notably
Pir Vilayat Inayat Khan, focus on the nature of healing. The
Sufi path is explored at weekend retreats and in a summer se-
ries of workshops and retreats.

Aegis brings together people from diverse walks of life in a
common quest for self-fulfillment and inner growth. You can
pitch a tent or work in the kitchen, join prayer sessions three
times daily, or enter your own personal retreat.

Aegis
R.D. 1, Box 1030D, New Lebanon, NY 12125
Tel. 518/794-8095 or 518/794-8090

Season   Year-round.

Accommodations   Log cabins with 2 beds, 1-person huts, and camping space in
the woods; rooms and dormitory shared in the Abode communi-
ty. Washhouses have hot showers and toilets for men and
women.

Rates $30 per night, including meals. Tuition for 3-day program $150,
3-day retreat with lodging and meals, $270 single, $240 per person sharing room; tent space $210 with meals. 50% advance
payment. Credit cards: MC, V.

Meal Plans   3 vegetarian meals a day, with dairy and nondairy choices.

**Services and
Facilities**   **Swimming Facilities:** Nearby lakes. **Recreation Facilities:** Hiking, cross-country skiing.

Getting Here   Located between Albany, NY and Pittsfield, MA, the Abode
provides pickup service at train and bus stations, and at Albany

airport. *From New York City.* By car, Taconic Parkway north to Rte. 295, Rte. 22 to Rte. 20 in New Lebanon.

Special Notes No smoking in communal areas. Remember to bring sleeping bag or bedding, warm clothing, insect repellent. No children.

Gurney's Inn

Luxury pampering

New York At the International Health and Beauty Spa the specialty is
Montauk seawater therapy by the sea. Located on the tip of Long Island, with all the amenities of a big beach resort, the spa at Gurney's Inn draws on the ocean for inspiration. The sybarite can revel in seaweed baths, swim in a 60-foot indoor seawater pool, have a seaweed facial, and dine on seafood while enjoying a view of the sea.

Modeled after European spas where ocean water is an integral part of advanced hydrotherapy, Gurney's adds aerobics, stress control, diet programs, and beauty-salon services. Executives can join a longevity program based on a health and fitness assessment; exercise buffs can concentrate on conditioning. Five packages, all with thalassotherapy, last from three days to a week; or you can put together an à la carte program.

Sea air and miles of white sandy beach come with your room at the inn. Brisk morning walks along the shore start the daily program. Add to that a 14-station parcourse, with instruction twice daily, for exercise at your own pace. Invigorated by the ocean, you can join an aquatics exercise class in the pool, relax in a sunken Roman bath, or swim in the surf.

The diversity of the seawater treatments makes Gurney's special among spas on this side of the Atlantic. Filtered and heated water from the ocean is pumped into whirlpools designed for underwater massage, mixed with volcanic mud from Italy, used in wraps with seaweed products from France, and added to body scrubs with salt from the Dead Sea. Treatments are scheduled 8 AM–10 PM. Spa-plan guests receive priority.

Massage choices include thalassotherapy, Swedish-style massage, Trager rhythmic rocking, Rolfing, polarity, reflexology, and shiatsu. Lymph drainage and deep facial work are offered. A full-service beauty salon is open to all guests.

The spa building is a world apart from the convention and timeshare vacation crowds that keep Gurney's Inn busy much of the year. The pool and classes are open to all guests, however, and this puts a strain on the facilities during the peak summer season. For peace and quiet, schedule your visit when the beach crowd goes home or during the winter, when you can take long walks, skate on the patio, and swim in the heated seawater pool while enjoying the seascape through the picture windows.

Gurney's Inn
Old Montauk Highway, Montauk, NY 11954
Tel. 516/668–2345 or 800/848–7639

Administration Keepers of the inn, Lola and Nick Monte; spa director, Margaret McNeill Byrnes

Season Year-round.

Accommodations Time-share apartments with 126 bedrooms including suites and cottages. None connect to the spa.

Rates Marine Renewal plan in summer, 4 days, $390 plus accommodations; fall-winter "Escape" 3-day/2-night package with room $448 single or double; 5-day/4-night Health and Beauty Plan package $1,119 single or double. Daily facility fee for non-residents $16.50; one-day package (nonresident) $150. Add 15% service charge, 7.5% tax. 25% payable in advance. Credit cards: AE, MC, V.

Meal Plans 3 spa meals daily included in packages. Spa cuisine in a private room and the main dining room. Calorie-controlled meals (1000–1200 calories per day) low in salt and sugar. Lunch can begin with tortellini en brodo or egg drop soup, three-bean salad; entree choice of manicotti, grilled salmon, steak stirfry, or whole wheat pasta. Dinner entrees include seafood brochette, paella vegetarian lasagna, chicken breast with asparagus. Herbal teas and espresso are available, as are vegetarian meals on request.

Services and Facilities **Exercise Equipment:** 15-station Universal gym, 4 Nautilus units, 2 Lifestep, 2 Lifecycle, Maxicam, 2 treadmills, dumbbells (3–75 lb), Olympic plates (2½–45 lb). **Services:** Massage, loofah scrub, herbal or seaweed wrap, facial, fango pack, aromatherapy, seawater private bath; health/fitness profile, biofeedback, private training. Full-service salon. **Swimming Facilities:** Indoor pool, ocean beach. **Recreation Facilities:** Hiking, jogging, disco dancing, yoga; tennis and horseback riding nearby; golf at Montauk Downs public course. **Evening Programs:** Lectures on health and nutrition; dancing and entertainment.

In the Area Historic homes, art galleries, whale-watching, museum, wineries, and boutiques in Montauk; summer theater; bird-watching.

Getting Here *From Connecticut and New England.* By ferry, at New London and Bridgeport. *From New York City.* By bus, Hampton Jitney and Montauk Express. By car, Long Island Expressway to Sunrise Highway (Rte. 27). By train, from Grand Central Station, the Long Island Railroad has daily round-trip schedules (tel. 212/526–0900). By air, USAir has scheduled flights to MacArthur Airport at Islip, private planes land at Montauk and East Hampton airports. Courtesy car meets trains and private planes. Rental car, taxi available.

Special Notes Children's swimming at midday and after 6 PM; under 18 not permitted in spa treatment areas. No smoking in the spa.

Living Springs Lifestyle Center

Preventive medicine
Vibrant maturity

New York **Putnam Valley** A budget-priced alternative to health resorts, the Living Springs Lifestyle Center is a residential retreat where you can improve your life and tone your body with spa-quality treatments. The medically supervised educational and conditioning programs focus on disease prevention, stress control, nutrition, weight management, and quitting smoking. Nondenominational and open to persons of all faiths, Living Springs offers a holistic health program for people past the age of 50 who want to recharge their lives.

The homelike atmosphere can be conducive to establishing lasting new habits. Healthy cooking is taught, and methods for preventing heart and other diseases are discussed. Daily exercise is geared to your level of fitness and personal goals.

Following a consultation with a doctor, you can schedule hydrotherapy treatments to promote healing or focus on relaxation. Saunas, alternating hot and cold showers, and exercise are also prescribed.

Natural foods and lots of spring water are key nutritional features. A community health service of the Seventh-day Adventists, the retreat specializes in vegetarian meals that are high in complex carbohydrates and fiber and free of fats and oil. The kitchen is kosher.

Living Springs Lifestyle Center
136 Bryant Pond Rd., Putnam Valley, NY 10579
Tel. 914/526–2800 or 800/729–9355

Administration	Manager, Herbert Poholka
Season	Year-round.
Accommodations	2-level modern lodge with 5 semiprivate rooms, 3 private rooms.
Rates	7-day program $750 per person, double occupancy. $100 payable in advance. Credit cards: MC, V.
Meal Plans	3 meals a day, buffet style. Lunch can include steamed vegetables, cashew chow mein, salad, fruit. No coffee or spices.
Services and Facilities	**Exercise Equipment:** Treadmill, rowing ergometer, 2 stationary bikes; outdoor parcourse. **Swimming Facilities:** Spring-fed lake. **Recreation Facilities:** Hiking and nature trails, boating; cross-country skiing; biking. **Evening Programs:** Lectures and films on health-related topics.
In the Area	West Point, Bear Mountain.
Getting Here	*From New York City.* By car, Taconic Parkway to Rte. 6 exit. By train, from Grand Central Station, Metro-North Commuter to Peekskill (free transfers). Pickup at airports on request. Courtesy car available.
Special Notes	No smoking.

Mohonk Mountain House

Sports conditioning
Life enhancement

New York
New Paltz

Nature walks have been a way of life at Mohonk Mountain House in the Hudson River Valley since 1875, and members of the founding family of Quakers are still active in organizing health and fitness weeks. Hikers, runners, and cross-country skiers choose from more than 100 miles of trails, paths, and carriage roads that link scenic sites within the 2,500 acres of private woodland. Others ride horseback or enjoy the crystal-clear lake.

What draws devoted guests back is an almost Zen-like detachment from reality. One writer known to science fiction fans calls it a private Shangri-la; time seems to stand still here.

In the hotel, a turreted and gabled Victorian structure that rambles an eighth of a mile and accommodates up to 500 guests, 19th-century manners and ambience are preserved. Choice rooms in the towers have original Victorian woodwork, working fireplace, balcony. There is no bar or smoking in public rooms, and a dress code is in effect for dinner.

Physiologists, sports trainers, and fitness buffs get together at Mohonk for exercise workshops and lectures. Scheduled throughout the year, they include weekend races, a five-day hiker's holiday covering four grades of terrain, and a week devoted to walking. Your pathmate could be an editor of *American Health* magazine or a professional boxer. Programs range from designing a personal fitness plan to nutrition and kinesiology. Weeks are devoted to quitting smoking, stress management, and the holistic way, combining Mohonk's natural setting with practical tools to enhance the quality of one's life.

Mohonk Mountain House
Lake Mohonk, New Paltz, NY 12561
Tel. 914/255–1000; 914/255–4500 or 800/772–6646

Administration	Fitness director, Geri Owens
Season	Year-round.
Accommodations	300 rooms, many with balcony and working fireplace, some with washbasin only, some sharing an adjoining bath. Rooms and bed-sitting rooms with private bath, double or twin beds.
Rates	Double rooms $245–$320 for 2 persons per day full American plan; tower room with fireplace $360–$390 for 2 persons. Midweek tennis packages $190 per person daily. Deposit: 1 night payable in advance. Credit cards: AE, DC, MC, V.
Meal Plans	3 meals and afternoon tea included with room. The menu follows the American resort tradition, with some light selections. Buffet-style lunch. Wine and alcoholic drinks available.
Services and Facilities	**Exercise Equipment:** 6-station Universal gym, 2 Schwinn Air-Dyne bikes, 2 Monark bikes, StairMaster, Lifecycle, Nordic-Track cross-country unit, hand weights. **Services:** Massage. **Swimming Facilities:** Mohonk Lake, ½-mile-long 60-foot-deep freshwater lake with swimming and diving areas. **Spa Facilities:** Separate saunas for men and women. **Recreation Facilities:** 6 tennis courts (4 clay, 2 Har-Tru), platform tennis courts; 9-hole golf course; ice skating and downhill skiing; croquet. **Evening Programs:** Concerts, films, dancing; speakers on health and fitness.
In the Area	Carriage rides, trail rides, hayrides.
Getting Here	By car, New York State Thruway (I-87) to New Paltz (Exit 18). By train, Amtrak to Poughkeepsie. By bus, New York City (Port Authority Terminal) and other cities served by Adirondack Trailways. Hotel transfer service to bus or train station and New York City and airports.
Special Notes	Weekday outdoor adventures and walks for children. No smoking in public areas indoors.

Mountain Valley Health Resort

Weigth management
Nutrition and diet
Luxury pampering

New York
Hunter Mountain

Shedding seven to ten pounds per week is the goal of most guests at the Mountain Valley Health Resort. The no-nonsense weight-loss program attracts both men and women. Set on 23 acres at the base of Hunter Mountain, the resort displays the backdrop and foreground of the majestic Catskill mountain range. Hiking trails lead into the Catskill State Park. The Hunter Mountain Ski Center is a mile from the resort. Relocated from New Jersey, where it was known as the Garden Spa, this new resort opened in 1992.

A brief medical background check and orientation is given for new arrivals. The spa director determines your level of fitness and your nutritional needs. This allows her to design a daily diet and exercise program for you. A computerized body-composition analysis (additional fee) may be recommended. The program includes daily massage, full fitness program with low-impact aerobics, step aerobics, swimnastics, stretching, toning, yoga, and guided walks. There is no mandatory schedule or arrival day.

Guests are given a list of daily activities and can start the day with a walk after breakfast. Other morning classes include toning and firming, fitness workout including step aerobics or swimnastics in the new indoor heated pool or heated outdoor pool. Each afternoon there are also toning ang stretching, yoga, or free time for the whirlpool and sauna or swimming.

Mountain Valley Health Resort
R. D. 214, Hunter, NY 12442
Tel. 800/232-2772

Administration Director, Natalie Skolnik

Season Year-round.

Accommodations 32 rooms, each with private bath, color TV (with cable and satellite), telephone. Some rooms are lofts with skylights, some have private saunas and whirlpools in a new chalet-style building.

Rates Weekly (7 nights) package rates $595–$995. 4-night packages $445–$795. Weekend packages (3 nights) $350–$695. Add tax and 15% service charge. Deposit $200–$300. Credit cards: AE, D, MC, V.

Meal Plans 3 meals daily based on 650-, 900-, or 1,200-calorie diets; optional juice fast, vegetarian meals, and special dietary requests. Breakfasts feature egg-white omelet, hearty grain cereals, and fresh fruit. Lunches offer tomato bisque, zuchini lasagne, spinach frittata. Dining-room service, candlelight dinners include Cornish game hen with apple glaze, chicken Parmesan, flounder Florentine, haddock with Creole sauce, chocolate mousse.

Services and Facilities **Exercise Equipment:** 3 treadmills, StairMaster, 2 recumbant bicycles, rowing machine. **Services:** Theraputic massage, reflexology, shiatsu, facial, seaweed and cellulite body wraps, exfoliating body polish, body waxing, manicure, pedicure. Individual nutritional fitness and stress counseling available. Body-composition analysis, cholesterol testing, Innerquest behavior-modification technology. **Swimming Facilities:** Indoor pool and heated outdoor pool. **Recreation Facilities:** 2 tennis courts, basketball and volleyball courts, hiking trails, cross-country skiing.

Getting Here New York Thruway to Exit 19 (Kingston), RD 28 west to Phoenicia, follow signs to Exit 214 north (Pine Hill). Mountain Valley Health Resort will be 15 minutes farther on the left.

Special Notes Ramps and some ground-floor rooms offer access for the disabled. No smoking in public areas but smoking and no-smoking rooms are available.

New Age Health Spa

Holistic health
Life enhancement
Weight management
Nutrition and diet
Sports conditioning

New York
Neversink
Committed to a holistic lifestyle, the New Age Health Spa is a country retreat that offers a wide range of physical treatments to enhance your new appearance. The tranquil, 160-acre farm estate in the Catskill Mountains is an ideal setting in which to balance body, soul, and mind.

Having undergone a rejuvenation itself, the farm is now a full-fledged spa with owners who supervised the redecoration of the pine-panelled guest rooms in five cottages surrounding the original farmhouse. They have added sophisticated pampering and astrological consultation to complement their serious weight-management program, plus an Outward Bound type of Challenge course popular for building corporate teamwork.

The chefs, graduates of the Culinary Institute of America, plan menus along guidelines set by the American Heart Association (high carbohydrates; low protein, fats, and salt; no sugar). For determined dieters, "juicing" is the recommended program for fast weight loss, and supervised participants are advised to sign up for an accompanying colonic cleansing, a water treatment that serves to speed up "detoxification" of the body. Other food plans include Spartan (700–800-calorie vegetarian) and Rotation (900- to 1,100-calorie plan consisting of vegetarian meals alternating with a fish, turkey, or chicken meal).

The program allows you to set your own pace; opt for exercises in Zen meditation, a tai chi class, the alpine tower ropes course, or a three- to five-mile aerobic walk before breakfast. Move on to a weight-management lecture followed by a series of innovative low-impact aerobics and floor-work classes that enable you to match activities to your energy level.

With the Catskill Mountains as a panoramic backdrop, the spa emphasizes outdoor activity—all-day and overnight hiking, cross-country skiing, snowshoeing, or a dip in the 30 # 60-foot outdoor swimming pool on those hazy days of summer.

Indoor spa services are housed in the barnlike Minisink building, where options include herbal baths, facials, treatments with paraffin or Dead Sea mud, and weight training.

The number of repeat participants testifies to the fact that this program produces results with an attentive staff and a verdant setting.

New Age Health Spa
Rte. 55, Neversink, NY 12765
Tel. 914/985–7601 or 800/682–4348
Fax 914/985–2467

Administration Owner/directors, Stephanie Paradise and Werner Mendel; fitness director, Sandra Lachaga

Season Year-round.

Accommodations 39 rooms in 2-story cottages, each with "country charm" decor, air-conditioning, no TV or phone, private bath.

Rates 1-week package, including diet and exercise program, $699–$969 per person double occupancy. Single and triple rooms available. Daily rate, $114–$154 per person double, $174–$214 single. Add 15% service charge, 8% tax. 25% payable in advance. Credit cards: AE, MC, V.

Meal Plans 3 meals daily included in package rates. Salad bar and fresh vegetables grown in the spa's greenhouses featured with such dinner entrees as poached fish and baked chicken. Special dietary requests accommodated. Juice fast available with staff consultation.

Services and Facilities **Exercise Equipment:** 2 StairMasters, 3 treadmills, rowing machine, NordicTrack, Cat's Eye and stationary bikes, free weights, weight training circuit. **Services:** Massage (Swedish, shiatsu, sports), herbal wrap, loofah scrub, colonic, Dea Sea mud body mask, paraffin body waxing, aromatherapy. Salon for hair, nail, skin care. **Swimming Facilities:** Indoor lap pool (30' × 50'), outdoor pool. **Spa Facilities:** Coed sauna and steam room. **Recreation Facilities:** Volleyball; cross-country skiing and snowshoeing. **Evening Programs:** Talks on healthy living and personal growth; workshops in astrology, psychology, awareness; movies, disco.

In the Area Guided hiking into the mountains 3 times a week.

Getting Here *From New York City.* By van, express service Fri. and Sun. morning and return ($40 each way). By bus, Short Line from Port Authority (2 hr). By car, New York State Thruway (I-87) to the Catskills, Rte. 17 to Liberty, Rte. 52 and 55E to Neversink (2 hr). Local taxi available.

Special Notes No children under 16; no alcohol, smoking, or drugs. Bring personal radio with earphones, clock, flashlight.

Omega Institute

Preventive medicine
Stress control
Holistic health
Spiritual awareness
Life enhancement

New York Call it a New Age mecca or a quest for higher consciousness; it's
Rhinebeck chiefly an adult summer camp where you can strive to develop physical and mental balance alongside people on the leading edge of preventive medicine and holistic health.

Sometimes referred to as Esalen East, the Omega Institute brings together people of different backgrounds—doctors, lawyers, housewives, college students—who want to function more positively as individuals and as members of society. More than 200 educational workshops, from Native American studies to wellness and stress control, last two to five days. The classes, including diet workshops and "Shamanic Journey, Power and Healing," are led by faculty and guest lecturers comprising a veritable *Who's Who* of the human potential movement.

Participants come away saying they achieved spiritual, emotional, and physical renewal. Even standard resort recreation is transformed: Tennis is choreographed with dance movements and music; archery becomes a Zen art.

Located about 100 miles north of Manhattan, the rustic, 80-acre campus features a new Wellness Center complete with sauna, massage rooms, flotation tanks, nutrition- and stress-reduction counseling, and holistic medical consultations. On campus are a theater, gift and bookshops, and cafe. Yet there's not a Nautilus gym in sight.

A Wellness Week integrates study and practice of a healthy lifestyle. Omega's core faculty offers a sound medical understanding of the roles that diet, nutrition, exercise, and fitness play in the ongoing development of health. Through experiential sessions in massage, yoga, tai chi chuan, group support, and games, each participant forms a positive attitude toward wellness.

Workshops scheduled throughout the summer at varying fees include clowning and play, creative problem solving, parenting, achieving high self-esteem, personal mythology, environmental awareness, and basketball.

On a typical morning, when as many as 350 people are camping out or living in the dormitories and cottages, groups assemble before breakfast for yoga and tai chi chuan sessions. The rolling Hudson Valley countryside provides an inspiring setting. Since it opened in 1977, Omega has nourished this environment as a safe place in which the concepts of transformation, New Age, and holism are rediscovered.

Omega Institute
Lake Drive, R.D. 2, Box 377, Rhinebeck, NY 12572
Tel. 914/266-4301 (May 15–Sept. 15), 914/338-6030
(Sept. 15–May 15), or 800/862-8890
(800/258-5353 in NY)
Fax 914/338-0474

Administration Program director, Thomas Valente; general manager, Skip Backus; medical director, Stephan Rechtschaffen, M.D.

Season June—mid-Sept. Winter programs in the Caribbean, New Mexico, and New England. No TV, phone, air-conditioning.

Accommodations Rooms in cottages, dormitory beds, camping facilities. Private rooms with shared bath.

Rates 5-day Omega Wellness Program $260 plus lodging. Private space in dormitory for 2-day program $144; cottage rooms for 2-day program $125–$157 per person, double occupancy (limited number of single rooms available). Campsites $30 per person, per day. Meals and tax included in lodging fee. 50% payment in advance. Credit cards: MC, V.

Meal Plans   Mainly vegetarian, with some fish and dairy products. Many locally grown fresh fruits and vegetables. Whole grains, beans, and bean products. No artificial sweeteners. 3 meals served daily, buffet style.

Services and Facilities   **Swimming Facilities:** Private lake. **Services:** Massage, aromatherapy, counseling in nutrition, antistress, wellness. **Recreation Facilities:** Basketball, canoeing, jogging, tennis, volleyball. **Evening Programs:** Concerts, films, lectures.

In the Area   The historic village of Rhinebeck, Old Rhinebeck Aerodrome.

Getting Here   *From New York City.* By car, New York State Thruway (I-87) or the Saw Mill River Parkway north to the Taconic Parkway, Bull's Head Rd. west to Lake Dr. (2 hr); By train, Amtrak from Grand Central Station stops at Rhinecliff, where Omega vans pick up guests (for train schedules, tel. 800/872–7245). By bus, Short Line from Port Authority Terminal to Rhinebeck (2 hr). Omega vans pick up in Rhinebeck at Beekman Arms Hotel.

Special Notes   Some cottages and facilities equipped for the disabled. Family Week in July with nature studies and creative games for children. No smoking indoors.

Omni Sagamore Resort & Spa

Luxury pampering

New York
Bolton Landing   Surrounded by the Adirondack Mountains and set on a 70-acre private island, the huge white clapboard Omni Sagamore Hotel suggests an escape to the quiet pleasures of a bygone era. Rejuvenated by new owners, the resort now includes a modern health club, indoor swimming pool, and indoor tennis and racquetball courts. Fitness classes are scheduled throughout the day, from walks and low-impact aerobics to water exercise, at no charge to hotel guests who book one or more spa treatments and services.

The health club has separate sauna, whirlpool, and steam-room facilities for men and women. There is a coed exercise area, with newly expanded space to accommodate the equipment, and a wet area specially equipped for body scrubs. Appointments are made for treatment on an à la carte basis, which includes the daily charge for use of the club. Joining the 8:30 AM fitness walk is free. If you simply want to swim and exercise with the equipment, a daily facilities charge is added to your account. Nonresident guests are also welcome.

In addition to massage, facials, and beauty makeovers, the specialty here is a full-body rubdown with a mixture of sea salt and massage oil that leaves your skin tingling. After the scrub with loofah sponges, the salt mixture is hosed off. Next, peppermint soap is applied, leaving you with a glowing feeling. The cost: $30. (A 17% gratuity is added to the cost of services.)

Omni Sagamore Resort & Spa
Box 450, Bolton Landing, NY 12814
Tel. 518/644–9400 or 800/358–3585

Administration   Manager, Robert MacIntosh; spa director, Damian Alessi

Season Year-round.

Accommodations 350 rooms, suites, and cottages. The main hotel's 100 rooms embody history and contemporary comfort. Condominium-style suites in new lodges.

Rates Daily: $150–$390 per room, single or double occupancy during summer season; meal plan $54 daily for breakfast and dinner. Spa package $55–$195 per day plus lodging. 2-night package $404–$496 per person, 4-night package $808–$992 per person, 7-night package $1,414–$1,736 per person. 1 night payable in advance. Add tax and gratuity. Credit cards: AE, MC, V.

Meal Plans Modified American Plan has Simply Healthy Cuisine menu. Dinner appetizers are seafood terrine or fresh berries, spinach consommé, green salad. Entree choices include poached salmon, grilled chicken breast, linguine. Desserts are apple strudel or blueberry cake, Grand Marnier Bavarian. 6 restaurants provide varied menus, emphasizing fish and local produce.

Services and Facilities **Exercise Equipment:** 12-station Universal gym, 3 Stair-Masters, Lifecycle, 10-unit Keiser weight training system, 2 Trotter treadmills, 3 Concept II rowers, Windracer, free weights. **Services:** Massage (Swedish, shiatsu, sports), loofah salt glow, reflexology, facials, herbal wrap, seaweed and mud wrap, aromatherapy. 4 aerobics classes daily including aquacise, step aerobics, stretching; beauty salon. **Swimming Facilities:** Indoor pool; lakeside docks. **Recreation Facilities:** 18-hole golf course, 4 outdoor lighted and 2 indoor tennis courts, jogging trails, hiking, boating, water sports; snowmobiling, ice skating, cross-country and downhill skiing, tobogganing; horseback riding and horse-drawn sleigh rides. **Evening Programs:** Dancing, jazz club, scheduled entertainment.

In the Area Cruises on Lake George aboard a classic wooden yacht; free transportation to golf course and ski areas; mineral baths at Saratoga Springs Spa by special arrangement. Saratoga Springs' Victorian area; summer season of concerts, ballet, and horse races; Colonial Fort William Henry; Lake George Village; hot-air balloon flights.

Getting Here Located about 65 miles north of Albany, NY. *From New York City.* By car, 4-hour drive on the New York State Thruway (I-87) to Exit 24 (Bolton Landing). By air, Albany is served by Eastern, USAir, and Continental airlines, among others. By train, Amtrak to Fort Edward, from Boston or New York City. A hotel car meets guests at Albany or the train station ($50 round-trip).

Special Notes No smoking in the spa. Facilities charge $10—includes shorts, T-shirts, robe, slippers.

Saratoga Spa State Park

Taking the waters
Luxury pampering

New York
Saratoga Springs
Once a rival of Europe's glamorous spas, Saratoga is better known today for Thoroughbred racing and the arts. But the mineral springs at Saratoga Spa State Park remain a major attraction, and plans are underway to develop a complete health and fitness center in some of the original buildings. Meanwhile,

the Roosevelt Bath operates year-round, and the Lincoln Baths are open during July and August.

The mineral-rich water bubbles up all around the town, where it is bottled for drinking as well as bathing. Here, however, it's free. Pick up a map from the Old Drink Hall, downtown, or the spa visitor center operated by the State of New York. If you park at the Geyser Picnic Area lot and follow the path, you will nencounter three of the best-known springs, all of the saline-alkaline variety. First is the Hayes Well, which has a breathing port at one side for inhaling carbon dioxide—said to be good for the lungs and sinuses. The gas also carbonates the water and powers geysers that spout up 10 feet or higher at this spot.

For a diuretic effect, try Hathorn Spring No. 1, a block east of Broadway on Spring Street. This water contains large amounts of sulfur, iron, lime, and other minerals. Dense, green-tinted, and faintly smelly, it has been prescribed for everything from sinus to complexion problems.

More palatable is the 90-minute relaxer offered spa visitors: a 15- to 25-minute mineral bath followed by a half-hour massage, then a 30-minute rest. Your float in the salty, effervescent warm mineral water induces relaxation by slowing breathing; studies have shown that some carbon dioxide is absorbed through the skin, where it dilates the blood vessels, improves circulation, and aids the flow of blood. Wrapped in warm sheets, you cool down after this treatment, which costs $15 during July and August, then book a relaxing massage.

To get a full taste of the town and its Victorian landmarks, stay at the venerable Adelphi Hotel on Broadway, built in 1870 and lovingly restored by the current owners. The Gideon Putnam Hotel, a sprawling, neo-Georgian hotel with old-fashioned country club charm, was built during the New Deal era and now adjoins the spa buildings.

Saratoga Spa State Park
The Gideon Putnam
Box 476, Ave. of the Pines, Saratoga Springs, NY 12866
Tel. 518/584–3000
Fax 518/584–1354

Administration Manager, Kenneth Boyles

Season Year-round.

Accommodations 132 rooms, 12 suites, with modern furnishings, flowered drapery, TV, air-conditioning.

Rates 2-night package $264 for 2, double occupancy (lower Nov.–Apr.). Program includes mineral baths, meals, raceway pass, gratuities, taxes. Daily rate $114–$236 single or double. Suites from $104. During racing season (Aug.), 3 meals per day required. Add tax, optional gratuity. 1 night payable in advance. Credit cards: AE, DC, MC, V.

Meal Plans Salads and light cuisine on the spa menu.

Services and Facilities Services: Swedish massage, baths, hot pack. **Swimming Facilities:** Victoria Pool in the spa park ($5), Great Scandaga Lake in nearby Adirondack State Park. **Spa Facilities:** Mineral-water baths in private tubs at the spartan facilities of Roosevelt Bath No. 1 (518/584–2011); semiprivate at Lincoln Baths (518/584–2010). Days and times of operation vary with season; call for reservations. **Recreation Facilities:** 8 free public tennis courts and 2 golf courses in the spa park; hiking trails at Spruce Mountain near town; guided history walks; jogging in Congress Park. **Evening Programs:** The Saratoga Performing Arts Center (tel. 518/587–3330) in Spa State Park presents the New York City Ballet in July, the Philadelphia Orchestra in Aug., and popular and jazz artists. Dance companies perform at the Little Theater (tel. 518/587–3330).

In the Area 900 buildings on the National Register of Historic Places; tours include the rose garden at the Yaddo artists' colony and the 1864 gable-roof clubhouse at the track. Polo matches and a harness-racing track nearby. Saratoga Battlefield National Historical Park has a scenic 9.5-mi drive open to bicyclists. Museums in former spa buildings are devoted to dance, racing, and local history.

Getting Here Located close to Albany; about 3½ hours from New York City. By car, New York Thruway (I–87). By train, Amtrak from Montreal, Boston, and New York City. By air, USAir and Pan Am schedule flights to Albany. By bus, Adirondack Trailways. Rental car at airport; taxi in town. Park admission: $3 per car, free for Gideon Putnam hotel guests.

Special Notes Specially equipped baths and rooms for the disabled. Nonsmoking rooms available. Remember to bring drinking cups.

Sivananda Ashram Yoga Ranch

Spiritual awareness

New York
Woodbourne
When stressed-out urbanites join members of the farm community to exercise and meditate or to jog through 80 acres of woods and fields, the effect is spiritual as well as physical. Guests from diverse social and professional lives around the world meet at Sivananda Ashram Yoga Ranch to share their interest in yoga.

Morning and evening, everyone participates in classes devoted to traditional yogic exercise and breathing techniques. The dozen *asana* positions range from a headstand to a spinal twist, and each has specific benefits for the body. You will be taught that proper breathing, *pranayama*, is essential for energy control.

The daily schedule includes meditation and chanting at 6 AM and 8 PM, yogic posture and breathing exercise classes at 8 AM and 4 PM, and vegetarian meals served at 10 AM and 6 PM. Participation in program activities is mandatory, including karma yoga classes and various talks on yogic practice and philosophy. The ideal is to become harmoniously balanced; the discipline can provide physical, psychological, and spiritual benefits.

Sivananda Ashram Yoga Ranch
Box 195, Woodbourne, NY 12788
Tel. 914/434–9242
Fax 914/434–1032

Administration Founder/director, Swami Vishnu Devananda; director, Swami Sankarananda

Season Year-round

Accommodations 50 small rooms: singles, doubles, apartments in the farmhouse and cottages. Apartments have private bath. Tent space.

Rates Room $35–$40 daily per person, including meals; 3-month work-study program $150. $25 payable in advance. No credit cards.

Meal Plans 2 meals daily, buffet style. Lacto-vegetarian diet with fresh vegetables grown on the ranch and dairy products. No coffee, eggs, alcohol.

Services and Facilities **Swimming Facilities:** Pond. **Spa Facilities:** Communal sweat lodge and sauna. **Recreation Facilities:** Woodland trail hiking. **Evening Programs:** Meditation, chanting, lectures.

Getting Here *From New York City.* By bus, Short Line (Port Authority Terminal) to Woodbourne, then arrange for pickup; during the summer, van service provided every weekend (243 W. 24th St., $20 round-trip). By car, Rte. 17N to Exit 105B, Rte. 42 to Woodbourne (2 hr).

Special Notes No smoking. Remember to bring towels and meditation mat.

Tai Chi Farm

Spiritual awareness
Sports conditioning

New York
New Milford

Martial arts and inner discovery bring harmony to participants in workshops at the Tai Chi Farm. Founded and led by Master Jou Tsung Hwa, the farm has a summer schedule devoted to understanding and perfecting the tai chi chuan postures and meditations. Specialists teach such exercises as Swimming Dragon Chi Kung, a complete muscle and organ toner that makes your body seem to flow like a swimming dragon. From the Creative Being Centre in England, a master teaches how to transform stress into self-discovery using Dragon Breath Energy.

The Chinese have been studying chi for 4,000 years. Here the concepts of leading, sticking, neutralizing, and attacking are discussed and practiced with experts in many specialized forms of tai chi chuan. Characterized by a spirited give-and-take, San Shou is an ingeniously choreographed set of 88 matched movements that refine your form and sensitivity. In the body mechanics of tai chi chuan, you discover how to root and balance the yin aspect of letting go with the yang aspect of connecting and projecting energy.

Tai Chi Farm
Box 630, New Milford, NY 10959
Tel. 914/986–9233

Administration Master, Jou Tsung Hwa; manager, David Pancarician

Season May–Oct.

Accommodations 10 wooden cabins with cots or mattresses for 2–10 persons. Bedding not supplied. No electricity or running water. Outhouse shared by campers. Campsites available.

Rates $30 per person for weekend lodging, $95 tuition; $50 per person for 5-day workshop lodging, $170 tuition. Campsites $10–$20.

Meal Plans No meal service. Participants prepare their own meals.

Services and Facilities **Services:** Individual and group instruction. **Exercise Facilities:** Indoor studio. **Swimming Facilities:** Pond.

Getting Here *From New York.* By bus, NJ Transit from Port Authority Terminal to Warwick (2 hr). By car, Rte. 80W, 23N to I-94N, exit 1 mile past NJ-NY state line in New Milford.

Zen Mountain Monastery

Spiritual awareness

New York
Mt. Tremper
Joining a group of Buddhist monks as they work in silence, meditate, and celebrate Zen rituals and arts is the unique experience at the Zen Mountain Monastery. You can sip green tea at a Zen tea ceremony, hear the broken notes of a Shakuhachi bamboo flute, learn Sumi-e ink painting or traditional wood carving, and explore the subtleties of Ikenobo flower arranging. There are weekends devoted to Taoist martial arts, poetry, and Zen photography.

Founded in 1980 by Zen priest John Daido Loori, who is addressed as *sensei* (teacher), it is the only monastery in America that offers concerts and programs for visitors throughout the year. Scheduled monthly retreats attract 60–100 participants.

Doing a retreat here seems to embrace almost every aspect of daily life. It blends monastic tradition with art and body practice, a characteristic of the golden ages in Japan and China. The hands-on experience can include working in a Japanese Zen garden, or learning a body-focusing technique called still point.

The day's activities move to a measured cadence, sometimes with chanting, often in silence. Everyone does caretaking, an hour of giving back to the buildings and land some of the benefits received from them. Periods of *zazen* (meditation) provide concentration during intensive *sesshin* silent retreat weeks.

Located in a state forest preserve, a 10-minute drive from Woodstock, the monastery seems to be of another time and world. It was, in fact, built at the turn of the century by Catholic monks and Norwegian craftsmen. There are endless mountain trails, ponds, and streams for hiking and recreation, and the atmosphere of peace and solitude is conducive to introspection.

Zen Mountain Monastery
Box 197PC, S. Plank Rd., Mt. Tremper, NY 12457
Tel. 914/688-2228

Administration Director, John Daido Loori; program director, Geoffrey Arnold

Season Year-round; scheduled weekend programs in summer, retreats in fall and winter.

Accommodations 4-story stone monastery with 175-bed dormitory. Main hall, classrooms, dining hall, library. All facilities shared on a communal basis. Rustic cabins available for couples.

Rates Weekend programs $150, retreats of 3–7 days (Tues.–Sun.) $150–$250 per person, including 3 meals daily. Advance payment of $50. Credit cards: MC, V.

Meal Plans Vegetarian meals and some fish or meat, served buffet style 3 times a day. Weekends begin with Fri. dinner (steamed fish with rice and vegetables) and end with Sun. lunch. Dairy products served. Much of the food from the monastery garden.

Services and Facilities **Services:** Zen training, intensive meditation, artist retreats. **Swimming Facilities:** Nearby mountain lakes. **Recreation Facilities:** Hiking; tubing on creek; skiing at Hunter Mountain. **Evening Programs:** Occasional concerts of contemporary and oriental music; an introduction to Zen.

In the Area Woodstock artists' colony, Catskill Mountain Forest Preserve, Beaverkill River scenic area.

Getting Here *From New York City.* By bus, Adirondack Trailways from Port Authority via Kingston to Mt. Tremper (about 3 hr). By car, New York State Thruway (I–87) to the Catskills, Rte. 28 and 212 to Mt. Tremper (2½ hr).

Special Notes No smoking.

The Equinox

Luxury pampering
Life enhancement

Vermont
Manchester Village

Tracing its history to a 1769 tavern still used as the resort's main dining room, The Equinox added a fitness center called The Evolution Spa in 1985. The comprehensive health and fitness facilities are open to all hotel guests on an à la carte basis. Three-night spa packages offer nutritional and beauty services. There is also a two-night Fun and Fitness package available.

An informal discussion of exercise physiology, nutrition, and stress management precedes a body composition analysis by the computer system to tailor your exercise schedule. Options include brisk walks and personalized training with weights.

The hotel and golf course's 1992 restoration gave guest rooms a fresh look, with Audubon prints and Vermont country charm. All bathrooms have been reconstructed with 18th-century tile, pedestal sinks, and natural finish beaded pine panelled ceilings.

The programs are limited to 16 participants, so early reservations and travel plans are suggested. Advance planning with the spa director will help you focus on weight loss, stress management, or behavior modification.

The Evolution facilities to which you have unlimited access include a coed Turkish steam bath, indoor and outdoor swimming pools, whirlpools, and a Swedish sauna. If you would rather explore the town or ski at Mt. Equinox, without a spa program, that's reason enough for visiting this historic resort.

The Equinox
Rte. 7A, Manchester Village, VT 05254
Tel. 802/362–4700 or 800/362–4747
Fax 802/362–1595

Administration General manager, S. Lee Bowden; fitness director, Susan Thorne-Thomsen

Season Year-round.

Accommodations 164 bedrooms and 6 suites, furnished in classic New England style with pine beds and dressers, flowered chintz fabrics, modern conveniences. Beds turned down at night; *New York Times* delivered. Lodging is in 17 buildings, with TV, phone, air-conditioning.

Rates $129–$375 single, $139–$375 for 2, double occupancy. Townhouses $250–$510 daily. Meal plan $45–$60 per day. Spa package 3 nights/4 days $755 single, $597 per person double. Fitness package for 2 nights $430 single, $295 double. Add 8% tax, gratuity. Deposit of 50% of the package price. Credit cards: AE, DC, MC, V.

Meal Plans Full American Plan in both formal and informal dining rooms. Spa breakfast includes choice of fruit, buttermilk pancakes with blueberry coulis, hot oatmeal or bran cereal with skim milk; lunch can be ceviche of sole with cilantro, grilled medallion of beef with shallots, or chilled asparagus with seasoned wild rice; dinner choices include herbed pasta with mushrooms, poached salmon, or veal medallion.

Services and Facilities **Exercise Equipment:** 8-station Nautilus circuit, free weights, 2 Lifecycles, 3 AMF semirecumbent bikes, NordicTrack, stairclimber, computerized rowing machine. **Services:** Massage, thalassotherapy, herbal wrap, loofah body scrub, pedicure, paraffin treatments, hair and skin care. **Swimming Facilities:** 47' indoor and 75' outdoor heated pools. **Recreation Facilities:** 3 tennis courts, golf course, hiking trails, bicycle rental, nearby downhill and cross-country skiing, horseback riding, canoeing, horse-drawn carriage rides. **Evening Programs:** Resort entertainment.

In the Area Antiques shops, shopping at factory outlets; summer theater, jazz concerts, Marlboro Music Festival; Brattleboro Museum, Norman Rockwell Museum, Bennington crafts center, Hildene (Robert Todd Lincoln's estate).

Getting Here *From New York City.* By car, New England Thruway (I–95) north to I–91, exit at second Brattleboro turnoff for Rte. 9 to Rte. 30 (4 hr). By bus, Greyhound from Port Authority Terminal (4½ hr). By air, scheduled flights to Albany, NY; bus service to Manchester by Vermont Transit. Taxis and rental cars available.

Special Notes No smoking in the spa.

Golden Eagle

Non-program resort facilities

Vermont
Stowe
In traditional mountain lodge with winter and summer activities, the Golden Eagle health spa is open daily year-round 9 AM–9 PM, at no cost to guests.

Toning and body shaping are what the spa does best. Popular with singles and families (most guests are between 30 and 60), this is a budget-priced alternative to luxury resorts.

You are free to order from menus in the resort's two dining rooms. Although there are temptations, the spa food is attractive enough to keep you on the set menu.

Golden Eagle
Box 1110B, Mountain Rd. (Rte. 108), Stowe, VT 05672
Tel. 802/253–4811 or 800/626–1010

Administration	Manager, Marc MacNamara; spa director, Sandy Morningstar
Season	Year-round.
Accommodations	80 rooms with private bath; suites, cottages, apartments with cooking facilities, color TV, air-conditioning, oversize beds. Some rooms with Jacuzzi and fireplace. Also a Bavarian-style chalet.
Rates	$89–$104 daily per room for 2, single occupancy $5 additional. 1-night deposit on booking. Credit cards: AE, DC, MC, V.
Meal Plans	Set menu totals 1,200–1,500 calories and includes veal marsala, fish rolled with vegetables, and broiled scrod. American plan menu available other times. Menus for diabetics are available.
Services and Facilities	**Exercise Equipment:** 8 Universal gym stations, Tunturi treadmills, stationary bikes, rowing machines, free weights. **Services:** Massage, reflexology. **Swimming Facilities:** Indoor and outdoor 50-foot pools. **Recreation Facilities:** Tennis courts, bicycles, scenic path for jogging. **Evening Programs:** Resort activities.
In the Area	Shelburne Museum, Cold Hollow Cider Mill, Trapp Family Lodge, Ben & Jerry's Ice Cream Factory.
Getting Here	*From Boston or New York City.* By train, Amtrak to Waterbury, VT (10 mi from Stowe). By car, I–91, I–89 to Stowe exit (3 hr from Boston, 6½ hr from N.Y.C.). By air, scheduled flights to Burlington, VT. Hotel limousine arranged on request to meet trains and planes; taxi, rental car in area.
Special Notes	Ground-floor rooms for the disabled. No smoking in the spa and areas of the dining rooms.

Green Mountain at Fox Run

Life enhancement   *Women only*
Weight management

Vermont
Ludlow

Located on over 20 acres of private land in the Green Mountain National Forest, overlooking the Okemo Valley and ski area, the resort works from an Aspen-like lodge tucked into a mountain ridge. Founded in 1972, it is the country's oldest all-women program devoted to developing a self-directed plan for eating and exercise that can be integrated into your life at home. Participants range in age from 17 to over 80 years, are from all parts of the world, and are united by a desire to really make lasting changes in their weight and health behavior.

For women with a serious weight problem, coming to Green Mountain at Fox Run is a commitment to change. The difference is not just a new diet or vigorous exercise, but a new lifestyle based on healthy habits. The program provides a practical approach to eating, exercise, and stress management that can ensure long-term success. Equally important are workshops and presentations on women's issues of personal growth and self-improvement. Over three-fourths of all participants are business and professional women who are highly stressed, driven and successful, but who "just don't have enough time to take care of themselves."

The first lesson is that diets don't work. Instead of deprivation, moderation becomes the key. Eating three balanced meals a day is required, and you are encouraged to give in, ever so slightly, to an occasional yearning for sweets. Guests learn to cope with food fads and are shown that being more active can be as pleasant as taking a walk down a country lane.

For women who have unsuccessfully attempted to manage their weight with liquid diets, there is a special program to overcome negative effects and resume a livable and enjoyable approach to eating.

Working with a team of registered dietitians, exercise physiologists, and behavioral therapists with specialties in weight, health, and addiction, you develop a personalized weight and health program that becomes part of your daily routine. A follow-up program helps you to maintain this routine at home. Tuition costs cover individual nutrition/dietary counseling, exercise prescription and modification, and private behavioral counseling sessions. The only extra expense, if desired, is for massage therapy.

The facilities are homelike, there is no high-tech gym equipment or luxury pampering. Exercise classes, running, walking, hiking, biking, and cross-country skiing in winter fill most of the day. Aerobic dance and body-conditioning sessions teach that exercise can be fun, something that fits easily into everyday life.

Green Mountain at Fox Run
Fox Lane, Box 164, Ludlow, VT 05149
Tel. 802/228–8885 or 800/448–8106
Fax 802/228–8887

Administration Program directors, Alan H. Wayler, Ph.D. and Thelma J. Wayler, M.S., R.D.

Season Year-round. Special seminars scheduled.

Accommodations 26 rooms: singles, doubles, and duplexes (2–4 persons), all with modern bath. Lounge with fireplace; high-ceiling, raftered dining room.

Rates 1-week session $1,075–$1,800; 2-week $1,900–$3,350; 4-week $2,800–$5,700. Rates based on type of accommodation, single or double occupancy (roommates matched on request). $500 deposit with application. Credit cards: MC, V.

Meal Plans 1,200-calorie (per day) diet low in fat and sodium, high in complex carbohydrates. Menus include a salad plate, pasta, eggplant Parmesan, tortilla dishes, liver and onions, baked potato with trimmings, even ice cream. Coffee and tea available throughout the day.

Services and Facilities **Exercise Equipment:** 2 Trotter treadmills, 2 Schwinn Air-Dyne bikes, NordicTrack, Concept II rower, free weights, mountain bikes. **Services:** Swedish massage; sports instruction. **Swimming Facilities:** Covered outdoor pool for all weather. **Spa Facilities:** Sauna. **Recreation Facilities:** 2 tennis courts, outdoor track, nearby golf course; downhill and cross-country skiing, snowshoeing. **Evening Programs:** Cooking classes, movies, group discussions, lectures.

In the Area   Trips into town for shopping, including antiques shops. Scenic mountain drives, summer stock theaters.

Getting Here   *From New York City.* By car, I–95 north to I–91, Exit 6 in Vermont (Rte. 103 North) to Ludlow (4½ hr). By bus, Vermont Transit from Port Authority Terminal to Ludlow. By air, scheduled flights to Lebanon, NH, on Delta, Northwest Airlines. Complimentary pick-up from airports and bus station. Transfers upon departure included in tuition.

Special Notes   Smoking only in specified areas. Remember to bring recent physical report, walking and aerobics shoes.

New Life

Nutrition and diet
Life enhancement
Holistic health

Vermont   Two vacations rolled into one is the concept of New Life fitness
Killington   guru Jimmy LeSage. His program attracts hikers who want to get in shape and enjoy the outdoors. Set in a picturesque alpine valley, the Inn of the Six Mountains houses New Life from mid-May through Thanksgiving, providing a healthy combination of nutritionally planned meals, fitness classes, and creature comforts. Days are filled with attractive options.

A former professional cook and hotel manager, LeSage caters to his guests' needs while exhorting them to learn ways to improve their habits. His philosophy on food and eating is published in a book given to each guest and experienced first-hand in a cheery dining room. Fresh fruit, herbal teas, decaffeinated coffee, and spring water are always on hand in the hospitality lounge.

Exercise classes are held in the Inn and are scheduled around outdoor activities. Sivananda-style yogic movements gently stretch muscles and prepare the body for vigorous outdoor activity; the afternoon program relaxes the body and works off fatigue. Other options are offered at the indoor complex with swimming, steam room, and heated whirlpool that guests can use at any time. Prebreakfast walks are also optional.

Hiking the lush valleys of the Green Mountain Range is a great way to strengthen your heart and muscles. Guided by New Life staff members, groups hike daily. The treks become more challenging as your stamina increases.

In an area where big, noisy resorts or quaint inns are the norm, this is a happy compromise: small enough so that guests get to know each other, and supported by a youthful staff eager to help you enjoy the area's attractions.

New Life
The Inn of the Six Mountains, Killington Rd.,
Killington, VT 05751
Tel. 802/422–4302 or 800/228–4676

Administration   Founder-director, Jimmy LeSage

Season   Mid-May through Thanksgiving.

Accommodations 100 rooms with double beds, private baths, color TV, and phone. Pine-paneled lobby, lounge with fireplaces and comfy chairs.

Rates Weekend sampler $400 single, $375 per person double; 6 day/5 night program (Sun.–Fri.) $1,025–$1,095 single, $895–$950 double; 7 day/6 night program (July–Sept.) $1,295 single, $1,150 double. $200 advance payment per person. Add 15% service charge, 8% tax. Credit cards: MC, V.

Meal Plans 3 meals served daily. Modified Pritikin diet (1,000–1,200 calories per day) low in fats and high in complex carbohydrates. Chicken, fish, vegetables, and fruit among the choices. Specialties include lentil loaf, chicken curry salad, sandwich with spicy tofu filling. Special diets accommodated.

Services and Facilities **Exercise Equipment:** Cardiovascular power circuit with Lifecycle rowing ergometer, rebounders, NordicTrack ski machine, stair climber, and stationary bikes. **Services:** Swedish massage, shiatsu, facials; classes in aerobics, yoga, tai chi chuan; aquacise. **Swimming Facilities:** Indoor lap pool, heated outdoor pool. **Recreation Facilities:** Outdoor tennis, racquetball courts; golf course and horseback riding nearby; mountain-bike rentals. **Evening Programs:** Discussions on healthy living, talks on beauty, lectures on nutrition and stress.

In the Area Antiques shops, summer theater, jazz concerts, Marlboro Music Festival.

Getting Here *From New York City.* By car, New England Thruway (I–95) north to Exit 24, Northway to Exit 120 (Fort Anne/Rutland), Hwy. 4 east via Rutland to Killington Rd., Rte. 100 (5 hr). By train, Amtrak to White River Jct. (4 hr). By bus, Vermont Transit to White River Jct. (5 hr). Complimentary pickup at bus station. By air, Delta Business Express or Northwest Link to Lebanon, NH (1 hr). Limousine, car rental available.

Special Notes No smoking in public areas. Remember to bring warm clothing, hats, walking shoes. Spa hours: daily 8 AM–10 PM.

Topnotch at Stowe

Luxury pampering
Sports conditioning
Nutrition and diet
Stress control

Vermont
Stowe

Perched in Vermont's Green Mountains, Topnotch is a classic country inn that caters to sports enthusiasts and weary urbanites seeking escape from civilization. Complementing its four-season outdoor activity, the resort opened a full-service spa in 1989. The combination of an intimate, charming mountain retreat and a state-of-the-art fitness program makes this an easygoing resort where you can learn new habits, maintain a healthy lifestyle, and enjoy your favorite sports.

Topnotch emphasizes health education by putting each guest through a "Fitness Profile" analysis. Based on your body composition, strength and flexibility, cardiovascular and blood tests, an exercise program is planned. Outfitted with a daily issue of shorts, T-shirt, robe and slippers, you have a choice of classes, one-on-one workouts, and circuit weight training.

Sport-specific fitness and conditioning classes get you in shape for tennis and skiing. The program for three to seven days includes instruction as well as time on the courts and slopes. The resort has an indoor tennis center with four lighted courts (Deco Turf II), and transports guests to nearby Mount Mansfield, Vermont's highest peak, top-rated for downhill skiing. Also, there are 50 kilometers of groomed cross-country trails winding through the 120-acre resort, which link with the Catamount Trail along the ridge of the Green Mountains.

For the riding enthusiast, the Topnotch Equestrian Center provides horses, trail rides, riding rings, lessons, and a gallop across the meadows and backwoods in the Vermont summer landscape.

In addition to brilliant fall foliage, there is trout fishing, mountain biking, and hiking along birch-lined trails. Golfers get guest privileges at the Stowe Country Club. A popular focal point for swimmers is the cascading waterfalls alongside the 60-foot heated indoor swimming pool. Tennis clinics and an Orvis school for fishermen are scheduled throughout summer.

With the accent on sports, the spa at Topnotch offers seminars catering to the athlete: Bodywork, skin care and nutrition, pampering, and relaxation are potential topics.

Dining here is a mix of spa cuisine and gourmet fare. An exclusive restaurant offers calorie-controlled meals. The package plans include three meals daily, based on 1,000–1,300 calories for women, 1,300–1,700 calories for men. A nutritionist is on staff for personal consultations.

For a romantic dinner in the main restaurant, gourmet spa cuisine is featured on the menu along with international specialties. Topnotch has long enjoyed acclaim from restaurant critics for the meals created by its master chef.

While the spa is sophisticated, the inn is comfortable and homey. Its 92 guest rooms are spacious, many with views of the mountains. A massive fireplace warms the living room, and there is a cushy sofa for reading by the fire. If you're not too sleepy after a day of sports and spa followed by evening-fitness rap sessions, there's a well-stocked library in your room for bedtime reading.

Topnotch at Stowe
Mountain Rd., Box 1458, Stowe, VT 05672
Tel. 802/253–8585 or 800/451–8686 (Eastern U.S.),
800/451–8686 (VT), 800/228–8686 (Canada)

Administration	General manager, Lewis Kiesler; spa director, Lynne Cantisano
Season	Year-round.
Accommodations	92 rooms furnished with antiques, fine wooden beds, some with canopy, and library. Modern bathroom with imported soaps and bath gels, plush towels. All have air-conditioning, cable TV. Also, suites, condominiums.
Rates	Double room $161–$234 per person per night; $166–$239 per night for 5-night program; $159–$270 per night for 3-night program. Program rates include 3 spa meals daily, use of facilities, screening, and selection of services. Add 17% service charge, 8% taxes. Credit cards: AE, DC, MC, V.

Meal Plans Menu served in spa cafe offers tofu omelet, buckwheat pancakes with fruit topping, hot or cold whole-grain cereals for breakfast. Lunch selections include mushroom-barley soup, salad of asparagus and roasted red peppers, whole-wheat pizza, chicken breast in cilantro-mint sauce. Dinner entrees can be seafood pasta in creamy 3-mustard sauce, or grilled chicken. Vegetarian meals, snacks available. Coffee, tea, milk served.

Services and Facilities **Exercise Equipment:** 9-station Eagle/Cybex weight training gym, 2 Schwinn Air-Dyne bikes, recumbent bike, Liferower, 2 StairMasters, 2 Lifecycles, Gravitron, free weights. **Services:** 2 aerobics studios with 13 scheduled classes, aquacise, yoga; massage (Swedish, shiatsu, reflexology), acupressure, aromatherapy, hydrotherapy, herbal wrap, loofah body scrub, facials; beauty salon for hair, nail, and skin care; instruction in tennis, skiing, riding. **Swimming Facilities:** Indoor 60-foot lap pool, outdoor pool. **Recreation Facilities:** 12 tennis courts (4 indoor), equestrian center, putting green, lawn croquet, bikes, table tennis, billiards, art studio; spa sauna, steam room, coed Jacuzzi. Nearby golf, downhill skiing, squash and racquetball. **Evening Programs:** bike rides and walks, nutrition seminars, scheduled events 5 nights per week.

In the Area Stowe Village (antiques shops), Trapp Family Lodge (concerts), Shelburne Museum (Americana), Cold Hollow Cider Mill, Ben & Jerry's Ice Cream Factory, Smuggler's Notch, Bingham Falls (swimming, picnics).

Getting Here *From Boston, MA.* By train, Amtrak to Waterbury, VT (4 hr). By bus, Greyhound and Vermont Transit (5 hr). By air, scheduled flights on USAir to Burlington, VT (1 hr), private-plane airport at Stowe. By car, I–93 to Concord, NH, I–89 north to Exit 10 (Stowe/Waterbury), Rte. 100N to Stowe, left on Rte. 108 (Mountain Rd.) 4 miles (4 hr). Taxi, car rental available; town trolley service, hotel limo.

Special Notes No smoking in spa or spa dining room. No-smoking guest rooms available. Limited access for the disabled. Spa hours: weekdays 8 AM–6 PM, weekends 8 AM–7 PM.

Woodstock Inn & Resort

Non-program resort facilities

Vermont
Woodstock
Picture the perfect New England town: the county courthouse and library facing an oval green, a covered bridge leading to immaculate farms, a cluster of fancy boutiques, and a Colonial inn. Add a $5-million sports center, 50 miles of cross-country ski trails, nearby mountains with more than 200 downhill trails, and you have the Woodstock Inn & Resort.

The current inn, the fourth on the site, spreads from the historic town center to the sports center. Included are a golf course and croquet lawn, outdoor and indoor swimming pools, tennis courts, and a 69-station parcourse. The weight equipment and aerobics studio are luxury-spa caliber, and they can be used for a nominal fee. Classes cost $5 each. A winter ski package includes lift tickets and equipment rental.

Traditions are alive at the inn from the dress code to the hearty New England menu. The nearby Billings Farm Museum has exhibits of early New England farm life, and offers visits to a prize-winning dairy barn. Phone and power lines were buried with a grant from a neighbor, Laurence Rockefeller, to preserve the view of the town green.

Woodstock Inn & Resort
14 The Green, Woodstock, VT 05091
Tel. 802/457–1100 or 800/448–7900

Administration General manager, Chet Williamson; sports director, Douglas Keleher

Season Year-round.

Accommodations 121 bedrooms with patch quilts, cable TV, air-conditioning, clock radio. Modern baths.

Rates In summer, $130–$495 for 2 persons. Meals not included. Midweek sports package (3 days, 2 nights) $207–$248 single, $341–$421 double, includes golf, tennis. 2 nights' deposit in advance. Credit cards: AE, DC, MC, V.

Meal Plans Modified American plan (breakfast and dinner) $44 per person per day. Courtside Restaurant in Sports Center serves a chicken salad plate or assorted melon slices with cottage cheese, sherbet, or yogurt sauce for lunch. The main dining room offers poached chicken, roast young pheasant, and sea scallops for dinner.

Services and Facilities **Exercise Equipment:** 11 Nautilus units, 2 Concept II rowing ergometers, 2 Monark bikes, Trotter treadmill, incline station, hyperextension station, free weights. **Services:** Swedish and deep-tissue massage, sports instruction, yoga and aerobics classes, aquatics for arthritics. **Swimming Facilities:** Indoor and outdoor pools. **Spa Facilities:** Coed steam room, separate men's and women's saunas, whirlpools in the Sports Center. **Recreation Facilities:** 10 outdoor and 2 indoor tennis courts, 2 indoor racquetball courts, 2 indoor squash courts; cross-country skiing, downhill skiing at Suicide Six, Killington, Ascutney Mountain, Okemo Mountain; horseback-riding center nearby, sleigh rides and nature walks. **Evening Programs:** Resort entertainment.

In the Area Walking tours of historic Woodstock. Quechee Village (crafts), Dartmouth College Hopkins Center (performing arts), Saint-Gaudens Studio (sculpture), Marlboro Music Festival (chamber music).

Getting Here *From Boston.* By car, I–90 to I–91 (100 mi). By air, scheduled flights to Lebanon, NH. Taxi, rental car available.

Special Notes Ramps and specially equipped rooms for the disabled. Tennis camp for children June–Aug. only. No smoking in the sports center.

Hawaii

Polynesian culture has given new dimensions to the pursuit of fitness. On the volcanic island of Hawaii, guests at Kalani Honua live in traditional lodges made of cedar logs or camp out among the palm trees. On Maui you can join MountainFit, a week-long trek in which participants encounter the natural features of the island as well as the Wellness Center at the secluded Hana Ranch.

At the same time, developers of luxury resorts have competed for the distinction of having the most opulent health club on the island. At the Grand Hyatt Wailea resort you can indulge in a combination of Japanese, Hawaiian, European, and American fitness fantasies, or work out in a two-level cardiovascular fitness and weight training center.

While the water sports of Hawaii are famous, the islands are full of more unexpected fitness opportunities, such as bicycle rides up the slope of Maui's extinct volcano, Mt. Haleakala. Local outfitters will drive you to the top of the 10,023-foot slope to see the sunrise and provide bikes for the leisurely ride down.

Home of the strenuous Iron Man Triathalon, Hawaii offers a full range of sports ventures for every taste—from horseback riding on ranches to kayaking up the Huleia River on Kauai through a wildlife refuge. Polo matches abound on Oahu and the Big Island; the Hawaii Polo Club even offers five-day training programs. For fishermen the waters off the Kohala coast are legendary for deep-sea catches, and the Kona coast has spectacular sites for scuba diving—Napoopoo Beach Park and Keei Beach are favored spots. In the winter, you can go skiing on the Big Island. From December through May, the upper slopes of Mauna Kea, 13,796 feet above the sea, frequently have enough snow to make for sun-baked skiing.

One word of caution, however, when venturing into secluded areas on any of the islands, because of the danger of happening upon some farmer's illegal crop. Check with local park-service officials before you start out on a hike or ride.

Global Fitness Adventures

Holistic health
Sports conditioning

Hawaii
Kauai Bali Hai is the backdrop for this Global Fitness Adventures week on the Garden Island. Organized by fitness trainer Kristina Hurrell, the program takes groups of 10–20 participants into the dramatic mountains and beach areas that have been used for filming *South Pacific*, "The Thornbirds," and other Hollywood productions. Escorts knowledgeable in the island's botany and geology add interest to the daily excursions.

Starting with a morning session of yoga and stretch class, a guided hike is outlined for experienced hikers and beginners. Ranging from 5 to 15 miles, the routes lead through nature preserves surrounded by volcanoes and miles-long beaches. The Kalalau Trail reveals breathtaking vistas as cliffs rise precipi-

Hawaii

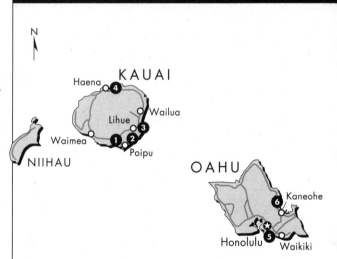

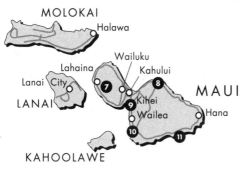

PACIFIC OCEAN

MOLOKAI
Halawa

Wailuku
Lahaina   Kahului
Lanai City   ⑦   ⑧   MAUI
LANAI   Kihei
              ⑨
              Wailea   Hana
KAHOOLAWE   ⑩
              ⑪

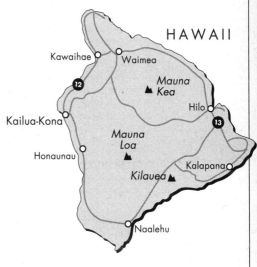

HAWAII

Kawaihae   Waimea

Mauna
▲ Kea

⑫   Hilo

Kailua-Kona   ⑬

Mauna
Loa
▲
Honaunau

Kilauea ▲   Kalapana

Naalehu

tously above the blue-green sea. Picnics are enjoyed at chosen scenic spots or on beaches. A private chef prepares meals for the group, usually a Hawaiian-style vegetarian menu. One evening is spent at a tiny restaurant in the town of Hanalei, and some meals are at the Bali Hai restaurant within the resort where the group is based.

An aura of "Old Hawaii" pervades the resort, which nestles on 22 acres of tropical hillside. The grounds are alive with waterfalls and pools, and eight tennis courts are available to guests. A championship golf course adjoins the resort, and guests receive massages every other day.

Sports conditioning options included in the program are kayaking, horseback riding, windsurfing, and snorkeling. A choice of three outings (weather and conditions permitting) takes you on a guided tour of the wetland bird refuge while viewing waterfalls from a kayak. Snorkeling excursions in a Zodiac boat take in a barrier reef and the dramatic Na Pali coast.

Completing this adventure is a helicopter tour over inaccessible parts of the island, which may include Wai'ale'ale crater, ancient sites of the Hawaiians, and Waimea canyon. At times, the sea comes alive with whales, dolphin, and flying fish.

Global Fitness Adventures
Box 1390, Aspen, CO 81612
Tel. 303/927-9593 or 800/548-2721
Fax 303/927-4793

Administration Founder/director, Kristina Hurrell

Season January–November, scheduled sessions.

Accommodations Hanalei Bay cottage rooms reflect the motif of a Hawaiian plantation guest house. All rooms have mountain or ocean view, air-conditioning, telephone, TV, bathroom, and maid service.

Rates $2,100 for the all-inclusive 8-day program. Included are 3 massages, choice of 3 excursions. Deposit: $500 check. Tax added, gratuities optional. No credit cards.

Meal Plans 3 meals daily included in program. Primarily vegetarian, the low-calorie daily menu includes some fish from local waters. Breakfast may be a power drink made from fruit, soy protein powder, and wheat germ, or a plate of papaya and pineapple with granola. Picnic lunch includes braised vegetable seitan kababs with spicy tai peanut sauce over rice, salad of sweet-and-sour cucumber, or baked lemon garlic tempeh and sprout sandwich and fruit. Dinner may be grilled mahimahi or tomato basil angelhair pasta with creamy mushroom tahini sauce.

Services and Facilities **Services:** Massage, yoga instruction, muscle toning class. **Swimming Facilities:** Freshwater outdoor pool, ocean beaches, and waterfalls. **Spa Facilities:** Jacuzzi, rock whirlpool. **Recreation Facilities:** 8 tennis courts, horseback riding, water sports; golf nearby. **Evening Programs:** Motivational workshops on nutrition, health, and detoxification; Hawaiian ceremony with island residents.

In the Area Na Pali Coast, Guava Kai Plantation, Ko Kee State Park, Princeville.

Getting Here *From U.S. mainland:* Scheduled airlines into Princeville or Lihue airports. Complimentary pickup at Princeville Airport. Rental car available.

Grand Hyatt Wailea Resort and Spa

Luxury pampering
Stress control
Preventive medicine
Nutrition and diet

Hawaii
Wailea (Maui)

Amid the splendor of the $600 million Grand Hyatt Wailea resort, the 50,000-square-foot Spa Grande offers the most extensive health and fitness facilities in Hawaii. In addition to 10 individual and private Jacuzzi areas, there are Roman-style whirlpools 20 feet in diameter located in the atriums of the men's and women's pavilions as well as 42 individual treatment rooms for everything from facials and loofah scrubs to mud treatments and massage.

Water sets the mood for the entire 40-acre resort. Located on Maui's south shore, 25 minutes from Kahului Airport, the eight-story hotel and spa overlooks formal gardens and a wide, crescent of Wailea beach. Try swimming through the system of locks, slides, and cascades that form a paradisiacal route of small islands and tropical grottoes among the outdoor pools.

Hydrotherapy comes with the spa's daily admission fee or as part of 4- to 7-night packages. The Terme Wailea circuit begins with a choice of two treatments designed to exfoliate and cleanse the skin: a loofah scrub or Japanese goshi-goshi scrub, sitting shower, and soak in a furo tub. Next you have a choice from five specialty baths in marble and gold mosaic tubs: aromatherapy for relaxation, Maui mud to remineralize, limu (Hawaiian seaweed) for detoxification, herbal for rejuvenation, and tropical enzyme bath for toning and softening the skin. Then a cascading waterfall massage in which stiff water jets focus on your thighs, calves, and back. In high-pressured jet-shower massage, you're subjected to spray from 20 high-pressure nozzles for periods of 30 seconds.

To stimulate circulation there are saunas, steam rooms, and cold-water plunges. Upstairs are private, oceanfront treatment rooms where seven types of massage and five different facials are offered. One room has a private tub for two and space for couples to be massaged together. And there is a unique Polynesian sand bath, where you are buried in moist ti plant leaves and volcanic sand heated to induce perspiration, detoxifying and relaxing the body.

Aerobics classes are held in a sprung-floored room several times daily. Also available is an air-conditioned racquetball court (convertible for squash) and weight training rooms. Before or after treatments, relax in the darkened Sonic Relaxation Room, cocooned in a futuristic longue chair that vibrates with music as you watch tranquilizing videos. Juices and waters are complimentary throughout your visit.

Water sports on the hotel beach include catamaran cruises, canoe rentals, snorkeling, windsurfing, and scuba diving. The Wailea resort area contains two 18-hole golf courses in its limits, and a tennis club with 14 courts, three of which are grass.

Guests at the neighboring Four Seasons resort also have access
to Spa Grande.

Grand Hyatt Wailea Resort and Spa
Wailea, Maui, HI 96753
Tel. 808/875–1234 or 800/233–1234

Administration Managing director, Jim Petrus; spa director, Darryll Leiman

Season Year-round.

Accommodations 787 rooms in an 8-story tower, all with ocean view, private
lanai, modern bath. Included are 53 suites and 100 rooms of Regency Club floors. Air-conditioned, telephones, TV, and full
amenities.

Rates Ocean front $400–$450 per night; Ocean view $375 per night;
Terrace $325 per night; Suites $700–$8,000 per night for 2; Regency Club-Ocean Front $500 per night; 7-night Grande Plan
spa package $4,275–$5,640 single, $6,590–$7,955 for 2 double
occupancy; 4-night Wailea Plan spa package $2,304–$3,084 single, $3,488–$4,268 for 2 double occupancy. Package rates include tax and service charge; tax added to room-only rate.
Deposit: 50%. Credit cards: AE, DC, MC, V.

Meal Plans 3 spa cuisine meals per day included in 4-night or 7-night
Grande Plan. Cafe Kula features organically grown island food
with Italian and Provençal touches: Grilled breast of chicken
with mango chili sauce, mahimahi with snap peas and roasted
red peppers, black-bean salad with cilantro. Breakfast and
lunch at cafe or main dining terrace. Optional Italian, Japanese, and Polynesian restaurants.

Services and Facilities **Exercise Equipment:** 14-unit Keiser system, 3 StairMasters, 4
Lifesteps, 4 WindRacer bikes, 2 Cybex cycles, 2 Biocycles, 2
Accufit, 5 StarTrac treadmills, Gravitron, LifeRower, Concept
II rower, free weights, and barbells. **Services:** Massage (Swedish, shiatsu, lomi-lomi, aromatherapy, sports, reflexology), facial, seaweed body pack, loofah scrub, wraps, healing baths.
Consultation on health, stress management, nutrition, fitness.
Full-service salon for hair, nail, skin care. **Recreation Facilities:** Ocean beach water sports, 2 swimming pools (1 Olympic
size), 2 18-hole golf courses, indoor racquetball/squash courts,
billiards, 14 tennis courts, 8,000 sq. ft. "Keiki"-land for kids.

In the Area Mt. Haleakala (volcano crater), Skyline Drive, Lahaina (old
port), Hana Highway, Seven Sacred Pools.

Getting Here *From the U.S. mainland.* Direct flights by United, Delta,
American, and Hawaiian Airlines to Maui's Kahului Airport.
By car, Hwy. 380 to Hwy. 350 via Kihei Hwy. 31. Complimentary transfers included in Grande Plan. Taxi, rental car, limousine available. *From Honolulu.* By interisland airlines and
American Hawaii cruises. Rental car available.

Special Notes Children's activities and lunch at Camp Hyatt, $35 daily. Accommodations for the disabled available. Separate spa facilities for men and women. Spa hours: daily 6 AM–8 PM.

Halekulani Hotel

Non-program resort facilities

Hawaii
Honolulu (Oahu)

Three mornings a week, at 7:30, guests gather on the beach for stretching exercises and a morning jaunt with Max Telford, fitness consultant for the Halekulani Hotel. Telford, holder of numerous world records for distance running, offers fitness tips as you jog along his favorite route; he adds a special dimension to the Waikiki routine.

The Halekulani fitness room, open since November 1987, is the focal point for daily activities. Free weights, multiple-exercise Paramount weight training gym, bicycles, rowing machines, and treadmill are available free of charge to all resort guests. For serious workouts, the hotel concierge arranges admission to the nearby Honolulu Club, where for a modest fee you can enjoy one of the best-equipped health clubs in the world.

The Halekulani is a small, private enclave, and the five-building complex and lush gardens have been meticulously restored. La Mer, a jewel-box restaurant open for dinner only, has an award-winning French chef. Best moments: afternoon tea in a tropical garden and evening entertainment in the House Without a Key (Charlie Chan's favorite spot on the island).

Halekulani Hotel
2199 Kalia Rd., Honolulu, HI 96815
Tel. 808/923–2311 or 800/367–2343
Telex 8382 HALE HR, Fax 808/926–8004

Administration Manager, Urs Aeby; fitness program director, Max Telford

Season Year-round.

Accommodations 456-room luxury hotel, 5 wings (1930s building and new additions). Rated best hotel in Hawaii. Rooms have sitting area, full bathroom with deep-soaking tub, glassed-in shower, marble vanity. Most have views of the beach and Diamond Head. 3 telephones, nightly turn-down service, cable TV (CNN), work desk.

Rates Rooms for 1 or 2 persons $245–$395 daily, suites $550–$3,000 single or double. Confirmation by credit card. Credit cards: AE, DC, MC, V.

Meal Plans Orchids Restaurant specializes in Pacific seafood and contemporary American cuisine. La Mer specialties include Lanai venison in a poivrade sauce, Norwegian salmon smoked over kiawe wood, onaga fish baked in herbed salt crust.

Services and Facilities **Exercise Equipment:** Paramount training gym, Ergo bike, Pritikin treadmill, free weights. **Services:** Shiatsu massage; aerobics class. **Swimming Facilities:** Outdoor pool, ocean. **Recreation Facilities:** At Honolulu Club: racquetball, volleyball, golf driving range; nearby tennis and golf. Water sports equipment on beach. **Evening Programs:** Resort entertainment.

In the Area The Plantation Spa, historic tours, Pearl Harbor, shopping.

Getting Here *From Honolulu International Airport.* Limousine, shuttle service, rental car, or taxi available (20 min).

Special Notes For the disabled, elevators, ground-floor lanai suites, and 14 specially equipped rooms are barrier free. Supervised activities and excursions for children. No smoking in designated dining areas; some nonsmoking rooms. Fitness room open daily 7 AM–10 PM.

Hawaiian Wellness Holiday

Holistic health
Life enhancement

Hawaii
Koloa (Kauai)

Combine a holistic approach to health and nutrition with a beach condominium resort, add therapeutic massage and chiropractic treatments, and you have Dr. Grady Deal's prescription for a fitness holiday. Dr. Deal—a psychologist, licensed massage therapist, gourmet cook, and practicing chiropractor—and his wife, Roberleigh, have created a warm, homelike atmosphere for their guests. Using facilities at the Sheraton Beach Resort, the Hawaiian Wellness Holiday is tailored to individual needs and interests. By keeping the group small—an average of 10 per week—the Deals aim for a high level of success in meeting each person's goals.

Yoga, aerobics, and aquacise in the swimming pool are part of the daily program. The cleansing diet helps correct underlying metabolic health problems. Included in the program cost are three massages or chiropractic therapy.

Detoxification, weight loss, and body toning are the primary objectives. Invigorating exercise and a cleansing diet are supplemented by natural therapies. Designed to clean out your digestive and eliminative tract and to reduce your appetite, the program can include such options as juice fasting, herbs, and self-administered colonic cleansing.

Spending most of the day outdoors, on scenic hikes and walks as well as at aerobics classes, guests quickly discover the natural healing effect of the island. Excursions included in the basic fee take the group to such scenic places as Waimea Canyon; the NaPali coast; Lumahai beach, where *South Pacific* was filmed; and the seven sacred pools.

Kauai is said to have a rare energy vortex, a metaphysical natural beauty that relaxes the mind and body. Exploring the island with a like-minded group of health seekers adds a special quality to the fitness holiday. Each person is encouraged to search for inner energy.

Rounding out the program are cooking demonstrations based on the macrobiotic and vegetarian meals that are served, workshops on nutrition and health, meditation, and deep-breathing exercises for relaxation. At the end of the day, you can unwind in the steam room, sauna, or Jacuzzi while awaiting yet another memorable sunset.

On this quiet crescent at the southern tip of the island, colors become almost magically intense. Where the sand ends, the lava rocks begin, black and shiny as wet coal, grouted with red soil. Surf hisses and spits at you from hidden spout holes. Compared with Waikiki, Poipu Beach is like switching from rock music to Debussy.

The caring program here has inspired many guests to adopt a healthy lifestyle. Highly structured, it is tailored to each guest's needs and interests.

Hawaiian Wellness Holiday
Box 279, Koloa, HI 96756
Tel. 808/332–9244 or 800/338–6977

Administration Program director, Roberleigh Deal; medical director, Grady A. Deal, Ph.D., D.C.

Season Year-round.

Accommodations Deluxe room or suite at Sheraton Kauai Beach Resort, with king- or queen-size beds, full bathroom, balcony, TV, telephone, air-conditioning, ceiling fans; choice of oceanfront or garden view.

Rates All-inclusive weekly program $1,195 single, $2,995 for 2 double occupancy in ocean-view room; $1,295 single, $2,295 for 2 in garden view room. Add 7% tax, gratuities optional. $500 on booking, balance due 30 days prior to arrival. Credit cards (5% surcharge): AE, MC, V.

Meal Plans Vegetarian, cleansing, or macrobiotic meals with whole grains, raw and cooked vegetables, fruit, juices, legumes, and fish. Breakfast can be wheatless waffles with berries; lunch, a vegetable stew or baked macaroni with cashew-pimiento cheeseless topping. Dinner includes green salad with oil-free dressing, brown rice cooked with sesame seeds, and herb tea. High in fiber and carbohydrates, meals include no dairy products, sugar additives, meat, free oils; eggs on request only. Optional diets: Fit for Life, full macrobiotic, low fat and cholesterol.

Services and Facilities **Exercise Equipment:** Cybex circuit with 10 variable resistance units, 3 Stairsteps, 2 Aerobicycles, 2 Monark bikes, computerized rower, Olympic free weights, dumbbells. **Services:** Massage (Swedish, shiatsu, deep tissue), reflexology, G-5 vibrator massage, chiropractic, physical therapy; hair, nail, and skin care (added fee). Nutritional counseling, cooking classes. Detoxification/colonic program ($250 additional). **Swimming Facilities:** 2 outdoor pools, ocean beach. **Recreation Facilities:** 2 tennis courts, water sports, hiking. Golf, horseback riding, bicycle rental nearby. **Evening Programs:** Talks and slide shows on health-related topics; Hawaiian cultural performances.

In the Area Scheduled group hiking and sightseeing trips to various parts of the island; botanical garden, fern grotto, Spouting Horn blowhole, Kokee State Park, Waimea Canyon. Optional: helicopter tour, scuba dives, day cruises.

Getting Here *From Koloa.* By car, Poipu Rd. to Poipu Beach (15 min). Transfers on arrival/departure at airport (and for all excursions) included in program fee. Taxi, rental car available.

Special Notes Accommodations for the disabled. Full program for children over 12; resort activity available. No smoking in program areas. Remember to bring medical or chiropractic records.

Sheraton Hotel Hana-Maui

Non-program resort facilities

Hawaii An aura of the Old West pervades the Hotel Hana-Maui, which
Hana (Maui) is set on an isolated coast in the middle of a cattle ranch. Hawaiian cowboys, called *paniolos*, lead white-faced Hereford in from pasture as you hike down the rocky coastal trail to catch

the sunset at Red Sand Beach; a session of yoga at the Wellness Center is a nice follow-up, topped off by a shiatsu massage.

Above all, Hana is a place of soothing seclusion. Lodging is in spacious one-story cottages with tropical furnishings and private lanais. During dinner in the Plantation Guest House, talented ensembles offer performances of Hawaiian music and dance in an authentic style not packaged for commercial shows.

The area has an ancient history of civilization, going as far back as AD 1100. From 1845 to 1945, the sugar industry thrived, then San Francisco baseball baron Paul Fagan transformed 4,700 acres into the Hana Ranch. Fagan's team, the Seals, used to train here; baseball is still played by town folk on a plush field next to the hotel.

Going upscale after a recent expansion, the hotel added a small health facility complete with panoramic views, mirrored aerobics studio, computerized workout equipment, and a swimming pool. For $10 per day, guests can get one-on-one training or participate in exercise classes. The schedule varies from day to day, offering low-impact aerobics, aquacise, and yoga at $10 per class. A nature walk begins the day at 9:30 AM, complimentary to all guests. The spa director's philosophy takes advantage of the island's natural beauty rather than emphasizing pampering attentions. For serious hikers, there is a four-hour trek into the lush tropical forest, with a stop to swim under the cascades of a waterfall.

Hana is not the kind of place for rigid schedules. Locals call their remote home the "heart of Hawaii." After the 53-mile roller-coaster ride from Kahului Airport on the Hana road, you'll understand why.

Sheraton Hotel Hana-Maui
Box 8, Hana, Maui, HI 96713
Tel. 808/248–8211 or 800/334–8484

Administration	General manager, Fred Orr
Season	Year-round.
Accommodations	97 cottages with wooden floors and walls, tropical furniture. Two queen-size beds, modern bathroom, private lanai, air-conditioning, ceiling fans.
Rates	Wellness 4-night package with meals, $1,690 single, $2,170 for 2 double occupancy. Daily $305–$2,000 per suite, single or double occupancy; no meals included. Add tax. Credit cards: AE, DC, MC, V.
Meal Plans	3 Wellness menu meals daily in spa package, or as à la carte.
Services and Facilities	**Exercise Equipment:** 2 Precor bikes, 2 Precor stairclimbers, Precor rowing machine, NordicTrack cross-country ski unit, 5-station Paramount gym. **Services:** Swedish and therapeutic massage, facial with coconut, honey, aloe vera; nature walk, hiking, aerobics classes, aquacise. **Swimming Facilities:** Outdoor lap pool, 80 # 40 ft.; ocean beaches. **Recreation Facilities:** Horseback riding, baseball, hay ride, breakfast cookout. **Evening Programs:** Folklore performances.
In the Area	Hana Museum and cultural center, Seven Sacred Pools, lava sand beaches, historic sites; boar hunts, rodeos.

Getting Here *From the U.S. mainland.* Direct flights by United, Delta, American, and Hawaiian Airlines to Kahului Airport. Transfers by van (1½ hr) or Aloha Island Air (15 min). *From Honolulu.* By interisland airlines and American Hawaii cruises. Rental car available.

Hyatt Regency Kauai

Non-program resort facilities

Hawaii
Poipu Beach
(Kauai)

Secluded within the Hyatt Regency Kauai resort is the full-service Anara Spa. ANARA stands for "A New Age Restorative Approach," best experienced while relaxing with a lomi-lomi massage followed by a facial using coconut oil scented with gardenias. Attentive staff members blend ancient Hawaiian healing therapies with state-of-the-art technology: this effective combination leaves guests feeling like a million bucks. There is a courtyard, lap pool, and lava rock showers, as well as a complete health facility, including steam room, sauna, sprung-floor aerobics studio, small fitness room with weights, and Jacuzzi. Scheduled daily are aerobics classes, weight training clinics, and aqua-trim water exercise.

Services worth noting include the Ti Leaf Cool Wrap, designed to alleviate the discomfort of sunburn and elevated body temperature. Guests are spread on a bed of the cooling leaves, covered with a gel made from aloe vera and comfrey, then covered with more heat-absorbing leaves and wrapped in a sheet for 20 minutes to sweat out any toxins. Another treatment is the Sacred Bath of Hawaiian elders or kapunas: red colloidal clay from the base of Kauai's Mt. Waialeale is mixed with sea salts and spread on the body after a session in the steam room. This treatment is followed with a botanical bath with a limu or seaweed and salt mixture, which simulates thalassotherapy in helping to stimulate blood circulation.

This plantation-style resort, set on 18 acres of lush beachfront, comes complete with a private jungle lagoon and includes a museum of Asian and Pacific art, a collection of wildlife, and fine restaurants. Joggers can enjoy a two-mile course on the beach.

Hyatt Regency Kauai
1571 Poipu Rd., Koloa, Kauai, HI 96756
Tel. 808/742–1234 or 800/228–9000

Administration General manager, Rick Riess; spa director, Judy Dixon

Season Year-round.

Accommodations Spread out on three floors, the 600-room resort includes concierge service floors in the Regency Club. Spacious, contemporary rooms, full bath, lanais, balconies; luxury amenities. Air-conditioning, TV, telephone.

Rates $195–$315 per day for one or two persons; Regency Club $390–$410. Pamper Yourself 1-day spa package $175, plus room. Ultimate spa package for 2 (including breakfast or lunch) $445; if reserved with 4-night Hyatt Vacation, $410 including rental car, tax, and gratuity. 2 nights' advance payment or credit-card confirmation. Credit cards: AE, DC, MC, V.

Meal Plans No special meal plan. Selected low-calorie, low-fat items for heart-healthy dining available daily.

Services and Facilities **Exercise Equipment:** Nautilus weight training units (6 stations), Lifecycle, treadmill, free weights. **Services:** Massage (shiatsu, Lomi-Lomi, Swedish, Esalen), beauty salon, tennis clinics, private lessons, scuba course. **Swimming Facilities:** Free-form ½-acre pool, ocean beach. **Recreation Facilities:** 5 tennis courts, hiking; bicycle rental. **Evening Programs:** Resort entertainment.

In the Area Hanalei National Wildlife Refuge (kayak tour), Kokee State Park (mountain lodge), Waimea Canyon (scenic drive), Waimea (Capt. Cook landed here in 1778), Na Pali Coast State Park (hiking trails), Fern Grotto.

Getting Here *From Lihue.* By car, Hwy. 50 to Poipu Beach Rd. (20 min). Rental car, taxi, airport shuttle van available.

Special Notes Sports clinics and day-camp programs (seasonal) for children. Ground-floor rooms for the disabled.

Hyatt Regency Waikoloa

Non-program resort facilities
Luxury pampering

Hawaii
Waikoloa (Hawaii) Created on a mammoth scale, the Hyatt Regency Waikoloa has a secluded spa called ANARA, which stands for A New Age Restorative Approach. Opened in 1988, it is part of a 62-acre resort that includes cavorting dolphins, horse-drawn carriages for rides into the countryside, and catamarans for surfing. Instead of walking to your room, you ride a canal boat or the "tubular tram." There is also a spiritual walk with guided meditation recalling the ancient kahunas.

ANARA offers European thalassotherapy in baths, herbal wraps, body masks, and loofah scrubs. Seaweed-based cosmetics and natural oils nourish the body and prevent sun damage to winter-weary complexions. Participants are provided with workout clothing and robes.

In one of the spa's posh, private massage rooms you can experience a traditional Hawaiian Lomi-Lomi massage, a form of lymphatic cleansing. With rhythmic rocking, the massage relaxes muscles while stimulating circulation.

Services are billed to your room on an à la carte basis, plus $15 for daily use of spa facilities; $10 after 4 PM if you include a massage or treatment. An alfresco cafe at ANARA serves "Cuisine Naturelle" from 8 AM to 2 PM.

Extensive facilities are at your disposal. In separate sections for men and women are Turkish steam rooms, Finnish sauna, outdoor whirlpool, showers and locker room with full amenities. A beauty salon, a gym for aerobics classes, and a weights room are all part of the freestanding spa building.

The spa's combination of Eastern and Western health philosophies includes daily tai chi chuan and yoga classes as well as stress reduction, water aerobics, and meditation. The ancient Chinese tai chi chuan movements are demonstrated on the beach at 7:30 and 9:30 in the morning. All guests are invited to join a power walk around the property, called the Sunrise Pacer (three to five miles). Classes are complimentary.

From the mile-long museum walkway filled with $3.5 million of Oriental and Pacific art to the acre-size swimming pool with its waterfalls, hidden grotto bar, and twisting waterslide, nonstop fantasy rather than fitness is the reason for vacationing here. Witness the Adventure Guide program with its own version of Indiana Jones leading intrepid guests into the island's lush flora and fauna preserves. The attraction most talked about is dolphins: Six tame Atlantic bottlenose cavort in the hotel's four-acre, beach-rimmed saltwater lagoon. Through a lottery system, guests have the opportunity to meet a dolphin for $65 under the supervision of experienced trainers. For $35, an educational dolphin encounter for children is available, with part of the proceeds supporting research to help endangered dolphins in the wild.

For more prosaic activities, the resort offers a par-72 golf course, tennis, sailing, fishing, and horseback riding. All can be booked along with spa appointments and restaurant reservations (there are eight places where you can eat, from Italian and Japanese to seafood and broiler specialties) through the "Vacations by Design" desk. Don't miss the luau.

Hyatt Regency Waikoloa
1 Waikoloa Beach Resort, Waikoloa, HI 96743
Tel. 808/885–1234 or 800/223–1234

Administration	General manager, Edward Crovo; spa director, Sylvia Sepielli
Season	Year-round.
Accommodations	1,241 guest rooms in 3 low-rise towers. Contemporary furnishings include king-size or 2 queen-size beds, marble-floored bathroom, full amenities. 75% of rooms have ocean view. Regency Club with 80 exclusive rooms, complimentary breakfast and beverage service.
Rates	From $215 a night, single or double occupancy. Day at ANARA $225; miniday at ANARA $150; spa sampler $99 (includes service charge and gratuity). Add 4.167% state sales tax. Deposit: Confirmation by credit card. Credit cards: AE, MC, V.
Meal Plans	No meal plan available. Lunch at the ANARA spa can include chili chicken salad with confetti of marinated rice and vegetables in cilantro vinaigrette; poached salmon with cucumber and tomato on Bibb lettuce with dill couli; vegetable antipasto with tuna. Also available at seafood and steak restaurants. Cuisine Naturelle menu with such specialties as Caribbean jerk chicken, clam linguine.
Services and Facilities	**Exercise Equipment:** 10-unit Keiser weight training gym, 2 StairMaster 4000 PT, Gravitron, 4 PTS turbo recumbent bikes, 2 Biocycles, 2 Precor treadmills, Concept II rowing machine, dumbbells (2½-50 lbs.). **Services:** Massage (Lomi-Lomi, aromatherapy, shiatsu, sports, Swedish), reflexology, seaweed pack, body facial, body mask, loofah buff, herbal wrap, herbal or aroma bath, hydrating facial. Beauty salon with French Phytomer products for hair, nail, and skin care. **Swimming Facilities:** Outdoor freshwater pools, seawater lagoon, ocean beach. **Recreation Facilities:** 8 tennis courts, 2 championship 18-hole golf courses plus 2 courses nearby, horseback riding, windsurfing, snorkeling, scuba diving, sailing.
In the Area	Hawaii Volcanoes National Park (2 active volcanoes, Kilauea and Mauna Loa), Kona coffee plantations, Captain Cook (fish-

ing port), Hilo (shopping), Mookini Heiau (royal palace), Puukohola Heiau (temple), Lyman House Museum (missionary home), downhill skiing (Jan.–Mar.).

Getting Here *From Honolulu.* Interisland air services to Keahole Kona Airport (45 min), transfer by hotel van ($17.50 each way) or rental car (20 min).

Special Notes Specially equipped rooms for the disabled. Children's day camp with lunch ($35). No smoking in spa. ANARA hours: daily 6 AM–8 PM.

Kalani Honua Retreat

Holistic health
Life enhancement
Weight management
Taking the waters

Hawaii Suspended between fire and water, the Kalani Honua Retreat
Pahoa (Hawaii) and Conference Center offers a full range of health-oriented activities. An intercultural program, with yoga and hula, complements workshops scheduled throughout the year. Visitors can participate or venture off to explore on their own.

The seaside ranch is surrounded by natural beauty. Lush jungle, black-sand beaches, and stark lava cliffs meet the ocean within the resort's 20 acres of seclusion. Nearby is the world's most active volcano, Kilauea, which provides spectacular scenery and nurtures orchids and hot springs.

The resort attracts an interesting mix of robust, healthy men and women, families hiking the volcano trails, and professional bodyworkers attending seminars, but it has no fixed program. If you're lucky, Aunty Margaret may be presenting a demonstration of Hawaiian Lomi-Lomi massage. Her historical perspective on native cleansing programs has been recognized by the State of Hawaii.

In keeping with the spirit of old Hawaii, guests are housed in *hales*, wood lodges made of cedar logs. Each hexagonal lodge has its own kitchen and ocean-view studio space, with dormitory rooms, but mostly private accommodations. Campers can sleep under the stars at 25 sites among the palm trees.

Therapeutic services and exercise classes are the focus of a Japanese-style spa. The wooden bathhouse has a communal hot tub, sauna heated by wood-burning stove, and private massage rooms. Four pavilions with suspended wooden floors are used for yoga, aerobics, and dance performances. Nearby are an 85-foot swimming pool and a Jacuzzi, plus a new fitness center.

Informal and laid-back, the days are totally unstructured. In addition to exploring craters and newly created beaches among the lava flows, you can soak at hot and warm springs, snorkel in a tidal pool, or join a scuba outing. Sunbathing on clothes-optional beaches is a major attraction, especially at nearby Kehena Beach.

The "Big Island" abounds with spiritual places, shrines to ancient gods, and mystical rain forests. Inner harmony and harmony with nature are qualities of ancient Hawaiian culture celebrated here.

Kalani Honua Retreat and Conference Center
Box 4500, Pahoa, HI 96778
Tel. 808/965-7828 or 800/367-6886

Administration Director, Richard Koob; program director, Michael Kraft

Season Year-round.

Accommodations 4 two-story lodges, 37 rooms double or multiple occupancy. Cedar walls and floors, minimal furniture, many windows; Hawaiian prints and fabrics, fresh flowers. Baths shared, except for 2 private suites in each lodge. Maid service daily; communal kitchen. Also available: private cottages with cooking facility, 25 tent sites. Amenities: coin-operated laundry, rental of water sports gear. No air-conditioning.

Rates Lodge room $65 per night single with private bath, shared bath $52; $75 for 2 persons double occupancy with private bath, shared bath $62. Suites on request. Tent site $15 single, $25 for 2. Cottages $85 for 2 in a duplex unit with private bath (rates 20% higher Dec. 15–May 1). Credit cards: AE, DC, MC, V.

Meal Plans Primarily vegetarian, meals at Cafe Cashew are à la carte. Hawaiian-style breakfast includes papaya, passion fruit, banana smoothies, buffet of tropical fruits, brown rice, French toast. Lunch can be sautéed vegetables with *tempeh* and *tahini* sauce, broiled mahimahi, or spinach lasagna. Dinner choices can be grilled chicken or mahimahi baked with mushrooms in lemon and garlic sauce; cream of papaya cashew soup, and a salad bar. Beer, wine, coffee, tea available. Special diet requests (Pritikin, macrobiotic) accommodated. Daily meal plan $22–$24.

Services and Facilities **Exercise Equipment:** Weight training units, stationary bike, treadmill, free weights. **Services:** Massage (shiatsu, Swedish, Esalen), acupressure, acupuncture, rolfing, chiropractic. Counseling on weight loss, diet, nutrition. **Swimming Facilities:** Outdoor pool (Olympic-size), ocean beaches. **Spa Facilities:** 2 Jacuzzi whirlpools, natural pools at nearby springs and steam baths. **Recreation Facilities:** Bicycle rental, tennis court, horseback riding, hiking, volleyball; golf course, ski slopes nearby. **Evening Programs:** Workshops on health and sports conditioning, yoga; cultural performances, traditional Hawaiian feasts.

In the Area Helicopter sightseeing tour of island; scuba trips (fee); Volcanoes National Park, Jaggar Museum (Volcanoes Park history), Kilauea caldera, lava tubes at Wahaula Visitor Center, Hawaii Tropical Botanical Garden, Parker Ranch resort area, Hawaii plantation town, King Kamehameha historic site, Mauna Kea observatory telescope, MacKenzie State Park (hiking, picnics, beach).

Getting Here *From Hilo.* By car, Rte. 11 to Keaau, Rte. 130 to Rte. 137 (45 min). Rental car, limousine, taxi available.

Special Notes No smoking in bathhouse area. Remember to bring sunscreen #15, mosquito repellent, and flashlight.

MountainFit

Sports conditioning

Hawaii
Kihei (Maui) Hiking through verdant rain forests and across a moonscape-like volcano crater, participants in the MountainFit program

explore the many contrasts that make Maui a popular Pacific paradise: Only this is like being a guest at a private estate with a dozen friends who enjoy getting off the beaten track.

Based in Kihei, participants are transported to trailheads, then picked up at the end of the hike without having to double back. The daily outings include swims in fern-rimmed pools beneath cascading waterfalls, snorkeling in crystal-clear water, and plenty of time to relax on the island's famed beaches. Designed for experienced hikers and beginners alike, the treks are geared to the average capacity of the group members. Each member sets his or her own pace.

The program (which also operates in Utah and Montana) attracts many repeaters, ranging in age from 30 to 70. Camaraderie develops quickly on the trails as staffers discuss local lore, geology, and horticulture while identifying plants and wildlife along the way. Supplied with fannypack, lunch, snacks, and a water bottle refilled and frozen nightly, the group sets out on new adventures daily during the eight-day program. Windsurfing, sea kayaking, snorkeling, and a boat trip to the neighboring island of Molokai are typical scheduled events. Trails will take you past ancient Hawaiian burial grounds and into Haleakala National Park. At day's end, you'll return for a well-earned sports massage to ease sore muscles.

Daily sessions of yoga and spa-type meals by a professional chef add to your sense of well-being. The setting does the rest.

MountainFit
Kihei, Maui, HI
Reservations: 633 Battery St. (5th floor), San Francisco, CA 94111
Tel. 415/397-6216 or 800/926-5700

Administration Owner/director, Diane Wechsler

Season Nov., Feb.–Mar.; 8 scheduled sessions.

Accommodations A residential compound in the cool uplands, with 7 guest rooms; 3-story main house has sauna, dining room, and kitchen, 4 bedrooms, some with private bath. Furniture is eclectic mix of beach retreat and Oriental pieces, mostly rattan chairs.

Rates $2,250 for the 8-day program (Saturday–Friday), includes meals, 2 hour-long massages, outings. $300 nonrefundable deposit with reservation by check or AE credit card; balance payable by check due 30 days prior to trip.

Meal Plans Private chef plans 1,200–1,500-calorie daily menu. Mostly vegetarian, meals include fresh fish from local waters, and poultry. Breakfast is buffet of cereals, fresh-baked muffins, tropical fruit, and pancakes or fruit-filled French toast. Trail lunch is cold fruit soup, pasta salad, peanut butter and jelly sandwiches, fruit. Coffee, herbal tea, milk available. Special diets accommodated.

Services and Facilities Services: Hiking guides, yoga, massage, laundry. **Swimming Facilities:** Freshwater pool. **Evening Programs:** Dinner at nearby cafe, lecture-demonstration on reflexology; VCR films.

In the Area Hana State Park, Haleakala volcano, shopping in Lahaina, Sugar Cane Train ride, Grand Hyatt Wailea Resort & Spa.

Getting Here *From U.S. Mainland:* Direct flights to Maui's Kahului Airport from Chicago and West Coast via United Airlines, or interisland services. Transportation provided on arrival and departure day (20 min) at airport.

Special Notes Smoking not permitted in residences. Lightweight hiking boots required, suggested clothing list supplied. Daily laundry service for personal items. Maid service and bathrobe provided. Gratuities for staff, $50–$100.

The Plantation Spa

Holistic health

Hawaii
Kaaawa (Oahu) Combine the Swedish approach to health and natural living with a Polynesian plantation set between Pacific beaches and rugged mountains, and you have a new breed of health resort.

The Plantation Spa was originally an old family estate where travelers watered horses. Now the carriage house is an aerobics studio, and guest cottages for up to 18 visitors are arranged on terraces leading to an airy therapy center. Recently expanded, the Orchid House now offers full-body cleansing with island fruits, vegetables, mud, and sea salt.

Surrounded by natural beauty and scenic splendor, the program takes you on canoeing trips and hikes to waterfalls through primal palm groves. Classes in hula dancing, as well as tai chi chuan, aerobics, and vegetarian cooking, are on the daily schedule. Beginning with a sunrise stretch and walk along the beach, the day is structured for exercise and relaxation.

An instructor leads a group through aquatic aerobics in the swimming pool equipped with water-resistant fins and support bars. After lunch there is free time for a massage or herbal wrap (one of each is included in your package price for the week). A 45-minute session of low-impact aerobics and circuit training is followed by yoga and sunset serenity. There is a coed sauna and outdoor Jacuzzi in the lush garden.

Although the days are well-balanced, you are not required to participate in all activities. The one-week program runs from Sunday afternoon through Saturday morning; extensions are possible if you fall in love with the place. It retains the peace and friendliness of old Hawaii and fosters positive thinking to rejuvenate you for today's world.

The Plantation Spa
51–550 Kamehameha Hwy., Kaaawa, HI 96730
Tel. 808/237–8685, 808/237–8442, or 800/422–0307
Fax 808/947–1866

Administration Director/owner, Bodil M. Anderson; managers, Chris and Lisa Potis

Season Year-round.

Accommodations Cozy cottages with 8 guest rooms. Furnished with rattan chairs, double beds, decorative Polynesian arts and crafts. Cottages cluster around farmhouse where meals are served. No TV, air-conditioning, or telephone in rooms. Most have private toilet with shower, 2 single beds, ceiling fan.

Rates 1 week $1,145 per person double occupancy, $1,490 single; 2-night retreat $357 double, $457 single. $500 advance payment per person, due within 14 days after reservation; nonrefundable. Add taxes and 15% gratuity. Credit cards: MC, V.

Meal Plans Lactovegetarian meals served from fixed menu. Breakfast is multigrain Muesli with fresh fruit, raisins, apricots, papaya with lime juice, herbal teas. Lunch is chilled lettuce cardamom soup, home-baked Spanish tomato bread, carrot salad, tropical fruit platter, vegetable juice. Dinner begins with slices of zucchini and tomato in pesto, an entree of ratatouille with fresh herbs and crème fraiche, brown rice. Special diets accommodated. Juice and broth fasts on request. No coffee or sugar.

Services and Facilities **Exercise Equipment:** Stairclimber, free weights, rowing machine, stationary bike. **Services:** Swedish massage, shiatsu, herbal wrap, pineapple body scrub, loofah salt scrub, mud mask, seaweed wrap, iridology, facial; fitness evaluation; arts and crafts instruction. **Swimming Facilities:** 17-meter outdoor pool; ocean beach. **Recreation Facilities:** Hiking, canoeing, croquet, badminton, volleyball. **Evening Programs:** Hawaiian folklore, palm reading, cooking class, meditation class.

In the Area Scheduled group hiking and canoe trips; Polynesian Cultural Center, Waimea Falls Park (botanical garden, nature trails), Byodo-in Temple (Japanese shrine) and Haiku Gardens, Sea World.

Getting Here *From Honolulu.* By bus, #5 from Ala Moana Shopping Center terminal (1 hr.). By car, Hwy. 63 (Likelike Hwy.) to coastal Hwy. 83 (Kamehameha Hwy.) via Kaneohe Bay (50 min). Rental car available. Transfers on request (fee).

Special Notes No smoking on property. Remember to bring medical records and hiking and exercise shoes. Program begins on Sundays. Roommate match on request. Day visitors welcome.

Strong, Stretched & Centered

Life enhancement
Holistic health
Sports conditioning

Hawaii
Kihei (Maui)

Working out with the instructors' instructor is a fitness buff's dream come true. Over 200 graduates of the professional certification course, an intensive six weeks, have spread the work of the body/mind training program originated here by Gloria Keeling to 17 countries.

This is not a quick-fix, so you probably should be in shape before joining Gloria's beach gang. The techniques used synthesize several cultures, from tai chi chuan to aquacize; in an East-West experience. Weight-reduction methods employ the notion of muscle definition as well as the concept of *ki*, the centered self.

Based at Kihei, the program participants work out at a fully equipped Powerhouse Gym. The staff instructors and advisers from the Maui Holistic Health Center work with you on a one-to-one basis to develop and expand your potential. Training sites include spectacular Haleakala crater (the world's sixth largest dormant volcano), the lush jungles of Hana, with its waterfalls and bamboo forests, and the numerous white-sand beaches for which Maui is celebrated.

Orchestrated for maximum body movement, you'll learn "gestalt dance" and African jazz rhythms with your aerobics. It's a high-powered experience in interdisciplinary training, with people devoted to nurturing a balance of mind and body fitness.

Strong, Stretched & Centered
Box 758, Paia, Maui, HI 96779
Tel. 808/575–2178
Fax 808/575–2275

Administration Program director, Gloria Keeling

Season Scheduled sessions year-round.

Accommodations Lanai-style apartments with 2–3 bedrooms shared by participants. Twin beds, modern bath, ocean-view balcony or terrace. Furnished informally, with white rattan seating, lots of big cotton pillows, tropical fabrics; color TV, completely equipped kitchen. Beach area has shaded Jacuzzi and swimming pool. No maid service; laundry unit in each apartment.

Rates 6-week program $4,185 per person double, $4,800 single. $1,000 advance payment. No credit cards.

Meal Plans 3 meals served family-style weekdays. Mostly vegetarian menu includes enchiladas with beans, choice of vegetables or chicken, eggplant Parmesan casserole, baked mahimahi fish, Thai satay noodles with oyster sauce, vegetables, and peanuts. On weekends, guests prepare their own meals.

Services and Facilities **Exercise Equipment:** Universal gym, free weights, treadmills, Lifecycles, StairMaster. **Services:** Sports conditioning, weightlifting training, massage, video analysis, instructor certification. **Swimming Facilities:** Outdoor pool, ocean beach. **Recreation Facilities:** Water sports, hiking; nearby tennis courts, golf course, bike rental, horseback riding, scuba and water sports, all for extra fees. **Evening Programs:** Workshops on health and fitness.

In the Area Group outings for snorkeling, overnight hike in Hana State Park, sunrise hike on Haleakala crater. Interisland cruises, helicopter sightseeing, shopping and nightlife in Lahaina, sugar-cane train ride, Grand Hyatt Wailea Resort & Spa.

Getting Here Direct flights to Maui's airport from Chicago and West Coast on United Airlines. *From Kahului.* About 20 min to Kihei by taxi or rental car. Rental car available for group use.

The Westin Kauai

Life enhancement
Nutrition and diet
Preventive medicine
Luxury pampering

Hawaii
Kauai Lagoons
(Kauai)

Fitness on a fantasy island is the theme of this Kauai Lagoons spa. The full 800-acre resort incorporates some older hotel blocks but is mainly developed as the first of Christopher Hemmeter's fantasies with Westin hotels. With huge reflecting pools, Athenian porticoes and columns, it's like a pleasure dome by Trajan as imagined by Sam Goldwyn. Pleasure, however, is not this resort's sole quest; the spa offers a comprehensive health and fitness evaluation, plus an overall wellness program for active participants.

The director is a registered dietitian who takes a serious approach to helping guests with nutrition and weight-loss problems. The low-fat, low-sodium food is spiced with enticing Hawaiian flavor. The average daily calorie intake of the seven-day plan is 1,500, with about 60% from carbohydrates, 20% from protein, and 20% from fat. The menu is low in sugar and high in fiber, and it's designed to ensure that you get the right amount of calories at the right time of day.

Activities begin early with a power walk at sunrise. Threading through lagoons bedecked with waterfalls, and seven life-size marble horses amid a 60-foot geyser, this is a good way to get your bearings. Unlimited classes are included in the spa's daily admission fee ($15; $10 after 4 PM) as well as packages that combine golf, tennis, fitness, and treatments. Morning and afternoon aerobics, aquacise, and toning and body sculpture are among six classes scheduled daily. A sunrise session of tai chi chuan on the beach is complimentary to all guests on Tuesday and Friday, as is the daily sunrise walk.

Sporting an extensive golf and tennis complex overlooking the beach, the Westin resort offers packages that include both spa services and emphasis on the game of your choice. There are two Jack Nicklaus signature courses, eight Plexi-pave tennis courts, and a 650-seat stadium court. Swimmers have a choice of the beach or a spectacular 96,000-square-foot swimming pool equipped with five whirlpool baths and dotted with palm-tree islands harboring a wallaby or two.

Located in the Golf & Racquet Club, the Spa and Wellness Center is a sybaritic retreat. Separate facilities for men and women include a Turkish steam room, Finnish sauna, whirlpool, weight training area, and locker-room lounge. You don't have to be a hotel guest to sign up for a one-day package. Your workout clothing (T-shirt, shorts) and a plush robe come with the fee.

The Westin Kauai
Kalakapi Beach, Lihue, HI 96766
Tel. 808/246–5050 or 800/228–3000
Telex 808/743–1211, Fax 808/246–5057

Administration	General manager, David Shackelton; Spa and Wellness Center manager, Terri Fields Hosler, R.D.
Season	Year-round.
Accommodations	850 rooms in mid-rise buildings surrounded by lagoons and tropical gardens. Modern furnishings, air-conditioned, with color TV, telephone, and full bath. The resort has 12 restaurants and lounges, 3-story discotheque, and a $2.5 million collection of Oriental and Pacific art.
Rates	$195–$400 daily per room, single or double occupancy; suites $400–$1,700 daily. 3-night spa and sports package with garden-view room, no meals, $1,662 per couple, including tax and gratuities; 7-night package $3,596 per couple. Day packages including massage, treatments, wellness screening $160–$200; Total Kauai Lagoons Experience $350. Credit cards: AE, DC, MC, V.

Meal Plans   Spa cuisine available à la carte at restaurants throughout the resort. Breakfast choices include cholesterol-free scrambled eggs, Bircher-Muesli cereal, bran muffin, yogurt, fresh fruit, orange-pineapple juice. Lunch can be grilled chicken fajitas, South Pacific bouillabaisse, or salad with poached chicken and shiitake mushrooms on romaine lettuce. Dinner entrees include chicken stir-fry with steamed brown rice, fettuccine with Manila prawns, baked mahimahi.

Services and Facilities   **Exercise Equipment:** Spring system (Men's Spa), Universal gym (Ladies Spa); StairMaster, 2 Lifecycles, 2 Monark bikes, dumbbells (3–50 lbs.) in each spa. **Services:** Massage (Swedish, Lomi-Lomi, shiatsu, sports), facials, herbal wrap and body buff, Hawaiian salt-glow rub, Pacific full-body mask, eyebrow shaping and tinting; fitness assessment, blood-cholesterol analysis, nutritional counseling, health-ad lifestyle appraisal. **Swimming Facilities:** Outdoor pool, ocean beach; indoor aquacise pool. **Recreation Facilities:** 2 18-hole golf courses, 8 tennis courts, jogging trails, horse-drawn carriage rides, outrigger canoe and mahogany launch cruises. **Evening Programs:** Luau.

In the Area   Waimea Canyon, Na Pali coastline, Alakai swamp, Awaawauhi hiking trail, Kokee State Park, Hanalei Beach County Park.

Getting Here   The hotel is 1 mile from Kauai Airport, outside Lihue on Rte. 56. Taxi, rental car available.

Special Notes   Spa hours: daily 6:30 AM–7:30 PM. Day camp for children under 12. Ground-floor accommodations and elevators for the disabled. No smoking inside spa.

The Westin Maui

Non-program resort facilities

Hawaii
Lahaina (Maui)   Breathtaking waterfalls, meandering streams, and a health club are among the attractions of this mega resort. The Westin Maui is set on 12 oceanfront acres and is bordered by two golf courses and a tennis complex; it has all the pleasures of paradise and none of the pain.

Take the wildlife and garden tour offered by Guest Services and you will learn that more than 650,000 gallons of water sustain the resort's aquatic needs. The pool area alone features five free-form swimming pools, two water slides, and a swimup Jacuzzi hidden away in a grotto. Swans, flamingos, and other charming characters roam freely, adding their individual personalities to the tropical atmosphere.

Pool activities include water volleyball and aquacize classes. Scuba instructors are on hand to give beginner and refresher courses as well as guided ocean beach dives. For other water sports you can rent a Hobie cat, Windsurfer, or snorkeling equipment.

The coed health club offers weight training and an exercise room where aerobics classes are held daily, at no charge. There is a steam room, sauna, and Jacuzzi for relaxing stiff, sore muscles. Massage therapy is available by appointment.

Tennis and golf enthusiasts have easy access to the island's finest facilities: the Royal Kaanapali Golf Course with 36 holes, the Royal Lahaina Tennis Ranch with 11 courts, stadium seating, and a massage therapist. During the winter months, golfers get a bonus as humpback whales play offshore in the warm waters within view of the links.

The Westin Maui

2365 Kaanapali Pkwy., Lahaina, HI 96761
Tel. 808/667–2525 or 800/228–3000
Fax 808/661–5764

Administration General manager, Steve Shalit; spa director, Karen Paresa

Season Year-round.

Accommodations 761-room resort has two towers, each 11 floors. Luxury rooms and suites, including the exclusive Royal Beach Club. Air-conditioned, private lanais, king-size or double beds, views of ocean or golf course.

Rates $195–$330 single or double occupancy, Royal Beach Club rooms $375–$395, suites from $500–$1,900. 2 nights' advance payment or credit-card confirmation. Credit cards: AE, DC, MC, V.

Meal Plans No special dining plan. 3 restaurants, snacks to Continental fare. Best choice: Sound of the Falls.

Services and Facilities **Exercise Facilities:** 10 Sprint weight training units, 2 StairMasters, 3 Lifecycles, Cybex rower, treadmill, dumbbells (to 40 lb). **Services:** Swedish massage, shiatsu, reflexology, acupressure, facial; beauty salon. **Swimming Facilities:** 5 outdoor pools, ocean beach. **Recreation Facilities:** 11 tennis courts (6 lighted), 218-hole golf courses, water sports. **Evening Programs:** Resort entertainment, Hawaiiana demonstrations.

In the Area Guided tours of the resort, includes art collection and gardens. Lahaina (old whaling capital) shops, bars, restaurants; Mt. Haleakala; up-country ranches and rodeos; Sugar Cane Train Ride; winery tour; Maui Tropical Plantation (botanic gardens).

Getting Here *From Kapalua-West Airport.* By car, Hwy. 30 (Honoapiilani Hwy.) via Lahaina (10 min). Complimentary transfers at airport. Rental car, taxi, shuttle van available.

Special Notes 10 barrier-free rooms specially appointed for the disabled. Children can enjoy Hawaiian arts and crafts classes and seasonal day camp (Easter, summer, Thanksgiving, Christmas). No smoking in designated areas of the dining room and in health club; two nonsmoking floors in Ocean Tower. Spa hours: daily 7 AM–8 PM. $6 daily facility fee.

Canada

Scenic splendor is an essential part of the fitness vacation in many areas of Canada. Two resorts in Alberta are set in the mountains of Banff National Park. British Columbia has a ski/spa in Whistler, a dude ranch with weight loss programs, and a holistic health retreat is on an island in the Strait of Georgia. The Gaspe Peninsula of Quebec, facing the Atlantic Ocean, is dotted with thalassotherapy centers catering mainly to French-speaking guests.

Western Canada is endowed with a number of hot springs where outdoor activity is oriented toward tennis, hiking, skiing, and horseback riding. The Hills Health Ranch adds weight-loss options and vegetarian meals.

While none are large destination spas, Canadian resorts provide all the elements for healthy escapes. They range from luxurious at The Inn at Manitou in Ontario to the demanding yoga regimen at the Sivananda ashram near Montreal.

Rates in Canada will include a room tax as well as a GST (guest tax).

Banff Springs Hotel

Taking the waters

Alberta
Banff
Before the railroad and hotel builders arrived in 1885, the hot springs were sacred, shrouded in clouds of steam. Today the spring-fed pools are open again, rebuilt by Parks Canada for the public, and a high-tech health club, where you can get a shiatsu massage or dine on sushi, has been added to the venerable Banff Springs Hotel.

The turreted hotel—the largest in Canada west of Toronto—looks like a castle out of Camelot, and it is equally majestic inside. No four rooms are alike, and many are historically furnished. But instead of English lords and ladies, the baronial halls may be filled with Japanese tour groups.

The hotel has 15 restaurants, bars, and lounges, 50 specialty shops, and a 24-hour deli, and abundant recreational facilities including saunas and whirlpools to boot. Were it not for the magnificence of the park and the town itself, you might never feel the need to leave this city within a city.

Golf and skiing are the main attractions. The park is at its best in summer when it's open to cyclers and horseback riders, backpackers and river rafters. Banff is a place to savor the scenery while bathing in the healthful, sulfurous waters.

Banff Springs Hotel
Box 960, Banff, Alta. T0L 0C0
Tel. 403/762–2211 or 800/828–7447
Telex 038–21705

Administration General manager, Ted Kissane

Season Year-round

Canada

Alberta
Banff Springs Hotel, **7**
Slim Inn at Lake Louise Inn, **6**

British Columbia
Chateau Whistler Resort, **2**
Fairmont Hot Springs Resort, **5**
Harrison Hot Springs Hotel, **3**
The Hills Health Ranch, **4**
Hollyhock Farm, **1**

New Brunswick
Manan Island Spa, **19**
Mozart Chalet, **18**

Ontario
The Eleanor Fulcher Spa, **9**
The Inn at Manitou, **10**
Wheels Country Spa at Wheels Inn, **8**

Quebec
Aqua-Mer Center, **16**
Auberge du Parc Inn, **17**
Auberge Villa Bellevue, **11**
Eastman Health Center, **14**
Gray Rocks Inn, **12**
Sivananda Ashram, **13**
Spa Concept at Le Chateau Bromont, **15**

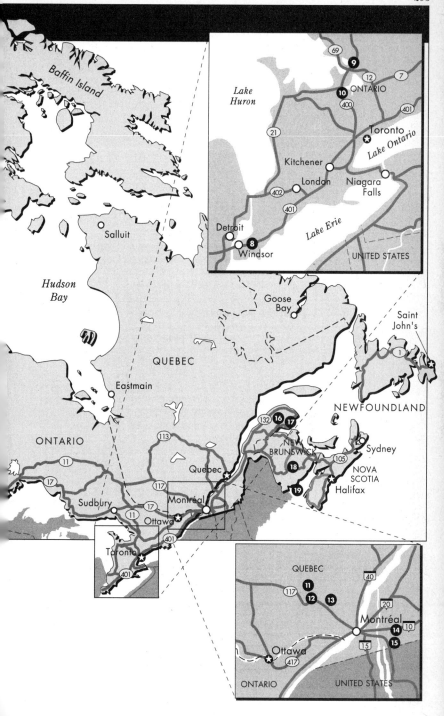

Baffin Island

Lake Huron

69
9
12
7
10
ONTARIO
400
401
21
Toronto
Lake Ontario

Kitchener
London
402
401
Niagara Falls

Detroit
8
Windsor
Lake Erie
UNITED STATES

Hudson Bay

Salluit

Goose Bay

Saint John's
1

QUEBEC

NEWFOUNDLAND

Eastmain

132
16
17
NEW BRUNSWICK
Sydney
105
18
NOVA SCOTIA
19
Halifax

ONTARIO

11
113
117
Québec
17
Montréal
11
Sudbury
17
Ottawa
401
Toronto
401

QUEBEC
40
117
11
12
13
20
Montréal
14
10
15
Ottawa
417
15
ONTARIO
UNITED STATES

Accommodations 867 rooms and suites in original hotel and annex, Banff Springs Manor. Suites in several sizes with nooks and antiques. 3-story VIP suite with private glass elevator, sauna, whirlpool, and lap pool.

Rates High season, mid-May–Sept., $155–$324 (Can.) daily single or double. Winter $100–$150, single or double. Suite with Jacuzzi (2–4 beds) $310–$860; VIP suite $1,500. Week-long ski packages from $302. Confirmation with credit card. Credit cards: AE, MC, V.

Meal Plans Traditional à la carte menu in main dining room. Japanese and Italian restaurants.

Services and **Exercise Equipment:** 10-station Universal gym weight training
Facilities circuit, 2 Lifecycles, 2 stationary bikes, rowing machine. **Swimming Facilities:** Large indoor and outdoor pools at Banff Springs Hotel. **Spa Facilities:** Large outdoor swimming pool fed by mineral hot springs at Cave and Basin Centennial Centre. Upper Hot Springs Pool on Sulphur Mountain. Both 1.5 mi from downtown Banff. **Recreation Facilities:** 3 ski areas: Mt. Norquay with 17 runs on 123 acres is closest and open till 9 PM Wed.–Sat. Sunshine Village has a 3,514-ft vertical drop and cross-country skiing on 20 mi of groomed trails. Bicycle rentals in Banff. Trail maps at the park information center. Horseback riding and guided treks arranged through outfitters.

In the Area Cave and Basin Centennial Centre with interpretive displays, self-guided boardwalk trails. Columbia Icefield tours (May–Sept., weather permitting); Banff Festival of the Arts at the Banff Centre and School of Fine Arts (May–Aug.); art of the Canadian Rockies at the Whyte Museum in Banff.

Getting Here By air, Calgary International Airport, about 80 mi east of Banff, serviced by Brewster Transportation and Tours and Pacific Western Transportation Ltd. By bus, Greyhound from Calgary and Vancouver. By train, VIA Rail transcontinental service from Vancouver and Calgary (tel. 204/949–1830). By car, Trans-Canada Hwy. to park entrances, where a 1-year vehicle pass must be purchased. Local taxi, limousine, airport shuttle bus available.

Special Notes No smoking in health club and Italian restaurant.

Slim Inn at Lake Louise Inn

Luxury pampering

Alberta Mountain hikes don't mean roughing it, nor do you have to give
Lake Louise up morning coffee to get fit at this alpine resort. In the spring and fall, the week-long Slim Inn program replaces the usual tourist routine at Lake Louise Inn. The daily mix of classes, walks, exercise, and sensible eating takes full advantage of the invigorating Rockies for inspiration and is designed to introduce you to the benefits of a healthy lifestyle.

From the sunrise eye-opener walk to an afternoon stretch-and-tone session, the emphasis is personal development. A team of instructors works with you in small, compatible groups. Activities are geared to the general energy of the group rather than to peak performance.

Breathtaking surrounding peaks come in view on walks around Lake Louise. Snow-covered Victoria Glacier is mirrored in the aqua-blue water. While one group does high-energy aerobics, another is in the pool for aquatic exercise. Two hour-long classes are scheduled each morning, and yoga is practiced before dinner. Massage and beauty services can be scheduled for an additional charge.

Slim Inn at Lake Louise Inn

Box 209, Lake Louise, Alta. T0L 1E0
Tel. 403/522–3791 (800/661–9237 in Western Canada)
Fax 403/522–2018

Administration Program director, Larry Hoskin; fitness director, Riki Jagar

Season 6-week sessions in both spring and fall.

Accommodations 91 motel-style rooms with double bed, private bath, and TV in a contemporary ski lodge hotel complex.

Rates $660 (Can.) single, $525 double per person. Add 5% provincial tax, 7% service charge, G.S.T. for Canadians. $100 check with reservation. Credit cards: AE, MC, V.

Meal Plans 3 daily meals prepared with Slim Inn recipes provided to guests on departure. Some vegetarian meals included in the 1,700-calorie diet (per day) plus between-meal refreshments. Nonalcoholic reception on Sun. evening.

Services and Facilities **Exercise Equipment:** Exercycles, Universal gym unit. **Services:** Massage (Swedish, sports), facial; beauty salon for hair, nail, and skin care. **Swimming Facilities:** Heated indoor pool. **Spa Facilities:** Whirlpool, sauna. **Recreation Facilities:** Bicycle rental, 3 outdoor tennis courts, nearby horseback riding, downhill and cross-country skiing. **Evening Programs:** Lifestyle lectures.

In the Area Trail hiking, gondola rides at ski area, 2½-mi trail to Lake Agnes teahouse.

Getting Here From Calgary by car, 110 mi on Trans-Canada Hwy. By bus, Greyhound and Brewster Transportation.

Special Notes Remember to bring hiking boots, warm clothing, gloves. Spa hours: daily 7 AM–10 PM.

Chateau Whistler Resort

Sports conditioning

British Columbia
Whistler/Blackcomb
Mountain

With year-round skiing on the greatest vertical rise in North America, alpine hiking in summer, horseback riding and water sports, the Whistler/Blackcomb vacation area continues to expand its fitness facilities. The baronial Chateau Whistler Resort, the largest hotel in Whistler Village, has a complete health club with a preski stretching program, tennis instruction, and licensed therapists for sports massage.

There are aerobics classes, a 30-foot indoor-outdoor pool, cardiovascular exercise equipment, coed sauna as well as separate sets of saunas and steam rooms for men and women.

Designed around a pedestrian plaza, Whistler Village has dozens of boutiques and restaurants within a short walk from the hotel. The 12-story Chateau was built on a grand scale in 1990.

The cathedral-ceilinged lobby offers unobstructed views of Blackcomb Mountain's famed slopes. The guest rooms feature folk art and carpets inspired by Mennonite hooked rugs. There are Quebec armoires, birdhouses, and baskets of apples. On an outdoor deck, a Jacuzzi beckons. A therapy center for treatment of sport-related problems with hydrotherapy, massage, and a flotation tank is in the village.

The facilities and mountain climate attract crowds from Vancouver and Seattle on weekends, but it's easy to get away from the throngs to the mountain meadows and hiking trails behind the golf course.

Chateau Whistler Resort

4599 Chateau Blvd., Box 100, Whistler, B.C. V0N 1B0
Tel. 604/938–8000 or 800/528–0444
Fax 604/938–2055

Administration General manager, David J. G. Roberts; health and tennis manager, Gary Winter

Season Year-round.

Accommodations 343-room high rise with standard rooms and deluxe suites, concierge club floor services. All with full bathroom and amenities, TV, telephone, radio, climate control.

Rates $140–$180 (Can.) daily in summer, single or double occupancy; winter rates $240–$275 daily, suites $350–$900. Add 7% GST, 10% tax. Deposit: one night's room and tax. Credit cards: AE, MC, V.

Meal Plans Innovative menu in the Wildflower Restaurant with natural, organic ingredients from the area; fresh seafood, wild boar, venison in season. There is also a tapas bar and a lounge for light meals.

Services and Facilities **Exercise Equipment:** 6-unit Keiser pneumatic weight training circuit, 3 ClimbMax stairclimbers, 2 Universal Aerobicycles, Universal treadmill, Concept II rowing ergometer, dumbbells. **Services:** Sports massage, one-on-one training, tennis lessons and camps. **Swimming Facilities:** Heated outdoor pool accessible from inside the health club. **Recreation Facilities:** Tennis courts and bike rental at the hotel; golf, canoeing, horseback riding nearby. 25 lifts and a gondola for downhill skiing; cross-country ski trails, glacier skiing (summer). Outdoor croquet court, fishing, paragliding school, ice skating. 2 18-hole golf courses. **Evening Programs:** sleigh rides.

In the Area Whistler Museum, ferry to Vancouver Island.

Getting Here *From Vancouver.* By car, Hwy. 99 past Horseshoe Bay, Squamish, and Howe Sound (70 mi; 90 min). By train, B.C. Rail daily at 7:30 AM (2½ hrs). By bus, Maverick Coach Lines from city terminal, Perimeter Airporter at 2 PM (tel. 604/261–2299). By air, B.C. Air or private plane to Pemberton Airport. Rental car, taxi, limousine available. Also Helijet service.

Special Notes Specially equipped guest rooms for the disabled. No smoking in therapy center and designated dining areas. 1 floor of nonsmoking rooms. Spa hours: daily 6 AM–11 PM.

Fairmont Hot Springs Resort

Taking the waters
Non-program resort facilities

British Columbia
Fairmont Hot
Springs

Canada's largest hot mineral pools are an attraction of this family-oriented vacation complex in the Rocky Mountains. There's golf, skiing, and a deluxe Sports Center where spa treatments and exercise equipment make it possible to assemble your own spa program. The privately owned Fairmont Hot Springs Resort has large swimming pools for day visitors who come for sports and relaxation. The beautifully landscaped grounds are surrounded by mountain forests.

The recently completed fitness facilities and a private pool are for guests in the lodge and villas. Two international racquetball courts, one squash court, coed saunas and whirlpools, and hydra-fitness exercise equipment are available. An optional spa-cuisine menu has been introduced to accompany fitness programs.

Fairmont Hot Springs Resort
Box 10, Fairmont Hot Springs, B.C. V0B 1L0
Tel. 604/345-6311 or 800/663-4979
Telex 041-45108; Fax 604/345-6616

Administration General manager, Gerard Gordon; therapist, Gordon Fraser

Season Year-round.

Accommodations 139 rooms with private baths in the main lodge. 75 deluxe villas, 5 cottages and 48 suites with cooking facilities. All with air-conditioning, TV, telephone, bath.

Rates $60–$105 (Can.) daily. 2-night/2-day spa package $139 (CAN) per person, double occupancy. Add 7% GST, 6% tax. Deposit: 1 night. Credit cards: AE, MC, V.

Meal Plans Health breakfast daily included in package. Breakfast buffet has fresh juices, bran muffins, yogurt, cottage cheese. Lunch menu is cold cucumber soup, salad of red cabbage and apple, pasta, curried chicken with yogurt dressing, fillet of sole with braised leeks. Dinner entrees include veal cutlet with wild mushrooms, breast of chicken stuffed with lobster, fillet of red snapper with curry sauce.

Services and Facilities **Exercise Equipment:** 9 Hydra-weight training units, stationary bike. **Services:** Swedish massage, fango, herbal wrap, loofah body scrub, salt-glow scrub; guided hikes, yoga, aerobics, aquacise classes. **Swimming Facilities:** Indoor and outdoor pools open year-round. **Spa Facilities:** Odorless mineral water for hot soaks and swimming pools, outdoor and indoor whirlpools. **Recreation Facilities:** 4 tennis courts, 2 racquetball courts, 1 squash court, 2 18-hole golf courses, water skiing, sailing, fishing, rafting; horseback riding; downhill and cross-country skiing; hiking.

Getting Here Located on BC Hwy. 93, north of Cranbrook (64 mi) and south of Banff (100 mi). By air, private airstrip (1.5 mi). By car, west of Calgary (190 mi), north of Spokane, WA (260 mi). By bus, service from Calgary on Greyhound. Spa hours: daily 8 AM–10 PM.

Harrison Hot Springs Hotel

Life enhancement
Taking the waters

British Columbia
Harrison Hot Springs

New fitness programs and refurbished guest rooms at the Harrison Hot Springs Hotel complement a large, modern hydrotherapy pavilion. A hot pool and a swimming pool are the main attractions. The pavilion is constructed of wood and brick and decorated with native carvings; it looks onto the garden where an Olympic-size swimming pool is filled with warm spring water year-round. The sulfurous, 140-degree spring water provides effective if temporary relief for aching muscles. The new owners, Itoman Canada, Inc., intend to introduce mud baths, Jacuzzis, herbal wraps, and oriental massage.

The pavilion has separate facilities for men and women, including private Roman baths with sunken seating. An exercise room and indoor tennis court are available. Aerobics classes are scheduled, and aquatic workouts are offered in the thermal pool. Joggers have the choice of running along the lake or on a Dynatrak paved circuit.

Lake Harrison looks scruffy when you arrive from the main road. The strip of rocky, gray beach is lined with parked cars and RVs, but beyond the tourist bars and souvenir stands are wilderness tracks for hiking and quiet country roads. The hotel, long popular with honeymooners and conventioneers, is being upgraded and refurbished, but afternoon tea is still served in front of the lobby fireplace.

Harrison Hot Springs Hotel
Harrison Hot Springs, B.C. V0M 1K0
Tel. 604/796–2244 (800/663–2266 in the western US and Canada)
Telex 04–361551, Fax 604/796–9374

Administration General manager, Gerald Hadway; fitness coordinator, Beverly Stoughton

Season Year-round.

Accommodations 300 motel-style rooms in main building, cottages in private garden area. Deluxe rooms in the new tower, some with lake view.

Rates $76–$160 (Can.) daily, double or single occupancy; 4 day/3 night package $318–$518 per person, double occupancy. Add 7% GST, 8% tax. Credit cards: AE, D, MC, V.

Services and Facilities **Exercise Equipment:** 5 Hydra-resistance units, Universal 15-station gym, 2 Lifecycles, 2 StairMasters. **Services:** Massage, one-on-one training. **Swimming Facilities:** Indoor pavilion and outdoor pool open 24 hours, 104 degrees for soaking, 94 degrees for swimming; lake. **Recreation Facilities:** Indoor and outdoor tennis courts, horseback riding, golf nearby; cross-country skiing. Bicycle rental. **Evening Programs:** Dinner dancing in the Copper Room.

In the Area Boat trips and fishing on the lake in summer. Minter Gardens showpieces in bloom Mar.–Oct.

Getting Here *From Vancouver.* By car, Trans-Canada Hwy. (Rte. 1) east to exit for Rte. 9 at Minter Gardens; continue to Lake Harrison (2 hrs). By bus, Cascade Lines (3 hrs).

Special Notes Some specially equipped rooms for the disabled.

The Hills Health Ranch

Luxury pampering
Weight management
Nutrition and diet

British Columbia
100 Mile House

Saddle up for a Western-style workout at The Hills Health Ranch in caribou country, in the heart of British Columbia. Facials and skin treatments mix with hayrides and massage, and options include summer trail rides or winter cross-country skiing.

Woodsy A-frame chalets fan out from the main lodge where the spa is located. Busy with skiiers in winter (several teams train here), the ranch is an all-season resort that offers special packages for weight management, beauty treatments, and an "Executive Renewal Week." Weekends and 11-day programs are available year-round; alternatively, you can schedule treatments and classes à la carte.

Trainers and beauticians cater to guests booked for the programs. After an initial fitness evaluation, you're scheduled for 3½ hours of guided brisk walks, classes (aerobics, aquacise, and stretch-and-flex), and training with weights each day. There's also yoga stretch, Jazzercise, and two-hour hikes.

Hearty fare is served in the dining room, but you can opt for low-cal meals that feature produce from local farms.

The Hills Health Ranch
C-26, 108 Ranch, 100 Mile House, B.C. V0K 2E0
Tel. 604/791–5225
Fax 604/791–6384

Administration President, Patrick Corbett; program director, Juanita Corbett; fitness director, Tim Cooper

Season Year-round.

Accommodations Private chalets with up to 3 bedrooms, kitchen, bath, TV, and balcony; alpine cottages for couples and singles. 10 deluxe rooms in the Ranch House have private bathroom, air conditioning, telephone.

Rates Weekend $236 (CAN) per person double occupancy, $328 single; 7-day package $892 double, $1,169 single; 2-night Spoiler package $276 per person double, $453 single. Deposit of $50 or 25% of total cost 2 weeks prior to arrival. Cancellations within 2 weeks of reservation not refundable. Add 10% service charge, 7% G.S. tax. Credit cards: MC, V.

Meal Plans 3 calorie-counted meals a day with health packages. 1,000–1,200 calories a day diet recommended for weight loss.

Services and Facilities **Exercise Equipment:** 2 Dynavit and 2 Monark bikes; 5-station Hydra-pressure gym; Quinton running machine; rowing ergometer; free weights. **Services:** Massage, facial, herbal wrap, loofah scrub, full-body mud pack, manicure, pedicure. **Swimming Facilities:** Indoor swimming pool. **Spa Facilities:** 2 whirlpools, 2 saunas. **Recreation Facilities:** Equestrian center; broomball, ice skating, tobogganing, 5 outdoor tennis courts with plexi-pave surface, lighted, golf, and lake fishing nearby.

Evening Programs: Western dancing with live local music; workshops on nutrition and wellness.

In the Area Cowboy-led full- or half-day rides.

Getting Here By air, Canadian Airlines International and Air Canada have daily flights to Williams Lake Airport. Complimentary transfers on arrival/departure. *From Vancouver.* By car, use main routes through the Rockies to the village of 100 Mile House. By train, BC Rail's Caribou Dayliner operates 3 times weekly on scenic route to 100 Mile House. Complimentary transfers on arrival/departure.

Special Notes Riding and skiing instruction and tepee parties for children. No smoking in designated areas of dining room and spa. Remember to bring warm clothing and 2 pairs of running shoes. Spa hours: daily 8 AM–10 PM.

Hollyhock Farm

Life enhancement

British Columbia
Cortes Island This secluded holistic community on an island in the Strait of Georgia, 100 miles north of Vancouver, welcomes summer visitors for weekend and five-day workshops in health and healing. Hollyhock Farm's wooden dormitories form an informal campus, surrounded by forest and beach, where discussion groups meet outdoors. You can jog, swim, or find the solitude to meditate.

Since 1982, faculty members from the Victoria Centre for Complementary Medicine and specialists in alternative therapies and spiritual health have drawn inspiration from each other in the island setting. Andrew Weill, from Arizona's Canyon Ranch, leads a workshop in total wellness that discusses vegetarian diets and nutrition and practices massage, chanting, and visualization. Another week is devoted to practicing tai chi chuan movements for longevity and peace of mind.

Many summer courses focus on spiritual health. Several sessions are devoted to the healing philosophies of Buddhism, others are for chanting or bodywork. An herbology workshop uses the garden where vegetables and herbs are grown for communal meals. Also scheduled are natural-history tours, bird walks, star talks, and ocean rowboating.

Mornings begin with yoga and meditation. Arrangements can be made for bodywork—Swedish massage or oriental techniques like shiatsu and Reiki. Mostly, you are free to take advantage of the forest trails and beaches, the water, and the hot tub.

Hollyhock Farm
Box 127, Manson's Landing, Cortes Island,
B.C. V0P 1K0
Tel. 604/935-6465

Administration Manager, Rex Weyler

Season Apr.–Oct.

Accommodations Semiprivate or dormitory rooms, a few private double rooms. Heated buildings with communal showers and toilets.

Rates 5-day programs $275–$645 (Can.). Children's programs, $28 a day. $100 check must accompany application. $25 cancellation charge up to 2 weeks before reservation, full fee after that. Add 7% GST. Credit cards: MC, V.

Meal Plans Buffet-style meals served 3 times a day. Organically grown vegetables, some seafood.

Services and Facilities **Exercise Equipment:** Outdoor bicycles, canoes on lake. **Services:** Massage, reflexology, acupressure; private counseling. **Swimming Facilities:** Private lake, ocean beaches.

Getting Here *From Seattle and Vancouver.* By car and ferries, via Vancouver Island. By air, Air BC has flights from Seattle and Vancouver to Campbell River for nearest ferry connection. Direct flights to Cortes Island from Seattle by float plane: book with Lake Union Air or Kenmore Air. Complimentary transfers on arrival/departure at Manson's Landing for 11-mi trip to Farm.

Special Notes No smoking indoors. Remember to bring warm clothes, flashlight, rainwear, sturdy walking shoes, and footwear that slips on and off easily. Children's program, $28 daily.

Manan Island Spa

Luxury pampering

New Brunswick
Grand Manan
New Brunswick is a corner of Canada's Atlantic provinces that combines the accents of New England, Scotland, and France. Day hikes abound in 76 provincial parks; La Manche has trails past working beaver dams and down to the sea, while a hike through Fundy National Park traverses steep wooded hills below which the world's highest tides surge upon cliffs and beaches. This island retreat takes advantage of sea air, seafood, and solitude. You bathe in dulse, an edible seaweed harvested on the island's shores, and stay in an elegantly refurbished 1840s house. There's a body wrap and dulse scrub, even a taste of dulse in your salad or soup at lunch.

Dulse is a Grand Manan Island export, sought by connoisseurs in Japan and America for its salty, iodine flavor and nutrients. Only here and at the Aurora House Spa in Ohio is it used in the treatments developed by an island native, Joanne Liuzzo, Aurora's director.

The eight-bedroom inn looks like a New England summer cottage. Antiques in the parlor and bedrooms belie the sophisticated hydrotherapy equipment for facials and the steam baths in the treatment rooms.

Staffed by aestheticians and a chef from the Aurora House, the program here is tailored to the guests' wishes. Walks or jogs along the beach and the wooded cliffs can be made with or without an escort. Group exercise or yoga is organized on request.

Naturalists have come here ever since James Audubon visited in 1832 and recorded over 250 different species of birds, including the bald eagle, which still nests here. Whale watching, photography, painting, and rock collecting are popular pastimes. Willa Cather, a frequent visitor during the 1930s, wrote that the island was "tranquilizing to the spirit and seemed to open up great space for it to roam in."

Manan Island Spa
North Head, Grand Manan, N.B. E0G 2M0
Tel. 506/662-8624 or 216/562-9171

Administration	Director, Joanne Liuzzo
Season	July–Aug.; May, June, Sept. by request (groups only).
Accommodations	8 bedrooms with private baths. Some king-size brass beds, upstairs views.
Rates	Daily B&B $59 (Can.), single, $69 for 2 double. Weekend retreat $225 single, $360 double. One-third advance payment. Cancellation charge for notification less than 48 hours in advance of arrival date. Credit cards: AE, MC, V.
Meal Plans	Breakfast cooked to order: Entree choice at lunch and dinner. Fresh seafood, local salmon, and boiled lobster specialties.
Services and Facilities	**Swimming Facilities:** Nearby ocean beaches and lakes. (Water tends to be cool.) **Recreation Facilities:** Bikes available to guests at the inn; canoeing by arrangement. 17 nature trails along the shore to landmarks such as Hole-in-the-Wall cave at Whale Cove, where dulse is harvested.
In the Area	Whale-watching expeditions; museum of over 300 island birds, local geological exhibits at Grand Harbour.
Getting Here	*From mainland.* By ferry, daily (2 hr). Reserve space in advance. Ferry lands at Blacks Harbour on the coastal road (Rte. 1) from St. John and the airport. Short walk from ferry dock to inn. *From Maine.* By car, border crossing at Calais/St. Stephen to Rte. 1. Free parking at both terminals.
Special Notes	No smoking in the spa or dining room.

Mozart Chalet

Nutrition and diet

New Brunswick *Cambridge*	The lakeshore wilderness and the European-style natural cooking are the specialties here. The owners, Rosel and Hans Neumann, emphasize healthy eating and living. No treatments are offered, but the beauty of New Brunswick's heartland can be explored on nature trails. There's a Finnish sauna and whirlpool.

The home cooking at the Swiss chalet is a treat. The Continental menu is prepared with reduced salt and sugar, and without chemicals or preservatives. Dinner with a view of the lake is served by candlelight with classical music.

The Neumanns share their enthusiasm for the outdoors with guests, who come for winter sports, and with summer and weekend vacationers. Maps, literature, equipment, and advice on how to enjoy yourself are available on request.

Mozart Chalet
Lakeview Rd., Cambridge, N.B. E0E 1B0
Tel. 506/488-3071

Administration	Manager, Hans Neumann
Season	Year-round; best times are June–Oct., Jan.–Mar.

Accommodations Lakeview rooms in European-style chalet, various sleeping and living quarters, private baths. Additional beds available for families.

Rates $59–$69 (Can.) daily per person double occupancy includes 2 sessions in the bathhouse. Midweek and weekend packages available. $100 deposit required. Add 7% GST. Credit cards: MC, V.

Meal Plans Breakfast and dinner served daily. Dinner menu features European specialties à la carte.

Services and Facilities **Exercise Equipment:** Bike and ski rentals. **Swimming Facilities:** Private beach on lake. **Recreation Facilities:** Hiking, boating, fishing, windsurfing, waterskiing, bicycle tours, deer- and bird-watching; cross-country skiing, snowshoeing, ice fishing, ice skating.

In the Area Car trips to the provincial capital, Fredericton; Beaverbrook Gallery's collection of Canadian art; Kings Landing historical village; the reversing falls, a tidal phenomenon at St. John seaport; restored Victorian landmarks; Gagetown riverside crafts community.

Getting Here By car, Trans-Canada Hwy. along the St. John River to Jemseg; Rte. 695 to Cambridge-Narrows. By air or train, to St. John and Fredericton. Car rentals available at both towns.

Special Notes No smoking in designated dining areas. Remember to bring bathrobe, hiking boots, and warm clothing.

The Eleanor Fulcher Spa

Holistic health *Women only*

Ontario
Gravenhurst Developing a new sense of awareness about your mind and spirit as well as your body is the goal of a week-long program for women only at Eleanor Fulcher's Spa. Strong on group dynamics, it includes plenty of personal pampering.

The program has the feel of a summer camp. Everyone is expected to join in aerobics, stretching, yoga, and hiking for 4½ hours every day. An indoor swimming pool is also used for exercise classes.

Eleanor Fulcher personalizes the program to suit her guests. Beauty treatments available include aromatherapy massage as well as facials, manicures, and pedicures. The exercise, diet, and stress-free environment are designed to help guests lose an average of five pounds each.

The Eleanor Fulcher Spa
*Gravenhurst, Ont., c/o Eleanor Fulcher, Ltd.,
Eaton Centre, 220 Yonge St., Box 606, Toronto M5B 2H1
Tel. 416/922–1945*

Administration Manager, Eleanor Fulcher

Season June–Sept.

Accommodations Country casual, with 7 bedrooms. 4 beds in each room.

Rates 1 week $995 (Can.) per person, sharing room, all-inclusive. Confirmation by credit card. Credit cards: AE, MC, V.

Meal Plans	3 meals a day, total of 800–1,500 calories. Emphasis on vegetables and fish, some meat.
Services and Facilities	**Swimming Facilities:** Indoor pool, private beach on lake. **Recreation Facilities:** Boating, nearby tennis and golf. **Evening Programs:** Health lectures.
Getting Here	*From Toronto.* By car, Hwy. 400 north (1½ hr). Rental car, limousine available.
Special Notes	No smoking indoors.

The Inn at Manitou

Luxury pampering
Life enhancement
Sports conditioning

Ontario
Lake
Manitouwubing

Tennis clinics have been a staple here since the early 1960s, but in the spring of 1990 The Inn at Manitou opened a full-service spa that provides cross-training as well as luxury pampering. Spa program guests may combine packages for three to seven days with the regular morning or afternoon tennis clinics, and choose from classic French cuisine or gourmet spa dining.

Having assembled a staff that includes aestheticians from Romania and Montreal, a Finnish masseuse, and the former director of a fitness club in Cannes, the founders/owners Sheila and Ben Wise opted for personal service in a luxurious setting rather than a large-scale spa. Only six persons per hour can be accommodated in the new building, which contains an indoor tennis court as well as an exercise room with a maple hardwood "Everflex" floating floor. Among the six private treatment rooms are two designed for wet therapies (mud masks, body wraps, and loofah scrubs) and furnished with a hydrotherapy tub boasting 47 underwater jets and a hand-operated hose.

In terms of massage and mud treatments, The Inn has an extensive menu. Shiatsu, aromatherapy, and Trager are a few of the specialties offered. Premassage facials involve cleansing the skin with a particular type of mud from the Rhine River. Mud, in fact, is used in several treatments: for body wraps, enabling the minerals and other active ingredients to be absorbed by the body, or for mud baths in the hydrotherapy tub. Known as Moor mud, it was used by monks during the 14th and 15th centuries to cure everything from rheumatism to asthma and depression. Rediscovered, the imported mud is said to contain 3,000 organic ingredients.

Natural therapies from leading European spas feature the French line of marine ingredients, Phytomer. A saltwater concentrate used in baths is said to aid slimming and eliminate water retained in tissues. Facials with molecular extracts from amniotic fluid are likewise said to enhance the structure of the skin, while collagen, elastogen, magnesium, and iodine produce similarly beneficial results.

Along with the rejuvenation process, the spa offers a daily menu that totals fewer than 1,600 calories. Breakfast and lunch are cooked to order; dinner, served in a formal dining room at The Inn, is a six-course affair—light yet elegantly French-inspired.

Fitness classes as well as a personal screening and consultation come with all spa packages. The daily schedule includes aerobics, stretching, body sculpting, aquaerobics, and dancercise classes. All guests are invited to join staff-led morning walks and nature hikes.

With a maximum capacity of 64 guests, the resort's sports services encourage private instruction. Horseback riding, kayaking, canoeing, windsurfing, and swimming instruction are offered in addition to private tennis and fitness sessions. Use of tennis courts, mountain bikes, and water-sports equipment is complimentary to all guests. Spa participants are provided with T-shirts, robes, and slippers.

Nestled on the shores of Lake Manitouwabing near Parry Sound, The Inn is a popular retreat for guests seeking peace and seclusion. About half the guests are Canadians who enroll as couples. A member of the prestigious Relais and Chateaux association, the northern Ontario resort was honored in 1990 with the group's Gold Prize for the best property outside France.

The Inn at Manitou
McKellar, Ontario P0G 1C0
Winter: 251 Davenport Rd., Toronto, Ontario M5R 1J9
Tel. 705/389-2171 (winter, 416/967-3466)
Fax 705/389-3818 (winter 416/967-6434)

Administration Owners/managers, Sheila and Ben Wise; spa director, Suzanne Letourneau

Season May–Oct.

Accommodations 32 chalet-style rooms, most lakefront, each with log-burning fireplace, modern bathroom; 11 suites with sunken living room, antique marble fireplace, dressing room, bathroom with whirlpool tub, private sauna, sun deck.

Rates $139–$289 (Canadian) per person daily, full American plan, double occupancy. Single supplement $35–$95 per day. 1-day spa sampler $160, 3-day package $180–$240 plus accommodations, 7-day package $350–$490 plus accommodations. Add 7% GST, 16% service charge. Deposit: $300 per person. Credit cards: DC, MC, V.

Meal Plans Choice of regular menu or spa cuisine. 3 meals daily, plus mid-morning and afternoon juice and fruit breaks. Spa menu is low in sodium, fat, and cholesterol. Breakfast can be a cold buffet of fresh fruit and juices, cereal, Muesli, granola, yogurt, muffins, brioche, croissants, plus individually cooked hot items. Lunch buffet specialties change daily, i.e., Oriental, Mediterranean. Dinner entrees include grilled breast of guinea hen with sesame seeds, Georgian Bay trout paper-baked with peaches, Provini veal chop; desserts are poached pears in Beaujolais with vanilla sauce, cream caramel flavored with Grand Marnier, or floating island perfumed with vervan.

Services and Facilities **Exercise Equipment:** 2 Trotter 575 treadmills, 2 Lifecycles, 2 Monark bikes, StairMaster, Legflex, free weights. **Services:** Massage (Swedish, Trager, shiatsu), reflexology, aromatherapy, herbal wraps, mud wraps, Moor therapy (scalp massage, body polish, body mask), facial, seaweed or mineral bath, hand or foot paraffin treatment, waxing, manicure, pedicure; nutrition and fitness consultation. **Swimming Facilities:** Outdoor heated pool 20 × 40 feet. **Recreation Facilities:** 12 outdoor tennis courts, 1 indoor court, horseback riding English style, mountain hiking, water sports, fishing, billiards, mountain bikes, lake cruises.

Getting Here *From Toronto.* By car, Hwy. 400 north to Parry Sound, right on Hwy. 124 to McKellar, right on McKellar Center Rd. for 5 miles (2½ hr). By plane, float-plane charter service; private planes land at Parry Sound District Airport. By limousine from Pearson International Airport ($250 each way). Taxi, rental car available. Shuttle bus $45 (min. 4 persons).

Special Notes Smoking permitted. Men requested to wear jacket at dinner. Tennis camp for teenagers (July-Aug.).

Wheels Country Spa at Wheels Inn

Luxury pampering

Ontario
Chatham
Total fun and fitness is the concept for Wheels Inn, a motel that grew into an indoor resort with seven acres of sports and spa facilities under one roof. Cavort with the kids in the outdoor-indoor swimming pool and water slide or choose from 42 revitalizing services in the European-style Wheels Country Spa.

Taking a serious approach to shape-ups, staff members have credentials for cardiovascular and muscular testing. They do basic body measurements, a wellness profile, and one-on-one training in a well-equipped fitness center.

Runners and joggers can set courses leading past the town's Victorian mansions and modern marina. There are 15 routes mapped out, ranging from 1.8 to 13.5 miles, and an indoor track where 22 laps equal one mile.

The variety of revitalizing body and skin treatments offered here, for men and women, is unique for Canada. Services are priced on an à la carte basis or on half-day or full-day packages. In this oasis of quiet luxury, stress melts away in the hands of certified masseurs and masseuses. There is also a fully equipped beauty salon. You can schedule a session of reflexology work on nerve centers or be cocooned in a fragrant herbal wrap. Therapeutic Swedish massage and invigorating body scrubs with a loofah sponge working sea salts and avocado oil into your skin are part of package offerings. There is a three-day deluxe spa program and a five-day "Super Tone-Up."

Aerobic exercise groups are scheduled according to your fitness level, from beginner to high-impact classes for the super-advanced, and run throughout the day, from 9 AM to 7 PM. A large number of club members from the community take advantage of the facilities and programs, so you'll never be at a loss for company, and the cushioned studio floor is easy on the feet.

All activities are coed, and you can join a group doing "aquabics" in the fitness pool, or the "renaissance" program for those with arthritis and circulatory problems. Then relax in the whirlpool and steam baths.

All this seems far removed from the family-oriented activity that fills the hotel atrium and dining room. Lunch is specially prepared and served in the privacy of the spa lounge for guests who want to avoid temptation. A supervised day-care center on the premises watches the children while parents are working out.

Wheels Country Spa at Wheels Inn
Best Western Wheels Inn
Box 637, Chatham, Ont. N7M 5K8
Tel. 519/351–1100, 436–5500 (spa); 800/265–5265 (in Canada); 800/265–5257 (in US)
Telex 64–7110

Administration Manager, Steven Bradley; spa director, Jeanette Tielemans

Season Year-round.

Accommodations Spa program limited to 30 participants. The inn has 354 rooms, standard motel amenities, and "club class" rooms.

Rates 3-day package $593 (Can.) per person double occupancy, $700 single. Program includes daily massage, herbal wrap, exercise periods, 3 spa meals, other services. 1-day Pamper Yourself package $150. Add 7% GST; deposit $100. Refundable upon 5-day notice. Rooms-only reservations through Best Western. Credit cards: AE, MC, V.

Meal Plans 3 meals total 1,000 calories per day for spa program participants. Low in salt and fat; choices include meat, fish, salads.

Services and Facilities **Exercise Equipment:** 10 Nautilus weight training units, 2 Windracer bikes, 2 StairMasters, Universal gym, 6 Schwinn Air-Dyne bikes, 3 Concept II rowers, free weights (5–200 lbs.), leg-lift benches. **Services:** Swedish massage, facial, loofah body scrub, herbal wrap, reflexology, relaxation body treatment; beauty salon for hair, nail, and skin care. **Swimming Facilities:** 4-lane lap pool in the Fitness and Racquet Club; Olympic-size pool with indoor and outdoor sections in the atrium. **Spa Facilities:** Saunas, whirlpools. **Recreation Facilities:** Indoor courts: 6 tennis, 9 racquetball, 4 squash; maps of area running and jogging trails; sailing and fishing; bowling alley.

In the Area Walks through Colasanti's Greenhouses, acres of tropical plants; wine tastings in nearby Blenheim at the Charral Winery. The Guy Lombardo Museum in his hometown, London; Uncle Tom's Cabin, home of Rev. Josiah Henson in Dresden, used on the Underground Railroad.

Getting Here *From border crossing at Detroit/Windsor.* By car, Hwy. 401 to Exit 81 North, then turn right and left at traffic lights (1 hr). *From London and Toronto.* By car, Hwy. 401. By train, VIA Rail serves Chatham from Toronto with 4 trains daily (5 on Thurs.). By air, Windsor/London airport, 1 hr from inn. Local taxi and bus available.

Special Notes Children's programs include day-care center and Kent Kiddie Kollege, with daily activity and special summer outings for children 6–12. No smoking in designated areas. Spa Hours: Mon.–Thurs. 9 AM–9, Fri 9 AM–7 PM, Sat. 9–5, Sun. 9–1.

Aqua-Mer Center

Taking the waters

Quebec The complete marine cure at this seaside auberge takes advan-
Carleton tage of natural elements—seawater, algae, mud—and a mild Atlantic climate charged with iodine and negative ions. A com-

bination of European and American therapies revitalizes your body while you relax and enjoy the Gaspé food and scenery at Aqua-Mer Center.

The sequence of treatments prescribed for you after consultation with the professional staff involves bathing and exercising in the indoor swimming pool filled with comfortably heated seawater. There are no cold plunges into the ocean, but brisk walks along the beach and a massage under alternating showers of warm and cold water are encouraged. To stimulate blood circulation and lymph drainage you will be massaged in underwater-jet baths; this will enhance the effect of algae added to seawater that has been heated to a high temperature. Follow this with a toning shower that focuses high-powered jets on every muscle in your body for invigorating results.

The Marine Cure Center interconnects with a residential building that has the ambience of New England beach cottages. Facilities and equipment, while small-scale, are similar to European thalassotherapy centers. Guests and staff are mainly French-speaking.

Aqua-Mer Center
868 Boulevard Perron, Carleton, Que. G0C 1J0
(Winter Office) 7541 rue St. Hubert, Montreal, Que. H2R 2N7
Tel. 418/364–7055 (514/273–3300 in winter)

Administration	Director, Yoland Dubois
Season	May 15–Nov. 1.
Accommodations	27 rooms in 3-story auberge and adjoining building. Program participants also stay in nearby hotels and guest houses. Day visitors accommodated on a space-available basis.
Rates	6-day/7-night marine cure single occupancy $1,045–$1,145 (Can.), double occupancy, $1,195–$1,350 (single). Includes meals and thalassotherapy treatments. 5-day package without room $550. Add 7% GST; gratuities extra. 25% deposit; balance on arrival. Refunds with notification 30 days prior to reserved dates. Credit cards: MC, V.
Meal Plans	3 meals a day in health cafe at the Marine Cure Center. Approximately 1,000 calories a day, including fish, chicken, fresh seasonal vegetables. Similar light cuisine at local inns.
Services and Facilities	**Exercise Equipment:** Balneotherapy tubs, aerobics studio, mountain bikes. **Swimming Facilities:** Indoor pool. **Recreation Facilities:** Nearby golf, tennis, sailing.
Getting Here	Transfers on arrival/departure Sun. at Charlo airport and Carleton train station.
Special Notes	Remember to bring bathing cap, slippers, 2 swim suits, beach towel, workout clothing, walking shoes.

Auberge du Parc Inn

Luxury pampering

Quebec
Paspebiac

Settle in for a relaxing week of seawater soaks and gourmet meals. This quiet retreat on the Baie des Chaleurs has a touch of Brittany and a style of its own.

Thalassotherapy is the main attraction. You are treated with mud, algae, and mineral-rich water pumped directly from the bay. Massage is part of the daily routine for guests on the one-week package.

Group activity is kept to a minimum. There are stretch-and-tone sessions, and in warm weather groups exercise in the outdoor swimming pool. But a large part of your day is occupied by treatments, a passive program that most of the men and women who come here regularly seem to prefer.

Small and self-contained, the 30-room inn books no more than 40 guests a week for treatments. French is spoken most of the time, though staff members are bilingual. Having some awareness of local customs helps, but with a sense of humor any problem can be solved.

After a walk in the countryside, appetite sharpened by the salty air, the low-calorie meals are a pleasant alternative to typical French-Canadian cooking.

Auberge du Parc Inn
C.P. 40, Paspebiac, Que. G0C 2K0
Tel. 418/752–3355 (800/463–0890 in Quebec)

Administration	Manager, Madame Le Marquand
Season	Year-round.
Accommodations	30 modern bedrooms with private bath in a country manor house.
Rates	7-day package $1,105–$1,245 (Can.) per person double occupancy; $1,225–$1,385 single. 10% advance payment on booking. Add 7% GST, and gratuities. Credit cards: MC, V.
Meal Plans	3 meals a day included in package. Seafood and fresh produce of local farms featured.
Services and Facilities	**Swimming Facilities:** Year-round heated outdoor pool; nearby beaches. **Recreation Facilities:** Hiking; golf, tennis, cross-country skiing nearby.
Getting Here	*From Quebec City.* Located on the main approach to the Gaspé Peninsula. By car, Hwy. 20 to Rivière-du-Loup, then Hwy. 132 east via Mt. Jolie through Matapedia (5 hr).
Special Notes	No smoking in spa.

Auberge Villa Bellevue

Non-program resort facilities

Quebec
Mont Tremblant

Located on a natural lake close to the provincial park, the Auberge Villa Bellevue recently added an indoor swimming pool, excrcise room, and sauna for year-round use by guests at no extra charge. Aerobics classes and water polo are scheduled daily. In addition, guests are teamed for volleyball and hockey. The Auberge, situated in one of Eastern Canada's most popular vacation playgrounds, is maintained and lived in by the owners and has the pleasant feeling of a country inn.

Open 8 AM–10 PM daily, the spa includes a coed whirlpool and a steam bath.

Auberge Villa Bellevue
Chemin Principal, Mont Tremblant, Que. J0T 2H0
Tel. 819/425-2734 or 800/567-6763

Administration	Owner/director, Serge DuBois; spa director, Sylvain Des-coteaux
Season	Year-round.
Accommodations	90 bedrooms including 14 deluxe rooms added in 1988.
Rates	1-week packages $418–$638 (Can.) per person double occupancy. Add 11.28% GST and local tax, plus gratuities. Credit cards: AE, DC, MC, V.
Meal Plans	Breakfast and dinner daily included in the weekly package. Health salad bar in the dining room; special diets accommodated with advance request.
Services and Facilities	**Exercise Equipment:** Circuit training Solaris units, StairMaster, 2 stationary bikes, free weights. **Services:** Swedish massage. **Swimming Facilities:** Private beach on Lake Ouimet; heated indoor lap pool at the fitness center. **Recreation Facilities:** Windsurfing and sailing on the lake, bicycles for country rambles. Ski instruction.
In the Area	Mont Tremblant Provincial Park, about 15 mi from the villa, with full range of winter and summer activities. Shopping and antiques hunting in St. Jovite.
Getting Here	*From Montreal and Quebec.* By bus, Voyageur lines from Montreal and Quebec City. By car, from Montreal airports and train station, about 1 hr drive on Route 117. Rental cars available at airport.
Special Notes	No smoking in designated areas.

Centre de Sante d'Eastman / Eastman Health Center

Life enhancement

Quebec *Eastman*	Occupying a farm nestled in the rolling countryside of the Eastern Townships, about an hour's drive southeast of Montreal, the Centre de Sante d'Eastman is a low-key retreat for body and mind. The setting may look bucolic, but the facilities are unquestionably up-to-date. Hydrotherapy is the specialty here, from algae body wraps to thalasso tub.

Seven buildings house up to 35 guests and the spa facilities. A barn is home to the kitchen and dining areas, and the stone farmhouse, complete with flared roof and jutting dormer windows, is the locale for the hospitality lounge. Exercise is optional, and not strenuous. Three guided walks are held daily, and yoga and tai chi chuan sessions are scheduled. A series of treatments designed to rid the skin of impurities is also available. The spa package includes a daily massage, three meals, and a snack.

Centre de Sante d'Eastman
895 Chemin des Diligences, Eastman, Que. J0E 1P0
Tel. 514/297-3009 or 800/665-5272 (Canada only)

Administration	Director/owner, Josena Dubuc; spa director, Jocelyne Veillette

Season Year-round.

Accommodations 20 rooms in main house and cottages, all with private bath. No TV, telephone. Comfortably furnished country rooms, some a short walk from spa and dining.

Rates $75–$250 (Can) daily per person, double occupancy, plus 7% GST. Credit cards: AE, MC, V.

Meal Plans 3 meals a day served family style. Vegetarian menu includes eggs, dairy products, decaffeinated tea and coffee. Breakfast can be an omelet with toast, cereal, yogurt, fruit, or herb power drink. Lunch is soup, plate of raw vegetables. Chinese stirfry is dinner specialty. Dessert is fruit crepe with maple syrup.

Services and Facilities **Swimming Facilities:** Outdoor pool, lake. **Services:** Massage, reflexology, body wrap, hydrotherapy tub, body scrub, facial. **Recreation Facilities:** horseback riding. **Evening Programs:** Sleigh rides, cooking class, lecture.

In the Area Quebec City, Gaspé Peninsula.

Getting Here *From Montreal.* By car, Hwy 10 (1 hr). *From Vermont.* Hwy. 55.

Gray Rocks Inn

Sports conditioning

Quebec With the addition of Le Spa in 1987, this historic ski and sum-
St. Jovite mer sports resort gained a full-service fitness program. Classes and personal services are offered on an à la carte basis, although there is no charge to guests for use of the exercise equipment, coed sauna, or whirlpools. Along with an active social schedule, there are lean cuisine options for dining, making the Gray Rocks vacation package one of the best values in this part of Canada.

If you start with a fitness appraisal to help establish your goals, staff members, including an exercise physiologist, will test your cardiovascular capacity, body composition, and muscle flexibility. A computerized model provides an in-depth analysis of factors that affect your overall wellness. The spa has gained certification for customized exercise programs on their equipment. There are also aerobic dance sessions, stretch classes, and water-supported exercise in the pool.

Après-ski beach parties are a Wednesday-night feature at the spa. During the summer, activity at the 2,000-acre resort focuses on the marine and private beach, the championship 18-hole golf course, riding stables, and tennis complex. There are two dining rooms and social lounges at the Inn.

Gray Rocks Inn
Box 1000, St. Jovite, Que. J0T 2H0
Tel. 819/425–2771 or 800/567–6767
Fax 819/425–3006

Administration General manager, Butch Staples; spa director, Kelly Orr

Season Year-round.

Accommodations	150 bedrooms with ski-lodge comforts. 24-room private, upscale "Le Chateau" located a short distance around the lake. 56 apartments (1–3 bedrooms).
Rates	Summer 6-night package with 3 meals daily, $672–$744 (Can.) per person double occupancy, $918 single. Daily rates: summer $135 per person double, winter $111–$137 per person double. Add 7% GST and 4.28% local tax. Credit cards: AE, DC, MC, V.
Services and Facilities	**Exercise Equipment:** 4 Nautilus weight training units, 3 Lifecycles, 2 ergometers, 2 Monark bikes, Liferower, free weights (5–50 lbs.), leg-extension and leg-curl benches, 2 NordicTracks. **Services:** Massage. **Swimming Facilities:** Outdoor pools (not heated); lap pool in the spa. Private beach on Lake Ouimet. **Recreation Facilities:** 22 tennis courts, horseback riding, golf, jogging and hiking trails. Ski school mid-Nov.–Apr. 30. **Evening Programs:** Dancing and theme parties.
In the Area	Sleigh rides, shopping in nearby villages. Mont Tremblant Provincial Park (15 mi) for hiking and skiing.
Getting Here	*From Montreal.* By train (2 hr). By air, 4,200-ft landing strip for private aircraft. By bus, Voyageur service direct to inn. Local taxi and rental cars.
Special Notes	No smoking in spa. Spa hours: 7 AM–10 PM daily in summer, 8 AM–8 PM in winter.

Sivananda Ashram

Spiritual awareness
Kid fitness

Quebec
Val Morin

Living and practicing yoga from dawn to sunset, vacationers come here to relax the mind and revitalize the body. Located just an hour from Montreal, the yoga camp is an oasis of peace and harmony. Yet there is time for skiing and family fun within the daily schedule of meditation and vegetarian diet that you are required to follow.

Aside from the bare essentials of lodging, campers revel in the natural beauty of 350 acres of unspoiled woodland. At dawn, you are called to meditation, followed by yogic exercise or *asanas* that stretch and invigorate the body. A first meal comes at mid-morning, peak energy time; supper follows the 4 PM *asana* session. In between, you are free to enjoy the recreational facilities, to hike, or to get a massage. Sunset meditation and a concert of Indian music and dance conclude most days.

Based on five principles for a long and healthy life prescribed by Swami Vishnu Devananda, the program teaches how to breathe and exercise, and how to combine diet with positive thinking and meditation. The crisp mountain air and tranquil setting complement the quest for inner stillness.

The ashram attracts a diverse group of participants, college students as well as seniors, and has an introduction to yoga for youngsters while their parents meditate. Anyone is welcome, regardless of religion or age, and can stay for a weekend, a week, or longer. Many come for several weeks of advanced training, but you don't need to be an expert in any aspect of yoga to participate in the program. A special two-week "Total

Health Intensive" focuses on yoga techniques for healthy and positive living.

The camp is also headquarters for an international nonprofit education organization that operates ashrams in New York State, California, and the Bahamas. Vacation opportunities at these retreats are detailed in chapters devoted to those areas.

Sivananda Ashram
Eighth Ave., Val Morin, Que. JOT 2R0
Tel. 819/322–3226

Administration Founder, Swami Vishnu Devananda; director, Swami Shanmugananda

Season Year-round.

Accommodations 2-story wood lodges with private and dormitory rooms. Simply furnished with beds, linens, chest of drawers. Some rooms with private bath. Tent space on grounds.

Rates Single-price all-inclusive policy $45 (U.S.) per person sharing room with private bath, $25–$35 in other rooms, $25 camping. Single room $50; dormitory bed $30. Reservations by mail, with deposit for $50 per person. Credit cards: AE, MC, V.

Meal Plans 2 vegetarian buffets daily. No meat, fish, eggs, alcohol, or coffee. Brunch has fruit, hot grain cereal, baked casserole of seasonal vegetables, rice, salad, herbal tea.

Services and Facilities **Swimming Facilities:** Large outdoor pool; lake. **Spa Facilities:** Sauna, massage. **Recreation Facilities:** Hiking, biking, volleyball; downhill and cross-country skiing. **Evening programs:** Traditional music and dancing of India; bonfires and silent walks.

Getting Here *From Montreal.* By car, Laurentian Autoroute (Rte. 15), Exit 76. By bus, chartered service for special weekends and peak periods from Centre Sivananda (tel. 514/279–3545); Voyageur lines to Val Morin daily. Taxi service available in Val Morin. Airport pickup arranged for $50 (Can.).

Special Notes Kids' Yoga Camp, for ages 4–14, is a month-long combination of yogic exercises, swimming, and other activities. No smoking. Remember to bring an exercise mat or blanket, sandals or shoes that can be slipped on and off easily, and warm clothing.

Spa Concept at Le Château Bromont

Luxury pampering
Nutrition and diet

Quebec
Bromont
Revitalization and beautification are the basis of the Spa Concept program at Château Bromont. Located 60 miles (100 kilometers) from Montreal, the resort is just 20 minutes from the U.S. border.

Emphasizing serious shape-ups, the Château has a fully equipped gymnasium, indoor and outdoor swimming pools, and an aerobics studio. The daily schedule includes aquafitness Jazzercise, stretch and tone, and low-impact aerobics classes. Also available are squash and racquetball courts, mountain biking, and horseback riding. In winter, the program includes optional downhill and cross-country skiing.

European-style treatments are a major attraction for cosmopolitan Montrealers, who make up the majority of the guests. Included in packages for one to seven nights are body peeling, herbal wraps, and an unusually wide choice of massages—from soothing Swedish to shiatsu, Trager, and reflexology. Special therapies include polarity, lymphatic drainage, and baths with mud, sea algae, or essential oils. There are indoor and outdoor whirlpools, and a sauna.

Health programs are based on an evaluation of your lifestyle and on an energy test. The spa directress may advise energy-balancing exercise and specific treatments if you are on a five-night program. Otherwise there is no minimum stay, and services can be booked à la carte.

Spa Concept at Le Château Bromont
90 Stanstead, Bromont, Que. J0E 1L0
Tel. 514/534–2717

Administration Owner/director, Yvette Pratte Marchessalt

Season Year-round.

Accommodations 127 rooms in a country lodge with rustic furnishings. All rooms with air-conditioning, private bath.

Rates 5-night package $1,190 (Can) per person double occupancy, $1,410 single; 1-night package $275 double, $320 single. Add 11.28% GST and local tax. Deposit: 1 night's accommodation. Credit cards: MC, V.

Meal Plans 3 meals daily included in packages. Meals are nutritionally balanced, low in calories. Herbal teas available.

Services and Facilities **Services:** Massage (Swedish, Esalen, Trager, shiatsu, aromatherapy, reflexology); lymphatic drainage, electro-puncture, polarity therapy, herbal wrap, body peel, facial; beauty salon for hair, nail, and skin care. **Swimming Facilities:** Indoor and outdoor swimming pools. **Recreation Facilities:** Tennis and squash courts, racquetball, shuffleboard, volleyball, horseshoes, mountain biking; nearby downhill and cross-country skiing, horseback riding, water slides.

Getting Here *From Montreal.* By car, Rte. 10E to Exit 78, right turn on Bromont Blvd. to ski-slope area (1 hr).

Mexico

Mexican spas can trace their origins to the ancient Aztecs, who bathed and worshipped spirits at the country's steaming hot springs. Throughout Mexico today, these *balnearios* (spa resorts) and *baños termales* (hot-spring baths) are a bargain, offering mud baths, thermal waters, and warm hospitality. The largest and most luxurious of them is in Ixtapan de la Sal, two hours' drive southeast of Mexico City.

A very different experience, and a success since it opened more than 50 years ago, is the Rancho La Puerta in Baja California, founded by Deborah Szekely and her late husband. This is the action-oriented counterpart to the Golden Door in California; its holistic health program, vegetarian meals, and the stress-free environment of the Sierra Madres blend into a seamless vacation experience.

The best equipped example of the new resort-based spas is the Avandaro Golf & Spa Resort, a mountain retreat that provides a good opportunity for contemplating nature or improving your golf game between visits to the spa. If the beach is more to your liking, try the Grand Spa at Puerto Vallarta. On the Caribbean coast, the Body & Sol package at the 900-acre Puerto Aventuras resort combines power walks amid Mayan ruins with open-water dives, massage, and aerobics.

Avandaro Golf & Spa Resort

Luxury pampering

Mexico
Valle de Bravo

Perhaps the last thing you'd expect to find 80 miles west of Mexico City is this miniature alpine village, set in the pines beside a vast lake. The cooler temperatures can be attributed to the area's high altitude, 6,000 feet above sea level. The climate allows for some very unlikely south-of-the-border experiences: crackling fires in guest suites at night to fend off the chill, and invigorating hikes over the hills to witness the annual migration of the monarch butterflies.

The spa is housed in a tile-roofed hacienda overlooking the golf course. The latest equipment for facials and anticellulite treatments is available in the salon on the lower level of the spa building, and separate facilities for men and women on the main level include Swiss showers and a set of plunge pools (hot and cold) equipped with a waterfall for an invigorating natural massage. Upstairs is a small aerobics studio used for scheduled classes or individual workouts accompanied by video instructors.

Avandaro Golf & Spa Resort
Valle de Bravo, Mexico
Reservations: Box 27424, San Diego, CA 92198
Tel. 800/654-3732 (U.S.) or (726)2-0626 (resort)
Fax 619/674-6661 (U.S.) or (726) 2-0627 (resort)

Mexico

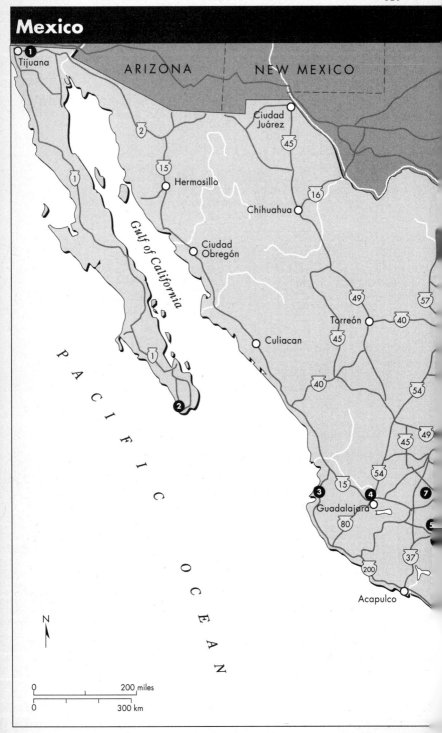

ARIZONA

NEW MEXICO

Tijuana **1**

Ciudad Juárez

2

45

15

Hermosillo

16

Chihuahua

Ciudad Obregón

Gulf of California

1

49

57

Torreón

40

45

Culiacan

1

40

54

PACIFIC

49

45

2

54

15

45

3

4

7

Guadalajara

80

5

OCEAN

37

200

N

Acapulco

0   200 miles

0   300 km

Avandaro Golf & Spa
Resort, **6**
Club Med
Huatulco, **10**
Hotel Balneario
Comanjilla, **7**
Hotel Balneario
San José Purua, **5**
Hotel Ixtapan, **8**
Melia Cabo Real, **2**
Puerto Vallarta
Grand Spa, **3**
Rancho La Puerta, **1**
Río Caliente, **4**
Villa Vegetariana, **9**

Administration General manager, Luis Labarca; spa director, Alexandra Simon

Season Year-round.

Accommodations 108 rooms within Spanish colonial–style cabins and adobe villas. Most have woodburning fireplace, TV, telephone, tiled modern bathroom. New buildings have 60 junior suites with sitting area, dining table, balcony or terrace.

Rates Daily spa plan (lodging, meals, 3 services) $250 per person double occupancy, $300 single. 7-day spa package $869 per person double, $1,069 single; gratuities, taxes, round-trip transfers from Mexico City included. Daily spa admission $25; cabin $80–$140 for 2, junior suite $110–$160 for 2; Avandaro Plan (lodging, breakfast, spa admission) $140–$160 for 2. Deposit: 50% advance payment. Credit cards: AE, MC, V.

Meal Plans 3 spa cuisine meals daily included in package rate; optional $30 credit for à la carte menu. Avandaro plan includes breakfast plus $10 dinner credit. Daily specials include grilled mountain trout, pasta, seafood, chicken, and steaks. Vegetarian meals on request.

Services and Facilities **Exercise Equipment:** 5 Paramount weight training units, 2 Lifecycles, 2 Trotter 540 treadmills, 2 Lifesteps, Precor rower, Tunturi stretch unit, Premier barbell bench, dumbbells (3–50 lb). **Services:** Massage (Swedish, sports, aromatherapy), loofah salt glow, facials, herbal wrap, electronic stimulation of facial and body liftings, anticellulite treatment, antistress biofeedback, nutritional analysis. Salon for hair, nail, and skin care. **Swimming Facilities:** Heated outdoor swimming pool. **Recreation Facilities:** 7 tennis courts, 18-hole golf course, hiking and nature trails, Ping-Pong; nearby horseback riding, water sports, hang gliding.

In the Area Lake Avandaro, Valle de Bravo (colonial pueblo), Toluca (Friday market, botanical garden, Spanish colonial architecture), trout farm, La Gavia (16th-century hacienda), volcano hike.

Getting Here *From Mexico City.* By car, Constituyendes Av. to Autopista (toll road) #15 via Toluca, Hwy. 134 through national forest, Hwy. 86, Hwy. 8 to Valle de Bravo (3 hr). By bus, Autobus Occidente from Observatorio Metro terminal (4 hr). Hotel provides complimentary round-trip transportation from Mexico City International Airport and hotels in Zona Rosa as part of 4- to 7-day packages.

Special Notes Ground-floor accommodations accessible for the disabled. Minimum age in spa is 16. No smoking in spa.

Balnearios

Taking the waters
Non-program resort facilities

A central belt cutting all the way to the Gulf of Mexico as well as the Pacific coast of Mexico comprises a vast volcanic zone. Hundreds of hot springs dot the region, and one entire state—Aguascalientes—has been named for the hot waters.

While most of the springs are not developed, some are popular with Mexican families, and within this volcanic area is Mexico's most beautiful mountain scenery. Here are some of the places where "taking the waters" can be enjoyed year-round.

Agua Blanca Hotel, Jungapeo, Michoacan
Carretera Zitacuaro, Cd. Hidalgo
Tel. #8 in Jungapeo.

Set deep in a canyon, the 10-room Agua Blanca hotel has three thermal pools fed by radioactive waters. Silence, manicured lawns, and luxuriant flower beds enhance this serene escape. Nearby are San Jose de Purua and the sanctuary of Monarch butterflies.

Aqua Hedionda
Av. Progreso s/n, Cuautla, Morelos
Tel. (735) 2–044

Sulfuric waters fill two public pools, wading pools, and eight private pools. Facilities include showers and dressing rooms, and the resort houses a restaurant with dancing on weekends. Located close to Cuernavaca.

El Almeal
Prolongacion Virginia Hernandez s/n. Cuautla, Morelos
Tel. (735) 2–1751

Two spring-fed pools, wading pools, playing fields, and a restaurant enhance this public spa. Dressing rooms and lockers provided for daily admission fee. Scenic railroad excursion Thursday, Saturday, and Sunday. Hiking trails nearby to Popacatepti and Ixtaccihuatl.

Hotel Balneario Atzimba
Av. Lazaro Cardenas, 58930 Zinapecuaro, Michoacan
Tel. (455) 5–0042 and 5–0050

A rustic 12-room hotel with thermal water baths, Atzimba is located about 30 minutes from Morelia, capital of the state. There is a small restaurant and lots of space for unwinding.

Hotel Balneario Chignahuapan
Km. 5 Carretera de Chignahuapan, Puebla
Tel. (777) 1–0313

Located at the edge of a canyon into which a cold-water stream plunges hundreds of feet and mixes with hot sulfur springs, the 40-room hotel has huge tiled bathing pools. All rooms with private bath, small balcony. Nearby are Tiaxcala, a colonial town noted for the Sanctuary of the Virgin of Ocotlan, and pre-Hispanic murals at the Cacaxtla archaeological site.

Hotel Balneario La Caldera
Km. 29 Libramiento, Carretera Abosolo, 36970,
Abasolo, Guanajuato
Tel. (460) 3–0020 and 3–0021

Private baths fed with thermal mineral water, an outdoor Jacuzzi, four tennis courts, soccer field, and extensive gardens are features of the 120-room La Caldera. All rooms have private bath, TV, air-conditioning. Located just west of Irapuato, Mexico's strawberry center.

Hotel Balneario Lourdes
Reservation office: Francisco Zarco 389, San Luis
Potosi, S.L.P.
Tel. (481) 2–3232 or 3–8065

Located 59 kilometers (37 miles) south of the picturesque colonial city of San Luis Potosi, this spa has 36 double rooms, a heated pool fed by mineral waters, horseback riding, squash and tennis courts.

Hotel Tainul
Km. 15 Carretera Cd. Valles—Tampico, Cd. Valles
Mailing Address: Box 87, CD. Valles, S.L.P.
Tel. (91–138) 2–0000
Fax (138) 2–4414

Located 15 minutes from Ciudad Valles and 62 miles (100 kilometers) from Tampico, the 3-star Hotel Taninul has 144 air-conditioned rooms, a thermal-water swimming pool fed by sulfur springs, and a freshwater pool. Restaurant and tennis are also available.

Oaxtepec Vacation Center, Oaxtepec, Morelos
Reservations: Apdo. 153, Oaxtepec, Morelos 62738
Tel. (91–735) 6–0101 or 6–0102

Located 35 miles east of Cuernavaca, near Cuautla, this was a favorite retreat of Moctezuma. The vast swimming pools, athletic fields, and restaurants are run by the Mexican Social Security Institute. Overnight accommodations available, in cottages or guest rooms for 6 persons.

Club Med-Huatulco

Sports conditioning

Oaxaca
Santa Cruz The green hills and emerald waters of Club Med's Huatulco village are located on the Pacific coast 525 kilometers (325 miles) from Acapulco. Sports-oriented activities are available year-round, and the modern fitness center is equipped with state-of-the-art Paramount workout machines.

Choose between exercise and aerobics classes to help work off the éclairs or chocolate mousse from last night's dinner. Sessions of low- and high-impact aerobics, and stretching (45–60 min), are offered throughout the day. You have unlimited access to three air-conditioned squash courts, tennis on 12 courts, and a practice golf course. Water-sports activities are popular, too.

Located on twin coves, Huatulco has casita-style lodgings terraced on the hillsides. There are three large freshwater swimming pools (one is Olympic-size) and a choice of five specialty dining rooms. The all-inclusive package, which is a Club Med tradition, takes the stress out of a week devoted to well-being.

Club Med-Huatulco
Bahia de Tangolunda, Santa Cruz, Oaxaca, Mexico
Tel. (011–52) 958–10033
Fax (011–52) 958–10101
(Reservations) 3 East 54th St., New York, NY 10019
Tel. 212/977–2100 or 800/258–2633

Administration Rotating Club Med manager

Season Year-round.

Accommodations 500 air-conditioned units furnished with twin beds, optional partition. Rattan furniture, local crafts and bedspreads; private sea-view terrace with hammock. Each casita has a bathroom and shower; electrical voltage is 110.

Rates All-inclusive weekly rate, $979–$1,219 per person double occupancy; add 10% for single room. Payment of 25% deposit due within a week of reservation, plus club membership fee ($50 annual, $30 initiation). Credit cards: AE, MC, V.

Meal Plans Buffets with unlimited choices for breakfast, lunch, and dinner. Choice of 5 restaurants serving Italian, Argentine, Moroccan, seafood, and Club Med salads, grilled chicken, and tropical fruits. Milk, coffee, tea, and dinner wine included; bottled water available.

Services and Facilities **Exercise Equipment:** 10-unit Paramount gym, free weights (3–70 lb), 2 bench presses, incline benches. **Services:** Scheduled classes aerobics, calisthenics, and water exercises; massage. **Swimming Facilities:** 3 outdoor pools, 2 ocean beaches. **Recreation Facilities:** sailing, kayaking, windsurfing, snorkeling, 12 tennis courts (7 lighted), 3 indoor squash courts, practice golf course, volleyball, basketball, softball, billiards, Ping-Pong. Golf course (9-hole) nearby (extra charge). **Evening Programs:** Nightly entertainment and dancing.

In the Area Monte Alban (Zapotec archaeological ruins), Oaxaca (16th-century colonial architecture, Indian marketplace), Mitla (Aztec ruins).

Getting Here Club Med flights on American Airlines via Dallas every Sunday. Transfers to club provided. Taxi one-way $25.

Special Notes No smoking restrictions. Registered nurse in residence. Airport fee required with proof of U.S. citizenship. Children 6 and over accommodated with parents.

Hotel Balneario Comanjilla

Taking the waters

Guanajuato
Leon Located in the heart of the fertile Bajio region, the pleasantly old-fashioned Hotel Balneario Comanjilla is a quiet, secluded resort convenient to beautiful nearby colonial Guanajuato and Leon (the leather capital of Mexico). Gardens surround the two-story guest buildings, one of which houses an aerobics studio and conference facilities.

Exercise programs are organized on request only, and massage appointments must be made well in advance. Medical and nutritional consultation is available to guests in Spanish only. Nevertheless, two swimming pools filled with warm thermal water, well-appointed guest rooms, tennis courts, and stables make the trip worthwhile for many honeymooners, Texas snowbirds, and, perhaps, you.

Hotel Balneario Comajilla
Carretera Panamericana #45, Km. 387
Apt. Postal 111, 37000 Leon, Gto.
Tel. (91–47) 16–5820 or 12–0942
Fax (91–47) 13–2479

Administration	Owner/director, Harold Gabriel Applet
Season	Year-round.
Accommodations	120 rooms in 2-story Spanish-colonial buildings. All with tiled private bathroom, phone, TV. Four suites have step-down Roman bath with thermal water. All with balcony or patio, view of forest or pool.
Rates	300,000–390,000 pesos for 2 people, 225,000–285,000 pesos single; suite, 420,000 pesos for 2 people, 320,000 pesos single.
Meal Plan	3 meals daily included in daily room rate. An à la carte menu is offered in the hotel dining room.
Services and Facilities	**Exercise Facilities:** 2 stationary bikes, free weights. **Services:** Massage, facial; medical evaluation. **Spa Facilities:** 2 outdoor pools. **Recreation Facilities:** 2 tennis courts, bicycles, horseback riding, billiards, Ping-Pong.
In the Area	San Miguel de Allende, Guanajuato (museums, university, fall festival), Leon (leather shopping, particularly for shoes)
Getting Here	*From Leon.* By car, Hwy. 45 (40 min). Taxi, rental car available at Bajio Regional Airport (20 min).
Special Notes	Ground-floor rooms provide access for the disabled.

Hotel Balneario San José de Purua

Taking the waters

Michoacán
San José Purua

Set on the edge of a small canyon, with spectacular views of the mountains and a nearby waterfall, the Hotel Balneario San José de Purua has been a popular watering place since the times of the Tarascan Empire (AD 1200). Lush gardens and giant trees bearing orchids surround the bathhouse where thermal waters from several springs on the hillside are piped into private bathing pools. Dipping into the fizzy water, which is highly carbonated, is a daily ritual that relaxes travelers' aches and pains. The mineral-radioactive water flows from springs at 89°F (32°C).

Mud packs are a specialty here. Facials using a mixture of the thermal water and highly mineralized mud are said to be beneficial to the complexion. Gently applied, the mud mask dries as you relax, and it is followed by a massage with herbal and fruit-based creams.

Treatments are booked on an à la carte basis. While there is no planned fitness program, the costs for a facial or massage are quite modest. And the resort offers a full complement of diversions, from golf and tennis to bowling and horseback riding.

Secluded and quiet, the hotel has the atmosphere of a colonial hacienda. Guest rooms with red-tile roofs, private terraces, and garden walks line the canyon to a small lake filled with ducks. The 55-year-old hotel was undergoing extensive renovations at press time.

Situated in the highlands between Guadalajara and Mexico City, the resort is near the town of Zitcuaro. Nearby attractions include stately old Morelia, a city richly endowed with museums, cultural and educational institutions, and crafts shops, and Lake Patzcuaro, where descendants of the Tarascan Indians still fish with butterfly nets and worship at the Virgin of Health statue in the town basilica. Nearby is the sanctuary of brilliantly colored Monarch butterflies.

Hotel Balneario San José de Purua

Apdo. Postal 43, Zitacuaro, Michoacán
Paseo de la Reforma, Esq. Colon, 06030 Mexico D.F.
Tel. 905/510-4949 in Mexico City; (52-725) 7-0200
Fax (52-725) 7-0150 at hotel

Administration	Director, Juan Gonzalez Rojas
Season	Year-round.
Accommodations	250 rooms in the hacienda-style hotel; heavy wood furniture, handwoven bedspreads, colorful decorations; all rooms with large private baths, modern facilities. Some small private terraces; 1 suite comes with private swimming pool. No air conditioning. TV lounge with programs by satellite.
Rates	Double room with 3 meals $60 per day for 2, $38 single. Credit cards: AE, MC, V. Spa package 270,000 pesos for 2; 180,000 pesos single. Add tips and taxes.
Meal Plans	Trained under German and Spanish master chefs, the restaurant staff takes a light approach to traditionally spicy Mexican cuisine. Fresh fish grilled over wood, without butter on request. Chicken, lamb, and beef usually well done. Lentil soup with plantain or baked zucchini are dinner choices.
Services and Facilities	**Services:** Massage, facials, mud packs. **Bathing Facilities:** Private bath, 5 outdoor pools. **Swimming Facilities:** Outdoor pool. **Recreation Facilities:** Minigolf, tennis, bowling, riding, game rooms for billiards, Ping-Pong, cards. **Evening Programs:** Folkloric groups.
In the Area	Michoacán Museum (Museo Michoacano) in an 18th-century palace on Morelia's main plaza houses Indian artifacts, a puppet collection, colonial furniture, and paintings; Museum of Contemporary Art (Museo de Arte Contemporaneo) in Morelia has changing exhibitions, as does the Casa de la Cultura; Church of the Christ of Health (Iglesia del Niño de la Salud) on Rte. 15 near Morelia, has an image of the Christ Child said to have healing powers.
Getting Here	*From Mexico City.* By car, Hwy. 15 northwest via Zitacuaro and Cd. Hidalgo, then 7 km to archway, 5 km south of Hwy. 15 (4 hr). By bus, from the Northern Bus Terminal, Transportes Norte de Sonora (tel. 567-9221, 567-9664, 587-5633), 4½ hr. By van, service costs $16 per person, one way. Rental car available.
Special Notes	Limited access for the disabled. Organized games for children. No smoking in the bathhouse.

Hotel Ixtapan

Luxury pampering
Taking the waters

Mexico
Ixtapan de la Sal

Hotel Ixtapan, largest and most luxurious thermal springs health resort in Mexico, is located in Ixtapan de la Sal, which has been a popular center for cures since the 16th-century Aztec emperor Móctezuma came to bathe. It is 70 miles (119 km) southeast of Mexico City, easily accessible from the capital by car or limousine service.

Its health and beauty programs are designed to revitalize, rejuvenate, and refresh the total person. The spa program is not regimented, but a typical day can include breakfast in bed, a nature walk, rhythmic gymnastics, aquatic exercises, and some pampering bodywork. Among the specialties are a facial with fresh fruit and vegetable oils, and a scalp massage.

Family-owned and run, the hotel has been extensively modernized. A water treatment plant and a power plant have been added, as have new, but somewhat limited facilities for aerobics classes and exercise equipment. The centerpiece of the new spa is the marble whirlpool, where you can relax while awaiting a facial or massage in private cubicles.

The thermal waters originate from an extinct volcano about an hour away and are piped into a huge lake in the Parque Acuatico as well as into a swimming pool in the hotel gardens. In a public bathhouse across from the gardens, you can have a private soak.

The hydrotherapy facilities include 20 private Roman baths. Marble-walled and mirrored, the sunken whirlpools are filled with warm mineral water, ideal for a late-afternoon soak or a Sunday indulgence when hotel masseuses have the day off.

Treatments are gentle and relaxing, and exercises are not strenuous. The masseuses work muscles by hand and utilize electric vibrators as well.

Among recreational facilities at this 35-acre family resort are a disco, bars, train rides, horse-drawn carriages, water slides, and a bowling alley. Avoid weekend crowds if possible.

Hotel Ixtapan
Ixtapan de la Sal, Mexico 51900
(Office) Tonala 177, Col. Roma, 06700 Mexico, D.F.
Tel. 905/564–5860 in Mexico City;
724/30073 at the hotel
(U.S. Reservation Center) 9311 San Pedro, Ste. 1140,
San Antonio, TX 78216
Tel. 512/341–8151 or 800/638–7950
Fax 512/342–9789

Administration Director, Roberto San Roman

Season Year-round.

Accommodations 200 rooms plus 50 private chalets; pre-Hispanic motifs, colorful native fabrics; rooms comfortable with king-size bed plus sofa bed standard; all suites with private baths and air-conditioning. Superior rooms with balcony face gardens.

Rates Full spa program, 1 week (Mon.–Sat.) $750–$850 per person double occupancy, $830–$995 single. 4-day program (Sun.–Thurs. or Wed.–Sun.) $530–$650 single, $420–$520 double. Add 10% tax and 15% service charge additional. 50% at time of booking, plus 1-way transfer if requested. No credit cards.

Meal Plans 900-calorie diet menu has fruit or juice with either tea or coffee for breakfast; cream of carrot soup, fresh fruit, and either chicken with mushrooms or plain tuna fish for lunch; dinner choices include fresh rainbow trout, omelet, and cheese plate.

Services and Facilities **Exercise Equipment:** 14-station CalGym, 2 Lifecycles, 2 Precor 9.5 treadmills, Precor X-country skier, free weights, benches. **Services:** Massage, reflexology, mud packs, facial; hair, skin, and nail treatments. **Bathing Facilities:** Indoor and outdoor pools, private whirlpools. **Swimming Facilities:** Outdoor pools. **Recreation Facilities:** Tennis courts, 9-hole golf course, horseback riding, volleyball, badminton. **Evening Programs:** Resort entertainment, movies, folkloric ballet.

In the Area Taxco (artisan center), archaeological sites.

Getting Here *From Mexico City.* By car, Hwy. 15 to Hwy. 55 via Toluca, then toll road (Cuota) (2 hr). By bus from Observatorio terminal. Transfers on arrival/departure at airport or downtown hotels $160 roundtrip, including tolls and tax. Taxi, rental car available.

Special Notes Elevators and ground-floor rooms provide access for the disabled. Minicamp and play areas for children. No smoking in the baths.

Melia Cabo Real

Non-program resort facilities

Baja California
San Jose del Cabo Found at the rugged tip of Baja California, where the Sea of Cortés meets the Pacific Ocean, the spa at the Melia Cabo Real resort is enjoyed by nature lovers and fitness buffs alike. Whale-watching in the Sea of Cortés is a popular pastime, as are desert cycling, mountain jogging, horseback riding, and a full range of water sports. Deep-sea fishing for marlin is also a major attraction.

Crowned by a unique glass-and-marble pyramid, the hotel is bordered by cactus gardens, flowering bougainvillea, and palms. A beachfront restaurant and two swimming pools are reached by cobblestone walkways. The health center's coed gym offers sessions of yoga and tai chi chuan, in addition to personalized exercise supervised by trained fitness instructors. Aquacise and weight training classes are scheduled in the pool. For relaxation, each locker room has a sauna, steam room, and Jacuzzi. Exercise equipment is minimal, and bodywork is limited to massage and wraps with herbs or mineral salts. Beauty salon services are available as part of the Avanti spa package, or à la carte.

Melia Cabo Real
Carretera Cabo San Lucas, Sector 5, Km 19.5
San Jose del Cabo, Mexico 23410
Tel. (011) 684/307–54 or 800/336–3542
Fax (011) 684/310–03

Administration General manager, Tomeu Alcina; spa director, Lucrecia M. Aguilar

Season Year-round.

Accommodations 292 double rooms and 7 suites, all with oceanfront view, air-conditioning, satellite TV, telephone, marble-floor bathroom with 110-volt (U.S.) electricity outlets. Garden-level rooms have landscaped private terrace: all others have private balcony.

Rates 5-day/4-night Health, Beauty and Pamper Package, including 3 meals daily, spa services, and airport transfers, $897 per person, double occupancy. One-day spa package (no lodging) $260 per person. Tax included. Daily room rate $110–$195 for 2 persons, $100–$185 single. Add 20% tax and gratuities. Deposit: guarantee by credit card. Credit cards: AE, DC, MC, V.

Meal Plans 3 meals daily included in spa package. The weight-loss menu for breakfast is eggwhite omelet or granola with low-fat milk, peach melva, juices, coffee, tea, and toast. Lunch can be soup, steamed broccoli and cauliflower, chicken breast, tossed salad, or broiled fish, zucchini and tomato. Dessert is an apple or apricot. Dinner entrees include broiled beef, fish, or chicken; vegetarian plate with cottage cheese; or spinach salad.

Services and Facilities **Exercise Equipment:** 2 Universal weights units, 2 stationary bikes, EZ Stepper, free weights, slant board. **Services:** Massage, herbal wrap, mineral salt wraps, reflexology; one-on-one instruction; salon for hair, nail, and skin care. **Swimming Facilities:** 2 outdoor freshwater pools, ocean beach. **Recreation Facilities:** Water sports, scuba, beach volleyball, table tennis, 2 tennis courts (lighted, $9 per hr); 18-hole golf course nearby, horseback riding, boat tours. **Evening Programs:** Live music and dancing nightly.

Getting Here *From Cabo San Lucas International Airport.* By car, Hwy. 1 southwest (25 km), resort entrance at Km 19 (30 min). Complimentary transfers included in 5-day spa package. Taxi, rental car available.

Special Notes Ground-floor rooms for the disabled. Ferry service to Puerto Vallarta scheduled daily.

Puerto Vallarta Grand Spa

Luxury pampering
Life enhancement
Nutrition and diet
Stress control

Jalisco
Puerto Vallarta While the steamy romance of Elizabeth Taylor and Richard Burton put Puerto Vallarta on the international tourist map, the personality of the Grand Spa is refreshing and healthful. Geared to staying fit, the program assesses lifestyle evaluations to curb stress-related and diet problems.

Located in a seaside complex of high-rise luxury hotels near the international airport, the spa is the site of eight exercise classes daily—from aerobics in a cushion-floored and air-conditioned studio to aquacise workouts open to all hotel guests. The well-equipped weight training room and suite of rooms for bodywork make this a bargain for day visitors as well as hotel guests.

For the spandex-suited fitness buff, the weights room and adjoining aerobics studio provide plenty of action. You don't have to be a guest at the hotel to register for the day. In addition to the daily charge ($10), services can be booked à la carte or with lunch as part of the Spa-Day package. Mexican food, prepared to be tasty yet light on calories and fat, is highlighted on the menu at the hotel's poolside Villa Linda restaurant.

Supervised by credentialed aerobics instructors, activities are scheduled from 8 AM to 7:30 PM. The morning begins with a walk along the beach, weekdays. Low-impact aerobics and a fit-and-firm class occur daily, as do afternoon sessions of abdominal workouts and high-energy aerobics. Spa director Diana Mestre holds a degree in physical education from California State Polytechnic University and was on the faculty there. With an international staff of 26, Mestre plans personalized regimens for guests participating in programs for three to seven days.

Fitness evaluations are conducted in specially equipped testing rooms. Staff members test your aerobic capacity, strength, flexibility, and blood pressure prior to starting you on a schedule of exercise and diet. Aided by computerized systems, they check your body-fat level, nutritional needs, and general health. A record of progress and recommendations to continue at home are provided at the end of your visit.

Stress reduction can begin with an analysis of sources of stress in your life; relaxing massages, herbal wraps, and facials soothe pressured areas. Guests are pampered with a complete regimen of body and beauty treatments using natural extracts and herbs. Even the mud in fango treatments has a history: It comes from a volcanic source in Michoacán, where it is purified for exclusive use here.

While the resort offers a full range of recreation from scuba diving to parasailing and has a tennis complex, the spa maintains a quiet calm that allows you to revitalize in style.

Puerto Vallarta Grand Spa
Km 2.5 Carretera Aeropuerto, Puerto Vallarta, Jal.,
Apdo. Postal 308, Puerto Vallarta, Jalisco, 48 300
Tel. (011–52) 322/23959
Fax (011–52) 322–26393

Administration Spa manager, Diana Mestre

Season Year-round.

Accommodations 248 deluxe rooms with balcony in a 4-star resort with two 5-story wings connected by a 14-story tower. Top floors are the Omni Club with 26 deluxe rooms, 4 master suites, 2 Presidential suites with private Jacuzzi and terrace. Club guests get complimentary Continental breakfast, afternoon cocktails, concierge service. All rooms are air-conditioned, with marble-floored bathroom, color TV, telephone.

Rates Daily rate, with spa meals, $91 per person double, $137 single. 2-night package $429 double, $519 single. 7-night program (Sun.–Sun.) includes 3 spa-cuisine meals daily, treatments, and unlimited exercise, $1,399 single, $1,069 double. Add 10%

gratuity, 15% tax. Deposit: prepay in full by 14 days after booking. Credit cards: AE, DC, MC, V.

Meal Plans 3 spa-cuisine meals plus juice and fruit snack daily. Breakfast choices include eggwhite omelet with steamed vegetables, yogurt, whole-grain cereal, tropical fruit. Lunch can be vegetarian chili, grilled fish, or sautéed vegetables. Dinner choices (available in the Villa Linda restaurant) include skinless chicken fajitas, pasta primavera, baked snapper, broiled chicken breast Florentine with steamed vegetables over spinach, or fish filet.

Services and Facilities **Exercise Equipment:** 22-unit Paramount weight training gym, 3 Lifecycles, 2 VersaClimbers, 2 recumbent bikes, Precor step machine, dumbbells, barbells (1¼–45 lb), benches. **Services:** Massage, herbal wrap, loofah body scrub, facial, fango, make-up application; computerized health and fitness evaluations, nutrition analysis, stress-management biofeedback, behavior modification for weight control; skin, nail care. **Spa Facilities:** Steam room, sauna, whirlpool. **Swimming Facilities:** Outdoor pool, ocean beach. **Recreation Facilities:** Tennis court (concrete surface, lighted) in spa, 8 courts nearby, water sports; Los Flamingos golf course (PGA par-72, designed by Percy Cliff), horseback riding on the beach.

In the Area Gringo Gulch (celebrity homes), Mismaloya (John Huston's setting for *Night of the Iguana*), Villa Vallarta Mall (shopping), Yelapa (beach restaurants, freshwater lagoon), Playa Las Animas (natural beach), ferry to Baja California.

Getting Here *From Mexico City.* By air, scheduled flights by Mexicana, Aeromexico, American (45 min). Also direct service from Dallas by Continental. Taxi, rental car available.

Special Notes Ground-floor accommodations, ramps, elevators for the disabled. Spa hours: Mon.–Sat. 7:30 AM–9 PM, Sun to 5 PM. Daily admission fee $10. Tennis shoes required in workout rooms.

Rancho La Puerta

Life enhancement
Weight management

Baja California The Rancho La Puerta regimen can be easy or challenging.
Tecate Hiking on sacred Mount Kuchumaa, a broad range of exercise classes (more than 60 daily), meatless meals spiced with Mexican specialties, and spa pampering are among your options.

The original formula for fitness has expanded since the resort opened 53 years ago, but the basic attractions endure: a nearly perfect year-round climate (an average of 341 sunny days) that's dry and pollen-free, the natural beauty of purple foothills ringed by impressive mountains, and the ovo-lacto vegetarian diet. "The Ranch," as old hands call it, has had a high percentage of repeaters. Newcomers quickly get into the swing of things.

Encouraged by instructors who use innovative techniques in workouts, and soothed by a massage or herbal wrap, you focus on recharging body and mind. Some classes are intense, others relaxing; counselors are on hand to help with your schedule.

Designed in the style of a Mexican village, there is a central complex of swimming pools, men's and women's health centers (each with sauna, steam room, Jacuzzi), library, and lounges, linked by brick-paved walkways to casitas and villas that accommodate 150 guests. Gyms dot the landscape: some open-air, others enclosed for cool days. No signup is required for any of the numerous classes, including aerobic circuit training, back-care workshop, better breathing, body awareness, hatha-yoga, self-defense, and a progressive series of fitness and stretching sessions for men combined with circuit training led by a former coach of Belgian Olympic teams. New additions include a Japanese-style bathhouse, a video room with VCR, and an olive press which guests may use to make their own virgin olive oil from the ranch's trees.

This flowering oasis, set amid 575 acres of seclusion, also gives you a taste of Mexican resort life. Accommodations vary from studiolike rancheras to luxury haciendas and villas decorated with native handmade furniture and rugs. Many feature tiled floors, fireplaces, and kitchenettes. (Large units can be shared by single guests on request.) The Ranch has its own style and personality thanks to the smiling staff who look after the rooms and run the kitchen. Special treats are poolside breakfast overlooking the mountain, and a breakfast hike to the 4-acre organic garden at Rancho Tres Estrellas.

Meals in the Spanish-colonial dining room become a communal exercise in stamina building. The low-fat, high-carbohydrate diet provides ample energy. Breakfast and lunch are buffet style, dinner a sit-down menu of four courses. In addition to dessert, you can have coffee, tea, homemade bread, and plenty of salads. One evening there is a gourmet dinner for the first 25 who sign up ($25).

After two or three days on this diet, without distractions from TV, newspapers, or telephone, guests usually discover that their appetite for food has decreased remarkably, while they look and feel healthier. Some do go "over the hill," tempted by Tecate's shops and burrito bars.

Learning the psychology of healthy living, pioneered here by Deborah and Edmond B. Szekely, is the real benefit of visiting the hemisphere's original fitness resort.

Rancho La Puerta
Tecate, Baja California
Tel. (011) 526–654–1155 at ranch
Reservations: Box 463057, Escondido, CA 92046
Tel. 619/744–4222 or 800/443–7565
Fax 619/744–5007

Administration	Manager, Jose Manuel Jasso; fitness director, Phyllis Pilgrim
Season	Year-round; special weeks for couples only during Mar. and Oct.
Accommodations	Single-level studios and suites (75) with bath in adobe haciendas and villas. Some large units with 2 bedrooms, 2 baths, southwestern-style beamed ceilings, fireplace, and dining-living area. The maximum number of guests is 150, cared for by a staff of more than 350. No air-conditioning, TV, telephone.

Rates The week-long program, Sat.–Sat., includes use of all fitness facilities, 3 meals a day. Rate varies according to accommodation. Treatments and personal services charged on an individual basis. Single accommodations $1,704–$2,130, double $1,357–$2,023 per person, including tax. Villa Studios have additional single bed, Villa Suites accommodate up to 4 persons. Gratuities optional. Minimum stay 1 week. Deposit: $250 per person within 14 days of request for accommodations; balance payable 30 days prior to arrival. Credit cards: MC, V.

Meal Plans The ovo-lacto-vegetarian diet includes fish 2 times a week; wine on Friday optional. Breakfast choices change daily: scrambled eggs and tofu with tortilla, hot and cold cereal, boiled egg, and fresh fruits are typically offered. The lunch buffet may include vegetables soup, tofu sandwiches, a vegetable platter, quesadillas of ricotta cheese and tofu, and garlic herbed pizza. Dinner entrees include lasagna, enchiladas, shrimp casserole, Thai spring roll, grilled swordfish, and steamed vegetables spiced with cilantro-based salsa. Fasting on liquified fruits fortified with fresh vegetables and nuts on Mondays.

Services and Facilities **Exercise Equipment:** Supervised weight training gym with 6 StarTrac treadmills, 15 CamStar weight units, 6 StairMasters (4000 PT), 8 Monark bikes, PTS recumbent bike, 4 Bio-Health computerized bikes, dumbbells, incline benches. **Services:** Massage, herbal wraps, beauty salon for hair, nail, and skin care daily by appointment. Charges will be added to your account. Golden Door hypoallergenic cosmetics used exclusively. **Swimming Facilities:** 3 outdoor pools, 1 heated, used primarily for aquatic exercise classes. **Recreation Facilities:** Tennis on 6 lighted courts, a putting green, volleyball and basketball courts. Hiking ranges from "moderate" to a challenging climb up Mt. Kuchumaa. Outdoor running track. **Evening Programs:** Movie and lecture scheduled nightly. Recreation hall is open for Ping-Pong and other games.

In the Area Tecate is 3 mi (5 km) from the ranch; Tijuana, 25 mi (40 km) west, bustles with curio shops, a cultural center, and, on summer Sundays, bullfights.

Getting Here *From San Diego airport.* Complimentary transfers on arrival/departure. By car, I–5 south to Hwy. 94, Tecate turnoff to Rt. 188, south to border crossing, right at 2nd light, onto Hwy. 2, 3 miles on right (1½ hr). Taxi, rental car available.

Special Notes Most facilities are barrier-free and ground-level for the disabled. Those with difficulty walking or seeing, or whose weight is 35% above normal for their height, are not accepted. Families are welcome, though no special activity for young guests is organized. No smoking inside buildings. Treatment facilities open daily 7 AM–noon; daily 2–8 PM except Sat.

Río Caliente

Life enhancement
Taking the waters
Nutrition and diet

Jalisco
Guadalajara For thousands of years, Indians used the meandering river of hot mineral water for curative purposes. Now the fertile valley around the tiny village of La Primavera is a national forest.

And the Rio Caliente Spa offers nature-oriented holidays, including vegetarian meals and convivial company.

The synthesis of therapies, diet, sun, and bathing is the key to enjoying this unique health resort. Entering the bathhouse, you encounter a 20-foot wall of volcanic rock, in front of which are wooden benches where guests relax while enjoying a sweat. A stream of hot thermal water snakes through the room, emitting occasional puffs of steam. Welcome to the Aztec steam room.

After about 10 minutes in this superheated room (130 degrees), you begin to sweat out the body's toxins. Then you can cool down in a plunge pool (separate facilities for men and women) and enjoy a 60-minute massage. In addition, there are pampering services at very reasonable rates.

Classes in yoga, tai chi chuan, and aquatics are scheduled for all guests who want to participate. No strict regimen is enforced; guests may join a group hike, trail ride, or meditation class, or may simply lounge on the sunny terrace. Spa services are provided by a well-trained staff, and acupuncture is available on request.

The therapeutic water used in the pools and baths contains 10 major elements. Odorless, the water is used for drinking as well as bathing.

Río Caliente
Apdo. Postal 1–1187, Guadalajara, Jalisco
No telephone at spa
Reservations: 480 California Terrace,
Pasadena, CA 91105
Tel. 818/796–5577, in Mexico 011–5/(236)343890, or
(236)157800

Administration Director, Caroline Durston

Season Year-round.

Accommodations 48 cabanas and rooms for 80 guests in the main buildings; hand-crafted beds and chairs; colorful fabrics by local artisans; small and simple rooms, all with private baths; no phones, TV, or air-conditioning.

Rates Daily rate $52 double occupancy, $52–$58 single. Rate includes vegetarian buffet meals, activity program, lodging. Personal services and trips range from $5 to $18. 10% discount for stays of 30 days or longer. Taxes and gratuity included. $100 deposit. No credit cards.

Meal Plans Vegetarian meals served buffet style 3 times daily. Tropical foods in season include guavas, jícama, zapote, and guanabana. Organically grown raw greens, raw and cooked vegetables, soups and home-baked grain casseroles supplement vegetarian platters.

Services and Facilities **Services:** Massage, reflexology, facial, manicure, pedicure, fango mudpacks. **Bathing Facilities:** Separate walled plunge pools for men and women, swimming pool; waterfall for nude bathing. **Swimming Facilities:** outdoor pool. **Recreation Facilities:** Hiking; horseback riding and golf are nearby.

In the Area Group trips into Guadalajara (crafts market, Orozco murals), Tlaquepaque (colonial architecture, crafts center), Tequila (brewery). Other attractions include Lake Chapala, Cabanas Institute (center for arts), and Plaza of the Mariachis in Guadalajara.

Getting Here *From Guadalajara.* By car, Hwy. 80 to La Primavera (60 min). Taxi, rental car available.

Special Notes Limited access for the disabled. No smoking indoors. Electrical voltage is 110 A.C. (compatable to U.S.).

Villa Vegetariana

Nutrition and diet
Weight management

Morelos
Cuernavaca
Emphasizing weight reduction and fasting cures, Villa Vegetariana health school was established by David and Marlene Stry as a center for nutrition and exercise. They serve tropical fruits and juices, vegetables raw and cooked. Low in cholesterol, and often grown organically on the property, the meals are included with consultation on diet and nutrition.

For recreation, there is a swimming pool, bicycles, a basketball court, and wall tennis. Walks and hikes in the countryside are arranged for groups of guests on request. Aerobics classes are scheduled in the gymnasium, and there is a coed sauna.

Yoga, Spanish classes, and organic gardening are among the activities scheduled. Surrounded by lush, tropical terrain, the villa is three miles from the center of one of the most interesting and colorful cities in Mexico.

Cuernavaca glitters in the sun, its plazas surrounded by baroque churches and palaces. One building, planned as a fortress by Hernán Cortés, is now a museum, exhibiting a collection of murals by Diego Rivera. There is also an herb museum (Museo de la Herbologia, Matamoros 200) with gardens.

Places to swim include rustic thermal springs and the recreation area at Oaxtepec, formerly the site of Móctezuma's botanical gardens. The warm, dry climate and caring staff at the villa add up to a healthy vacation.

Villa Vegetariana
Reservations: Apdo. 1228, Pino 114,
Sta. Maria Ahuacatilan 62058
Cuernavaca, Morelos
Tel. (011) 91–73–131044

Administration General manager, Isidoro Morales; program director, Maria de los Angeles Uvillado

Season Year-round.

Accommodations 20 guest rooms, some with private terrace. Simply furnished; no TV, air-conditioning, or telephone.

Rates Daily rate with meals 16,500,000–17,500,000 pesos for 2 persons, 11,000,000–12,500,000 pesos single; without meals, 5,000,000–6,000,000 pesos for one or two persons. 5-day package with meals, 12,000,000–130,000,000 pesos for 2 persons, 75,000,000–85,000,000 pesos single. Add tax and gratuity. No credit cards accepted.

Special Notes Medical services available.

The Caribbean, the Bahamas, Bermuda

The current trend in the Caribbean is to import European thalassotherapy and American fitness programs. At a seaside estate on St. Lucia, the body holiday at Le Sport provides the fitness buff's counterpart to Club Med. On the seafront malecón of the Dominican Republic's capital city, a high-tech European spa adjoins the casino at the Jaragua Resort; the new Port de Plaisance resort on St. Martin also has a casino, as well as a spa and tennis clinic. In the vicinity of Puerto Rico's Loquillo Beach, the La Casa de Vida Natural offers holistic health programs, while the nearby El Conquistador sports a new spa and casino.

Jamaica has the widest range of options, among them the luxurious Charlie's Spa at the Sans Souci resort, the rustic mineral water baths at Milk River Spa, and Negril's sports-oriented Swept Away resort, all outstanding opportunities for combining a Caribbean holiday with a health regime.

Hyatt Regency Aruba Resort

Non-program resort facilities

Aruba
Palm Beach

Set on 12 acres of powdery white sand, two miles from the island's pastel-colored capital of Oranjestad, the $52 million Hyatt Regency Aruba Resort & Casino opened in 1990. An 8,000-square-foot three-level swimming pool with cascading waterfalls and tropical lagoons graces this water-sports-oriented resort. Canoe rentals, sailboats, and a 50-foot luxury catamaran for sunset cruises are all available, and two dive boats ferry guests to coral reefs and sunken shipwrecks.

The health and fitness facilities—including exercise room, coed sauna, steam room, outdoor whirlpool, and sun deck for aerobics classes—are open to hotel guests without charge. For those who don't want to get wet or sweat, the gardens feature a 5,000-square-foot saltwater lagoon replete with native fish and wildlife; a poolside restaurant fashioned out of native coral stone is good for lounging.

Arubans are naturally friendly and welcome visitors with suggestions for hiking, water sports, and golf. Drive to the old capital, San Nicolas, to play the oiled-sand links of the Aruba Golf Club. Along the way, stop at the fish market in Savaneta, the island's first settlement, and later dine on Dutch Creole dishes at the Brisas del Mar restaurant. Charlie's Bar, a tavern on Main Street in San Nicolas, provides local color.

Beaches are public throughout the island. Hike from the natural bridge (carved by the sea), on the rugged coast near Boca Prins, to Andicouri for a romantic picnic on a secluded beach surrounded by a coconut plantation.

Aruba's volcanic origins are revealed at Casi Bari, a rock garden of giants, and at tall, unusual rock formations called *Ayo*.

The Caribbean, the Bahamas,

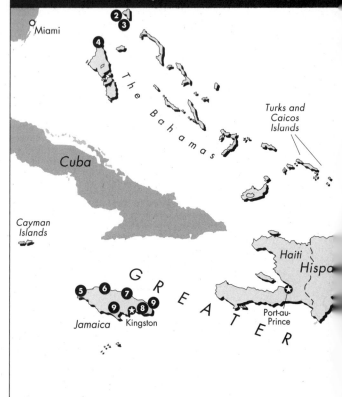

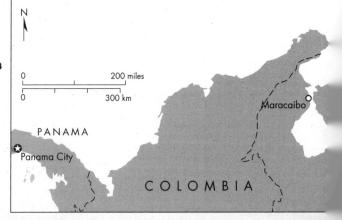

Bermuda

Bermuda

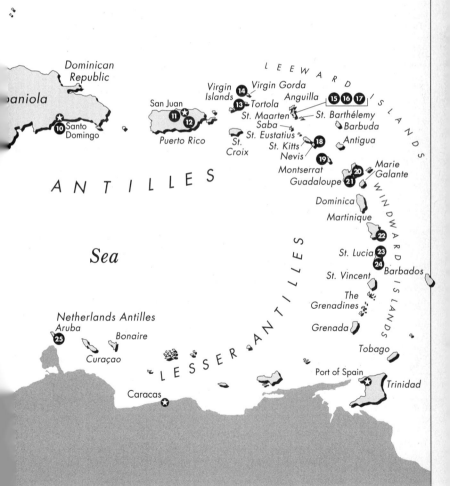

ATLANTIC OCEAN

LEEWARD ISLANDS

Dominican
Republic

aniola

10 Santo
Domingo

San Juan

Virgin
Islands

Virgin Gorda

Anguilla

15 16 17

11 ★

12

13 Tortola

St. Maarten

St. Barthélemy

Barbuda

Puerto Rico

Saba

St. Eustatius

Antigua

St.
Croix

St. Kitts

18

Nevis

19

Montserrat

Marie
Galante

Guadeloupe

20

21

A N T I L L E S

Dominica

Martinique

W I N D W A R D   I S L A N D S

Sea

22

St. Lucia

23

24 Barbados

St. Vincent

L E S S E R   A N T I L L E S

The
Grenadines

Netherlands Antilles

Grenada

Aruba

25

Bonaire

Curaçao

Tobago

Port of Spain ★ Trinidad

Caracas ★

V E N E Z U E L A

Hikers can enjoy panoramic, breezy views from paths cut into the rock.

Hyatt Regency Aruba Resort
L. G. Smith Blvd., Aruba
Tel. 29/783–1234 or 800/233–1234

Administration General Manager, Carlos Cabrera

Season Year-round.

Accommodations 360 rooms and suites in 9-story tower and 2 wings of 4 and 5 stories. Regency Club has 27 deluxe rooms, lounge, concierge service. All rooms are spacious, with balcony and full modern bath, queen-size beds. Air-conditioning, TV, telephone, maid service.

Rates $170–$430 daily, single or double occupancy, suite $450–$600; Credit-card confirmation. Credit cards: AE, DC, MC, V.

Meal Plans New heart-healthy options on main dining room menu. No special meal plan is available. Vegetarian dishes, fruit salad, grilled fish among daily selections. Snack bar in health spa has herbal teas, protein drinks, fruit.

Services and Facilities **Exercise Equipment:** Universal gym, StairMaster, Precor treadmill, Lifecycle, Concept II rowing machine, free weights. **Services:** Massage (Swedish, shiatsu, acupressure, reflexology). Beauty salon for hairstyling, manicure, pedicure. **Swimming Facilities:** Outdoor pool, ocean beach. **Recreation Facilities:** 2 tennis courts, water sports, cruiser and mountain bikes. **Evening Programs:** Carnival costume show and barbecue; casino.

In the Area Boats to underwater gardens; scuba and snorkeling. Marlab marine biology tour (3 hr) booked through DePalm Tours. Trail riding at Rancho El Paso (tel. 23310). Boca Prins (sand dunes, secluded beach), Chapel of Alto Vista (1750), Fort Zoutman (history museum) and Olde School Straat (colonial architecture) in Oranjestad, DePalm Island (recreation), Santa Anna Church (carved altar) in Noord, Cas di Cultura (concerts, art exhibits).

Getting Here *From airport.* By car, coastal road to L. G. Smith Blvd. (20 min). Bus, taxi, rental car, moped available.

Special Notes Ground-floor accommodations and elevators for the disabled. Children under 12 stay with parents free. No smoking in spa.

Sivananda Ashram Yoga Retreat

Spiritual awareness

The Bahamas
Paradise Island,
Nassau
A few steps from one of the best-known beaches in the Bahamas, secluded in a grove of pines and palm trees, is a unique combination of spiritual retreat and tropical holiday. Based on the teachings of Swami Vishnu Devananda, the yogic discipline and vegetarian diet at the Sivananda Ashram Yoga Retreat are identical to Sivananda ashrams in Canada, New York, and California, but the sunny climate and beach make this one of the best bargains anywhere.

The regimen is intensive; attendance at classes and meditations is mandatory for all guests. Mornings begin at 6 with a session of yogic exercises, or *asanas*, to stretch and invigorate the body. Brunch is served at 10, then you are free to enjoy the beach or a relaxing massage until the 4 PM yoga session.

The retreat attracts an international eclectic group of vacationers and yoga disciples. New students are given personal coaching in the 12 basic asanas, from headstands to spinal twists. Children are encouraged to join in.

Although there are glitzy hotels and casinos a short walk away, the environment here is totally suffused with a mystical quality—partly due to the quaint appearance of the buildings, some on stilts, some on houseboats. The main house, once the retreat of a wealthy family and leased since 1967 to the Sivananda group in appreciation for healing services, might have sunk into the sand long ago without the volunteer labor of the retreat members. Many guests prefer to bring their own tent and camp among the tropical shrubbery. Arrival can be any day; average stay is two weeks.

The retreat's informal atmosphere sharply contrasts with the structured schedule of classes. Based on five principles for a long and healthy life, the program focuses on proper exercise, breathing, diet, relaxation, and meditation techniques. The regimen demands total self-discipline and is designed to develop a better understanding of the mind-body connection.

The daily routine is gentle and, once you get accustomed to rising at 5:30 AM, can be quite stimulating. In a sense, it is preventive medicine, a way of warding off psychological and physical problems through rigorous training. People come here to recuperate from job burnout or to heal after surgery.

To provide the proper nutritional balance, there is an organic garden in which herbs and vegetables are grown. Coconuts come gratis from the palm trees that shelter the 4½-acre compound. For snacks and sweets, a canteen is tucked into a building near the communal laundry and shower facilities. After meals, guests wash their own plates and utensils and dry them on open-air racks. There's no air-conditioning at this retreat, but a new filtration system provides plenty of cool, chemical-free drinking water.

Sivananda Ashram Yoga Retreat
Box N7550, Paradise Island, Nassau, Bahamas
Tel. 809/363–2902
Fax 809/363–3783

Administration	Program director, Swami Shanmugananda
Season	Year-round.
Accommodations	Wooden huts on the beach, dormitory rooms, and cottages provide 103 beds. Furnished with 2–6 beds and table; linens and towels provided. Communal shower and toilet facilities, laundry equipment. Tent space: 50 sites.
Rates	$40–$55 daily, rooms shared by 2–6 persons. Single cabin $75. Beachfront meditation huts are preferred location. Tent space $30 per night. $200 advance payment. Credit cards: MC, V.
Meal Plans	The lacto-vegetarian diet includes midmorning meal of wholegrain cereal, fresh fruit, homemade yogurt and wheat bread. Dinner dishes include stirfried tofu and rice, steamed vegetables, green salad. No fish, meat, fowl, eggs, or coffee served.

Services and Facilities	**Services:** Massage (shiatsu, reflexology), personal counseling. **Swimming Facilities:** Ocean beach. **Recreation Facilities:** Tennis court, volleyball, walks. **Evening Programs:** Workshops in Hindu culture, philosophy. Concerts.
In the Area	Boat trips; botanical gardens, Colonial and Victorian architecture.
Getting Here	*From Nassau airport.* Shared taxi van (fixed fee) to Mermaid Marina, Bay and Deveaux streets. Shuttle service by Ashram boat operates on daily schedule.
Special Notes	Yoga training for children. No smoking on premises. Remember to bring beach towel, blankets during winter months.

Le Meridien Hotel & Villas

Luxury pampering
Non-program resort facilities

The Bahamas
Cable Beach,
Nassau

This grand manor, reeking of Colonial decadence, is stylishly managed by Le Meridien, and has one of the best little spas in the Bahamas. Created as part of a $9 million renovation in 1985, the Royal Bahamian Hotel & Villas facilities include mud baths and a large whirlpool, sauna and steam rooms, and an aerobics studio with exercise equipment.

The resort was originally a private reserve for the rich and titled and is still an oasis for those who seek peace and quiet. A modest strip of powdery sand, manicured gardens abloom with bougainvillea, and a parlor where tea is served with cucumber sandwiches are among the attractions enjoyed by its international clientele.

Tarted up but showing its age, the six-story hotel offers more spacious rooms than any of the fancier neighbors down the road. And for those with a taste for privacy (and the means) there are 10 villas, all pink with sugar-white roofs. Three are individual town houses—each boasting three bedrooms, a private pool, sun room, and a whirlpool in the master suite.

The spa can be reached by elevator in the main building or by a private entrance alongside the swimming pool terrace. Chrome and mirrors add a sleek, modern look to the smallish spaces where you can work out at leisure or book private treatments. Services are offered à la carte, billed to your account, or payable with credit card. Aerobics classes are complimentary to all guests weekdays at 10:30 AM and 6:30 PM.

Try a luxurious mud bath for the ultimate in body-stimulating treatments. The ancient therapy of soaking in herbs and algae has been re-created here with a mixture of peat mud taken from deposits in the Neydharting Valley Basin of northern Austria. The therapeutic effect soothes nerves, eliminates sleeplessness, improves circulation, and rejuvenates the skin.

Soaking in the mud bath is like stepping into a tub of yogurt. Dark in color—almost black—the formula leaves no stain while opening and closing the pores. Mixed with tap water, the odorless liquid easily showers off, leaving a visible sheen on the skin.

The mud treatment should be followed with a brief nap. An early dinner and full night's rest enhance the effect, as the body reacts to the healing substances absorbed during the bath.

The physiotherapy specialist Charles Bowleg is both manager and head masseur; a graduate of Dr. Swanson's School of Swedish Massage in Chicago, he returned to the Bahamas more than 30 years ago to work on the muscles of such notables as the Duke of Windsor, the prime minister of the Bahamas, and the screen star Sidney Poitier.

The facilities are designed to pamper and relax rather than give a serious workout. Outside guests can drop in for a day by making advance reservations for treatments. With one of the classiest restaurants on the island, the resort is the kind of place that makes you yearn for an extra day in which to do nothing.

For more active pursuits, try the sports center at the Crystal Palace complex. Just a few minutes' walk from the Royal Bahamian, the indoor, air-conditioned facilities include squash and racquetball/handball courts. Nearby is a championship 18-hole (par 72) golf course. Guests at both hotels get special rates. For a taste of Jamaican cooking, the Casuarinas Round House restaurant just across from the hotel entrance has a "Fit for Life" menu.

Le Meridien Hotel & Villas
Box N 10422, Cable Beach, Nassau, Bahamas
Tel. 809/327-6400 or 800/543-4300
Telex 20317

Administration	General manager, Abel Damergi; recreation director, Don Williams; fitness director, Charles Bowleg
Season	Year-round.
Accommodations	Beachfront main building has 145 rooms; villas and town houses offer suites with 25 bedrooms. Ocean view, twin queen-size beds, dressing room, twin baths with shower or bathtub, balcony. Cable TV, air-conditioning, bathrobes.
Rates	In winter, $165–$306 daily, single or double occupancy; summer $135–$200. Tariffs for suites/town houses depend on length of stay and include butler or maid service. First-night confirmation by credit card. Credit cards: AE, DC, MC, V.
Meal Plans	Buffet breakfast and dinner in Cafe Royale, dinner only (jacket and tie required) in Baccarat pavilion. Dinner offers innovative crossovers of Continental and island fare: Gâteau de Conch et Saint-Jacques au Safron is a mousse of Bahamian conch and scallops baked in delicate saffron sauce. Other specialties include grouper baked in pastry shell with sabayna sauce and rack of lamb dusted with herbs, roasted and broiled.
Services and Facilities	**Exercise Equipment:** Universal weight system (6 stations), 2 digital stationary bikes, treadmill. **Services:** Swedish massage, mud bath, facial, manicure, pedicure, waxing. **Swimming Facilities:** Outdoor freshwater pool, ocean beach. **Recreation Facilities:** 2 tennis courts, chess tables. Nearby bicycle rental, golf course, indoor sports center. **Evening Programs:** Casino and theater nearby, with complimentary transportation.
In the Area	Island tours, interisland flights, charter boats for fishing and scuba; Seafloor Aquarium (performing dolphins and sea lions),

Fort Charlotte, botanic garden, Adastra Gardens (performing flamingos), Junkanoo Art Gallery.

Getting Here *From airport.* By car, coastal road (10 min). Jitney minibus for trips into town. Taxi, rental car available.

Special Notes Elevator to all floors of main building. No smoking in spa or designated dining areas. Spa hours: daily 9 AM–7:30 PM.

Silver Reef Spa

Luxury pampering
Weight management

The Bahamas
Freeport, Grand Bahama
New in 1990, the Silver Reef Spa is set on a 10-acre bayside estate complete with fishing dock, water sports, and aerobics studio. The emphasis is on exercise, weight loss, and beauty treatments—all included in programs lasting from two days to a week.

Cottages surrounding the main house provide accommodations for a maximum of 24 guests. Decorated by a local artist, each cottage has floral motifs to complement antiques and island handcrafted furnishings. In the large house there is a library, dining room with outdoor terrace, and music room where evening programs are presented. Housed in one of the cottages are massage rooms, a sauna, and special equipment for treatments.

Staff members offer the most extensive selection of services in the Bahamas; employees trained in European therapies, usher guests through a carefully balanced regimen. While the scheduled classes range from low-impact aerobics and aquacise to yoga, the instructors give each guest one-on-one training. Beginning with a fitness evaluation and an analysis of your nutritional needs, a personal schedule is developed. Diet options include supervised juice fasting.

Workouts on gym equipment are less important than participating in the program. Free time is provided for use of the water-sports equipment and optional outings by private plane and boat. Staff members provide transportation to shopping, beaches, and a golf course.

Silver Reef Spa
Box F–773, Freeport, Grand Bahama
Tel. 809/373–7761
Reservations: 188 Eagle Rock Ave., Roseland, NJ 07068
Tel. 800/458–9772

Administration Owner/manager, Cay Gottlieb; spa director, Dana Hall

Season Year-round.

Accommodations 27 guest rooms in cottages and main house. Furnished with antiques, twin beds, each with private bath. Air-conditioned, TV, telephone. Penthouse suite with private Jacuzzi.

Rates All-inclusive 7-night package $1,000–1,300 per person double, $1,600–2,300 single. 2-night package $245–$475 per person double occupancy, $355–$775 single; 4-night package $490–$750 double, $1,000–$1,350 single. Taxes added; gratuities optional. Deposit: 2-nights' accommodation. Credit cards: AE, MC, V.

Meal Plans 3 spa-cuisine meals daily included in program. Menu offers choice of entree for lunch and dinner. Featured are fish from local waters, home-grown vegetables. Optional juice fast.

Services and Facilities **Exercise Equipment:** Universal gym units, stationary bike. **Services:** Swedish massage, shiatsu, facial, collagen treatment, mud pack, anticellulite treatment; hair, nail, and skin care; fitness evaluation, nutrition analysis. **Swimming Facilities:** Outdoor pool, dock. **Recreation Facilities:** Tennis and croquet courts, volleyball, bicycles, rowboats, sailboat. **Evening Programs:** Musical entertainment, talks on health.

Getting Here *From Miami.* By air, Bahamasair and commuter services (30 min). By sea, SeaEscape one-way cruise (4 hr). Transfers provided. Taxi, rental car available in Freeport.

Sonesta Beach Hotel & Spa

Life enhancement
Luxury pampering
Non-program resort facilities

Bermuda
Southampton

Weight maintenance is the principle at the Sonesta Beach Hotel & Spa. You can drop in between business meetings or after a round of golf or plan a comprehensive schedule of treatments and exercise classes for three to seven days. Package plans can begin any day of the week.

The flexibility of planning your own program is a plus, but only if you are prepared to work with the spa staff. They will do a preliminary fitness assessment; don't expect counseling. The emphasis is on relaxation and beauty treatments, not strenuous exercise. Even the diet plan is optional.

Aerobics are moderate or vigorous, plotted over 30- or 40-minute periods, alternating active and passive exercise with relaxing stretches. You can select from early morning walks (moderate), circuit training (vigorous), workouts in the water, and yoga. And don't miss the loofah body scrub.

If you simply want to be pampered and left alone to swim or shop, there is a three-day "spa refresher break." For women who want to learn nutrition, exercise, and beauty skills, an exclusive eight-day program is offered. Spouses get a discount when they aren't participating in a spa program.

For a person who wants to try many different activities and treatments, there are dance exercise routines and easy aerobics, hiking and walking on the beach, and clinics devoted to awareness of proper posture for exercise and running. All can be included in a spa package, or you can simply pay a daily facility charge ($15) and use the whirlpool baths, Finnish sauna, Turkish steam bath, and Universal equipment room.

Separate facilities for men and women offer privacy when you want to soak and relax. Workout clothing is provided daily; a leotard, warm-up suit, gym shorts, shirt, robe, and slippers.

Sonesta Beach Hotel & Spa
Southampton, Bermuda
Tel. 809/238–8122 or 800/766–3782
Fax 809/238–8463

Bersalon Co. Ltd.
Box HM1044, Hamilton HM EX, Bermuda
Tel. 809/292–8570 or 809/238–1226
Fax 809/295–2506

Administration	Spa director, Michael J. Ternent; general manager, David Boyd; assistant spa manager, Diane Horbacewicz
Season	Year-round.
Accommodations	25-acre peninsula setting. 6-story hotel and Bay Wing suites with 403 guest rooms, ocean or bay view. Spacious split-level units have sitting area and dressing room, full bath, modern rattan furniture, floor-to-ceiling windows, balcony or patio (all rooms). Queen- or king-size beds, full carpeting, air conditioning, color TV, telephone.
Rates	3-night Spa Sampler package $953 per person double occupancy; $1,296 single. 3-night Couples or Mother/Daughter package, $2,022 for 2, double occupancy; 4-night Eurospa package $1,435 per person double, $1,892 single; 5-night Inch Away Slimming Plan $1,894 double, $2,466 single. 2-night payment at booking. Credit cards: AE, DC, MC, V.
Meal Plans	Breakfast and dinner daily included in 3- and 4-night packages, 3 meals daily in Inch Away package. Optional diet plan, 800–1,000 calories per day; can be developed by staff nutritionist after a personal consultation. Spa meals in separate section of the main dining room. Breakfast may be a wholegrain cereal with fruit; lunch, a garden salad or cold seafood platter. Dinner entrees include grilled swordfish, vegetarian lasagna, and skewers of vegetables broiled with sea scallops. 2 juice breaks are included in the daily program.
Services and Facilities	**Exercise Equipment:** Universal weight training gym (8 stations), aerobicycle, computerized bicycle. Total Hip machine. **Services:** Massage (Swedish, aromatherapy, reflexology, G-5 mechanical), facials for men and women, loofah body scrub, herbal wrap, manicure, pedicure, cellulite control treatments, European facial treatments. Hairstyling and beauty-salon services. Consultation on fitness, nutrition, and makeup; skin-fold test, facial skin analysis. Passive reducing treatments with Vivatone; Therabath treatments for hands and feet; depilatory treatments. **Swimming Facilities:** Outdoor freshwater pool, indoor pool, 3 ocean beaches. **Recreation Facilities:** 6 lighted tennis courts, volleyball, badminton, croquet, shuffleboard, table tennis. Golf and bicycle rental nearby. Water sports include helmet and scuba diving, windsurfing. Horseback riding available at Spicelands Riding Centre, Warwick. **Evening Programs:** Resort entertainment.
In the Area	Island tours; St. George's (replica of colonists' ship *Deliverance*), Blue Grotto (dolphin show), Verdmont House (Georgian antiques), Hamilton (shopping, museums), Maritime Museum (ship replicas).
Getting Here	*From airport.* By taxi, North Shore Rd. to South Rd. (45 min). Public bus for trips to town. Frequent ferry service to points on the island. Moped available.

Special Notes Play area in gardens for children; under 18 not permitted in spa. No smoking in spa or designated sections of the dining room.

Renaissance Jaragua Resort

Luxury pampering

Dominican Republic
Santo Domingo

The Jaragua Resort is an impressive Caribbean casino-cum-spa in the center of the hemisphere's oldest capital city. A few minutes' drive from the flashy ocean boulevard is the colonial capital founded by Bartholomew Columbus, the brother of the Discoverer. Vacationers can combine culture and fitness with casino action.

The new and the old meet on Avenida George Washington, a lively strip of hotels, restaurants, and shops fronting the ocean. There is no beach here, but spa goers hardly notice; with an oversize swimming pool surrounded by tropical gardens, Scandinavian saunas, Turkish steam bath, Roman whirlpool, and cold plunge, the resort complex has an ample supply of water sports. Daily beach trips are complimentary.

The freestanding fitness facility is a world unto itself. All marble and glass, it is an oasis of aerobics and bodywork. You work out on the latest in exercise equipment or join a calisthenics class. Exercise is scheduled in the Olympic-size swimming pool, as well as in the air-conditioned cushion-floored aerobics studio.

Pampering services come in several packages or à la carte. You can get an herbal wrap, a body scrub, a facial, or a massage. Grandly titled the European Spa, the facilities include no thalassotherapy tubs or seawater treatments, but you may bliss out in a private Jacuzzi, then get a surge of energy from the cold plunge.

The daily entrance fee of $10 is waived when you book a Jaragua Energizer, with massage, for $25 or a 4-day/3-night Tropical Tone-Up. With this come robe and slippers, and snacks of fresh fruit and juices throughout the day.

Secluded on 14½ palm-fringed acres, the resort has a tennis stadium with four clay courts and spectator seating. During the day this facility can be used by spa guests free of charge. From your room it's a pleasant walk or jog through the garden and alongside the lagoon to the spa. Serious spa buffs may find the program too loose; your best bet is to relax and join the merengue beat.

Renaissance Jaragua Resort
367 George Washington Ave., Santo Domingo
Tel. 809/221–2222 or 800/228–9898

Administration General manager, Alvaro Soto; spa manager, Donna Perez-Mera

Season Year-round.

Accommodations New 10-story Jaragua Tower and an older 2-level wing of garden suites provide 355 luxury rooms. 6 suites with butler, marble baths. All rooms with modern rattan furniture, large bath with magnified makeup mirror, hair dryer. Air-conditioned, carpeted; 3 telephones with direct dial, color cable TV, decorative works by Dominican artists.

Rates $108–$135 daily for 2 persons. 3-night Custom Spa Vacation package $734 single, $530 per person double occupancy; 6-night $1,357 single, $916 double. Tax and gratuities included in packages. Payment for 1 night at time of booking. Credit cards: AE, DC, MC, V.

Meal Plans   3 daily spa-cuisine meals included in packages. Choice of four restaurants: Latin American Cafe for meats char-broiled, grilled, or cooked on a spit; Oriental Cafe for stirfry specialties; fresh homemade pasta in the Italian Cafe; New York deli.

Services and Facilities   **Exercise Equipment:** Nautilus gym (10 stations), stationary bicycles, treadmills, rowing machine, free weights. **Services:** Swedish massage, loofah body scrub, herbal wrap, facial. Fitness evaluation. Beauty salon for hair, nail, and skin care. **Swimming Facilities:** Olympic-size outdoor pool. **Recreation Facilities:** 4 lighted tennis courts. **Evening Programs:** Casino theater; National Theater for concerts and opera.

In the Area   Daily beach trip (complimentary), walking tour of the colonial area, Columbus lighthouse museum. Cathedral of Santa Maria la Menor (oldest in the Hemisphere, Columbus monument), Museum of the Royal Houses in the colonial quarter; Gallery of Modern Art and Natural History Museum downtown; National Botanical Gardens (train ride) in northern section of the city; Altos de Chavon (artisans, museum of Taino Indian artifacts) near La Romana. Baseball (Oct.–Feb.), Merengue Festival (July), Polo (Casa de Campo).

Getting Here   *From airport.* By taxi (45 min). Public bus, rental car available.

Special Notes   Elevators and ramps to all levels for the disabled. No smoking in the spa. Spa hours: daily 7 AM–8 PM.

Centre Thermal Harry Hamousin

Taking the waters
Non-program resort facilities

Guadeloupe
Saint-Claude   Christopher Columbus saw the volcano La Soufrière erupting when he stepped ashore November 4, 1493, at Sainte-Marie, a fishing village along the road to the island's present-day capital, Basse-Terre. The native Caribs were not hospitable to the Discoverer. All that's left of that time are primitive drawings scratched into black rocks at Trois-Rivières, where the road branches toward a nature preserve around La Soufrière.

The new discovery is Centre Thermal Harry Hamousin, a therapy center that taps the natural healing power of the mineral springs. French hydrotherapy equipment and therapists trained at leading French spas provide treatments for rheumatism, asthma, and dermatology problems. The classic "cure" has come to the Caribbean.

As an overseas department of France (not a colony or an independent country), Guadeloupe offers its citizens all the benefits of the mother country, including health coverage for the cost of spa therapy. Thus the Centre Thermal Harry Hamousin, a private institution, enjoys a steady stream of visitors from Europe and other islands in the French Antilles. Opened in 1978 with state-of-the-art facilities, the center now welcomes any visitors needing massage or special therapy.

Physical training to aid recovery from injuries includes exercise in shallow pools of mineral water and on special equipment in the gymnasium. Respiratory problems are treated with aerosol-like inhalations of mineral water. There are douches with high-powered jets of water and sulfur baths.

The thermal center is open every morning except Sunday and accepts reservations for one-time treatments. Serious problems require consultation with a doctor at the nearby clinic Les Eaux Vives. Arrangements can be made by your hotel or directly with the clinic, and medical records should be brought along for the interview with *le médecin thermal*. Several doctors speak English if your French isn't sufficient.

Hotel arrangements are not provided by the center. One of the most interesting places to stay is the Hotel Relais de la Grande Soufrière. Located at the base of the volcano, it reflects the old-world charm of the banana plantations that cover nearby fields. Once a government-owned *relais*, or country inn, the hotel is now under private management. The dining room is popular with local families and businessmen who escape from the city for lunch.

The attractions of the island include the Nature Park; the spectacular three-tiered Carbet Falls near Capesterre, reached by a moderately difficult hike that starts at the end of Habituée Road; the Grand Etang (Great Pond), surrounded by luxuriant vegetation; and La Grivelière, an atmospheric old coffee plantation near Vieux Habitants.

Guadeloupe cuisine is a fascinating mixture of Gallic and African flavors. Among the best places to sample this spicy food is La Canne a Sucre (tel. 83–58–48), near the fashionable Point-à-Pitre shops, and La Plantation (tel. 90–84–83), overlooking the marina at Bas du Fort. Wherever you go on this butterfly-shaped island there are wonderful native cooks offering inexpensive homemade meals.

On market days the stalls are filled with herb sellers hawking natural seasonings and medicines: *matriquin*, Marie-Perrine, *zhèbe-gras*, *fleupapillon*, *bois-de l'homme*, *bonnet-carré*, and the like. All the tastes and stimulations of the old Carib Indian flavorings and remedies are still on sale, alongside modern pharmacies and boutiques laden with Parisian fashions.

Centre Thermal Harry Hamousin
97120 Saint-Claude, Guadeloupe
Tel. 590/89–53–53
Fax 590/80–06–08

Hotel Relais de la Grande Soufrière
97120 Saint-Claude, Guadeloupe
Tel. 590/80–01–27, Fax 590/8001–025

Administration Director, Harry Beaubois; medical director, Dr. Henri Corenthin

Season Year-round.

Accommodations 22-room plantation great house decorated with fine antiques. Spacious and airy rooms have no air-conditioning, telephone, or TV. All have private bath.

Rates Daily hotel tariff is 250–300 French francs, single, 200–250 francs per person double occupancy. Clinique Les Eaux Vives 21-day rheumatism therapy 1,330 francs. Breakfast 30 francs; meal plans additional 150–270 francs daily. 1 night advance payment. Credit cards: AE, MC, V.

Meal Plans No diet plan available. Creole cooking specialties include spicy fritters, *accras de morue* (salt cod), stuffed land crab, called crabs *farcis;* goat stew; classic *boudin* sausage.

Services and Facilities **Exercise Equipment:** Weight training units, treadmills. **Services:** Massage, underwater massage, steam cabinet, loofah body scrub, Scotch douche, skin peeling, acupuncture, physical therapy. **Swimming Facilities:** Outdoor pool. **Spa Facilities:** Therapy pool, hydrotherapy tubs. **Recreation Facilities:** Hiking, nearby beaches.

In the Area Ferry to Les Saintes (natural bathing), organized hiking with Friends of the Nature Park, scuba at Club Med.; Basse-Terre gardens and Prefecture, botanical garden, Fête des Cuisinères (mid-Aug.), Neuf Château (experimental orchard).

Getting Here *From airport.* By car, coastal road to Trois Rivières, Allée Dumanoir, Route de la Traversée (50 min). Rental car, taxi, public bus available.

Special Notes No smoking in the center. Remember to bring passport and medical certificate.

Hotel PLM Azur-Marissol

Luxury pampering

Guadeloupe
Gosier
French and American fitness regimens merge at the large and popular Hotel PLM Azur-Marissol beach resort. Set in a tropical garden perfumed by blossoms, the facilities include a "hammam" steam room and private rooms for massage and thalassotherapy. Light gymnastics on the beach and stretching exercises in the swimming pool are offered at no extra charge for all guests.

The Gym Tropique is open daily, except Sunday, 8 AM–8 PM. There is a coed steam room, aerobics studio, and hydrotherapy tubs but no exercise equipment. Workout clothing is provided daily.

European spa treatments included in the week-long fitness package are a plus: underwater massage, steam baths, a facial, and whirlpool treatment with seaweed and oils. Classes are scheduled for yoga and aerobics, all optional.

The program, which can begin any day of the week, includes group hiking in the Parc Natural. Most of the guests are French, with an interesting mix of Canadians and Americans. Designed for fun and fitness, the program rejuvenates strung-out bodies and souls with a blend of Gallic style and disco routines.

Hotel PLM Azur-Marissol
Bas-du-Fort, 97190 Gosier, Guadeloupe
Tel. 590/909398 or 800/221–4542
Telex 919855 GL; Fax 590/938332

Administration	Manager, Nicole Duval
Season	Year-round.
Accommodations	200 air-conditioned rooms (50 bungalows) with terrace or loggia. Modern furniture accented with island fabrics and prints. All rooms have private bath, radio, direct-dial telephone, color TV with satellite programs.
Rates	7-night package $994–$1,199 per person double occupancy, $1,245–$1,450 single. Daily rate $160–$204. 25% payment at time of booking. Credit cards: MC, V.
Meal Plans	Fitness package includes breakfast and dinner. Breakfast buffet includes yogurt, croissants, granola, fresh fruit. Selections from the dinner menu include steamed vegetables, fresh grilled fish, salads. Grilled specialties: veal scallops, entrecote steak, seafood brochette.
Services and Facilities	**Services:** Massage, body wrap with seaweed, underwater massage, whirlpool bath with seaweed, skin and nail care. **Swimming Facilities:** Outdoor freshwater pool, ocean beach. **Recreation Facilities:** Tennis, hiking, water sports.
In the Area	Scuba, mountain hiking; thermal mineral-water treatments at Centre Harry Hamousin, Nature Park, La Soufrière (volcano).
Getting Here	*From airport.* Complimentary transfers on arrival and departure. Taxi, rental car available.
Special Notes	No smoking in fitness center.

Charlie's Spa at the Sans Souci

Luxury pampering
Taking the waters
Life enhancement
Weight management

Jamaica *Ocho Rios*	Charlie's Spa takes a fresh approach to island holidays. More hedonistic than health-oriented, the resort atmosphere up on the hill complements vigorous workouts on the beach. It's a pleasant combination if you're interested in toning up or taking off a few pounds.

With the sea on one side and a cascade of mineral water on the other, the spa provides instant stress reduction. The waters, however, are not used for therapy or beauty treatments; you can soak or swim at leisure, and you may join an exercise class in the pool.

Long noted as a luxurious hideaway, Sans Souci came under new management a few years ago and revamped the facilities— and its image. Sans Souci upgraded all guest rooms, adding marble bathrooms with whirlpool tubs and amenities such as hair dryers and robes. New cottages and an open-air aerobics pavilion were designed to blend with the old-world ambience of the hotel. Introduced for the first time in the Caribbean were beauty treatments and a nutritious diet that work together.

The result is a program that offers more than the sum of its parts.

Begin with a fast-paced walk through the terraced gardens and along the curve of beach where tennis courts and water sports await your pleasure. After Blue Mountain coffee, freshly squeezed orange juice, and a muffin or banana porridge, you have a wide variety of options to fill your day—within the program at Charlie's Spa or on your own. Anyone staying at the resort can join in the group activities and take treatments à la carte.

Appointments are scheduled in the tiny spa office alongside a pool that's home to mascot Charlie, a huge sea turtle who thrives in the mineral water. The Hideaway is a charming gazebo on the rocks, just big enough for a private massage. Facials and other treatments are given inside a tiny wooden cottage.

The grotto conceals a dry sauna next to steps entering the sea. The shallow water here is a mix of saltiness and refreshingly cool mineral water from the springs. It's ideal for washing off oils and salts used for body scrubs (depending on your skin type, it can be aloe, peppermint, or coconut, plus cornmeal).

Sybarites can enjoy a secluded soak, free of charge, by climbing down a wooden ladder at a second grotto where the springwater seeps into a sand-bottom pool; or sunbathing on an upper-floor terrace among the treetops.

Charlie's Spa at the Sans Souci
Box 103, Ocho Rios, Jamaica
Tel. 809/974-2353 or 800/237-3237 or 800/654-1337
Telex 7496; Fax 809/974-2544

Administration | General manager, Werner Dietl; spa director, Margaret Spencer

Season | Year-round.

Accommodations | 111 suites and rooms in villa-style buildings overlooking gardens and the sea. All are air-conditioned, with private balcony. Main building nearby houses the Casanova Restaurant and bar/lounge. New wing of beach terrace suites, French restaurant.

Rates | Charlie's Spa Program, $398 daily per person (4 night minimum); 7-night package for 2, $3,579, $2,323 single. L'Espirit de' Sans Souci all-inclusive package per week, $1,400–$1,640 per person, double; European Plan (no meals) $200–$470 per night, double. Tax and service charge included with packages. 3-night deposit due within 2 weeks after reservation; cancellation must be received 30 days prior to scheduled arrival to avoid charges. Credit cards: AE, DC, MC, V.

Meal Plans | Breakfast, lunch, and dinner included in spa package. Calorie-counted spa menu includes breakfast of sliced pineapple, granola, or eggwhite omelet with wholewheat toast; lunch can be a grilled tuna sandwich, shrimp ceviche, tagliartelle primavera, or Niçoise salad; dinner includes seafood fettuccine, smoked marlin appetizer, broiled lobster or vegetarian lasagna.

Services and Facilities | **Exercise Equipment:** 2 Tunturi bikes, barbells (15–44 lbs.), benches, free weights, 4-station Universal unit on the beach beneath the aerobics studio. **Services:** Massage, aromatherapy, reflexology, fango mud body and face treatment, paraffin wax hand and foot treatment, seaweed wrap, body scrub, facial;

beauty salon for hair, nail, and skin care. **Swimming Facilities:** 2 pools and a private beach. **Spa Facilities:** Mineral springwater swimming and soaking pools. **Recreation Facilities:** Complimentary greens fee at Upton Country Club (18-hole golf course), St. Ann Polo Club; horseback riding at Chukka Cove, tennis and instruction on Sans Souci's 4 courts (2 lighted); croquet lawn; complimentary use of sailboat, snorkeling, surfboard, and scuba equipment. **Evening Programs:** Folkloric groups, combo for dancing on terrace.

In the Area Tour operators in Ocho Rios offer group and private car trips to area attractions. At Prospect Plantation (agricultural training center), a guided tour and horseback trail rides are available.

Getting Here *From Montego Bay Airport.* Transfers (about 2 hr) are included in package plans. Air Jamaica has frequent nonstop flights from U.S. cities and Canada. Taxi or limousine available at all times.

Special Notes For the disabled, elevator connects guest rooms with spa facilities on the beach. (Hillside location of the hotel requires considerable stair climbing.)

The Enchanted Garden

Non-program resort facilities

Jamaica Set amid 20 acres of rain forest, botanical gardens, waterfalls,
Ocho Rios and rolling lawns, this all-inclusive, leafy retreat was designed as an alternative to the island's other, more active beach resorts. Activities include spa services, golf, and horseback riding; guests may float in a natural pool, get massaged under a waterfall or in one of the private garden nooks where a masseuse awaits with aromatherapy.

The spa is a cheerful, air-conditioned hideway. Ambitious plans for beauty and fitness services are listed, but only the basics, (massage, facial, manicure, pedicure) are available regularly. The limited selection of exercise equipment may be a disappointment for fitness buffs, though the facilities do include a Turkish steambath, Finnish sauna, outdoor whirlpools, and Swiss showers with multiple heads.

Organized outings include trips to nearby Prospect Plantation for trail rides, minigolf, and guided tours in an open-air tram. The golf course is also nearby, and a daily excursion to the beach comes complete with lunch and drinks. Climbing the falls at the Enchanted garden can be just as challenging as at Dunn's River, and less crowded.

The Enchanted Garden
Box 284, Ocho Rios, Jamaica W.I.
Tel. 809/974–1400 or 800/323–5655
Fax 809/974–5823

Administration Owner/director, Edward Seaga; general manager, Richard Mercer

Season Year-round.

Accommodations 129 bedrooms in 87 hillside suites. 40 deluxe, modern town houses include sunken living room, private patio with plunge pool, kitchen. TV with satellite channels, telephone, air-conditioning, maid and turndown service.

Rates Weekly all-inclusive package $900–$1,400 per person, double occupancy May–Dec. 14, $1,100–$1,500 Dec. 15–Apr. 30. Taxes and gratuities included. 50% advance payment. Credit cards: AE, MC, V.

Meal Plans 3 meals, snacks, afternoon tea, and open-bar included in daily rate. Specialty restaurants feature pasta, Middle Eastern, and Far Eastern cuisine. Continental fare at L'Eau Mirage includes tropical fruit, omelet, cereal, and Jamaican specialties at breakfast and lunch, seafood at dinner prepared to order. Vegetarian meals available on request.

Services and Facilities **Exercise Equipment:** 2 stationary bikes, rowing machine, free weights. **Services:** Aromatherapy massage, facial, body scrub, herbal wrap, manicure, pedicure. **Swimming Facilities:** 3 outdoor swimming pools, nearby ocean beach. **Recreation Facilities:** Tennis, aviary, nearby golf and riding, water volleyball, reggae lessons. **Evening Programs:** Nightclub, Jamaican show and buffet dinner (Friday).

Getting Here Complimentary transfers from Montego Bay airport. Taxi, rental car available.

Special Notes Minimum age 16. No tipping allowed.

Jamaican Mineral Springs

Taking the waters

Jamaica
Milk River and Bath

Getting off the beaten track is easy, but you need a car to explore some of the most scenic areas of the hilly island of Jamaica. In addition to breathtaking vistas there are botanical gardens, a bird sanctuary, and two spas built around mineral springs that have been attracting cure seekers for nearly two centuries.

Legend holds that an African slave, wounded in an uprising, was healed by bathing in pools of water fed by hot springs located high in the lush valleys between Kingston and Port Antonio. English plantation owners seeking respite from the coastal heat spread the word. By the beginning of the 18th century there was a spa hotel, church, and botanical garden for cultivation of medicinal herbs in the town of Bath. What remains today is primitive, nothing like its Georgian namesake in England. The waters, however, still gush forth in a setting of tropical splendor enjoyed by hill people and an occasional visitor.

From the town, a narrow road cuts through fern gulleys alongside the Sulphur River to reach Bath Fountain Hotel. Cut into rocks beneath the hotel are private chambers where you can soak in the sulfurous warm water. European spa experts have confirmed high levels of radioactivity, equal to the best springs on the continent.

The hotel's 10 guest rooms are airy, simply furnished. Meals are prepared to order in the public dining room (no credit cards). *Bath Fountain Hotel, Bath, St. Thomas Parish. Rooms cost $350 (Jam.) per night, without private bath; $420–$473 (Jam.) with bathroom, for 2 persons.*

West of Kingston's high-rise government center, past agricultural and industrial developments, is the former capital city, Spanish Town, and from there you can reach the Milk River spa in about two hours. Stop to admire the main square, surrounded by Georgian buildings that date from 1762. One now houses the Jamaican People's Museum of Craft and Technology. A classical statue of Admiral George Rodney commemorates his 1792 naval victory over the French that saved the British colony.

Continuing westward on Route B12 past the market town of May Pen, you reach the Milk River near a crossroads called Toll Gate. Built on a hillside, the spa hotel has private cubicles hewn from stone that are filled directly from the springs. Here, too, an analysis of the water in 1952 confirmed a high degree of radioactivity and minerals, similar to that of the best European spa waters.

Although there are no special treatments or exercise equipment, the hotel has a large outdoor swimming pool filled with the cool mineral water. Ocean beaches and citrus groves are a few miles away. Trout Hall, which produces *ugli* fruit, can be visited on request.

Most of the guests at Milk River come to soak three times a day, reserving cubicles with the receptionist. Bottles of mineral water are on the tables in the dining room. The hotel has seen better days (and may again); the 22 guest rooms are simple, clean, and inexpensive, with two meals included in the daily tariff.

Milk River Spa and Hotel
Milk River Post Office, Clarendon, Jamaica
Tel. 809/924–9544

Administration General manager, Desmond Edwards

Rates Double room with private bath $900 (Jam.) for 2 persons, single room with private bath $600 (Jam.) with 2 meals daily, tax and service included. Credit cards: MC, V.

Pine Grove Guest House

Non-program resort facilities

Jamaica Hiking the mist-shrouded vales and jungle-lined rivers that
The Blue crisscross the rugged Blue Mountains is an adventure for back-
Mountains packers and experienced walkers. The Pine Grove Hotel is a convenient base, easily reached by car from Kingston. The chalets and dining room command breathtaking views of the mountains and the city far below. Outings can be arranged to the Mavis Bank Coffee Factory, where beans are sorted by hand before roasting, and to Charlottenburg House, an antiques-filled example of a coffee plantation Great House. Naturalists will discover rare specimens of Asam tea plants and the cinchona tree (whose bark is a source of quinine) cultivated since 1868 at the Cinchona Botanical Gardens.

The hotel owners, Marcia and Ronald Thwaites, will arrange for guides if you want to see the sun rise above the island's tallest peak. This difficult trek reaches 5,402 feet and requires proper personal gear.

Pine Grove Guest House
c/o 62 Duke St., Kingston, Jamaica
Tel. 809/922–8705

Administration	General manager, Marcia Thwaites
Season	Year-round.
Accommodations	12 rooms in single-level lodges. Private bathrooms, no air-conditioning.
Rates	$70 daily per room for 2 persons, including tax. Meals à la carte. No credit cards. 10% Service charge added.

Swept Away

Sports conditioning   *Couples only*

Jamaica As a counterpoint to the laid-back pace of life on the beach at
Negril Jamaica's westernmost point, the new Swept Away resort
stresses a sports and fitness regimen within its 20-acre complex. Included in the rates are unlimited use of the island's first
indoor air-conditioned racquetball and squash courts, tennis
lessons with resident professionals, and a fully equipped dive
shop.

From the open-air reception area, paths lead to 26 two-story
villas set rather close together in beachside gardens. The standard villa has four minisuites arranged on two levels around a
plant-filled atrium. It is a quiet environment, far removed from
the frenetic pace of most vacation villages, but plenty of action
vibrates at the tennis complex and around the beach bar and
pool. Most guests are young couples, some are honeymooners.

Set apart from the villas by the island's main road is the sports
center. At the reception desk you can book courts, massages,
and check on scheduled classes in the aerobics pavilion. An
Olympic-length lap pool is used for aquacise sessions.

Tennis buffs get workouts with such pros as Noel Rutherford.
There is a ball machine and racquet stringing equipment. If you
haven't brought a racquet, there's no problem; equipment can
be loaned.

Massage therapy is close at hand; two rooms are in a thatch-roofed pavilion in the center of the sports complex, complete
with outdoor Jacuzzi. (Massage is not part of the all-inclusive
package; charges go on your account.)

The weights room here is an open-air pavilion with high-tech
German equipment. Instructors are on hand throughout the
day to coach you on proper use of the equipment.

In the clubhouse are men's and women's locker rooms with
steam rooms and saunas. A sports-theme bar with big-screen
TV opens at noon, and there is an open-air restaurant. Resort
guests can dine here at no extra charge.

With the fitness facilities comes unlimited use of water-sports
equipment: Windsurfing, kayaking, sunfish sailing, paddle-boating, and water skiing are all featured. Snorkeling gear is
also provided, as well as outings in a glass-bottom boat. For certified divers, scuba trips to nearby reefs depart three times daily in the resort's own dive boat. A certification course is
available for an extra fee.

With the ambience of a private club, Swept Away allows you to set your own pace. Bicycles are available when you want to explore the area's more lively beaches at leisure. Relax on your veranda and enjoy the sunset. Room service delivers afternoon tea or Continental breakfast at your bidding while you soak up the romantic vista. In the two-level beachside dining pavilion, diversions range from billiards and a piano bar to a games room with a big-screen color TV that brings in stateside programs. Many guests seem content to simply lounge by the seaside freshwater pool; snacks are always available at the juice and veggie bar.

Swept Away
Box 77, Long Bay, Negril, Jamaica
Tel. 809/957-4040 or 800/545-7937;
in U.S., 212/941-9239
Fax 809/957-4060

Administration General manager, Freddie DePass; spa manager, Susan Rodehaver

Season Year-round.

Accommodations 134 suites housed in 2-story villas. Jamaican handwork adds to the tropical look of rooms with wooden louvered walls, furnished with rattan rocker and wicker chairs, and plush cushions. King-size beds have cedar headboard; warm colors and earth-toned materials include decorative clay masks, lamps, and floor tiles. Private veranda; air conditioner, ceiling fan, telephone.

Rates Per couple daily rates range from $357–$486. Choice of villa: garden, sea view, beachfront. Packages for 4 days/3 nights from $855 to $1,080; 8 days/7 nights $2,500–$3,500 per couple. Rates include all meals, use of sports equipment and fitness facilities with instruction, alcoholic beverages, gratuities, and hotel taxes. Airport transfers provided. Deposit: Payment of 50% with confirmation. Credit cards: AE, DC, MC, V.

Meal Plan Buffet breakfast and lunch, dinner served by candlelight. Spa-cuisine options include egg-white omelet cooked to order, hot and cold cereals for breakfast. Lunch can be steamed vegetables, skinless chicken breast, baked fish. Dinner entrees include goat chops in phyllo dough, curried-goat stew, grilled fish in fruit sauce, homemade fish pâté, pasta. Jamaican buffet on Friday evening includes ackee strudel made with native applelike vegetable. Beach bar serves pita sandwich with tuna fish or chicken, fruit, vegetables, juices, beer, and bottled water. Italian restaurant at sports complex open for lunch and dinner has calorie-controlled pizza and pasta.

Services and Facilities **Exercise Equipment:** 22-unit weight training gym, free weights and dumbbells (5–100 lbs), 2 Lifecycles, Liferower, Stairclimber. **Services:** Swedish massage (extra charge); tennis clinics and private lessons, introduction to scuba. **Swimming Facilities:** 2 outdoor freshwater pools, ocean beach, clothing-optional beach. **Recreation Facilities:** 10 tennis courts (4 hard-surface, 5 clay), jogging track, basketball court, 2 racquetball courts, 2 squash courts; dive shop with 3 trips daily. **Evening Programs:** Nightly dancing, band and show weekends.

In the Area Paradise Park (18th-century plantation), Great Morass (bird sanctuary), Savanna-la-Mar (19th-century sugar port), Milk River Bath (geothermal springs).

Getting Here *From Montego Bay.* By car, round-trip transfers provided (1½ hr). By air, scheduled air taxi service. Rental car, taxi available.

Special Notes Ground-floor accommodations for the disabled. No children.

Centre de Thalassothérapie du Carbet

Taking the waters
Life enhancement

Martinique Seawater and kinesitherapy are the basis of an aquatic workout
Carbet   at the indoor pools of the Centre de Thalassothérapie near Fort-de-France, capital city of the island. Considered effective in the treatment of rheumatism, the four-step procedure takes about 2½ hours and costs 300 francs.

Beginning with a plunge into heated seawater (33°C), you may participate in group exercise or simply relax. The pool has built-in underwater jets to massage sore muscles. A more intense underwater massage is next, in a private tub with jets designed to effect lymphatic drainage. The third step is a *douche à affusion*, a full body massage by a therapist working under a continuous shower of seawater.

The massage therapist devotes special attention to relieving tension in the vertebrae of your spine. The water pressure helps relax muscles. The final douche is in a shower stall lined with high-pressure jets aimed at cellulite points, the abdomen, and the vertebrae.

Supplementary services available include electrotherapy to recondition muscles after injury, an algae body mask, and antiarthritis and antiaging treatments for the skin. Inhalation of seawater mist is advised for asthma sufferers, and negative ions are introduced to relieve nervous tension.

While the center is open to the public every day with the exception of Sunday, there is no fitness program in conjunction with a hotel. Located nearby is the beachfront Hotel Marouba (tel. 596/78–00–21; telex 912138), which has single rooms at 745F to 1,000F for 2 persons daily, including Continental breakfast. Also within a short walk is the 10-room Hotel Christophe Colomb (tel. 596/78–05–38) with single rooms 182F, double 275F per day, but no meals.

Popular in France, this is spa therapy that sybarites can combine with a Caribbean holiday.

Centre de Thalassothérapie du Carbet
Grand'Anse
97221 Carbet, Martinique
Tel. 596/78–08–78

Administration General manager, Dr. Jacques-Joseph Louisia

Season Year-round. Open Mon.–Fri. 7 AM–6 PM, Sat. 7 AM–1 PM; closed Sun.

Getting Here *From Fort-de-France.* By car, coastal road toward St. Pierre, 16 miles (25 min). Taxi, rental car available.

Special Notes Bring bathing cap, sandals, swimwear. Robe and towels provided.

The Hard & the Soft

Sports conditioning

Montserrat
Vue Point Hotel

When the New York Road Runners Club searched for a fitness vacation site, it found an ideal combination of challenges on tiny Montserrat. Using the villas at the Vue Point Hotel as a base, the program offers clean and sparkling dove-gray obsidian beaches for running and a stark volcanic island marine ecosystem for hiking. Add workshops on health and nutrition, plus a natural, healthy diet, and you have a daily regimen for total fitness training.

Developed as an alternative to the traditional vacation by Beryl Bender Birch, wellness director for the NYRRC, the program is designed for people of all ages and fitness levels. Included is training in Ashtanga yoga, an ancient hatha-yoga exercise for health, strength, and personal growth. Daily workouts are precise and vigorous and individualized to purify the body. The Ashtanga system builds intense heat and energy in the body through static muscular contraction, increased circulation, and concentration on a powerful breathing technique, which brings about a cleansing effect.

Daily options are hiking, swimming, snorkeling, sailing, tennis, and golf. Nearby are natural pools fed by a soufrière (volcanic vein) where mineral waters soak away muscular pain.

Limited to 35 participants, the week-long program is designed to balance exercise and nutrition with the simpler pleasures of life. The focus is on increasing your knowledge of the positive effects of exercise and good nutrition. A natural high-complex carbohydrate and low-fat menu includes local fruits and vegetables, and fish or meat specialties of the region.

Your reward for hiking in the lofty green mountains only 30 minutes from the island's capital, Plymouth, is a lush setting for picnics. Also nearby is the Foxes Bay Bird Sanctuary, which can be visited. The ultimate challenge is a road race, held at the end of the week's program.

Far from the beaten path of Caribbean holidays, the island is a mélange of African, Irish, and other European influences that contribute to an overriding sense of peace and tranquility.

The Hard & the Soft
New York Road Runners Club
9 E. 89th St., New York, NY 10007
Tel. 212/661–2895

Administration Program director, Beryl Bender Birch

Season Jan.–Feb. only.

Accommodations Modern villas with 3–4 bedrooms shared by program participants; modern furniture, twin or king-size beds, private bath, living room with balcony. Air-conditioning, VCR and cassette player, TV. Maid service daily.

Rates 1-week program including round-trip airfare from New York, $1,595–$1,695; 2nd week $1,100. 50% payment with registration. Credit cards: AE, MC, V.

Meal Plans 2 meals daily included in program. Hotel caters breakfast buffet of blue-corn muffins or blue-corn pancakes, oatmeal; fresh fruit is accompanied by "smoothies" made of whipped juices from banana, papaya, mango, coconut. Eggs, low-fat homemade yogurt, freshly baked whole-grain breads available. Dinner (at hotel) includes steamed vegetables, green salad, choice of grilled fish or chicken; vegetarian meals and West Indian barbecue are other options.

Services and Facilities **Services:** Lectures and workshops on health, fitness, nutrition; personal consultation on nutrition, fitness; analysis of body biomechanics, posture; yoga training, Swedish massage, ayurvedic treatments. **Swimming Facilities:** Outdoor freshwater pool, ocean beaches. **Spa Facilities:** Hot springs. **Recreation Facilities:** Tennis courts, horseback riding, hiking. **Evening Programs:** Workshops alternate with reggae and disco nights.

In the Area Group hiking (optional).

Getting Here *From airport.* Transfers provided. Taxi, car rental, bicycle rental available.

Special Notes No smoking in the villas.

Four Seasons Resort

Non-program resort facilities

Nevis
Pinney's Beach Pristine beaches, aquamarine seas, and tropical rain forests set the scene for the 12-cottage Four Seasons Resort on tiny Nevis. Guests set their own pace, choosing between golf, sunbathing, tennis, and a number of water sports incorporating motorized inner tubes, giant bicycle-like pedda vehicles, and snorkeling equipment.

The Health Club, located in the Sports Pavilion, incorporates a whirlpool and saunas, a unisex hair salon, two massage rooms, and an air-conditioned workout room. Aerobics classes, stretch-and-tone sessions, aqua-aerobics, and early morning walks and beach jogs are open to all guests, free of charge. Croquet, volleyball, and shuffleboard are also offered. The dining room is reminiscent of a plantation great house, with a plank floor, high ceiling with rafters, cut-stone fireplace, ceiling fans, and a small dance floor. The menu selection changes daily, and West Indian nights are staged every Wednesday. Plantation-style guest-cottages are luxurious and oversized, each with a large veranda and a view.

Four Seasons Resort
Box 565, Charlestown, Nevis, West Indies
Tel. 809/469–1111; Reservations (U.S.) 800/332–3442,
(Canada) 800/268–6282
Fax 809/469–1040

Administration General Manager, John Strauss; tennis director, Greg Smith

Season Year-round.

Accommodations 196 rooms in 2-story plantation-style cottages. Oversize marble tiled bathrooms with full amenities. All air-conditioned, with ceiling fans, TV and VCR, refrigerator, telephone.

Rates $225–$450 daily per room, single and double; suites $425–$900. Add 17% tax and gratuity. Credit cards: AE, DC, MC, V.

Meal Plans The breakfast buffet features tropical fruits and juices in season, Grenadian spice muffins, omelets, meats, and grills. Lunch can be a West Indian rotis with curried breadfruit and chicken, herbed lobster, or gingered pork. Dinner choices include grilled Caribbean fish, seafood gumbo, Caesar salad, and rotisserie specialties such as local range hen and lamb.

Services and Facilities **Exercise Equipment:** 4 Trotter treadmills, 2 StairMasters 4000 PT, 5 Lifecycles, 1 rowing machine, free weights and incline board. **Services:** Swedish massage; salon for hair, nail, and skin care. **Swimming Facilities:** Freshwater swimming pool, ocean beach. **Recreation Facilities:** 18-hole golf course, 10 tennis courts (6 Har-Tru, 4 red clay; 4 lighted), water sports, volleyball, croquet, scuba, fishing. **Evening Programs:** Dancing, folklore show.

In the Area Nevis Peak (wild monkeys), Charlestown (shopping, crafts, colonial architecture), coral fields, and underwater caves.

Getting Here *From San Juan.* American Eagle flights to St. Kitts, resort shuttle by car and 40-passenger launch ($40 round-trip for 30-minute cruise). Also, scheduled flights from St. Martin and Antigua directly to Nevis.

Special Notes Ground-floor rooms accommodate the disabled. Complimentary day-long program for children ages 3–10.

La Casa de Vida Natural

Holistic health
Preventive medicine

Puerto Rico
Luquillo
Secluded in the foothills of the Caribbean National Forest, practically in the shadow of towering El Yunque, the highest peak on the island, La Casa de Vida Natural has carved out a 10-acre center for natural health. Vegetarian meals, mud, herbal, and seaweed treatments, and psychological counseling are offered.

With one of the island's best ocean beaches just down the hill at Luquillo, and hiking trails leading into the lush rain forest of El Yunque, the institute is an ideal getaway, winter and summer. The informal accommodations consist of an old farmhouse and guest house, with space for a dozen guests and staff.

The health center offers nonintrusive diagnostic procedures as well as kinesiology and massage. Workshops on physical and mental health are scheduled periodically, and individual counseling is available by appointment. The focus may be on building a psychological immune system, love and hate in health, or organic farming. Specialists on staff include a naturopathic doctor and a certified acupuncturist.

Taking an integrated biological and psychological approach to prevention and cure of disease, the center's services are geared to serve a wide range of interests. Therapies such as cleansing the body with burial in sand and immersion in mud can be combined with colonics and urine analysis. Aerobics classes and Jazzercise are organized in an open-air pavilion.

The program developed by New York-based psychoanalyst Jane G. Goldberg was introduced in 1988. At present, only 16 guests can be accommodated, and plans are to keep the center small, emphasizing personal attention to each guest.

Surrounded by natural beauty, panoramic views of the ocean, and the mountains, the pristine air and water are in natural harmony with the earth. Luquillo Beach, once a thriving coconut plantation, is protected by barrier reefs. The crescent-shaped, white-sand beach is perfect for swimming and picnics. Roadside stands sell slices of *coco frio*, the island's sweet pineapple. One morning is devoted to kayaking on the Santo Spiritu river.

El Yunque, protected by the U.S. National Park Service, encompasses 28,000 acres. Reaching an elevation of 3,526 feet, its rain forest includes 240 different tree species, as well as orchids and wildflowers. Brief tropical showers keep things lush, moist, and cool.

Hot sulfur springs, known to the earliest Taino Indians, are an hour's drive from the center. At the Parador Baños de Coamo you can bathe in the same pool where Franklin D. Roosevelt, Thomas Edison, Alexander Graham Bell, and Frank Lloyd Wright took the waters. Now a modern mountain inn, the Parador offers Puerto Rican meals as well as overnight lodging. (Rte. 546; tel. 825–2186).

The institute's workshops bring together specialists in mind/body health, herbalistics, and natural cures. Thalassotherapy here is as pure as it can get: Seaweed harvested in the morning is brewed in a big vat with herbs picked fresh from the garden.

La Casa de Vida Natural
Rio Grande, Luquillo, Puerto Rico 00673
(Reservations) 222 Park Ave. S, New York, NY 10003
Tel. 809/887–4359 or 212/260–5823

Administration Director, Jane Goldberg

Season Year-round.

Accommodations Renovated farmhouse and cottage have 6 guest rooms, simply furnished with 2 beds or queen-size bed; no air-conditioning; shared baths.

Rates $100 daily with meals; 5-day workshop $495. Advance payment $125 for workshops or 2 nights' lodging. Nonprogram lodging $60 per couple, without meals. Credit cards: MC, V.

Meal Plans 3 meals daily included in program fee. Vegetarian diet emphasizes raw fruits and vegetables grown on the property; wholegrain home-baked bread, sprouts, juices, salads. Special diets are accommodated. No coffee is served; herbal teas available.

Services and Facilities **Services:** Massage (full body, $40; reflexology), colonics, mud pack, sand burial, polarity, herbal/seaweed wrap, facial. Holistic medical counseling, nutritional and psychological consultation. **Swimming Facilities:** Outdoor pool; ocean beaches nearby. **Spa Facilities:** Baños de Coamo (60-min drive). **Recreation Fa-**

cilities: Hiking, river boating. **Evening Programs:** Informal workshops.

In the Area Fajardo (marina, ferry to Vieques and St. Thomas); National Park Service interpretive program at El Yunque.

Getting Here *From San Juan.* By car, Rte. 3 east to Luquillo Beach, Carr. 186 to El Verde (60 min). Rental car, taxi, public car (*publico*) available. Complimentary airport transfers.

Special Notes No smoking on property.

Spa Caribe at the Hyatt Resorts

Non-program resort facilities

Puerto Rico Talking back to the exercise machines might improve your fit-
Dorado ness rating during a workout at the new health clubs in Hyatt's sports-oriented resorts. Like a personal coach, the computerized system monitors your progress. Powercise machines converse not only with the users but with each other. Their composite rating is handed to you at the end of the exercise circuit, with suggestions for additional improvement.

These high-tech shape-ups are featured at both the Hyatt Regency Cerromar Beach and the Hyatt Dorado Beach, sister resorts two miles apart, on the north shore of the island, 22 miles west of San Juan. In addition to computerized equipment, they offer aerobics classes and aquaerobics, jogging trails, sauna, and a parcourse. Plus professional pampering.

Lifestyle-management prescriptions that you can take home are also computer-generated. Based on medically approved models, the programs evaluate your body composition, diet, exercise profile, and general fitness level. The spa's fitness specialist can then work up an exercise program tailored to your needs and schedule.

Geared to serve large groups at conferences and conventions in the resort, the spa also caters to the health club regular. A full day of exercise and bodywork, with facial as well as computerized evaluation, is available for $160. Groups meeting at both resorts are offered corporate games, seminars, workshops, and spouse programs, all supervised by experts.

Spa services are available daily on an à la carte basis. In addition to the usual body and skin care, the specialties include neuromuscular therapy, sports massage, herbal wraps, and loofah body scrub. Peter Burwash Tennis Pros offer a full agenda on 21 courts.

Spa Caribe at the Hyatt Resorts
Hyatt Resorts in Puerto Rico, Dorado, P.R. 00646
Tel. 809/796–1234 or 800/233–1234
Telex 3859758, Fax 809/796–4647

Administration Director, Marietta Fridjohn; program manager, Patricia Lach

Season Year-round.

Accommodations Low-rise construction, luxurious landscaping, and vast swimming pools are hallmarks of these resorts. Hyatt Regency Cerromar Beach has 506 rooms on 7 floors, the Dorado Beach has 300 rooms on 2 floors. Both hotels feature sleek new tropical looks: rattan furniture, pastel fabrics, island prints on bedcovers and window drapery; baths have marble-top counters, tile floors, contemporary lighting.

Rates At Cerromar Beach, $190–$380 daily, at Dorado Beach $225–$550 daily, single or double occupancy. Suites and Regency Club rooms higher. Add tax, gratuities. Guarantee by credit card. Credit cards: AE, MC, V.

Meal Plans No special diet available. Modified American Plan (breakfast and dinner) $53 per person for adults, $27 for children.

Services and Facilities **Exercise Equipment:** Powercise system (8 machines), 2 Lifecycles, Liferower, Hydra-Fitness muscular and cardiovascular training units. Outdoor parcourse with Dynacourt equipment. **Services:** Massage (Swedish, reflexology, sports, neck and shoulder), herbal wrap, loofah body scrub, facial cleansing treatments, aromatherapy. Hair, nail, and skin care. **Swimming Facilities:** Outdoor freshwater pools, ocean beaches. **Recreation Facilities:** Tennis courts, golf courses, bicycling, volleyball, pool volleyball, water sports. **Evening Programs:** Resort entertainment; casino.

In the Area Scuba, deep-sea fishing, sightseeing tours; Old San Juan (colonial architecture, art galleries, boutiques, museums), El Yunque rain forest, Camuy caves, Aricebo Observatory, San German (architecture, university).

Getting Here *From San Juan.* By car, Hwy. 22 (De Diego Expwy.), Rte. 693 to Dorado (30 min). By air, Dorado Airport. By public car (*publico*) from Old San Juan (60 min). Airport transfers ($45) by Dorado Transport Van. Rental car, taxi available. Shuttle service between hotels.

Special Notes Specially equipped rooms by advance request for the disabled. Elevators to all levels. Supervised day camp for children June 1–Labor Day. No smoking in spa and designated dining areas; nonsmoking rooms available. Remember to bring a medical certificate of fitness.

Jalousie Plantation

Luxury pampering
Taking the waters

St. Lucia Nestled between the Piton Mountains and a 320-acre nature
Soufriere preserve, the new Jalousie Plantation resort is an intimate hideaway for the rich and famous. The spa program features a daily 25-minute massage, aerobics classes, and use of the health club. The fitness center complex has separate saunas for men and women, a Jacuzzi, hot and cold plunge pools, a squash court, and massage rooms. Optional services include facials, seaweed bodywraps, mud wraps, hydrotherapy, and aromatherapy. Stress management and relaxation classes are held each afternoon.

Spa cuisine is served at each of the resort's four restaurants, including the bar at the spa, where nonalcoholic drinks are featured. The one-price all-inclusive policy covers meals, sports, and the basic spa package. The guest accommodations range from private cottages, each with a private plunge pool, to suites in a former sugar mill.

Nearby are the thermal baths. The baths, built for French forces in the 17th century, still bear the crest of Louis XVI.

Jalousie Plantation
Box 251, Soufriere, St. Lucia
Tel. 809/459–7666 or 800/877–3643
Fax 809/459–7667

Administration	General manager, Robert Stewart; spa director, Linda Brewer
Season	Year-round.
Accommodations	115 one- and two-bedroom cottages and Sugar Mill junior suites. Each cottage has a covered veranda, air-conditioning, TV, coffeemaker, refrigerator; full bathroom with hair dryer, robes; direct-dial phone, FM radio; private plunge pool in garden.
Rates	All-inclusive daily rate $215–$240 per person double occupancy in suite, $315–$340 single; cottages $265–$325 per person double, $365–$425 single. Tax and gratuities included. Deposit: One night's guarantee by credit card. Credit cards: AE, DC, MC, V.
Meal Plans	3 meals daily included in tariff. Spa cuisine options on all menus.
Services and Facilities	**Exercise Equipment:** Treadmill, Windracer, Liferower, Schwinn Air-Dyne stationary bike, Conquest weight training system, StairMaster. **Services:** Swedish massage, aromatherapy massage, hydrotherapy, seaweed or mud wrap, loofah body scrub, facial; salon for hair, nail, and skin care. **Swimming Facilities:** Outdoor freshwater pool, ocean beach. **Recreation Facilities:** 4 tennis courts (Plexicushion; 3 lighted), squash court, Sunfish and Hobie Cat sailing, windsurfing, watercycles, floats, waterskiing, scuba, snorkeling, kayaking. Charter yachts at Jalousie Cove Marina.
In the Area	Thermal springs near Diamond Falls, Pigeon Island National Park (Fort Rodney), Castries (colonial fortifications, Saturday market). Aqua Action festival and boat races (May) at Reduit Beach. Carnival parades in July.
Getting Here	*From Hewanorra International Airport.* Complimentary transfers on arrival and departure (1 hr).
Special Notes	Ground-floor accommodations for the disabled. Passport required. Supervised daily activity for children.

Le Sport

Sports conditioning
Luxury pampering
Taking the waters

St. Lucia *Cariblue Beach*	Thalassotherapy has come to the tiny nation of St. Lucia in a big way. At the all-inclusive Le Sport resort, an elegant bathhouse with sophisticated European equipment for seawater therapy is part of a vacation program completely devoted to health and fitness. They call it the Body Holiday.

The beneficial properties of seawater used to massage joints and muscles and the culinary pleasures of a diet based on meals created by famed chef Michel Guerard are the main features of the Body Holiday; its tonic part is complemented by the friendly nature of the St. Lucians and the balmy seaside resort.

Thermal-jet baths and seaweed wraps beautify the body. Image-enhancing treatments for men and women—facials, loofah body scrubs, and skin care—are included in the basic program price. Tipping is not permitted. The daily schedule offers aerobics classes, toning, and physical culture workshops, and an array of land and water sports. All come with expert instruction, at no additional charge.

The food part of the Body Holiday is called "cuisine legère," which simply means that calories don't count. In emulating the renowned Michel Guerard, the chefs provide meals balanced in complex carbohydrates, low in sodium and sugar, and full of options if you want to indulge. They even include wine with lunch and dinner, an open bar stocked with premium brands, fresh fruit juices, and mineral waters.

Before any treatments, a checkup is scheduled with the staff physician. Stress-linked fatigue and muscle tension, poor circulation, and lymphatic drainage are noted, and measurements are taken for blood pressure, heart rate, and weight. A prescribed course of treatments can include the "hydrator," a bubbling bath with herbs and sea algae, in which underwater jets needle away at the fatty tissue found on the upper arms, thighs, and calves. Another pool fitted with underwater jets is for exercise in seawater, which is denser than fresh water and thus gives greater support for the body. And the therapeutic nutrients of seaweed act as catalysts to create changes in the skin as you are wrapped, cocoonlike, in a coating of algae and sea mud.

St. Lucia's natural resources also include sulfur baths. Twin volcanic peaks called Petit Piton and Gros Piton rise dramatically above the tiny village of Soufrière on the southwest coast where signs point to the baths. From bubbling, underground springs, the sulfurous water flows into natural pools. Bathing here is said to cure whatever ails you.

A short jaunt up into the hills, across the ridge, brings you into the rain forest. Located between Soufrière and Fond St. Jacques, it's a three-hour trek through a tropical wonderland of dense foliage, flowering plants, and colorful birds.

Situated on an 18-acre estate, the new thalassotherapy center is a marble-walled oasis, with sauna, hot and cold plunge pools, and Swiss needle showers. It is a rejuvenating combination of restorative treatments, luxurious privacy, fine food, and lazy days at the beach. Like the local Creole patois, liberally sprinkled with French, this is a resort that blends the best of many worlds.

Le Sport
Box 437, Castries, St. Lucia
Tel. 809/450–8551 (800/257–9713 in USA)
Telex LC 6330; Fax 809/450–0368

Administration Owner/director, Craig Bernard; manager, Michael Mathews; spa director, Anne Hurrell

Season Year-round.

Accommodations 102 rooms oceanfront or with garden view in pavilions linked to dining room and lounge. Rooms have tropical contemporary look, rattan furniture. Air-conditioning, private balcony or patio, full modern bath with hair dryer, robes; all rooms with telephone, radio.

Rates $195–$340 daily per person double occupancy, single occupancy supplement $40 per day. No minimum stay. Suite $250–$380 per person, double. Estate House $350–$450, single supplement $200. Credit-card guarantee for first night. Tax and gratuities included in rates. Credit cards: AE, DC, MC, V.

Meal Plans 3 meals daily included in program price. Breakfast: fresh fruits and juices, bran and Meusli cereals, omelets, smoked salmon, pastries, coffee, milk, tea. Lunch selections include fresh salads, stuffed chicken legs in leek-and-cream sauce, boiled wild rice, julienne of carrots and zucchini. Dinner options broccoli soufflè, scallop of veal with champagne sabayon, fresh asparagus. Desert offerings include homemade pear sherbet. Selected wines with lunch and dinner at no additional charge.

Services and Facilities **Exercise Equipment:** Nautilus-type units, bicycles, fencing outfits. **Services:** Massage, hydrotherapy, facials, beauty and rejuvenation treatments. **Swimming Facilities:** Outdoor freshwater pool, seawater pool, ocean beach. **Spa Facilities:** Therapy tubs in private rooms. **Recreation Facilities:** Tennis courts, bicycling, archery, volleyball, scuba diving, windsurfing, waterskiing. **Evening Programs:** Live entertainment nightly, disco.

In the Area Pigeon Island National Park (museum), Rodney Bay marina, Castries market (built 1894), Government House. Aqua Action Festival in early June.

Getting Here *From Castries.* By car, coastal road to Gros Ilet (15 min). Complimentary transfers on arrival/departure. Taxi, rental car available.

L'Aqualigne

Life enhancement
Preventive medicine
Luxury pampering

St. Maarten
Simpson Bay At L'Aqualigne, European beauty and rejuvenation therapies can be combined with aerobic exercise and a weight-loss diet in programs designed and developed by the cosmetologists Claire and Marc Van Thielen, who researched natural healing and cosmetic products used at leading spas throughout the world. The focus ranges from anticellulite French body-sculpting massage and injections to the antiaging cell therapies created in Romania by Dr. Ana Aslan. For relaxation, a week of fitness training is interspersed with body peeling, postural reeducation, and soothing massage. The sophisticated equipment for beauty treatments can produce a total experience of revitalization.

Located within a large time-share resort on the Dutch side of the half-French, half-Dutch island, this is a small, private oasis. Guests from many nations mix with local residents who come for workouts and therapy. Treatments can be scheduled over one or two weeks. Aerobics and yoga classes are scheduled daily and can be booked along with massage or use of the weights room equipment on an à la carte basis. Locker rooms are available for day guests.

The medically oriented programs are structured to achieve serious results; facials and massage are included. A thorough examination, including blood analysis, precedes some therapies. Plastic and reconstructive surgery, sclerosis injections, liposuction, collagen implant for facial scars and wrinkles, and injections of Gerovital H3 are offered here. The advanced equipment for aesthetic treatments is based on techniques created by plastic surgeons and dermatologists. L'Aqualigne technicians are joined by specialists who participate in the scheduled programs.

Dieters are treated to foods that satisfy the appetite and appeal to a sense of being well fed. Planned individually by a nutritionist who works with guests throughout the week, the weight-loss program is geared to taking off inches and pounds. Daily anticellulite massages and the metabolism-balancing oligo therapy are intended to enhance your new look.

Refreshing breezes, gentle surf, and the relaxed atmosphere of island life complete the stress-reduction process, and naturalist beaches and a casino are nearby.

L'Aqualigne
Pelican Resort, Simpson Bay, St. Maarten
Tel. 011/599-5-42426
Fax 011/599/5-43319

Administration	Program director, Marc Van Thielen; medical director, Paul Musarella, M.D.
Season	Year-round.
Accommodations	The Pelican Resort has 655 suites $105–$320, with air-conditioning, king-size beds, spacious closets, kitchenette, cable TV, direct-dial telephone, large balcony. Cool white walls, tile floors, rattan furniture, island fabrics, prints by native artists.
Rates	1-week beauty and fitness program $2,545; 2-week anticellulite program (with special diet and lipoplasty surgery) $5,630; 2-week electroridopuncture program $5,816; 1-week rejuvenation program (with Gerovital therapy) $2,570. All prices per person, not including hotel or meals. 1-day revitalizer (includes lunch) $180. Use of facilities (only) $30 day, $60 week, $100 week for a couple. 50% payable in advance. Credit cards: AE, MC, V.
Meal Plans	Fresh fish and fruit salads at the hotel restaurant. Grilled snapper, sautéed aubergine, other island specialties at lunch and dinner. Breakfast selections include cereal, yogurt, home-baked whole-wheat bread. Juice bar.
Services and Facilities	**Exercise Equipment:** 16-station Weider circuit, 2 Tunturi bicycles, free weights and bench; aerobics exercise area with special flooring. **Services:** Massage, acupressure, hydrotherapy, aromatherapy, algotherapy, herbal wrap, facial, body peel, pedicure; ozone therapy, liposuction, cell therapy, hair implant. **Swimming Facilities:** Outdoor freshwater pool, ocean beach. **Spa Facilities:** Coed sauna, steam room, hot and cold whirlpools. **Recreation Facilities:** Marina, 6 tennis courts (Astroturf, asphalt; lighted). **Evening Programs:** Resort entertainment, casino.

In the Area Duty-free shopping in Philipsburg, French boutiques in Marigot, boat trips to St. Bart, water sports, horseback riding.

Getting Here *From Juliana Airport.* By taxi, Union Road to Simpson Bay (15 min). Taxi, rental car available at resort.

Special Notes Limited access for the disabled. No smoking in the therapy center, which is open weekdays 9 AM–6 PM, weekends 10 AM–6 PM.

Port de Plaisance

Luxury pampering

St. Maarten Sprawling Port de Plaisance, the newest resort on the Dutch
Simpson Bay side of the island, offers one of the Caribbean's major tennis programs in addition to a full-service health club. Tennis is under the watchful eye of Peter Burwash, and instruction is by American-trained pros; the tennis center, with its seven lighted courts, is also home to the health club, which has four massage rooms, two facial rooms, a fitness room, and a beauty salon, as well as separate men's and women's saunas, steamrooms, and locker rooms with whirlpool and showers.

The resort complex, which faces a vast bay, also includes a marina and a casino, where you'll find the La Belle Vie restaurant, serving spa cuisine; a French master chef is in charge of the spa menu, which is low in salt, fat, and cholesterol. Accommodation is currently in luxury apartments, but a huge Sheraton hotel is now rising back from the marina between the tennis center and the planned 18-hole golf course. A medical center and additional sports facilities are also in the offing.

Port de Plaisance
Box 2089, Phillipsburg, Sint-Maarten, N.A.
Tel. 5995–45222 or 800/732–9480
Fax 5995–42390

Administration Spa Director, Jeffrey Bliss

Season Year-round.

Accommodations 82 marina apartments (studio, 1-, and 2-bedroom); 592-room Sheraton Hotel (scheduled to open in 1994). All rooms air-conditioned, with telephone, TV.

Rates Studio $200–$275 daily, single or double occupancy, one-bedroom apartment double occupancy, $265–$375. Daily Spa admission included.

Meal Plans A la carte menu featuring spa cuisine.

Services and Facilities **Exercise Equipment:** Paramount multistation gym, 3 Lifesteps, 5 Lifecycles, 2 Precor treadmills, 2 rowing machines, free weights. **Services:** Massage, facial; personal training, fitness analysis; salon for hair, nail, and skin care. **Swimming Facilities:** Outdoor freshwater pool (23.5 meter); bay beach on property; ocean beaches nearby. **Recreation Facilities:** 7 all-weather tennis courts (lighted), deep-sea fishing, charter boats. Aquacize class daily.

Getting Here *From Juliana Airport.* By taxi, 10 minutes. Rental car available only at resort.

Special Notes Spa Hours: Mon.–Sat. 7 AM–9 PM, Sun. 7 AM–5 PM. Daily admission $35 refunded with treatment. Member I/SPA.

L'Habitation

Non-program resort facilities

St. Martin
Anse Marcel
For the sports enthusiast, L'Habitation offers the most comprehensive facilities on the French side of binational St. Martin/St. Maarten. With 150 acres of beautifully landscaped grounds, private white-sand beach, and 60-slip marina, the activity is nonstop on land and water.

Topping a hill overlooking the resort, Le Privilege is a combination fitness center and social club. Exercise equipment is housed in open-air pavilions next to one of the island's hottest discos. Lunch is served at a poolside restaurant that features grilled fish, salads, and spa cuisine.

L'Habitation has an airy, marbled lobby, and a French flair is noticeable throughout. Rooms and suites are decorated in Creole style, and bathrooms come with bidet as well as hair dryer. The sports program includes your choice of water skiing and use of the facilities at Le Privilege each day.

Yachting enthusiasts can mingle with luxury craft from many parts of Europe and the Caribbean at the Port Lonvilliers complex adjoining the main hotel. Also nearby are the Caid & Isa stables, with eight horses for rides into the hills and a helicopter landing pad for island excursions.

L'Habitation
Box 581 Anse Marcel, 97150 St. Martin, French West Indies
Tel. (590) 87–33–33
Telex 919355; Fax (590) 87–30–38
Reservations: Le Meridien L'Habitation, 888 Seventh Ave., New York, NY 10106
Tel. 212/245–2920 or 800/543–4300

Administration General manager, Renaud Legey

Season Year-round.

Accommodations 407 rooms and 50 marina suites in low-rise buildings connected by a 2-story rotunda with restaurant. Rooms have French Provincial furniture, air-conditioning, TV, telephone. All with private bathroom equipped with bidet, hair dryer.

Rates $177–$599 per room, double or single occupancy. Rate includes full American breakfast buffet, taxes, and $25 daily food or bar credit. Prepayment in full required 30 days prior to arrival. Credit cards: AE, DC, MC, V.

Meal Plans Breakfast buffet included in daily and package rate. Spa cuisine served at Le Privilege, à la carte.

Services and Facilities **Exercise Equipment:** Weight training units, free weights, stationary bike. **Swimming Facilities:** Outdoor pool, ocean beach. **Recreation Facilities:** 2 tennis courts, squash, racquetball, horseback riding, water sports. **Evening Programs:** Disco dancing.

In the Area Marigot (shopping), day trip by boat to St. Bart, Anguilla.

Getting Here *From Queen Julianna Airport.* Taxi (30 min); complimentary transfers included in some packages. Rental car available at resort. Helicopter service.

Special Notes Children's playground and pool, supervised activity daily for ages 5 to 12.

Hyatt Regency St. John

Non-program resort facilities

U.S. Virgin Islands
St. John
Set on a wide stretch of beach at Great Cruz Bay, the 34-acre Hyatt Regency St. John (formerly Virgin Grand Beach Hotel) sports a completely new health club. A first for the island, the fitness facility includes weight training equipment, saunas, and a whirlpool. Aerobics classes scheduled throughout the day are free to guests.

Designed around an 11,000-square-foot free-form swimming pool, the resort's accommodations are in two-story villas. Terraced down to the beach are the main reception area and restaurant. For informal dining, there is an open-air seaside restaurant and a poolside snack bar.

Equipment for windsurfing, scuba diving, snorkeling, and deep-sea fishing is available. Close by are hiking trails into the National Park, which is the main attraction of St. John. For scheduled nature walks and talks on the history of the area, check with the rangers at the park's visitor center near the ferry landing in the little town of Cruz Bay.

Hyatt Regency St. John
Great Cruz Bay, St. John, U.S. Virgin Islands
Tel. 809/776–7171 or 800/233–1234

Administration General manager, Mark Heinzelman; sports manager, Lisa Johnson

Season Year-round.

Accommodations 285 deluxe rooms with balcony, modern bath. All are air-conditioned, have color TV, telephone.

Rates $155–$498 daily, single or double occupancy. 2-bedroom town house $855 per day. Add 15% gratuity, 7% tax. $55 daily for breakfast and lunch, $30 children.

Meal Plans À la carte menu.

Services and Facilities **Exercise Equipment:** Air-conditioned gymnasium with weight training and cardiovascular exercise equipment. **Services:** Massage. **Swimming Facilities:** Outdoor pool, ocean beach. **Recreation Facilities:** 6 lighted tennis courts, windsurfing equipment, snorkeling gear; scuba trips and deep-sea fishing; golf course nearby. Aquacise class daily.

In the Area Virgin Islands National Park, Tortola.

Getting Here *From St. Thomas.* Ferry service from Red Hook to Cruz Bay (40 min). Complimentary transfers from airport.

Omega Journeys at Maho Bay

Holistic health
Spiritual awareness

U.S. Virgin Islands
Maho Bay, St. John

Workshops in health, music, movement, and personal growth are mixed with fun in the sun during four week-long programs planned by the New York–based Omega Institute. The annual migration to the sunny beaches of St. John is joined by faculty members who lead explorations into the body, mind, and spirit. Living close to nature in a tent village, the workshop participants experience many dimensions of natural healing.

Early birds can start the day with sunrise meditation, tai chi chuan, or yoga. Workshops run two hours each morning and afternoon, allowing a choice of several subjects. Informal and experimental, the group sessions are devoted to bringing health, aliveness, and peace into the many dimensions of contemporary life.

Drawn from a variety of professions, ages, and backgrounds, the participants find common ground in the open-minded, natural atmosphere. Maho Bay Camp Resort is a unique tent-cottage community dedicated to the concept of simple comforts and life in harmony with nature. Perched in thickly wooded hillsides, the canvas-walled cottages are set on plank decks that cantilever over the forest. The 16-by-16-foot units blend in so naturally that they seem to be part of the environment.

Located within the Virgin Islands National Park, the campground has unrestricted access to miles of pristine beaches and well-marked hiking trails, where you may pursue both ecological and historical interests. The National Park Service conducts free tours and lectures on island flora, fauna, and marine biology, as well as on St. John's colorful history and culture.

St. John remains the sleepiest and most tranquil of the three islands (with St. Thomas and St. Croix) the United States bought from Denmark for $25 million. Its main town, Cruz Bay, isn't very sophisticated, but it is delightful just for that reason and is much loved by Virgin Island visitors.

A good place to begin an island tour is the National Park Service visitor center next to the pier where ferries carry passengers and cargo from St. Thomas. Scheduled hikes are posted, brochures on trails are free for the asking. Panoramic views and lush foliage reward hikers and photographers. For those who prefer to ride, open-sided vans pick up passengers along the main Northshore Road to Caneel Bay and a string of public beaches around Maho Bay.

Thanks to the efforts of preservationists, about two-thirds of the island was designated a national park in 1956. Although the Caneel Bay Resort developed by Laurence Rockefeller is still extremely popular with those who like to experience some luxury with their wilderness, Maho Bay welcomes those who are serious about exploring the natural wonders of St. John.

A must, if time permits, is a drive over Bordeaux Mountain, with its rain forest and spectacular views, to Coral Bay and East End, where descendants of the Danish settlers still farm in the old style. En route you will have to be patient with the wildlife, especially the prolific mongooses. Imported to deal with rats on the sugar plantations, they consider the road to be their own playground.

Surrounded by mahogany and bay trees (from which bay rum is derived), the campground is alive with large and small birds and with brilliant flowers including tamarind and flamboyant. Underwater at Trunk Bay, snorkelers can explore a marked trail of sealife: flora, coral, and brilliantly colored fish.

Omega Journeys at Maho Bay
Maho Bay, St. John
Reservations: Omega Institute, RD 2, Box 377,
Rhinebeck, NY 12572
Tel. 914/338–6030 or 800/862–8890

Administration Director, Stephan Rechtschaffen, M.D.; program director, Jan Deleics

Season Jan.–mid-Feb.

Accommodations 96 tent/cottages tucked into foliage on 14 acres overlooking white-sand beach. Wooden floors, 2 beds, living/dining area (equipped with 2-burner propane stove), lounge chairs, sofa. Linens and bedding supplied, no maid service. Boardwalks connect to toilets, showers, dining pavilion, commissary.

Rates 1 week with workshops, lodging, meals, and round-trip airfare from New York, $1,275 per person double occupancy. Lodging for single persons and children available. 50% payment at time of booking. Credit cards: MC, V.

Meal Plans Vegetarian meals 3 times daily. Omega's natural-food chefs prepare sumptuous buffets of vegetables and tropical fruits. Some fish and dairy products are available. Lunch includes salads, home-baked whole-wheat bread. Dinner menus offer vegetarian lasagna, baked eggplant Parmesan, tofu casserole.

Services and Facilities **Services:** Personal consultation on nutrition, body movement, energy training. Yoga instruction. **Swimming Facilities:** Ocean beaches. **Recreation Facilities:** Tennis, hiking, volleyball. **Evening Programs:** Informal workshops, concerts.

In the Area National Park Service interpretive tours, ferry to Tortola, catamaran trips. Annaberg Plantation (Danish-era ruins, special programs), Trunk Bay (underwater trail), Caneel Bay Plantation, Virgin Grand Beach Hotel (water sports).

Getting Here *From Cruz Bay.* By bus, shuttle service from ferry landing or along Northshore Rd. (15 min). Car rental, taxi, minimoke, bicycle rental available.

Special Notes No smoking indoors. Remember to bring flashlight, insect repellent, hiking shoes.

3 Health & Fitness Cruises

Staying fit at sea is no longer a matter of doing 10 laps around the promenade deck. Today's luxury liners feature fitness facilities and programs that are the equal of anything ashore. Seagoing spas were an innovation of the 1970s. Since water is the basic ingredient in many spa cures, it was argued, a spa on the high seas should only make the experience more enjoyable. With abundant fresh air and sunshine, pools filled with filtered sea water, and aerobics classes on deck, the cruise would be an invigorating escape from health club routines at home.

For cruise connoisseurs, however, diet was a dirty word. And the gourmet meals and lavish buffets aboard ship have been the downfall of many calorie counters. Then came the American Heart Association's "Eating Away From Home" program adapted for shipboard dining by Royal Cruise Line, followed by the Golden Door menu selections offered on Cunard cruises. Your travel agent can provide details on lean and light shipboard cuisines offered by 22 members of the Cruise Lines Industry Association (CLIA).

Advance planning is important for those on a special diet. Specific foods and general preferences can be discussed with a travel agent, who can then secure a confirmation of your meal plan from the cruise line. All the leading lines offer such services at no extra charge.

Smoke-free cruising is a new option. Introduced by the Majesty Cruise Line in cooperation with the Smoke Free Travel Council, cruises from Miami aboard the new *Royal Majesty* offer no-smoking cabins as well as a totally smoke-free dining room.

For the committed fitness buff, cruising can provide the best of both worlds. Norwegian Cruise Line has annual Fitness and Beauty cruises in October. Guest lecturers on nutrition, sports medicine, hairstyling, and makeup make the trip along with football, golf, and tennis stars. Basketball cruises, baseball cruises, and football cruises allow passengers to team up for fun and fitness aboard the *Seaward* and its sister ship the *Norway*, which has the largest seagoing spa and fitness center.

Shore excursions on these cruises offer more than shopping and sightseeing. Several lines, including Norwegian Cruise Line and the *Cunard Countess*, provide entree to local racquet clubs, golf courses, and fitness centers. Some ships have access to private ports of call, islands where passengers may swim, snorkel, and sunbathe on their own "deserted island." Others have scheduled nature walks and bicycle tours.

While the Caribbean and the Bahamas account for 60% of all cruise destinations, a steadily growing fleet of ships sails from California and Canadian ports. Alaska, the Mexican Riviera, and the Hawaiian islands offer exciting variations on the cruise theme. And there is little problem in maintaining a reduced fat and cholesterol diet while traveling when your meals are planned and scheduled aboard ship.

As a new wave of luxury liners comes into service by the mid-1990s, look for more adventure cruises exploring off-the-beaten track ports and nature preserves. Small, specially designed expedition vessels are sailing to Alaska and along the Pacific coast for Clipper Adventure Cruises, Seaquest Cruises, and Windstar Cruises.

For newcomers to fitness programs, the cruise may be a good way to inaugurate a personal fitness routine that can then be continued effectively at home. Staff instructors offer one-on-one workouts that teach proper exercise routines—perhaps the best bargain in fitness education. And there's a healthy bonus from mother nature: The bracing effect of the fresh air generated by sea water and sun may be just what the doctor ordered for our high-pressure society.

CostaClassica

The ancient Roman rituals for relaxation and revival of the body and mind are updated with modern technology in the Caracalla Spa aboard Costa Cruise Lines' new ship, the *CostaClassica*. The 6,500-square-foot spa rivals land-based resorts in the variety of treatments offered, including thalassotherapy, aromatherapy, and hydrotherapy. The luxuriously appointed top-deck fitness center offers both complimentary group instruction an one-on-one sessions in aerobics, strength training, stress conditioning, and relaxation. A steam bath, saunas, Jacuzzis, and beauty salon are part of spa complex, and treatments with rejuvenating Moor mud, seaweed, and essential oils can be reserved in advance of sailing (call 800/462–6782). Packages range from a half-day treatments to the six-day ($625) Bellisima program. Runners, joggers, and power walkers enjoy a dedicated track overlooking the pool deck. **Costa Cruise Lines.** *World Trade Center, 80 S.W. 8th St., Miami, FL 33130, tel. 305/358–7325 or 800/462–6782.* Deluxe outside staterooms, inside cabins, with 2 lower beds that convert to a queen-size bed; shower and toilet. Launched 1992. 1,300 passengers. Italian registry, Italian officers and dining room staff, European stewardesses.

Fitness Facilities: Complete line of weight training equipment, 3 Lifecycles, free weights. **Services:** Massage, reflexology, body wrap, body scrub, hydrotherapy bath, deep-cleansing facial, rehydrating facial, personal training.

Cruises weekly from Ft. Lauderdale: Fares, including airfare, are $995–$3,395 per person, double occupancy.

Crown Odyssey

The largest of the three ships in the Royal Cruise Line, the 34,250-ton *Crown Odyssey*, sports a lavish health center complemented by a healthful alternative dining program approved by the American Heart Association. Principal attractions are an indoor swimming pool, whirlpools, gymnasium, saunas, and a health bar. Reminiscent of a sumptuous Roman bath with its tile walls and floors in shades of green, coral, and white, the health center offers the latest in exercise equipment and programs. Choices include classes in yoga, aerobics, dancercise, walk-a-thon, aquacise workouts, Body Shop for strengthening and tightening muscles, and Sit and Be Fit, which incorporates exercises that can be done while sitting in a chair. In addition, two outdoor whirlpools and a parcourse walking track complement the outdoor pool. Programs include lectures and workshops with guest experts on subjects ranging from stress management to nutrition and self-esteem. The *Crown Odyssey* (and her sister ship the *Golden Odyssey*), offers an expanded New Beginnings program that has included a pain clinic and workshops on retirement adjustment.

Royal Cruise Line. *Maritime Plaza, San Francisco, CA 94111, tel. 415/956-7200 or 800/227-4534.* Launched in 1988. 1,000 passengers (most have outside staterooms with picture windows). Exclusive suites have private Jacuzzis, balconies, butler service. Bahamian registry and crew.

Fitness Facilities: Universal 8-station gym, 4 LifeFitness computerized bikes, Fitstep stair/climber, computerized treadmill, 2 Precor rowers, aquacourse, free weights, ballet bar. **Services:** Massage, herbal wraps, facials; hair, nail, and skin care. **Sports:** Golf driving instruction; tennis and golf ashore.

Cruises to Canada, New England, the Panama Canal, the Mexico Riviera, the Caribbean, Hawaii. Fares for a 10-day Acapulco–San Juan cruise from $2,339 per person double occupancy.

Crystal Harmony

This 960-passenger liner has a 3,000-square-foot oceanview spa and fitness center that offers aerobic and Jazzercise instruction and treatments that include thalassotherapy, moortherapy, and aromatherapy. Passengers relax in men's and women's saunas and steam rooms, tee-off at a golf simulator, jog on a full promenade deck, play on paddle tennis or volleyball courts, swim in a lap pool, soak in Jacuzzis, or socialize in an indoor/outdoor swimming pool with built-in bar. A fitness trainer is aboard, and there are special slimming programs using the DeCleor program. The spa also offers a salon for hair, nail, and skin care, and a men's barbershop.

Crystal Cruises. *2121 Avenue of the Stars, Los Angeles, CA 90067, tel. 310/785-9300 or 800/446-6645.* 8 passenger decks with 480 deluxe staterooms, including 62 penthouse suites. All outside accommodations except 19 inside cabins; many have private verandas; all have king- or queen-size beds. Bahamian registry, Norwegian and Japanese officers, Italian dining staff, international crew.

Fitness Facilities: 3 treadmills, 3 Lifecycles, 2 StairMasters, 2 rowing machines, 4 Lifecircuit weight training machines, free weights. **Services:** massage, facials, body scrub, herbal wrap; foot, hand and eye treatments; personal trainer; beauty salon.

Cruises from Los Angeles and New York City; fares including airfare for 17-day trans-Canal cruise $3,925–$18,740 per person, double occupancy. Average per diem $421 per person, double, not including air.

Cunard Countess

Active vacationers aboard the *Cunard Countess* can take advantage of a state-of-the-art fitness center and the shore excursions offered through "SeaSports" TM program. The 2,000-square-foot exercise facility is packed with the latest in LifeFitness equipment. Trainers are on hand daily to assure proper form in your workout. Aerobics class, weight training seminars, and nutritional lectures are part of the program at no additional charge for all passengers.

When your workout is over, you can relax in one of two adjacent Jacuzzis, a European-style sauna, and an outdoor swimming pool. Ashore, you can enjoy beach facilities at Cunard resorts and sign up for water skiing, golf, tennis, horseback riding, 5K "fun runs" and hikes in remote jungles. (Shore excursions are booked aboard ship for an additional fee.)

Cunard Line. *555 Fifth Ave., New York, NY 10017, tel. 212/880–7304 or 800/221–4770.* Commissioned in 1976, refurbished 1986. 790 passengers. British registry and officers, international staff.

Fitness Facilities: Lido Deck fitness center with 12-station Paramount circuit, 2 LifeRowers, 5 Lifecycles, 2 Lifesteps, computerized weight training system; outdoor swimming pool, 2 whirlpools. **Services:** Massage, one-on-one training, barbershop/beauty salon. **Sports:** Golf driving range, basketball practice, paddle tennis court, table tennis, shuffleboard.

Cruises from San Juan every Saturday, alternating itineraries. Fares for a 7-day cruise from $1,680 per person double occupancy, including air fare from U.S. Also available, "Sail 'n Stay" resort packages.

Fantasy and Ecstasy

First of a new generation of megaships for Carnival Cruise Lines, the upscale *Fantasy* and sister ship *Ecstacy* have spas that are bigger than the casinos (another first!). In the Nautica Spa, with a view of the sea, you work out with row upon row of exercise machines reflected in a mirrored ceiling. Behind the gym are whirlpools (also with a sea view), saunas, steam rooms, massage rooms, showers, and lockers. Also active throughout the day is a large glass-and-mirror-enclosed aerobics studio. Classes include "Cardio-Funk" and "Cardio-Pump," as well as organized walks on the ships' upper decks. Familiarizations with the equipment and talks by the spa staff are offered regularly throughout each cruise.

A beauty salon completes the enclosed portion of the 12,000-square-foot spa; a ⅛th-mile jogging track circles the deck.

Calorie-conscious passengers can take advantage of a Nautica Spa Selection on the menu at each meal. In addition, a circular salad bar in the grill area is open for lunch and dinner.

While the spa has separate saunas for men and women, the two coed whirlpools made of red-and-black ceramic tile allow passengers to bask in bubbling water while gazing up to the heavens through a skylight. This is, after all, a fun ship.

Carnival Cruise Lines. *3655 NW 87th Ave., Miami, FL 33178. Tel. 305/599–2600 or 800/327–7353 (800/325–1214 in FL).* Commissioned in 1990. 2,600 passengers. Liberian registry, Italian officers, international staff.

Fitness Facilities: 35 weight training units and computerized exercise machines, ranging from bikes to bench press. **Services:** Massage, loofah scrub, facial, anticathiodermie facial, herbal pack, aromatherapy, pressotherapy (air bags), G5 weight loss massage, eucalyptus steam inhalation. **Sports:** 2 outdoor pools, trapshooting, table tennis, shuffleboard.

Fares include airfare from major cities: $459–$1,149 for 3-day cruise to the Bahamas, aboard the Fantasy; $999–$2,439 for 7-day cruise aboard the Ecstacy.

Special Notes: Two identical sister ships, *Fascination* and *Sensation*, are scheduled to begin service in late 1993 and 1994. Children's playroom and facilities for the disabled are available on all ships.

The Horizon

A newcomer in 1990, the $175 million *Horizon* features the Olympic Health Club. Located on the sun deck, it has a window-walled weights room, cushion-floored aerobics studio, three outdoor whirlpools, and a coed sauna. Dieters choose between a full vegetarian menu and the regular menu with highlighted items that are low in sodium and cholesterol.

The extensive selection of beauty services is provided by a professional staff, who also provide fitness classes that range from cardio-funk low impact aerobics to designer body conditioning and a 30-minute session of aqua-aerobics in the outdoor swimming pool.

Chandris Celebrity Cruises. *900 Third Ave., New York, NY 10022, tel. 212/750–0044, 800/621–3446, or 800/423–2100 (800/432–4231 in FL).* Deluxe staterooms and outside cabins; most cabins are compact, all have private shower and toilet. 1,354 passengers. Liberian registry, Greek officers and European staff.

Fitness Facilities: Universal 5-station gym, 2 Trendex treadmills, NordicTrack cross-country ski machine, 3 Aerobicycles, 2 rowing machines, free weights. 2 outdoor swimming pools, whirlpools. **Services:** Massage, Cathiodermie revitalizing facial, Ionithermie slimming treatment, bodybrushing; personal fitness analysis, body fat analysis, personal training; Salon for hair, nail, and skin care.

Cruises Saturdays from San Juan; fares for 7-day cruise including airfare, $1,295–$3,160 per person double occupancy. Bermuda cruises from New York (May–Sept.) $1,165–$2,995 for 7-day cruise including airfare, per person, double.

Special Notes Wheelchair-equipped staterooms for the disabled.

SS *Independence* and SS *Constitution*

American Hawaii Cruises' vessels feature two of the most complete fitness centers afloat in the Pacific. Added in 1990 atop the SS *Constitution* was a 2,000-square-foot Health and Fitness Center with StairMasters, Lifecycles, treadmill, weight training equipment, and free weights. A large open area is used for aerobics classes scheduled several times during each day at sea. A sauna and massage room are located near the barbershop/beauty salon.

The Solarium aboard the SS *Independence* has a full-size gym and health spa, with over 20 pieces of weight training equipment, plus free weights. The spa has two saunas and massage rooms.

The Hawaiian way to watch your waistline on these cruises is, of course, the hula. Lessons are offered in hula dancing as well as dancercise and water aerobics. In the mornings you can join the sports director in "walk-a-mile," followed by exercise in one of the two freshwater swimming pools.

Menus have been updated to include lighter fare. The new *Pu'uwai* ("heart") program offers healthy options at breakfast, lunch, and dinner for passengers who wish to limit their intake of fats and cholesterol, but you have to skip the chocolate-macadamia-nut cream pie for dessert if you have the Herculean resolve, and opt for fresh pineapple.

American Hawaii Cruises. *550 Kearny St., San Francisco, CA 94108, tel. 415/392–9400 or 800/765–7000.* Commissioned in 1951, rebuilt 1974. 798 passengers. U.S. registry and officers. 7-day cruise from Honolulu every Saturday evening; fare $1,095–$3,690 per person double occupancy. Also available are cruise-resort combinations via Hilo, with cruise and 3–4 day stay at selected hotels, transfers included, $669–$1,549 per person, double.

MS Mermoz

Thalassotherapy is the specialty aboard Paquet French Cruises' 530-passenger MS *Mermoz*. Outfitted with hydrotherapy tubs and a multihead "grande douche" Swiss shower, the spa also takes advantage of a watery view from its location on the uppermost deck. The thalasso course, designed to help with circulatory problems and muscular aches, begins with a 7-minute douche, bubbling baths, and an underwater massage, and finally, a 20-minute manual massage. This spa was added to this elegant, Old World ship in 1989, and while the facilities are limited, the French-trained and certified therapists are completely professional. In addition, there are exercise classes in the seawater swimming pool on deck, and a coed sauna and Roman bath whirlpool for relaxation. Regularly scheduled exercise and fitness classes are held on deck.

Paquet French Cruises. *1510 S.E. 17th St., Ft. Lauderdale, FL 33316; tel. 305/764–3500.* Large staterooms, inside cabins, with shower or bathtub. 530 passengers. French registry, French officers and staff. **Fitness Facilities:** Hydrotherapy center with tubs and showers. **Services:** Swedish massage, underwater massage, facial, skin analysis; salon for hair, nail, and skin care, including body waxing, manicure, pedicure, makeover.

Cruises from Guadeloupe, Ft. Lauderdale, and San Juan. Fares for a 7-day French Caribbean cruise $1,450–$3,495 per person, double occupancy, including free airfare from Miami.

Nieuw Amsterdam and Noordam

With a Passport to Fitness program aboard their twin luxury liners the *Nieuw Amsterdam* and the *Noordam*, Holland America Line offers one of the best values in health and fitness cruises year-round. Passengers pick up a passport aboard the ship to earn stamps for fitness classes, team sports, and beauty treatments. Even ordering lunch and dinner from the Perfect Balance menu in the dining room earns a stamp. Prizes are awarded for 20–40 stamps. Aerobics classes and aquatic workouts are available to all passengers. A newly introduced spa menu has such healthful selections as Thai chicken salad and fresh Pacific snapper. Tennis and golf programs and a scuba certification course are offered on shore excursions. The twin luxury liners, immaculately maintained and decorated with an extensive collection of art and antiques, offer services and amenities in the grand tradition of transatlantic travel.

Holland America Line. *300 Elliott Ave. W, Seattle, WA 98119, tel. 206/281–3535. Nieuw Amsterdam* built 1983, *Noordam* built 1984. 1,214 passengers each. Netherlands Antilles registry, Dutch officers, Indonesian and Filipino staff.

Fitness Facilities: Gymnasium with Ultra Mac multipurpose 9-way muscular exercise unit, stationary bicycles, rowing machines, free and pully weights, slant boards, treadmills; 2 outdoor swimming pools (1 has whirlpool jets), 2 saunas. **Services:** Massage, facials, manicure, pedicure, hairstyling, makeup consultation. **Sports:** Tennis courts, shuffleboard, scuba instruction, volleyball.

The *Nieuw Amsterdam* cruises from Tampa, Florida, on Saturdays; fares for 7-day Caribbean cruise, including airfare, $1,640–$2,420 per person, double occupancy. The *Noordam* cruises from Ft. Lauderdale (Port Everglades); fares for 10-day Caribbean cruise, including airfare, $2,175–$3,470.

Special Note: Program also available aboard the recently enlarged and refurbished *Westerdam,* which has a HydroFitness circuit and dome-covered swimming pool. Also, four staterooms for the disabled.

Norway

The 14-room, 6,000-square-foot Roman Spa, which opened in 1990, aboard the SS *Norway* launched a new era of spa luxury at sea. Featuring the first hydrotherapy baths on a cruise ship, the spa employs European-trained specialists in thalassotherapy, shiatsu, reflexology, aromatherapy, thermal body wraps, and a wide range of beauty services. Services can be booked à la carte; five package programs are available for a complete spa vacation. Ranging from a half-day introductory workout and herbal massage for $99 to a 6-day customized regime for $689, packages always include a calorie-controlled luncheon served in the spa lounge, which has a juice bar.

Located on Dolphin Deck, the new Roman Spa is a sybaritic enclave of soothing treatment rooms (each equipped with shower), men's and women's saunas and steam rooms, a seawater aquacise pool and Jacuzzi, and an exercise room with computerized cardiovascular equipment. The *Norway's* spa treatments incorporate ancient Roman philosophy and a sea theme with Phytomer marine algae, by moor mud products by Remé Laure, and Sir Anthony Kaye hairstyling products. Advance appointments prior to sailing can be made by calling 800/327-0712 (in Dade County, 305/445-1679).

For more active passengers there is a "Fit with Fun" program on the ship's Olympic Deck, where state-of-the-art exercise equipment and a 360-degree jogging/walking track have been installed. Team games are organized in the *"Norway* Olympics," and snorkeling is offered at a beach party on NCL's private uninhabited island in the Bahamas. Added features during the Fitness and Beauty Cruise at the end of October include workshops on nutrition, sports medicine, and skin care; running clinics; and workouts with sports personalities. During the rest of the year, golf and tennis Pro-Am cruises have professionals aboard to help improve your game, and opportunities for play abound on shore. Fitness walks are organized in each port.

Norwegian Cruise Line. *95 Merrick Way, Coral Gables, FL 33134, tel. 305/447–9660 or 800/262–4625.* Entered service as the *France,* in 1962, refitted as the *Norway* in 1979, renovated and expanded in 1990. 2,044 passengers. Norwegian registry and officers, international staff.

Fitness Facilities: Gymnasium with Universal equipment, 2 Liferowers, 3 Lifecycles, 2 Lifesteps, free weights; Roman Spa with Bally cardiovascular equipment; 2 outdoor swimming pools; outdoor jogging track. **Services:** Massage, facials, hydrotherapy bath, bodywrap, makeup cleansing; hair, nail, and skin care. **Sports:** Racquetball, basketball, volleyball courts, golf putting and driving areas, skeet shooting.

Cruise fares from $1,245 to $5,645, including air fare and transfers. Year-round 7-night cruises departing from Miami on Saturday. Roman Spa open daily 9AM–7 PM, until 10 PM port days. Spa packages from $99 plus 12% gratuity, includes facility charge, toga. Massage (50 min.) $60.

SSC Radisson Diamond

The entire top deck of the SSC *Radisson Diamond* is devoted to a spa and jogging track, and there is a marina that descends into the sea, and a wide range of fitness activites. Designed for upscale cruising, the ship has just 177 staterooms. New technology called SSC (Semi-Submersible Craft) minimizes engine and propeller noise and maximizes deck space. From the 5-story atrium, you are whisked up a glass elevator to three decks of suites (there are 12 decks total) and a glass-walled dining room. All cabins are suite-size with private balcony, queen-size bed, TV, VCR, stereo, and a full bath with shower. The spa and health club feature European beauty treatments, separate saunas and steam rooms for men and women, and exercise equipment. The open-air swimming pool and Jacuzzi are tiny, but in port you can swim in a floating marina equipped for snorkeling, windsurfing, and water jet boats.

With an open-seating policy in the main dining room, you can order off the menu, request a special diet, or select from the "Simplicity" menu. Evening entertainment is limited to the casino and TV. The ship's rates do not cover personal services in the spa and salon.

Radisson Diamond Cruises. *Box 1732, Minneapolis, MN 55440, tel. 612/540–5451, fax 612/449–3400.* Debut in 1992. 354 passengers. Finnish registry, international crew.

Fitness Facilities: Exercise room with 4 David cam weight machines, 2 Lifesteps, 2 Liferowers, 4 Lifecycles, free weights.

Services: Massage, facials, body wraps, hand and foot treatment, aromatherapy. Salon for hair, nail, and skin care.

Cruises from San Juan and other Caribbean ports on 4-, 5-, and 7-day itineraries. Fares approximately $600 per person, per day, double occupancy. Spa packages $140–$465.

Royal Majesty

The *Royal Majesty* debuted in 1992 as the first ship to ban smoking in the dining room. 132 of the cabins are also smoke-free.

A well-equipped seaview spa is situated high atop the ship, and healthful Regal Bodies spa cuisine is available in the dining room. The spa has an aerobics studio with wooden floor where aerobics and tai chi classes are scheduled daily. There are massage rooms, 2 saunas, a smallish outdoor swimming pool, and a pair of whirlpools.

Majesty Cruise Line. *901 S. America Way, Miami, FL 33132, tel. 305/536–0000 or 800/532–7788.* Commissioned in 1992. 1,056 passengers. Panamanian registry, Greek officers, international crew.

Fitness Facilities: Gymnasium with 2 StairMasters, Lifecycle, Fly, recumbent bike, 4 weight training machines, free weights, NordicTrack cross-country machine, rowing machine. **Services:** Massage, personal training; hair, nail, and skin salon.

Cruises from Miami. Fares for 3-night Bahamas cruise, including airfare, $489–$969 per person, double occupancy; 4-night cruise to Nassau, Key West and private island, $599–$1,099 per person.

Royal Princess

Located high atop the *Royal Princess* on the Sun Deck, a well-equipped gymnasium affords panoramic views of the sea and excursion scenery to those working out. A quarter-mile cushioned jogging track circles the Promenade Deck. The dining room menu offers heart-healthy items that are low in sodium and cholesterol, prepared according to American Heart Association guidelines.

The *Princess's* fleetwide Cruisercise (R) program was designed by Kathy Smith, fitness trainer for the Stars & Stripes U.S. sailing team. On all ships a daily schedule of classes includes walk-a-mile, stretch and tone, high- or low-impact aerobics, and aquacise. Participation earns you prizes.

Princess Cruises. *10100 Santa Monica Blvd., Los Angeles, CA 90067, tel. 213/553–1770.* Commissioned in 1984. 1,200 passengers. British registry and officers, Italian dining room staff, British stewards.

Fitness Facilities: Gymnasium with Hydro-fitness 11-station multipurpose weights unit, rowing machines, treadmill, Paramount Uniflex sports trainer, Lifecycles, slant boards, free weights; aerobics studio with classes at all levels scheduled daily; 4 outdoor swimming pools (with a 33-foot pool for laps), 2 whirlpools, sauna. **Services:** Massage, facials; hair, skin, and nail care, moortherapy facial mask, leg and back treatment, throat and decolette treatment, foot and hand treatment, body wrap, eye treatment.

Cruises include Alaska, Trans-Panama Canal, Caribbean. Fares for 10-night cruise, Acapulco–San Juan, $2,650–$7,390 including round-trip air connections. Wheelchair accommodations in 10 staterooms.

Royal Viking Sun

The *Royal Viking Sun* upholds Royal Viking Line's reputation for luxury. Among its features are a computerized indoor golf simulator that enables passengers to play some of the world's most challenging courses and—breaking new ground—the first croquet court on a cruise ship. The elaborate Viking Spa overlooks the ship's pool area, where a swim-up bar permits you to combine exercise and socializing. This liner also has a library with fireplace, and butlers for the penthouse suites.

Royal Viking Line. *95 Merrick Way, Coral Gables, FL 33134. Tel. 305/460–4761 or 800/422–8000.* Launched 1988. 740 passengers. Bahamian registry, Norwegian officers, European crew.

Fitness Facilities: Gym equipped for toning muscles and building endurance; 2 heated outdoor saltwater swimming pools, saunas for men and women; aerobics studio with classes at all levels. **Services:** Massage; facials; moortherapy facial mask; back and leg treatment; thermal or herbal body wrap; throat and decollete treatment; eye, foot, and hand treatment; exfoliation. Salon for hair, nail and skin care. **Sports:** Badminton, tennis practice court, Ping-Pong, quoits, darts.

Fares for 16-day trans–Panama Canal cruise, New York–San Francisco via the Caribbean, $4,435–$12,355 per person double occupancy including air connections (shorter segments available). Wheelchair accommodations in 4 cabins.

Special Notes: Bermuda cruises aboard the *Royal Viking Star*, another Viking ship, feature a new health and fitness center equipped with Lifecycles, Liferowers, saunas, and steambaths. Weekly from New York (May–August).

Seabourn Pride and *Seabourn Spirit*

With almost an entire upper deck devoted to a seagoing spa, the *Seabourn Pride*—the creation of an experienced team of Norwegian and American designers—and sister ship *Seabourn Spirit*, take aim at the upscale cruiser who demands service and spaciousness. The all-suites ships have six passenger decks, open-seating dining rooms where meals are prepared to order, and many attractive features such as marble baths, 5-foot windows, and walk-in closets in every stateroom. The spa program includes a full range of aerobics and activities. Passengers may request a personalized fitness evaluation and dietary guidance. Treatments include body firming and silhouette refining with marine algae body wraps and baths, herbal massages, and facials. Shore excursions include ports rarely visited by large cruise ships, such as Soufrière Bay in St. Lucia, where a visit to the thermal baths can be arranged.

Seabourn Cruises. *55 Francisco St., San Francisco, CA 94133, tel. 415/391-7444.* Debut season 1988–1989. 212 passengers. Norwegian registry and officers, European staff.

Fitness Facilities: Gymnasium with Nautilus exercise units, computerized exercycles, rowing machines, isotonic exercisers, free weights; outdoor swimming pool and twin whirlpool baths, sauna, steam room, aerobics studio. **Services:** Massage, body wraps, moortherapy facial mask, back and leg treatments, hand and eye treatments, throat and decollete treatment. Salon for hair, nail, and skin care, personal fitness consultation. **Sports:** Swimming from the ship's marina deck.

Fares average $460–$989 per day, plus tips. Seasonal destinations include Montreal, New York, and the Caribbean. A 14-day cruise from Fort Lauderdale costs $7,780–$12,400 per person double occupancy. Airfare included from selected cities.

Seaward

The *Seaward*, a Finnish-built addition to the Norwegian Cruise Line fleet, is a 42,000-ton beauty complete with cascading waterfall, cushioned running track, and basketball court. Although smaller than her big sister the *Norway*, she has a quarter-mile promenade deck that encircles the ship—a detail missing on many new liners. The top-deck spa, all glass and gleaming chrome, affords panoramic views of the sea to those working out. Separate saunas and showers are provided for men and women, and massage is available. The accent is on sports: The ship's two swimming pools and adjacent whirlpools have splash areas surrounded by Astroturf, where a "dive-in" center offers snorkeling equipment and instruction. Excursions in port take in some of the finest golf courses and tennis courts in the islands. Pro-Am cruises team passengers with golf and tennis pros on designated weeks throughout the year. Racquet Club cruises and Tee-Up golf cruises offer clinics and workshops at sea and special games and matches ashore. As host to the annual NCL Fitness and Beauty cruise, the ship will become a seagoing spa with lectures and classes on nutrition, sports medicine, fitness, exercise, and personal image, jogging and running clinics, and a nature walk on a Bahamian out island. Dining alternatives include a choice of lighter meals at an informal cafe and an à la carte restaurant where meals are prepared to order.

Norwegian Cruise Line. *95 Merrick Way, Coral Gables, FL 33134, tel. 305/447-9660 or 800/327-7030.* Inaugurated in 1988. 1,534 passengers. Bahamian registry, Norwegian officers, international crew.

Fitness Facilities: Health spa with Universal equipment, stationary bicycles, aerobics studio with daily scheduled classes, rowing machines, free weights; 2 outdoor swimming pools, whirlpools, sauna, no steam room. **Services:** Massage, facials; moortherapy facial mask; throat and decollete treatment; eye, foot, and hand treatments; exfoliation; herbal or thermal body wrap; salon for hair, nail, and skin care. **Sports:** Volleyball, snorkeling, skeet shooting, golf driving.

Cruises on Sun. from Miami, calling at Great Stirrup Cay, Ocho Rios in Jamaica, Grand Cayman, and Cozumel. Cruise fares $1,245–$2,680 per person double occupancy. Airfare included from major gateways.

Seawind Crown

Sailing from Aruba, the 632-passenger *Seawind Crown* offers features not found on larger ships, such as squash and volleyball courts, as well as a fitness center. In addition to the coed sauna and cold plunge pool, there are two outdoor swimming pools (one heated) and a jogging track for deck exercise.

Seawind Cruise Line. *1750 Coral Way, Miami, FL 33145; tel. 305/285–9494 or 800/258–8006.* Commissioned as TSS *Vasco da Gama*, rebuilt 1989. Panamanian registry, Portugese and Greek officers, European dining room staff, Portugese cabin service. 632 passengers. Cabins have color TV, terry cloth robes, bathroom with hair dryer.

Fitness Facilities: Fitness Center with stationary bikes, rowing machine, free weights, whirlpool. **Services:** massage, salon for hair, nail, and skin care.

Cruises from Aruba every Sunday. Fares $895–$2,695, including airfare or discount from U.S. cities. Accommodations for the handicapped in 2 cabins.

Sovereign of the Seas

Sovereign of the Seas, the world's largest ship, sports a central lobby area, the Centrum, that spans five decks. Located one step down from the Sports Deck, the ShipShape exercise and relaxation facility features the latest in weight training equipment, sauna, massage, and whirlpool. Passengers participate in activities that range from yoga and aerobics classes to shooting basketball free throws. The program offers 12 activities, beginning with a morning Walkathon of timed laps; other choices include aquacise in the swimming pools and team sports. Muscle tension can be soothed away with a cleansing sauna followed by a relaxing massage by qualified therapists. Dining options include a selection of light items that are highlighted on the regular menu as being low in sodium and cholesterol, in line with the American Heart Association guidelines.

Royal Caribbean Cruise Line. *903 South American Way, Miami, FL 33132, tel. 305/379–2601 or 800/327–6700 (800/245–7225 in Canada).* Commissioned in 1988. 2,690 passengers. Norwegian registry and officers, international staff.

Fitness Facilities: Gymnasium with David pneumatic pressure exercise units, abdominal board, 5 Lifecycles, 6 Liferowers, StairMaster, Boland dumbbells; two outdoor swimming pools. **Services:** Massage, facials; hair, nail, and skin care; personalized exercise program. **Sports:** PGA sanctioned "Golf Ahoy" program aboard and ashore, tennis clinics, basketball, golf putting, shuffleboard, skeet shooting.

Cruises from Miami on Sat., calling at San Juan, St. Thomas, and a beach resort. Fares $1,245–$2,945 per person double occupancy. Airfare included from selected cities.

Windjammer Figaro

The *Windjammer Figaro* provides an unusual opportunity for vegetarians and yoga devotees to sail among the islands of Maine aboard a 51-foot yawl that offers programs in nutrition, nature studies, and seamanship. With accommodations for just six passengers, this ocean racing ship cruises from the storybook harbor of Camden, Maine, to secluded coves of Acadia National Park. Meals are based on whole grains, fresh garden vegetables, and fruit, in the macrobiotic tradition, with dairy products and coffee as desired. Passengers can participate in sailing the ship, and yoga for all levels, with a week for intermediate students of the Iyengar style, is taught on scheduled cruises during the summer and by request in winter. Special weeks are devoted to men's and women's issues. Life aboard is informal; smoking is not permitted.

Figaro Cruises. *Box 1336, Camden, ME 04843, tel. 800/473–6169.* Built in 1965, rebuilt in 1987. 6 passengers (2 double-berth cabins, 2 semiprivate berths). U.S. registry, Coast Guard inspected. Crew of 4. Owners/skippers: Jennifer Martin, Barry King.

Cruises on Mon. for 6 days, fares $399–$675 per person double occupancy; Sails Monday morning, with sleep-aboard privilege the night before sailing. 3-day weekender cruise $295–$350.

Wind Spirit

A blend of modern technology and the romance of cruising under sail, the yachtlike *Wind Spirit* offers a fitness center and a full program of water sports. While under sail, a computerized system raises the six sails automatically in less than two minutes. While anchored in secluded coves, away from the routes of the large cruise ships, the vessel's crew members organize waterskiing and snorkeling expeditions. For certified divers there is scuba equipment aboard. Shore excursions to golf and tennis resorts can be arranged through the ship's purser.

Windstar Cruises. *300 Elliott Avenue West, Seattle, WA 98119. Tel. 206/286–3210 or 800/258–7245 (Canada, 800/263–0844).* Commissioned in 1988. 148 passengers. Bahamian registry, international crew.

Fitness Facilities: Exercise room with 2 rowing machines, stationary bikes; outdoor swimming pool, sauna. **Services:** Massage. **Sports:** Water sports program, shore excursions for golf and tennis.

Cruises from St. Thomas on Sun., calling throughout the Virgin Islands. (A sister ship, the *Wind Star*, departs Barbados on Sat. for 7-day cruises of the Leeward islands.) Fares for 7-day cruise $2,795 per person double occupancy.

Glossary

A **Acupressure.** Finger massage intended to release muscle tension by applying pressure to the nerves.

Acupuncture. A Chinese system that inserts fine needles at key points of the body that relate to different organs as a means of relieving muscular, neurological, and arthritic problems.

Aerobics. Exercise routines orchestrated to enhance cardiovascular and muscular strength.

Aerobics studio. A gymnasium used strictly for floor exercise; a cushioned or suspended floor aids in avoiding injury.

Air-Dyne Bicycle. See *Schwinn Air-Dyne Bicycle.*

Alexander Technique. A massage system created in the 1890s by the Australian actor F. M. Alexander to correct physical habits that cause stress and help improve posture.

Algotherapy. Seaweed bath. See *Thalassotherapy.*

Aquaerobics. Aerobics workouts in a swimming pool; stretch, strength, and stamina exercises that combine water resistance and body movements. Also *aquafit* and *aquacise.*

Aromabath. See *herbal wrap.*

Aromatherapy. Massage with oils from essences of plants and flowers intended to relax the skin's connective tissues and stimulate the natural flow of lymph.

Ayurvedic. 4000-year-old Indian treatments with oils, massage, and herbs.

B **Bach Cures.** Healing with flowers.

Balneology. Traditional study and practice of water-based treatments using geothermal hot springs, mineral water, or seawater.

Barre. Balance bar or rail used during exercise.

Behavior modification. Change in personal habits brought about through counseling and psychological conditioning.

Bindi. Bodywork combining exfoliation, herbal treatment, and light massage.

Bioenergetics. Exchange of energy between persons giving and receiving massage.

Biofeedback. Monitoring and control of physical functions such as blood pressure, pulse rate, digestion, and muscle tension with an electronic sensing device.

Body composition test. Evaluation of lean body mass and percentage of body fat, using standard weight charts; a computerized system compares personal data with standard percentages to determine whether an individual is overweight.

Body sugaring. Hair-removal process said to date from the time of Cleopatra.

C **Calipers.** Measuring device used in determining the percentage of fat in the body.

Cardiovascular endurance. Oxygen utilization by the body.

Cathartic. Laxative of natural or organic substances.

Chiropractic. Realignment of the spine and bone/body mechanics to relieve backache and postural problems.

Circuit training. The combination of aerobics and high-energy workout with weight-resistance equipment. Also *Cross training*.

Circuit weight work. See *Circuit training*.

Cold plunge. Deep pool for the rapid contraction of the capillaries, stimulates circulation after sauna.

Colonic irrigation. Enema to cleanse high into the colon with water.

Contour. Calisthenics for deep toning of muscle groups.

Coordination. Connection and integration of parts of the body during movement.

Cross-country ski machine. A device that simulates the motions of cross-country skiing.

Cross-training. Alternating high-stress and low-stress exercise or sports to enhance physical and mental conditioning.

Crystal Healing. Healing energy believed to be generated by quartz and other minerals.

Cybex. Patented equipment for isokinetic strength testing and training.

D **David System.** Pneumatic weight training units in which air is pumped. See *Circuit training*.

Drinking cure. Medically prescribed regimen of mineral water consumption.

E **Ergometer.** Exercise machine designed for muscular contraction.

F **Facial.** Deep-cleansing of the face and/or upper body with steam, light scrub.

Fango. A mud pack or body coating intended to promote the release of toxins and relieve muscular and arthritic pain.

Fast. Supervised diet of water, juice, nuts, seeds; intended to produce significant weight loss.

Feldenkrais. System of bodywork developed by Moshe Feldenkrais that attempts to reprogram the nervous system through movement augmented by physical pressure and manipulation.

Flex and stretch. Continuous movement exercises intended to increase endurance, flexibility, and muscular strength.

Flexibility. Muscular elasticity; the ability to stretch over joints.

Free weights. Hand-held dumbbells or barbells.

G **Gestalt.** Sensory awareness; the inner experience of being.

Guided imagery. Visualization to stimulate the body's immune system.

H **Haysack wrap.** Kneipp treatment with steamed hay intended to detoxify the body.

Hellerwork. A system of deep tissue bodywork, stress reduction, and movement reeducation developed by Joseph Heller.

Herbal bath. See *herbal wrap.*

Herbal wrap. A treatment in which moisture, heat, and herbal essences penetrate the skin while the body is wrapped in hot linens, plastic sheets, and blankets; it is intended to promote muscle relaxation and the elimination of toxins. Also *aromabath, herbal bath.*

Herbology. The therapeutic use of herbs in treatments and diet.

Holistic health. A nonmedical approach to the healing and health of the whole person that seeks to integrate physical and mental well-being with lifestyle factors.

Homeopathy. Treating disease with tiny doses of natural substances.

Hot plunge. Deep pool for the rapid dilation of the capillaries.

Hot tub. A wooden soaking pool.

Hydromassage. See *hydrotub.*

Hydrotherapy. Underwater massage; alternating hot and cold showers; and other water-oriented treatments.

Hydrotub. Underwater massage in deep tubs equipped with high-pressure jets and hand-manipulated hose. Also *hydromassage.*

Hypnotherapy. Clinical use of hypnotism to stimulate positive habits.

I **Inhalations.** Hot vapors, or steam mixed with eucalyptus oil, inhaled to decongest the respiratory system; breathed through inhalation equipment or in a special steam room.

Interval training. A combination of high-energy exercise followed by a period of low-intensity activity.

Iridology. A theory that links markings in the iris of the eye to the condition of organs of the body.

Isometrics. Pushing against a stable object to tone muscles.

Isotonics. Muscles are lengthened and shortened against a source offering constant resistance, such as barbells, known as free weights, or controlled weight-lifting stations.

Isokinetic exercise. Resistance balances effort applied against a device.

Iyengar yoga. Exercise system developed in India by B.K.S. Iyengar.

J **Jacuzzi.** A patented design of a whirlpool bath with underwater jets.

K **Keiser Cam II.** A patented system of pneumatic weight training units. Also, Keiser Cam III.

Kinesiology. The testing and strengthening of muscles through exercise and diet, intended to achieve better balance in the body.

Kneipp cures. Treatments combining hydrotherapy, herbology, and a diet of natural foods, developed in Germany in the mid-1800s by Pastor Sebastian Kneipp.

L **Lap pool.** A shallow swimming pool with exercise lanes; the standard lap length is 50 feet.

Lifecycle. A computer-programmed exercise bike, made by Bally.

Liferower. A computer-programmed exercise machine that simulates rowing, made by Bally.

Lomi-Lomi. Hawaiian rhythmical rocking massage.

Loofah body scrub. Cleansing of the body with a mixture of sea salt, warm almond or avocado oil, and a loofah sponge.

Low-impact aerobics. A dancelike exercise in which one foot is always on the floor; intended to avoid muscle fatigue and to enhance cardiovascular fitness.

M **Macrobiotics.** A vegetarian diet low in fat and high in antioxidant vitamins.

Manicure. Nail care.

Massage. Soothing, energizing deep-muscle manipulation, usually by hand, intended to reduce stress and fatigue while improving circulation. Various methods.

Maximal heart rate. An individual's highest attainable heart rate (the number of heartbeats per minute). It is best determined by means of a graded maximal exercise test, but an estimate can be made by subtracting one's age from 220. See *target heart rate.*

Mineral bath. A soaking in hot or cool water from thermal springs that contains mineral salts, natural elements, and gases.

N **Naturopathy.** Natural healing prescriptions that use plants and flowers.

Nautilus. Patented strength training equipment designed to isolate one muscle group for each exercise movement that contracts and lengthens against gravity.

NordicTrack. A patented design of cross-country ski machine.

Nutrition counseling. The analysis of an individual's eating habits and dietary needs.

O One-on-one training. Personal instruction on exercise equipment from a professional exercise therapist.

Orthion. Stretching device for neck, spine.

Ovo-lacto diet. A regimen that includes eggs and dairy products.

P Parafango. Combination of mud and paraffin wax. See *fango*.

Parcourse. A trail, usually outdoors, equipped with exercise stations. Also *parcours, vitacourse*.

Pedicure. Nail care and treatment of the feet to remove dead skin with a pumice stone or razor; involves soaking feet, scraping, and massage.

Pilates. Strength training movements developed in Germany by Dr. Joseph Pilates during the 1920s.

Plyometrics. Jumps and push steps to strengthen leg muscles. See also *Step aerobics*.

Polarity therapy. Balancing the energy within the body through a combination of massage, meditation, exercise, and diet; created by Dr. Randolph Stone.

Power. Anaerobic force exerted by a muscle.

R Radiance technique. See *Reiki*.

Rebirthing. A yoga breathing technique combined with guided meditation to relax and clear the mind. Also, reliving the experience of birth.

Rebounder. A miniature trampoline.

Reiki. An ancient healing method that teaches universal life energy through the laying on of hands and mental and spiritual balancing. Intended to relieve acute emotional and physical conditions. Also *Radiance technique*.

Reflexology. Massage of the pressure points on the feet, hands, and ears; intended to relax the parts of the body.

Rolfing. A bodywork system developed by Ida Rolf that improves balance and flexibility through manipulation of rigid muscles, bones, and joints. It is intended to improve energy flow and relieve stress (often related to emotional trauma).

Roman pool. A step-down whirlpool bath, for one or two persons.

Rowing machine. An exercise machine that simulates rowing; it can include computer graphics.

Rubenfeld Synergy. A method of integrating body and mind through verbal expression and gentle touch, developed by Ilana Rubenfeld.

Russian bath. Steam bath to flush toxins from the body.

S Salt glow. A cleansing treatment, using coarse salt to remove dead skin, similar to the loofah body scrub. Also *salt rub*.

Salt rub. See *salt glow*.

Sauna. A wood-lined room with dry-heat generated at temperatures of 160–210 degrees, intended to induce sweating to cleanse the body of impurities. In the Finnish tradition, which seeks even higher temperatures, heat is generated by a stove containing a heap of stones (*kiuas*) over which water is thrown to produce vapor (*löyly*).

Schwinn Air-Dyne Bicycle. A stationary exercise bike that works the upper and lower body simultaneously.

Scotch douche. A treatment with high-pressure hoses that alternate hot and cold water, intended to improve circulation through rapid contraction and dilation of the capillaries.

Shamanism. Spiritual and natural healing performed by medicine men.

Shiatsu. A massage technique developed by Tokujiro Namikoshi that uses finger (*shi*) pressure (*atsu*) to stimulate the body's inner powers of balance and healing.

Sitz bath. Immersion of the hips and lower body in herbal hot water, followed by cold water, to stimulate the immune system. Also a Kneipp treatment for constipation, hemorrhoids, prostate problems, menstrual problems, and digestive upsets.

Spa cuisine. Fresh, natural foods low in saturated fats and cholesterol, with an emphasis on whole grains, low-fat dairy products, lean protein, fresh fruit, fish, and vegetables and an avoidance of added salt and products containing sodium and artificial colorings, flavorings, and preservatives.

StairMaster. A patented exercise machine that simulates climbing stairs.

Steam room. A ceramic-tiled room with wet heat generated at temperatures of 110–130 degrees, intended to soften the skin, cleanse the pores, and calm the nervous system.

Step aerobics. Rhythmic stepping on and off a small platform.

Stress management. A program of meditation and deep relaxation intended to reduce the ill effects of stress on the system.

Sweat lodge. Native American body-purification ceremony.

Swedish massage. A treatment that duplicates gymnastics movements with stroking, kneading, friction, vibration, and tapping to relax muscles gently; devised at the University of Stockholm early in the 19th century by Henri Peter Ling.

Swiss shower. A multijet bath that alternates hot and cold water.

T **Tai chi chuan.** Movements intended to unite body and mind; an ancient oriental discipline for exercise and meditation.

Target heart rate. The number of heartbeats per minute an individual tries to attain during exercise; the figure is 60% to 90% of one's maximal heart rate. The American College of Sports Medicine recommends maintaining this rate for 20–30 minutes during exercise three to five days a week. See *maximal heart rate*.

Thalassotherapy. Water-based treatments that use seawater, seaweed, algae, and sea air; an ancient Greek therapy.

Trager massage. A technique developed by Milton Trager that employs a gentle, rhythmic shaking of the body to release tension from the joints. Intended for sensory repatterning.

Treadmill. An exercise machine that simulates walking.

U **Universal Gym.** A patented weight training system.

V **Vegetarian diet.** A regime of raw or cooked vegetables and fruit, grains, sprouts, and seeds; natural foods with no additives.

VersaClimber. A patented exercise machine that simulates the climbing of a ladder.

W **Water volleyball.** The net game played in a pool.

Whirlpool. A hot pool with water rushing from jets on the sides at temperatures of 105–115 degrees, used to stimulate the system and relax sore muscles.

Y **Yoga.** A discipline of stretching and toning the body through movements or asana postures, controlled deep breathing, relaxation techniques, and diet. A school of Hindu philosophy that advocates physical and mental discipline for the unity of mind, body, and spirit.

Z **Zen shiatsu.** A Japanese acupressure art intended to relieve tension and balance the body.

Fodor's Travel Guides

U.S. Guides

Alaska

Arizona

Boston

California

Cape Cod, Martha's
Vineyard, Nantucket

The Carolinas & the
Georgia Coast

Chicago

Disney World & the
Orlando Area

Florida

Hawaii

Las Vegas, Reno,
Tahoe

Los Angeles

Maine, Vermont,
New Hampshire

Maui

Miami & the Keys

New England

New Orleans

New York City

Pacific North Coast

Philadelphia & the
Pennsylvania Dutch
Country

San Diego

San Francisco

Santa Fe, Taos,
Albuquerque

Seattle & Vancouver

The South

The U.S. & British
Virgin Islands

The Upper Great
Lakes Region

USA

Vacations in New York
State

Vacations on the
Jersey Shore

Virginia & Maryland

Waikiki

Washington, D.C.

Foreign Guides

Acapulco, Ixtapa,
Zihuatanejo

Australia & New
Zealand

Austria

The Bahamas

Baja & Mexico's
Pacific Coast Resorts

Barbados

Berlin

Bermuda

Brazil

Budapest

Budget Europe

Canada

Cancun, Cozumel,
Yucatan Penisula

Caribbean

Central America

China

Costa Rica, Belize,
Guatemala

Czechoslovakia

Eastern Europe

Egypt

Euro Disney

Europe

Europe's Great Cities

France

Germany

Great Britain

Greece

The Himalayan
Countries

Hong Kong

India

Ireland

Israel

Italy

Italy's Great Cities

Japan

Kenya & Tanzania

Korea

London

Madrid & Barcelona

Mexico

Montreal &
Quebec City

Morocco

The Netherlands
Belgium &
Luxembourg

New Zealand

Norway

Nova Scotia, Prince
Edward Island &
New Brunswick

Paris

Portugal

Rome

Russia & the Baltic
Countries

Scandinavia

Scotland

Singapore

South America

Southeast Asia

South Pacific

Spain

Sweden

Switzerland

Thailand

Tokyo

Toronto

Turkey

Vienna & the Danube
Valley

Yugoslavia

WHEREVER YOU TRAVEL, *H*ELP IS NEVER FAR AWAY.

From planning your trip to providing travel assistance along the way, American Express® Travel Service Offices* are always there to help. For the office nearest you in the United States, call **1-800-YES-AMEX**